Economic Growth and Structural Reforms in Europe

In contrast to the United States, Europe has struggled to return to the growth path it was on prior to the financial crisis of 2007–2011. Not only has the recovery been slow, it has also been variable, with Europe's core countries recovering more quickly than those on the periphery. It is widely believed that the best way to address this slow recovery is through structural reform programmes whereby changes in government policy, regulatory frameworks, investment incentives and labour markets are used to encourage more efficient markets and higher economic growth. This book is the first to provide a critical assessment of these reforms, with a new theoretical framework, new data and new empirical methodologies. It includes several case studies of countries such as Greece, Portugal and France that introduced significant reforms, revealing that such programmes have very divergent, and not always positive, effects on economic growth, employment and income inequality.

NAURO F. CAMPOS is professor of economics at the University College London and research professor at ETH-Zürich. His main fields of interest are political economy and European integration. He has taught at the Universities of Bonn, Brunel, CERGE-EI (Prague), Newcastle, Paris 1 Sorbonne and Warwick. He was a Fulbright Fellow at Johns Hopkins University, a Robert McNamara Fellow at the World Bank and a CBS Fellow at Oxford University. He is a research fellow at the Institute for Labour Economics (IZA)–Bonn, a member of the Scientific Advisory Board of the (Central) Bank of Finland, a senior fellow of the Economic and Research Council (ESRC) Peer Review College and was a visiting scholar at the International Monetary Fund (IMF), World Bank, European Commission, University of Michigan, ETH, University of Southern California (USC), Bonn, University College London (UCL) and Stockholm.

PAUL DE GRAUWE is professor of economics at the London School of Economics. He was a member of the Belgian parliament from 1991 to 2003. He is honorary doctor of the University of Sankt Gallen, the

University of Turku, the University of Genoa, the University of Valencia, and Maastricht University. He has taught at the universities of Paris, Amsterdam, Berlin, Kiel, Milan, Pennsylvania and Michigan. He is a research fellow at the Centre for European Policy Studies in Brussels and a Centre for Economic Policy Research (CEPR) fellow in London. His research interests are in the economics of monetary unions and behavioural macroeconomics. He is the author of *The Limits of the Market* (2017), *The Economics of Monetary Union* (11th edition, 2016) and *Lectures on Behavioral Macroeconomics* (2012).

YUEMEI JI is associate professor of economics at the University College London. She was a visiting fellow at the European Institute at LSE and the Centre for European Policy Studies (CEPS) in Brussels. She gives lectures on European macroeconomics and international macroeconomics. Her research interests cover international macroeconomics in general and the European Monetary Union during the postcrisis period in particular, and she has done intensive research on the causes of Eurozone debt crisis and its impact on the austerity policies in the Eurozone.

Economic Growth and Structural Reforms in Europe

Edited by

NAURO F. CAMPOS
University College London

PAUL DE GRAUWE
London School of Economics and Political Science

YUEMEI JI
University College London

CAMBRIDGE
UNIVERSITY PRESS

CAMBRIDGE
UNIVERSITY PRESS

University Printing House, Cambridge CB2 8BS, United Kingdom

One Liberty Plaza, 20th Floor, New York, NY 10006, USA

477 Williamstown Road, Port Melbourne, VIC 3207, Australia

314–321, 3rd Floor, Plot 3, Splendor Forum, Jasola District Centre, New Delhi – 110025, India

79 Anson Road, #06–04/06, Singapore 079906

Cambridge University Press is part of the University of Cambridge.

It furthers the University's mission by disseminating knowledge in the pursuit of education, learning, and research at the highest international levels of excellence.

www.cambridge.org
Information on this title: www.cambridge.org/9781108479110
DOI: 10.1017/9781108782517

First published 2020

Printed in the United Kingdom by TJ International Ltd. Padstow Cornwall

A catalogue record for this publication is available from the British Library.

Library of Congress Cataloging-in-Publication Data
Names: Campos, Nauro F., editor. | Grauwe, Paul de, editor. | Ji, Yuemei, editor.
Title: Economic growth and structural reforms in Europe / edited by Nauro F. Campos, Brunel University, Paul De Grauwe, London School of Economics and Political Science, Yuemei Ji, University College London.
Description: Cambridge, United Kingdom ; New York, NY : Cambridge University Press, 2019. | Includes bibliographical references and index.
Identifiers: LCCN 2019038188 (print) | LCCN 2019038189 (ebook) | ISBN 9781108479110 (hardback) | ISBN 9781108749336 (paperback) | ISBN 9781108782517 (epub)
Subjects: LCSH: Economic development–Europe. | Europe–Economic policy. | Europe–Economic conditions–21st century.
Classification: LCC HC240 .E2735 2019 (print) | LCC HC240 (ebook) | DDC 338.94–dc23
LC record available at https://lccn.loc.gov/2019038188
LC ebook record available at https://lccn.loc.gov/2019038189

ISBN 978-1-108-47911-0 Hardback

Contents

Figures

Tables

Contributors

Mirko Abbritti is Associate Professor in the Department of Economics of the University of Navarra. He holds a PhD and a master's in international economics from the Graduate Institute of International and Development Studies in Geneva. He previously received a BSc (Hons) in economics from the University of Perugia. His research is at the intersection between monetary policy, labour economics, international macroeconomics and finance.

Nauro F. Campos is Professor of Economics at University College London and Research Professor at ETH-Zürich. His main fields of interest are political economy and European integration. He has taught at the universities of Bonn, Brunel, the Centre for Economic Research and Graduate Education–Economics Institute (CERGE-EI) (Prague), Newcastle, Paris 1 Sorbonne and Warwick. He was a Fulbright fellow at the Johns Hopkins University (Baltimore), a Robert McNamara fellow at the World Bank and a CBS fellow at Oxford University. He is a research fellow at the Institute of Labour Economics (IZA)-Bonn, a member of the Scientific Advisory Board of the (Central) Bank of Finland, a senior fellow of the Economics and Social Research Council (ESRC) Peer Review College and was a visiting scholar at the International Monetary Fund (IMF), the World Bank, the European Commission, the University of Michigan, ETH, the University of Southern California (USC), Bonn, University College London (UCL) and Stockholm. From 2009 to 2014, he was seconded as senior economic advisor to the chief economist of the Department for International Development. He received his PhD from the University of Southern California (Los Angeles) in 1997.

Mariarosaria Comunale is a principal economist in the Applied Macroeconomic Research Division, Economics Department at the Bank of Lithuania and recently she was also working as economist in

Directorate General International & European Relations at the European Central Bank (ECB). She holds a PhD in money and finance from the University of Rome Tor Vergata. Previously, she worked at the Italian Trade Agency and at the European Union (EU) Commission and spent a period at the University of Cambridge, Trinity College Dublin, ECB and De Nederlandsche Bank. Recently she was visiting the Oesterreichische Nationalbank within the European System of Central Banks (ESCB) Schuman Programme. Comunale's main area of research pertains to applied international macroeconomics, for analyses on EU integration, growth, macroeconomic imbalances, financial cycles and exchange rate pass-through.

PAUL DE GRAUWE is John Paulson Professor at the London School of Economics. He was a member of the Belgian parliament from 1991 to 2003. He is honorary doctor of the University of Sankt Gallen (Switzerland), the University of Turku (Finland), the University of Genoa, the University of Valencia and Maastricht University. He was a visiting professor at various universities: Paris, Amsterdam, Berlin, Kiel, Milan, Pennsylvania and Michigan. He obtained his PhD from the Johns Hopkins University in 1974. He is a research fellow at the Centre for European Policy Studies in Brussels and Centre for Economic Policy Research (CEPR) fellow in London. His research interests are in the economics of monetary unions and behavioural macroeconomics. His book publications include *The Limits of the Market* (2017), *The Economics of Monetary Union* (11th ed., 2016) and *Lectures on Behavioral Macroeconomics* (2012).

BALÁZS ÉGERT is a senior economist at the Organisation for Economic Cooperation and Development (OECD), where he heads the workstream on the quantification of structural reforms. He previously worked at the Austrian Central Bank (2003–2007). He was visiting researcher at the South African Reserve Bank (2007), Bruegel (2006), Centre for Economic Studies and Ifo Institute for Economic Research (CESifo) (2006), the Czech National Bank (2006), the Central Bank of Hungary (2005), the Bank of Finland/Bank of Finland Institute for Economies in Transition (BOFIT) (2004–2005) and the Bank of Estonia (2002). He earned his PhD at the University of Paris X-Nanterre (2002). Balázs has published articles in many publications, including the *American Economic Review*, *Journal of Banking and*

Finance, *Journal of Comparative Economics*, *Journal of Economic Surveys*, *Journal of Macroeconomics*, *Macroeconomic Dynamics*, *Open Economies Review* and *The World Economy*.

DAVIDE FURCERI is a senior economist at the Research Department of the International Monetary Fund. He holds a PhD in economics from the University of Illinois and a doctoral degree in regional economics from the University of Palermo. He previously worked as economist at the Fiscal Policy Division of the European Central Bank and at the Macroeconomic Analysis Division of the Organisation for Economic Cooperation and Development. His research covers a range of issues in the area of macroeconomics, public finance and international macroeconomics.

MICHAEL GANSLMEIER is currently a doctoral student in social policy at the Department of Social Policy and Intervention (DSPI) at St Antony's College, Oxford. He studied economics at Zeppelin University and Columbia University, and continued his postgraduate studies in international political economy at the London School of Economics and Political Science (LSE). His major research interest lies in analysing the effects of labour market reforms on growth, employment and inequality in European countries. He is also interested in applying new big data and machine learning techniques to improve the measurement of structural reforms.

MICHAEL HUME is managing director and head of strategy and research at MKP Capital Management L.L.C. in London. Before joining MKP, he was head of the Capital Markets Division at the Bank of England. His other roles at the bank included senior adviser on international issues and monetary policy adviser to the Monetary Policy Committee (MPC). Michael started his career at Lehman Brothers, where he became chief European economist. He read philosophy, politics and economics at the University of Oxford and took an MSc in economics at the University of Warwick. He is currently researching the Euro-area crisis at the LSE.

JOÃO TOVAR JALLES is an economist in the Research Department of the IMF. Previously, he spent four years in the Fiscal Affairs Department. Before joining the IMF, João was the economist at the OECD and before that a fiscal economist at the ECB. Academically, he was an invited lecturer at Sciences Po and assistant professor at the University of Aberdeen, and he also taught at the University of Cambridge and Universidade Nova de Lisboa. João holds a BSc in economics from Universidade Nova de Lisboa, an MSc in economics from the University of Warwick and a PhD in economics from the University of Cambridge.

Yuemei Ji is an associate professor in economics at the University College London. She obtained her PhD in economics from the University of Leuven. She was a visiting fellow at the European Institute at LSE and the Centre for European Policy Studies (CEPS) in Brussels. She gives lectures on European and international macroeconomics. Her research interests cover international macroeconomics in general and the European Monetary Union during the postcrisis period in particular. She has done intensive research on the causes of the Eurozone debt crisis and its impact on the austerity policies in the Eurozone.

Nikolitsa Lampropoulou holds a PhD in economics from the Department of Economics at the University of Patras. She has worked as a Hellenic Bank Association postdoctoral fellow at the Hellenic Observatory, European Institute at the London School of Economics. She has also taught at the Department of Economics at the London School of Economics and the University of Patras. Her research interests lie in the fields of labour economics, applied microeconometrics, unemployment, labour mobility, discrimination and migration. She has also participated in several research projects, such as the 'Social Situation Monitor' for the European Commission and 'Unemployment Duration in Greece' for the University of Patras.

Corrado Macchiarelli is an associate professor in economics and finance at Brunel University London and a research fellow at the London School of Economics' European Institute. In the past, he worked at the European Central Bank and the International Monetary Fund and consulted for the European Commission, the European Central Bank, the Swedish Riksbank and the European Parliament. His interests mainly lie in the fields of international macro and finance, financial economics, expectation modelling, business cycles and European economic governance. He holds a PhD from the University of Torino (Collegio Carlo Alberto).

Pasquale Marco Marrazzo is an economist at the European Central Bank in the Risk Management Directorate. He is currently pursuing his doctoral programme in economics at Goethe University in Frankfurt. Marco holds a BSc and MSc in economics and finance from Bocconi University. During his studies, he spent a semester at EDHEC Business School and at Schulich School of Business. His academic research revolves around issues of financial econometrics and risk management. Marco has also worked at the Bank of Italy in the risk management department and at Innocenzo Gasparini Institute for Economic Research on financial econometrics research projects.

Angelo Martelli is an assistant professor at the LSE European Institute, where he works on the Economic and Social Research Council project 'Structural Reforms and European Integration: Theory, Measurement and Econometric Evidence'. He is also a consultant for the Jobs Group of the World Bank and a policy fellow for the Open Innovation Team of the UK Cabinet Office and HM Treasury. His research interests span labour economics and European political economy, with a particular focus on the impact of technology on the evolution of employment structures across Europe and the implications for labour market institutions and income inequality.

Kieran McQuinn is a research professor at the Economic and Social Research Institute who works on the quarterly economic commentary (QEC) and housing-related projects. His research interests include house prices, economic growth and household finance. Dr McQuinn spent more than eleven years working in the Irish Central Bank, and before that he worked as an economist with Teagasc, the Irish agriculture and food development authority. He is adjunct professor of economics at both Trinity College Dublin and University College Cork. Dr McQuinn is also a current council member of both the Economic and Social Studies and the Economic and Social Research Institute.

Vassilis Monastiriotis is Associate Professor of Political Economy at the European Institute, London School of Economics (UK). He is director of the LSE Research Unit on Southeast Europe and holds affiliations with LSE's Department of Geography and Environment and the Hellenic Observatory. His research focuses on economic policy and performance at the regional, national and supranational levels, with emphasis on labour markets, economic growth and the macroeconomy. His publications include articles in *Oxford Economic Papers*, the *British Journal of Industrial Relations*, the *Journal of Regional Science*, *Regional Studies* and others. He is currently a member of the Minimum Wage Committee of Greece.

Francesco Paolo Mongelli is Senior Adviser in the Directorate Monetary Policy at the ECB and Honorary Professor at the Johann Wolfgang Goethe University of Frankfurt. He holds a BA in economics from the Free University for Social Studies (LUISS) in Rome and also a master's degree and a PhD in economics from the Johns Hopkins University in Baltimore. He has worked at the ECB since 1998. Prior to that, he spent several years as an economist at the International Monetary Fund in Washington. Mr Mongelli also teaches economics of monetary unions. His papers have been published in various outlets, including the *Journal of Money Credit and Banking*, the *Journal of Common Market Studies*, *Comparative Economic Studies*, *Economie Internationale*, *Bancaria* and the *Journal of Economic Integration*.

Fabian Mushövel is a Max Weber Fellow at the European University Institute. He completed his PhD at the European Institute and International Inequalities Institute, London School of Economics and Political Science. His research has been funded by the Leverhulme Trust and focuses on the political economy of inequality, the welfare state, labour markets and political reforms. He previously worked as a consultant for Chatham House and was a visiting scholar at the Department of Economics at the University of California, Berkeley, and the Department of Government at Harvard University.

Orkun Saka is an assistant professor in finance at the University of Sussex, a visiting fellow at the LSE and a research associate at the Systemic Risk Centre. His research revolves around financial crises and political economy of finance. He holds a PhD in finance from Cass Business School, City University of London, and an MSc (finance) from LSE.

Alessio Terzi is an affiliate fellow at Bruegel. He has also worked for the macroeconomic forecasting unit of Directorate-General for Economic and Financial Affairs (DG ECFIN) of the European

Commission, the European Central Bank and BMI Research (Fitch Group), a country risk and forecasting firm in the city of London. He holds a bachelor's degree in international economics from Bocconi University and an MPA in economic policy from the London School of Economics. He is currently pursuing a PhD in political economy at the Hertie School of Governance in Berlin. Between 2016 and 2018, Alessio was a visiting Fulbright fellow at the Kennedy School of Government of Harvard University.

PETROS VARTHALITIS is a research officer in macroeconomics at the Economic and Social Research Institute (ESRI) and adjunct assistant professor at the Department of Economics at Trinity College Dublin. He works on the macromodelling at ESRI. His main academic research focus is on theoretical and applied macroeconomics. He has published papers on fiscal and monetary policy in dynamic stochastic general equilibrium (DSGE) models (open and closed economy), fiscal and currency unions, public and tax reforms and debt consolidation policies in international academic journals.

SEBASTIAN WEBER currently works at the International Monetary Fund, where he held positions in the Research, European and African departments. He holds a PhD and a master's in international economics from the Graduate Institute of International and Development Studies in Geneva and has previously studied politics and economics at the University of Cape Town and the University of Hamburg, where he obtained a BSc (Hons) in economics. His research mainly focuses on labour markets, monetary policy and international macroeconomics and finance.

Introduction

Since the financial crisis started in 2007–2008, many advanced economies have struggled to return to their precrisis growth path. Although the recovery in the United States was relatively rapid, Europe's wasn't. A sovereign debt crisis led to a double-dip recession in the euro area. Unemployment soared, particularly youth unemployment in the periphery countries, and private and public investment experienced an extremely slow and protracted recovery with its precrisis level still not being reached in many countries. The experience has also been uneven across Europe's core and periphery countries: from the form in which reforms were designed and implemented to the depth and speed of the recovery.

It has been incessantly repeated that structural reforms are key to the recovery. This view has been influential and led many countries into adopting structural reforms programmes. Although there seems to be wide agreement on structural reforms' potential positive effects on output, they have been captured to such an extent by politicians that a candid assessment is warranted. In the meantime, the research interest on reforms is fast growing among academics and much research work has been conducted.

The objective of this book is to put forward a comprehensive, detailed, yet critical assessment of the state of the art in this burgeoning literature. The book will cover most recent work related to economic impacts of structural reforms on growth (recovery), unemployment, investment, imbalances and inequality in the background of the 2007 financial crisis in Europe. This volume has a collection of chapters that show the progress made in this field: new theoretical framework, new data and new empirical methodologies. These are also discussed and illustrated by several case studies of countries that introduced significant reforms.

The book is divided in three main parts. The first part focuses on economic growth and structural reforms in Europe. Chapter 1 by

Comunale and Mongelli looks at a wide range of real, financial, monetary and institutional variables as possible factors behind fluctuations and differences in growth rates among euro area countries since 1990. When they split the European institutional integration in its main components, they observe a significantly positive role for financial and political integration in the long run.

What is the growth payoff from structural reforms? Chapter 2 by Terzi and Marrazzo quantifies the impact of wide-reaching reform packages implemented in twenty-three countries worldwide and then examines the role that reforms had in contributing to spark growth accelerations, i.e. positive up-breaks in growth patterns. They show that economic reforms can have an important impact on a country's growth rate but, often, they fail to deliver their benefits and, in some instances, they can even be detrimental. In achieving economic growth, there are no silver bullets. They advocate that economic reforms should be framed as an opportunity that, if appropriately tailored to country-specific needs and well implemented, could yield important benefits.

In Chapter 3, Égert uses the Organization for Economic Cooperation and Development's (OECD) newly created dataset Structural Policy Indicators Database for Economic Research (SPIDER) to study the impact of regulation and institutions on economic growth. Using a large sample of countries, he investigates the extent to which product and labour market regulations influence per capita income levels. His results indicate that more business-friendly product market regulations are associated with higher per capita income levels, while the effects from labour market regulation are much less precise.

The second part of the book focuses on the macroeconomic implications of reforms. Chapters 4 and 5 examine convergence and imbalances, Chapters 6 and 7 examine crises and fiscal sustainability and Chapters 8 and 9 look at the reform implications in terms of labour markets.

Chapter 4 by Abritti and Weber examine the effects of product and labour market regulations on adjustment to shocks and on long-term growth in a two-country currency union dynamic stochastic general equilibrium (DSGE) model with endogenous growth. They show that under symmetric shocks, heterogeneous regulation can cause persistent divergence of output and inflation, which is consistent with the disappointing productivity growth and inflation rates that some countries in the euro area have experienced. Chapter 5 by Hume focuses on macroeconomic imbalances in euro area. He uses a Bayesian Structural vector autoregression (VAR) model to assess the feasibility of managing macroeconomic imbalances in the euro area focusing on four macroeconomic policy tools: fiscal policy, macroprudential policy, product market structural reforms and labour market reforms. One of the more striking conclusions of this chapter is that once macroeconomic imbalances have emerged, the introduction of product and labour market structural reforms is unlikely to help to restore equilibrium. This is especially the case for labour market structural reforms, which may even run the risk of making preexisting macroeconomic imbalances worse.

Saka et al. in Chapter 6 study the effects of financial crises as a determinant of reforms. Using a comprehensive dataset on financial liberalization over a large sample of countries from 1973 to 2015 and difference-in-differences and local projection estimations, they formally test the crises-beget-reforms hypothesis for the member states of the European Union (EU) as well as for a global sample. For the global (but not for the EU) sample, they find governments react to crises by reducing the degree of liberalization in financial markets. Yet, in a dynamic setting with impulse responses, they show that such interventions are only temporary and the liberalization process restarts after a financial crisis to reach its precrisis level after five to ten years. In Chapter 7, Furceri and Jalles examine the effect of structural reforms (domestic and external finance, trade and product market) on public debt again using the local projection method for a large sample of advanced and developing countries between 1973 and 2003. The results suggest that over the medium term, reforms contribute to lower the debt-to-GDP ratio, but this effect depends crucially on the initial debt-to-GDP ratio at the time of the reform.

These are followed by two chapters focusing on labour markets. In Chapter 8, Macchiarelli et al. study the role of structural reforms in speeding up transitions (across three key labour market statuses of employment, unemployment and inactivity) in the EU labour market before and after the crisis. Using EU–Labour Force Survey (EU-LFS) data over the period 2004–2016, they construct country-specific measures of transition rates and a synthetic index of mobility that allows comparisons across countries over time. They examine how country-specific patterns relate to key institutional characteristics, both microeconomic (e.g., employment protection legislation) and macropolitical (e.g., welfare regimes) and how this evolved over time since the crisis. Chapter 9 by Martelli et al. focuses on the complementarity between labour market regulation and tax reforms in terms of employment. They use a dynamic model of employment growth for a yearly panel of EU countries from 1990 to 2015 and show reform complementarity between labour market regulation and taxation through substantial and significant interaction effects. Thus, labour market reforms have enhanced positive effects on employment when they occur simultaneously with reductions of the wage wedge.

The third part of the book contains a series of case studies covering six different countries. Chapter 10 examines early product and labour market reforms in Denmark, France, Greece and Portugal. Chapter 11 studies fiscal consolidation and inequality in Greece and Portugal. Chapter 12 examines trade reforms in Ireland, while Chapter 13 focuses on labor market reforms in Hungary.

In Chapter 10, Saka et al. use the synthetic counterfactual method to study the largest early labour market reforms in Denmark, France, Greece and Portugal. They find that these early reforms generally have a negative (or at least nonpositive) relationship to several macro variables including economic growth and inequality. They conclude that reforms, especially when introduced all at once as a big bang, do not seem to produce the intended results on economic growth. This chapter comes to the important conclusion that structural reforms are not good predictors of subsequent changes in economic growth and inequality. In Chapter 11, Mushövel studies the effects of fiscal consolidation reforms on income inequality. While the previous literature suggests that phases of fiscal consolidation correlate with increases in inequality levels, he finds that this was not the case in Greece and Portugal. Examining the Greek and Portuguese programmes, he finds strikingly that inequality outcomes were very different in these two counties. In the case of Greece, the Troika-steered austerity programmes were accompanied by a redistribution towards the lowest income decile, while in Portugal these programmes seemed to have led to a redistribution to the middle classes. Again, it appears that similar structural reforms programmes can have very different effects, in this case on income inequality.

McQuinn and Varthalitis in Chapter 12 study how trade liberalization had a transformative effect in the Irish economy. Focusing on the postcrisis period from 2008 to 2014, they examine whether the recovery was due to the successful adoption of structural reforms in labour and product markets or whether the improved performance was due to a rebalancing of the Irish economy. The rebalancing they study was the move away from the disproportionate influence of the construction sector (nontradable) in the run-up to the crisis and back towards the more productive tradable sector. They offer evidence supporting the latter. Their results suggest that the financial crisis acted as a rebalancing mechanism for the Irish economy, with the tradable sector contracting less and recovering quicker than the nontradable sector. They conclude that the Irish recovery was mostly export driven, with structural reforms playing a minor role in the immediate period after the crisis. In Chapter 13, Campos investigates structural labour market reforms in Hungary from 1986 to 2016, a period encompassing the collapse of the Soviet Union, EU accession in 2004 and the global financial crisis. Using the narrative approach, he identifies three major structural reforms: in 1992 and in 2002 aimed at increasing and the one 2012 at decreasing employment protection. He studies the effects of these reforms using a unique micro dataset and finds that over 1986–2016 the skill premium almost doubled, the gender wage gap declined by two-thirds and gender discrimination practically halved. The conclusions of the book by Campos, De Grauwe and Ji distil the main lessons from these various chapters.

This book would not have come about without the intellectual inputs from our contributors who attended our workshop on 11 May 2018 in London. We would like to thank Wendy Carlin for her stimulating keynote speech, and all the other participants of the workshop for the new ideas and interesting discussions they brought. We are grateful to the organizational support of the workshop from the European Institute at the London School of Economics. We also would like to thank the superb research assistance and suggestions from Nicolas Andreoulis and Michael Ganslmeier, Angelo Martelli and Orkun Saka. Finally, we would also like to thank the UK Economic and Social Research Council for its financial support under research grant ES/P000274/1.

PART I

Economic Growth and Structural Reforms in Europe

1 *Euro Area Growth and European Institutional Reforms*

MARIAROSARIA COMUNALE AND
FRANCESCO PAOLO MONGELLI

1.1 Introduction

Over the last three decades, euro area (EA) countries have experienced profound economic, financial and institutional changes, as well as diverse shocks.[1] This is the period with the run-up to the launch of the euro, and the initial twenty years with the single currency. Gross domestic product (GDP) growth has been very volatile and uneven across countries. Which factors played a role in stirring growth and/or reducing it? We assemble a large set of real, financial, monetary and institutional variables covering the period between 1990Q1 and 2016Q4 for euro area countries. Each of these blocks contains diverse variables. Our goal is to investigate which played a role and at which frequency. This is a novelty in the growth literature, which normally focuses on determinants largely based on the classic Solow exogenous growth model (Solow, 1956) or on the endogenous growth theory pioneered by Romer (1990). Our aim and main contribution is to provide an atheoretical toolkit looking at the 'usual suspects' in the policy debate, which are also rather 'unusual' in the academic literature, as possible factors behind fluctuations and differences in growth rates among euro area countries since 1990.

We focus on euro area countries because they were bound by the process of European economic and monetary integration that started in the 1970s; experienced nominal convergence along the Maastricht convergence criteria; and have shared a single currency and monetary

[1] The views expressed in this chapter are those of the authors and not necessarily those of the institutions with which they are or have been affiliated. We are very thankful to Katrin Assenmacher, Matteo Ciccarelli, Istvan Szekely, Manfred Kremer, Nauro Campos, Paul De Grauwe, and the participants to the 2018 workshop 'European Integration and Structural Reforms' at the London School of Economics and the participants at the seminar at the European Central Bank (ECB) and at the Oesterreichische Nationalbank for their comments and suggestions.

policy, and faced the same nominal exchange rate since 1999. Upon the launch of the euro, money markets and sovereign bond markets rapidly converged. Thus, several forces narrowed differences across countries, i.e., a catching-up process. Or, to be more precise, a three-layered economic, financial and institutional convergence process.

At the same time, euro area countries have also experienced diverse shocks: some slow moving and some fast, some exogenous and some endogenous to the euro area. At the risk of oversimplifying, since 1990 we have witnessed, among others, the last nominal exchange rate gyrations during 1992–1993; the burst of the Dot-Com Bubble and September 11; the great Moderation and a broad financial cycle spurred by globalization, financial innovation and securitization; the financial turmoil starting in August 2007; and the Global Financial Crisis starting in September 2008 followed by the Great Recession. The latter episode spread around the world exacerbating euro area imbalances that contributed to the Sovereign Debt Crisis (SDC) of the euro area (May 2010).[2] Breakup risks were acute until summer 2012 and the announcement of outright monetary transactions (OMT) in September 2012. This followed a period of low inflation with risks of deflation.

During this prolonged and mutating crisis, the European Central Bank (ECB) implemented exceptional standard and nonstandard monetary policies (already since the start in August 2007). Moreover, there were institutional reforms throughout the crisis, and we witnessed an enhanced pace of structural reforms. Structural reforms support steady growth by increasing price and wage flexibility and by supporting the swift reallocation of resources within and across sectors and countries and, more generally, by encouraging innovation. Institutional reforms improve the governance and steady convergence. Thus all reforms strengthen resilience. Hence, what do we see in terms of growth dynamic over the last three decades? Which are the different dynamics in growth's *variance*? Which factors played a role in stirring growth and/or reducing it? Were they real, financial, monetary and/or institutional? For now, ours is a broad-brush detective story.

[2] There was a lack of financial backstops for sovereigns and banks. The incompleteness of the Economic and Monetary Union (EMU)'s architecture and governance emerged. For an account of the factors underlying the SDC of the euro area crisis and the contagion, see Mongelli (2013).

The different growth rates across the considered period (1990–2016) are clearly shown in both our nine considered member states (Figure 1.1)[3] and it is even more so for the entire euro area (this includes new member states). Not only growth rates are heterogeneous across countries, but also they differ depending on the time subsamples, i.e., until 1999 (launch of the euro), before the Global Financial Crisis (GFC) in 2008 and before/after the SDC in the second half of 2010.

We also look at two subgroups, defined in a very simple way as the euro area 'core' (Belgium, Germany, Finland, France, Luxembourg, Netherlands) and 'periphery' (Spain, Italy, Portugal).[4] The core countries had high growth rates before the launch of the euro. This is especially true for Finland in the 1990s, in which the country changed trade partners and most of its industrial policies after the collapse of the USSR. From the mid-2000s, Germany has experienced the most rapid increase in GDP, thanks to many structural reforms under Schröder's government period. Later on, the euro area core recovered faster and then stabilized at around 2 per cent. Luxembourg is instead an outlier, having a very volatile and generally higher GDP growth over the period. Within the periphery group, Italy has a stagnating GDP growth since the beginning of the 1990s and the weakest recovery after the GFC and sovereign crisis (Papadia, 2017). Spain, on the other hand, had a boom period lasting a decade, from the mid-1990s to mid-2000s, fuelled by reforms and an increase in the magnitude of the credit cycle (Comunale, 2017b).

[3] The countries are Belgium, Germany, Spain, Finland, France, Italy, Luxembourg, the Netherlands and Portugal. The reason is that we rely on the database from the European System of Central Banks (ESCB) Working Group on Economic Remodelling (WGEM) on real and financial cycles (ECB WGEM Team on Real and Financial Cycles, 2018), based on ECB, Bank for International Settlements (BIS) and national data sources. The data for the other euro area countries are either not included in this database – e.g., Austria and Ireland – or have very limited time dimension (Greece and new member states).

[4] This subsampling includes in the core more countries than the seminal paper by Bayoumi and Eichengreen (1993), following the idea of two groups' members somehow changing over time (see Campos and Macchiarelli, 2018). Our subgroups refer indeed to country performances after the global financial crisis and the sovereign debt crisis. This can be also described as member states with high versus low spreads or ratings. As a robustness check, we also provided a different splitting based on high versus low growth volatility. The differences between the groups in the latter case are not significant (see the robustness check).

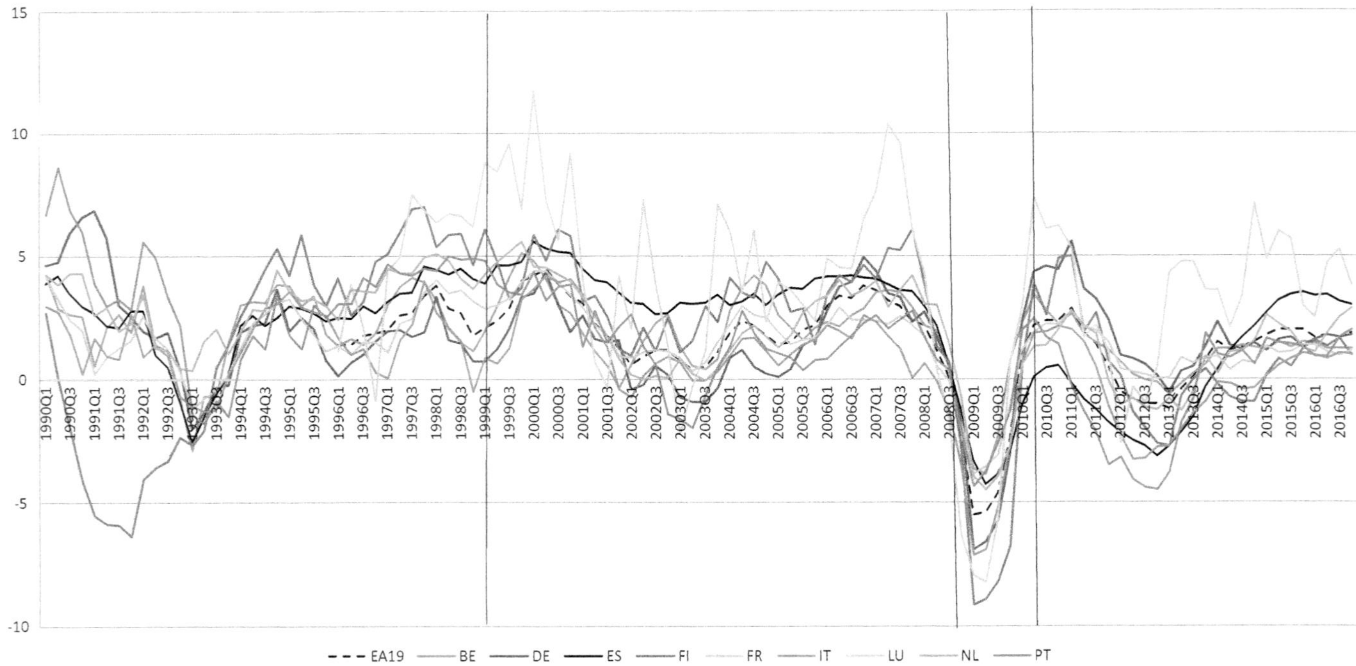

Figure 1.1 Growth rates of euro area countries and EA 19.
Note: These are the real growth rates compared to the same quarter of previous year.

Overall, the drop-in growth for the periphery was less substantial during 2008–2009. Only after 2014 we can see a further increasing growth trend for periphery as well. We expect, therefore, differences in the changes of growth rates and in their volatilities over time. Not only the growth rates themselves performed differently, but we can see also specific paths in the second moments. Finland and Luxembourg experienced the higher volatilities, especially before the introduction of the euro, and this is in line with the findings shown in Figure 1.1. France, Italy and Belgium seem more stable. The largest volatilities are found if we include the Global Financial Crisis (2008Q3–2013Q4), as expected.

Given these heterogeneities, we provide an atheoretical tool to track them among euro area countries trying to look at 'usual suspects' in the policy debate. Our study is clearly at the intersection of a rich literature on growth models as well as the determinants of real convergence and heterogeneity in the euro area, as also recently analysed in Alcidi et al. (2018) and Diaz del Hoyo et al. (2017). We make use of several techniques to select the relevant factors, which may have influenced growth based on the events and situations previously mentioned. The Weighted-Average Least Squares (WALS) is a statistical method by Magnus et al. (2010) and Magnus and De Luca (2016) that provides us with clues about the variables to select. Then we apply a heterogeneous panel Error Correction Model (ECM) to quantify their contributions to growth in the short and long run.[5]

The main outcomes stress the important positive role for long-run growth of institutional reforms at the EU level overall and for the periphery in specific, and it is a robust result across specifications and setups. If we split our institutional index in its main components, we can see a big and significant positive role for financial and political integration, while economic and financial integration are ineffective in boosting growth. A deeper financial integration seems to have beneficial effects on the core only, while such integration is not significant in the periphery. The opposite holds for political integration, as an increase in the latter boosts long-run growth only for the periphery of the euro area.

[5] A panel Vector Autoregression (VAR) model and country-by-country VARs for a subset of determinants, to count for endogeneities and transmissions, are also provided in the companion working paper by Comunale and Mongelli (2019). We do not claim any causality here in the single equation setup.

As for the other factors taken into account, an improvement in competitiveness seems to matter for growth in the euro area in the long run as well as a decline in sovereign and systemic stress. A decrease in systemic stress matters even more for growth. The debt over GDP influences negatively growth for the periphery only in the short run. The equity price cycle affects positively GDP growth only precrisis and in the short run, while the loans to nonfinancial corporations (NFCs) had a positive impact for core in a longer perspective. An increase in global GDP is also positive for growth.

This chapter is organized as follows. Section 1.2 describes our set of data and the econometric setup. Section 1.3 shows the main results. Section 1.4 concludes.

1.2 Data Description and Econometric Analysis

1.2.1 Data

We consider several possible factors that may have influenced GDP growth in euro area countries in the short and in the long run. This analysis tries to include real, financial, monetary and institutional factors in order to explain GDP growth in the euro area, various subsamples as well as pre- and postcrisis. This section describes these variables, while more details are provided in a companion paper (Comunale and Mongelli, 2018).[6] The *real GDP growth* data for the countries as well as the real and financial cycles come from the database of the European System of Central Banks (ESCB) WGEM team (see ECB WGEM Team on Real and Financial Cycles, 2018).[7]

We firstly include our main variable of interest as a regressor: a *European Index of Regional Institutional Integration* (EURII), which maps developments in European integration for six euro area founding members on the basis of a monthly dataset from Dorrucci et al. (2015), extended to include 2016.[8] This index is common across all the countries, and it is time varying. This index represents a novelty in this type

[6] More details on data and also econometrics are available in Comunale and Mongelli (2019, forthcoming).

[7] Updating these series from the ESCB WGEM team is a complex exercise and would require the collaboration of all the national central banks involved in the team. This is the main reason why our panel data ends in 2016Q4.

[8] A concise explanation is in Dorrucci et al. (2015).

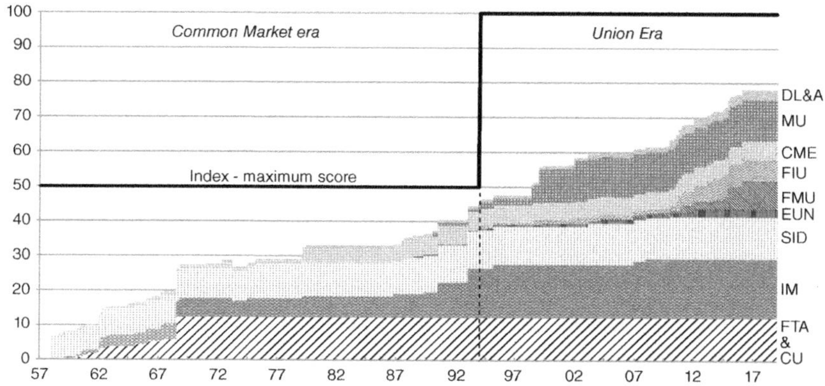

Figure 1.2 The EURII index.

Source: Authors' updated series from Dorrucci et al. (2015). Free trade area (FTA) and customs union (CU), internal market (IM), coordination of monetary and exchange rate policies (CME), supranational institutions and decision-making (SID), Economic Union (EUN), Financial Markets Union (FMU), Fiscal Union (FIU), Monetary Union (MU), democratic legitimacy and accountability (DL&A)

of studies (see Figure 1.2). The EURII index captures the path of institutional integration in Europe since the launch of the EU in 1958. We define two overarching periods. The first is the 'Common Market Era', from 1958 to 1993. During this overarching period, integration advanced along five stages (originally identified by Balassa, 1961, 1964). They are a free trade area and customs union; the gradual build-up of the European internal market; some degree of coordination of, for instance, exchange rate policies or monetary policies; and a number of institutions, laws and decision-making processes that can be defined – though to different degrees – as supranational in nature (such as the EU Parliament and Court of Justice). The second overarching period is the 'Union Era', which starts after 1993. This era has four main components, which are the economic union, the fiscal union, the financial union and the political union.[9] Conceptually, the Union Era became the centre of the European debate at the end of 2012, with the Four Presidents' Report and in 2015 with the Five Presidents' Report. These reports postulated the need to complement the monetary union with the other four unions. A maximum score of 50 is assigned to each of these eras, with the index starting at 0 on 1 January 1958 (when the

[9] A check by using these four components separately is also provided.

Treaty of Rome entered into force) and then making progress up to the current cumulated value of slightly above 76 as of 1 January 2015. The gap between 100 – i.e., the maximum total score that would be assigned in the index if all objectives of the Common Market and Union eras were fully accomplished – and the current total score gives an indication of the distance still to be covered until a 'new perceived steady state' is achieved in the process of integration. The EURII index exhibits a discontinuity in the integration process that was implied by the start of stage two of EMU in 1994. That is when the nature of institutional integration profoundly changed in the EU/euro area. In our sample, we start from the period just before the latter (starting in 1990) until 2016.

Then we include other possible factors that can affect growth. For the *financial variables,* we use several measures of the financial cycle based on credit, house prices and equity prices. We also make use of a new set of within-country synchronicity indices between real and financial cycles from Comunale (2017b). Each index results in a value of either 1 or –1, where 1 means that the cycles are perfectly synchronized at time *t,* and therefore they have the same sign (either positive or negative). In the set of *real variables*, we include fiscal variables, such as (seasonally adjusted) fiscal deficit and debt over GDP, and a proxy for price competitiveness represented by the growth rate of the real effective exchange rate (REER) vis-à-vis forty-one partners and deflated by the Consumer Price Index (CPI). Lastly, we make use of global GDP growth in the robustness checks, to look at possible global/spillover effects on growth in the euro area countries. For the *monetary factor*, with the ECB policy rate constrained by the zero-lower bound (ZLB) over a significant portion of the sample under investigation, we use shadow interest rates of Wu and Xia (2016) to represent both conventional and unconventional monetary policy actions.[10] We include indicators for *sovereign and systemic stress*, especially important for the last ten years of data. We have the country-specific Composite

[10] We decided to apply the specific Wu and Xia (2016) shadow rate because it has been already widely used in the literature and it is constantly updated. Moreover, if we use a simple VAR with GDP and inflation adding several different shadow rates, the results of the transmissions are very much alike. Results based on shadow rates series described in Comunale and Striaukas (2017). The results are available on request. There are other shadow rates or methods used in the literature in order to capture the unconventional monetary policy phase. However, all have pros and cons, and there is no consensus on the best to be used (see once more Comunale and Striaukas, 2017).

Indicator of Sovereign Stress (SOVCISS)[11] and the common Composite Indicator of Systemic Stress (CISS) as computed by Holló at al. (2012).

1.2.2 Selection of Variables and Econometric Analysis

Given our atheoretical approach to the analysis, we first test for the relevance of each of our regressors in explaining GDP growth (over the short and long term). We use methods that combine information taken from parameters of each model using weighted average of conditional estimates. This incorporates the uncertainty we have of models and of estimations together. We apply as a preferred way to do so the WALS method by Magnus et al. (2010) and Magnus and De Luca (2016). This is a more flexible approach and reduces the computational burden compared to other methods, especially when we include synchronicity indices. This method combines Bayesian weights with frequentist, i.e., (constraint) least squares, estimations. Thereafter, the Bayesian Model Averaging (BMA) method, which relies fully on Bayesian weights and estimates, has been applied as a robustness check.

Summing up (Table 1.1), by means of what overlaps in the WALS and the BMA techniques, we can have some robust factors that need to be added as regressors: debt over GDP, CISS and SOVCISS, REER growth, the EURII and shadow rates. Among the cycles, we will add the cycles for house prices and loan to NFCs and lastly one representative for synchronicity, i.e., the one between long-term rates and loan to households.[12] This is our baseline setup. Our alternative baseline is without the synchronicity measure, which is not captured in BMA. This results in an especially robust set of factors, which is in line with the findings in Magnus et al. (2010). One clear cut is that, by using either of these techniques, the fiscal deficit should not be included and only some specific financial cycles.

In order to select the most proper empirical setup for the estimations, we tested for cross-sectional dependence (CSD), nonstationarity and

[11] See Garcia-de-Andoain and Kremer (2017) for more details.

[12] If we do not include the lagged GDP growth, we find that other synchronicity indices could be also one of the factors to take into account. Among the cycles, the business cycle seems to capture what was given by the lagged GDP growth in the previous specification. More checks are available in Comunale and Mongelli (2019, forthcoming).

Table 1.1 *Comparison and selection of baseline.*

	BMA		WALS	
	Posterior inclusion probability	Posterior inclusion probability	*t*-values	*t*-values
L.GDP growth	1.0		20.45	
Fiscal deficit	0.1	0.1	−0.91	0.79
Debt/GDP	0.9	1.0	−3.73	−6.64
REER growth	1.0	1.0	−5.52	−5.32
CISS	1.0	1.0	−5.49	−2.39
SOVCISS	0.2	1.0	−1.99	−3.83
Shadow rates	0.1	1.0	2.11	7.34
EURII institutional index	0.1	1.0	2.33	8.15
Equity price cycle	0.8	0.1	1.66	1.30
Long-term rates cycle	0.1	0.2	−0.59	−1.05
Real GDP cycle	0.1	1.0	0.31	3.62
Credit to households cycle	0.1	0.1	0.88	−0.83
Credit to NFCs cycle	0.1	1.0	−2.04	−4.33
Property price cycle	0.2	1.0	2.23	3.82
Total credit to private sector cycle	0.1	0.1	−1.19	−2.18
Synchronicity: long-term rates and credit to households cycles	0.1	0.0	−1.76	−1.02
Synchronicity: long-term rates and credit to NFCs cycles	0.1	0.1	1.62	−0.02

Note: The cycles are based on data from real GDP (YER), equity price indices (EQP), real total credit to private nonfinancial sector (TCN), real credit to nonfinancial corporations (LNF), real credit to households (LHH), property prices (RPP) and nominal long-term rates (LTN). The synchronicities are based on a cycle's pairs. In case of WALS, only *t*-values greater than 1.5 in absolute terms are included (dark grey). The light grey areas for the WALS only indicate *t*-values greater than 1.0 (but smaller than 1.5), as in the literature. For BMA, we include only regressors for which the posterior inclusion probability (pip) is minimum 0.8 (dark grey); instead, in light grey we have the minimum pip equal 0.5, as in the literature.[13]

[13] As reported by Magnus et al. (2010), we can consider as a rough guideline for 'robustness' of a regressor if it does have a value posterior inclusion probability

also cointegration, finding that our dynamic panel experiences all of these. On the basis of these findings, we reparametrized our single equation setup from an Autoregressive Distributed Lag (ARDL) form (Equation 1.1) into a panel error correction model (PECM), as shown in Equation (1.2)[14]. Another reason for the choice of the PECM is also that this framework allows us to study both the short-term and the long-term influence of factors on growth. In this case, the estimators we can use are three, namely the Mean Group (MG), the Pooled Mean Group (PMG) and the Dynamic Fixed Effects (DFE). The MG estimator is the only one that gives heterogeneous coefficients in both the short- and long-run analysis, and we decide to use it to keep the information coming from the heterogeneity of our sample.

$$GDPG_{i,t} = \beta_{1i} GDPG_{i,t-1} + \beta_{2i} X_{i,t} + \varepsilon_{i,t} \tag{1.1}$$

$$\Delta GDPG_{i,t} = \phi_i \left(GDPG_{i,t-1} - \theta'_{0i} - \theta'_{1i} X_{i,t-1} \right) + \delta'^{*}_{11i} \Delta X_{i,t} + \mu_i + \varepsilon_{i,t} \tag{1.2}$$

The coefficients θ capture the long-run effects, while the coefficients δ correspond to the impact of the variables in the short run. The X is the vector of the factors taken into account. Lastly, ϕ_i represents the error correcting speed of adjustment term. This parameter is expected to be significantly negative and signals that the variables show a return to a long-run equilibrium (Blackburne and Frank, 2007).

1.3 Results

1.3.1 Main Results

The comparison between the two baselines by using the ECM and with or without the synchronicity between real GDP and equity prices is in

(pip) of 0.5 (Raftery, 1995) in the BMA, corresponding approximately with an absolute t-ratio of abs(t) = 1 (Masanjala and Papageorgiou, 2008) for instance in WALS. Initially, we opt for a more restrictive case for BMA, adding only regressors for which the pip is close to one (minimum of 0.8). If pip is exactly equal to one, the regressor needs to be included by probability one. In case of WALS, only t-values greater than 1.5 in absolute terms are included.

14 A panel VAR and country-by-country VARs for a subset of determinants, to count for endogeneities and transmissions, are also provided in the companion working paper by Comunale and Mongelli (2019, forthcoming). We do not claim any causality here in the single equation setup.

Table 1.2. We also look at two subgroups (Table 1.3), defined as euro area 'core' (BE, DE, FI, FR, LU, NL) and 'periphery' (ES, IT, PT) and if the difference in the coefficients is significantly nonzero[15].

The key outcome of our analysis is the important positive role for long-run growth of the European Index of Regional Institutional Integration before and after the crisis and above all the positive impact on the periphery overall. This finding is very robust across specifications including a panel VAR.[16] This is in line with the literature showing that countries with stronger institutions (see Acemoglu et al., 2005, among others) grow faster in the long run than their counterparts. Moreover, our finding confirms the results coming from studies on the positive long-run effect of economic integration on growth (Henrekson et al., 1997). In the short run, instead, we do see a negative impact only prior to the crisis. We only look at the cumulative index for EURII in the baseline reported in Table 1.2 and 1.3, but we also run a specification in which the four main components of EURII, namely the economic integration, the fiscal integration, the financial integration, and the political integration, are taken into account separately. As shown in Table 1.4, we also provide the split in core and periphery.

An interesting narrative comes out from the different EURII components and the difference between core and periphery.[17] For the full EA sample, we can see a big and significant positive role for financial and political integration, while economic and financial integration are ineffective in boosting growth. In the short run, we do not see any positive outcomes coming from the components, and even the political integration seems to affect growth negatively in the very short run.

[15] The results for the data until 2010Q1 (the European sovereign debt crisis) are available in Comunale and Mongelli (2019, forthcoming). In this case, we did not split the samples into core and periphery because we have too few observations. The results for the data until 2008Q3 are available on request. In a nutshell, the factors seem to matter mostly only in the short run, and equity prices and competitiveness are key. The sample from 2010Q2 to 2016Q4 also lack of degree of freedom in the time series to perform an error correction model in a proper way, so we compare the precrisis rather with the entire sample.

[16] In a nutshell, in the VAR analysis, we find that the European Index of Regional Institutional Integration has a negative impact on growth only in the short run (up to one year), while in the long run it is always positive and significant. Interestingly, in Spain and Portugal, we don't see any negative impact in the short run of the institutional EU index, and the long-run positive impact is bigger in magnitude and far more persistent over time.

[17] The main findings from the other factors are confirmed in this specification.

Table 1.2 *Baseline results for the whole sample.*

	Short run	Long run
Error correction term	−0.501***	
	(0.052)	
EURII institutional index	**0.058**	**0.523*****
	(0.141)	**(0.121)**
Debt/GDP	−0.069**	−0.039
	(0.0323)	(0.081)
CISS	0.028	−0.070
	(0.020)	(0.049)
SOVCISS	0.041***	−0.037
	(0.011)	(0.042)
REER growth	0.088	−0.509***
	(0.096)	(0.121)
Short-term rates and shadow rates	0.057	1.098**
	(0.163)	(0.446)
Equity prices cycle	0.061	−0.011
	(0.046)	(0.017)
House prices cycle	0.413*	0.160
	(0.226)	(0.223)
Credit to NFCs cycle	−0.108	0.239*
	(0.307)	(0.133)
Synchronicity credit households (HH) and rates	2.73e-05	−0.002
	(0.000)	(0.001)
Constant	−0.137**	
	(0.066)	
Observations	535	535

Notes: Standard errors in parentheses. The EURII index is in bold. *** $p < 0.01$, ** $p < 0.05$, * $p < 0.1$. The cycles are based on data from real GDP (YER), equity price indices (EQP), real total credit to private nonfinancial sector (TCN), real credit to nonfinancial corporations (LNF), real credit to households (LHH), property prices (RPP) and nominal long-term rates (LTN). The synchronicities are based on the cycle's pairs.

Looking instead at the subsample of core and periphery, the latter result holds, but what is good noting in the short run is the opposite sign for the economic integration. While it is strongly positive for the periphery, it goes negative for the core. In the short run, we can also see

Table 1.3 *Baseline results for core and periphery.*

	Core	Periphery	Core	Periphery
	Short run	Short run	Long run	Long run
Error correction term	–0.581***	–0.341***		
	(0.049)	(0.034)		
EURII institutional index	**0.088**	**–0.002**	**0.442*****	**0.684****
	(0.216)	**(0.037)**	**(0.115)**	**(0.300)**
Debt/GDP	–0.077	–0.053*	-0.050	–0.015
	(0.048)	(0.027)	(0.123)	(0.048)
CISS	0.037	0.010***	–0.061	–0.087***
	(0.031)	(0.001)	(0.075)	(0.025)
SOVCISS	0.048***	0.027***	-0.003	–0.106*
	(0.017)	(0.002)	(0.053)	(0.058)
REER growth	0.140	–0.015	–0.431***	–0.665***
	(0.134)	(0.116)	(0.136)	(0.254)
ST rates and shadow rates	0.067	0.037	1.072*	1.150**
	(0.244)	(0.146)	(0.642)	(0.569)
Equity prices cycle	0.069	0.045	–0.009	–0.014
	(0.069)	(0.033)	(0.021)	(0.036)

House prices cycle	0.452	0.336	0.166	0.148
	(0.334)	(0.231)	(0.340)	(0.127)
Credit to NFCs cycle	0.0775	–0.479	0.255**	0.209
	(0.378)	(0.558)	(0.112)	(0.384)
Synchronicity credit HH and rates	0.000	–0.000	–0.004*	0.001
	(0.001)	(0.001)	(0.002)	(0.003)
Constant	–0.145	–0.123**		
	(0.099)	(0.050)		
Observations	357	178	357	178

Notes: Standard errors in parentheses. The EURII index is in bold. *** $p < 0.01$, ** $p < 0.05$, * $p < 0.1$. The cycles are based on data from YER, EQP, TCN, LNF, LHH, RPP and LTN. The synchronicities are based on the cycle's pairs.

Table 1.4 *Results with separated EURII components.*

	EA countries	Core	Periphery	EA countries	Core	Periphery
Variables	Short run	Short run	Short run	Long run	Long run	Long run
Error correction term	−0.542***	−0.642***	−0.343***			
	(0.0731)	(0.0827)	(0.00353)			
Financial integration	−0.0352	0.129	−0.363***	1.322***	1.239*	1.489
	(0.204)	(0.289)	(0.0537)	(0.509)	(0.641)	(1.017)
Economic integration	−0.125	−0.432**	0.489***	−0.326	0.209	−1.397
	(0.202)	(0.192)	(0.152)	(0.550)	(0.527)	(1.175)
Fiscal integration	−0.0743	−0.233	0.244***	0.541	0.490	0.644
	(0.162)	(0.216)	(0.0836)	(0.414)	(0.433)	(1.055)
Political integration	−2.483**	−3.052**	−1.347*	2.749**	1.822	4.603*
	(1.034)	(1.504)	(0.745)	(1.308)	(1.570)	(2.374)
Debt/GDP	−0.0693*	−0.0806	−0.0468	0.0280	0.0413	0.00136
	(0.0415)	(0.0621)	(0.0318)	(0.128)	(0.191)	(0.118)
CISS	0.00912	0.00819	0.0110***	−0.0254	−0.000411	−0.0754***
	(0.0194)	(0.0301)	(0.00299)	(0.0510)	(0.0766)	(0.00722)
SOVCISS	0.0447**	0.0537*	0.0267**	−0.0759	−0.0519	−0.124**

	(0.0191)	(0.0283)	(0.0114)	(0.0490)	(0.0699)	(0.0514)
REER growth	0.0996	0.167	–0.0348	–0.291*	–0.220	–0.432*
	(0.128)	(0.187)	(0.0878)	(0.169)	(0.236)	(0.221)
ST rates and shadow rates	–0.561*	–0.804*	–0.0753	1.883***	2.244***	1.161*
	(0.304)	(0.429)	(0.102)	(0.532)	(0.726)	(0.606)
Equity prices cycle	0.112**	0.136*	0.0641	–0.0218	–0.0247	–0.0160
	(0.0566)	(0.0803)	(0.0670)	(0.0254)	(0.0365)	(0.0323)
House prices cycle	0.611	0.979*	–0.125	0.0599	0.0186	0.143
	(0.446)	(0.584)	(0.527)	(0.233)	(0.351)	(0.169)
Credit to NFCs cycle	–0.0397	0.0508	–0.221	0.447**	0.562*	0.218
	(0.283)	(0.425)	(0.181)	(0.218)	(0.309)	(0.233)
Synchronicity credit HH and rates	0.00156*	0.00224**	0.000198	–0.00604***	–0.00746***	–0.00322
	(0.000822)	(0.00110)	(0.000837)	(0.00185)	(0.00239)	(0.00256)
Constant	–0.253***	–0.373***	–0.154*			
	(0.0905)	(0.102)	(0.0875)			
Observations	535	357	178	535	357	178

Note: Standard errors in parentheses. The grey shaded figures stress the different components of the EURII index when they are significant. *** $p < 0.01$, ** $p < 0.05$, * $p < 0.1$.

a positive effect of fiscal integration on periphery countries, which, however, does not translate to any long-run effects. For the long run, instead, a deeper financial integration seems to have beneficial effects on the core, while it is not significant in the periphery. The opposite holds for political integration, as an increase in the latter boosts long-run growth only for the core members of the euro area.

As for other factors, in the long run also an improvement in competitiveness seems to matter as well as a decline in sovereign and systemic stress.[18] The link between competitiveness and growth in the EU has been found in the literature, and our results are in line with these studies. It is good to stress that, as reported in Berg and Miao (2010), the REER is not a policy instrument, but mainly a result of policy actions and externalities. So, the direction of funding the appropriate, more productive sectors can increase competitiveness and then long-run growth (Comunale, 2017a).[19] The debt over GDP influences negatively growth for the periphery only in the short run (and this drives the same results for the entire sample) but the result is not significant when EURII components are used. This is somehow in line with the general empirical literature on the relationship between public debt and economic growth, which is far from being conclusive on this issue (Panizza and Presbitero, 2013, 2014, and Mika and Zumer, 2017). The equity price cycle affects positively GDP growth just pre-crisis, when some countries experienced a substantial increase in the magnitude of the positive side of the cycle. This affected growth only in the very short run, and it did not have a persistent effect on the overall performance. The loan to NFCs instead had a positive and robust role for growth in the long run for the core countries. This result may depend on how the funding has been used in the different economies, i.e., for more productive or less productive sectors. As reported in Hassan et al. (2017), the differences in the efficient allocations of funds

[18] An increase in REER and REER growth means a decrease in competitiveness and vice versa.

[19] Results of Gala and Lucinda (2006) and Rodrik (2008) indicate that a real depreciation, i.e., increase in competitiveness, is associated with higher GDP growth. Comunale (2017a) find that the REER misalignments associated with foreign capital inflows in the EU were a further cause of declining GDP, in a long-run perspective, while they played no role in the short run. Indeed, situations of protracted or recurrent REER misalignments have been associated with lower economic growth mostly over the medium and long run in the literature (Edwards and Savastano, 2000).

could have mattered. In Italy, the credit is allocated less efficiently than in France and Germany. Lastly, the monetary policy, proxied by the shadow rates,[20] has a very different impact in the short and long run, as well as pre- and postcrisis. The sign is as expected over the period, because monetary policy is set endogenously: when GDP rises, interest rates are set to go up. In fact, in the early part of the sample, GDP leads interest rates. Stagnation after the Great Recession gives the reason for the monetary policy stance to react to the situation. From the sovereign debt crisis, the transmission mechanism broke down and monetary policy has been most accommodating (to increasing degrees).[21]

1.4 Additional Robustness Checks

Having checked for the presence of CSD in our panel, we add, as a further determinant, a measure of global GDP growth.[22,23] The global GDP growth seems to positively spillover to euro area GDP growth in the short run. The main result is once again robust: the institutional index is crucial in the long run.

As a further check, we also added the fiscal deficit, to go deeper into the fiscal side of growth, which we expect to be crucial after the Sovereign Debt Crisis. The positive and significant role for the institutional index is here confirmed in almost all the checks. This gives a very robust factor that helps growth in the longer-run perspective. The fiscal deficit does not have a clear role on influencing growth in the short run, while we find a significant negative effect only in some cases in the long run.

[20] We use pre-1992 country-specific short-term interest rates and then the Euro Overnight Index Average (EONIA).

[21] There was a strong comovement between EONIA (in levels) and GDP growth before the rate reached the ZLB. Afterwards, a lower shadow rate signals a further use of unconventional monetary policy measures. This causes the coefficient to be positive and significant in the long run (or not significant after 2010), while in the short run, when we use the changes, we do experience a negative effect when the sample is split.

[22] We also check for the importance of global GDP growth with WALS, and this method confirmed that the variable could be indeed included. Results are available on request.

[23] A more complete way to deal with CSD would be using a dynamic factor model á la Pesaran and Tosetti (2011) instead of adding a global proxy. However, we cannot disentangle between short- and long-run effects, which are at the core of this work, in the dynamic factor models.

Lastly, we applied a different way to split the sample, not based on level of debt or sovereign stress (core vs. periphery), but rather on low vs. high volatilities of growth in the whole period. The first group is composed by Belgium, Germany, France, Italy and the Netherlands. The high growth volatility group includes the other four countries, namely Spain, Finland, Luxembourg and Portugal. With this alternative way of dividing the sample, the coefficients for the institutional index and REER growth are very similar and extremely robust in comparison to the baseline for the entire sample (Table 1.2). When we had core vs. periphery (Table 1.3), they mattered more for the latter group of countries. This means that institutional reforms at EU level and competitiveness may be more substantial factors in affecting growth for countries with higher debt or more affected by the sovereign crisis. SOVCISS, the country-specific index of stress in sovereign bond markets, has a negative impact on growth in the short run when growth volatility is high. However, it impacts negatively growth in the long run for countries with lower volatilities in GDP growth.

We thus calculated the contributions of each of the factors in determining changes in the growth rates during the years before 2010 and then from 2010 to 2016. These two periods are chosen to stress possible differences in the contribution between before and after the sovereign debt crisis and in order to have a clearer idea of the magnitudes. We do so by using the long-run coefficients (group-specific coefficients as in Table 1.3) multiplied by the difference in the factors in the considered period.[24] The REER growth has been recalculated here to the reader convenience and an increase means a better competitiveness performance. The results for the two periods, before 2010 and then from 2010 to 2016, are provided respectively in Figure 1.3 and 1.4.

The institutional factor is again the main one associated with higher GDP growth. The contribution is bigger in magnitude in the first period, given the major advancement in the Economic and Monetary Union (EMU) design from the 1990s to the 2000s; however, the positive contribution for increase in GDP growth is very evident also after the Sovereign Debt Crisis. For Spain, Italy and Portugal, both before and after 2010, the magnitude of the contribution of EURII to

[24] This is because the index is always equal to 1 or −1.

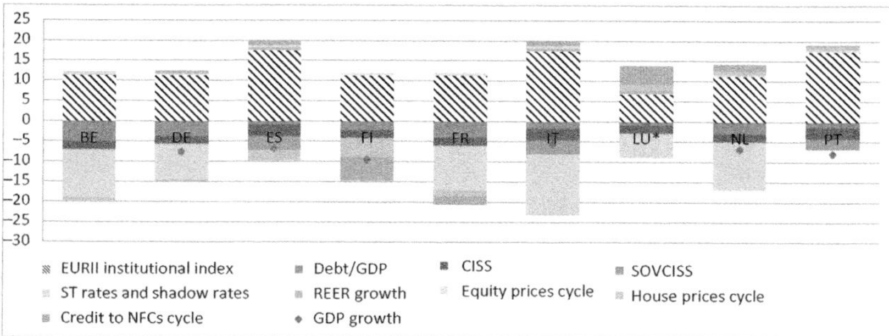

Figure 1.3 Factor analysis until 2010.

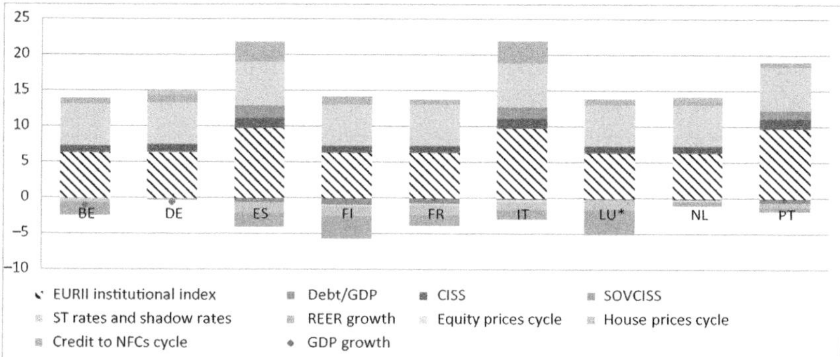

Figure 1.4 Factor analysis from 2010 to 2016.
Note: The data for Luxembourg (LU*) are only from 1996Q1.

growth is bigger compared to the core countries by 6pp before the GFC and by around 3pp afterwards.[25]

Ultimately, as for the other factors, from 2010 to 2016, we also see a decrease in the CISS, which captures systemic stress, and this has had a positive influence for growth. To a lesser extent, we see in 2016 a positive contribution to growth of a decrease in the sovereign stress indicator. We can see an increase in the important positive role of price competitiveness between 2010 and 2016. The role of cycles is mostly negative but small in relative terms. Lastly, the impact of the short-term interest rates could be somehow counterintuitive. This is because the coefficients are for the

[25] We use the different coefficients for the EURII for core and periphery (as in Table 1.3), but the overall index is the same across countries because it represents the common advancements in EU institutional integration.

whole period positive, and only after the ZLB a more accommodative monetary policy means a decrease in the shadow rate.[26]

1.5 Policy Conclusions

Over the last three decades, euro area countries have experienced profound economic, financial and institutional changes, plus diverse shocks. Growth has been volatile, and almost missing, in some countries. In this study, we have assembled a rich panel to find which factors played a more important role in stirring growth, and/or reducing it in the short vs. long term and pre- vs. postcrisis. After excluding several variables with no bearing on growth, we apply a series of time series techniques for large panels of heterogeneous data.

Our main findings are that further institutional integration at EU level supports long-run growth for all countries, and in particular in the periphery. This finding is robust across specifications and setups, a fact for which there might be diverse complementary explanations. One possible explanation might be a rising confidence in the evolving European governance and institutional framework. Another explanation might lie in a convergence of policy preferences and lesser policy activism, and greater financial stability (until the sovereign crisis!). The contribution is bigger in magnitude in the first period, given the major advancement in EMU design from the 1990s to the 2000s; however, the positive contribution for increase in GDP growth is evident also after the Sovereign Debt Crisis. If we split our institutional index in its components, we can see a big and significant positive role for financial and political integration, while economic and financial integration are ineffective in boosting growth. A deeper financial integration seems to have beneficial effects on the core only, but is not significant in the periphery. The opposite holds for political integration, as an increase in the latter boosts long-run growth only for the periphery.

We also find that an improvement in competitiveness matters for sustained growth in the long run. A decline in systemic stress is also associated with growth. An increase in global GDP is also positive for growth, generally in the medium run. The debt over GDP influences negatively growth for the periphery but only in the short run.[27] Surprisingly, the

[26] Again, for reader's convenience, the sign is here reversed in the analysis for 2010 onwards.

[27] This is less clear by using the VARs, and it is in line with the lack of consensus in the literature about the impact of public debt on economic growth.

deficit plays no role. Instead, higher sovereign stress is associated with lower growth. Prior to the zero-lower bound, higher monetary policy rates are associated with growth. These relations turn past the ZLB and when using the shadow rate that captures exceptional standard and nonstandard monetary policies. The equity price cycle affects positively GDP growth only precrisis and only in the very short run, while the loans to NFCs had a positive impact for the core euro area.

Our results need to be seen as preliminary. Correlations and associations are no causations. Evidence in this chapter needs to be corroborated by model-based analysis. We cover a very intense and mutating period in European economic, financial, monetary and institutional history. Hence, our findings should be refined in several directions. For most countries in the sample, there were switches in policy regimes. Hence, national paths matter. Future research might also consider the role of net contributions to the EU budget and the role of EU funds. We have not included this aspect because of a (still) limited availability of data. Similarly, we are especially constrained in reflecting the improved quality of the euro area governance that unfolded in recent years. A case in point is the launch of the Single Supervisory Mechanism (SSM), which brought a cleanup of bank balance sheets, better bank management and in fact coincides with rising credit growth (in combination with exceptional monetary policies).

References

Acemoglu, D., Johnson, S. and Robinson, J. A. (2005). 'Institutions as a Fundamental Cause of Long-Run Growth', *Handbook of Economic Growth*, in Philippe Aghion and Steven Durlauf (ed.), *Handbook of Economic Growth*, 1st ed., Vol. 1, chap. 6. Elsevier, pp. 385–472.

Aikman, D., Haldane, A. G. and Nelson, B. D. (2015). 'Curbing the Credit Cycle', *Economic Journal*, Vol. 125, pp. 1072–1109.

Aixala, J. and Fabro, G. (2008). 'Does the Impact of Institutional Quality on Economic Growth Depend on Initial Income Level?', *Economic Affairs*, Vol. 28, No. 3, pp. 45–49.

Alcidi C., Núñez Ferrer, J., Di Salvo, M., Musmeci, R. and Pilati, M. (2018). 'Income Convergence in the EU: A Tale of Two Speeds', CEPS Comments, January. www.ceps.eu/ceps-publications/income-convergence-eu-tale-two-speeds/.

Arbia, G., Battisti, M. and Di Vaio, G. (2010). 'Institutions and Geography: Empirical Test of Spatial Growth Models for European Regions', *Economic Modelling*, Vol. 27, No. 1, January, pp. 12–21.

Balassa, B. (1964). 'The Purchasing Power Parity Doctrine: A Reappraisal', *Journal of Political Economy*, Vol. 72, No. 6, pp. 584–596.

Balassa, R. (1961). *The Theory of Economic Integration*. Irwin.

Bayoumi, T. and Eichengreen, B. (1993). 'Shocking Aspects of European Monetary Integration', in F. Giavazzi and F. Torres (ed.), *Adjustment and Growth in the European Monetary Union*. Cambridge University Press, pp. 193–235.

Berg, A. and Miao, Y. (2010). 'The Real Exchange Rate and Growth Revisited: The Washington Consensus Strikes Back?' IMF Working Paper 10/58.

Blackburne III, E. F., and Frank, M. W. (2007). 'Estimation of Non-Stationary Heterogeneous Panels', *Stata Journal*, Vol. 7, No. 2, pp. 197–208.

Borio, C., Disyatat, P. and Juselius, M. (2017). 'Rethinking Potential Output: Embedding Information about the Financial Cycle', *Oxford Economic Papers*, Vol. 69, No. 3, July, pp. 655–677.

Buti, M. and Turrini, A. (2015). 'Three Waves of Convergence: Can Eurozone Countries Start Growing Together Again?', *Vox.EU*, 17 April.

Campos, N. and Macchiarelli, C. (2018). 'A History of the European Core and Its Periphery: How an Optimal Currency Area Forms', *Vox.EU*, 12 March.

Checherita-Westphal, C. and Rother, P. (2010). 'The Impact of High and Growing Government Debt on Economic Growth: An Empirical Investigation for the Euro Area', Working Paper Series 1237, European Central Bank.

Comunale, M. (2017a). 'Dutch Disease, Real Effective Exchange Rate Misalignments and Their Effect on GDP Growth in EU', *Journal of International Money and Finance*, Vol. 73, Part B, May, pp. 350–370.

(2017b). 'Synchronicity of Real and Financial Cycles and Structural Characteristics in EU Countries', Centre for Economic and International Studies (CEIS) Working Paper No. 414.

Comunale, M. and Mongelli, F. P. (2019). 'Who Did It? A European Detective Story Was it Real, Financial, Monetary and/or Institutional? Tracking Growth in the Euro Area with an Atheroretical Tool', Bank of Lithuania Working Paper Series.

Comunale, M. and Striaukas, J. (2017). 'Unconventional Monetary Policy: Interest Rates and Low Inflation. A Review of Literature and Methods',

Centre for Applied Macroeconomic Analysis (CAMA), Australian National University, WP Series 29/2017.

Crespo Cuaresma, J., Ritzberger-Grünwald, D. and Silgoner, M. A. (2008). 'Growth Convergence and EU Membership', *Applied Economics*, Vol. 40, No. 5, pp. 643–656.

Cristina, F. and Garcia Perea, P. (2015). 'The Impact of the Euro on Euro Area GDP per Capita', Banco de España Working Paper No. 1530.

De Luca, G. and Magnus, J. R. (2011). 'Bayesian Model Averaging and Weighted-Average Least Squares: Equivariance, Stability, and Numerical Issues', *Stata Journal*, StataCorp LP, Vol. 11, No. 4, December, pp. 518–544.

Diaz del Hoyo, J. L, Dorrucci, E., Ferdinand Heinz, F. and Muzikarova, S. (2017). 'Real Convergence in the Euro Area: A Long-Term Perspective', *Occasional Paper Series*, No. 203, ECB.

Dorrucci, E., Ioannou, D., Mongelli, F. and Terzi, A. (2015). 'The four unions "PIE" on the Monetary Union "CHERRY": A New Index of European Institutional Integration', *Occasional Paper Series*, No. 160, ECB.

Drehmann, M., Borio, C. and Tsatsaronis, K. (2012). Characterising the Financial Cycle: Don't Lose Sight of the Medium Term!', Bank for International Settlements, Working Paper No. 380.

ECB (2007). 'Determinants of Growth in the EU Member States of Central and Eastern Europe', *Monthly Bulletin*, May.

(2015a). 'Real Convergence in the Euro Area: Evidence, Theory and Policy Implications', *Economic Bulletin*, No. 5, pp. 30–45.

(2015b). 'Progress with Structural Reforms across the Euro Area and Their Possible Impacts', *Economic Bulletin*, No. 2, pp. 59–71.

(2016). 'Increasing Resilience and Long-Term Growth: The Importance of Sound Institutions and Economic Structures for Euro Area Countries and EMU', *Economic Bulletin*, No. 5, pp. 76–96.

(2017a). 'The Importance of Firm Heterogeneity for Competitiveness in the European Union', *Economic Bulletin*, No. 2, March, pp. 83–102.

(2017b). 'The Slowdown in Euro Area Productivity since the Crisis in a Global Context', *Economic Bulletin*, No. 3, May, pp. 47–67.

ECB WGEM Team on Real and Financial Cycles (2018). 'Real and Financial Cycles in EU Countries: Stylised Facts and Modelling Implications', *ECB Occasional Paper Series*, No. 205.

Edwards, S. and Savastano, M. (2000). 'Exchange Rates in Emerging Economies: What Do We Know? What Do We Need to Know?', in A. Krueger (ed.), *Economic Policy Reform: The Second Stage*. University of Chicago Press, pp. 453–510.

European Commission (2013). 'Catching-Up Processes in the Euro Area', *Quarterly Report on the Euro Area*, Vol. 12, No. 1, March, pp. 7–18.

(2014). 'The Drivers of Total Factor Productivity in Catching-Up Economies', *Quarterly Report on the Euro Area*, Vol. 13, No. 1, April, pp. 7–19.

Gala, P. and Lucinda, C. R. (2006). 'Exchange Rate Misalignment and Growth: Old and New Econometric Evidence', *Revista Economia*, vol.7, n.4, pp. 165–187, December 2006.

Garcia-de-Andoain, C. and Kremer, M. (2017). 'Beyond Spreads: Measuring Sovereign Market Stress in the Euro Area', *Economics Letters*, Vol. 159, October, pp. 153–156.

Gómez-Puig, M. and Sosvilla-Rivero, S. (2016). 'Debt-Growth Linkages in EMU across Countries and Time Horizons', Instituto Complutense de Estudios Internacionales, Universidad Complutense de Madrid, WP 02/16.

Han, X., Khan, H. and Zhuang, J. (2014). 'Do Governance Indicators Explain Development Performance? A Cross-Country Analysis', *Economics Working Paper Series*, No. 417, Asian Development Bank.

Hassan, F., di Mauro, F. and Ottaviano, G. I. P. (2017). 'Banks Credit and Productivity Growth', Working Paper Series 2008, European Central Bank.

Henrekson, M. , Torstensson, J. and Torstensson, R. (1997). 'Growth Effects of European Integration', *European Economic Review*, Vol. 41, No. 8, August, pp. 1537–1557.

Holló, D., Kremer, M. and Lo Duca, M. (2012). 'CISS – a Composite Indicator of Systemic Stress in the Financial System', Working Paper Series 1426, European Central Bank.

IMF (2017). 'Real Income Convergence in the Euro Area', Euro Area Policies, Selected Issues, *IMF Country Report*, No. 17/236, pp. 4–14.

Ivanov, V. and Kilian L. (2005). 'A Practitioner's Guide to Lag Order Selection for VAR Impulse Response Analysis', *Studies in Nonlinear Dynamics & Econometrics*, Vol. 9, No. 1, March, pp. 1–36.

Kempa, B. and Khan, N. S. (2017). 'Spillover Effects of Debt and Growth in the Euro Area: Evidence from a GVAR Model', *International Review of Economics & Finance*, Vol. 49, May, pp. 102–111.

Magnus, J. R. and De Luca, G. (2016). 'Weighted-Average Least Squares (WALS): A Survey', *Journal of Economic Surveys*, Vol. 30, pp. 117–148.

Magnus, J. R., Powell, O., and Präufer, P. (2010). 'A Comparison of Two Model Averaging Techniques with an Application to Growth Empirics', *Journal of Econometrics*, Vol. 154, pp. 139–153.

Masanjala, W. and Papageorgiou, C. (2008). 'Rough and Lonely Road to Prosperity: A Reexamination of the Sources of Growth in Africa Using

Bayesian Model Averaging', *Journal of Applied Econometrics*, Vol. 23, pp. 671–682.

Mauro, P. (1995). 'Corruption and Growth', *Quarterly Journal of Economics*, Vol. 110, No. 3, pp. 681–712.

Mika, A. and Zumer, T. (2017). 'Indebtedness in the EU: A Drag or a Catalyst for Growth?', Working Paper Series 2118, European Central Bank.

Milano, V. and Reichlin, P. (2017). 'Risk Sharing across the Euro Area: The Role of Public Institutions', *Vox.EU*, 23 January.

Mongelli, F. P. (2013). 'The Mutating Euro Area Crisis: Is the Balance between "Sceptics" and "Advocates" Shifting?', Occasional Paper Series 144, European Central Bank.

Owoundi, F. (2016). 'Do Exchange Rate Misalignments Really Affect Economic Growth? The Case of Sub-Saharan African Countries', *International Economics*, Vol. 145, No. C, pp. 92–110.

Panizza, H. and Presbitero, A. F. (2013). 'Public Debt and Economic Growth in Advanced Economies: A Survey', *Swiss Journal of Economics and Statistics*, Vol. 149, pp. 175–204.

(2014). 'Public Debt and Economic Growth: Is There a Causal Effect?', *Journal of Macroeconomics*, Vol. 41, 21–41.

Papadia, F, (2017). 'Italian Economic Growth and the Euro', Bruegel Blog post, 26 July. http://bruegel.org/2017/07/italian-economic-growth-and-the-euro/

Pesaran, M. H. (2003). 'A Simple Panel Unit Root Test in the Presence of Cross Section Dependence', Cambridge Working Papers in Economics 0346, Faculty of Economics (DAE), University of Cambridge.

(2004). 'General Diagnostic Tests for Cross Section Dependence in Panels', CESifo Working Paper Series No. 1229; IZA Discussion Paper No. 1240.

Pesaran, M. H. and Tosetti, E. (2011). 'Large Panels with Common Factors and Spatial Correlation', *Journal of Econometrics*, Vol. 161, pp. 182–202.

Raftery, A. E. (1995). 'Bayesian Model Selection in Social Research', *Sociological Methodology*, Vol. 25, pp. 111–163.

Rodrik, D. (2008). 'The Real Exchange Rate and Economic Growth', Brookings Papers on Economic Activity, Fall.

Romer, P. M. (1990). 'Endogenous Technological Change', *Journal of Political Economy*, Vol. 98, No. 5, October, pp. 71–102.

Solberger, M. (2011). 'Demeaning the Data in Panel-Cointegration Models to Control for Cross-Sectional Dependencies', *Economics Letters*, Vol. 110, No. 3, pp. 252–254.

Solow, R. (1956). 'A Contribution to the Theory of Economic Growth', *Quarterly Journal of Economics*, Vol. 70, No. 1, pp. 65–94.

Sondermann, D. (2012). 'Productivity in the Euro Area: Any Evidence of Convergence?', Working Paper Series, No 1431, ECB, April.

Westerlund, J. (2007). 'Testing for Error Correction in Panel Data'. *Oxford Bulletin of Economics and Statistics*, Vol. 69, No. 6, pp. 709–748.

Wu, J. C. and Xia, F. D. (2016). 'Measuring the Macroeconomic Impact of Monetary Policy at the Zero Lower Bound', *Journal of Money, Credit and Banking*, Vol. 48, No. 2–3, pp. 253–291.

2 Structural Reforms and Growth

The Elusive Quest for the Silver Bullet

ALESSIO TERZI AND PASQUALE MARCO MARRAZZO

2.1 Introduction

My German mother-in-law once said: everything is better with butter. In economics, everything is better with growth. Even a few tenths of a percentage point gain in growth makes everything easier: fiscal consolidation, debt reduction, and poverty alleviation.[1]

With these words, Nemat Shafik, then deputy managing director of the International Monetary Fund (IMF), kicked off the Brussels Economic Forum in 2012, speaking to a multitude of concerned European economic policy-makers. At a time when the Eurozone was plunging into the second trough of a double-dipped recession and public debt levels were running high, everybody was looking for a growth silver bullet. In order to raise their growth potential, Dr Shafik continued, 'countries will need to implement comprehensive structural reforms'. Since then, European Union (EU) policy makers have deeply internalised the message, constantly reiterating calls for structural reforms. In a speech in 2015, European Central Bank (ECB) President Mario Draghi acknowledged himself that the term 'structural reforms' appeared in all of his Press Conference Introductory Statements, and in roughly one out of three of all ECB board member speeches, compared to only 2 per cent of speeches from US Federal Reserve governors.[2]

The term structural, or economic, reforms is a catch-all expression that refers to 'policy recommendations based on their ability to improve long-term material living standards through higher productivity and labour utilisation' (OECD, 2012, p. 18). In practical terms, and slightly dependent on the decade or region of interest, the term usually implies some form of liberalisation of trade, agriculture, current, capital, labour and product market. An original listing of these

[1] http://ec.europa.eu/economy_finance/bef2012/media/files/speeches/bef-speech-nemat-shafik-s2.pdf.
[2] www.ecb.europa.eu/press/key/date/2015/html/sp150522.en.html.

measures is usually traced back to Williamson (1994), and is generally referred to as 'Washington Consensus'. This is due to the fact that Williamson's book covered the proceedings of a conference that took place in the US capital, summarising the experience of policy makers in the 1980s and 1990s. Later on, the so-called second-generation reforms were added to the listing, to include education, innovation, research and development (R&D) or institutional capacity (Krueger, 2005).

However, these policy recommendations do not simply originate from anecdotal evidence of closed policy circles, but are rather the standard outcome of canonical economic models (Rodrik, 2009). In the 1990s, at a time when central bank independence was being presented as the silver bullet that would bring inflation under control (Alesina and Summers, 1993), and fiscal rules as the silver bullet that would keep fiscal profligacy in check (Kopits and Symansky, 1998), 'structural reforms' were put forward as the silver bullet that would ensure growth.

The surprising paradox that emerged since then is that, while the model-based literature is relatively unanimous in finding a positive impact of structural reforms, the empirical evidence is much more nuanced or even controversial. Looking at some of the standard measures that would fall under the 'structural reform' headline, as for example trade liberalisation, the evidence suggesting a positive effect on growth dates back to the 1990s (Dollar, 1992; Dollar and Kraay, 2004; Frankel and Romer, 1999; Sachs and Warner, 1995; Wacziarg and Welch, 2008). However, these results have been challenged in several instances (DeJong and Ripoll, 2006; Rodriguez and Rodrik, 2001).

Looking at domestic financial liberalisation, Levine (1997, 2005) reviews the literature and shows how the preponderance of studies on the topic finds positive effects, albeit with some nuances (Abiad et al., 2008; Aghion et al., 2005; Beck et al., 2000; Galindo et al., 2007; Rajan and Zingales, 1998). Dervis and Page (1984) argued in favour of product market reforms and policies promoting competition, for which several authors find positive effects, particularly in developed economies (Barro, 1991; Easterly, 1993; Frischtak et al., 1989; Jalilian et al., 2007; Nicoletti and Scarpetta, 2003). Rodrik (1995), however, preserves a degree of scepticism: while the theoretical channels are clear, the empirical aggregate impact of these industrial policies seems rather small. Looking at agricultural reforms, Gollin (2010) offers a mixed picture, as does Rodrik (1995). Aside from Anderson (2010), this empirical literature has generally focussed on specific countries, finding strong positive effects in China (Gulati et al., 2005; Lin 1992) and Vietnam (Pingali and Xuan, 1992). The evidence points, however, in a different direction for former Soviet countries, which saw collapsing output and productivity (Macours and Swinnen, 2000; Rozelle and Swinnen, 2004).

Perhaps the most contentious reform among those considered is capital account liberalisation (Eichengreen, 2001). While several authors find positive effects on growth (Bekaert et al., 2005; Dell'-Ariccia et al., 2007; Kose et al., 2009; Quinn, 1997; Quinn and Toyoda, 2008), these results tend to be rather weak (Rodrik 1998). Klein and Olivei (2008) and Edwards (2001) suggest that these unsatisfactory empirical findings, which clash with the strong theoretical case in favour of financial globalisation, are driven by developing countries. A point later echoed by Prasad et al. (2007) and Rodrik and Subramanian (2009).

Since then, a lot of the focus in trying to solve what we frame here as the 'structural reforms dilemma' has been on developing and employing more advanced empirical methodologies of estimation. If practice did not match theory, the argument went, it must have meant that the identification strategy was weak. These new techniques include, but are not limited to, Bayesian Model Averaging (Moral-Benito, 2012; Sala-i-Martin et al., 2004), Synthetic Control Methods (Adhikari et al., 2018; Billmeier and Nannicini, 2013) and Local Projection Methods (Bordon et al., 2016; Duval et al., 2017).

While saluting any effort to devise new econometric techniques that allow a more accurate impact analysis of policies, our contention is that polishing estimation techniques will ultimately fail in reconciling model-based blanket positive predictions, with the heterogeneity of ex post evaluation results. The reason is that, in our view, the original question itself is ill posed. Asking what the growth impact of a specific measure (e.g., labour market liberalisations) is crucially begs for the corollary question: on whom. In other words, different countries respond to a similar shock in different ways, depending on a multiplicity of factors. It therefore comes as no surprise that in the literature review we have presented, similar measures such as an agricultural liberalisation seemed to have very different impacts: positive when evaluated for China and Vietnam, negative when evaluated for post-Soviet economies.

To draw a medical comparison, looking empirically for the unconditional average impact of a specific type of reform is like wondering what the impact of aspirin is. The answer will obviously crucially depend on what group is being tested. If it is among people with a fever, it is likely to be positive on average. If it is among people with stomach ulcers, it is likely to be negative. If it is among a random group of the population, it is probably close to neutral or insignificant.

Interestingly, most growth economists and experts from multilateral institutions, as a general point, would be willing to subscribe to the mantra that 'every country is different'. However, often in their research, they fall prey to the quest for the definite determinants of growth or the unconditional impact of a specific type of reform.[3]

On the other hand, we believe there are two research avenues that are more likely to prove prosperous. The first focusses on identifying what factors determine the success and failure of a specific reform. Recent examples of this are Duval et al. (2017), who look at job protection deregulation depending on the business cycle conditions; Eggertsson et al. (2014), who explore the interaction between product and labour market reforms and monetary policy; and Prati et al. (2013), who condition reform impact on institutional quality.

The second avenue brings the concept of 'every country is different' to a higher level, by postulating that the structural reform dilemma is due to the fact that each economy displays multiple distortions at the same time, and these interact with each other (Hausmann et al., 2007). This point is empirically corroborated by Levine and Renelt (1992). As such, the argument goes, the savvy researcher should use the model-based literature as a set of guiding principles, but employ a so-called diagnostics framework to identify which model is relevant and which reforms are more likely to yield a positive and significant impact (Hausmann et al., 2008; Rodrik, 2015).

[3] This line of criticism does not necessarily classify all studies on the impact of a specific reform as irrelevant. In several instances, authors have limited their scope of analysis to a particular set of countries, as for example OECD-only. These countries will clearly share a set of characteristics, such as income level or administrative quality, limiting the potential interactions in the economy, and making an impact assessment of a specific reform more informative.

2.2 Reform Waves and Economic Growth

We fall squarely within the 'growth diagnostics' worldview or research stream, and our research questions originate from that. In Marrazzo and Terzi (2017), we explore whether governments in general, independently of their constraints and economic cycle, are capable of correctly identifying their economic shortcomings, and implementing well reforms to address them. In practice, this research question implies testing empirically whether countries implementing wide-reaching reforms, defined in a sufficiently loose way that allows for country-specificity, experience an improvement in their growth prospect.

To do so, we build on a global dataset of structural reforms originally developed by Ostry et al. (2009) and later updated by Giuliano et al. (2013) covering 156 countries between 1960 and 2005. One of the appealing features of this dataset is its breadth, spanning six policy dimensions: domestic financial sector, capital account, product market, agricultural market, trade and current account (see Table 2.1).As we have discussed, our aim is to set up a sufficiently flexible framework that ensures country-specificity, in order to avoid the quantification of a specific measure fallacy, but at the same time identifies episodes of reforms that were (i) wide-reaching, (ii) deep and (iii) not immediately

Table 2.1 ***Policy indices.***

	Domestic financial sector
Securities market	This indicator assesses the quality of the securities market framework, including the existence of an independent regulator and the extent of legal restrictions on the development of domestic bond and equity markets
Banking	This indicator captures reductions or removal of interest rate controls (floors or ceilings), credit controls (directed credit and subsidised lending), competition restrictions (limits on branches and entry barriers in the banking market, including licensing requirements or limits on foreign banks) and public ownership of banks. It also captures a measure of the quality of banking supervision and regulation, including the power and independence of bank supervisors, the adoption of Basel capital standards and the presence of a framework for bank inspections.

Table 2.1 (*cont.*)

	Domestic financial sector
	Capital account This indicator aims to measure the extent of the external capital account liberalisation. The index contains information on a broad set of restrictions, including, for example, controls on external borrowing between residents and nonresidents, as well as approval requirements for foreign direct investment
	Product market This indicator covers the degree of liberalisation in the telecommunication and electricity markets, including the extent of competition in the provision of these services, the presence of an independent regulatory authority and privatisation
	Agriculture market This indicator measures the extent of public intervention in the market going from total monopoly or monopsony in production, transportation or marketing (i.e., the presence of marketing boards), the presence of administered prices, public ownership of relevant producers or concession requirement to free market.
	Trade This indicator is based on tariff liberalisation and is measured by average tariffs.
	Current account This indicator captures the extent to which a government is compliant with its obligations under the IMF's Article VIII to free from government restriction the proceeds from international trade in goods and services.

Source: This table presents a brief description of the variables. For a more comprehensive treatment, including data sources, refer to Giuliano et al. (2013).

reversed. To do so, we build on a methodology first formulated by IMF (2015, pp. 59–60). In particular, we identify large and stable jumps, which reflect a positive break (improvement) in the six policy fields contained in our reform database.

It is worth mentioning upfront that, along the lines suggested by Rodrik (2015), we build on the model-based literature in defining the direction of policy change that we call reform. Effectively, our analysis is asymmetric, as we look only at reductions in the policy indicators, i.e., liberalisations. We therefore leave out the debate on whether unorthodox policies might at times be beneficial (Hausmann and Rodrik, 2003).

In order to formalise the flexible framework that we have laid out, we look at the three-year differences, $\Delta I_t^i = I_{t+3}^i - I_t^i$, where i refers to the country and I is a specific policy indicator, out of the six contained in Giuliano et al. (2013). We subsequently pool together the three-year differences over the entire time and country sample $\mathsf{A}{:=}\Delta I_t^i \in \mathsf{A}, \forall i, t$. We then identify breaks $\forall I \in [1,6]$ based on three criteria:

(i) The three-year difference ΔI_t^i belongs to the top 3 percentile of the distribution of all ΔI_t^i.
(ii) The three-yearly difference that composes ΔI_t^i is all nonnegative: $I_{t+1}^i - I_t^i \geq 0$, $I_{t+2}^i - I_{t+1}^i \geq 0$ and $I_{t+3}^i - I_{t+2}^i \geq 0$.
(iii) If conditions (i) and (ii) occur more than once consecutively, we consider only the first observation.

We then identify wide-reaching reform episodes (or 'reform waves') as instances when, within a three-year interval, at least two out of our six variables present a break as defined in the preceding. By doing so, we obtain a list of events, consisting of twenty-nine episodes distributed over five decades. Looking at the temporal distribution, we identify one episode in the 1960s, three in the 1970s, thirteen in the 1980s, eleven in the 1990s and one in the early 2000s. This intuitively makes sense, as the period 1980–2000 is when wide-reaching reforms were implemented in several Latin American countries and Asia. Figure 2.1 offers a geographical visualisation of the distribution of reform waves.

The countries displaying reform waves are twenty-eight, with Argentina being prominently featured twice, in the 1970s and 1980s. As is clear from Figure 2.1, many of our countries are located in Latin America and the Caribbean (LAC). Given that more than half our events are to be found outside of the LAC region, we would resist the temptation of considering our results as only pertinent to one continent. At the same time, our methodology selects what might look like a remarkably low number of Asian economies. However, as underlined by Rodrik (2009), many of these countries, including South Korea,

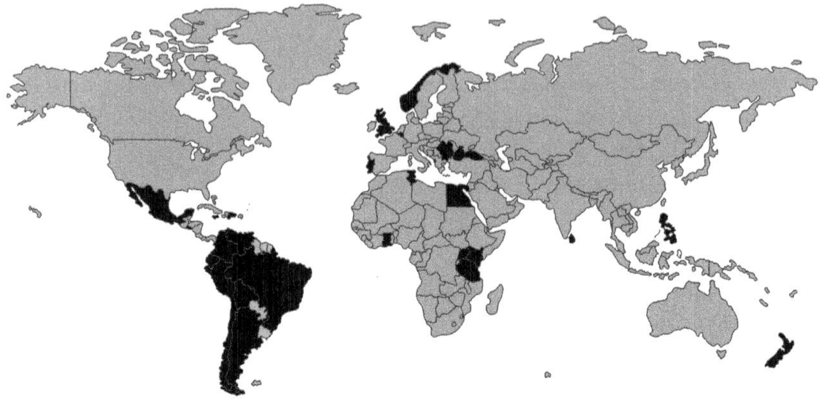

Figure 2.1 Countries experiencing reform waves between 1960 and 2005.
Source: Marrazzo and Terzi (2017).

Vietnam and China, did not develop as a result of an economic reform wave across the board, but rather by opening up their economy gradually while retaining export subsidies, a closed capital account and other 'heterodox' measures. Moreover, during the Asian Crisis of the early 1990s, reforms were introduced, but they were rather focussed on the banking and financial sector, therefore failing to classify as 'reform waves' in our setting.

Before engaging in more formal empirical assessments of the impact of reform waves, we run a simple statistical exercise. In particular, we collect real gross domestic product (GDP) per capita data for all the reform episodes from the Penn World Table 9.0 (Feenstra et al., 2015), rebase it to set the prereform period equal to 100 and then compute the standard deviation across reform episodes for each year over the period $t - 10$ to $t + 10$, where t is the midpoint of a reform wave. Figure 2.2 displays the result of this exercise. Interestingly, in the decade that precedes a reform wave, countries' GDP per capita among various episodes has a certain degree of heterogeneity, but that heterogeneity is broadly constant.[4] However, following the implementation of wide-reaching reforms, the heterogeneity of GDP performance shoots up. We take this as prima facie evidence that structural reform

[4] It can be shown that this finding is not conditional on the specific rebasing of gross domestic product per capita (GDPpc) that we employ, and remains true also in the case in which we set GDPpc = 100 at $t - 10$.

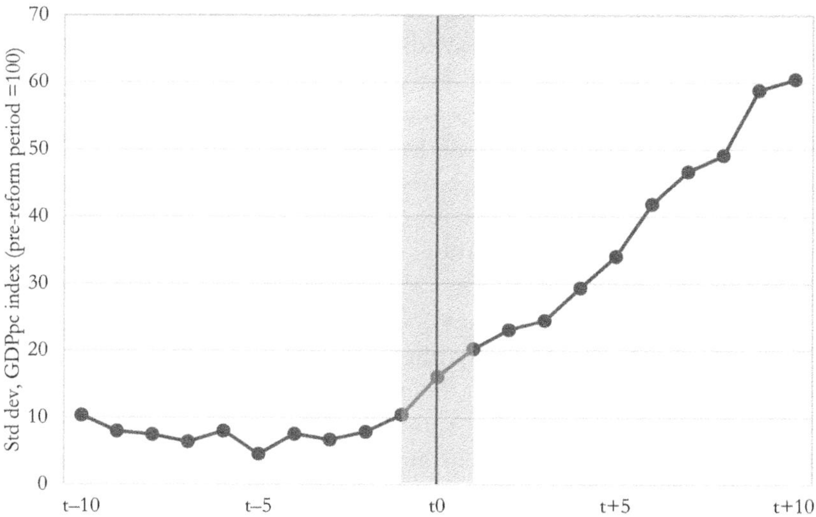

Figure 2.2 Variability of GDP per capita across countries, pre- and postreform wave episodes.
Source: Own calculations based on Marrazzo and Terzi (2017)

waves tend to have a highly heterogeneous impact on growth. Once again, this vindicates the view that looking at (some form of) average treatment effects is likely to prove, in a sense, not very informative.

Moving beyond descriptive statistics, we then track reform wave countries over the ten years following adoption and estimate the dynamic impact of reforms by employing the Synthetic Control Method (SCM), a technique first developed in Abadie and Gardeazabal (2003) and later refined in Abadie et al. (2010, 2015). The reason that led us to choose the SCM over other recent econometric techniques is that it has the desirable feature of allowing us to quantify the individual impact of a country's reform package. Our technique therefore caters for the fact that each country is different, displaying the heterogeneity thereby associated.

In a nutshell, this nonparametric data-driven approach creates a control for each individual reform wave country, as a linear combination of other countries displaying similar prereform characteristics. In Marrazzo and Terzi (2017), we formally illustrate how synthetic controls are built for each country. In this setting, we will simply mention that the SCM is generated solving a double-minimisation problem, whereby the algorithm identifies a set of weights, whose sum adds to 100 per cent, such that the synthetic control replicates as close as possible the evolution of GDP per capita of our country of interest in the ten years preceding the reform wave. Moreover, it will try to match as closely as possible a set of macroeconomic covariates that the literature has identified as important predictors of long-term growth. These include investment rates, the degree of openness of the economy, secondary and tertiary education, population growth and the value added of industry.

We call the set of countries from which the algorithm can pick potential components of the synthetic control a 'donor pool'. Clearly, a necessary condition to be in the donor pool is that for the period of interest the candidate donors should not have experienced a reform wave, both in the pretreatment and in the posttreatment phase. For example, a country that has experienced a reform wave in 1982 can be a candidate for another country experiencing a reform wave in 2000, but not in 1989. Furthermore, extremely small countries (less than 1.5 million people) are excluded from our analysis because of their limited contribution and high volatility in GDP per capita. Moreover, using the Correlates of War database (Pevehouse et al., 2004), we excluded from the donor pool all countries affected by war in the time period of interest, given that such a factor is likely to affect in an extreme (negative) way the donor and be unrelated to the reforming country, hence presenting the risk of distorting our impact estimates.[5]

In principle, the countries considered in the donor pool of each individual reform episode should be similar to the reforming country, to avoid the risk of running in a so-called interpolation bias (Abadie et al., 2010). Intuitively, what this means is that, for example, it would not be desirable to replicate Greece as a weighted mix of Sweden and Angola, which, by averaging, could yield a good prereform match, but at the same time are more likely to fail the parallel trend assumption. To avoid this, we restricted each reform wave episode's donor pool

[5] In practice, this meant excluding the following countries from selected donor pools: Azerbaijan 1993–1994; Cambodia 1977–1979; Cyprus 1974; Democratic Republic of the Congo 1975–1976; Ethiopia 1998–2000; Iraq 1980–1988, 1990–1991 and 2003; Jordan 1973 and 1991; Rwanda 1994; Sierra Leone 1991– 2002; South Africa 1975–1976; Syrian Arab Republic 1973; Uganda 1978–1979; and Vietnam 1979.

only to countries that have a GDP per capita of ±50 per cent that of the reformer.

While many of these conditions might look arbitrary, we note how these practices are generally used in the SCM literature to increase the credibility of the estimating assumptions. By shrinking the size of the donor pool, we are actually reducing the risk of overfitting the model. And indeed, partly as a result of this, not every country's performance can be replicated using the SCM. In some instances, the synthetic control will simply display a limited replication power of the country of interest in the pretreatment period. When this happened, we decided to exclude the reform episodes from our sample.[6] The underlying reason is that if our empirical methodology is unable to track accurately enough our country of interest before the reform wave, then the assumption that the country would have behaved like its synthetic control had it not been for the reform shock becomes untenable. By doing so, we cut down our units of analysis to twenty-three reform wave episodes.

Before exploring in detail the country-specific results, we deem it worthwhile aggregating the individual SCM results by computing something similar to an average treatment effect, in order to allow a benchmarking with the literature results. For each reform episode, we looked at the difference in the average across the six policy indicators contained in the Giuliano et al. (2013) database and the respective synthetic control policy indicators (reform gap). We then looked at the difference in GDP per capita between each reformer and its respective synthetic control (GDP gap). Finally, we took the average of these two metrics across the twenty-three instances considered, effectively computing an average change in policy stance in the reformers vis-à-vis counterfactuals and the average impact on GDP. Figure 2.3 displays these two indicators over the period $t - 10$ to $t + 10$. Interestingly, over the period $t - 10$ to t0, on average reformers and their counterfactuals display a similar policy stance, and their GDP per capita behaved broadly in a similar way. At t0 and for the following few years, we see a notable departure in terms of policy stance: this is the effect of the reform wave. Following that, the policy gap remains broadly unaltered. In turn, on average, GDP per capita reacts negatively

[6] In Marrazzo and Terzi (2017), we detail how the appropriate threshold is determined, largely building on Adhikari et al. (2018).

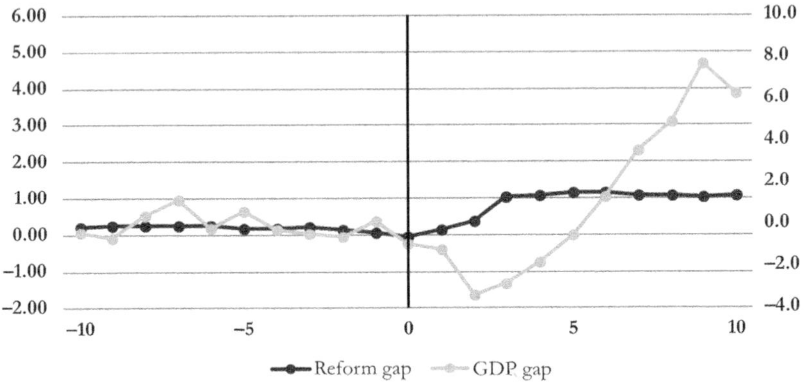

Figure 2.3 Change in average policy indicator (left-hand scale) and impact on GDP (right-hand side scale).
Source: Own calculations based on Marrazzo and Terzi (2017)

during the reform implementation period, and then accelerates vis-à-vis counterfactual. Ten years after the kickoff of a reform wave, GDP per capita is roughly 6 percentage points higher. In the original Marrazzo and Terzi (2017) paper, we use multiple estimation techniques to cross-check this result, including more standard parametric estimations based on Acemoglu et al. (2014), a modified difference-in-difference (diff-in-diff) estimator, and a local polynomial fit.

Albeit with different and often fancier econometric estimation techniques, this is the kind of research question several papers in the literature aim to answer and therefore where the analysis often stops. On the other hand, for the reasons detailed in Section 2.1, we aim to dissect this result and fully grasp the potential heterogeneity of impacts thereby associated. As such, taking advantage of the granular nature of the SCM, we analysed also the country-specific results. To do so, we effectively fit a diff-in-diff estimator through the GDP gap data points. The diff-in-diff estimator so computed is therefore the average growth differential between 'reformer' and 'counterfactual' over the postreform period, net of the growth differential between the two in the prereform period. A positive coefficient would then imply that in the postreforms phase, the gap vis-à-vis the synthetic had a tendency to widen in favour of the reformer. The converse is true for negative values. Figure 2.4 displays the country-specific coefficients for the twenty-three reform wave episodes considered.

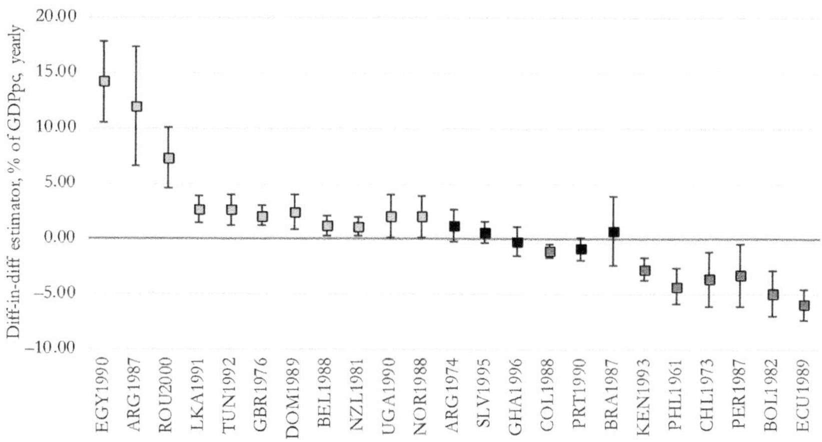

Figure 2.4 Country-specific average impact of reform waves on GDP growth over the ten years after reform implementation.

Note: This figure displays the average yearly growth rate differential between 'reform episode' and 'synthetic control' over the period t0 and $t + 10$. Brackets display 95 per cent confidence intervals based on robust standard errors. Light grey implies positive and statistically significant impact of reform wave, dark grey negative and statistically significant and black statistically insignificant.

Source: Own calculations based on Marrazzo and Terzi (2017)

The most interesting finding is that reform waves can have a highly heterogeneous impact. While it might be true that a majority of cases displayed a positive and significant effect, there are also several instances of no or even negative impact. In the Philippines in the 1960s, Chile in the 1970s, Ecuador, Bolivia, Colombia and Peru in the 1980s and Kenya in the 1990s, large economic reforms failed to deliver their strong economic dividend. Within our setting, this could be due either to a wrong selection of reforms, along the lines of what Hausmann et al. (2007) would possibly argue, or implementation problems within reforms.

This obviously opens the scope for differentiating between advanced economies and emerging markets, as in the former both the selection and implementation is likely to be carried out by a more highly qualified bureaucratic apparatus. As a matter of fact, Prati et al. (2013) are among those who have detailed how the impact of reforms is heterogeneous and depends on the quality of institutions. While refraining from engaging in a full-blown multivariate regression in a small-n setting like ours, quick eyeballing of Figure 2.4 already shows that the four advanced economies in the selection tended to fall more in the positive side of the spectrum, with the exception of Portugal, where the impact was not significant. As such, one could be inclined to conclude that, even if based on thin evidence of large structural reform waves, in Europe they tend to have a positive or at most nonnegative effect.

One interesting point is clearly how to reconcile positive and significant aggregate average effects with this more heterogeneous country-specific picture. Looking at Figure 2.4, in this respect, we would side with Easterly (2005), who made the point that average results are potentially driven by positive outliers. In our setting, these would be Egypt, Argentina and Romania. This is not to say that outliers are irrelevant, and rather they carry interesting information per se. For example, we know that both Egypt and Argentina experienced sharp economic corrections in the order of magnitude of 25–30 per cent of GDP shortly after our horizon of assessment. What this suggests is that, in a way, we could postulate that economic liberalisations in these countries contributed to the buildup of large bubbles. This should come as no surprise, and has been shown extensively to be particularly true for capital account liberalisations, for instance (Rodrik, 1998). All in all, our analysis would suggest that large economic reforms should perhaps be presented more as an economic double-edged sword rather than a growth silver bullet.

Understanding under which conditions economic reforms paid out, or failed to do so, requires in our view not only cross-country econometric studies for general principles, but also in-depth country-by-country approaches, either quantitatively along the lines discussed by Hausmann at al. (2008), or qualitatively through case studies. In the words of Rodrik (2003, p. 10), this can be particularly valuable when speaking about growth processes as 'case studies and cross-national econometrics are not substitutes for each other. [...] Any cross-national empirical regularity that cannot be meaningfully verified on the basis of country studies should be regarded as suspect'.

2.3 Growth Accelerations and Economic Reforms

One standard critique of the literature and econometric approaches detailed hitherto is that using some form of long-term average as the dependent variable could be misleading as growth is a highly unstable variable over time (Easterly et al., 1993; Pritchett, 2000). In particular, aside from the most advanced economies, countries tend to experience frequent up- and down-breaks in their growth time series. As such, the argument goes, it is more important to focus on explaining the origin of these turning points.

Following Pritchett (2000)'s seminal contribution, many in the literature have tried to identify the determinants of 'growth accelerations'," i.e., positive up-breaks in growth patterns. Unsurprisingly, many have tried to link them to economic reforms. Hausmann et al. (2005) were the first to use structural break analysis to identify these turning points in a data-driven way and predict growth take-offs based on a set of covariates. Using the Sachs and Warner (1995, p. 317) index of economic liberalisation, they concluded that 'standard economic reform packages have marginal effects on the probability that a growth transition will be initiated'. However, that finding has not gone uncontested. Improving the structural break methodology, Jong-A-Ping and De Haan (2011) find on the contrary that economic liberalisations are a significant contributor to spark a growth take-off. This finding is in tune with Aizenman and Spiegel (2010).

In a recent contribution (Peruzzi and Terzi, 2018), one of us took aim at revising this finding leveraging on the more granular Giuliano et al. (2013) structural reform database illustrated in the previous section, and on a longer list of growth accelerations recently identified by Kar et al. (2013). The intuition behind the paper is that growth accelerations are ultimately structural breaks in a growth time series. As such, in these countries one would expect to observe significant fluctuations in standard growth determinants around the acceleration years, flagging which growth channel was unlocked or category of binding constraint relaxed. The statistical framework developed to detect these channels falls under the name of Systemic Diagnostics Framework (SDF), as its aim is to replicate across countries in a data-driven, more basic manner, some of the ideas that Hausmann et al. (2008) outlined in their handbook on how to do country-specific growth diagnostics in practice. As the purpose of the Peruzzi and Terzi (2018) paper was wider, namely to characterise a standard growth acceleration process across countries and time, several growth determinants and channels on top of structural reforms are considered, including inflation control, exchange rate depreciation, export demand boosts, terms of trade shocks, end of conflict situations, institutional

Table 2.2 *Growth determinants considered in Peruzzi and Terzi (2018).*

Theory	Subtheory	Variable
Institutions		Freedom House Index Conflict (domestic/external)
Economic policy	Macroeconomic policies	Inflation Effective exchange rate
	Structural policies	Agriculture market liberalisation Product market liberalisation Trade liberalisation Capital account liberalisation Current account liberalisation Domestic financial liberalisation
Endowments		Natural resource rent
Luck		Terms of trade Export demand
Solow–Swan		Investment (public and private)

Source: Peruzzi and Terzi (2018).

reform and so on (see Table 2.2). Crucially, the SDF is designed in a flexible way that caters for the fact that world countries – for example, natural resource intensive or not, rich or poor, autocratic or democratic – have different growth models, and might therefore have exploited different strategies in achieving a take-off. At the same time, it allows to detect potential common patterns. In the original paper, we went at length to illustrate the mechanics of the SDF and how it does a good job at identifying intrinsic characteristics of the take-off process. In this setting, for the purposes of our argument, we will focus on the construction and findings relating to structural reforms.

In line with the view outlined in the introduction that trying to pin down the effect of specific typologies of reform is of marginal interest, in the growth acceleration setting we used a similar approach to the one followed in Marrazzo and Terzi (2017). That is, for each of the six policy indicators contained in our database, and for each country's time series, we flagged a liberalisation if it fell in the top fifth percentile of reforms ever implemented. Evidently, identifying large reforms in this manner allows for country-specificity, rather than applying arbitrary global thresholds (e.g., one standard deviation). In the original paper, we also show how reforms identified in this fashion are corroborated by country-specific reports.[7]

The first interesting finding is that, out of 135 growth acceleration episodes that took place between 1962 and 2002 worldwide, almost half (45 per cent) were preceded by at least one sharp structural reform. We call this metric 'incidence'. Economic reforms display the highest incidence among all other potential growth determinants and channels. If we zoom in on Europe only, actually 100 per cent of growth accelerations (or nine out of nine) were preceded by a structural reform shock. These include Portugal in the 1960s; Cyprus in the 1970s; the United Kingdom, Portugal and Ireland in the 1980s; and Poland, Albania, Finland and Bulgaria in the 1990s. All in all, these results seem to resonate with the findings outlined in the previous section, and would suggest that reforms do have a role to play in engendering large and sustained positive shifts in growth trajectories.

However, in the previous section we observed that often large reform waves fail to boost output significantly. To check whether this was the case in the growth acceleration setting, and in line with Hausmann et al. (2007), we computed the so-called effectiveness indicator. This metric is computed as the ratio between the number of growth accelerations preceded by large structural reform episodes, and the number of times large structural reform episodes occurred over the whole time series.[8] Intuitively, if incidence relates to a necessary condition, effectiveness relates to a sufficient condition. The latter is a characteristic you would expect from a growth silver bullet.

The effectiveness of large structural reforms does not outperform other growth predictors. Moreover, it is only around 10 per cent (see Figure 2.5). What this implies is that nine out of ten times, at global level, sharp changes in policy failed to engender a large positive

[7] In a robustness check in the paper, we also show how applying a global threshold on top of our country-specific definition does not invalidate our findings.

[8] We acknowledge that one potential criticism of this metric could be that not all reforms are designed with the objective of boosting aggregate GDP. At times, they might be implemented to generate some redistribution within sectors and parts of society. However, given that we are only looking at deregulations, this is less likely to be an issue in our setting.

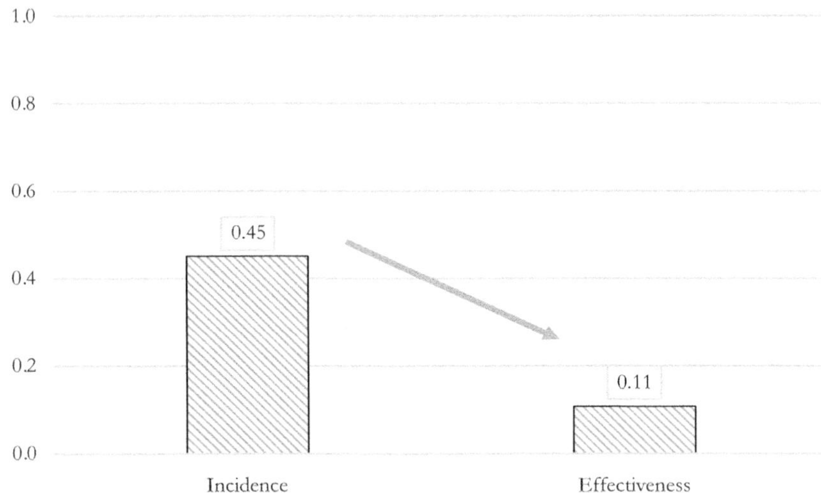

Figure 2.5 Incidence and effectiveness of large structural reforms.
Note: Incidence indicates the share of growth acceleration episodes preceded by large structural reform episodes. Effectiveness is computed as the ratio between the number of growth accelerations preceded by large structural reform episodes, and the number of times large structural reform episodes that occurred over the whole time series. See text for further details.
Source: Own calculations based on Peruzzi and Terzi (2018).

structural change in long-term growth rates.[9] This value is not far from the 18 per cent effectiveness result in the original Hausmann et al. (2007) paper.

Pushing the logic of this exercise further, we also constructed a two-way table looking at the effectiveness score of different combination and sequence of growth levers. For example, the most successful combination of events to spark a growth acceleration was macroeconomic policies such as bringing hyperinflation under control, followed by a boost in natural resource extraction. The interesting findings for the purposes of our discussion here are twofold. First, there is no

[9] The reader should note that here the bar is set higher vis-à-vis the estimation in the previous section, as we are no longer debating whether reforms have a positive impact on growth, but rather whether this is sizeable and sustained. Possibly only our three positive outliers in Figure 2.4 would qualify as a growth acceleration, with 3/23≈13 per cent, in line with the structural reform effectiveness.

strictly dominant strategy to spark a growth take-off. This goes in line with the idea that every country has its own characteristics, and that there are no clear panaceas or silver bullets. Second, that being said, in most instances structural reforms seem to be the best bet as a first move to ignite a growth acceleration, if supporting measures will follow suit. This supports the idea that they might be seen as a necessary, more than sufficient condition to yield a growth acceleration. However, even in the best case, this brings effectiveness to roughly 12 per cent. This implies that complementarity-related explanations will only go so far in explaining why reforms sometimes work, and sometimes do not.

All in all, these results would seem once again to point to the fact that deep economic reforms can have an important impact on a country's growth rate, but often times, they fail to deliver their benefits. As underscored by Rodrik (2018), when talking about the recent Eurozone crisis experience and Troika programme countries, in achieving economic growth there are no silver bullets. Rather, economic reforms should be framed as an opportunity that, if tailored to country-specific needs and well implemented, could yield important benefits.

2.4 Concluding Remarks

The sarcastic witticism goes that whenever asked a thorny question, economists will tend to reply with a statement that starts with 'it depends'. To us, structural reforms mark no exception from this rule. Over the past three decades, many have tried to verify empirically whether deep or wide-reaching economic reforms are a key determinant of growth. In line with much of the literature, our analyses would lead us to side with the idea that structural reforms on average do have a positive contribution to growth. Countries implementing wide-reaching structural reform waves saw their GDP per capita expand on average by more than 6 percentage points in ten years vis-à-vis a no-reform counterfactual scenario. Likewise, almost half of the 135 growth acceleration episodes registered in postwar history were preceded by some form of deep economic reform. Based on historical evidence, this seems to be particularly true in Europe, or in settings where the quality of institutions is comparatively higher. As such, if we were called to advise hastily on what to do to reignite growth behind a veil of ignorance, we would probably push for economic reforms.

However, we also show how economic reforms tend to have highly heterogeneous effects that range from extremely positive to mildly negative. In some cases, even the positive instances ended up proving to be the buildup of a bubble that ended up in burst, as was the case in Argentina in the 1990s. When looking at growth acceleration episodes, while it is true that roughly half of the accelerations were preceded by important economic reforms, in nine out of ten instances, deep reforms failed to spark a take-off.

What this suggests is that asking unconditionally whether structural reforms work is rather misleading. This is particularly relevant given that these measures tend to be highly unpopular. In presence of high heterogeneity, if we had to put our political career on the line and burn large amounts of political capital, we would want to work with more than a positive effect on average. Rather, we would want that our reform package had a decent chance of boosting output in our specific country setting. What this underscores is the importance of carrying out a thorough growth diagnostics exercise rather than implementing checklists based on international best practices and indicators. Given the potential for negative impacts, experimenting policies before fully phasing them in at the national level becomes all the more important. This principle is encapsulated by China's economic reformer Deng Xiaoping's recommendation to 'cross the river by feeling for the stones'.

Structural reform should not be seen or presented as a growth silver bullet. This is because there is no such thing. If there is one general principle that by now goes widely uncontested in the growth field, it is that every country is different and that therefore there is no one-size-fits-all growth strategy. The Soviet Union in the 1950s, South Korea and Taiwan in the 1960s, Japan in the 1970s and 1980s and China in the 1990s all experienced sharp growth accelerations while implementing different, often heterodox, policy mixes, which were evidently tailored to the local conditions (Rodrik, 2009). In 2008, a World Bank Commission on Growth and Development composed of nineteen high-level economic policy makers and two Nobel Prize winners qualitatively reviewed decades of experience to reach similar conclusions (World Bank, 2008). Our own quantitative characterisation of growth accelerations confirms these findings. Resorting to a medical parallel, saying 'countries with low growth potential need structural reforms' is like saying 'sick people need treatment'. The key is the diagnostics of the problem and the design of the solution. If chosen well, treatment can be beneficial and lead to healing. If chosen poorly, it can fail to heal or even worsen the condition. Perhaps unsurprisingly, countries displaying growth problems tend to be very different from one another. To quote Lev Tolstoy's Anna Karenina, 'all happy families look alike, unhappy families are unhappy in different ways'.

References

Abadie, A., Diamond, A. and Hainmueller, J. (2010). 'Synthetic Control Methods for Comparative Case Studies: Estimating the Effect of California's Tobacco Control Program', *Journal of the American Statistical Association*, Vol. 105, No. 490, 493–505. doi:DOI 10.1198/jasa.2009.ap08746.

Abadie, A., Diamond, A, and Hainmueller, J. (2015). 'Comparative Politics and the Synthetic Control Method', *American Journal of Political Science*, Vol. 59, No. 2, 495–510. doi:10.1111/ajps.12116.

Abadie, A. and Gardeazabal, J. (2003). 'The Economic Costs of Conflict: A Case Study of the Basque Country', *American Economic Journal: Economic Policy*, Vol. 93, No. 1, 114–132. doi:10.1257/000282803321455188.

Abiad, A., Oomes, N. and Ueda, K. (2008). 'The Quality Effect: Does Financial Liberalization Improve the Allocation of Capital?' *Journal of Development Economics*, Vol. 87, No. 2, 270–282. doi:10.1016/j.jdeveco.2007.12.002.

Acemoglu, D., Naidu, S., Restrepo, P. and Robinson, J. A. (2014). 'Democracy Does Cause Growth'. *NBER Working Paper*, (20004), 1–64.

Adhikari, B., Duval, R., Hu, B. and Loungani, P. (2018). 'Can Reform Waves Turn the Tide? Some Case Studies Using the Synthetic Control Method', *Open Economies Review*, Vol. 29, No. 4, 879–910.

Aghion, P., Howitt, P. and Mayer-Foulkes, D. (2005). 'The Effect of Financial Development on Convergence: Theory and Evidence', *Quarterly Journal of Economics*, Vol. 120, No. 1, 173–222. doi:10.1162/qjec.2005.120.1.173.

Aizenman, J. and Spiegel, M. M. (2010). 'Takeoffs', *Review of Development Economics*, Vol. 14, No. 2, 177–196.

Alesina, A. F. and Summers, L. H. (1993). 'Central Bank Independence and Macroeconomic Performance: Some Comparative Evidence', *Journal of Money, Credit and Banking*, Vol. 25, No. 2, 151–162. doi:10.2307/2077833.

Anderson, K. (2010). 'Krueger, Schiff, and Valdes Revisited: Agricultural Price and Trade Policy Reform in Developing Countries since 1960',

Applied Economic Perspectives and Policy, Vol. 1, No. 2, 195–231. doi:10.1093/aepp/ppq005.

Barro, R. J. (1991). 'Economic Growth in a Cross Section of Countries', *Quarterly Journal of Economics*, Vol. 106, No. 2, 407–443. doi:10.2307/2937943.

Beck, T., Levine, R. and Loayza, N. (2000). 'Finance and the Sources of Growth', *Journal of Financial Economics*, Vol. 58, No. 1–2, 261–300. doi:10.1016/S0304-405X(00)00072-6.

Bekaert, G., Harvey, C. R. and Lundblad, C. (2005). 'Does Financial Liberalization Spur Growth?' *Journal of Financial Economics*, Vol. 77, No. 1, 3–55. doi:10.1016/j.jfineco.2004.05.007.

Billmeier, A. and Nannicini, T. (2013). 'Assessing Economic Liberalization Episodes: a Synthetic Control Approach', *Review of Economics and Statistics*, Vol. 95, No. 3, 983–1001. doi:10.1162/REST_a_00324.

Bordon, R., Ebeke, C. and Shirono, K. (2016). 'When Do Structural Reforms Work ? On the Role of the Business Cycle and Macroeconomic Policies', IMF Working Paper, (62).

DeJong, D. N. and Ripoll, M. (2006). 'Tariffs and Growth: An Empirical Exploration of Contingent Relationships', *Review of Economics and Statistics*, Vol. 88, No. 4, 625–640. doi:10.1162/rest.88.4.625.

Dell'Ariccia, G., Giovanni, J., Faria, A., et al. (2007). 'Reaping the Benefits of Financial Globalization', IMF Occasional Paper Series.

Dervis, K. and Page, J. M. J. (1984). 'Industrial Policy in Developing Countries', *Journal of Comparative Economics*, Vol. 8, No. 4, 436–451. doi:10.4337/9781781000267.

Dollar, D. (1992). 'Outward-Oriented Developing Economies Really Do Grow More Rapidly : Evidence from 95 LDCs', *Economic Development and Cultural Change*,Vol. 40, No. 3, 523–544.

Dollar, D. and Kraay, A. (2004). 'Trade, Growth, and Poverty', *Economic Journal*, Vol. 114, No. 493, F22–F49. doi:10.1111/j.0013-0133.2004.00186.x.

Duval, R., Furceri, D. and Jalles, J. (2017). 'Job Protection Deregulation in Good and Bad Times', IMF Working Paper, 277.

Easterly, W. (1993). 'How Much Do Distortions Affect Growth?' *Journal of Monetary Economics*, Vol. 32, No.2, 187–212. doi:10.1016/0304-3932(93)90002-W.

(2005). 'National Policies and Economic Growth: A Reappraisal', in Philippe Aghion and Steven N. Durlauf (ed.), *Handbook of Economic Growth*, Vol. 1A, Elsevier B.V., pp. 1015–1059. doi:10.1016/S1574-0684(05)01015-4.

Easterly, W., Kremer, M., Pritchett, L. and Summers, L. H. (1993). 'Good Policy or Good Luck – Country Growth-Performance and Temporary

Shocks', *Journal of Monetary Economics*, Vol. 32, No. 3, 459–483. doi:10.1016/0304-3932(93)90026-C.

Edwards, S. (2001). 'Capital Mobility and Economic Performance: Are Emerging Economies Different?' NBER Working Paper 8076, 1–34. doi:10.3386/w8076.

Eggertsson, G., Ferrero, A. and Raffo, A. (2014). 'Can Structural Reforms Help Europe?' *Journal of Monetary Economics*, Vol. 61, 2–22. doi:10.1016/j.jmoneco.2013.11.006.

Eichengreen, B. (2001). 'Capital Account Liberalization: What Do Cross-Sections Studies Tell Us?' *World Bank Economic Review*, Vol. 15, No. 3, 341–365.

Feenstra, R. C., Inklaar, R. and Timmer, M. P. (2015). 'The Next Generation of the Penn World Table', *American Economic Review*, Vol. 105, No. 10, 3150–3182. doi:10.1257/aer.20130954.

Frankel, J. and Romer, D. (1999). 'Does Trade Cause Growth?' *American Economic Review*, Vol. 89, No. 3, 379–399.

Frischtak, C., Hadjimichael, B. and Zachau, U. (1989). 'Competition Policies for Industrializing Countries', Policy and Research Series.

Galindo, A., Schiantarelli, F. and Weiss, A. (2007). 'Does Financial Liberalization Improve the Allocation of Investment? Micro-Evidence from Developing Countries', *Journal of Development Economics*, Vol. 83, No. 2, 562–587. doi:10.1016/j.jdeveco.2005.09.008.

Giuliano, P., Mishra, P. and Spilimbergo, A. (2013). 'Democracy and Reforms: Evidence from a New Dataset', *American Economic Journal: Macroeconomics*, Vol. 5, No. 4, 179–204. doi:10.1257/mac.5.4.179.

Gollin, D. (2010). 'Agricultural Productivity and Economic Growth', in Philippe Aghion and Steven Durlauf (ed.), *Handbook of Agricultural Economics*, 1st ed., Vol. 4, Elsevier B.V., pp. 3825–3866. doi:10.1016/S1574-0072(09)04073-0.

Gulati, A., Fan, S. and Dalafi, S. (2005). 'The Dragon and the Elephant: Agricultural and Rural Reforms in China and India', MTID Discussion Paper No 87.

Hausmann, R., Klinger, B. and Wagner, R. (2008). 'Doing Growth Diagnostics in Practice: A "Mindbook"', Center of International Development at Harvard University – Working Papers, (177).

Hausmann, R., Pritchett, L. and Rodrik, D. (2005). 'Growth Accelerations', *Journal of Economic Growth*, Vol. 10, No. 4, 303–329. doi:10.1007/s10887-005-4712-0.

Hausmann, R. and Rodrik, D. (2003). 'Economic Development as Self-Discovery', *Journal of Development Economics*, Vol. 72, No. 2, 603–633. doi:10.1016/S0304-3878(03)00124-X.

Hausmann, R., Rodrik, D. and Velasco, A. (2007). 'Growth Diagnostics', in D. Rodrik (ed.), *One Economics Many Recepies*, Princeton University Press, p. 280.

IMF. (2015). 'Structural Reforms and Macroeconomic Performance: Initial Considerations for the Fund'.

Jalilian, H., Kirkpatrick, C. and Parker, D. (2007). 'The Impact of Regulation on Economic Growth in Developing Countries: A Cross-Country Analysis', *World Development*, Vol. 35, No. 1, 87–103. doi:10.1016/j.worlddev.2006.09.005.

Jong-A-Ping, R. and De Haan, J. (2011). 'Political Regime Change, Economic Liberalization and Growth Accelerations', *Public Choice*, Vol. 146, No. 1–2, 93–115.

Kar, S., Pritchett, L., Raihan, S. and Sen, K. (2013). 'Looking for a Break: Identifying Transitions in Growth Regimes', *Journal of Macroeconomics*, Vol. 38, No. PB, 151–166. doi:10.1016/j.jmacro.2013.09.022.

Klein, M. W. and Olivei, G. P. (2008). 'Capital Account Liberalization, Financial Depth, and Economic Growth', *Journal of International Money and Finance*, Vol. 27, No. 6, 861–875. doi:10.1016/j.jimonfin.2008.05.002.

Kopits, G. and Symansky, S. (1998). 'Fiscal Policy Rules', IMF Occasional Paper Series, 1–45.

Kose, M. A., Prasad, E., Rogoff, K. and Wei, S.-J. (2009). ‚Financial Globalization: A Reappraisal', *IMF Staff Papers*, Vol. 56, No. 1, 8–62. doi:10.1057/imfsp.2008.36.

Krueger, A. O. (2005). 'De Tocqueville's "Dangerous Moment": The Importance of Getting Reforms Right', *World Economy*, Vol. 28, 749–763. doi:10.1111/j.1467-9701.2005.00705.x.

Levine, R. (1997). 'Financial Development and Economic Growth: Views and Agenda', *Journal of Economic Literature*, Vol. XXXV, . June, 688–726. doi:10.1126/science.151.3712.867-a.

(2005). 'Finance and Growth: Theory and Evidence', in P. Aghion and S. N. Durlauf (ed.), *Handbook of Economic Growth*, Vol. 1, Elsevier B.V., pp. 865–934. doi:10.1016/S1574-0684(05)01012-9.

Levine, R. and Renelt, D. (1992). 'A Sensitivity Analysis of Cross-Country Growth Regressions', *American Economic Review*, Vol. 82, No. 4, 942–963.

Lin, J. Y. (1992). 'Rural Reforms and Agricultural Growth in China', *American Economic Review*, Vol. 82, No. 1, 34–51.

Macours, K. and Swinnen, J. F. M. (2000). 'Causes of Output Decline in Economic Transition: The Case of Central and Eastern European Agriculture', *Journal of Comparative Economics*, Vol. 28, No. 1, 172–206. doi:10.1017/CBO9781107415324.004.

Marrazzo, P. M. and Terzi, A. (2017). 'Structural Reform Waves and Economic Growth, ' ECB Working Paper Series, (2111).

Moral-Benito, E. (2012). 'Determinants of Economic Growth: A Bayesian Panel Data Approach', *Review of Economics and Statistics*, Vol. 94, No. 2, 566–579.

Nicoletti, G. and Scarpetta, S. (2003). 'Regulation, Productivity and Growth: OECD Evidence', Policy Research Working Paper Series, 1–26. doi:10.1111/1468-0327.00102.

OECD (2012). 'Economic Policy Reforms: Going for Growth 2012'.

Ostry, J. D., Prati, A. and Spilimbergo, A. (2009). 'Structural Reforms and Economic Performance in Advanced and Developing Countries', IMF Occasional Paper Series, 268.

Peruzzi, M. and Terzi, A. (2018). 'Growth Acceleration Strategies', Harvard CID Working Paper Series, (91).

Pevehouse, J., Nordstrom, T. and Warnke, K. (2004). 'The Correlates of War 2 International Governmental Organizations Data Version 2.0', *Conflict Management and Peace Science*, Vol. 21, No. 2, 101–119. doi:10.1080/07388940490463933.

Pingali, P. L. and Xuan, V.-T. (1992). 'Vietnam: Decollectivization and Rice Productivity Growth', *Economic Development & Cultural Change*, Vol. 40, No. 4, 697–718.

Prasad, E. S., Rogoff, K., Wei, S. and Kose, M. A. (2007). 'Financial Globalization, Growth and Volatility in Developing Countries', in A. Harrison (ed.), *Globalization and Poverty*, University of Chicago Press, pp. 457–516. doi:10.1016/j.jmoneco.2006.08.001.

Prati, A., Onorato, M. G. and Papageorgiou, C. (2013). 'Which Reforms Work and under What Institutional Environment ? Evidence from a New Data Set on Structural Reforms', *Review of Economics and Statistics*, Vol. 95, July, 946–968.

Pritchett, L. (2000). 'Understanding Patterns of Economic Growth: Searching for Hills among Plateaus, Mountains, and Plains', *World Bank Economic Review*, Vol. 14, No. 2, 221–50.

Quinn, D. (1997). 'The Correlates of Change in International Financial Regulation', *American Political Science Review*, Vol. 91, No. 3, 531–551.

Quinn, D. and Toyoda, A. M. (2008). 'Does Capital Account Liberalization Lead to Growth?' *Review of Financial Studies*, Vol. 21, No. 3, 1403–1449. doi:10.1093/rfs/hhn034.

Rajan, R. G. and Zingales, L. (1998). 'Financial Dependence and Growth', *American Economic Review*, Vol. 88, No. 3, 559–586. doi:10.1017/CBO9781107415324.004.

Rodriguez, F. and Rodrik, D. (2001). 'Trade Policy and Economic Growth: A Skeptic's Guide to the Cross-National Evidence', in K. Bernanke, Ben

S. Rogoff (ed.), *NBER Macroeconomics Annual 2000*, Vol. 15, MIT Press, pp. 261–338. doi:doi:10.1086/654419.

Rodrik, D. (1995). 'Trade and Industrial Policy Reform', in J. Behrman and T. N. Srinivasan (ed.), *Handbook of Development Economics*, Elvisier, pp. 2925–2982. doi:10.1016/S1573-4471(95)30022-8.

(1998). 'Who Needs Capital-Account Convertibility?' in P. Kenen (ed.), *Should the IMF Pursue Capital Account Convertibility?* Princeton University Press, pp. 55–65.

(2003). 'What Do We Learn from Country Narratives?' In D. Rodrik (ed.), in *Search of Prosperity: Analytical Narratives on Economic Growth*, Princeton University Press, pp. 1–20.

(2009). *One Economics, Many Recipes: Globalization, Institutions, and Economic Growth*. Princeton University Press.

(2015). *Economics Rules: The Rights and Wrongs of The Dismal Science*. W. W. Norton.

(2018). *Straight Talk on Trade*. Princeton University Press.

Rodrik, D. and Subramanian, A. (2009). 'Why Did Financial Globalization Disappoint?' *IMF Staff Papers*, Vol. 56, No. 1, 112–138. doi:10.1057/imfsp.2008.29.

Rozelle, S. and Swinnen, J. F. M. (2004). 'Success and Failure of Reform: Insights from the Transition of Agriculture', *Journal of Economic Literature*, Vol. 42, No.2, 404–456. doi:10.1257/0022051041409048.

Sachs, J. D. and Warner, A. (1995). 'Economic Reform and the Process of Global Integration', *Brookings Papers on Economic Activity*, Vol. 26, No. 1, 1–118. doi:10.2307/2534573.

Sala-i-Martin, X., Doppelhofer, G. and Miller, R. I. (2004). 'Determinants of Long-Term Growth: A Bayesian Averaging of Classical Estimates (BACE) Approach', *American Economic Review*, Vol. 94, No. 4, 813–835. doi:10.1257/0002828042002570.

Wacziarg, R. and Welch, K. H. (2008). 'Trade Liberalization and Growth: New Evidence', *World Bank Economic Review*, Vol. 22, No.2, 187–231. doi:10.1093/wber/lhn007.

Williamson, J. (ed.) (1994). *The Political Economy of Policy Reform*. Institute for International Economics.

World Bank. (2008). *The Growth Report: Strategies for Sustained Growth and Inclusive Development*.

3 Regulation, Institutions and Economic Growth in Advanced, Emerging and Developing Countries

BALÁZS ÉGERT

3.1 Introduction

The general interest in structural reforms has increased in the aftermath of the 2007–2008 financial and economic crisis.[1] The crisis impacted negatively economic growth, and the world economy has been in a low-growth regime ever since. Monetary and fiscal policies have reached their limits in reviving growth. As a result, policy makers have started looking at structural reforms as a way to boost economic growth.

There is a large body of literature aimed at studying the effect of structural reforms on economic outcomes. Many studies employ sectoral or micro data to understand the relation between regulation and economic outcomes, typically one of the supply-side channels of growth including multifactor productivity (MFP), capital deepening or employment.[2] Proponents of sectoral and micro data studies argue that (i) the effects of countrywide policies can be better identified econometrically, and (ii) policy effects can be better understood in terms of sectoral and firm characteristics. But these studies have some

[1] The views expressed in this chapter are those of the authors and do not necessarily reflect those of the Organisation of Economic Cooperation and Development (OECD) and its member countries. An earlier version of this chapter was presented at the Association for Comparative Economic Studies (ACES)/American Economic Association (ASSA) meetings held in Chicago in January 2016. Many thanks go to Iikka Korhonen for his useful comments.

[2] Examples for firm-level studies on MFP are Andrews and Cingano (2014), Andrews et al. (2015) and Arnold et al. (2008); for industry-level studies on MFP, see Cette et al. (2013, 2014, 2016) and Nicoletti and Scarpetta (2003). For investment, Alesina et al. (2005), Égert (2009) and Vartia (2008) use sector-level data, Araujo (2011), Autor et al. (2007), Cingano et al. (2010, 2016) and Vartia (2008) analyse firm-level data. For employment, examples are Bassanini and Garnero (2013) and Micco and Pages (2006) for sectoral data and Bjuggren (2015), Bottasso (2016) Chaurey (2015), Kaplan (2009) and Kugler and Pica (2008) for micro-level data for firm-level data and Cette et al. (2013, 2014, 2015) for sector level data.

drawbacks as well. First, these studies use the difference-in-difference approach, which help pin down whether some sectors or firms react differently to a given policy change than others. Some specific assumptions are needed to pin down the overall macroeconomic effects.[3] Second, only one or a limited number of policies are studies at the same time. Hence, estimated policy effects are unconditional on the effect of other policies.

Estimation results derived from aggregate macroeconomic data have the straightforward advantage that they can be used directly to obtain macroeconomic policy effects. Examples for such an approach are Bassanini et al. (2001) and Bouis et al. (2011), who analysed how innovation, financial and trade policies relate to per capita income levels in OECD countries.[4] Another appeal of growth regressions over sector- and firm-level studies is that it is easier to estimate policy effects by including a larger number of policies in the regressions. Hence, the estimated policy effects will be conditional on a number of other policy areas. Yet few studies explored this avenue. Égert and Gal (2016) come the closest by aggregating up various product and labour market policy effects to the per capita income level from econometric estimates obtained for various product and labour market policies and regulations obtained for MFP, capital deepening and employment.

A separate branch of the literature has been studying how institutions influence economic outcomes, and more specifically economic growth and development. As data on institutions do not change much over time and/or they are observed at very low frequencies, pure cross-country regressions composed of a large number of countries are the empirical workhorse of this literature. They tend to show that weaker institutions are usually associated with lower growth and lower per capita income levels.[5]

This chapter seeks to contribute to the literature in several ways. First, we run growth regressions, including a considerable number of product and labour market policies. Earlier studies typically used

[3] It is assumed that policies have no effects on the worst-performing sectors/firms. Another assumption is that policy effects transit only though the industry/firm characteristics used to figure out the impact of economywide regulations.

[4] Such panels are composed of annual country-level observations for about three decade for about twenty to thirty OECD countries.

[5] See, e.g., Acemoglu et al. (2004, 2014), Barro (2015), Hall and Jones (1999), Mauro (1995), Nawaz (2015) and Rodrik et al. (2004).

indirect measures of mostly financial and trade regulations (such as research and development [R&D] expenditures and trade openness) but not product and labour market regulations and certainly not simultaneously. Second, we would like to figure out the influence of a large number of regulations and institutions on per capita income levels. Third, we seek to understand whether policy effects are different for developing, emerging and advanced economies. Fourth, and somewhat relatedly, we assess the extent to which the level of institutions determines the magnitude and direction of various regulations. Our final question is to see how product and labour market regulations interact with each other, whether they are complementary or whether they substitute for each other.

The remainder of the paper is organised as follows. Section 3.2 discusses conceptual issues related to growth regressions. Section 3.3 describes our estimation strategy. Section 3.4 deals with data issues and presents a preliminary data analysis. Section 3.5 reports the estimations results. Finally, Section 3.6 provides some concluding remarks.

3.2 Conceptual Issues

The large body of literature aimed at analysing the drivers of long-term economic output (growth) can be split into three major branches depending on the modelling approach.

A first strand of growth regressions relies on *purely cross-sectional data for a large number of countries*. Many papers have been using cross-country data to analyse the covariates of economic growth.[6] A typical example is Sala-i-Martin et al. (2004): single observations per variable per country are used for eighty-eight countries. The typical regression estimated in Sala-i-Martin et al. (2004) is the following:

$$\Delta \log (Y_{60-96}) = f(\log (Y_{60}), P\_INV_{60-64}, HCAP_{60}, HEALTH_{60}, OPEN_{60}, \sum_{i=1}^{n} CHARACTERISTICS_i) \qquad (3.1)$$

where Y is per capita income in constant purchasing power parity (PPP) and HCAP is human capital. The Sala-i-Martin regression uses

[6] Examples are Crespo-Cuaresma (2002), Crespo-Cuaresam and Doppelhofer (2007), Durlauf et al. (2000), Fernandez et al. (2001), Levine and Renelt (1992), Sala-i-Martin (1997) and Sala-i-Martin et al. (2004).

relative investment prices (P_INV) rather than the investment-to-gross domestic product (GDP) ratio and a large number of indicators capturing country characteristics related to geography, history, religion, culture and institutions.

A second strand of growth regressions uses *multiyear averages for a large number of countries*. Barro (2001, 2003, 2013, 2015) are examples for such growth regressions for around ninety countries, using five- and ten-year averages. The main drivers of long-term growth are very similar in growth regressions à la Barro and à la Sala-i-Martin: the rate of growth of per capita income is usually regressed on a measure of physical and human capital, population growth and drivers of MFP growth such as openness (capturing the degree of technology diffusion); measures of macroeconomic stability; and a variable reflecting the health status of the working-age population. These measures are averaged over thirty to forty years in the Sala-i-Martin-type of regression. By contrast, these variables are allowed to vary over time in Barro regressions. Beyond that, the main difference is that Sala-i-Martin et al. (2004) incorporate a larger number of time-invariant country characteristics (such as geographical, political, cultural and historical differences). The Barro regressions can be best captured by the following equation (as in Barro, 2015):

$$\Delta \log\left(Y_{j,t}\right) = f\Bigg(\log\left(Y_{j,t-1}\right), \frac{INV_{j,t}}{Y_{j,t}}, HCAP_{j,t}, \Delta \log\left(POP_{j,t}\right) \\ HEALTH_{j,t}, \frac{GC_{j,t}}{Y_{j,t}}, OPEN_{j,t}, \sum_{i=1}^{n} INSTITUTIONS_{i,j,t}\Bigg) \tag{3.2}$$

where *dlogPOP* is population growth,[7] and *INV/Y* is the investment-to-GDP ratio. It also includes a variable capturing the health status of the population (life expectancy at birth), the government consumption-to-GDP ratio, trade openness and a measure for the quality of the institutional environment (rule of law and democracy).

Finally, other studies employ *annual data for a relatively small number of countries*. Examples are Arnold et al. (2007), Bassanini et al. (2001) and Bouis et al. (2011), who run growth regressions for

[7] The Barro equation uses the fertility rate to proxy population growth.

about thirty years for around twenty OECD countries. Arnold et al. (2007) estimates the following specification:

$$\Delta \log\left(Y_{j,t}\right) = f\left(\log\left(Y_{j,t-1}\right), log\left(\frac{INV_{j,t}}{Y_{j,t}}\right),\right.$$
$$\left.\log\left(HCAP_{j,t}\right), \Delta \log\left(POP_{j,t}\right), ST\ dynamics\right) \qquad (3.3)$$

where ST dynamics stand for the first-differenced long-term variables.[8]

While Equations 3.1–3.3 are typically referred to as ‘growth’ regressions in the literature, they are all variants of an error correction specification.[9] In this sense, error-correction specification implies that in the long run, only the level of GDP per capita is affected by the independent determinants. Growth rates are only changed during the transition period to the new steady-state level, which, however, depending on the speed of convergence and the short-term dynamics, can last for many years.

3.3 Estimation Issues

Given our interest in the long-run impact of policies and institutions on output, the level rather than the growth rate of output is regressed on the variables capturing institutions and policies. Adjustment to the long-run and short-term effects is analysed in a separate second step in the framework of a two-step error correction modelling approach.

In accordance with the existing literature reflected in Equations (3.1)–(3.3), the starting point is a growth regression including the following explanatory variables: (i) physical capital (investment as a per cent of GDP, K), (ii) human capital (HK) and (iii) population growth ($\Delta \log (POP)$). All growth regressions are estimated by regressing these variables on the log level of per capita income ($\log(Y)$) such as in Equation (3.4):

$$\log(Y_{j,t}) = f(K_{j,t}, HK_{j,\ t}, \Delta \log (POP_{j,t})) \qquad (3.4)$$

[8] Arnold et al. (2007) use population aged fifteen to sixty-four years and investment excluding residential investment.

[9] Equations (3.1) and (3.2) are reduced error correction models excluding short-term dynamics. They are mostly single-step error correction models whereas a two-step approach could also be used.

Equation (3.4) could be extended by adding macroeconomic stability (proxied by the inflation rate, dP), life expectancy (*LifeEXP*) and trade openness (measured as export and imports over GDP, *OPEN*):

$$\log(Y_{j,t}) = f(K_{j,t}, HK_{j,t}, \Delta \log (POP_{j,t}), \Delta P_{j,t}, LifeEXP_{j,t}, OPEN_{j,t}) \tag{3.5}$$

3.3.1 *Incorporating Regulation and Institutions in Growth Regressions*

Studies that investigate how policies influence per capita income levels enter the policy variables as additional regressors into (3.4). For instance, Bassanini et al. (2001) and Bouis et al. (2011) add a measure of financial development or financial liberalisation, trade openness or trade liberalisation and innovation intensity. Along these lines, it would be straightforward to add product and labour market policies and regulations to Equations (3.4) and (3.5).

But more policies could be added to the regression. In a production function framework, output can be decomposed into (i) MFP, (ii) physical capital, (iii) human capital and (iv) employment. Each factor could be modelled separately and the policy effects added up to derive to aggregate effects. But these policies, in a reduced-form equation, could enter directly the growth regressions.

MFP, capital deepening and the employment rate can be typically modelled as follows:

$$MFP_{j,t} = f(OPEN_{j,t}, INNOVATION_{j,t}, PMR_{j,t}, LMR_{j,t}, FMD_{j,t}, INSTITUTION_{j,t}) \tag{3.6a}$$

where innovation and openness foster the creation, adoption and diffusion of new technologies. PMR, LMR and FMD stand for product market regulation, labour market regulation and financial market development. These policies determine how efficiently resources can be reallocated within and across firms and how easy it is to finance new and incumbent businesses. Institutions capture the overall institutional framework (see, e.g., Égert, 2017a).

Capital deepening can be written as in Equation (3.6b):

$$(K/Y)_{j,t} = f(UCC_{j,t}, PMR_{j,t}, LMR_{j,t}, FMD_{j,t}, INSTITUTION_{j,t}) \tag{3.6b}$$

where UCC denotes the user cost of capital, which can be further broken down into the real interest rate, the relative price of investment and corporate taxes (see, e.g., Égert, 2017b).

The employment rate equation is given by Equation (3.6c):

$$L_{j,t} = f(PMR_{j,t}, LMR_{j,t}) \tag{3.6c}$$

where LMR denotes a variety of labour market regulations and policies (see, e.g., Gal and Theising, 2015).

Taking into account the policies in Equations (3.6a) to (3.6c) yields the following empirical specification:[10]

$$\log(Y_{j,t}) = f(OPEN_{j,t}, INNOVATION_{j,t}, PMR_{j,t}, LMD_{j,t}, FMD_{j,t}, INSTITUTION_{j,t}) \tag{3.7}$$

3.3.2 *Heterogeneous Effects in the Output-Regulation Nexus*

3.3.2.1 Threshold Models

Threshold models aim to capture nonlinear effects that can occur abruptly when the variable of interest has different coefficients below and above a given value of the threshold variable (threshold nonlinearity). For instance, the impact of product market regulation could depend

[10] Physical and human capital and employment (population growth) are typically used as explanatory variables in growth regressions. MFP is not included in Equations (3.4) and (3.5). It is actually the residual of these regressions. Adding policies and institutions to Equations (3.4) or (3.5) would therefore imply that the effects of policies would transit only through MFP but not via capital deepening and employment. Policies would only capture variation in the residual, e.g., variation in MFP. Policy effects going through capital deepening and employment are directly captured by these variables themselves. Hence, including measures of capital and labour will reduce the overall estimated effects of policies. If one would like to allow policies to impact output through the three channels, then it would be more appropriate to leave investment and population growth out of the regression. This would lead to entering policy variable to a reduced Equation (3.4). Nevertheless, not including capital and labour into the regressions would most probably introduce omitted variable bias: policies not included in the regressions and transiting through capital and labour would not be captured. In this chapter, we follow the conventional approach and add policies on top of capital and labour. In future research, however, we will compare how excluding capital and labour would alter the estimated policy effects.

on the level of another policy. The threshold value is determined endogenously through a grid search. In this chapter, a grid search with steps of 1 per cent of the distribution is carried out to identify the value of the threshold variable that minimises the sum of squared residuals of the estimated two-regime model. The grid search starts at 15 per cent of the distribution and stops at 85 per cent to ensure that a sufficient number of observations fall into each regime. There is evidence for nonlinearity if the null hypothesis of $\beta_1 = \beta_2$ can be rejected against the alternative hypothesis of $\beta_1 \neq \beta_2$ (Hansen, 1996, 1999).

$$Y_{j,t} = \begin{cases} \alpha_1 + \beta_1 non-linear\_variable_{j,t} + \varepsilon_t & if \ \ threshold\_variable < T \\ \alpha_1 + \beta_2 non-linear\_variable_{j,t} + \varepsilon_t & if \ \ threshold\_variable \geq T \end{cases} \tag{3.8}$$

where T is the threshold value of the threshold variable.

3.3.2.2 Parameter Heterogeneity: Does Economic Development Matter?

One question we seek to answer in this chapter is whether various product and labour market policies have the same impact in all countries or whether different countries may face different policy impacts. One obvious way that policies could differ across countries is through the development channel: policies could have a different impact for developing, emerging and advanced economies. Per capita income will be used in this chapter to measure economic development. Adjusting Equation (3.8) to per capita income levels as the threshold variable gives Equation (3.9a):

$$Y_{j,t} = \begin{cases} \alpha_1 + \beta_1 policy\_variable_{j,t} + \varepsilon_t & if \ \ per\_capita\_income < T \\ \alpha_1 + \beta_2 policy\_variable_{j,t} + \varepsilon_t & if \ \ per\_capita\_income \geq T \end{cases} \tag{3.9a}$$

where T is the tipping point of the per capita income variable.

3.3.2.3 Parameter Heterogeneity: Does the Quality of Institutions Matter?

Another question addressed in this chapter is the extent to which institutions matter for per capita income levels. Institutions could enter the country-time panel regressions as a time-varying variable. If country fixed effects are included into the regressions, the impact will be identified through the within dimension, that is, through the time variation in these variables. However, institutions tend to change very slowly over time. Hence, it would be interesting to see whether the cross-country variation in institutions is correlated with cross-country differences in per capita income levels. One way to look at this issue is to replace country fixed effects with constant terms capturing institutions. In such a setting, institutions would be measured as their period averages. Obviously, such an approach runs the risk of an omitted variables bias. But if the overall fit (adjusted R-squared) of the regressions excluding country fixed effects and including institutional constants comes close to that of regressions including country fixed effects, such a bias can be substantially reduced.

3.3.2.4 Parameter Heterogeneity: Does the Quality of Institutions Matter for Regulation?

Institutions may matter for per capita income levels not only on their own right but also through the way they influence the impact of other policies. For instance, better institutions could increase the negative impact of more restrictive regulations via better enforcement. But better institutions could also decrease the negative impact of more binding regulations via reducing regulatory uncertainty. This hypothesis could be tested as follows:

$$Y_{j,t} = \begin{cases} \alpha_1 + \beta_1 policy\_variable_{j,t} + \varepsilon_t & if \quad institutions < T \\ \alpha_1 + \beta_2 policy\_variable_{j,t} + \varepsilon_t & if \quad institutions \geq T \end{cases} \tag{3.9b}$$

3.3.2.5 Parameter Heterogeneity: How Do Product and Labour Market Regulations Interact?

Threshold regressions are well suited to provide insights for the last question to be answered in this chapter: do different policies interact with each other? More specifically, we would be interested to figure out whether the level of labour market policies amplify or attenuate the effect of product market regulations on output levels and vice versa. Equation (3.9c) will be employed to test for this hypothesis:

$$Y_{j,t} = \begin{cases} \alpha_1 + \beta_1 product\_market\_regulation_{j,t} + \varepsilon_t \\ \qquad if \quad labour\_market\_regulation < T \\ \alpha_1 + \beta_2 product\_market\_regulation_{j,t} + \varepsilon_t \\ \qquad if \quad labour\_market\_regulation \geq T \end{cases} \tag{3.9c}$$

3.3.2.6 Estimation Method

Given the trending nature of the data (even if country and year fixed effects are accounted for), cointegration techniques are needed to estimate the level relationships linking output with its long-term drivers. If the variables are not related through a cointegrating vector, the estimated level equations may be spurious.

We have two panels. The first panel covers around 100 countries for about ten years. For this panel, standard ordinary least squares (OLS) are used to estimate the long-term coefficients. The second panel covers the OECD countries for about thirty years. As the time series dimension of the second panel is large enough, the long-term coefficients are estimated on the basis of the dynamic OLS (DOLS) estimator: over the standard OLS estimator, it has the advantage that it corrects for the possible endogeneity of the regressors and autocorrelation in the residuals by incorporating leads and lags of the regressors in first differences (Stock and Watson, 1993):

$$Y_{j,t} = \beta_0 + \sum_{i=1}^{n} \beta_n X_{j,i,t} + \sum_{i=1}^{n} \sum_{l=-k_1}^{k_2} \gamma_{i,l} \Delta X_{j,i,t-l} + \varepsilon_t \tag{3.10}$$

where Y_t is per capita income and $\bar{X}$ is a vector of the independent variables. j stands for individual countries, i for the regressors and k1 and k2 represent respectively leads and lags. Equation (3.10) can be estimated using country and time fixed effects. In the empirical analysis, one lead and one lag of the covariates will be used.

Whether or not the variables of interest are cointegrated can be tested in two ways. First, the residuals obtained from the long-term relationship (ε_t) can be used to estimate the error correction model in the second stage. Weak evidence for the presence of cointegration is if the error correction term in this second stage is statistically significant and has a negative sign. This implies an error correction mechanism to be in place. A second and more formal test of cointegration is when the estimated residuals from the long-term relationship are tested for the presence of a unit root. The rejection of the null hypothesis of a unit root can be interpreted in favour of cointegration, in the spirit of the Engle and Granger residual-based cointegration approach. This chapter uses Kao's residual-based panel cointegration tests (Kao, 1999), which, along Equation (3.10), allow for country-specific intercepts but imposes homogeneous coefficients.

3.4 Data Issues

This section describes the database we use for the estimations. It describes the data and gives data definitions. Finally, it gives an overview of the statistical properties of the data series used for the econometric analysis and provides some stylised facts.

3.4.1 The SPIDER Database

The data used in this chapter were obtained from the OECD's SPIDER database. SPIDER stands for Structural Policy Database for Economic Research. SPIDER contains four main types of indicators:

i. Legal and political institutions.
ii. Framework conditions and regulations that determine the overall business environment in which businesses operate. They determine, for instance, how costly it is to start, run and close a business and reallocate resources within and across firms.
iii. Very specific regulations and intermediate outcomes. They cover policies and regulations affecting only a specific segment of a supply-side channel such as elderly workers or female workers. Examples are family benefits or policies aimed at influencing the effective retirement age. The frontier between framework conditions and very specific policies is not always very clear-cut.
iv. Outcome variables. They cover variables that are influenced by institutions and policies such as per capita income, various measures of productivity, investment, employment, unemployment and the participation rate.

SPIDER is a compilation of data from forty-three existing data sources. It draws heavily on a large number of existing OECD databases. It includes a number of non-OECD databases such as the World Bank's Doing Business and World Development Indicators databases of the Penn World Table 8.0. The final source of data in SPIDER are individual research papers, either academically published articles or working papers (for more details, see Égert et al., 2017).

3.4.2 Country and Time Dimensions

Two different panels are used in this chapter:

- The first panel covers around 100 countries. The time coverage of this dataset goes from 2002 to 2012. The data coverage is largely dictated by the data availability of the regulation indicators and to a lesser extent the institutional indicators. The Doing Business indicators covering the cost and time of starting a business, contract enforcement and insolvency procedures cover about ten years. The same applies to the business and labour market regulation indicators by Economic Freedom of the World (EFW).
- The second panel covers most of the OECD countries. For this panel, we use regulatory indicators developed and collected by the OECD. They include the energy transport and communication regulation (ETCR) indicator, an annual (and narrower) version of the main product market regulation (PMR) indicator, the employment protection legislation (EPL) indicator for regular contracts and spending on active labour market policies (ALMP). These indicators are typically available for more than thirty years.

3.4.3 Measures of Regulation and Institutions

This section presents the initial set of regulatory and institutional variables used in this chapter.

3.4.3.1 General Business Environment

Two sets of indicators describing the general business environment are used:

- ○ Doing business indicators: the cost and time of starting a business, contract enforcement and insolvency procedures
- ○ EFW: general business regulation

These indicators are available for a very large number of countries but they only cover about ten years.

3.4.3.2 Product Market Regulation

Two types of indicators specific to product market regulation are available for OECD countries:

- The OECD's overall ETCR indicator and its subcomponents, including (i) barriers to entry and (ii) state ownership. These indicators are available at an annual frequency. They cover the energy, transport and communications sectors from 1975 to 2013.

- The OECD's PMR indicator and its subcomponents, including (i) barriers to entry, (ii) scope of government and (iii) barriers to trade and investment. These indicators are available every five years and cover 1998, 2003, 2008 and 2013. They are used as constants in the regressions, obtained as averages over 1998–2013.

3.4.3.3 Labour Market Regulations

For the worldwide panel, the EFW's labour market regulation indicator is employed. For the panel of OECD countries, two labour market indicators are used: (i) the OECD's EPL indicator for regular (permanent) contracts and spending on ALMP. Spending on ALMP is measured as spending per unemployed as a ratio to per capita income (see Gal and Theising, 2015, for more details in this indicator).

3.4.3.4 Institutions

Variables capturing the quality of institutions cover the worldwide sample and come from a variety of sources. The major source is the World Bank's World Governance Indicators database. Variables covering the legal system, the rule of law and the degree of corruption are obtained from this database and cover the period after 1996. Civil liberty is obtained from Freedom House. Political stability comes from the Polity 2 database.

3.4.4 Descriptive Statistics and Preliminary Data Analysis

Tables 3.1a and 3.1b give an overview of the data series used in the empirical estimations. A striking observation is that the standard deviation of the raw data is considerably larger than that of the data purged of country and time fixed effects.[11] This implies that the cross-country variation in the data is considerably larger than the variation over time.[12] Hence, panel data analysis relying country and time fixed effect will not be able to explain cross-country variation in the data. Another observation displayed in Table 3.1b is that the cross-country variation of the institutional and regulation variables is

[11] The original data series are regressed on country and time fixed effects only. The residual of these regressions gives the series without country and time fixed effects.

[12] Not reported here are the data series purged only of country fixed effects. The overall differences are due mostly to taking the country fixed effects rather than the time fixed effects.

Table 3.1a *Descriptive statistics: time varying variables.*

	Raw data				Data purged of country and time fixed effects			
	Min	Max	Mean	Sdev	Min	Max	Mean	Sdev
					Worldwide sample			
Per capita income	5.29	11.62	8.75	1.31	–0.50	0.38	0.00	0.08
Openness	0.31	449.99	91.94	51.78	–93.67	118.80	0.00	12.28
Log openness	–1.18	6.11	4.40	0.52	–0.61	0.63	0.00	0.12
Log openness (size adjusted)	–4.93	1.99	0.24	0.49	–0.60	0.62	0.00	0.12
R&D spending % GDP	0.01	4.52	1.00	0.99	–0.65	0.99	0.00	0.14
Patents/capita	1.31E-08	2.96E-03	1.37E-04	3.78E-04	–8.45E-04	5.00E-04	5.25E-22	5.31 E-05
Rule of law	–2.67	2.00	0.00	0.99	–1.15	0.94	0.00	0.15
Cost of starting a business	0	1,540	67	143	–653	783	0	69
Time of starting a business	1	697	41	59	–193	82	0	15
Labour market regulation – EFW	2.34	9.73	6.31	1.49	–2.19	2.19	0.00	0.42
Business regulation – EFW	2.86	8.89	6.01	1.04	–2.16	2.26	0.00	0.45
Finance – bank branches per capita	0.13	237.07	19.38	23.96	–29.12	70.76	0.00	4.31
Stock market capitalisation % GDP	0.04	606.00	54.91	62.54	–134.33	336.15	0.00	24.07

					OECD sample			
	7.38	11.05	9.76	0.58	−0.85	0.84	0.00	0.16
Openness	5.73	371.44	68.15	43.87	−57.61	128.77	0.00	14.47
Log openness	1.75	5.92	4.04	0.61	−1.05	0.67	0.00	0.18
Log openness	−2.12	1.32	0.03	0.49	−1.11	0.66	0.00	0.18
(size adjusted)	0.00	0.00	0.00	0.00	0.00	0.00	0.00	0.00
patents/capita – World Bank								
Business spending on R&D % GDP - OECD	0.01	3.76	1.05	0.73	−1.23	1.27	0.00	0.27
General spending on R&D % GDP – OECD	0.15	4.48	1.68	0.88	−1.03	1.50	0.00	0.31
General spending on basic R&D % GDP – OECD	0.05	0.90	0.31	0.16	−0.19	0.23	0.00	0.06
ETCR – overall	0.79	6.00	4.08	1.47	−1.04	1.40	0.00	0.40
ETCR – entry barriers	0.43	6.00	3.77	1.84	−1.55	1.75	0.00	0.52
ETCR – public ownership	0.83	6.00	4.29	1.43	−2.10	2.09	0.00	0.53
EPL regular contracts	0.26	5.00	2.18	0.83	−1.16	0.75	0.00	0.17
ALMP spending	0.45	182.86	22.00	21.53	−49.15	101.86	0.00	12.56

Table 3.1b *Descriptive statistics: time-invariant variables (period averages).*

	Worldwide sample				OECD sample			
	Min	Max	Mean	Sdev	Min	Max	Mean	Sdev
Institutions								
Legal system	2.23	8.93	5.53	1.61	4.86	8.54	7.27	1.07
Legal system – enforcement	0.00	8.11	4.46	1.75	3.22	8.11	5.75	1.29
Legal system – judicial independence	0.60	9.15	4.80	2.15	3.85	9.17	7.06	1.74
Rule of law	-2.38	1.94	0.01	0.99	-0.53	1.94	1.27	0.60
Civil liberties	1.00	7.00	4.78	1.81	4.02	7.00	6.29	0.86
Polity2 – political stability	-10.00	10.00	3.78	6.17	0.27	10.00	8.01	3.17
Corruption	-1.71	2.45	0.01	0.98	-0.31	2.44	1.33	0.80
Government effectiveness	-2.18	2.18	0.00	0.99	0.16	2.14	1.36	0.56
Business environment								
Cost of contract enforcement	8	163	35	26	8	39	21	8
Time of contract enforcement	133	1715	628	305	216	1332	517	260
Cost of insolvency procedures	1	76	17	12	1	23	10	6
Time of insolvency procedures	0.40	6.97	2.75	1.21	0.40	5.84	1.92	1.16
Cost of starting a business	0.00	991.49	66.32	121.40	0.05	20.69	6.80	6.42
Time of starting a business	2.78	690.71	41.86	60.34	2.71	61.08	16.83	11.68
OECD PMR indicator								
PMR indicator – overall					1.18	2.80	1.73	0.35
PMR indicator – barriers to entry					1.49	3.07	2.06	0.37
PMR indicator – barriers to trade and investment					0.20	2.09	0.74	0.41
PMR indicator – scope of state control					1.51	3.92	2.41	0.54

smaller for OECD countries compared to the worldwide sample. This is another reason to motivate us to look at cross-country regressions.

The first column in Table 3.2a shows the large number of variables we have for the empirical analysis. The major problem with so many variables is that they are very likely correlated with each other. This may give rise to the problem of multicollinearity in the regression analysis. To preempt this problem, we proceed in two stages. First, for the panel data analysis including time and cross-country data, we calculate bivariate correlations for the data series purged of country and time fixed effects. We first group variables in thematic clusters and select one or more variables from each cluster. We then look at the correlation for the selected variables and retain only those, which have correlation coefficients lower than 0.3 with the other variables. Table 3.2a reports the selected variables. Variables within each group are indeed strongly correlated. In the final stage, we are left with one variable per group. An exception is made with the EFW's business regulation indicator, which has a correlation coefficient of higher than 0.3 with the variables measuring the cost and time of starting a business. These two variables will be entered separately into the regressions.

For the pure cross-country data (period averages), a similar two-stage selection procedure is applied (Table 3.2). There was a degree of arbitrariness in the selection of the institutional variables. All institutional variables are very strongly correlated among each other. We selected three of them – the quality of the legal system, the rule of law and the level of corruption – because we are interested in the effect of these variables on the level of per capita income. But because they are related to each other, they cannot enter the regressions at the same time. A further complication is related to the World Bank's Doing Business indicators. Within the group, three variables can be selected, broadly independent from each other. But it turns out that they are very strongly correlated with the aforementioned institutional variables. Variables in boldface in Tables 3.2a and 3.2b indicate that they are strongly interrelated with each other. Therefore, they will used only one by one in the regression analysis.

3.4.5 Stylised Facts

Eyeball econometrics applied to Figures 3.1 and 3.2 sheds light on a number of features of the regulatory and institutional indicators. First, plotting per capita income (in logs) against two measures of business regulation (the cost of starting a business; the EFW's business regulation

Table 3.2a *Variable selection – time series variables, worldwide sample.*

Starting categories	Group-specific selection	Final selection
Trade Openness		
Openness	Log openness – size adjusted	Log openness – size adjusted
Log openness	Trade liberalisation – EFW	
Log openness – size adjusted		
Trade liberalisation – EFW		
Innovation intensity		
R&D % GDP	Patents/capita	Patents/capita
Patents/capita		
Institutions		
Legal system	Rule of law	Rule of law
Legal system – enforcement		
Legal system – judicial independence		
Rule of law		
Civil liberties		
Poliy2 – political stability		
Corruption		
Government effectiveness		

Business regulation		
Cost of contract enforcement	Cost of starting a business	**Cost of starting a business**
Time of contract enforcement	Time of starting a business	**Time of starting a business**
Cost of insolvency procedures		
Time of insolvency procedures		
Cost of starting a business		
Time of starting a business		
EFW regulation indicators		
Labour market regulation – EFW	Labour market regulation – EFW	**Labour market regulation – EFW**
Business regulation – EFW	Business regulation – EFW	**Business regulation – EFW**
FINANCIAL DEVELOPMENT		
Financial liberalisation – EFW	Financial liberalisation	Bank branches per capita
Domestic credit % GDP	Bank branches per capita	
Domestic private credit % GDP	Stock market capitalisation % GDP	
Bank branches per capita	Stock market turnover % GDP	
Stock market capitalisation % GDP		
Stock market turnover % GDP		

Note: Variables in bold indicate that they are strongly interrelated with each other.

Table 3.2b *Variable selection – cross-country variables (period averages), worldwide sample.*

Starting categories	Group-specific selection	Final selection
Trade openness		
Openness	Log openness – size adjusted	Log openness – size adjusted
Log openness		
Log openness – size adjusted		
Trade liberalisation – EFW		
Innovation intensity		
R&D % GDP	R&D % GDP	Patents/capita
Patents/capita	Patents/capita	
Institutions		
Legal system	Legal system	**Legal system**
Legal system – enforcement	Rule of law	**Rule of law**
Legal system – judicial independence	Corruption	**Corruption**
Rule of law		
Civil liberties		
Poliy2 --political stability		
Corruption		
Government effectiveness		

Business regulation		
Cost of contract enforcement	Cost of contract enforcement	**Cost of contract enforcement**
Time of contract enforcement	Cost of insolvency procedures	**Cost of insolvency procedures**
Cost of insolvency procedures	Cost of starting a business	**Cost of starting a business**
Time of insolvency procedures		
Cost of starting a business		
Time of starting a business		
EFW regulation indicators		
Labour market regulation – EFW	Labour market regulation – EFW	Labour market regulation – EFW
Business regulation – EFW	Business regulation – EFW	
Financial development		
Financial liberalisation – EFW	Financial liberalisation	Bank branches per capita
Domestic credit % GDP	Bank branches per capita	Stock market capitalisation % GDP
Domestic private credit % GDP	Stock market capitalisation % GDP	
Bank branches per capita		
Stock market capitalisation % GDP		
Stock market turnover % GDP		

Note: Variables in bold indicate that they are strongly interrelated with each other.

indicator) for the worldwide panel suggests a possible negative correlation between less business-friendly regulation and economic development (Figure 3.1a). For the panel of OECD countries, a tighter ETCR indicator is possibly related in a negative fashion to per capita income (upper part of Figure 3.1b). There appears a positive correlation between higher spending on active labour market policies (unlmp_110) and per capita income. By contrast, there is no straightforward correlation between employment protection legislation on regular contracts (EPL) and per capita income (lower part of Figure 3.1b)

Looking at purely cross-sectional data shows a fairly convincing positive correlation between better institutions (the quality of the legal system, the strength of the rule of low and the level of corruption) and per capita income for the worldwide sample. Also, more business-friendly regulations (captured by lower costs of contract enforcement, insolvency procedures and starting a business) appear to go hand in hand with higher per capita income. But the correlation between labour market regulation (the EFW's labour market regulation indicator) and economic development is not very appealing (Figure 3.2a). The picture

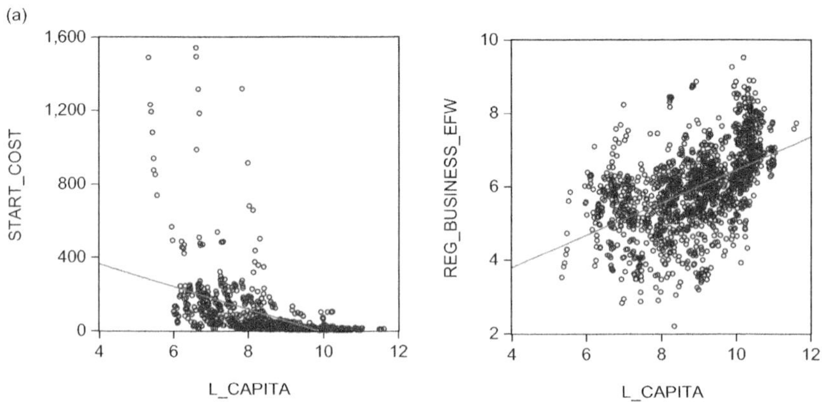

Figure 3.1 Per capita income (in logs) and selected policies, time and cross section.

Note: START_COST = cost of starting a business; REG_BUSINESS_EFW = EFW's business regulation indicator, higher values indicate more business-friendly regulation. ETCR_AGG, ETCR_EN and ETCR_PO refer to the overall ETCR indicator and its subcomponents, entry regulation and public ownership, respectively. EPL_EPRV1 and UNEMPL_110 are the indicators of employment protection legislation for regulator contracts and spending on active labour market policies, respectively.

(b)

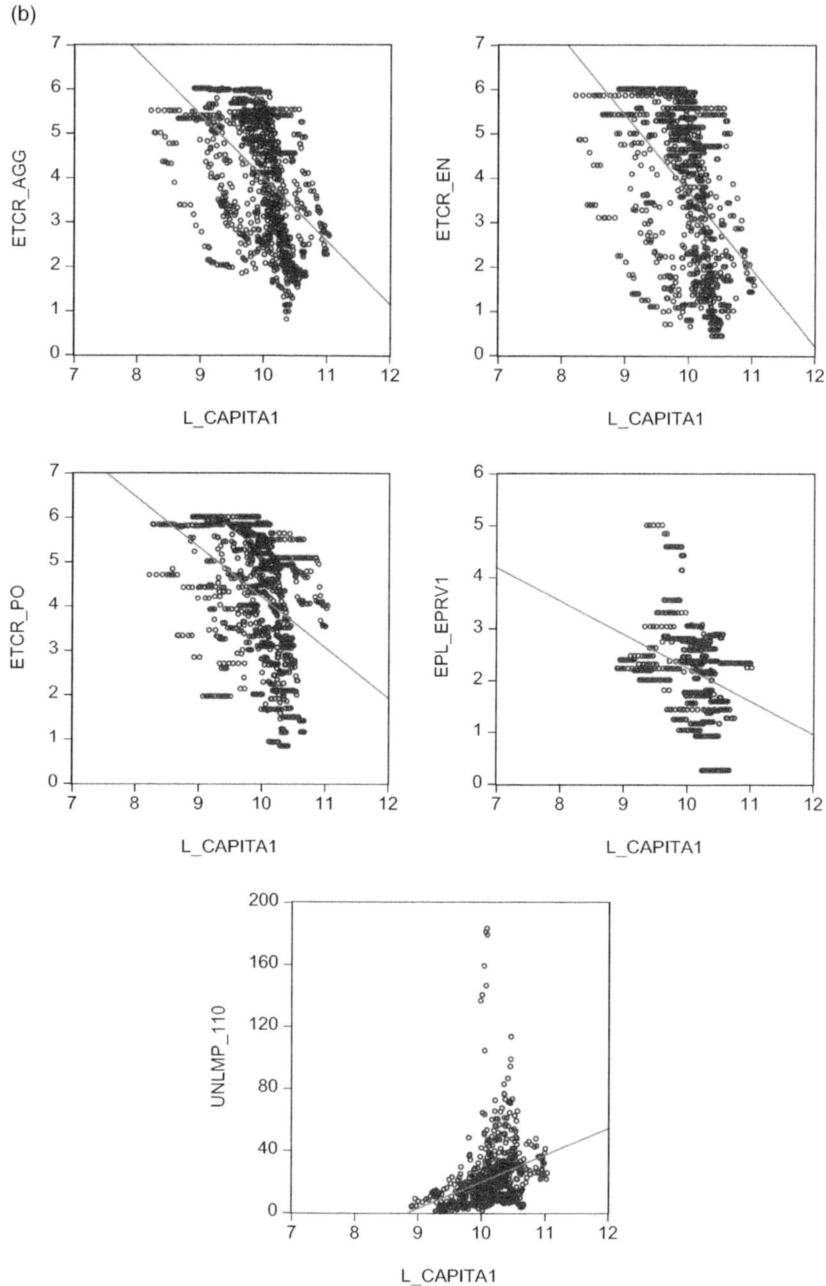

Figure 3.1 *(cont.)*

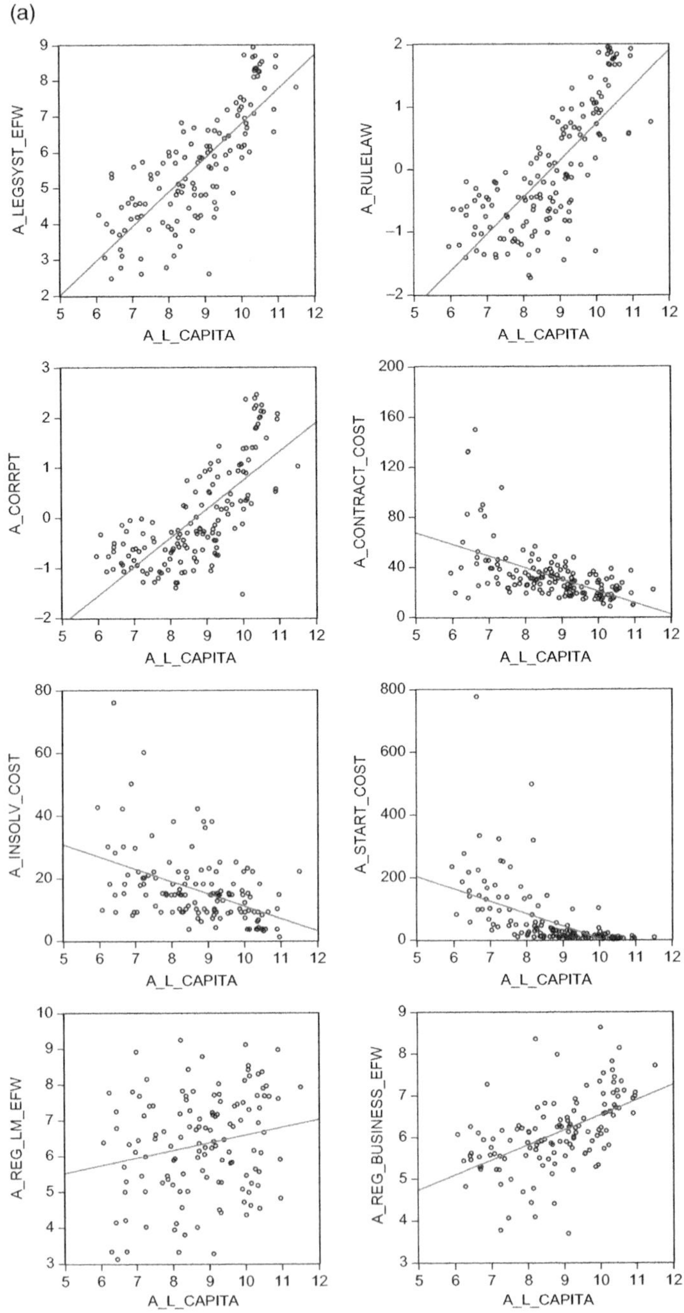

Figure 3.2 Per capita income (in logs) and selected policies, pure cross-section. (a) Worldwide sample. (b) OECD sample institutions. (c) OECD sample, product market regulation.

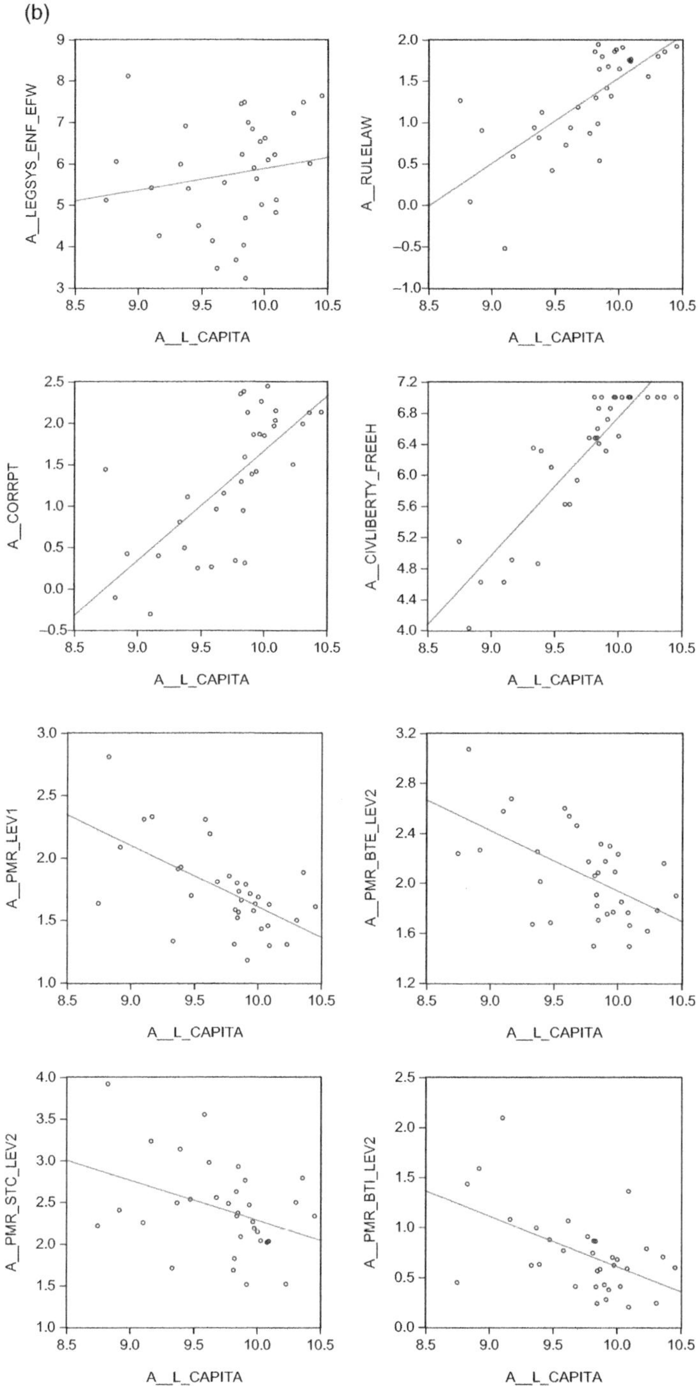

Figure 3.2 (*cont.*)

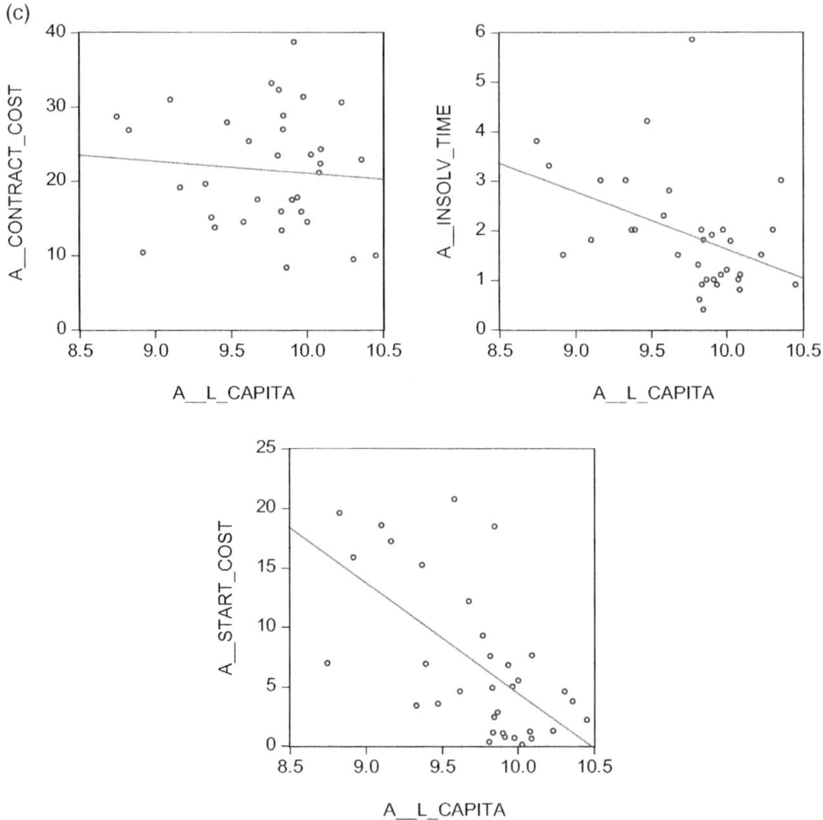

Figure 3.2 *(cont.)*

Note: In Panel A, A_LEGSYST_EFW, A_RULELAW and A_CORRPT denote the quality of the legal system, the strength of the rule of law and the degree of corruption, respectively. Higher values indicate better quality legal systems, a stronger rule of law and less corruption. A_CONTRACT_COST, A_INSOLV_COST and A_START_COST are the cost of contract enforcement, the cost of insolvency procedures and the cost of starting a business. A_REG_LM_EFW and A_REG_BUSINESS_EFW refer to the EFW's labour market regulation and business regulation indicators. Higher values indicate less regulation.

In Panel B, A__LEGSYST_ENF_EFW, A__RULELAW, A__CORRPT and A__CIVLIBERYT_FREEH denote the strength of the enforcement of the legal system, the strength of the rule of law, the degree of corruption and civil liberty, respectively. Higher values indicate stronger law enforcement, and rule of law, emerging from scatterplots obtained on the basis of cross-section data for OECD countries is blurred. Various measures of institutional quality are correlated to per capita income to a varying degree if at all. Also, scatterplots do not always suggest a reasonably strong correlation between business regulations and development. Finally, there seems to be some negative correlation between barriers to entry and barriers to trade and investment on the one hand and per capita income on the other. But the negative correlation between the scope of government control in the economy and income per capita is very loose.

3.5 Results

3.5.1 The Effect of Product and Labour Market Regulations and Policies

Let us now turn to the estimation results. For the worldwide panel including country and time fixed effects, variables capturing the stance of business sector regulation tend to have a strong relation with per capita income (Table 3.3). A more business-friendly regulatory environment goes in tandem with higher per capita income. The time of starting a business is a very robust driver of per capita income levels even when used to explain cross-country variations in per capita income levels (Tables 3.4 and 3.5). Other measures of doing business, including the cost of contract enforcement and insolvency procedures, are less robust drivers of income levels.

The income boosting effect of more lenient business sector regulation can be confirmed on the sample of OECD countries, using different measures of regulation, namely the OECD's ETCR indicator. Less

---

Figure 3.2 (*cont.*)
less corruption or greater civil liberty.. A_CONTRACT_COST, A_INSOLV_COST and A_START_COST are the cost of contract enforcement, the cost of insolvency procedures and the cost of starting a business. A_REG_LM_EFW and A_REG_BUSINESS_EFW refer to the EFW's labour market regulation and business regulation indicators. Higher values indicate less regulation.

In Panel C, A__PMR_LEV1, A__PMR_BTE_LEV2, A_PMR_STC_LEV2 and A_PMR_BTI_LEV2 denote the OECD's overall PMR indicator and its three subcomponents: barriers to entry (BTE), the scope of state control (STC) and barriers to trade and investment (BTI), respectively. Higher values indicate more restrictive regulation.

Table 3.3 *Estimation results with country and time fixed effects, world sample dependent variable: log per capita income.*

	(1)	(2)	(3)	(4)	(5)	(6)	(7)	(8)	(9)
Business regulation – EFW	0.017**			0.031**			0.034**		
Cost of starting a business – WB		2.00E-05			−0.001**			−0.001**	
Time of starting a business – WB			-0.0001			3.00E-05			−0.0001
Labour market regulation – EFW	−0.007	−0.006	−0.006	−0.009	−0.006	−0.004	−0.008	−0.008	−0.007
Rule of law	0.04**	0.048**	0.047**	0.058**	0.068**	0.071**	0.068**	0.114**	0.111**
Finance – bank branches	0.002**	0.002**	0.002**	0.002**	0.002**	0.002**	0.002**	0.001	0.001
Log trade openness – adjusted for size	−0.096**	−0.138**	−0.138**	−0.077**	−0.134**	−0.145**	−0.086**	−0.132**	−0.135**
R&D - patents per capita				104.3**	180.7**	176.3**			

R&D spending % of GDP							−0.019	−0.014	−0.018
Error correction term	−0.227**	−0.233**	−0.226**	−0.19**	−0.218**	−0.198**	−0.189**	−0.18**	−0.182**
Cointegration test, null hypthesis of no coint. p-value	0.006	0.023	0.029	0.282	0.487	0.374	0.452	0.299	0.105
Adj. R-squared	0.999	0.999	0.999	0.998	0.998	0.998	0.998	0.999	0.999
No. observations	888	770	770	597	500	500	545	463	463
No. countries	122	109	109	93	81	81	96	85	85
Country fixed effects	Yes	Yes	Yes	Yes	Yes	Yes	Yes	Yes	Yes
Time fixed effects	Yes	Yes	Yes	Yes	Yes	Yes	Yes	Yes	Yes

Note: * and ** denote statistical significance at the 10 per cent and 5 per cent levels, respectively, based on heteroscedasticity-robust standard errors.

Table 3.4 *Estimation results with constants and time fixed effects, world*

	(1)	(2)	(3)	(4)	(5)
Time-varying variables					
Business regulation – EFW	−0.039	−0.01	−0.05*	−0.025	−0.003
Cost of starting a business – WB					
Labour market regulation – EFW	0.016	−0.007	0.008	−0.016	−0.023
Rule of law	0.328**	0.302	0.13**	0.53**	0.553*
Finance – bank branches	0.004	0.003	0.003*	0.003	0.002
Log trade openness – adjusted for size	E-0.118	−0.123	−0.148	−0.141	−0.122
Time-invariant variables (period averages)					
Log trade openness – adjusted for size	0.18	0.212	0.306	0.222	0.191
R&D – patents per capita	70.173**	79.062**	108.931**	* 0.515	21.888
Labour market regulation – EFW	−0.167**	−0.137**	−0.141**	−0.122**	−0.123*
Finance – bank branches	0.005*	0.005**	0.005**	0.005**	0.006*
Finance – stock market capitalisation % GDO0	0.002**	0.002**	0.002**	0.002**	0.002*
Legal system	0.142**				
Rule of law		0.204			
Corruption			0.392**		
Cost of contract enforcement				−0.003	
Cost of insolvency					0.004
Cost of starting a business					
Error correction term	0.013	−0.008	−0.018	0.008	−0.002
Cointegration test, null hypthesis of no coint. p-value	0.006	0.006	0.006	0.006	0.006
Adj. R-squared	0.855	0.851	0.860	0.830	0.830
No. observations	650	650	650	573	573
No. countries	87	87	87	77	77
Country fixed effects	No	No	No	No	No
Time fixed effects	Yes	Yes	Yes	Yes	Yes

Note: * and ** denote statistical significance at the 10 per cent and 5 per cent levels,

sample dependent variable: log per capita income.

(6)	(7)	(8)	(9)	(10)	(11)	(12)
−0.032						
	−0.008**	−0.008**	−0.007**	−0.008**	−0.008**	−0.002
0.012	−0.022	−0.027	−0.016	−0.027	−0.028	−0.013
0.494**	0.449**	0.415**	0.251**	0.491**	0.5**	0.491**
0.007**	0.006**	0.006**	0.006**	0.006**	0.006**	0.008**
−0.102	−0.037	−0.032	−0.052	−0.033	−0.032	−0.079
0.186	0.156	0.156	0.221	0.156	0.158	0.203
112.73**	75.109**	82.002**	95.33**	77.641**	81.319**	100.413**
−0.143**	−0.13**	−0.121**	−0.131**	−0.117**	−0.12**	−0.132**
0.001	0.002	0.002	0.002	0.002	0.002	0.001
0.001*	0.0004	0.0004	0.0001	0.0005	0.0005	0.0003
	0.039					
		0.089				
			0.245**			
				−0.002		
					−0.0003	
−0.01**						−0.007**
0.039*	0.004	0.0005	−0.004	0.002	0.001	0.027
0.006	0.023	0.023	0.023	0.023	0.023	0.023
0.859	0.858	0.858	0.862	0.858	0.858	0.861
573	543	543	543	543	543	543
77	75	75	75	75	75	75
No	No	No	No	No	No	No
Yes	Yes	Yes	Yes	Yes	Yes	Yes

respectively, based on heteroscedasticity-robust standard errors.

Table 3.5 *Estimation results based on pure cross-section data, world sample dependent variable: log per capita income.*

	(1)	(2)	(3)	(4)	(5)	(6)
R&D – patents per capita	71.768	77.958	109.756	102.09	96.353	357.051*
Log trade openness – adjusted for size	0.013	0.08	0.149	0.076	0.083	0.083
Finance – bank branches	0.01**	0.009**	0.009**	0.011**	0.013**	0.012**
Finance – stock market capitalisation % GDP	0.002**	0.002**	0.001*	0.004**	0.005**	0.004*
Labour market regulation – EFW	−0.161**	−0.143**	−0.131**	−0.062	−0.129**	−0.102**
Legal system	0.325**					
Rule of law		0.506**				
Corruption			0.472**			
Cost of contract enforcement				−0.025**		
Cost of insolvency					−0.013	
Cost of starting a business						−0.016**
Adj. R-squared	0.807	0.808	0.812	0.696	0.660	0.725
No. observations	88	88	88	77	77	77
No. countries	88	88	88	77	77	77

Note: * and ** denote statistical significance at the 10 per cent and 5 per cent levels, respectively, based on heteroscedasticity-robust standard errors.

stringent regulation in the energy, transport and communications sectors are associated with higher per capita income levels. This finding holds true when breaking down the overall ETCR indicator into barriers to entry and public ownership (Table 3.6). This finding holds very strongly for the between dimension as well: the PMR indicator and its subcomponents measuring barriers to entry and barriers to trade and investment. Lower costs of contract enforcement and starting a business and shorter times of insolvency procedures are also related to higher per capita income levels across OECD countries. The only surprising result is that more government involvement in the business sector (through ownership and other controls) correlates positively with per capita income (Table 3.7).

Estimation results show a weak link between labour market regulation and policies and per capita income levels. For the worldwide sample, the EFW's labour market regulation indicator is systematically not significant. But once this variable is entered as a time-invariant variable, it is precisely estimated and has a negative sign, implying that more regulation is better (Tables 3.4 and 3.5).

For the OECD sample, the coefficient estimates on the EPL indicator on regular contracts also tend to be imprecisely estimated and switches sign across specifications (Table 3.6). While its sign is mostly negative when used as a time-invariant variable, it is often not significant statistically (Table 3.7).

Spending on ALMP usually has a positive sign but it is significant at the 5 per cent level only if a specific measure of innovation intensity (spending on basic R&D as a share of GDP) and the DOLS estimator is used (Table 3.6). For alternative measures of innovation intensity and when the OLS rather than DOLS is used, the standard errors are large.[13]

[13] Some of the results are controversial. First, the openness variable has an unexpected negative sign for the worldwide sample. The sign does not change even if using alternative measures of openness (size unadjusted and in logs). But openness works as expected for the sample of OECD countries. Second, variables capturing innovation intensity can have puzzling results. Per capita patents are linked via a positive relationship to per capita income. But R&D spending as per cent of GDP is not significant for the large panel. For OECD countries, general expenditures on basic R&D have a positive relationship to per capita income. The coefficient estimates are, however, significant only when using the OLS estimator. Even worse, general and business expenditures on R&D are estimated to have a strong negative relation to per capita income. These findings warrant further investigation in future research.

Table 3.6 *Estimation results with country and time fixed effects, OECD*

	(1)	(2)	(3)	(4)	(5)	(6)
ETCR overall	−0.032**	−0.033**	−0.056**			−0.057**
ETCR entry barriers				−0.038**		
ETCR – public ownership					−0.031**	
EPL – regular contracts	−0.039**	−0.042**	−0.001	−0.009	−0.009	−0.005
ALMP	0.0002	0.0002	0.001*	0.001*	0.002**	0.001
Log trade openness - size adjusted on world sample	0.2**	0.197**	0.169**	0.189**	0.196**	
Log trade openness - size adjusted on OECD sample						0.169**
Trade liberalisation index- EFW						
General expenditures on basic R&D % GDP			0.177"	0.169**	0.163*	0.184**
General expenditures on R&D % GDP		−0.052**				
Business expenditures on R&D % GDP	−0.06**					
Error correction term	−0.054**	−0.05**	−0.071**	−0.074**	−0.059**	−0.071**
Cointegration test, null hypthesis of no coint. p-value	0.012	0.015	0.000	0.000	0.001	0.000
Adj. R-squared	0.975	0.975	0.981	0.981	0.98	0.981
No. observations	655	657	410	410	410	407
No. countries	32	32	27	27	27	27
Estimation method	OLS	OLS	OLS	OLS	OLS	OLS
Country fixed effects	Yes	Yes	Yes	Yes	Yes	Yes
Time fixed effects	Yes	Yes	Yes	Yes	Yes	Yes

Note: * and ** denote statistical significance at the 10 per cent and 5 per cent levels,

But it is more statistically significant across alternative specifications once constants (period averages) of selected variables are used by replacing country fixed effects (Table 3.7).

Finally, our measure of financial development comes across as a very robust variable. It has a positive sign and is always statistically significant in various settings reported in Tables 3.3, 3.4, 3.5 and 3.7.

countries dependent variable: log per capita income.

	(7)	(8)	(9)	(10)	(11)	(12)	(13)	(14)
	−0.05**	−0.03**	−0.035**	−0.046**			−0.046**	−0.106**
					−0.032**			
						−0.034**		
	−0.008	0.008	0.005	0.035	0.027	0.04*	0.035	0.06
	0.0005	1.00E-05	−2.0E-05	0.005**	0.005**	0.006**	0.005**	0.009**
		0.261**	0.269**	0.208**	0.223**	0.243**		
							0.208**	
	0.07**							0.079**
	0.152*			0.089	0.046	0.086	0.089	−0.04
			−0.054**					
		−0.059**						
	−0.109**	−0.059**	−0.06**	−0.067**	−0.071**	−0.066**	−0.067**	−0.019
	0.000	0.012	0.015	0.000	0.000	0.001	0.000	0.000
	0.986	0.979	0.979	0.988	0.988	0.987	0.988	0.997
	267	559	561	323	323	323	323	160
	27	32	32	26	26	26	26	24
	OLS	DOLS	DOLS	DOLS	DOLS	DOLS	DOLS	DOLS
	Yes	Yes	Yes	Yes	Yes	Yes	Yes	Yes
	Yes	Yes	Yes	Yes	Yes	Yes	Yes	Yes

respectively, based on heteroscedasticity-robust standard errors.

3.5.2 *The Effect of Institutions*

An interesting finding emerging from Table 3.3 is that the coefficient on the rule of law is precisely estimated and is correctly signed. An increase in the strength of the rule of law is associated with an increase in per capita income. Plugging institutional variables as time-invariant variables into the regressions yield similar results. The

Table 3.7 *Estimation results with constants and time fixed effects, world*

	(1)	(2)	(3)	(4)
Time-varying variables				
ETCR overall	−0.111**	0.006	−0.017	−0.025*
ETCR entry barriers				
ETCR – public ownership				
EPL – regular contracts	0.104**	−0.075*	0.032	0.022
ALMP	0.004**	0.002**	0.001	0.001
Log trade openness – size adjusted on world sample	−0.006	0.227**	0.262**	0.206**
Business expenditures on R&D % GDP	0.177**	0.097**	0.067**	0.101**
Time-invariant variables (period averages)				
Log trade openness – size adjusted on world sample	0.088	−0.223**	−0.204**	−0.151*
R&D - patents per capita	3.53	117.553**	112.106**	90.229**
EPL – regular contracts	−0.095*	0.053	−0.045	−0.028
Finance – bank branches	0.003**	0.0003	0.002**	0.002**
Legal system – enforcement	0.07**			
Civil liberty		0.332**		
Rule of law			0.45**	
Corruption				0.274**
Cost of contract enforcement				
Time of insolvency procedures				
Cost of starting a business				
PMR overall				
PMR – barriers to entry				
PMR – barriers to trade and investment				
PMR – scope of state ownership				
Error correction term	−0.018**	−0.037**	−0.048**	−0.046**
Cointegration test, null hypthesis of no coint. p-value	0.012	0.012	0.012	0.012
Adj. R-squared	0.569	0.724	0.723	0.654
No. observations	655	655	655	655
No. countries	32	32	32	32
Country fixed effects	No	No	No	No
Time fixed effects	Yes	Yes	Yes	Yes

Note: * and ** denote statistical significance at the 10 per cent and 5 per cent levels,

sample dependent variable: log per capita income.

(5)	(6)	(7)	(8)	(9)	(10)	(11)
−0.165**	−0.095**	−0.071**	−0.037**	−0.056**	−0.089**	−0.148**
0.148**	0.092**	0.028	0.028	0.035	0.07*	0.097**
0.004**	0.003**	0.003**	0.003**	0.004**	0.002**	0.004**
0.009	−0.147	0.128	0.093	0.087	0.182**	−0.005
0.175**	0.217**	0.133**	0.187**	0.198**	0.16**	0.197**
0.08	0.2**	−0.09	−0.088	−0.055	−0.18**	0.051
111.982**	−100.777**	102.08**	23.421	51.238	82.864**	40.579
−0.199**	−0.07	−0.017	−0.018	−0.035	−0.081*	−0.105**
0.003**	0.003**	0.003**	0.002**	0.003**	−0.0003	0.002**
−0.018**						
	−0.128**					
		−0.017**				
			−0.374**			
				−0.276**		
					−0.379**	
						0.083**
−0.017**	−0.014	−0.027**	−0.026**	−0.025**	−0.03**	−0.017**
0.012	0.012	0.012	0.012	0.012	0.012	0.012
0.626	0.612	0.568	0.57	0.564	0.623	0.534
655	655	655	655	655	655	655
32	32	32	32	32	32	32
No	No	No	No	No	No	No
Yes	Yes	Yes	Yes	Yes	Yes	Yes

respectively, based on heteroscedasticity-robust standard errors.

quality of the legal system, the control of corruption and the strength of rule of law are associated, for most of the time, with higher per capita income, both for the worldwide and the OECD panel (Tables 3.5, 3.6 and 3.7).

3.5.3 Nonlinear Effects

The estimation results are not very conclusive regarding the influence of the level of development on the impact of regulations on per capita income. It is true that the threshold value of the level of development below and above which policy effects can differ is estimated to be very similar, around 10.000 USD per capital for the two samples and various measures of business and product market regulation. But the policy effects themselves around the tipping point are diverging. For the worldwide sample, the EFW's business regulation indicator has a stronger impact above the tipping point. At the same time, the opposite holds true for the cost of starting a business. For the OECD sample, a decrease in the ETCR indicator and its subcomponents has a milder positive effect on per capita income above the 10.000 USD level (Tables 3.8 and 3.9).

As for the effect of regulations conditional on the level of institutions, the results differ for the two country samples. For the sample covering around 100 countries, stricter business regulation has more negative impacts on per capita income if the rule of law exceeds a given level. For OECD countries, the opposite effect holds true. Nevertheless, the estimated threshold values for the rule of law are fairly different. This suggests that several a multiple-regime relationship might exist. Business regulations become more binding as laws are more strictly applied but the increase in the rule of law reduces uncertainty above a certain level, which makes the negative effect of business regulation fade away.

Finally, an increase in the stringency of business regulation tends to be more biting at higher level of labour market regulation both for our large sample (cost of starting a business) and the sample of OECD countries (ETCR indicator). An additional and interesting finding is that stricter product market regulations become less binding at higher levels of ALMP spending. This suggests that spending on ALMP above a given level may attenuate the negative effect of product market regulation on per capita income levels.

Table 3.8 *Estimation results with nonlinear effects, world sample dependent variable: log per capita income.*

		(1)	(2)	(3)	(4)	(5)	(6)
Threshold variable		Per capita income		Rule of law		Labour market regulation	
Threshold value		9,814	9,814	0.60	0.60	5.67	5.79
Test of nonlinearity, p-value	Null of absence of nonlinearity	0.000	0.000	0.000	0.000	0.008	0.000
Business regulation	When threshold var < threshold value	0.022**		0.025**		0.031**	
	When threshold var > threshold value	0.035**		0.04**		0.027**	
Cost of starting a business	When threshold var < threshold value		−0.001**		−0.001**		−0.0002
	When threshold var > threshold value		0.002**		0.003**		−0.002**
Error correction term		−0.22**	−0.254**	−0.2**	−0.265**	−0.201**	−0.229**
Cointegration test, p-value	Null hypthesis of no coint.	0.138	0.496	0.123	0.339	0.300	0.164
Adj. R-squared		0.998	0.999	0.999	0.999	0.998	0.998
No. observations		597	500	597	500	597	500
No. countries		93	81	93	81	93	81
Country fixed effects		Yes	Yes	Yes	Yes	Yes	Yes
Time fixed effects		Yes	Yes	Yes	Yes	Yes	Yes

Note: * and ** denote statistical significance at the 10 per cent and 5 per cent levels, respectively, based on heteroscedasticity-robust standard errors.

Table 3.9 *Estimation results with nonlinear effects, OECD countries dependent*

		(1)	(2)	(3)	(4)
Threshold variable		**Per capita income**			**Rule of law**
Threshold value		10,335	10,335	10,335	0.93
Test of nonlinearity, p-value	Null of absence of nonlinearity	0.000	0.000	0.000	0.000
ETCR all	When threshold var < threshold value	−0.05**			−0.078**
	When threshold var > threshold value	−0.024**			−0.007
ETCR entry barriers	When threshold var < threshold value		0.049**		
	When threshold var > threshold value		−0.024**		
ETCR public ownership	When threshold var < threshold value			−0.042**	
	When threshold var > threshold value			−0.015**	
Error correction term		−0.053**	−0.057**	−0.051**	−0.066**
Cointegration test, p-value	Null hypthesis of no coint.	0.016	0.043	0.067	0.046
Adj. R-squared		0.976	0.977	0.976	0.979
No. observations		655	655	655	655
No. countries		32	32	32	32
Country fixed effects		Yes	Yes	Yes	Yes
Time fixed effects		Yes	Yes	Yes	Yes

Note: * and ** denote statistical significance at the 10 per cent and 5 per cent levels,

3.6 Conclusions

This chapter set out to investigate a number of questions relating to the drivers of per capita income levels for a large set of countries and a narrower set of OECD countries. First, we tried to figure out whether and if so to what extent product and labour market regulations and policies impact per capita income levels. We find very robust empirical evidence for the existence of a strong relationship between product

variable: log per capita income.

(5)	(6)	(7)	(8)	(9)	(10)	(11)	(12)
		EPL regulat contracts			**ALMP**		
0.93	1.12	2.23	2.23	2.23	21.22	21.22	21.22
0.000	0.000	0.000	0.000	0.000	0.000	0.000	0.000
		−0.008			−0.045**		
		−0.039**			−0.03**		
−0.055**			−0.008			−0.038**	
−0.004			−0.034**			−0.022**	
	−0.084**			0.002			−0.024**
	−0.001			−0.027**			−0.013**
−0.068**	−0.063**	−0.069**	−0.074**	−0.066**	−0.059**	−0.066**	−0.055**
0.089	0.196	0.023	0.055	0.088	0.039	0.114	0.074
0.98	0.978	0.978	0.978	0.977	0.977	0.978	0.976
655	655	655	655	655	655	655	655
32	32	32	32	32	32	32	32
Yes	Yes	Yes	Yes	Yes	Yes	Yes	Yes
Yes	Yes	Yes	Yes	Yes	Yes	Yes	Yes

respectively, based on heteroscedasticity-robust standard errors.

market regulations and a country's level of development. More precisely, more business-friendly product market regulations were found to be associated with higher per capita income levels. At the same time, we could not identify precisely estimated effects of labour market regulation and policies, perhaps with the exception of spending on ALMP, which tends to have a positive relation to per capita income. The second question we sought to understand related to whether policy effects are different for developing, emerging and advanced economies. This chapter cannot give a clear answer. But we were more successful in finding out how institutions relate to economic development and whether they interact with other policies. We found, as have many more before us, that on average, institutions are very strongly correlated with a country's level of development. And importantly, we showed that institutions interact with product market regulations. The final issue we sought to raise was to show whether how product and labour market regulations interact with each other. We showed that labour market regulation and policies may attenuate or accentuate the impact of product market regulations on per capita income levels.

References

Acemoglu, D., Gallego, F. and Robinson, J. A. (2014). 'Institutions, Human Capital and Development', NBER Working Paper No. 19933.

Acemoglu, D., Johnson, S. and Robinson, J. (2004). 'Institutions as the Fundamental Cause of Long-Run Growth', NBER Working Paper No. 10481.

Alesina, A., Ardagna, S., Nicoletti, G. and Schiantarelli, F. (2005). 'Regulation and Investment', *Journal of the European Economic Association*, Vol. 3, 791–825.

Andrews, D. and Cingano, F.,(2014). 'Public Policy and Resource Allocation: Evidence from Firms in OECD Countries', *Economic Policy*, Vol. 29, 253–296.

Andrews, D., Criscuolo, C. and Gal, P. N. (2015). 'Frontier Firms, Technology Diffusion and Public Policy: Micro Evidence from OECD Countries', OECD Productivity Working Paper No. 2.

Araújo, S. (2011). 'Has Deregulation Increased Investment in Infrastructure? Firm-Level Evidence from OECD Countries', *OECD Economics Department Working Paper* No. 892.

Arnold, J., Bassanini, A. and Scarpetta, S. (2007). 'Solow or Lucas?: Testing Growth Models Using Panel Data from OECD Countries', OECD Economics Department Working Paper No. 592.

Arnold, J., Nicoletti, G. and Scarpetta, S. (2008). 'Regulation, Allocative Efficiency and Productivity in OECD Countries: Industry and Firm-Level Evidence', OECD Economics Department Working Paper No. 616.

Autor, D. H., Kerr, W. R. and Kugler, A. D. (2007). 'Does Employment Protection Reduce Productivity? Evidence from US States', *Economic Journal*, Vol. 117, 189–217.

Barro, R. J. (2001). 'Human Capital and Growth', *American Economic Review*, Vol. 91, 12–17.

(2003). 'Determinants of Economic Growth in a Panel of Countries', *Annals of Economics and Finance*, Vol. 4, 231–274.

(2013). 'Education and Economic Growth', *Annals of Economics and Finance*, Vol. 14, 301–328.

(2015). 'Convergence and Modernisation', *Economic Journal*, Vol. 125, 911–942.

Bassanini, A. and Garnero, A. (2013). 'Dismissal Protection and Worker Flows in OECD Countries: Evidence from Cross-Country/Cross-Industry Data', *Labour Economics*, Vol. 21, 25–41.

Bassanini, A., Scarpetta, S. and Hemmings, P. (2001). 'Economic Growth: The Role of Policies and Institutions: Panel Data. Evidence from OECD Countries', OECD Economics Department Working Paper No. 283.

Bjuggren, C. M. (2015). 'The Effect of Employment Protection on Labor Productivity', Working Paper Series No. 1061.

Bottasso, A., Conti, M. and Sulis, G. (2016). 'Firm Dynamics and Employment Protection: Evidence from Sectoral Data', Working Paper CRENoS No. 201606.

Bouis, R., Duval, R. and Murtin, F. (2011). 'The Policy and Institutional Drivers of Economic Growth across OECD and Non-OECD Economies: New Evidence from Growth Regressions', OECD Economics Department Working Papers 843, OECD Publishing.

Cette, G., Lopez, J. and Mairesse, J. (2013). 'Upstream Product Market Regulations, ICT, R&D and Productivity', Working paper No. 441.

(2014). 'Product and Labor Market Regulations, Production Prices, Wages and Productivity', NBER Working Paper No. 20563.

(2016). 'Market Regulations, Prices, and Productivity', *American Economic Review*, Vol. 106, 104–108.

Chaurey, R. (2015). 'Labor Regulations and Contract Labor Use: Evidence from Indian Firms', *Journal of Development Economics*, Vol. 114, 224–232.

Cingano, F., Leonardi, M., Messina, J. and Pica, G. (2010). 'The Effects of Employment Protection Legislation and Financial Market Imperfections on Investment: Evidence from a Firm-Level Panel of EU Countries', *Economic Policy*, Vol. 25, 117–163.

(2016). 'Employment Protection Legislation, Capital Investment and Access to Credit: Evidence from Italy', *Economic Journal*, Vol. 126, 1798–1822.

Crespo Cuaresma, J. and Doppelhofer, G. (2007). 'Nonlinearities in Cross-Country Growth Regressions: A Bayesian Averaging of Thresholds (BAT) Approach', *Journal of Macroeconomics*, Vol. 29, 541–554.

Crespo-Cuaresma, J. (2002). 'Some Million Thresholds: Nonlinearity and Cross-Country Growth Regressions', Vienna Economics Paper No. 210.

Durlauf, S. N., Kourtellos, A. and Minkin, A. (2000). 'The Local Solow Growth Model', Working paper No. 21.

Égert, B. and Gal, P. (2016). 'The Quantification of Structural Reforms in OECD Countries: A New Framework', OECD Economics Department Working Paper No. 1354

Égert, B. (2009). 'Infrastructure Investment in Network Industries: The Role of Incentive Regulation and Regulatory Independence', OECD Economics Department Working Paper No. 688.

(2017a). 'Regulation, Institutions, and Productivity: New Macroeconomic Evidence from OECD Countries', OECD Economics Department Working Paper No. 1393.

(2017b). 'Regulation, Institutions and Aggregate Investment: New Evidence from OECD Countries', OECD Economics Department Working Paper No. 1392.

Égert, B., Gal, P. and Wanner, I. (2017). 'Structural Policy Indicators Database for Economic Research (SPIDER)', OECD Economics Department Working Paper No. 1429.

Fernandez, C., Ley, E. and Steel, M. (2001). 'Benchmark Priors for Bayesian Model Averaging', *Journal of Econometrics*, Vol. 100, 381–427.

Gal, P. and Theising, A. (2015). 'The Macroeconomic Impact of Policies on Labour Market Outcomes in OECD Countries: A Reassessment', OECD Economics Department Working Paper No. 1271.

Hall, R. E. andJones, C. I. (1999). 'Why Do Some Countries Produce So Much More Output per Worker than Others?', *Quarterly Journal of Economics*, Vol. 114, 83–116.

Hansen, B. E. (1996). 'Sample Splitting and Threshold Estimation', Boston College Working Papers in Economics No. 319.

(1999). 'Threshold Effects in Non-Dynamic Panels: Estimation, Testing, and Inference', *Journal of Econometrics*, Vol. 93, 345–368.

Kao, C. (1999). 'Spurious Regression and Residual-Based Tests for Cointegration in Panel Data', *Journal of Econometrics*, Vol. 90, No. 1, 1–44.

Kaplan, D. S. (2009). 'Job Creation and Labor Reform in Latin America', *Journal of Comparative Economics*, Vol. 37, 91–105.

Kugler, A. and Pica, G. (2008). 'Effects of Employment Protection on Worker and Job Flows: Evidence from the 1990 Italian Reform', *Labour Economics*, Vol. 15, 78–95.

Levine, R. and Renelt, D. (1992). 'A Sensitivity Analysis of Cross-Country Growth Regressions', *American Economic Review*, Vol. 82, 942–963.

Mauro, P. (1995). 'Corruption and Growth', *Quarterly Journal of Economics*, Vol. 110, 681–712.

Micco, A. and Pagés, C. (2006). 'The Economic Effects of Employment Protection: Evidence from International Industry-Level Data', IZA Discussion Paper No. 2433.

Nawaz, S. (2015). 'Growth Effects of Institutions: A Disaggregated Analysis', *Economic Modelling*, Vol. 45, 118–126.

Nicoletti, G. and Scarpetta, S. (2003). 'Regulation, Productivity and Growth: OECD Evidence', *Economic Policy*, Vol. 18, 9–72.

Rodrik, D., Subramanian, A. and Trebbi, F. (2004). 'Institutions Rule: The Primacy of Institutions over Geography and Integration in Economic Development', *Journal of Economic Growth*, Vol. 9, 131–165.

Sala-i-Martin, X. (1997). 'I Just Ran Two Million Regressions', *American Economic Review*, Vol. 87, No. 2, 178–183.

Sala-i-Martin, X., Doppelhofer, G. and Miller, R. I. (2004). 'Determinants of Long-Term Growth: A Bayesian Averaging of Classical Estimates (BACE) Approach', *American Economic Review*, Vol. 94, 813–835.

Stock, J. and Watson, M. (1993). 'A Simple Estimator of Cointegrating Vectors in Higher Order Integrated Systems', *Econometrica*, Vol. 61, No. 4, 783–820.

Vartia, L. (2008). 'How Do Taxes Affect Investment and Productivity? An Industry-Level Analysis of OECD Countries', OECD Economics Department Working Paper No. 656.

PART II

Macroeconomic Implications of Reforms

4 Heterogeneous Market Regulation and Divergence in a Currency Union

MIRKO ABBRITTI AND SEBASTIAN WEBER

4.1 Introduction

The euro area was created almost twenty years ago, increasing from its initial eleven members in 1999 to nineteen members since 2015.[1] The experience has been mixed: compared to the pre-1999 period, inflation rates have been stable, close to target, and similar across countries. But differences have persisted. Progress on real income convergence has not materialized as hoped for (Brinke et al., 2015; Franks et al., 2018). At the onset of the euro creation, it was known that real income convergence would be difficult to attain. However, together with standard Solow-growth considerations, increased trade was seen as a potential driver in allowing lagging countries to converge to the productivity frontier by adopting the best technologies. This idea may be formalized with a simple production function with constant returns to scale technology for the overall economy:

$$Y_t = TFP_t \cdot K_t^{\alpha} L_t^{1-\alpha} \tag{4.1}$$

where Y_t denotes output, K_t physical capital, L_t labor, and TFP_t total factor productivity. Assuming identical functional forms in the member countries of the union and using lower cases to denote log deviations from the respective union value, e.g., $y - pop = log((Y)/(POP)) - log((Y^U)/(POP^U))$, real income divergence can be broken down into three drivers: TFP differential (tfp), the difference in the capital–labor ratio ($k - l$), and the difference in the labor-to-population rate ($l - pop$):

$$y_t - pop_t = tfp_t + \alpha(k_t - l_t) + (l_t - pop_t)$$

[1] The views expressed are those of the authors and do not necessarily reflect those of the International Monetary Fund (IMF).

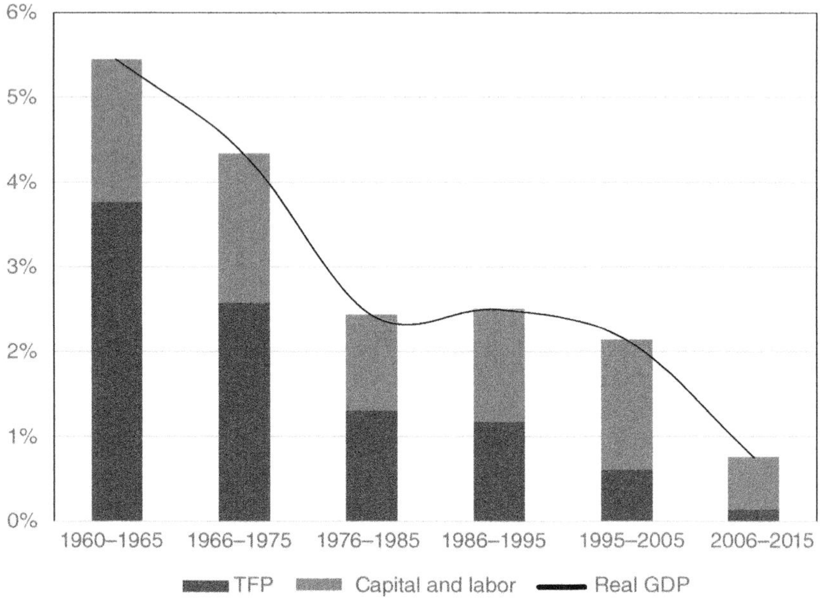

Figure 4.1 Euro area: TFP contribution to growth since 1960.

Over the medium term, there are reasons why capital–labor ratios and labor-to-population rates fluctuate and diverge. The traditional Solow-growth catch-up reflects one important aspect why the capital–labor ratio varies over time as it adjusts to the optimal level during a country's convergence process. However, in the long run, the capital–labor ratio should be constant when resources are allocated optimally (or adjust to changes in TFP), and the labor-to-population rate has a natural upper bound. Hence, long-term divergence would largely be driven by TFP.

According to European Commission estimates, TFP has indeed been the main driver of the long-run growth decline and growth divergence in the euro area. Figure 4.1 shows the contribution of capital, labor, and TFP to gross domestic product (GDP) growth for the first twelve euro area member countries. GDP growth has declined substantially in the last sixty years, from more than 5 percent in the 1960s to less than 1 percent in the last decade. The decline in measured TFP has been the main cause behind this slowdown in GDP growth. Average TFP growth declined from close to 4 percent in the early 1960s to a meager 0.1 in the last decade. Thus, the figure suggests that if we want to understand the dismal economic performance, we need to understand TFP dynamics. In addition, the top panel of Figure 4.2 shows the

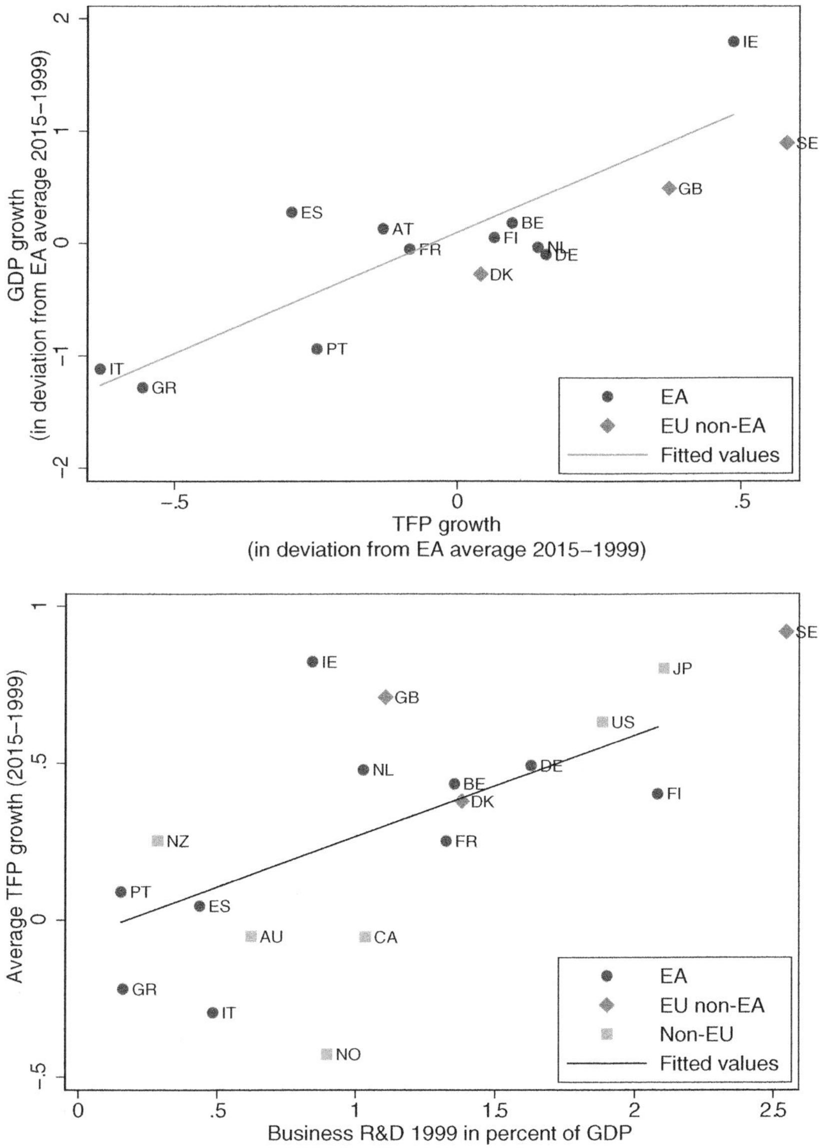

Figure 4.2 Long-run relationships among TFP, regulation, and growth.

correlation between GDP growth and TFP growth for individual euro area member countries, which is, not surprisingly, strongly positive. Variation in TFP accounts for half of the GDP growth differential among euro area members since the creation of the euro area. Thus,

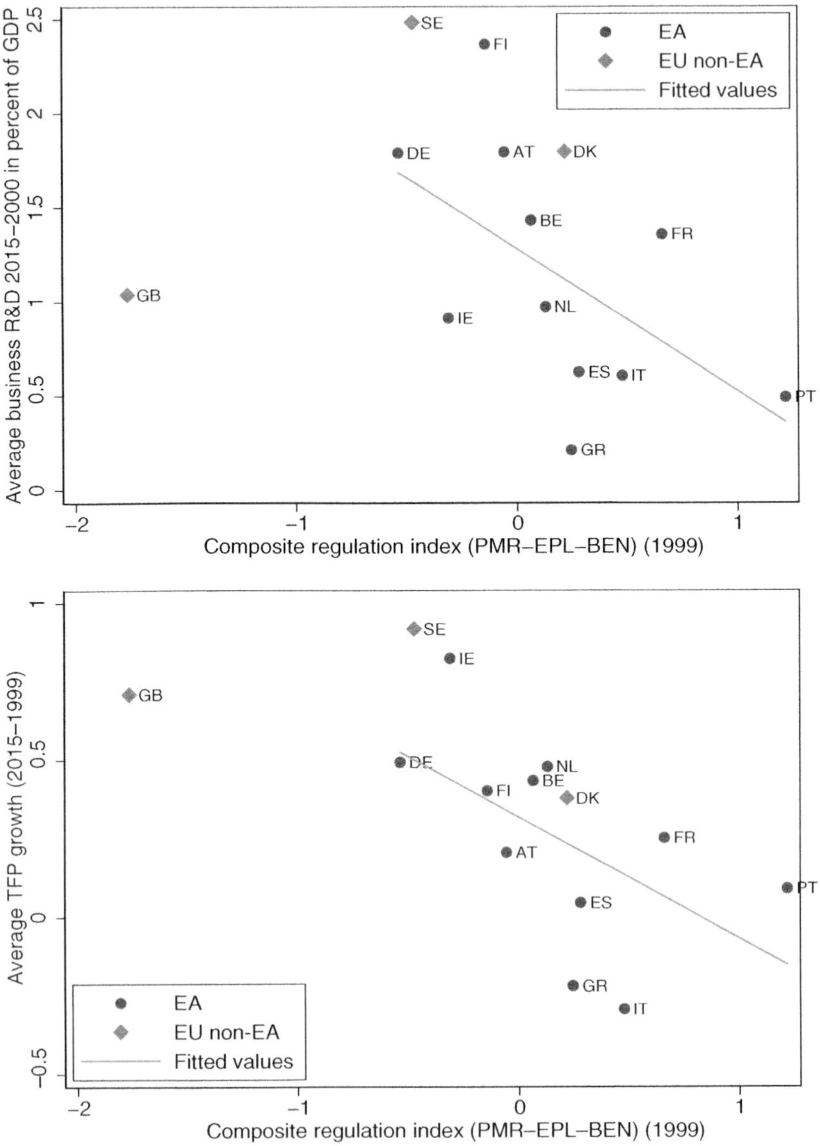

Figure 4.2 *(cont.)*

differences in TFP growth explain time and cross-country variation of GDP growth in the euro area.

The objective of this chapter is to analyze the potential role of different product market (PMR) and labor market (LMR) regulations in explaining such differences in TFP growth in a currency union. To this aim, we build a currency union endogenous growth dynamic stochastic general equilibrium (DSGE) model with product and labor market frictions.[2] The model differs from most existing two-country models because TFP growth is endogenous and depends on the state and on the regulation of the economy. Labor and product market institutions affect not only the adjustment of member countries to shocks, but also their long-run growth prospects. The model features three main elements. First, the labor market is modeled using search and matching frictions and Nash bargaining over sticky wages. This gives rise to involuntary unemployment and allows us to capture the effects of two key labor market regulations: employment protection legislation and unemployment benefits.[3] Second, we assume imperfect competition in the retail goods sectors. This allows us to measure product market regulation with the price markups of the economy. And third, building on Kung and Schmidt (2015) and Romer (1990), we assume that productivity growth is endogenous and sustained by innovation through research and development (R&D).

Using the three extensions, we study how reforms to the product and labor markets affect the short-run and long-run dynamics of the currency union. Synchronized labor and product market reforms are found to be strongly beneficial for the union as a whole: symmetric reductions in employment protection legislation, unemployment benefits, or price markups lift output and consumption and reduce unemployment in the long run. This is in line with the effects found in standard closed economy models and reflects the supply enhancing effect of such reforms. However, different to standard New Keynesian models without endogenous TFP growth, the effect here goes beyond a level shift in output, because the higher level of demand triggers higher R&D expenditure. This increases the intangible stock of capital, which is the driver of TFP and output growth.

When reforms are implemented only by one union member, their effects crucially depend on the degree of technology spillovers across countries. In the absence of technology spillovers, asymmetric reforms imply a competitiveness effect and are unambiguously beneficial only

2 See Abbritti and Weber (2019) for more details on the model.

3 Here we focus on these two dimensions of the labor market. An extension to include the labor tax wedge or union bargaining power is relatively simple.

for the reforming country. In the reforming country, higher production triggers higher R&D investment, which in turn increases TFP growth. This increases output growth and leads to a lower inflation rate in the reforming economy, as part of the productivity gain is passed on through lower prices. The member that is not reforming experiences lower long-term output growth and a higher inflation rate, although unemployment and consumption growth remain broadly unaffected. As unionwide output and consumption growth increase and unemployment rates decrease, asymmetric reforms remain beneficial for the currency union as a whole. However, this equilibrium is also consistent with long-run real income divergence. The situation is ameliorated in the presence of positive technology spillovers. In this case, reform efforts in one country also benefit the foreign country, because new discoveries in the domestic economy facilitate TFP growth also abroad. Consequently, consumption growth increases in both member countries, and real income divergence is reduced.

Concerning the cyclical properties of the model, we find that LMR and PMR have a sizable effect on the adjustment of member countries to shocks. Consistent with the evidence in Abbritti and Weber (2018), the model implies that less restrictive employment protection legislation increases the employment response but decreases the price response to shocks. Higher competition in the retail sector and lower unemployment benefits have the opposite dynamic effect, as they reduce employment volatility and increase inflation volatility. Correspondingly, symmetric monetary policy shocks tend to increase the response of inflation in countries with higher competition in product markets and higher employment protection legislation, while the opposite is true for the response of employment.

While a full empirical analysis is beyond the scope of this chapter, we provide evidence on the interactions among market regulation, R&D investment, and TFP dynamics in the euro area that supports the relevance of the main channels of the model. Specifically, we document that less regulated countries are characterized, on average, by higher R&D investment rates, stronger TFP and output growth, and lower inflation rates.

The findings of this chapter are related to the literature studying the effects of euro area membership on economic convergence. At least since the Delors Report (1989), income convergence has been an explicit objective of the euro area. The creation of the Single Market was expected to facilitate income convergence by reducing obstacles to trade, labor, and capital mobility, by fostering competition and by favoring technology diffusion. Recent research has analyzed the experience of the first years of the euro along different dimensions. There is little evidence of income convergence among the original member countries: real convergence of per capita income levels has stagnated in the early years of the common currency, while the North has diverged from the South since the start of the financial crisis (Franks et al., 2018). The synchronization of business and financial cycles has improved, but the amplitudes of those cycles have diverged. Moreover, there are growing signs that German financial cycles have become more delinked from other member countries' financial cycles (Franks et al., 2018). This has led some to ascribe the divergent patterns to the creation of the common currency. For instance, Estrada et al. (2013) notice that following the Great Recession the increase of dispersion in unemployment rates has been much larger for euro area countries than for noneuro area countries. De Grauwe and Yuemei (2013) argue that the sovereign spread increase in some euro area countries in 2010–2011 was delinked from fundamentals and associated with negative self-fulfilling market sentiments – not present in countries with independent monetary policy. Taking a longer-term view, Diaz del Hoyo et al. (2017) argue that certain member countries began to face a "convergence trap" well before the launch of the euro. While it is still unclear whether sharing a common currency may have played a central role in accounting for the increase in income divergence inside the union, studies generally point to the crucial role of total factor productivity in driving real convergence/divergence in the euro area over time.

On the theoretical side, our results are related to the literature studying the effects of market regulation on economic activity. Theoretical studies have mostly relied on calibrated business cycle models. Recent papers have studied the transitional dynamics following labor and product market reforms. For instance, Eggertsson et al. (2014) analyze the effects of structural reforms that increase competition in labor and product markets when monetary policy is constrained by the zero lower bound and find that these reforms can generate large output losses in the short run. Andres et al. (2017) analyze similar reforms in a small open economy model with credit restrictions and long-term debt and find that these reforms can reduce the short-run output and employment losses caused by deleveraging shocks. Cacciatore and Fiori (2016) develop a real business cycle model with endogenous product creation and labor market frictions to study the effects of deregulation of labor and product markets on economic activity. They find that reforms can have short-run recessionary effects, despite being expansionary in the long run. Cacciatore et al. (2016) develop a similar model for the case of a two-country monetary union and study the implications of structural reforms for the conduct of optimal monetary policy. They find that highly regulated product and labor markets generate sizable static and dynamic distortions that call for active monetary policy. Importantly, all these studies build on standard business cycle models with exogenous growth or no trend, and do not allow to fully account for the medium and long-run growth implications of different LMR and PMR.[4]

The remaining sections of this chapter are structured as follows. Section 4.2 describes the model. Section 4.3 provides model simulations showing how labor and product market regulations affect dynamics of the currency union under symmetric and heterogeneous market regulations. Section 4.4 presents related evidence on the relationship among investment in R&D, TFP, and output growth in the euro area. Finally, Section 4.5 concludes.

4.2 The Model

This section describes briefly the model used to simulate the currency union effects of different product and labor market regulations in the presence of endogenous growth through R&D accumulation. A detailed description of the model is provided in Abbritti and Weber (2019). The monetary union is assumed to consist of two countries, Home (H) and Foreign (F), of equal

[4] Empirical studies on the effect of structural reforms have either focused on long-run effects, e.g., through the use of averages of dependent variables of interest across several years (e.g., , Masuch et al., 2016; Nickell, 1997) or cyclical effects (see, e.g., Abbritti and Weber, 2018, and the references therein). The effect of market structures may be different in the short compared to the long run. For instance, higher employment protection legislation (EPL) is often found to limit employment adjustment in a downturn, but it is also frequently associated with lower long-run growth.

size. There is no migration across countries and, for simplicity, we abstract from population growth. The only traded asset across borders is a one-period nominal bond denominated in the common currency.

4.2.1 Households

The representative household in a country can be thought of as a large extended family that insures household members against fluctuations in consumption due to employment status. The household maximizes utility and saves in riskless bonds to smooth consumption. A preference for liquidity is reflected by incorporating bonds in the utility function (Anzoategui et al., 2018; Kryshnamurty and Vissing-Jorgensen, 2013). Households consume a bundle of differentiated domestic and foreign final goods in constant fractions of their income. A fraction of household members work while others are unemployed. In addition to the income from labor and unemployment benefits, households receive interest income on their holding of the international bond and their share of aggregate profits from firms net of any government taxes or lump-sum transfers. Even though the law of one price holds, absolute purchasing power parity does not hold, because the two countries consume domestic and foreign produced goods in different proportions with a home bias.

4.2.2 The Product Market

The production side of the monetary union builds on Kung and Schmidt (2015). There are four sectors in each economy. New patents are generated by innovation through R&D in the innovation sector. These patents are sold to intermediate good producers, which produce a differentiated good. Firms in the wholesale sector use these domestic patented goods, labor, and physical capital to produce the homogeneous wholesale good. Monopolistically competitive retailers buy homogeneous wholesale goods and transform them one for one into differentiated retail goods at no additional cost. Price rigidities, in the form of convex adjustment costs, arise in the retail sector, while search frictions together with convex wage adjustment costs create labor market rigidities in the wholesale sector. The introduction of these rigidities is the main difference to Kung and Schmidt (2015).

4.2.2.1 Retail Sector

Firms in the retail sector purchase wholesale goods and convert them one for one into differentiated goods that they sell to households and domestic firms. The presence of quadratic costs of adjusting prices á la Rotemberg (1983) yields, in each country, a standard price inflation Phillips curve, which gives a role to monetary policy. In addition, the government charges a tax, which limits the competitiveness of the retail sector as it increases the markup retail producers charge over marginal costs. Consequently, this tax is used to simulate the effect of PMR in the economy.

4.2.2.2 Wholesale Sector

In each country i ($i = H$ *or* F), firms in the wholesale sector combine physical capital, labor, and a composite of patented goods to produce output according to a standard Cobb–Douglas technology:

$$Y_{it} = ((Z_{it}L_{it})^{1-\alpha}(K_{it})^{\alpha})^{1-\xi}G_{it}^{\xi}$$

where Z_{it} is an exogenous AR(1) technology shock and G_{it} is a CES composite of patented goods defined over the varieties of domestically produced patents.

Search frictions are introduced by assuming that, to find a new worker, firms in the wholesale sector must actively search in the unemployment pool and incur the associated cost of posting a job vacancy. Workers are separated each period from an existing work relationship with an exogenous probability. The number of workers in the wholesale firms is therefore given by the sum of nonseparated workers and successful matches of job vacancies with job seekers. Wages are negotiated by Nash bargaining between the firm and the worker.[5]

4.2.2.3 Intermediate Good Sector

Patented goods are produced in the intermediate good sector, where firms have monopoly power due to product differentiation. These firms get the exclusive right to produce the patented variety by buying new patents from firms in the innovation sector. Each differentiated good is produced by transforming one unit of the final good into one unit of

[5] To improve the ability of the model to match the data, we also allow for quadratic costs of changing nominal wages and adjusting investment. These, however, have no bearing on the main results.

their patented good. Profit maximization leads to set the price as a constant markup over marginal costs. Hence, profits depend on the demand for patented goods and are procyclical.

4.2.2.4 Innovation Sector

Innovations (new patents) are developed by conducting R&D. Innovators use the domestic final good as input and sell their innovation to patent producers.[6] Because the innovation sector is competitive, the total amount of R&D investment is determined by a free entry condition that equates the costs of investment with the expected benefits of R&D. By determining the amount of R&D investment, this free entry condition pins down the equilibrium growth rate in the economy given by the growth rate of the intangible capital stock. Denoting by $N_{i,t}$ the aggregate stock of intangible capital (patents) in country i, the aggregate growth rate of $N_{i,t}$ evolves according to the following:

$$\Delta N_{i,t} = (N_{i,t+1})/(N_{i,t}) = \vartheta_{i,t}(S_{i,t})/(N_{i,t}) + (1 - \delta_N) \qquad (4.2)$$

where $S_{i,t}$ is the R&D expenditure, δ_N is the patent obsolescence rate, and $\vartheta_{i,t}$ captures the productivity of the R&D sector, which is taken as given by innovating firms. For the Home country, its functional form is as follows:

$$\vartheta_{H,t} = \chi((S_{Ht})/(N_{Ht}))^{\varkappa - 1}((S_{Ft})/(N_{Ft}))^{\sigma_R}$$

where $\varkappa \in [0, 1]$ is the elasticity of innovations with respect to R&D and $\chi > 0$. Following Kung and Schmidt (2015), this specification implies decreasing marginal returns to R&D investments, $\partial\vartheta_H / \partial S_H < 0$ (a congestion effect). Moreover, we allow for the possibility of positive technology spillovers ($\sigma_R > 0$) or negative congestion externalities ($\sigma_R < 0$) at the unionwide level. Intuitively, stronger R&D investment in Foreign can have both a positive effect on domestic R&D, by facilitating new inventions at Home, or negative effects, by increasing the difficulty of discovering and registering new patents. When $\sigma_R > 0$, we are implicitly assuming that positive externalities are dominating, so that technology spillovers from R&D are positive.

[6] The main force behind the cyclicality of R&D investment is the value of innovation, which is the present discounted value of profits that an innovator expects to obtain by selling the new discovery.

The opposite happens when $\sigma_R < 0$. Therefore, this functional form allows us to study in a simple way the effects of different assumptions about technology spillovers on the dynamics of the currency union.

4.2.3 The Labor Market

Labor markets in each country are characterized by search and matching frictions á la Diamond–Mortensen–Pissarides, which affect the choice of labor input in the wholesale sector. Total employment evolves following a process of job matching and destruction. A fraction s_i of employment relationships is destroyed in each period t, while a number of new matches m_{it} becomes immediately operative. As standard in this literature, the number of new matches is determined by a constant returns to a scale-matching function that combines searching workers with the job vacancies posted by wholesale good firms.

Nominal wages are determined according to standard Nash bargaining. Specifically, the firm and the worker choose nominal wages to maximize the Nash product of the value to the firm of an employment relationship and the corresponding value for the household, subject to the bargaining power of the workers. This bargaining over nominal wages yields the optimal sharing rule, whereby a higher weight is given to the firm's value of the employment relationship when workers have stronger bargaining power. The resulting bargained wage is increasing in the marginal product of labor, the continuation value of the employment relationship, and the outside option of the worker, given by the unemployment benefits.

4.2.4 Monetary Policy and Long-Run Equilibrium

The model is closed with a standard Taylor monetary policy rule, whereby the monetary authority targets average output growth and inflation in the currency area. This together with the specifications of household's preferences and firms' technologies allows finding a balanced growth path for the monetary union – even in the case in which the two countries grow at different steady-state growth rates.[7]

[7] To obtain the balanced growth certain parametric restrictions need to be imposed. See Abbritti and Weber (2019) for more details. Notice also that since the aggregate consumption baskets are Cobb–Douglas in the domestic and

Using equilibrium conditions, one can rewrite Home's output analogous to the standard production function in Equation (4.1):

$$Y_{Ht} = TFP_{Ht} \cdot K_{Ht}{}^{\alpha} L_{Ht}{}^{1-\alpha} \tag{4.3}$$

Importantly, the TFP term is endogenously determined and given by:

$$TFP_{Ht} = \theta_{Ht}(Z_{Ht}N_{Ht})^{1-\alpha} \tag{4.4}$$

where θ_{Ht} is a wedge that depends on the parameters of the model and the markups of the retail and intermediate good sectors. TFP is increasing in the exogenous forcing process Z_H as is the case in any standard model. More importantly, TFP is driven by the domestic stock of intangible capital, N_H, which is in turn determined by investment in R&D. Through this channel, innovation and R&D endogenously affect the dynamics of productivity and lead to persistent swings in output and consumption rates. In particular, the introduction of endogenous technological progress has two main advantages for our purposes. First, it breaks down the dichotomy between growth and cycle of most macroeconomic models: adverse temporary shocks not only lower the level of consumption and economic activity today, but also reduce the resources and the incentives to innovate, which in turn impact long-term prospects. Second and most importantly, TFP dynamics depend on the state and institutions of the economy. Therefore, labor and product market institutions affect not only the adjustment of member countries to shocks, but also their long-run growth prospects. The model, thus, provides a rigorous, unified framework to study the effect of heterogeneous market regulation on short-, medium-, and long-run dynamics.

While the growth rate of domestic production depends on the domestic stock of intangible capital, $\Delta Y_H = \Delta N_H$, the growth rate of consumption reflects both domestic and foreign technological progress. This happens because households in each country consume goods produced in both countries. In particular, it can be shown that, along the balanced growth path, the growth rate of home consumption

foreign goods, the differences in real growth rates in consumption are exactly neutralized by the secular trend in relative prices.

is proportional to the growth rates of the stock of intangible capital embodied in the aggregate home consumption basket:

$$\Delta C_H = (\Delta N_H)^{1-\gamma}(\Delta N_F)^{\gamma} \tag{4.5}$$

where γ is the weight of foreign goods in domestic consumption. A corresponding equation holds for Foreign. Differences in trend growth in turn translate into different steady state inflation rates, where the country growing faster has a lower inflation rate. This in turn leads to a secular trend in the equilibrium real exchange rate, which depreciates for the fast-growing country:

$$\Delta RER = (\pi^*)/(\pi) = ((\Delta N_H)/(\Delta N_F))^{1-2\gamma} \tag{4.6}$$

where π and π^* denote respectively home and foreign inflation. In summary, the model implies that member countries with higher R&D investment enjoy higher average TFP growth, which translate into higher GDP growth, lower average inflation rates, and a secular real exchange rate depreciation.

4.3 Market Regulation and Currency Union Dynamics

Drawing on the outlined model, we analyze how different labor and product market institutions affect the dynamics of the currency union. To perform this quantitative assessment, we first calibrate the parameters of the model in line with the standard values used in the literature and to capture the main structural features of the euro area.[8] Then we consider the effects of three reforms. The first reform is product market deregulation. Following Eggertsson et al. (2014), we model this policy as a reduction of the tax rate on the retail sector, which decreases the markup and increases competition. Specifically, we reduce the tax rate from $\tau_{it}^{p} = 0.2$ to $\tau_{it}^{p} = 0.185$. This translates into a reduction of the net markup of the retail sector by 7 percent, from 0.375 to 0.35.

Regarding labor markets, we focus on two institutions. In the first exercise, we reduce permanently unemployment benefits by 20 percent,

[8] In the baseline calibration, we assume that the Home and Foreign countries are perfectly symmetric. The model is calibrated at the quarterly frequency and solved by second-order perturbation methods using Dynare ver. 4.5.1. Full details on the calibration strategy can be found in Abbritti and Weber (2019).

which lowers the equilibrium benefits over wage ratio from 0.523 to 0.431. In the second exercise, we change the overall degree of rigidity of labor market flows. Specifically, following Blanchard and Galí (2010), we define a labor market as "flexible" when the job-finding and the separation rate are high. The opposite holds in a "rigid" labor market. In practice, to attain a more flexible labor market, we change the efficiency of matches and the exogenous separation rate such that in the steady state the job-finding rate is higher, and the unemployment rate is lower than in the baseline calibration.[9]

4.3.1 *Steady-State Growth under Varying Market Regulation*

In the model, TFP is an endogenous variable, and the steady-state growth rates of output, consumption, prices, and other endogenous variables are a function of the deep parameters of the model. Therefore, by changing the corresponding parameters of the model, we can analyze the effect of reforms on the long-run equilibrium of the currency union.

Table 4.1 shows the effects of varying labor and product market parameters on the steady state of the economy. The exercise is performed by fixing all the deep parameters of the model to their values of the baseline calibration and allowing all the endogenous variables to adjust to changes in the policy parameters of interest. We consider symmetric reforms, where both countries are characterized by more flexible markets, and asymmetric reforms, in which case we assume that there is deregulation in the Home economy, but not in the Foreign economy.

First, we discuss the effects of symmetric reforms. The results are in line with those from conventional models capturing LMR and PMR. All three reforms increase the long-run growth of the economy, and lower the unemployment rate, although to different extents. A reduction of the markup of retailers (column τ_t^p in the table) increases the growth rate of union output and reduces the unemployment rate. Intuitively, higher competition in the retail market reduces monopolistic distortions and the price of retail goods and improves the overall efficiency of the retail sector. This in turn increases the demand for wholesale goods and thus for intangible goods. The higher profit opportunities for new discoveries stimulate investment in R&D, which

9 As shown in Abbritti and Mueller (2013), this calibration of labor market rigidities captures, in a reduced form, the effect of lower hiring and firing costs.

Table 4.1 ***Comparative statics analysis of the steady-state growth rate for different values of product and labor market institutions.***

Long run		Baseline	Symmetric reforms			Asymmetric reforms		
Mean		Calibration	τ_i^p	b_i	LMR_i	τ_H^p	b_H	LMR_H
Union	Δy^U	1.60	2.34	2.12	1.93	1.97	1.86	1.76
	Δc^U	1.60	2.34	2.12	1.93	1.97	1.86	1.76
	u^U	8.00	6.62	3.30	5.00	7.28	5.13	6.35
	π^U	2.00	2.00	2.00	2.00	2.00	2.00	2.00
Home	Δy^H	1.60	2.34	2.12	1.93	2.68	2.34	2.06
	Δc^H	1.60	2.34	2.12	1.93	2.33	2.10	1.91
	u^H	8.00	6.62	3.30	5.00	6.51	3.32	5.09
	π^H	2.00	2.00	2.00	2.00	1.28	1.53	1.71
Foreign	Δy^F	1.60	2.34	2.12	1.93	1.25	1.39	1.47
	Δc^F	1.60	2.34	2.12	1.93	1.61	1.63	1.62
	u^F	8.00	6.62	3.30	5.00	8.14	7.92	7.93
	π^F	2.00	2.00	2.00	2.00	2.72	2.48	2.29
Rel. prices	ΔToT	0.00	0.00	0.00	0.00	1.44	0.95	0.58
	ΔRER	0.00	0.00	0.00	0.00	0.72	0.48	0.30

leads to higher steady-state growth in the number of patents. As described by Equations (4.2), (4.3), and (4.4), this is the source for higher TFP and output growth.

Similarly, a reduction in unemployment benefits lowers the unemployment rate and increases long-run growth (column b_i in the table). A reduction of unemployment benefits worsens the outside option of workers and lowers the equilibrium wage. At the lower wage, demand for labor and consequently production increases. As with deregulation in the product market, the higher production triggers more demand for wholesale goods and R&D investment, leading to higher growth. Finally, a more flexible labor market (LMR_i in the table) implies, by definition, lower unemployment rates and higher job-finding rates. The lower costs of production and higher employment rates increase the resources available for R&D and stimulate further demand for patented goods, leading to higher production and output growth.

When reforms are asymmetric, the impacts on unemployment, production and growth of the Home country (i.e., the country affected by the reform) are qualitatively similar, but even larger under the baseline calibration. The impact on the Foreign country depends crucially on the degree of technology spillovers. Several authors suggest that increased trade and integration through value chains help the diffusion of innovation and productivity-enhancing technologies (e.g., Cameron et. al., 2005; Coe and Helpman 1995; Piermartini and Rubínová, 2014). Hence, currency member countries that are trading more heavily among each other are more likely to benefit from another member's productivity enhancing R&D investment. Negative spillovers would instead arise if there is no technology transfer and a country's R&D investment reduces another country's return to R&D investment, as it becomes more difficult to innovate beyond the existing stock of patents, which cannot be copied abroad.

Let us consider first the baseline case in which there are neither positive nor negative spillovers of Home country's R&D intensity on the productivity of foreign R&D, i.e., $\sigma_R = 0$ (see Table 4.1). At Home, the positive effect of the reform on output growth is amplified by the inaction of the Foreign country because the reform improves the competitiveness of home firms at the expense of foreign firms. In response to the changed relative price, demand shifts to home goods. R&D activity in Foreign declines, and output growth is reduced. However, unemployment is only weakly affected. Consumption growth of foreign households remains almost constant, because the lower growth rate of foreign production is compensated by a much higher growth rate of home production and by an improved terms of trade of Foreign. Thus, in the absence of technology spillovers, a country that undertakes no reform is expected to exhibit relatively lower TFP growth if other union members liberalize labor or product markets. Different steady-state output growth rates translate into different inflation rates and an equilibrium depreciation of the Home country's terms of trade and real exchange rate.[10]

[10] We compare the long-run properties of a currency union with different product and labor market regulations here, but not the transition dynamics from the old to the new equilibrium or the role of monetary policy in facilitating the adjustment process following a reform. For related work on the role of monetary policy in the context of product and labor market reforms (though not necessarily in the context of monetary unions), see Aghion et al. (2018), Ahn et al. (2018), and Cacciatore et al. (2016). Their work suggests that optimal monetary policy should be more expansionary in response to deregulation to support demand, which would limit the negative spillover from asymmetric reforms.

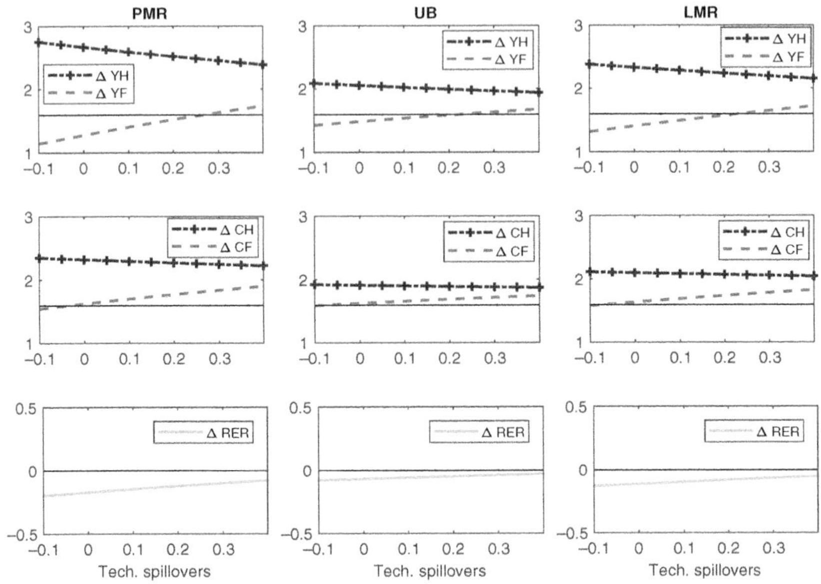

Figure 4.3 The effects of asymmetric reforms on the long-run equilibrium and the role of technology spillovers. This graph shows how the steady-state growth rates of output, consumption, and the real exchange rate change with different values of the technology spillover parameter σ_R.

Figure 4.3 shows how technology spillovers can affect this long-run equilibrium of the Home and Foreign country, following a reform in the Home country. When technology spillovers are negative, asymmetric reforms are beggar-thy-neighbor, i.e., detrimental for the nonreforming country. For $\sigma_R < -0.05$ reforms at Home reduce not only output growth, but also consumption growth in the Foreign country. Instead, for positive technology spillovers, higher R&D intensity at Home increases the productivity of R&D in the foreign country. Thus, the asymmetric reform increases output growth at Home and abroad. This is possible because the negative competition effect from the asymmetric reform is compensated (partly) by the positive productivity enhancing effect from the technology spillover. As a consequence, inflation, output, and consumption growth differentials among union members are strongly decreasing in σ_R: the higher the degree of integration through technology spillover in the currency area, the lower the degree of real income and consumption divergence among union members, even under asymmetric labor and product markets.

4.3.2 Regulation and Monetary Policy Shocks

To further analyze the effects of market structures on the functioning of the currency union, we analyze how a common monetary policy shock is transmitted across countries when member countries have heterogeneous product or labor markets. For simplicity, we focus on two regulatory differences: product market regulation (i.e., a lower markup of retailers compared to the baseline) and employment protection legislation, represented by lower hiring and firing costs.[11] We consider three calibrations: (a) the baseline calibration, (b) a currency union where the Home country has low product market regulation, and (c) a currency union where the Home country has low employment rigidities. The Foreign country is throughout calibrated as in the baseline economy. Figure 4.4 shows the effect of a common monetary policy shock in such an asymmetric currency union. When market structures are heterogenous, symmetric shocks can have large asymmetric effects and lead to long-lasting inflation and employment differentials. A lower degree of product market regulation increases the response of inflation to shocks (home inflation goes down by more on impact, which induces an increase in the inflation differential) but reduces the employment response. A lower degree of employment rigidities has exactly the opposite effect: employment reacts by more and inflation is more muted in a flexible region. The effects are large and persistent, especially in the case of employment rigidities.

We thus find that product market rigidities and employment rigidities have opposite dynamic effects on inflation and employment. This happens because a higher degree of product market regulation flattens the Phillips curve, while higher employment rigidities steepen it. To understand this, it is helpful to recall that the slope of the Phillips curve captures the sensitivity of inflation to variation in marginal costs, which in turn are driven by variation in economic activity. An increase

[11] The effects of lower unemployment benefits are qualitatively similar to the ones of lower PMR.

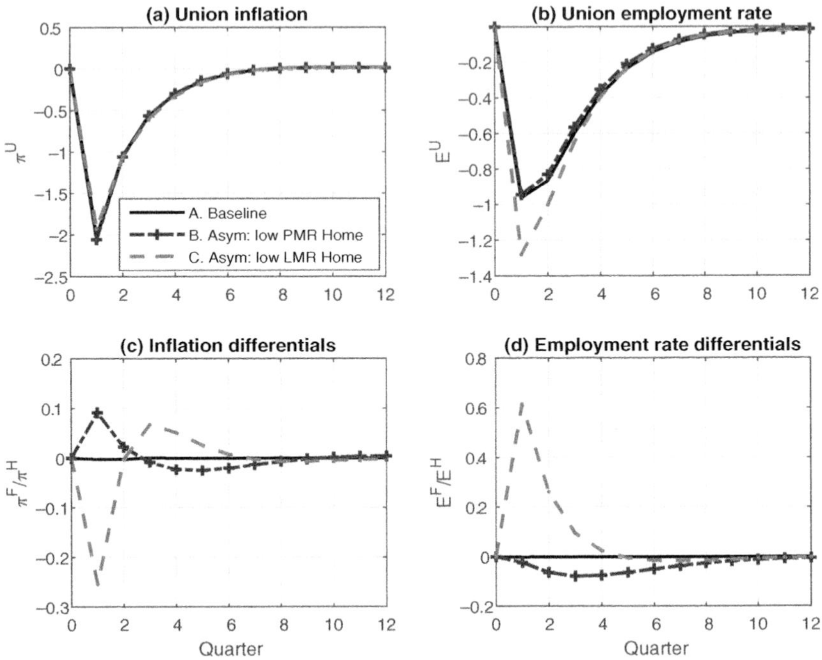

Figure 4.4 Monetary policy and labor and product market asymmetries.

in PMR reduces the elasticity of inflation to marginal costs. Hence, the slope of the Phillips curve is decreasing in the extent of product market regulation. Put differently, higher competition in the product market implies a more direct link between the development of prices and marginal costs.

To understand the effect of employment rigidities, notice that in a flexible labor market, average job finding and separation rates are large, and changes in employment lead to small variations in labor market tightness. This translates into a lower elasticity of marginal costs and inflation to changes in employment. Hence, the Phillips curve gets flatter. Intuitively, as the employment regulation becomes more flexible, changes in output and corresponding changes in demand for labor put less pressure on changes in wages as it is easier to hire or fire workers. Consequently, inflation reacts less to variation in employment.[12]

[12] See also Abbritti and Mueller (2013).

To get an idea of the quantitative effects of different labor and product market institutions on business cycle dynamics, Table 4.2 shows how the moments of the model at business cycle frequencies change with different calibrations of the model. Specifically, we simulate the model for different calibrations of the product and labor markets and show the standard deviation of the filtered time series of the macroeconomic variables. The volatility of inflation is annualized.

Less regulated product markets reduce the volatility of employment, but slightly increase the volatility of inflation. As a consequence, the volatility trade-off, which we define as the ratio between the inflation volatility and employment volatility, increases after liberalizing the product market. This trade-off has a direct economic interpretation, as it is related to the slope of the Phillips curve and represents how much inflation volatility needs to be afforded in order to reduce the volatility of employment by 1 percent.[13]

A reduction of hiring and firing costs (LMR_i) has the opposite effect on business cycle fluctuations: the volatility of employment increases, while the responsiveness of inflation is reduced. As a consequence, the volatility trade-off is strongly reduced in a more flexible labor market, as the Phillips curve gets flatter. In this sense, a reform reducing hiring and firing costs is steady-state efficient because it increases the long-run growth prospect of the economy, but dynamically inefficient, because it flattens the Phillips curve, which makes macroeconomic stabilization costlier.

4.4 Evidence on Market Regulation and TFP in the Euro Area

In this section, we analyze the data for the euro area on the relationships among market regulation, R&D investment, TFP, and output

[13] Similarly, reducing the generosity of the unemployment benefits system increases the volatility of inflation and reduces the volatility of employment, leading to an increase in the volatility trade-off. Intuitively, this reform increases the flexibility of real wages and facilitates the possibility of firms to absorb shocks using this margin: when real wages are more flexible, the firms' share of the match surplus does not change that strongly with shocks and hence hiring and employment react more smoothly to changing economic conditions.

Table 4.2 *Second moments for different values of product and labor market institutions.*

Second moments		Euro area	Baseline	Symmetric reforms			Asymmetric reforms		
(HP-filtered)		Data	Calib.	τ_i^p	b_i	LMR_i	τ_H^p	b_H	LMR_H
Union	$\sigma(\pi_U)$	1.25	1.03	1.06	1.08	0.95	1.05	1.06	0.99
	$\sigma(L_U)$	0.50	0.60	0.57	0.43	0.90	0.59	0.51	0.75
	$\sigma(\pi_U)$ / $\sigma(L_U)$	2.49	1.72	1.86	2.51	1.06	1.78	2.08	1.32
Home	$\sigma(\pi_H)$	–	1.12	1.15	1.18	1.03	1.16	1.20	1.02
	$\sigma(L_H)$	–	0.67	0.63	0.47	0.98	0.63	0.48	0.98
	$\sigma(\pi_H)$ / $\sigma(L_H)$	–	1.67	1.83	2.51	1.05	1.84	2.50	1.04
Foreign	$\sigma(\pi_F)$	–	1.12	1.15	1.18	1.03	1.11	1.10	1.13
	$\sigma(L_F)$	–	0.67	0.63	0.47	0.98	0.67	0.65	0.67
	$\sigma(\pi_F)$ / $\sigma(L_F)$	–	1.67	1.83	2.51	1.05	1.66	1.69	1.69
Differentials	$\sigma(\pi_F)$ / $\sigma(\pi_H)$	–	1.00	1.00	1.00	1.00	0.96	0.92	1.11
	$\sigma(L_F)$ / $\sigma(L_H)$	–	1.00	1.00	1.00	1.00	1.06	1.35	0.68

growth. For this purpose, we draw on the AMECO database for TFP growth and the Organization for Economic Cooperation and Development (OECD) database for data on R&D investment, employment protection legislation, product market regulation, and unemployment benefit generosity.

Evidently, there are several reasons that can explain diverse dynamics of growth and productivity among euro area members. The described model suggests that the level of R&D investment is an important factor. Empirical evidence since the creation of the euro area supports this. The bottom panel of Figure 4.2 shows a positive relationship between investment in R&D as a percentage of GDP in 1999 and average TFP growth between 1999 and 2015. For example, since 1999, TFP (GDP) growth in Italy and Greece has been more than 0.5 (1) percent lower than the simple euro area average. Both countries entered the euro area with the lowest level of business R&D in 1999 (See also, e.g., Cameron et al., 2005, and Griffith et al., 2004, and, for evidence on the importance of R&D for growth.)

To understand the effect of labor and product market regulation on growth and TFP dynamics, we build a composite regulation index, which is measured as the sum of standardized product market regulation index, employment protection legislation index, and the unemployment benefit generosity in deviation from the euro area average.[14] The top panel of Figure 4.2 (cont.) shows a negative correlation between market regulation and investment in R&D (see also Ciriaci et al., 2016). Relatedly, countries that entered the monetary union with a less regulated product and labor market experienced higher TFP growth since the existence of the euro (bottom panel of Figure 4.2 (cont.)). The top panel in Figure 4.5 suggests that this relationship is also true in a dynamic sense: countries that made stronger reform efforts relative to the union average, i.e., that moved

[14] Several authors have either used interaction terms or principal components of regulation indicators. See, for instance, Berger and Danninger (2007). Recent research has shown that EPL and PMR may have ambiguous effects on innovation activities depending on the nature of the productive sector affected (see, e.g., Amable et al., 2016; Cette et al., 2016; Franco et al., 2016; Griffith and Macartney, 2014; Griffith et. al, 2010, for different views).

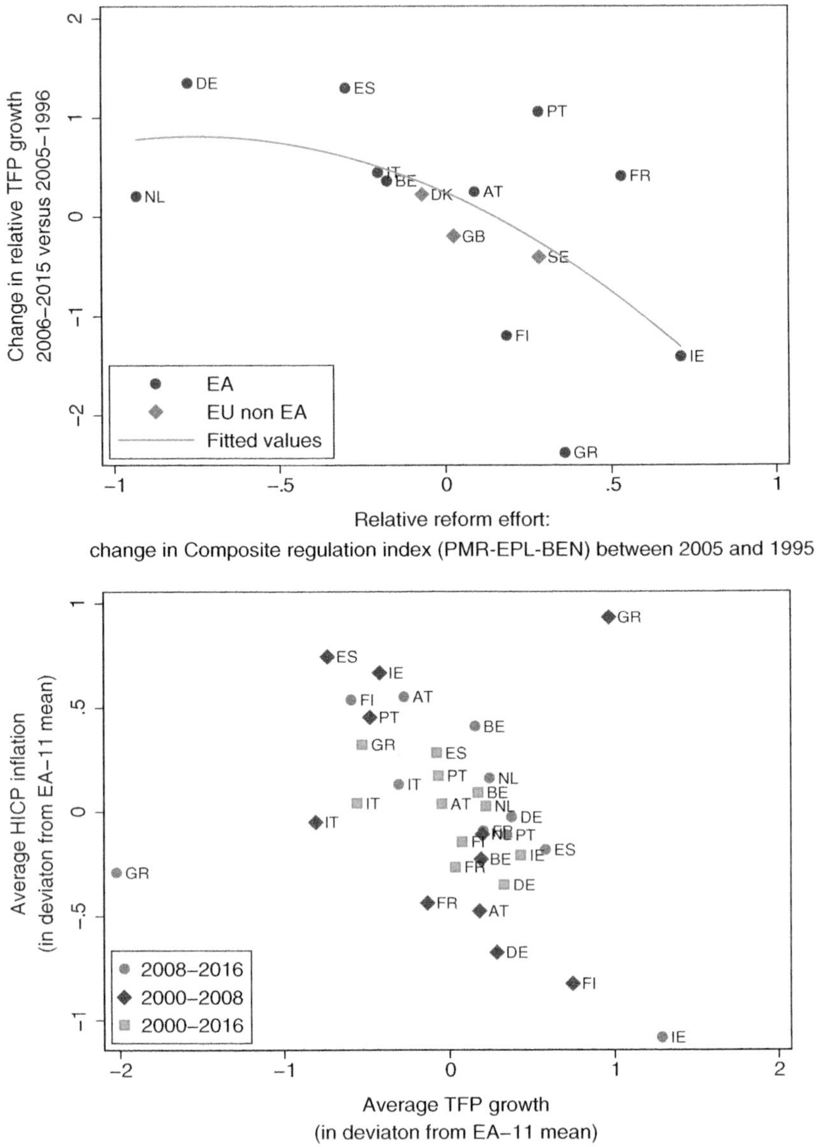

Figure 4.5 Short- and medium-term dynamics of TFP.

toward less regulated markets, experienced a stronger acceleration in average TFP growth compared to the average of the union. These patterns are consistent with the results of the model, establishing that countries with higher levels of market regulation exhibit lower levels of

R&D spending and lower steady-state TFP growth.[15] These results seem to provide a plausible underpinning for the role of the regulatory environment in supporting innovative activity and TFP growth as suggested by the model.[16]

Euro area member countries with higher TFP growth have on average experienced lower inflation rates (bottom panel of Figure 4.5). This is true when looking at two equal length subperiods (2000–2008 and 2008–2016) or at the entire sample period. Notably, Greece (and to a much lesser extent Italy) appears not to follow this pattern. While the inflation rates in the subperiods are undoubtedly driven by a multitude of factors, it is striking that even for the overall period of more than fifteen years, the negative correlation between TFP and inflation remains. This suggests that part of the TFP gain (or loss) translated into lower (higher) prices as opposed to moving wages to offset TFP gains. Labor market institutions that generate wage rigidities may have contributed to this pattern.

Finally, Figure 4.6 suggests that the unconditional ratio of employment volatility to inflation volatility is increasing in the extent of product market regulation and decreasing in the extent of effective employment protection legislation.[17] This is consistent with the two regulations' varying impact on the slope of the Phillips curve.[18]

Summing up, a simple look at the evidence of euro area countries in the last two decades seems to support the potentially significant effect of labor and product market regulations on union member dynamics present in the model, with different institutions affecting long-run growth and inflation prospects.

[15] Even though we attempted to limit possible reverse causality by using past values of R&D investment and market regulation in building these correlations, results are no evidence of causality.

[16] While discoveries from research may support productivity globally, diffusion of knowledge is unlikely to be immediate and returns from innovation are likely to accrue with a home bias (Coe and Helpman, 1995).

[17] Effective EPL is measured by multiplying the OECD EPL index for regular contracts with one minus the fraction of those in temporary contracts that couldn't find permanent contracts. See also IMF (2016) for a similar approach.

[18] The results regarding unemployment benefits are instead inconclusive. This may be due to the simplicity of the exercise, the limited time period considered, and the small number of countries in our sample. Using more countries and a longer time period, Abbritti and Weber (2018) find that a more generous unemployment benefit system reduces the responsiveness of inflation to aggregate fluctuations but increases unemployment volatility.

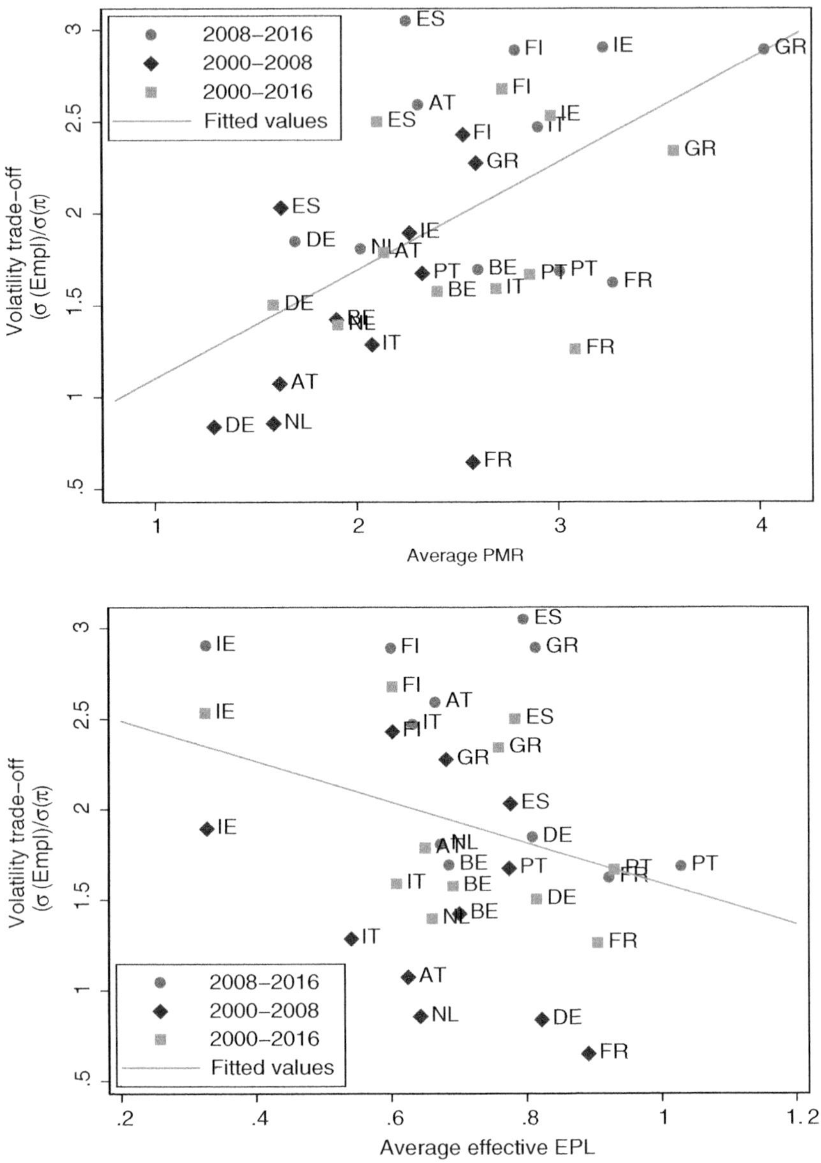

Figure 4.6 Effect of EPL and PMR on volatility trade-off between employment and inflation.

4.5 Concluding Remarks

We have described a DSGE currency union model where productivity grows endogenously through R&D investment. The model provides a tool to study short-term business cycle and long-term growth effects of different product and labor market regulations. As an illustration of the properties of the model, we have analyzed three different institutions: product market regulation, unemployment benefits, and employment rigidities. The analysis suggests three main conclusions. First, symmetric reforms in a currency union aimed at making product and labor markets more flexible are likely to be welfare enhancing in the long run, because they have a positive effect on long-run growth and the natural unemployment rate. Second, we show that in a currency union with endogenous productivity and heterogeneous market regulation, there is no reason to expect real income convergence among member countries. Countries with relatively more flexible market structures benefit from higher long-term growth. Thus, some members can remain on a permanently lower output trajectory, as their lower level of innovation makes them less competitive and demand for their output grows by less, reducing their real income relative to other union members' income. Finally, we show that while product market deregulation and unemployment benefit reductions make the Phillips curve steeper, a lower degree of employment rigidities tends to flatten the Phillips curve and make macroeconomic stabilization more difficult. Data from the euro area supports these findings as euro area countries with more regulated labor and product markets have lower levels of investment in business R&D, lower average TFP growth, and higher average inflation rates. Hence, higher rigidities in labor and product markets provide one explanation for lower growth trajectories in the euro area.

These three conclusions provide support to one relatively established and three relatively newer policy insights. In line with previous research, the findings provide a case for policy coordination because the highest unionwide return from deregulation of product or labor markets is attained from symmetric policy reforms. Different from previous work relying on standard New Keynesian models, this return is significantly higher because reforms have long-lasting growth effects by unleashing productivity enhancing R&D investment. In addition, coordinated regulation, by limiting divergence of Phillips curves among union members, facilitate macroeconomic stabilization by the unionwide central bank. In the absence of policy coordination, real income divergence among union members with different market regulations can still be reduced through policies that foster integration and enable technology spillovers.

References

Abbritti, M. and Fahr, S. (2013)."Downward Wage Rigidity and Business Cycle Asymmetries," *Journal of Monetary Economics*, Vol. 60, No. 7, 871–886.

Abbritti, M. and Mueller, A. I. (2013). "Asymmetric Labor Market Institutions in the EMU and the Volatility of Inflation and Unemployment Differentials," *Journal of Money, Credit and Banking*, Vol. 45, No. 6, 1165–1186. doi:10.1111/jmcb.12048.

Abbritti, M. and Weber, S. (2018). "Reassessing the Role of Labour Market Institutions for the Business Cycle," *International Journal of Central Banking*, Vol. 14, No. 1, 1–4.

(2019). 'Market Regulation, Cycles and Growth in a Monetary Union', IMF Working Paper No. 19/123.

Aghion, P. , Farhi, E. and Kharroubi, E. (2018). "Monetary Policy, Product Market Competition, and Growth," mimeo.

Ahn, J., Duval, R. and Sever, C. (2018). "Macroeconomic Policy, Product Market Competition and Growth: The Intangible Investment Channel," mimeo.

Amable, B., Ledezma, I. and Robin, S. (2016). "Product Market Regulation, Innovation, and Productivity," *Research Policy*, Vol. 45, No. 10, 2087–2104.

Andrés, J., Arce, O. and Thomas, C. (2017). "Structural Reforms in a Debt Overhang," *Journal of Monetary Economics*, Vol. 88, No. C, 15–34.

Anzoategui, D., Comin, D., Gertler, M. and Martinez, J. (2018). "Endogenous Technology Adoption and R&D as Sources of Business Cycle Persistence," *American Economic Journal: Macroeconomics*, Vol. 11, No. 3, 67–110. DOI: 10.1257/mac.20170269.

Berger, H.and Danninger, S. (2007). "The Employment Effects of Labor and Product Market Deregulation and Their Implications for Structural Reform," *IMF Staff Papers*, Vol. 54, No. 3, 591–619.

Blanchard, O. and Gali, J. (2010). "Labor Markets and Monetary Policy: A New Keynesian Model with Unemployment," *American Economic Journal: Macroeconomics*, Vol. 2, No. 4, 1–30.

Brinke, A., Enderlein, H. and Fritz-Vannahme, J. (2015). *What Kind of Convergence Does the Euro Area Need?* Bertelsmann Stiftung und Jacques Delors Institut.

Cacciatore, M. and Fiori, G. (2016). "The Macroeconomic Effects of Goods and Labour Markets Deregulation," *Review of Economic Dynamics*, Vol. 20, 1–24.

Cacciatore, M., Fiori, G. and Ghironi, F. (2016). "Market Deregulation and Optimal Monetary Policy in a Monetary Union," *Journal of International Economics*, Vol. 99, 120–137.

Cameron, G., Proudman, J. and Redding, S. (2005). "Technological Convergence, R&D, Trade and Productivity Growth," *European Economic Review*, Vol. 49, No. 3, 775–807.

Cette, G., Lopez, J. and Mairesse, J. (2016). "Market Regulations, Prices, and Productivity," *American Economic Review*, Vol. 106, No. 5, 104–108.

Ciriaci, D., Grassano, N. and Vezzani, A. (2016). "Regulation, Red Tape and Location Choices of Top R&D Investors," European Economy – Discussion Papers 2015 – 031, European Commission.

Coe, D. T. and Helpman, E., (1995) "International R&D Spillovers," *European Economic Review*, Vol. 39, No. 5, 859–887.

Comin, D. and Gertler, M. (2006). "Medium-Term Business Cycles," *American Economic Review*, Vol. 96, No. 3, 523–551.

De Grauwe, P. and Yuemei, J. (2013). "Self-Fulfilling Crises in the Eurozone: An Empirical Test," *Journal of International Money and Finance*, Vol. 34, No. C, 15–36.

Diaz del Hoyo, J. L., Dorrucci, E., Heinzand, F. and Muzikarova, S. (2017). "Real Convergence in the Euro Area: A Long-Term Perspective," Occasional Paper Series 203, European Central Bank.

Eggertsson, G., Ferrero, A. and Raffo, A, (2014). "Can Structural Reforms Help Europe?" *Journal of Monetary Economics*, Vol. 61, No. C, 2–22.

Estrada, Á., Galí, J. and López-Salido, D. (2013). "Patterns of Convergence and Divergence in the Euro Area," *IMF Economic Review*, Vol. 61, 601.

Franco, C., Pieri, F. and Venturini, F. (2016). "Product Market Regulation and Innovation Efficiency," *Journal of Productivity Analysis*, Vol. 45, No. 3, 299–315.

Franks, J., Bergljot, B., Rodolphe, B., William, O. and Hanni, S. (2018). "Economic Convergence in the Euro Area: Coming Together or Drifting Apart?" IMF Working Paper No. 18/10.

Griffith, R. and Macartney, G. (2014). "Employment Protection Legislation, Multinational Firms, and Innovation," *Review of Economics and Statistics*, Vol. **96**, No. 1, 135–150.

Griffith, R., Harrison, R. and Simpson, H. (2010). "Product Market Reform and Innovation in the EU," *Scandinavian Journal of Economics*, Vol. 112, No. 2, 389–415.

Griffith, R., Redding, S. and Van Reenen, J. (2004). "Mapping the Two Faces of R&D: Productivity Growth in a Panel of OECD Industries," *Review of Economics and Statistics*, Vol. 86, No. 4, 883–895.

IMF (2016). "Time for a Supply-Side Boost? Macroeconomic Effects of Labour and Product Market Reforms," World Economic Outlook, chapter 3, April.

Krishnamurthy, A. and Vissing-Jorgensen, A. (2012). 'The Aggregate Demand for Treasury Debt', *Journal of Political Economy*, Vol. 120, 233–267.

Kung, H. and Schimdt, L. (2015). "Innovation, Growth, and Asset Prices," *Journal of Finance*, Vol. 70, 1001–1037.

Masuch, K., Moshammer, E. and Beatrice, P. (2016). "Institutions, Public Debt and Growth in Europe," ECB Working Paper No. 1963, September 19.

Nickell, S. (1997). "Unemployment and Labor Market Rigidities: Europe versus North America," *Journal of Economic Perspectives*, Vol. 11, No. 3, 55–74, Summer.

Piermartini, R. and Rubínová, S. (2014). "Knowledge Spillovers through International Supply Chains," WTO Staff Working Papers ERSD-2014-11, World Trade Organization (WTO), Economic Research and Statistics Division.

Romer, P. (1990). "Endogenous Technological Change," *Journal of Political Economy*, Vol. 98, No. 5, S71–102. www.jstor.org/stable/2937632.

Rotemberg, J. J. (1982). 'Monopolistic Price Adjustment and Aggregate Output', *Review of Economic Studies*, Vol. 49, 517–531.

5 *Macroeconomic Imbalances in the Euro Area*

Can They Be Managed?

MICHAEL HUME

5.1 Introduction

Over recent years, a consensus has emerged among economists concerning the root causes of the euro-area crisis. More than seventy leading economists across academia, public sector institutions, the private sector and think tanks have subscribed to a 'consensus narrative' suggesting that the causes of the crisis were 'imbalances and a lack of crisis management' (Baldwin and Giavazzi, 2015)). In particular, it highlights the contribution of 'policy failures that allowed imbalances to get so large'. Given this consensus view, it would appear essential that macroeconomic imbalances are managed more effectively in the future. This chapter contributes to this policy imperative by providing an assessment of the effectiveness of different macroeconomic and structural policies for managing macroeconomic imbalances.

The European Commission defines a macroeconomic imbalance as '*any trend giving rise to macroeconomic developments which are adversely affecting, or have the potential to adversely affect, the proper functioning of the economy of a Member State or of the Economic and Monetary Union, or of the Union as a whole*'. This definition is motivated by the macrofinancial risks that such macroeconomic developments present, and as such an important aspect is the accumulation of net financial claims between economic sectors. Reflecting this, economic phenomena that have historically been associated with the accumulation of these claims and generated macrofinancial risks, such as current account deficits, competitiveness, asset price surges and private-sector credit expansions, are viewed by the European Commission as evidence of macroeconomic imbalances.

The precrisis policy for dealing with external imbalances in the euro area can be described as one of benign neglect, driven by a belief in the disciplining effects of membership of the single currency on wage and price setters in national economies. This is not to suggest that external imbalances were not expected to arise from time to time. To the extent that financial integration was expected to spur greater income convergence among the members of the euro area and lead to the emergence of imbalances, it was thought that they were structural, sustainable and desirable. To the extent that asymmetric shocks hit national economies and led to imbalances, it was thought that they would be cyclical, temporary and a price worth paying for establishing the euro. In other words, it was thought that economic mechanisms were in place to ensure that external imbalances would smoothly self-correct and that there was little need for policy to assist the process.

The precrisis policy for dealing with other macroeconomic imbalances was only slightly more developed and targeted mostly at delivering the broader objective of monetary and financial stability. It consisted of three principal mechanisms. First, monetary stability would be maintained at the euro-area level by the politically independent European Central Bank (ECB) pursuing a two-pillar strategy oriented around monetary aggregates and consumer price inflation. Second, financial stability would be achieved through microprudential supervision of financial institutions and infrastructure at the national level. Third, to overcome the common pool problem created by monetary union and prevent 'fiscal laxity' undermining the euro, the Stability and Growth Pact limited the public debt of euro members to 60 per cent of GDP and public borrowing to 3 per cent of GDP.

It is now clear that this precrisis policy framework was flawed. While the ECB delivered monetary stability in terms of its inflation target, the Stability and Growth Pact was honoured mostly in the breach and microprudential supervision completely missed the emergence of major macroprudential risks. The disciplining effects of euro membership also proved less powerful than anticipated with changes in competitiveness and external imbalances proving more persistent than originally envisaged. The result was that structural and cyclical forces put economies on a path of external debt accumulation that were left largely unmanaged, creating a dangerous vulnerability to a change in economic circumstances.

The precise nature of these structural and cyclical forces remains hotly debated with several explanations advocated. One of the more controversial explanations is that macroeconomic imbalances were driven by an optimistic growth story in which animal spirits drove a decline in savings and increase in investment in periphery countries. De Grauwe (2010, 2012a) has suggested that this led to self-fulfilling but ultimately unsustainable national credit cycles. There is certainly a clear empirical relationship between optimism about growth and macroeconomic imbalances. For example, Lane and Pels (2012) have shown a strong relationship between growth expectations and external imbalances in a panel regression framework. Crucially, this view does not depend on either income convergence or financial integration, although they may have initiated them or amplified them in some cases. Rather, at the heart of this view is the contention that euro-area countries will always be vulnerable to the possibility of national credit cycles driven by animal spirits and that these need to be managed with policy.

An alternative postcrisis view is that they were driven by fiscal policy. This view is held by the German government, and as a result the role of fiscal policy continues to feature prominently in discussions concerning the management of macroeconomic imbalances. There is some evidence to suggest that fiscal policy may have a larger impact on current accounts in a monetary union. In particular, Bluedorn and Leigh (2011) have shown that traditional estimates of the impact of fiscal policy on the current account are probably underestimated due to endogeneity problems, especially in the case of monetary unions. And Abbas et al. (2010) have shown that public-sector debt affected the current account in euro-area countries. But this explanation is not typically seen as being a quantitatively significant explanation. Paul Krugman speaks for many when he argues that the only country for which fiscal policy was an important contributor to macroeconomic imbalances was Greece.

Most economists acknowledge that the introduction of a common interest rate was also a factor explaining the emergence of macroeconomics imbalances. But it is mostly seen as being of secondary importance relative to other explanations and is generally thought to have run its course by the early to mid-2000s. The Walters' critique is sometimes invoked to suggest that even if the initial shock from monetary union may have played itself out after a few years, subsequent inflation divergence resulted in procyclical movements in real interest rates that could have contributed to the persistence of macroeconomic imbalances over a longer period. Finally, it has been suggested that financial integration and divergent financial liberalisation may have led to divergence in bank interest rates and credit conditions also fuelling macroeconomic imbalances.

The main supply-side view, advanced primarily by the European Commission, suggests that the persistence of macroeconomic imbalances was a consequence of slow nominal adjustment and the prevalence of structural rigidities in the euro area. The argument here is that if prices and wages adjusted more flexibly then, through changes in the real exchange rate, demand shocks would be neutralised by real income and expenditure switching effects. In particular, Kennedy and Slok (2005) show that external imbalances are more persistent when market rigidities are high. Relatedly, Biroli et al. (2010) and Zemanek et al. (2010) find that higher price and wage rigidities are associated with slower adjustment in real exchange rates while Berger and Nitsch (2010) and Ju and Wei (2007) find that labour market rigidities are more important than product market rigidities.

An alternative supply-side explanation is that macroeconomic imbalances were driven by divergent labour market institutions (Hancké and Soskice, 2003; Soskice and Iversen, 2000). In recent contributions, Hancké (2013) has argued that the roots of competitiveness divergences can be found in the different responses of public-sector unions to the launch of the euro. Prior to the euro, national central banks had contained wage demands across countries. But following the launch of the euro, this disciplining device was no longer operative. As a consequence, public-sector wages increased and also put upward pressure on wages in the export-competing manufacturing sectors via a 'reverse Balassa–Samuelson effect'. More generally, many observers have emphasised the role played by wage restraint of large German manufacturing unions in helping to improve the competitiveness of German firms and contributing to the large increase in the German current account surplus.

Despite the continuing uncertainty as to what exactly was the origin of macroeconomic imbalances, a number of governance reforms have still been agreed and implemented to improve their management. They aim at identifying macroeconomic imbalances at an early stage and enforcing policy actions to correct them in a timely manner. The most important reform in this regard is the Macroeconomic Imbalances Procedure (MIP). This applies to all European Union (EU) member states and includes an Annual Alert Mechanism (AAM) report that will use standardised metrics to detect imbalances in current accounts, competitiveness, housing and credit markets. For those countries where macroeconomic imbalances are identified, an In-Depth Review (IDR) will be triggered. Based on that review, there is the possibility of corrective measures, backed up with fines in the case of euro-area members.

The MIP's task of identifying and correcting macroeconomic imbalances in real time will not be easy. An emerging consensus[1] is that managing macroeconomic imbalances in a monetary union may not be possible. For some, this is because it rests on national governments attempting to manage capital flows using policies for which they are only loosely related. Capital controls, monetary and exchange rate policies are simply not available to national governments whose economies are part of the euro area. The policies available include fiscal policy, microprudential and macroprudential policies and structural policies. Daborwski (2015) reviews these policy instruments and concludes that there is 'limited potential of national policies in regulating [current account imbalances] within a monetary union and single market with unrestricted capital movement'. Even those who see some hope in these policies still question whether they will be sufficient. According to Kincaid and Watson (2015), 'reliance cannot be placed solely on the timeliness and adequacy of national fiscal and macroprudential measures, even when coordinated across borders, to prevent financial stress arising under EMU [Economic and Monetary Union]'.[2]

1 Some analysts are optimistic that the MIP would have made a difference in the 2000s. For example, Kamps et al. (2014) has argued that, had the MIP framework been in place before the crisis, it would 'most certainly have facilitated an earlier identification of macroeconomic and budgetary imbalances. Euro area countries thus would have been obliged to take preventative and corrective action at an earlier stage, provided that the stricter rules had been effectively implemented'.

2 Political economy considerations point in a similar direction but are not addressed in this chapter. Benassy-Quere and Ragot (2015) argue that the European Semester has 'ended up in a complicated, bureaucratic process rather than a fully-fledged coordination of macroeconomic policies', raising important questions about its likely effectiveness. There is also widespread criticism of the MIP's asymmetric design. Nine of the eleven thresholds used in the MIPs scorecard for the AMA only signal excessive deficits with no threshold for an emerging excessive surplus, and there are different thresholds used in the AMA depending on whether the country has an external surplus (+6 per cent of gross domestic product) or a deficit (–4 per cent). This has led to claims that the MIP could lead to a deflationary bias in euro-area macroeconomic policy (Benassy-

The aim of this chapter is to enhance the evidence base concerning the feasibility of managing macroeconomic imbalances in the euro area. It provides a formal analysis of the impact on a wide range of macroeconomic imbalances of four different policy shocks: fiscal policy, macroprudential policy, product market policy and labour market policy. Although the results do tend to confirm the pessimistic conclusions of the emerging consensus, there are two important exceptions. First, there is clear evidence that labour market policies could be effective at addressing employment imbalances. Second, macroprudential policies could be effective at addressing a wide range of macroeconomic imbalances. Importantly, these include the trade imbalances that the consensus narrative views as the root cause of the crisis.

The chapter is organised as follows. Section 5.2 describes the theoretical framework and empirical strategy used to model macroeconomic imbalances. Section 5.3 presents the main results from the model. Section 5.4 offers conclusions and policy implications.

5.2 Modelling Macroeconomic Imbalances

5.2.1 Theoretical Framework

In the years following the launch of the euro, there was a large volume of work that sought to measure the extent to which euro-area financial integration had increased.[3] This showed substantial integration, in terms of both prices and quantities, and especially in wholesale markets but also to a more limited extent in retail markets. For most, these trends were seen to be a consequence of monetary union, although the effects of financial deregulation that took place not only in the euro area but across most advanced economies in the 1990s were also emphasised. Around the same time, macroeconomic imbalances

Quere and Ragot (2015);), Ederer (2015); Kincaid and Watson (2015). And according to Alcidi and Gros (2013) the country-specific recommendations that have been made since the MIP has been in place have been 'too vague to allow one to judge implementation. The politically and financially strong countries tend to ignore them. The politically and financially weaker countries usually respond to recommendations on structural policies by taking many measures, but it is often difficult to say whether these measures will achieve the intended result'.

3 See, for example, Adam et al. (2002); Baele et al. (2004); Cabral et al. (2002); Coueurdacier and Martin (2007); Galati and Tsatsaronis (2003); Lane and Milesi-Ferretti (2005); Pagano and von Thadden (2004); Santos and Tsatsaronis (2003).

emerged in euro-area countries with relatively low per capita incomes, notably in Portugal and Greece where there were current account deficits of between 8 to 10 per cent of gross domestic product (GDP) and public- and private-sector deficits of roughly 4 to 5 per cent of GDP.

The seminal paper in the field of euro-area macroeconomic imbalances – a Brookings paper by Blanchard and Giavazzi (2002) (hereafter BG) – was the first theoretically and empirically substantive explanation for the coexistence of rapid financial integration and macroeconomic imbalances in the low per capita income countries of the euro area. Eichengreen (2010) provides a helpful summary and sets out some of its normative implications:

> The authors focused on savings-investment differentials in the run-up and immediately after the transition to the euro. They showed that savings-investment correlations fell significantly even before but especially with the advent of the euro, which they interpreted in terms of increased financial integration that comes with the adoption of a single currency. They demonstrated that the current account balances of the member states increased with per capita income. This showed capital to be flowing 'downhill' from more advanced, capital-abundant countries to their less advanced, capital-scarce euro-area partners.
>
> This in turn reflected the scope that existed within the euro-area periphery for catch-up and convergence. This, then, was an example of a 'good' imbalance of countries with attractive investment opportunities and outstanding growth prospects capitalising on the advent of the euro and the deeper financial integration it entailed to undertake additional investment, tapping foreign saving by running current account deficits while at the same time boosting their consumption to reflect the positive permanent income effect of faster growth and the positive wealth effect of lower interest rates.

The theory underpinning the BG hypothesis follows straightforwardly from the intertemporal theory of the current account (Obstfeld and Rogoff (1996)). This model suggests that agents' decisions to borrow and lend across economies reflects the efficient allocation of capital towards the most profitable investment opportunities and to households wishing to smooth their consumption over time. BG argued that for Portugal and Greece it was the impact of integration on the scope for income convergence that had driven the fall in their current account balances, and that the main channel through which this took place was consumption smoothing leading to lower saving.

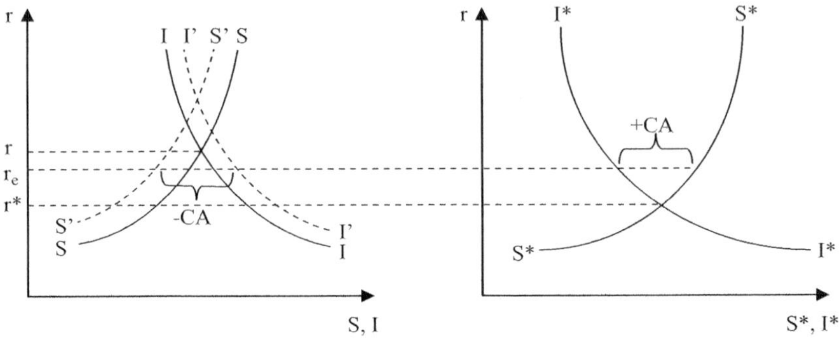

Figure 5.1 The Metzler diagram.

An important feature of the intertemporal model is the absence of an explicit role for competitiveness. This is not to say that competitiveness does not matter. But as Blanchard and Giavazzi (2002) acknowledge separating out the roles of competitiveness on the trade account from those of consumption smoothing on the capital account 'is far from straightforward, both conceptually and empirically'. An important breakthrough of the new open economy macroeconomics developed over the past decade is that both these channels are incorporated into the analysis. Within this framework, consumption smoothing households determine demand but they are also affected by changes in relative costs through effects on real incomes and competitiveness.

In these models, the relative importance of the real income and competitiveness channels will depend on how prices are set across economies. If firms set traded goods prices according to levels prevailing in the foreign economy – known as Local Currency Pricing (LCP) – then there will be no competitiveness effects but there will be real income effects from changes in relative costs. If firms set prices according to the level of costs in the home economy – known as Producer Currency Pricing (PCP) – then there will be competitiveness effects but no real income effects from changes in relative costs. The consensus view has been that LCP is the predominant pricing strategy of firms, suggesting a limited role for competitiveness effects. This puts the emphasis back on intertemporal demand rather than changes in competitiveness as being the main determinant of current accounts.

A simple graphical representation of the BG model is the Metzler diagram shown in Figure 5.1. The left-hand graph shows the relationship between interest rates and the saving and investment schedules of the periphery economy, while the right-hand graph shows the same for the core economy. Euro membership leads to a common interest rate as a consequence of a single monetary policy and the elimination of exchange rate risk. Assuming pre-euro interest rates are higher in the periphery this interest rate convergence leads to excess investment in the periphery and excess saving in the core. In addition, if expected future productivity increases in the periphery as a consequence of broader economic integration, then the saving and investment schedules will undergo shifts that lead to further falls in the periphery current account balance. Taken together, the result is a current account deficit in the periphery and a current account surplus in the core.

After BG was published, the tendency for capital to flow 'downhill' in this way was confirmed by a number of empirical studies. Abiad et al. (2009) shows that Europe has been unusual in seeing this 'downhill' flow of capital not only with regard to euro-area economies but also those in emerging Europe that have been part of the European Union. These flows have also been associated with a significant acceleration of income convergence. Ca'Zorzi and Rubaszek (2008) show that expectations of real income convergence and consumption smoothing explain the pattern of current account imbalances. Lane (2010) finds evidence for both differences in income levels and growth expectations. And Waysand et al. (2010) depart from the focus on external imbalances and create a new database on bilateral external financial assets and liabilities. They note that creditor and debtor positions within the EU have tended to increase between 2000 and 2008 with capital largely flowing from wealthier to catching-up economies. Schmitz and von Hagen (2011) find similar results.

The BG analysis suggested that for the periphery economies, an initial period of strong consumption and current account deficits would be followed seamlessly by a period of strong output growth and current account surpluses. This was a consequence of a dynamic optimisation process in which households responded rationally to a combination of access to euro-area capital markets and expectations of stronger income growth in the years ahead. But subsequent events can be viewed as consistent with the BG analysis only if the crisis is seen as a consequence of a very large and unforeseeable shock to national balance sheets that had nothing at all to do with the accumulation of the imbalances themselves.

Few economists today are willing to subscribe to such a view, and even before the crisis there were many economists who did express concern about the buildup of macroeconomic imbalances. For example, in direct response to the BG analysis, Pierre-Olivier Gourinchas (2002) raised the concern that although capital may be flowing 'downhill', it did not seem to be leading to income convergence, and this reflected the tendency for saving to fall rather than for investment to rise. Presciently, he worried that 'real overvaluation may happen relatively slowly in Portugal and Greece. But there are signs that it is coming. In time, this will require an adjustment in relative prices, which may prove painful'.

As explained in the introduction, since the crisis, a consensus narrative has emerged that highlights the major policy failure of 'allowing' imbalances to get so large. This is consistent with the idea that, in the absence of a stabilising policy framework, economic agents cannot be relied upon to ensure that the economy converges upon a stable equilibrium path as suggested by the BG analysis. On this view, the mainstream theory of current account determination remains valid but that it may be inevitable in a monetary union that shocks will come along and cause not only temporary disturbances but also risk putting some economies on a path of unsustainable debt accumulation. This is can be viewed primarily because of nonrational expectations that lead agents to deviate from their intertemporal budget constraint for an extended period until a later date when there is a day of reckoning with creditors.

Reflecting this, the chapter adopts the theoretical framework of the BG model but without assuming rational expectations and is described in detail in Appendix A. It adapts an open economy New Keynesian model to a core–periphery framework where the euro area as a whole is assumed to be a large closed economy and macroeconomic imbalances are determined endogenously but have no implications for the general equilibrium. Overall, the theoretical model consists of six variables (output, prices, interest rates, fiscal balance, employment and the current account balance) with four policy shocks (fiscal policy, macroprudential policy, product market structural reforms and labour market structural reforms).

5.2.2 Empirical Strategy

Empirical modelling of macroeconomic imbalances is not straightforward. By their nature, imbalances are determined simultaneously, leading to problems of endogeneity. This makes inference problematic in a field dominated by research that has relied to a large extent on cross-country analysis. Consider, for example, the debate concerning the role of fiscal policy as a contributor to macroeconomic imbalances. Does the absence of an empirical cross-country association between fiscal balances and external balances prior to the crisis demonstrate that fiscal policy has not contributed to macroeconomic imbalances? The truth is that it is impossible to say without controlling for the shocks that have affected both. A positive demand shock, for example, will tend to produce a negative correlation between the fiscal balance and the external balance. This will even be the case if the fiscal authorities were to take advantage of the positive effect the demand shock has on the public finances by raising government expenditures, boosting imports and contributing to external imbalances.

Another case in which correlations shed more heat than light concerns the role of competitiveness, which may be amendable to being influenced through structural policies. To what extent does the empirical association between competitiveness measures and external imbalances indicate that changes in relative prices have been the main driver of macroeconomic imbalances? Again, it is impossible to say without controlling for the shocks hitting the economy. Given the existence of a Phillips curve relationship between demand and prices, a positive demand shock that contributes to external imbalances primarily by boosting imports will nevertheless tend to produce a positive correlation between prices and the external balance. Yet in this case, the change in prices may be of secondary importance. In other words, correlations can only take the analysis of macroeconomic imbalances so far.

Endogeneity problems of this sort are, of course, common in empirical macroeconomics, and there are well-established methods for overcoming them. One approach is to use a dynamic stochastic general equilibrium (DSGE) model in which the structure of the economy is fully articulated and hence capable of decomposing past outturns into a full array of shocks to the deep parameters that comprise the model. There have been some attempts in recent years to apply this approach to understanding the origins of macroeconomic imbalances within a monetary union. But not only have these attempts produced conflicting results, indicating sensitivity to the precise structure of the economy being articulated, these models are incompatible with the consensus narrative of the crisis and postcrisis explanations about the origins of macroeconomic imbalances, which reject the idea that they were the result of optimising behaviour by agents who are assumed to form their expectations rationally.

An alternative and less rigid method for overcoming the endogeneity problem is to estimate a Structural Vector Auto Regression (SVAR) in which the structure of the economy is not fully articulated but reflected in the key properties of a small-scale model. With this more limited economic structure, a subset of the structural shocks that hit the economy can be identified and used to provide estimates of their impact. This method has the advantage of not presuming any knowledge of the decision rules followed by agents and so is compatible with the consensus narrative of the crisis and postcrisis explanations that eschew rational expectations. It has also been applied extensively to a wide range of important macroeconomic issues, including the related issue of global macroeconomic imbalances,[4] but to the best of the author's knowledge this is the first time it has been applied to the issue of euro-area macroeconomic imbalances.

5.2.2.1 Reduced Form

The Vector Auto Regression (VAR) used in estimation is based on the theoretical model described in the previous section and is estimated using Bayesian methods. The derivation of the VAR representation of the model and method of estimation is set out in detail in Appendix B. The reduced-form VAR is as follows:

$$VAR = [\Delta y; \Delta p; \Delta g; \Delta r; \Delta n; \Delta x]$$

where Δy is output growth; Δp is the inflation rate of the GDP deflator at market prices; Δg is change in the fiscal balance as a percentage of GDP; Δr is the change in the interest rate on bank loans; Δn is employment growth; and Δx is the change in the current account balance as a percentage of GDP.

[4] There are two papers in the global imbalances literature that this chapter is related to. The first considered the role of shocks to technology, monetary policy and fiscal policy as a driver of US financial imbalances (Bems et al., 2007). The second identified shocks to real savings, real investment and monetary policy as drivers of US and Asian current account balances in the late 1990s and 2000s (Bracke and Fidora, 2008).

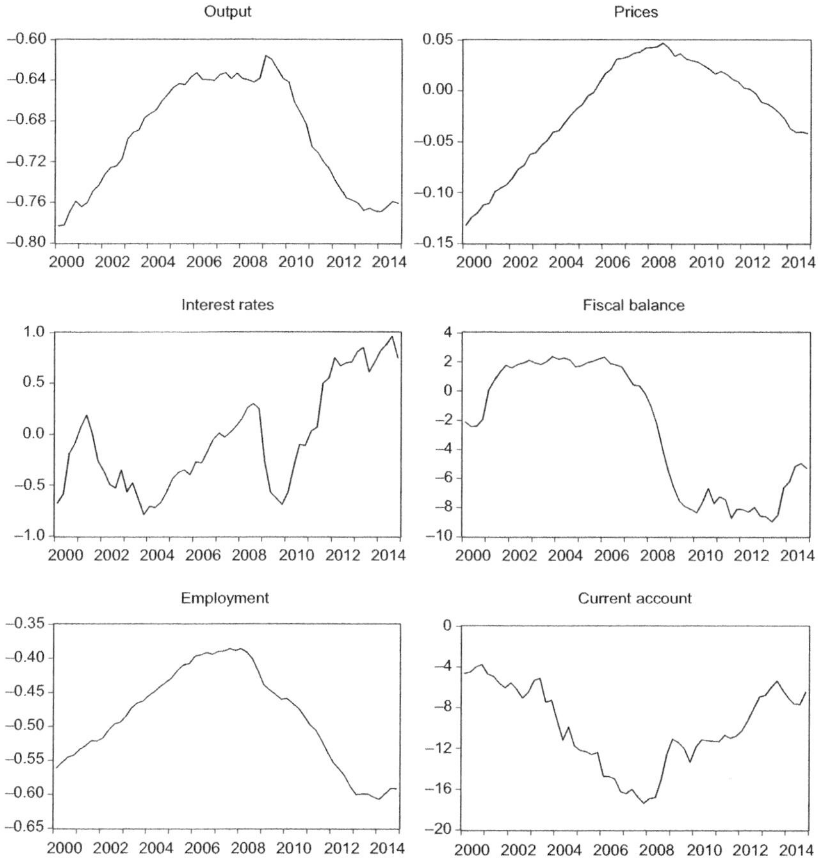

Figure 5.2 Data used in estimation.
Note: The data shown are the log difference between periphery and core variables weighted by GDP. Core countries are Germany and the Netherlands while periphery countries are Spain, Portugal, Ireland and Greece.

The raw data are shown in Figure 5.2 and consist of the log differences between periphery and core aggregate variables. The data are aggregated using GDP weights of national series of Eurostat data. The countries comprising the core aggregate are Germany and the Netherlands, while the countries comprising the periphery are Spain, Portugal, Ireland and Greece. These groupings were selected on the basis that they showed persistent widening of current account surpluses and deficits since the early 2000s until the financial crisis. The benchmark model was estimated over a sample period from 2000Q1 to 2015Q2 using four lags. The model was estimated in first differences to prevent the results from being impacted by cointegrating relationships arising from the impact of the financial crisis.

5.2.2.2 Structural Form

There are many methods for identifying the structural form of the VAR model. Appendix C sets out the most common methods and their principal advantages and disadvantages. This chapter adopts the method of sign restrictions in which economic theory is used to establish what the initial impact of shocks on the variables should be. Sign restrictions are set when they are compatible with candidate models that could be said to characterise the structure of the economy. Where there is uncertainty about the correct sign that a shock will have on a variable, it can be left unrestricted. Canova and Paustian (2011) have shown that sign restrictions are a robust method of identification that has good properties, even in small samples, and even when the class of models is incorrectly specified. It requires no knowledge of either the data generation process or the decision rules of agents. These properties are particularly suited to the case of euro-area macroeconomic imbalances, where, as explained in the introduction, there remains considerable uncertainty about the precise nature of the cyclical and structural shocks hitting the economy and about how expectations are formed.

Figure 5.3 illustrates the choice of sign restrictions used in this chapter with the set of restrictions shown in dark grey consistent with the macroeconomic imbalances model in Appendix A. Positive demand-side policy shocks lead to higher growth, higher inflation, and a lower current account balance. In addition, a positive fiscal policy shock – i.e., an easing of fiscal policy – leads to a decline in the fiscal balance,[5] while a positive macroprudential policy shock – i.e., an easing of bank capital requirements – leads to a decline in the interest rate. This decline in the interest rate is a consequence of a

[5] The identification of fiscal shocks using sign restrictions is not without controversy. For example, Leeper et al., 2012, 2013) have shown that anticipation effects complicate identification and that additional information is needed to avoid contamination issues. However, there is clear precedent for identifying fiscal shocks in an SVAR framework (e.g., Dalsgaard and de Serres, 2001; Straub and Peersman, 2009) and the estimates of the impact of fiscal policy shocks were found to be within the range found in the literature.

Shock/variable		Δy	Δp	Δr	Δg	Δn	Δx
Demand	Fiscal policy	+	+		–		–
	Macroprudential policy	+	+	–	+		–
Supply	Product market structural reforms	+	–			–	+
	Labour market structural reforms	+	–			+	+

Signs consistent with the macroeconomic imbalances model specified in Appendix A

Signs required for unique identification

Figure 5.3 Identifying sign restrictions for contemporaneous impact effect.

reduced cost of funding for the banking system enabling them to lower their lending spreads and is consistent with the effects found in the emerging literature on the impact of macroprudential policies, including in a monetary union (Brzoza-Brzezina et al., 2015; Quint and Rabanal, 2014). Positive supply-side shocks lead to higher growth, lower inflation and a higher current account balance. Additionally, a positive labour market structural reform shock leads to an increase in employment. This is a consequence of labour market reforms being assumed to target improving labour market efficiency and reducing unemployment.

The restrictions shown in light grey are required for unique identification of the four policy shocks. The first restriction is that a positive macroprudential policy shock leads to an improvement in the fiscal balance. This is justified by the positive sign restrictions on growth and inflation, which would be expected to lead to an improvement in the cyclical fiscal balance via an increase in the level of nominal output. The second restriction is that a product market reform shock leads to a fall in employment. This is a consequence of product market reforms being assumed to target increasing competition and reduced profit margins, leading firms to reduce costs. One way for firms to do this is to lay off workers.

It is important to stress that within this framework the exact nature of the policy shocks is not specified, even though there can be significant differences between subtypes of each policy shock. For example, tax- and spending-based fiscal policy shocks and capital- and leverage-based macroprudential policy shocks are unlikely to have identical impacts. And there is a particularly wide range of possible policy options in the case of product market and labour market structural reform shocks. Also, because the model does not include directly observed policy variables, shocks originating from a change in policy are not distinguished from those originating from some alternative source. For example, a fiscal policy shock from an exogenous change in the composition of the tax base cannot be distinguished from that of a discretionary change in tax rates. Consequently, the results from this chapter should be interpreted as generic and only an approximate guide to the likely macroeconomic impact of specific shocks pertaining to each policy type.

5.3 Results

This section reports and provides analysis of the results both in terms of the steady-state impact and the impulse response functions (IRFs). It also considers a number of robustness checks. The steady state shows the impact on the levels of the variables after a period of five years while the IRFs show the impact on the growth rates of the variables over a period of twenty quarters.

5.3.1 Steady State

The steady-state impacts of one standard deviation structural shocks are shown in Figure 5.4. There are several noteworthy features indicating that the results are consistent with findings in the literature regarding the behaviour of the economy. First, there is a consistent negative relationship between relative prices and current account imbalances across the different shocks. The macroprudential shock has a larger impact on the current account for a given change in prices, while the fiscal policy shock has a smaller impact, but all of them are within the range of estimates of the relationship between prices and the current account suggested in the literature. Second, the Phillips curve relationship is stable across the two demand-based policy shocks at around 0.8. This too is within the range of estimates of the Phillips curve slope found in the literature. Third, the fiscal multiplier is around

Steady-state impact of a 1 SD shock	**Fiscal policy**	**Macroprudential policy**	**Product market structural reform**	**Labour market structural reform**
Output	0.36	0.99	0.26	0.89
Prices	0.27	0.78	–0.34	0.21
Interest rates	–0.01	–0.06	–0.07	–0.07
Fiscal balance	–0.41	0.48	–0.16	0.11
Employment	0.10	1.37	–0.38	1.15
Current account	–0.23	–0.94	0.39	–0.23
Response of current account to prices	*–0.85*	*–1.21*	*–1.15*	*–1.10*
Implied Phillips curve slope	*0.75*	*0.79*		
Implied fiscal multiplier	*0.88*			
Fiscal passthrough to current account	*0.56*			

Figure 5.4 Steady-state impacts.

0.9 while fiscal passthrough to current account imbalances is just over 0.5. Again, these are results that are broadly consistent with the findings in the literature. That these findings on the behaviour of the economy appear consistent with the literature suggest that the model is well specified.

It is in this context that there are two noteworthy findings. The first is the finding that there is a strong response from the macroprudential policy shock in response to relatively small movements in interest rates. The effect of a change in interest rates is approximately four times as powerful in terms of its impact on output and six times as powerful in terms of its impact on prices as is typically found in the literature. If correct this could suggest an important role for macroprudential policy for managing macroeconomic imbalances. The second finding is that the counterintuitive result that a labour market structural reform shock leads to deterioration in the current account imbalance. This may be a consequence of strong output and employment response leading to an increase in relative prices despite the shock having been identified via a contemporaneous negative impact effect on relative prices. This raises important questions about the role of structural reforms to labour markets in addressing current account imbalances.

5.3.2 Impulse Response Functions

The most striking feature of the impulse response functions is that in most cases the confidence bounds indicate a low level of statistical significance, as shown in Figure 5.5. This result applies to most of the impulse response functions from the fiscal, labour market structural reform, and product market structural reform shocks. This would seem to add weight to emerging consensus view that managing macroeconomic imbalances within the euro area using policy may not be possible. However, there are two important exceptions.

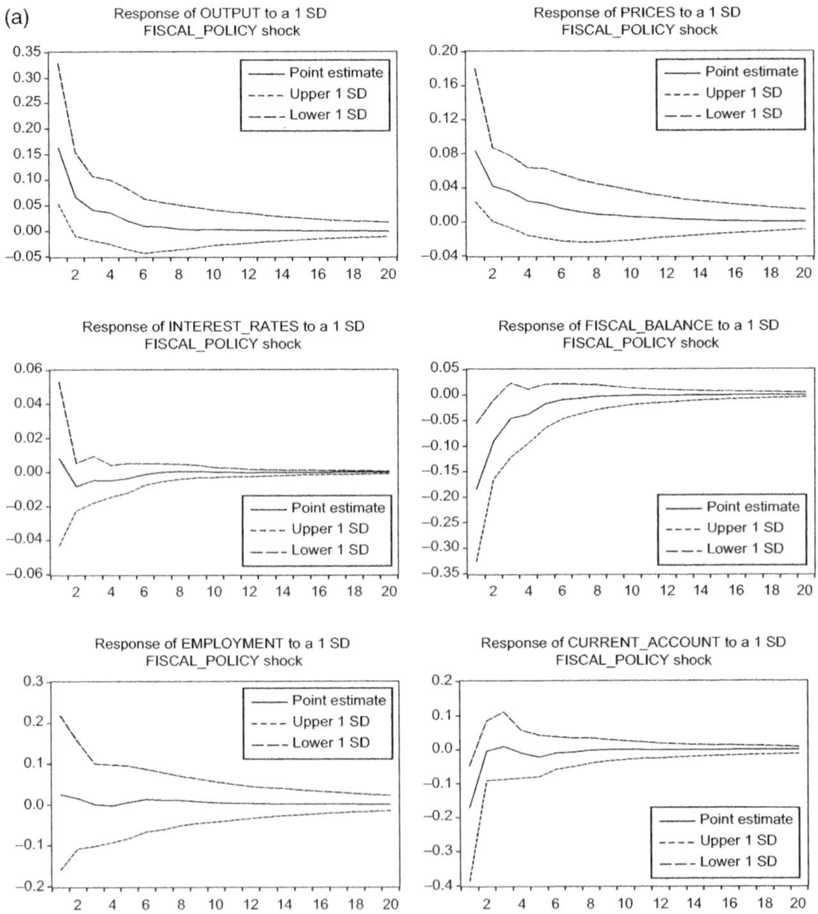

Figure 5.5a Demand – fiscal policy shock IRFs.

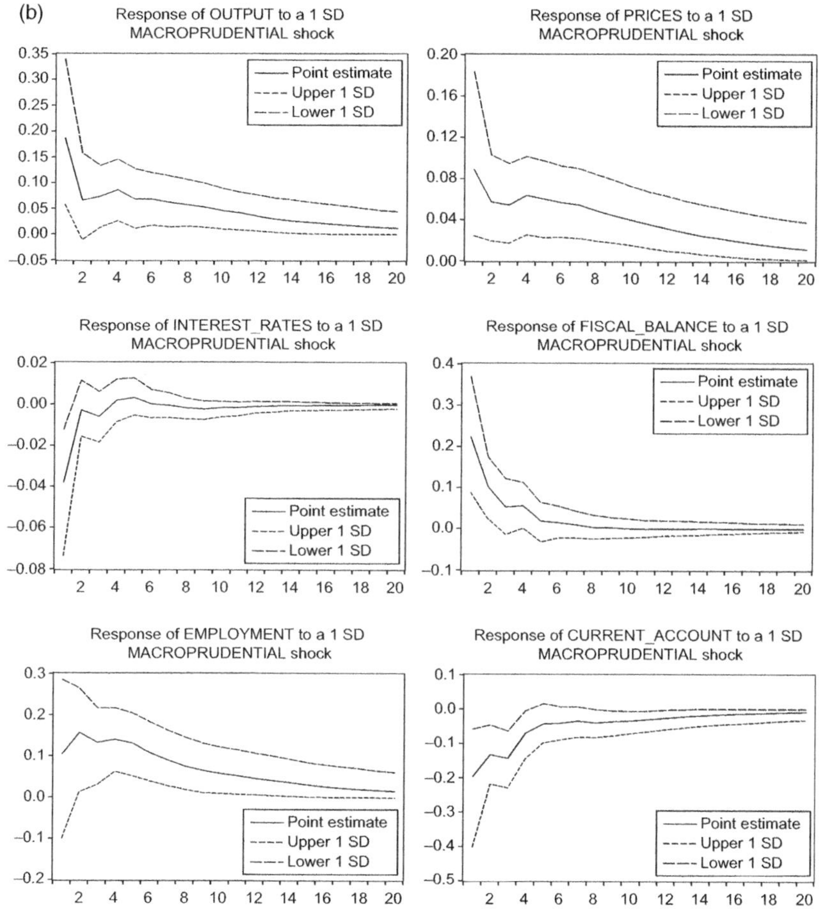

Figure 5.5b Demand – macroprudential policy shock IRFs.

The first is the impact of a labour market structural reform shock on employment. In this case, the impact on employment is statistically significant for the first three years. So, we can say with some confidence that labour market structural reforms would have a positive effect on addressing employment imbalances in the euro area. However, it remains the case that success in employment outcomes does not translate into other measures of macroeconomic imbalances. As noted in the steady-state analysis, the impact on the current account could well be perverse. And for all the other measures of macroeconomic imbalances, there is no statistically significant impact.

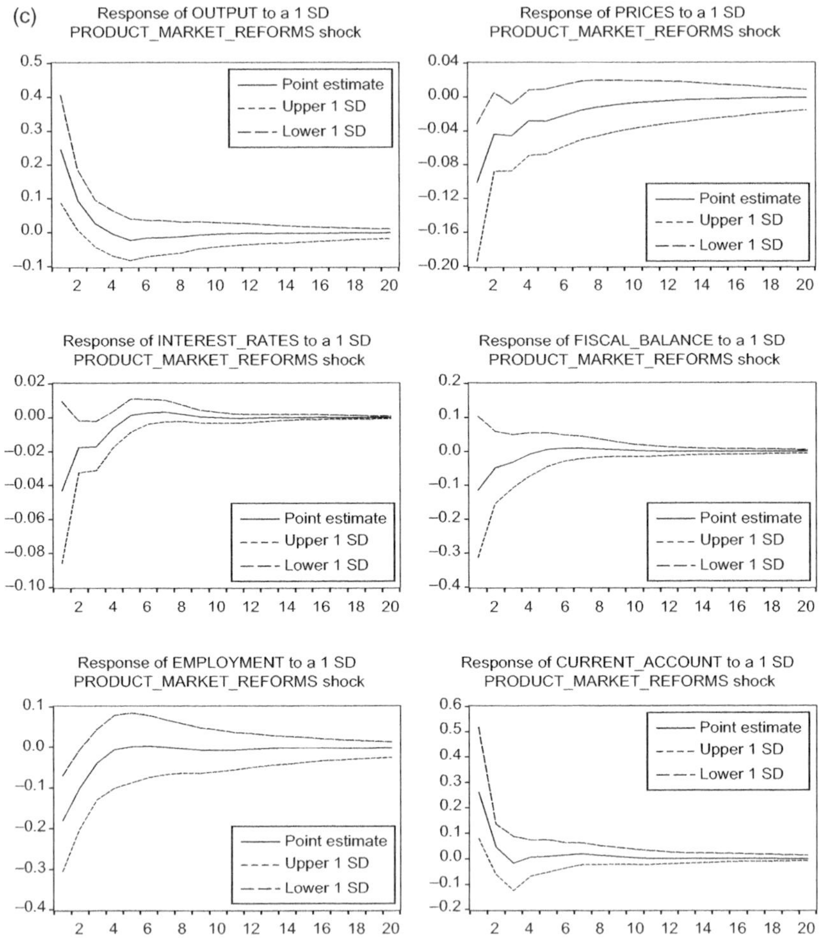

Figure 5.5c Supply – product market structural reform shock IRFs.

The second exception concerns the impact of the macroprudential policy shock. In addition to having a powerful impact in terms of the steady-state impact it also has a statistically significant impact on the various measures of macroeconomic imbalances. This is true not only for a few quarters but in some cases, such as for prices, the entire five-year period. It is worth noting that the profile of the impulse response function for the macroprudential policy shock is also very similar to that of a monetary policy shock in that the peak effect on growth and inflation takes place with a lag of one-to-two years. The impact on the current account is powerful and is statistically significant for several quarters.

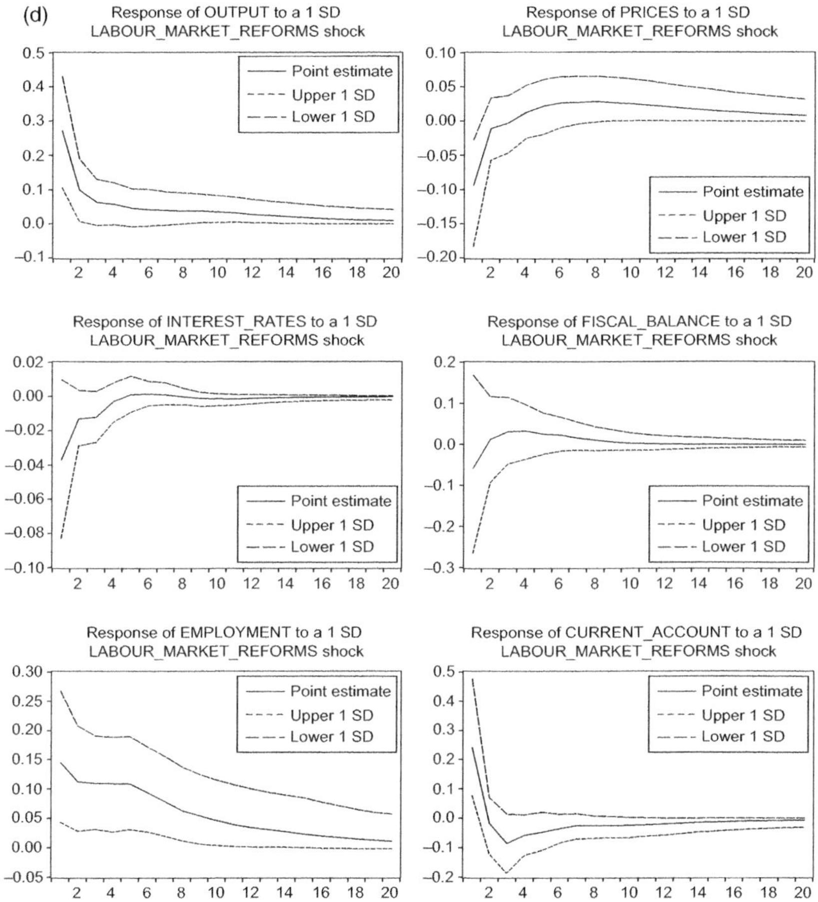

Figure 5.5d Supply – labour market structural reform shock IRFs.

5.3.3 Robustness Checks

Several robustness checks were conducted. First, the IRFs from nine alternative models with different lag lengths and sample periods were estimated. The lag lengths ranged from one to six quarters and sample periods were truncated by two years at the start and the end of the benchmark sample period. The results from these nine alternative models are shown in Figure 5.6 with the IRFs from these models represented by a light grey swathe. These swathes are generally narrow and closely aligned with the IRF from the benchmark model, which is shown as dark black line, indicating that the results appear to be

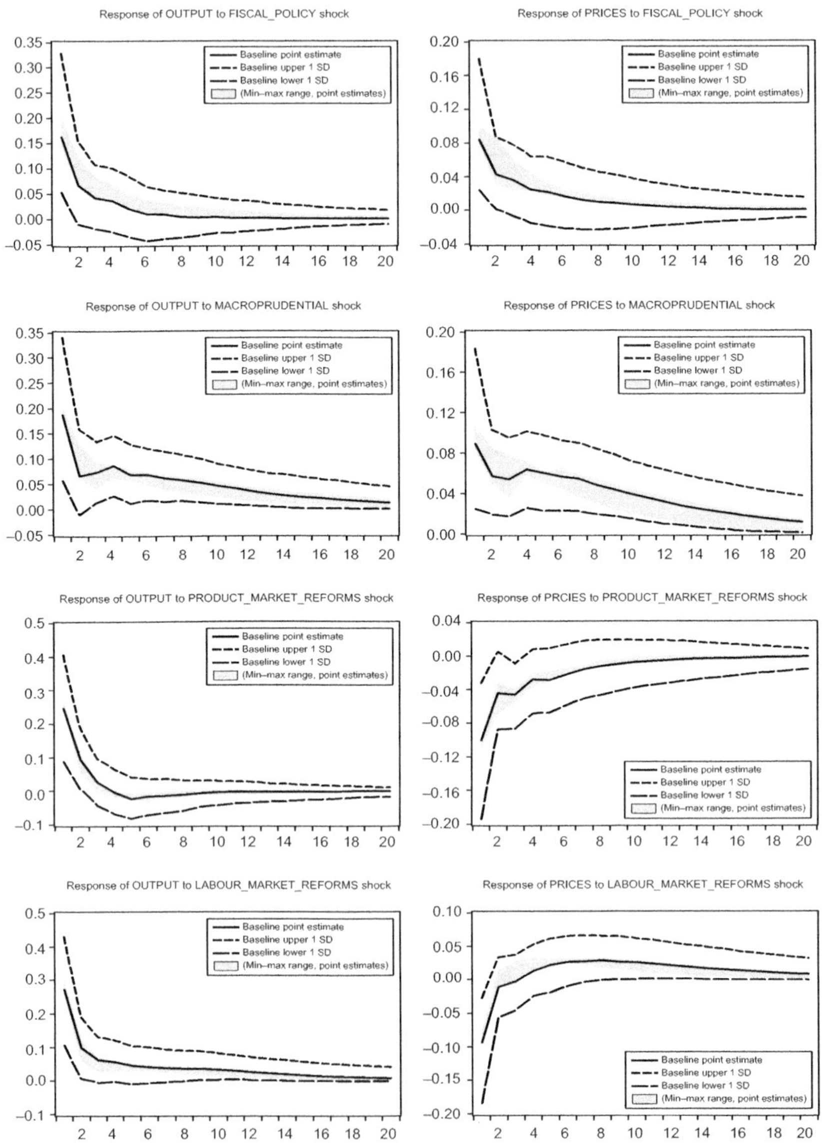

Figure 5.6 Robustness – impulse responses.

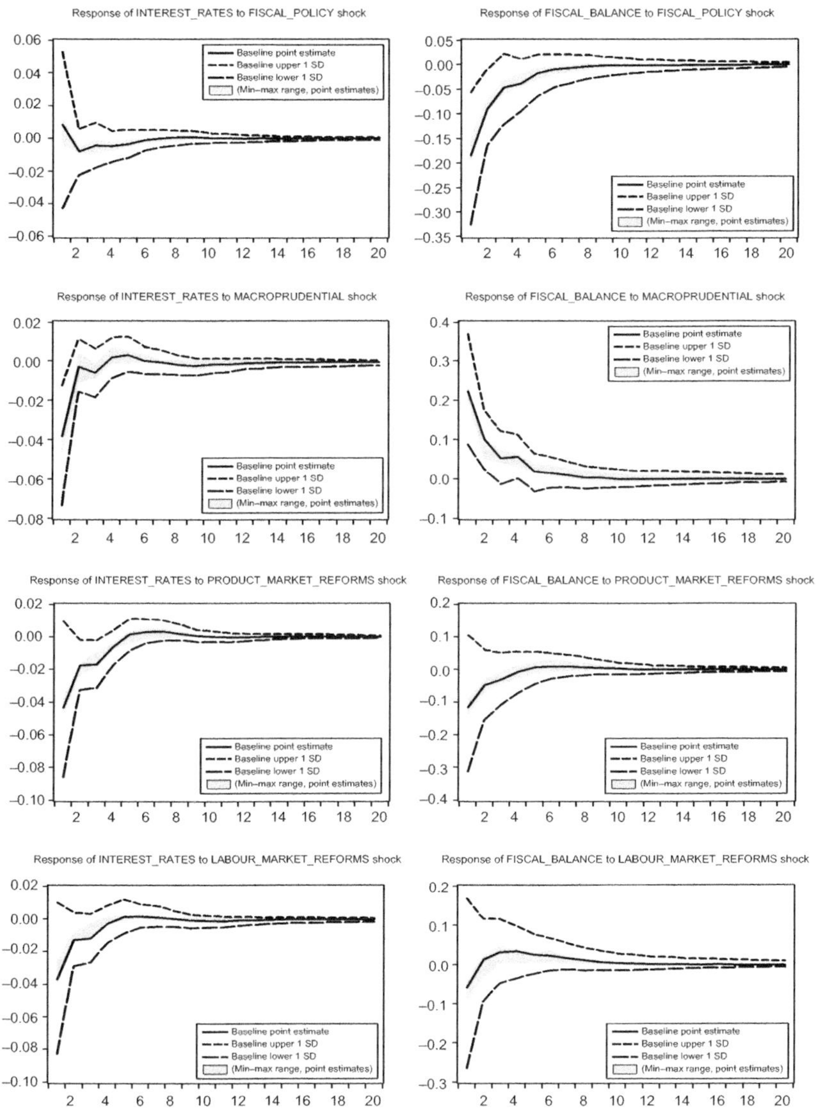

Figure 5.6 (*cont.*)

generally robust to alternative sample periods and lag lengths. The steady-state results were also found to be robust to these different sample periods and lag lengths.

A second robustness check was to use alternative sign restrictions to identify the product market and labour market reform shocks. In the

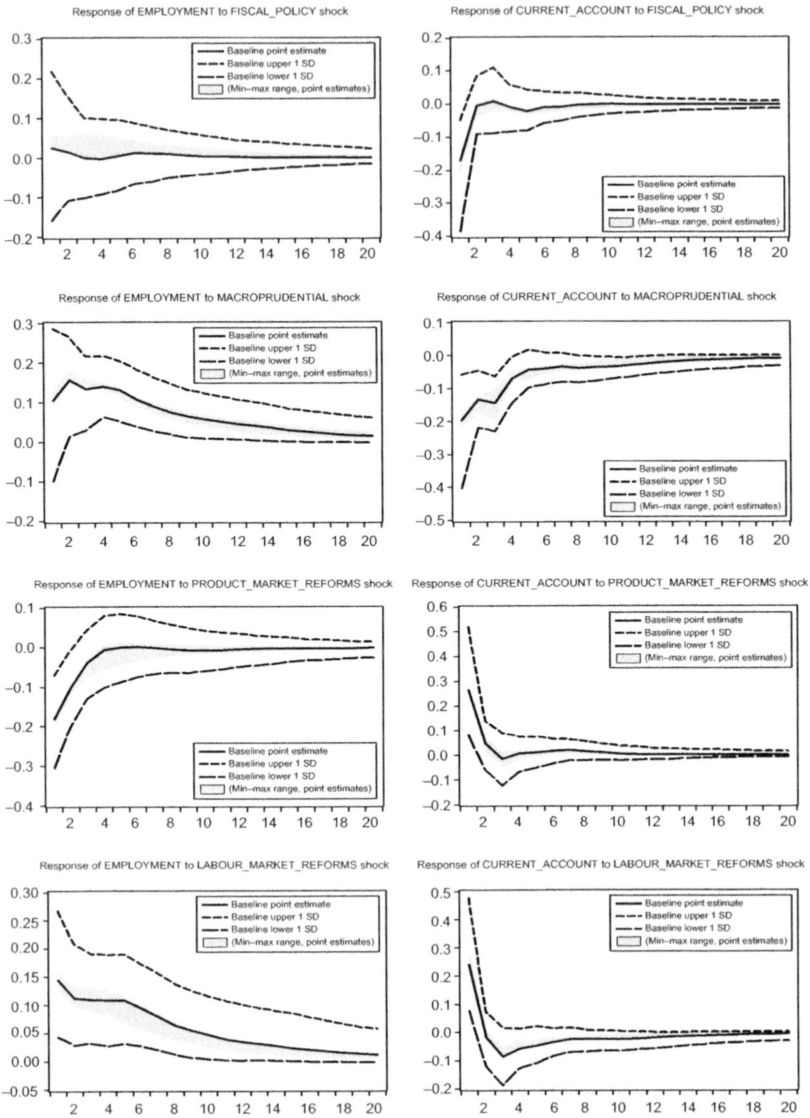

Figure 5.6 (*cont.*)

benchmark model, these shocks are distinguished from each other by the employment response. However, it is possible that the initial impact of some type of labour market reforms – such as those making it easier to dismiss employees – could be to reduce employment rather than increase it as required in the benchmark model. To check this, an alternative model in which the employment variable is replaced by a real wage variable was estimated. Product market structural reforms were identified by a rise the real wage, and labour market structural reforms were identified by a fall in the real wage. This alternative specification was not found to alter the main results.

A third robustness check was to use data from different countries in the macroeconomic imbalances model. In principle, the model results should be the same for any two countries or two groups of countries that, together, can be considered as a large, closed economy and where there are macroeconomic imbalances present. Consistent with this principle, an alternative 'large two-country' macroeconomic imbalances model between Germany and Spain was estimated. This alternative specification was also not found to alter the main results.

5.4 Conclusions and Policy Implications

This chapter has investigated the feasibility of using four policy shocks to manage macroeconomic imbalances in the euro area. It considered two demand-side policy shocks – fiscal policy and macroprudential policy and two supply-side policy shocks – labour market policy and product market policy. Although the steady-state impacts suggest that most of these policies could play some role in managing macroeconomic imbalances, in most cases the results are not found to be statistically significant beyond the first quarter or two. This would appear to add weight to the emerging consensus in the literature that managing macroeconomic imbalances in the euro area may not be possible.

However, there are two policy shocks that are identified as being of possible policy significance. The first is labour market policy shocks, which appear to have a persistent and statistically significant effect on employment imbalances. This would suggest that there is an important role for national labour market structural reforms in determining labour market outcomes. However, the impact on employment imbalances was not found to carry over into measures of macroeconomic imbalances such as relative prices and current accounts. This may reflect that labour market policies were also found to have a strong effect on relative output and price imbalances. If anything, the results would seem to suggest that pursued in isolation labour market policy could serve to make other macroeconomic imbalances worse.

The second policy shock of significance concerns macroprudential policy shocks. This was found to have persistent and statistically significant effect on a wide range of measures of macroeconomic imbalances. Crucially, it was found to have a particularly large and persistent impact on current account imbalances. The question remains as to how plausible this finding is. On the one hand, the profile of the impulse response functions is found to be consistent with that of a monetary policy shock for both output and prices, and the implied Phillips curve slope is within the range of estimates found in the literature. On the other hand, the magnitude of the responses for a given change in interest rates is several times larger than is typically found in the literature on monetary policy shocks.

There are reasons to think that in a monetary union relatively small changes in interest rates could be expected to be associated with outsized effects on economies. For example, owing to the common interest rate in money markets, an easing in credit supply within the banking system is more likely to manifest itself in terms of easier credit conditions available to households and firms than lower interest rates. This could take the form of lower fees and less stringent credit checks. As a result, the easing of credit supply may show up more strongly in terms of credit and money growth than in changes in interest rates. Certainly, credit and money growth was markedly higher in the periphery than the core during the period of widening macroeconomic imbalances.

It is important to emphasise that the findings in this chapter have little to say about the European Commission's approach of managing macroeconomic imbalances by eliminating structural rigidities. This approach relies on flexible price and wage setting so that demand shocks are neutralised by real income and expenditure switching effects. Once macroeconomic imbalances have emerged, however, the findings in this chapter would suggest that the introduction of product and labour market structural reforms is unlikely to help. This is especially the case for labour market structural reforms, which may even run the risk of making preexisting macroeconomic imbalances worse.

While this chapter has tended to confirm the emerging consensus view that managing macroeconomic imbalances in the euro area may be difficult, it raises the tantalising prospect that a combination of eliminating structural rigidities before macroeconomic imbalances emerge plus using macroprudential policy to manage emerging macroeconomic imbalances could be effective. Further research is undoubtedly needed to confirm the results found in this chapter and to calibrate the likely the scale of macroprudential intervention required to see whether it is feasible within existing regulatory frameworks.

Appendix A Theoretical Model

We start with a simple open economy New Keynesian (NK) model comprising a production function, open economy dynamic IS equation, an open economy New Keynesian Phillips Curve and an equation relating the trade balance equation to competitiveness that reflects the impact of relative price changes on both consumption in the Euler equation and expenditure switching effects:

$$\bar{y}_t = a_t + n_t$$

$$y_t = E_t\{y_{t+1}\} - \rho(r_t - E_t\{\Delta p_{t+1}\} - \overline{rr}_t) + \theta g_t - \vartheta q_t$$

$$\Delta p_t = E_t\{\Delta p_{t+1}\} + \lambda\{y_t - \bar{y}_t\} - \delta q_{t-1}$$

$$x_t = -\phi q_t$$

$\bar{y}$ is potential output, a is technology, n is employment, y is output, r is the effective interest rate, p is prices, $\overline{rr}$ is the neutral interest rate, g is the fiscal balance, q is the real exchange rate and x is the trade balance.

To adapt the NK model to the issue of macroeconomic imbalances, we make three simplifying assumptions: (i) the euro area as a whole is a large closed economy; (ii) members of the euro area are small open economies that share an identical economic structure; and (iii) throughout the euro area inflation expectations are anchored at the ECB's inflation target. This enables the model to be rewritten in terms of imbalances in output, prices and trade, where the subscript i denotes a variable expressed in differences across two sets of euro-area members:

$$y_{it} = E_t\{y_{it+1}\} - \rho r_{it} + \theta g_{it} - \vartheta p_{it}$$

$$p_{it} = (1 - \delta)p_{it-1} + \lambda\{y_{it} - (a_{it} + n_{it})\}$$

$$x_{it} = -\phi p_{it}$$

We then close the model by identifying four policy shocks:

$g_{it} = g_{it-1} + u_{it}^f$ [fiscal policy shock]
$r_{it} = r_{it-1} + u_{it}^c$ [macroprudential policy shock]
$a_{it} = a_{it-1} + u_{it}^p$ [product market structural reform shock]
$n_{it} = n_{it-1} + u_{it}^w$ [labour market structural reform shock]

These equations constitute the equilibrium dynamics.

Appendix B VAR Representation and Method of Estimation

The model is estimated in first differences and represented in matrix form by the following:

$$\boldsymbol{B}_0 \begin{bmatrix} \Delta y_t \\ \Delta p_t \\ \Delta g_t \\ \Delta r_t \\ \Delta n_t \\ \Delta x_t \end{bmatrix} = \boldsymbol{B}_1 \tilde{\boldsymbol{E}}_{t-1}\left[\Delta y_{t+1}\right] + \boldsymbol{B}_2 \begin{bmatrix} \Delta y_{t-1} \\ \Delta p_{t-1} \\ \Delta g_{t-1} \\ \Delta r_{t-1} \\ \Delta n_{t-1} \\ \Delta x_{t-1} \end{bmatrix} + \begin{bmatrix} u_{1t} \\ u_{2t} \\ u_{3t} \\ u_{4t} \\ u_{5t} \\ u_{6t} \end{bmatrix}$$

Or more compactly:

$$\boldsymbol{B}_0 \boldsymbol{Z}_t = \boldsymbol{B}_1 \tilde{\boldsymbol{E}}_{t-1}\left[\Delta y_{t+1}\right] + \boldsymbol{B}_2 \boldsymbol{Z}_{t-1} + \boldsymbol{u}_t$$

The bold characters refer to matrices and vectors; $\boldsymbol{Z}_t$ is a vector of potentially endogenous variables; and $\boldsymbol{u}_t$ is a vector of white noise disturbances. $\tilde{\boldsymbol{E}}_t$ is an expectations operator where the tilde denotes that these are expectations that are not formed rationally, as required by the consensus narrative of the crisis and the animal spirits explanation of macroeconomic imbalances.

There are several ways in which expectations might be formed nonrationally. De Grauwe (2012a) proposes a behavioural formulation in which agents use heuristics to form their expectations. Such heuristics include fundamentalist and extrapolative rules that are weighted according to performance into a single 'market forecast'. But it might be that they are formed in many other ways, such as assuming a random walk for each of the variables or with some proportion of agents forming their expectations rationally while others form them adaptively. In estimation, we simply model them adaptively:

$$\tilde{\boldsymbol{E}}_{t-1}\left[\Delta y_{t+1}\right] = \boldsymbol{C}_1 \boldsymbol{Z}_{t-1}$$

With this simple formulation, the preceding structural equation can now be rewritten as follows:

$$A_0^{-1}Z_t = A_1 Z_{t-1} + u_t$$

where $A_0^{-1} = B_0$ and $A_1 = [B_1 C_1 + B_2]$. Premultiplying by A_0 then gives the following:

$$Z_t = A_0 A_1 Z_{t-1} + A_0 u_t$$

Or:

$$Z_t = \Gamma_0 Z_{t-1} + v_t$$

where $\Gamma_0 = A_0 A_1$ and $v_t = A_0 u_t$. This final equation gives the reduced-form VAR representation of the model that is estimated.

To improve precision of the estimates given the relatively small sample size, this chapter utilises Bayesian methods to obtain the reduced-form VAR. The Bayesian reduced-form VAR (the 'posterior VAR') is a weighted average of a VAR estimated by maximum likelihood (the 'sample VAR') and a VAR assumed to follow a particular form and statistical distribution (the 'prior VAR').[6] The prior VAR is that the vector of variables, X_t, is modelled as an $AR(1)$ prior mean for the D matrix:[7]

$$X_t = DX_{t-1}$$

The Bayesian reduced-form VAR therefore takes the same form as a standard maximum likelihood VAR in which a vector of variables, Z_t, is a function of their own lags, $D(L)Z_{t-1}$, with the reduced-form errors, v_t, having a covariance structure of Σ:

$$Z_t = D(L)Z_{t-1} + v_t, \quad VAR(v) = \Sigma$$

[6] The weighting procedure was implemented using the dummy variables approach with hyperparameters $\tau = 1$ (prior tightness on own lag) and $c = 10$ (prior tightness on constant).

[7] The coefficient matrix B is assumed to follow a normal-inverse Wishart distribution.

Appendix C Alternative Methods of Structural Identification

A VAR includes only a constant and lags of the vector of variables included in estimation. Consequently, a structural (i.e., economic) shock will lead to residuals in the reduced-form error vector, v_t. The errors will not be random but reflect the structure of the economy and how it responds contemporaneously to the structural shocks hitting the economy. By making assumptions about the structure of the economy, the reduced-form errors can be used to recover from the structural shocks that have hit the economy and what their impact on the variables in the VAR has been.

Formally, this is done by decomposing the reduced-form errors, v_t, into a $N \times N$ contemporaneous impact matrix, A_0, and an $N \times 1$ structural shock vector, u_t:

$$v_t = A_0 u_t, \qquad VAR(u_t) = I$$

In effect, the A_0 matrix summarises the structure of the economy assumed by the econometrician. Note that the condition $VAR(u_t) = I$ means that the structural shocks are assumed to be orthogonal to each other, i.e., there is no relationship between them, and they occur independently of each other and are normalised to have unit variance.

There are several ways of imposing an economic structure on the A_0 matrix. The challenge is to ensure that the imposed structure, when combined with the recovered structural shocks, results in the same covariance structure as seen in the reduced-form residuals, i.e., $VAR(A_0 u) = VAR(v) = \Sigma$. Because the structural shocks are normalised to have unit variance, this condition amounts to finding a matrix that satisfies $A_0 A_0' = \Sigma$. The most basic solution to this problem is to use a Cholesky decomposition of the reduced-form errors. Its lower triangular structure means it automatically satisfies the $VAR(A_0 u) = VAR(v) = \Sigma$ condition. But it requires a unique causal chain that runs through the variables with at least one variable being invariant to structural shocks in the other variables. It is doubtful whether the structure of the economy can ever be characterised in this way and as a consequence the results of such an interpretation are usually economically meaningless.

Alternative approaches include imposing restrictions on some combination of the short-run and long-run impact of specific structural shocks. This can be motivated by economic theory, e.g., that the effect of a monetary shock on real variables is neutral in the long run (i.e., zero). However, in order to meet the condition $VAR(A_0u) = VAR(v) = \Sigma$, an arbitrary number of restrictions is still required to identify the contemporaneous impact matrix. This may require imposing restrictions that are hard to justify on economic grounds purely for the purposes of identification. Experience has also shown that the results from these approaches are very sensitive to the model's specification, such as lag length.

Owing to the inherent weaknesses of these approaches, a method of identification that has become popular in recent years is the sign restrictions approach (Canova and De Nicolo [2002]; Faust [1998]; Uhlig [2005]). This method is much more flexible and requires only that each shock has a unique sign pattern of effects on the variables in the VAR. The basic idea is that the econometrician should establish from economic theory what the effect of the shocks on the variables should be. For example, in a three-variable model of demand, supply and interest rates, a wide class of models would suggest that a positive demand shock would raise all three and that a negative interest rate shock would raise demand and prices but lower interest rates. This signing pattern meets the condition of being unique in the sense that they have the same signed impact on demand and inflation but a different signed impact on interest rates.

Numerical techniques are then used to find all the decompositions that are compatible with the imposed sign restrictions. This is implemented using the Rubio-Ramirez et al. (2010) algorithm. First an $N \times N$ matrix, K, is drawn from the standard normal distribution and the matrix Q is calculated from the QR decomposition of K. The Cholesky decomposition of the current draw of $\Sigma = \tilde{A}_0'\tilde{A}_0$ is then found. The A_0 matrix is obtained as $A_0 = Q\tilde{A}_0$. Note that the QR decomposition implies $Q'Q = I$ and, therefore that $\Sigma = A_0'A_0$. In other words, the new A_0 matrix is a random rotation of the old $\tilde{A}_0$ matrix that also satisfies the requirement that $\Sigma = A_0'A_0$. The signs of this new A_0 matrix are checked to ensure that the contemporaneous impacts are in accordance with the sign restrictions derived from economic theory. If they are, the draw is kept; if they are not, the draw is discarded. This process is repeated until a distribution of the A_0 matrices that is compatible with the economic theory underlying the model is obtained.

A disadvantage of this approach relative to the Cholesky approach and short-run and long-run restrictions approaches is that a whole distribution of decompositions is obtained. To simplify analysis, however, the decomposition that produces IRFs that are closest to the mean response is the one that is used to summarise the model. The IRFs that this decomposition generates are referred to as the Fry–Pagan median (Fry and Pagan, 2011). An indication of the uncertainty can be given by reporting intervals from the distribution of IRFs (usually one standard deviation either side of the median).

References

Abbas, S., Bouhga-Hagbe, J., Fatas, A. J., Mauro, P. and Velloso, R. C, (2010). 'Fiscal Policy and the Current Account', IMF Working Papers, No. 10/121.

Abiad, A., Leigh, D. and Mody, A. (2009). 'Financial Integration, Capital Mobility, and Income Convergence', *Economic Policy*, Vol. 24, No. 4, 241–305.

Adam, K., Jappelli, T., Menichini, A., Padula, M. and Pagano, M. (2002). 'Analyse, Compare, and Apply Alternative Indicators and Monitoring Methodologies to Measure the Evolution of Capital Market Integration in the European Union', CSEF Paper, University of Salerno.

Alcidi, C. and Gros, D. (2013). 'Economic Policy Coordination in the Euro Area under the European Semester', CEPS Special Report, No. 123, December.

Baele, L., Ferrando, A., Hordahl, P., Krylova, E. and Monnet, C. (2004). 'Measuring European Financial Integration', *Oxford Review of Economic Policy*, Vol. 20, No. 4, 509–530.

Baldwin, R. and Giavazzi, F. (2015). The Eurozone Crisis: A Consensus View of the Causes and a Few Possible Solutions, VoxEU ebook.

Bems, R., Dedola, B. and Smets, F. (2007). 'US Imbalances: The Role of Technology and Policy', *Journal of International Money and Finance*, Vol. 26, No. 4, 523–545.

Benassy-Quere, A. and Ragot, X. (2015). 'A Policy Mix for the Euro Area', Les notes du conseil d'analyse economique, no 21, March.

Berger, H. and Nitsch, V. (2010). 'The Euro's Effect on Trade Imbalances', IMF Working Papers, No. 10/226, October.

Biroli, P., Mourre, G. and Turrini, A. (2010). 'Adjustment in the Euro Area and Regulation of Product and Labour Markets: An Empirical Assessment', European Economy, Economics Papers No. 428, October.

Blanchard, O. and Giavazzi, F. (2002). 'Current Account Deficits in the Euro Area: The End of the Fedlstein-Horioka Puzzle?' *Brookings Papers on Economic Activity*, Vol. 33, No. 2, 147–210.

Bluedorn, J. and Leigh, D. (2011). 'Revisiting the Twin Deficits Hypothesis: The Effect of Fiscal Consolidation on the Current Account', *IMF Economic Review*, Vol. 59, No. 4, 582–602.

Bracke, T. and Fidora, M. (2008). 'Global Liquidity of Global Savings Glut? A Structural VAR Approach', ECB Working Papers, No. 911.

Brzoza-Brzezina, M., Kolasa, M. and Makarski, K. (2015). 'Macroprudential Policies and Imbalances in the Euro Area', *Journal of International Money and Finance*, Vol. 51, No. C, 137–154.

Cabral, I., Dierick, F. and Vesala, J. (2002). 'Banking Integration in the Euro Area', ECB Working Papers, No. 6, December.

Canova, F. and De Nicolo, G. (2002). 'Monetary Disturbances Matter for Business Fluctuations in the G-7', *Journal of Monetary Economics*, Vol. 49, No. 6, 1131–1159.

Canova, F. and Paustian, M. (2011). 'Business Cycle Measurement with Some Theory', *Journal of Monetary Economics*, Vol. 58, 345–361.

Ca'Zorzi, M. and Rubaszek, M. (2008). 'On the Empirical Evidence of the Inter-Temporal Current Account Model for the Euro Area Countries', ECB Working Papers, No. 895.

Coeurdacier, N. and Martin, P. (2007). 'The Geography of Asset Holdings: Evidence from Sweden', Riksbank Research Paper Series, No. 202, January.

Daborwski, M. (2015). 'Monetary Union and Fiscal and Macroeconomic Governance', mimeo.

Dalsgaard, T. and de Serres, A. (2001). 'Estimating Prudent Budgetary Margins', in A. Brunila, M. Buti and D. Franco (ed.), *The Stability and Growth Pact*. UK: Palgrave MacMillan, pp. 204–234.

De Grauwe, P. (2010). 'The Financial Crisis and the Future of the Eurozone', Bruges European Economic Policy Briefings, No. 21.

(2012a). 'Lessons from the Eurocrisis for East Asian Monetary Relations', *World Economy*, Vol. 35, No. 4, doi: 10.1111/j.1467-9701.2012.01443.

(2012b). *Lectures on Behavioural Macroeconomics*. New Jersey, USA: Princeton University Press.

Ederer, S. (2015). 'Macroeconomic Imbalances and Institutional Reforms in the EMU', WWWforEurope Working Papers, No. 87, March, www.ac.at.

Eichengreen, B. (2010). 'Imbalances in the Euro Area', mimeo, November.

Faust, J. (1998). 'The Robustness of Identified VAR Conclusions about Money', *Carnegie–Rochester Conference Series on Public Policy*, Vol. 49, No. 1, 207–244.

Fry, R. and Pagan, A. (2011). 'Sign Restrictions in Structural Vector Autoregressions: A Critical Review', *Journal of Economic Literature*, Vol. 49, No. 4, 938–960.

Galati, G, and Tsatsaronis, K. (2003). 'The Impact of the Euro on Europe's Financial Markets', *Financial Markets, Institutions & Instruments*, Vol. 12, No. 3, 165–222.

Gourinchas, P. (2002). 'Comments on Current Account Deficits in the Euro Area: The End of the Feldstein–Horioka Puzzle?' *Brookings Papers on Economic Activity*, Vol. 33, No. 2, 147–210.

Gros, D. (2012). 'Macroeconomic Imbalances in the Euro Area: Symptom or Cause of the Crisis?', CEPS Policy Brief, No. 266, April.

Hancke, B. (2013). *Unions, Central Banks and EMU: Labour Market Institutions and Monetary Integration in Europe*. Oxford University Press.

Hancke, B. and Soskice, D. (2003). 'Wage-Setting and Inflation Targets in EMU', *Oxford Review of Economic Policy*, Vol. 19, No. 1, 149–160.

Ju, J. and Wei, S. (2007). 'Current Account Adjustment: Some New Theory and Evidence', NBER Working Papers, No. 13388.

Kamps, C., De Stefani, R., Leiner-Killinger, N., Ruffer, R. and Sonderman, D. (2014). 'The Identification of Fiscal and Macroeconomic Imbalances: Unexploited Synergies under the Strengthened EU Governance Framework', ECB Occasional Paper Series, No. 157, November.

Kennedy, M. and Slok, T. (2005). 'Are Structural Reforms the Answer to Global Current Account Imbalances', *OECD Economic Studies*, No. 41, 47–73.

Kincaid, R. and Watson, M. (2015). 'Avoiding Another Crisis in the Euro Area: Public and Private Imbalances and National Policy Responses', *Journal of European Integration*, Vol. 37, No. 2, 787–801.

Lane, P. (2010). 'A European Perspective on External Imbalances', Swedish Institute for Policy Studies Report, May.

Lane, P. and Milesi-Ferretti, G. (2005). 'Financial Globalization and Exchange Rates', IMF Working Papers, No. 05/03.

Lane, P. and Pels, B. (2012). 'Current Account Imbalances in Europe', CEPR Discussion Papers, No. 8958, May.

Leeper, E., Richter, A. and Walker, T. (2012). 'Quantitative Effects of Fiscal Foresight', *American Economic Journal: Economic Policy*, Vol. 4, No. 2, 115–144.

Leeper, E., Walker, T. and Shu-Chun, S. (2013). 'Foresight and Information Flows', *Econometrica*, Vol. 81, No. 3, 1115–1145.

Obstfeld, M. and Rogoff, K. (1996). *Foundations of International Macroeconomics*. MIT Press.

Pagano, M. and von Thadden, E. (2004). 'The European Bond Markets under EMU', CSEF Paper, University of Naples.

Peersman, G. and Straub, R. (2009). 'Technology Shocks and Robust Sign Restrictions in a Euro Area SVAR', *International Economic Review*, Vol. 50, No. 3, 727–750.

Quint, D. and Rabal, P. (2014). 'Monetary and Macroprudential Policy in an Estimated DSGE Model of the Euro Area', *International Journal of Central Banking*, Vol. 10, No. 2, 169–236.

Rubio-Ramirez, J., Waggoner, D. and Zha, T. (2010). 'Structural Vector Autoregressions: Theory of Identification and Algorithms for Inference', *Review of Economic Studies*, Vol. 77, No. 2, 665–696.

Santos, J. and Tsatsaronis, K. (2003). 'The Cost of Barriers to Entry: Evidence from the Market for Corporate Bond Underwriting', Bank for International Settlements Working Paper No. 134, September.

Schmitz, B. and von Hagen, J. (2011). 'Current Account Imbalances and Financial Integration in the Euro Area', *Journal of International Money and Finance*, Vol. 30, 1676–1695.

Soskice, D. and Iversen, T. (2000). 'The Non-Neutrality of Monetary Policy with Large Price or Wage Setters', *Quarterly Journal of Economics*, Vol. 115, No. 1, 265–284.

Uhlig, H. (2005). 'What Are the Effects of Monetary Policy on Output? Results from an Agnostic Identification Procedure', *Journal of Monetary Economics*, Vol. 52, 381–419.

Waysand, C., Ross, K. and de Guzman, J. (2010). 'European Financial Linkages: A New Look at Imbalances', IMF Working Papers, No. 10/295, December.

Zemanek, H., Belke, A. and Schnabl, G. (2010). 'Current Account Balances and Structural Adjustment in the Euro Area', *International Economics and Economic Policy*, Vol. 7, 83–127.

6 *Financial Crises and Liberalization*

Progress or Reversals?

ORKUN SAKA, NAURO F. CAMPOS, PAUL DE GRAUWE, YUEMEI JI AND ANGELO MARTELLI

6.1 Introduction

It is difficult to overestimate the economic and political turbulence in the aftermath of financial crises.[1] What usually starts as a panic in a single financial market or institution usually propagates in a rapid pace to other agents of the economy and necessitates an urgent reaction from the policy makers. However, it is not easy to predict, a priori, whether the reaction of the policy makers to such news would be in the direction of further reforms; that is, the optimal policy change during/after a financial crisis may not necessarily aim to further liberalise the markets. As financial institutions and markets become dysfunctional in the midst of a crisis, governments may feel the urge to intervene in the sector, for instance bailing out the failed banks and/or increasing the ex-post efforts to better regulate the misbehaving institutions. This could be politically unavoidable especially when the cause of the crisis is commonly perceived to be the 'free markets', and the public sentiment turns against the financial industry as well as the bankers at its helm. On the other hand, such periods of instability may act as a catalyst for pushing forward the otherwise impossible but necessary liberalization agendas that might have been stuck due to private interests or lack of political enthusiasm. In that case, financial crises could open a window of opportunities to make sharp changes in policy space, in line with the more general crises-beget-reforms hypothesis (Drazen and Easterly, 2001; Drazen and Grilli, 1993).

[1] This work was supported by the Economic and Social Research Council grant ES/P000274/1. We are grateful to the participants of the conference on 'Integration and Structural Reforms: The European Experience' (London School of Economics) for their useful comments and suggestions. Nicholas Andreoulis provided superb research assistance for this chapter. All remaining errors are ours.

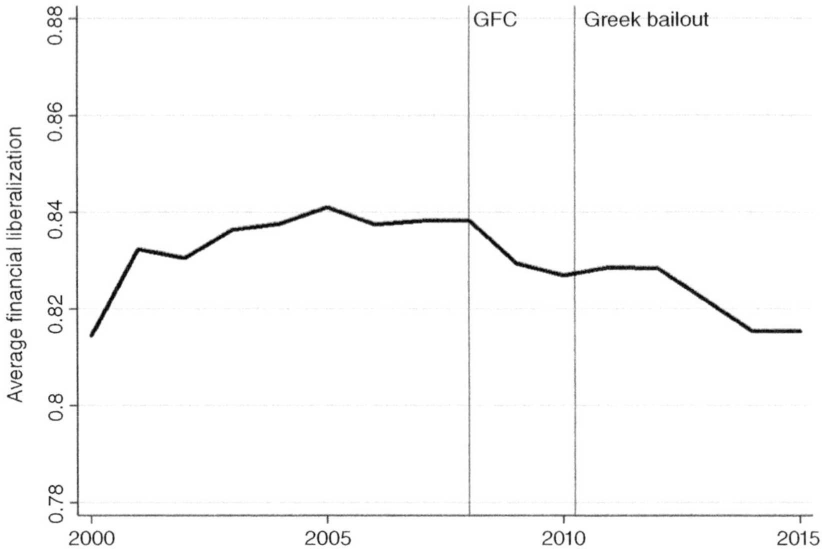

Figure 6.1 Average financial liberalization in EU countries between the years 2000 and 2015. The figure shows the aggregate financial liberalization index averaged over the following twenty-two EU countries: Austria, Belgium, Czech Republic, Denmark, Estonia, Finland, France, Germany, Greece, Hungary, Ireland, Italy, Latvia, Luxembourg, Netherlands, Poland, Portugal, Slovakia, Slovenia, Spain, Sweden and the United Kingdom. The first vertical line corresponds to the start of the Global Financial Crisis and the second to the announcement of the first bailout package for Greece.
Liberalization data come from Denk and Gomes (2017)

The experience of the European Union (EU) in the last two decades suggests that the first argument might be closer to the truth. Using the latest indexes of financial reform from the Organization for Economic Cooperation and Development (OECD), Figure 6.1 shows that the overall level of financial liberalization in EU countries had a slightly upward trend before the Global Financial Crisis (GFC), after which it reversed and had a sharp drop especially during/after the recent Eurozone debt turmoil. Hence, in fifteen years and after two major financial crises, it appears that there has been no progress in Europe regarding financial liberalization as the region went back to the levels it had around 2000.

When the EU is separated into euro and non-euro members, one observes in Figure 6.2 that the initial upward trend in liberalization

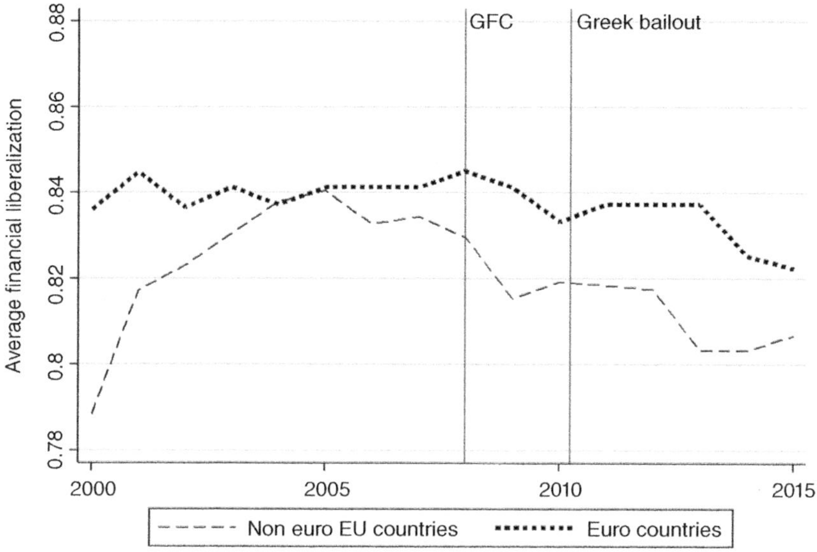

Figure 6.2 Average financial liberalization in euro and non-euro EU countries between the years 2000 and 2015. The figure shows the aggregate financial liberalization index averaged over twelve euro and ten non-euro EU countries. The euro sample includes Austria, Belgium, Finland, France, Germany, Greece, Ireland, Italy, Luxembourg, Netherlands, Portugal and Spain. The non-euro EU sample includes the Czech Republic, Denmark, Estonia, Hungary, Latvia, Poland, Slovakia, Slovenia, Sweden and the United Kingdom. The first vertical line corresponds to the start of the Global Financial Crisis and the second to the announcement of the first bailout package for Greece.
Liberalization data come from Denk and Gomes (2017)

efforts mainly came from the EU countries that were not part of the Eurozone during that period. This group is mostly comprised of East European countries that had to reform their economies to gain EU membership. However, once the convergence between these new members and the old ones was completed and EU access was granted, new members started diverging again, the speed of which seems to have only accelerated with the Global Financial Crisis.

Better identifying the impact of the Eurozone debt crises on the liberalization process requires dividing the Eurozone sample further into the countries that were and were not struck by the crises. Figure 6.3 illustrates the evolution of the reform process in crisis-stricken (Greece, Italy, Ireland, Portugal and Spain, or GIIPS) and

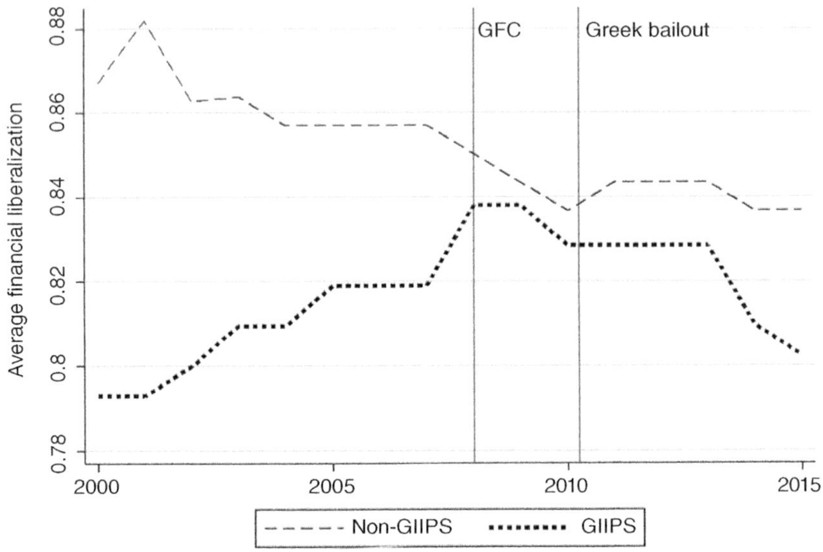

Figure 6.3 Average financial liberalization in GIIPS and non-GIIPS euro countries between the years 2000 and 2015. The figure shows the aggregate financial liberalization index averaged over five GIIPS and seven non-GIIPS euro countries. The GIIPS sample includes Greece, Ireland, Italy, Portugal and Spain. The non-GIIPS euro sample includes Austria, Belgium, Finland, France, Germany, Luxembourg and Netherlands. The first vertical line corresponds to the start of the Global Financial Crisis and the second to the announcement of the first bailout package for Greece.
Liberalization data come from Denk and Gomes (2017)

other (non-GIIPS) euro member states. It is obvious that both groups have been converging towards each other until 2008, which is what one would expect among the members of a financially integrated currency union. However, when the global financial crisis struck, this convergence gradually stopped and both groups started deliberalizing their financial markets. This negative trend continued later only in the countries experiencing debt crises, which led to further reform divergence within the currency union.

Are these experiences unique to Europe? Is there a case to be made that financial crises lead countries to deliberalize their financial markets? If so, are these policy changes temporary and aimed at curbing the imminent financial crisis or rather do they represent the long-term choices permanently changed by the policy equilibrium in the country? In this chapter, we shed light on these questions and show that while financial crises lead to more government intervention (i.e., less liberalization) in the short term, reform efforts kick in afterwards and countries gradually liberalize their financial markets again, catching up with the others in the medium to long term.

What is special about financial liberalization? Why is it a particularly appropriate setting to test the crises-beget-reforms in general and in the EU specifically? We think this is a particularly appropriate setting because financial liberalisation changes relatively quickly. Other reforms (consider labour market reforms) respond much more slowly, with considerable implementation lags. This fast response allows us to disentangle short- from long-run effects (a subject that has gained huge importance, as demonstrated by the voluminous literature surveyed by Loayza et al., 2018). Moreover, the financial reform–financial crisis combination yields a setting that is favourable to confirm the hypothesis. In other words, we should be extra confident if we don't find a strong positive effect from crisis to reforms in this setting. Additionally, contrasting the global sample with the EU is of interest in light of the literature that posits that the positive effect of financial integration on the speed of convergence is indeed one of the factors that makes Europe different from the rest of the world (Friedrich et al., 2013).

We employ two strategies in our empirical framework. First, by using a quasi–difference-in-differences methodology in a panel setting, we compare the level of financial liberalization between the two periods immediately before and after a financial crisis, which helps us capture the causal impact of the financial crisis itself. Our findings suggest that, even though small on average in terms of their economic magnitude, all types of financial crises have a negative effect on the reform process. Moreover, we also find that reversals are strongest after the sovereign debt defaults followed by currency crises, whereas banking crises seem to have a relatively more modest impact.

Second, we explore the dynamic relationship between financial (banking) crises and various areas of financial reform by using a flexible methodology estimating the impulse-response functions via local projections (Jordà, 2005). On average, we find that a banking crisis leads to a rapid reduction in the degree of overall financial liberalization in the first two years after the shock. However, after the second year, governments restart the reform efforts and fully catch up with other countries in a duration of two to four years, sometimes even ending up with a more liberalized financial market at the end of a ten-year-long window after a crisis.

This result is also obtained for various aspects of the reform process. We show that government ownership in the banking sector increases substantially as bailouts become necessary. Controls on the domestic credit as well as on the international capital flows are introduced in the very short term, possibly to stop potential bank runs and restore confidence in the financial system. Moreover, negative public and policy sentiment during banking crises seem to spread even towards the alternative sources of finance as asset (security) markets also suffer from the deliberalization process. Nevertheless, in the medium to long term, countries gradually catch up with the others, and the initial effect of state interventionism disappears in each and every reform area.

These findings contribute to the literature by providing systematic evidence for the argument that financial crises might spur reform progress using a new and up-to-date dataset and a novel methodological approach. Thus, we conclude that crises often generate reform dynamics that change the current level of liberalization first by making the policy makers more likely to restrict the market activities in order to contain the crisis and then restarting the liberalization process to catch up with others.

The evidence here builds on the somewhat ambiguous – and not always consistent – results provided by a long stream of papers in the literature. Bruno and Easterly (1996), in possibly the first empirical attempt to tackle the question of whether crises feed reforms,[2] show that countries experiencing high-inflation periods are also more likely to undertake efforts for subsequent macroeconomic stabilisation. Perotti (1999) illustrate that fiscal adjustments are more likely to be successful during times of fiscal stress than in normal times. Although they fail to find consistent evidence for all types of economic underperformance, Drazen and Easterly (2001) point out that the positive relationship between high inflation (or black market premium) today and in the future turns negative in extreme cases, which is consistent with the idea that only sufficiently high economic turbulence leads to

[2] Earlier literature treating crises as a precondition for reform mostly depends on country-specific case studies. For seminal examples, see Krueger (1993), Nelson (1990) and Williamson (1994).

subsequent corrections in macroeconomic policies. Alesina et al. (2006) analyse the interaction between crises and political environment and provide evidence that inflation and budget crises lead to better macroeconomic performance later, especially when the government has strong popular support.

Beyond the studies that investigate the stabilization processes after difficult economic periods and simply treat such cases of adjustment as reforms, Lora (1998) is one of the first to construct actual policy indices in five main reform areas. Although his sample is limited in coverage (i.e., only Latin American economies), he finds some evidence that certain reform efforts respond to certain types of crises. Specifically, trade and labour reforms seem to be triggered by drops in growth and income, whereas financial reforms are pushed by inflationary problems. Following a similar de jure policy measurement approach, Abiad and Mody (2005) construct a more granular index of financial reforms for a global set of countries and support the view that financial crises drive policy changes, though not always in the same direction. While balance-of-payment crises are likely to be proliberalization, banking crises turn out to act in the opposite way, encouraging reversals. However, using an instrumental-variables approach to deal with the potential reverse causality problem between crises and reforms, Pepinsky (2012) shows that currency crises lead developing countries to close their capital accounts as a form of self-help. In a recent contribution, Mian et al. (2014) focus on the political fragmentation and how voters adopt more extreme ideological views in the aftermath of financial crises. In parallel with voter polarization and the resulting weak coalition governments, they argue that financial liberalization seems to experience a deadlock and rather reverse in most postcrisis episodes.

We add to these studies by providing robust evidence (for any crisis or reform type) that financial crises lead to policy changes, with more government intervention in the short term and a gradual liberalization in the medium to long term. Hence, by taking a more nuanced view, we can try to reconcile the previous evidence in the literature and point out the relative importance of the time horizon in the crises-beget-reforms debate.

The chapter proceeds as follows. The next section describes the construction of the dataset. Section 6.3 explains the methodology we employ. Section 6.4 presents the results alongside the related discussion. Section 6.5 concludes.

6.2 Data

The objective of this section is to describe how we assemble a most up-to-date and comprehensive dataset of financial crises and financial reforms, respectively.

In the literature, the standard dataset on various areas of financial reform in the cross-country setting has been the one constructed by Abiad et al. (2010; henceforth, ADT), which in turn builds on the earlier and smaller set of observations compiled by Abiad and Mody (2005).[3] ADT assesses seven dimensions of financial policy in ninety-one countries over the years from 1973 to 2005. Specifically, it includes five indices directly related to the domestic banking sector (credit controls, interest rate controls, entry barriers, privatization, and supervision), one index on restrictions in international capital movements and one on asset markets (security market regulation). Each of these variables is constructed through a set of standardized questions for which responses can be coded discretely and then aggregated to represent the extent of liberalization in each reform area. They take values between 0 and 1, higher values implying more liberalization, except in the area of banking supervision, where an increase implies more government intervention, and thus less liberalization. For this reason, we use the banking supervision index in the reversed form (1–x) in our estimations to make sure that our sign interpretations are consistent across different indices.[4]

One major setback in the empirical research after the Global Financial Crisis has been the fact that these indices have not been updated by the authors, preventing economists from analysing the financial reform dynamics since 2005. Fortunately, Denk and Gomes (2017; henceforth, DG) have recently attempted to fill in this gap by extending the original ADT until 2015. These authors follow the same methodological approach for the years from 2005 to 2015 and keep the original coding rules when aggregating responses to individual questions. One exception they make is to change the index on capital account restrictions where, instead of posing the original questions in ADT, they directly input the index built by Chinn and Ito (2006), which is

[3] Some of the recent studies employing this dataset include Giuliano et al. (2013), Mendoza et al. (2009) and Prati et al. (2013).

[4] For the details on the specific questions used for each index, see Abiad et al. (2010).

probably the most widely used measure of capital account openness in the literature.[5] Compared to the original methodology of Abiad et al. (2010), DG also drops one question in the credit controls section, which is not a material change given that half of the observations for this question in the original ADT were missing in the first place.[6] Their data also goes five more years back in time to 2000, where the original ADT series already exist, and they confirm that their scores are very comparable to the ones obtained in the original dataset. For the few cases in which there is little divergence, they keep their own scores for consistency.

As a result, DG is composed of seven financial reform indices for the years from 1973 to 2015 for forty-three countries. Thirty-eight of these already existed in the original ADT, and five new countries were added by DG; hence the new ones only have observations for the years from 2000 to 2015.[7] For our analysis, we first take the full panel created by DG and then merge it with the remaining (fifty-three) country-time-series from ADT. Hence, we obtain an unbalanced panel consisting of ninety-six countries over the period from 1973 to 2015. To our knowledge, this is the first study analysing this most comprehensive and recent dataset of financial reforms.

Table 6.1 presents the summary statistics for the seven subindices as well as the overall financial reform variable, which is the simple average of these subindices.[8] Both the full sample at the global level and the subsample at the European Union level are shown. It is obvious that within our sample period in the full sample there has been at least one country that was not liberalized at all (0) or fully liberalized (1) at some point for each reform area. This is a reassurance that policy questions composing the de jure measures do not specify unachievable targets for liberalization. However, for the average financial reform, these

[5] As Denk and Gomes (2017) puts it, Chinn–Ito index is highly correlated with the original index in ADT (up to 2005) and other commonly used capital account indices in the literature.

[6] The next section (on methodology) describes how we control for the possible biases that may arise due to these differences between the two datasets.

[7] These new countries are Iceland, Luxembourg, Saudi Arabia, Slovakia and Slovenia.

[8] Table 6.1 is constructed only with the observations that remain in the analysis after merging the reform database with financial crises. Less than 2 per cent of the full reform dataset is dropped after the merging process.

Table 6.1 *Summary statistics for main variables. The table outlines the summary statistics for variables related to financial reforms and crises. Reform database is obtained by merging two subsets of observations from Abiad et al. (2010) and Denk and Gomes (2017). Data on financial crises is obtained from Laeven and Valencia (2018).*

	Variables	*Mean*	*Median*	*Std. deviation*	*Min*	*Max*	*Observations*
Global sample							
	Financial liberalization (average)	0.59	0.63	0.23	0.14	0.96	3,046
	Credit controls	0.58	0.67	0.38	0.00	1.00	3,046
	Interest rate controls	0.63	1.00	0.43	0.00	1.00	3,082
	Entry barriers	0.65	0.67	0.39	0.00	1.00	3,082
	International capital controls	0.56	0.67	0.37	0.00	1.00	3,082
	Privatization	0.47	0.33	0.40	0.00	1.00	3,082
	Banking supervision	0.66	0.67	0.37	0.00	1.00	3,082
	Security markets	0.57	0.67	0.39	0.00	1.00	3,082
	Financial crises	0.08	0.00	0.27	0.00	1.00	3,082
	Banking crises	0.04	0.00	0.19	0.00	1.00	3,082
	Sovereign debt crises	0.02	0.00	0.13	0.00	1.00	3,082
	Currency crises	0.04	0.00	0.19	0.00	1.00	3,082

European Union sample							
	Financial liberalization (average)	0.77	0.81	0.14	0.27	0.95	600
	Credit controls	0.83	1.00	0.30	0.00	1.00	600
	Interest rate controls	0.92	1.00	0.22	0.00	1.00	604
	Entry barriers	0.88	1.00	0.25	0.00	1.00	604
	International capital controls	0.83	1.00	0.27	0.00	1.00	604
	Privatization	0.72	1.00	0.34	0.00	1.00	604
	Banking supervision	0.32	0.33	0.36	0.00	1.00	604
	Security markets	0.92	1.00	0.18	0.33	1.00	604
	Financial crises	0.06	0.00	0.23	0.00	1.00	604
	Banking crises	0.05	0.00	0.22	0.00	1.00	604
	Sovereign debt crises	0.03	0.00	0.16	0.00	1.00	604
	Currency crises	0.00	0.00	0.06	0.00	1.00	604

extreme points have never been reached by any country, implying that there is no country in our sample that receives all 0s or 1s simultaneously at each dimension. On average, liberalization seems to have been highest in banking supervision, followed by entry barriers and interest rate controls. Privatization turns out to be the least liberalized area on average with significant state presence in domestic banking sectors. As expected, the overall financial liberalization in EU is much higher than the global average within our sample period.

For the dating of the financial crises, we resort to the classic dataset from the IMF (Laeven and Valencia, 2013) which has recently been updated by the original authors (2018). This includes the starting dates for three different types of financial crises, namely banking, currency and sovereign debt crises. Coverage is quite large compared to alternative datasets (such as Reinhart and Rogoff, 2011), covering 165 countries between the years 1970 and 2017. All types of crises are represented with a dummy variable taking the value of 1 in the initial year of the crisis and 0 for the rest (see Table 6.1). Hence, we are unable to trace the length of a crisis (or depth for that matter) in general. However, we can observe the end dates for the banking crises only, which helps us create a continuous dummy for this type and use it in the later part of the analysis with local projections.

In addition, for the EU sample, we update the IMF dataset by manually adding the following country-years for sovereign debt crises: Greece (2010, 2011, 2012, 2013, 2014, 2015); Cyprus (2012, 2013, 2014); Ireland (2010, 2011, 2012); Italy (2011, 2012); Portugal (2010, 2011, 2012); and Spain (2011, 2012). Similarly, we add the following country-years in EU for the banking crises: Greece (2011, 2012, 2013, 2014, 2015); Cyprus (2012, 2013, 2014); Ireland (2011, 2012); Italy (2011, 2012); Portugal (2011, 2012); and Spain (2011, 2012).[9]

After merging financial crises with the reform database previously constructed by joining two separate datasets (ADT and DG), we end up with 105 banking, 121 currency and thirty-eight sovereign debt crises within the global sample as well as thirty banking, sixteen sovereign and two currency crises within the EU subsample.

[9] We use TARGET2 balances and government bond spreads to track down these specific country-year crisis observations.

6.3 Methodology

We are first interested in the causal impact of financial crises on the process of financial liberalization, which is not an easy task to accomplish given the possible reverse causality in this kind of a relationship. It has long been suspected that liberalization processes themselves may lead to economic/financial crises, with many anecdotal examples, especially from Latin American countries (Green, 1995). Another empirical problem is that countries experiencing crises may have a different reform pace (too fast or too slow), or they may be at a different stage of their liberalization process when they get hit by a financial crisis. If that is the case, one might accidentally capture the country-specific nature of the liberalization process rather than the effect of the crisis itself.

Despite these possibilities, very few papers explicitly tackle the identification issue in a cross-country setting.[10] We attempt to solve this problem in three steps. First, we do not only estimate what happens to the reform process after a crisis, but we also check if the countries had any diverging reform trends before the crises struck so as to make sure that any precrisis trends are controlled. Hence, we obtain a quasi-diff-in-diff estimate by directly comparing the country's liberalization levels just before and after a financial crisis.

Second, we implicitly control for the pace of the liberalization process specific to each country by including country-varying time trends in our estimations.

Third, we benefit from the high dimensionality of our dataset (with multiple reform areas) and include a full set of fixed effects with interactions across dimensions in order to nonparametrically control for potentially omitted variables.

Specifically, we estimate the following equation:

$$FinancialLiberalization_{i,t,r} = \beta_1 * POSTcrisis_{i,t} + \beta_0 * PREcrisis_{i,t} + \sum_i \mu_i * d_t + \delta_i + \alpha_t + \lambda_r + \varepsilon_{i,t,r} \quad (6.1)$$

[10] Two exceptions are Pepinsky (2012), who uses an instrumental-variables approach to analyse the impact of currency crises on capital account liberalization, and Mian et al. (2014), who use a panel diff-in-diff setting similar to ours comparing the level of reforms before and after the crises.

where i represents country, t year and r specific reform index. μ_i is a dummy for each country, and d_t is a linear time trend. In the baseline estimation, we include the basic set of fixed effects at the country (δ_i), year (α_t) and reform (λ_r) levels and saturate the specification at later estimations. *POSTcrisis* is a binary dummy variable turning on in the first five years after any crisis in the sample including the starting year itself. *PREcrisis* is a binary dummy for the five years immediately preceding the same financial crisis. Therefore, our diff-in-diff estimate (average treatment effect of a crisis) is given by the test of the following difference:

$$ATE = \beta_1 - \beta_0$$

Next our focus shifts to the dynamic aspects of the relationship between crises and reforms. Specifically, we would like to observe the persistence of the average treatment effect in the aftermath of financial crises. For this purpose, we utilize a flexible methodology, namely local projections (LPs), popularized by Jordà (2005).[11]

The main tenet of this method is to estimate the average treatment effect at changing horizons of interest rather than extrapolating it from a given model that heavily depends on the correct specification of the data generating process (as in VARs). Hence, local projections are more robust to misspecification and their analytic inference is simpler.

Formally, we run the following model to generate impulse response functions via LPs:

$$FL_{i,t+p} = \beta^p * C_{i,t} + \sum\nolimits_{k=1}^{4} \emptyset_k^p * C_{i,t-k} + \sum\nolimits_{k=1}^{4} \omega_k^p * FL_{i,t-k} + \sum\nolimits_i \mu_i^p * d_t^p + \delta_i^p + \alpha_t^p + \varepsilon_{i,t}^p \tag{6.2}$$

where FL stands for the financial liberalization index, C for crisis, and p for changing horizons into the future. We reiterate the model up to ten years after year t (p = [1.10]) and obtain the impulse responses by plotting the β^p coefficients from each iteration.

Here, instead of using the postcrisis dummy as an independent variable of interest (as in Equation [6.1]), we resort to the time-continuous variable of banking crises for which we can see the end dates in Laeven and Valencia (2018) and thus can locate the exact

[11] For recent papers making use of local projections, see Mian et al. (2017), Ramey and Zubairy (2018) and Romer and Romer (2017, 2018).

length of the crisis in time. This helps us avoid making assumptions regarding the length (persistency) of the average shock, which may distort our estimates for the dynamic relationship between crises and reforms.

6.4 Results

6.4.1 Panel Difference-in-Differences

Results from the estimation of Equation (6.1) on the global full-sample are reported in Table 6.2. The first column shows the baseline model with a set of fixed effects at country, year and reform levels. Our concern for the existence of diverging reform trends prior to the average financial crisis is confirmed here. However, contrary to the argument that crises themselves may be caused by the liberalisation process, the *PREcrisis* variable produces a significantly negative coefficient. Hence, the usual reverse causality issue in the literature (i.e., liberal reforms causing crises), which would predict a positive coefficient for *PREcrisis,* is not confirmed here, and the difference between two coefficients before and after the financial crisis (*PREcrisis* vs. *POSTcrisis*) is estimated to be approximately –0.02 at the 8 per cent significance level. On the other hand, these pretrends still constitute a concern for identification since it is possible that crises only strike countries when they have low levels of liberalization or the countries that are too slow (or fast) reformers might experience financial crises with different probabilities.

In order to check whether the pace of reforms (or any unobserved country-level factor with a trend) could explain this pattern, we turn to the second column, where we add country-specific linear time trends into the baseline specification. It turns out that the diverging pretrends disappear after this addition, confirming our earlier concern that crises may be hitting the countries with a particular reform speed or level. The diff-in-diff coefficient is even stronger with an estimate lower than –0.03 at 0.1 per cent significance level. Nevertheless, the magnitude of this average treatment effect is quite modest compared to the average financial liberalization in the sample (which is 0.58; see Table 6.1). This constitutes our first evidence showing that policy makers react to financial crises by increasing government intervention in financial markets.

Table 6.2 *Global sample: difference-in-differences estimates for the effect of a financial crisis on average financial liberalization. The table summarizes the estimation results with the specification in Equation (6.1). Dependent variable is* Financial Liberalization *varying over countries, years and reform areas.* POSTcrisis *is a binary dummy variable turning on in the first five years after any financial (banking, sovereign debt or currency) crisis in the sample including the starting year itself.* PREcrisis *is a binary dummy for the five years immediately preceding a financial crisis. Robust standard errors are clustered at the country level and standard errors are reported in brackets. Diff-in-diff estimates test the difference between the coefficients estimated for* POSTcrisis *and* PREcrisis, *and p-values are reported underneath. The reform database is obtained by merging two subsets of observations from Abiad et al. (2010) and Denk and Gomes (2017). Data on financial crises are obtained from Laeven and Valencia (2018).* *$p < 0.1$, **$p < 0.05$, ***$p < 0.01$.

Dependent variables:			*Financial liberalization*		
Models:	*I*	*II*	*III*	*IV*	*V*
POSTcrisis	−0.046***	−0.035***	−0.035***	−0.035***	−0.035***
	[0.009]	[0.008]	[0.008]	[0.008]	[0.008]
PREcrisis	−0.028**	−0.004	−0.004	−0.004	−0.004
	[0.011]	[0.009]	[0.009]	[0.009]	[0.009]
Diff-in-diff	**-0.017***	**−0.031*****	**−0.031*****	**−0.031*****	**−0.031*****
P-value	0.075	0.001	0.001	0.001	0.001
N	21,538	21,538	21,538	21,538	21,538
Adj-R-sq	0.177	0.200	0.474	0.534	0.746
Clustering	Country	Country	Country	Country	Country
Country FE	Yes	Yes	Yes		
Reform FE	Yes	Yes			
Year FE	Yes	Yes		Yes	
CountryTime trend		Yes	Yes	Yes	Yes
Country × reform FE				Yes	Yes
Reform × year FE			Yes		Yes

One more concern for our empirical strategy is the possibility of breaks in the data and how these may bias the estimates in one way or another, especially if the different authors preparing the two datasets had in mind different criteria when judging the countries' liberalization levels in the more subjective parts of the questionnaire. It is hard to imagine a test to check for such differential biases between the two datasets; however, what we can do is that, assuming that such biases would apply to all countries by the specific researchers, we could add fixed effects at the interaction of reform types and years. This ensures that any systematic bias in any index at any year (conditional on it being applied against or towards all countries for that reform year) is taken into account. The third column in Table 6.2 reports the results with these fixed effects, and there does not seem to be any material change compared to the previous column, confirming that the combination of indices from two different sources has a minimal impact on our estimates.

The fourth and fifth columns in Table 6.2 add interacted fixed effects of country and reform dummies, meaning that any systematic component of liberalization that may have been missed or not captured constantly over time for a specific country and reform area would be subsumed by these dummies. The results again confirm that such potential mismeasurement issues do not seem to be important in our sample. Overall, we have sufficient evidence to conclude that the average effect of a crisis on financial liberalization is significantly negative.

An important additional investigation can be pursued by separating this average effect for different types of crises. Table 6.3 reestimates Equation (6.1) with separate dummies for banking, sovereign debt and currency crises in the full sample. Again, our conclusions for different models are very similar to those previously discussed. Diff-in-diff estimates turn out to be significantly negative for fourteen out of fifteen estimations, with the exception of the baseline model (column I) for banking crises, which apparently suffers from the existence of diverging trends prior to the crisis events. In terms of economic magnitude, the largest effect comes from sovereign debt crises (0.064), followed by currency (0.036) and banking crises (0.021).

We repeat the previous analyses on the EU subsample and report the corresponding results in Tables 6.4 and 6.5. Despite still being negative, the diff-in-diff estimates reported here are generally smaller and statistically indistinguishable from zero. Hence, it seems that we cannot obtain much evidence from the EU subsample regarding the relationship

Table 6.3 *Global sample: difference-in-differences estimates for the effect liberalization. The table summarizes the estimation results with the* liberalization *varying over countries, years and reform areas.* POST *a financial (x = banking, sovereign debt or currency) crisis in the sample the five years immediately preceding a financial crisis. Robust standard in brackets. Diff-in-diff estimates test the difference between the coefficients underneath. The reform database is obtained by merging two subsets of financial crises are obtained from Laeven and Valencia (2018). *p < 0.1,*

Dependent variables:			*Financial liberalization*			*Financial liberalization*	
Models:	*I*	*II*	*III*	*IV*	*V*	*I*	*II*
POSTcrisis_banking	–0.036***	–0.024***	–0.024***	–0.024***	–0.024***		
	[0.010]	[0.0081	[0.008]	[0.009]	[0.009]		
PREcrisis_banking	–0.026**	–0.001	–0.001	–0.001	–0.001		
	[0.011]	[0.009]	[0.009]	[0.009]	[0.009]		
POSTcrisis_debt						–0.066***	–0.040**
						[0.019]	[0.015]
PREcrisis_debt						-0.007	0.022
						[0.021]	[0.016]
POSTcrisis_currency							
PREcrisis_currency							
Diff-in-diff	–0.010	–0.023**	–0.023**	–0.023**	–0.023**	–0.059”*	–0.062***
P-value	0.314	0.015	0.016	0.017	0.017	0.000	0.000
N	21,538	21,538	21,538	21,538	21,538	21,538	21,538
Adj-R-sq	0.175	0.199	0.473	0.533	0.745	0.175	0.199
Clustering	Country	Country	Country	Country	Country	Country	Country
Country FE	Yes	Yes	Yes			Yes	Yes
Reform FE	Yes	Yes				Yes	Yes
Year FE	Yes	Yes		Yes		Yl”i	Yes
CountryTime Trend		Yes	Yes	Yes	Yes		Yes
Country × Reform FE				Yes	Yes		
Reform × year FE			Yes		Yes		

between crises and reforms. On the one hand, it is possible that the small sample size here prevents us from reaching statistical significance. On the other hand, the EU, as an institutional anchor, might prevent its members from reducing market liberalization after financial crises, thus decreasing

of banking, sovereign debt and currency crises on average financial specification in Equation (6.1). The dependent variable is **financial crisis_x** ***is a binary dummy variable turning on in the first five years after including the starting year itself.*** **PREcrisis_x** ***is a binary dummy for errors are clustered at the country level, and standard errors are reported estimated for*** **POSTcrisis_x** ***and*** **PREcrisis_x** ***and p-values are reported observations from Abiad et al. (2010) and Denk and Gomes (2017). Data on*** $^{**}p < 0.05$, $^{***}p < 0.01$.

			Financial liberalization				
III	*IV*	*V*	*I*	*II*	*III*	*IV*	*V*
−0.040**	−0.040**	−0.040**					
[0.016]	[0.016]	[0.016]					
0.022	0.022	0.022					
[0.016]	[0.016]	[0.016]					
			−0.056***	−0.044***	−0.044***	−0.044***	−0.044***
			[0.011]	[0.011]	[0.0111	[0.011]	[0.011]
			−0.033**	−0.009	−0.009	−0.009	−0.009
			[0.012]	[0.011]	[0,011]	[0.011]	[0.011]
−0.062***	−0.062***	−0.062***	−0.023**	−0.035"“	−0.035***	−0.035***	−0.035***
0.000	0.000	0.000	0.030	0.001	0.001	0.001	0.001
21,538	21,538	21,538	21,538	21,538	21,538	21,538	21,538
0.474	0.533	0.746	0.177	0.200	0.474	0.534	0.746
Country	Country	Country	Country	Country	Country	Country	Country
Yes			Yes	Yes	Yes		
			Yes	Yes			
	Yes		Yes	Yes		Yes	
Yes	Yi-s	Yes		Yes	Yes	Yes	Yes
	Yes	Yes				Yes	Yes
Yes		Yes			Yes		Yes

the size of the estimates in this subsample. A contributing factor could be the potentially large lobbying power of commercial banks in Europe since the banking sector composes a big chunk of the overall financial system in many European countries, a phenomenon called ‘bank bias’ in

Table 6.4 *European Union sample: difference-in-differences estimates for the effect of a financial crisis on average financial liberalization. The table summarizes the estimation results with the specification in Equation (6.1). The dependent variable is* financial liberalization *varying over countries, years and reform areas.* POSTcrisis *is a binary dummy variable turning on in the first five years after any financial (banking, sovereign debt or currency) crisis in the sample, including the starting year itself.* PREcrisis *is a binary dummy for the five years immediately preceding a financial crisis. Robust standard errors are clustered at the country level, and standard errors are reported in brackets. Diff-in-diff estimates test the difference between the coefficients estimated for* POSTcrisis *and* PREcrisis, *and p-values are reported underneath. The reform database is obtained by merging two subsets of observations from Abiad et al. (2010) and Denk and Gomes (2017). Data on financial crises are obtained from Laeven and Valencia (2018).* *$p < 0.1$, **$p < 0.05$, ***$p < 0.01$.

Dependent variables:			*Financial liberalization*		
Models:	*I*	*II*	*III*	*IV*	*V*
POSTcrisis	–0.023*	–0.022	-0.022	–0.022	–0.022
	[0.013]	[0.015]	[0.015]	[0.015]	[0.015]
PREcrisis	0.013	–0.005	–0.005	–0.005	–0.005
	[0.023]	[0.015]	[0.015]	[0.015]	[0.015]
Diff-in-diff	**–0.037**	**–0.017**	**–0.018**	**–0.018**	**–0.018**
P-value	0.219	0.223	0.237	0.229	0.244
N	4,224	4,224	4,224	4,224	4,224
Adj-R-sq	0.406	0.440	0.678	0.605	0.832
Clustering	Country	Country	Country	Country	Country
Country FE	Yes	Yes	Yes		
Reform FE	Yes	Yes			
Year FE	Yes	Yes		Yes	
CountryTime Trend		Yes	Yes	Yes	Yes
Country × Reform FE				Yes	Yes
Reform × Year FE			Yes		Yes

the literature (Langfield and Pagano, 2016). It is possible that a stronger banking sector might have more resources to resist potential government interventions in the aftermath of financial crises. More research will be necessary to confirm these hypotheses.

6.4.2 Baseline Local Projections

Impulse responses of the level of financial liberalization to a banking crisis shock (Equation [6.2]) are shown in Figure 6.4. The initial shock has a significantly negative contemporaneous effect on liberal reforms, the size of which (0.02) is similar to the diff-in-diff estimates reported in Table 6.4. The effect stays at approximately the same level for the next three years, after which a gradual reliberalization process starts and countries catch up in five to six years with the liberalization levels of the countries that did not experience a crisis. This illustrates that, on average, banking crises have sudden but short-term negative effects on financial market liberalization. Such evidence supports the view that these temporary interventions stem from the policy makers' efforts to curb the crisis; and once the crisis is over, reforms reverse back to their long-term equilibrium.

In the next step, our aim is to trace these dynamics in various subareas of financial liberalization. Figure 6.5 presents the results from the estimation of Equation (6.2) with various financial reform subindices as dependent variables. First, we find that credit controls are introduced in the same and the following year after a banking crisis, but later disappear, supporting the claim that this financial policy might be used for curbing the crisis in the immediate aftermath rather than being part of a long-term policy agenda.

Second, there is no evidence that interest rates are deliberalized. Though the contemporaneous response seems to be negative, confidence bands are too large to be conclusive.

Third, there is some evidence that entry barriers to the domestic banking sector are temporarily increased, though not immediately but two to three years after the crisis. Out of the four questions that comprise this subindex, it is likely that the effect comes from the restrictions on banks pushing them to engage only in banking activities rather than becoming universal.[12]

[12] The other three questions are on foreign bank entry, domestic bank entry and restrictions on bank branching (see Denk and Gomes, 2017).

Table 6.5 *European Union sample: difference-in-differences estimates for financial liberalization.*

Dependent variables				*Financial liberalization*			
Models	*I*	*II*	*III*	*IV*	*V*	*I*	*II*
POSTcrisis_rankmg	0.047	−0.017	−0.017	−0.017	−0.017		
	[0.027]	[0.013]	[0.013]	[0.013]	[0.013]		
PREcrisis_banking	0.070*	−0.014	−0.014	−0.014	−0.014		
	[0.038]	[0.014]	[0.014]	[0.014]	[0.015]		
POSTcrisis_debt						0.069*	−0.029
						[0.039]	[0.023]
PREcrisis_debt						0.087*	0.000
						[0.043]	[0.012]
POSTcrisis_currency							
PREcrisis_currency							
Diff-in-diff	−0.021	−0.003	−0.003	−0.003	−0.003	−0.018	−0.029
P-value	0.163	0.835	0.839	0.834	0.84	0.454	0.149
N	4,224	4,224	4,224	4,224	4,224	4,224	4,224
Adj-R-sq	0.408	0.440	0.678	0.605	0.832	0.410	0.440
Clustering	Country	Country	Country	Country	Country	Country	Country
Country FE	Yes	Yes	Yes			Yes	Yes
Reform FE	Yea	Yes				Yes	Yes
Year FE	Yes	Yes		Yes		Yes	Yes
CountryTime trend		Yes	Yes	Yes	Yes		Yes
Country × reform FE				Yes	Yes		
Reform × year FE			Yes		Yes		

Note: The table summarizes the estimation results with the specification in Equation (6.1). Dependent binary dummy variable turning on in the first five years after a financial (x = banking, sovereign debt or five years immediately preceding a financial crisis. Robust standard errors are clustered at the country the coefficients estimated for *POSTcrisis_x* and *PREcrisis_x* and p-values are reported underneath. Denk and Gomes (2017). Data on financial crises are obtained from Laeven and Valencia (2018).

Fourth, additional capital controls stay in place up to four years after the shock, which could be due to the fear of capital flights even after the end of a crisis.

Fifth, privatization is the reform area where the initial deliberalization process is the strongest. This subindex is only comprised of the degree of government ownership in the domestic banking sector.

the effect of banking, sovereign debt and currency crises on average

	III	IV	V	I	II	III	IV	V
	−0.029	−0.029	−0.029					
	[0.024]	[0.023]	[0.024]					
	0.000	0.000	0.000					
	[0.013]	[0.012]	[0.013]					
				−0.136**	−0.030	−0.031	−0.031	−0.031
				[0.053]	[0.030]	[0.031]	[0.030]	[0.031]
				−0.196***	0.027	0.027	0.027	0.027
				[0.046]	[0.021]	[0.022]	[0.022]	[0.022]
	−0.029	−0.029	−0.029	0.061	−0.017*	−0.057	−0.057	−0.057
	0.160	0.150	0.163	0.122	0.099	0.109	0.104	0.115
	4,224	4,224	4,224	4,224	4,224	4,224	4,224	4,224
	0.678	0.605	0.832	0.412	0.440	0.678	0.605	0.833
	Country	Country	Country	Country	Country	Country	Country	Country
	Yes			Yes	Yes	Yes		
				Yes	Yes			
		Yes		Yes	Yes		Yes	
	Yes	Yes	Yes		Yes	Yes	Yes	Yes
		Yes	Yes				Yes	Yes
	Yes		Yes			Yes		Yes

variable is *financial liberalization* varying over countries, years and reform areas. *POSTcrisis_x* is a currency) crisis in the sample, including the starting year itself. *PREcrisis_x* is a binary dummy for the level and standard errors are reported in brackets. Diff-in-diff estimates test the difference between reform database is obtained by merging two subsets of observations from Abiad et al. (2010) and *$p < 0.1$, **$p < 0.05$, ***$p < 0.01$.

Hence, the change of hands in the banking sector from private to state is clearly visible during the immediate aftermath of a banking crisis, possibility due to bailouts of the failing banks and government takeovers after the initial shock. However the liberal reform process seems to restart after three years and governments fully privatize in six years the additional banks they had acquired during the crisis. This tendency

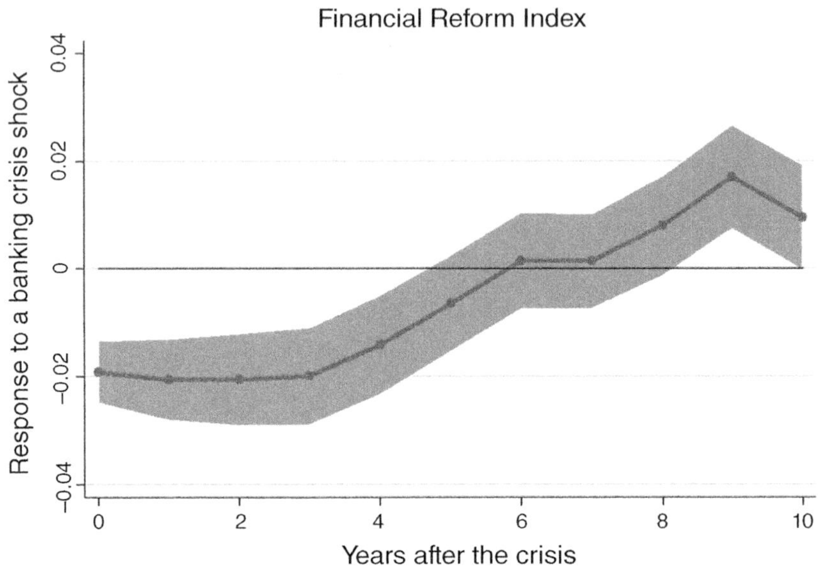

Figure 6.4 Global sample: impulse-response functions of average financial reform to a banking crisis shock. The figure shows the estimated LPs from Equation (6.2) using the average financial reform as the endogenous variable and banking crises as the exogenous shock. The shaded area represents the 90 per cent confidence intervals.

even goes a bit further in the other direction, meaning that countries struck by crises may end up with a more privatized banking sector in the very long term.

An additional insight in Figure 6.5 comes from the observation that banking supervision does not seem to suffer much after a banking crisis. In fact, after the immediate insignificant negative response to the crisis, there is weak evidence that banking supervision is relaxed in the medium term, possibly due to the lobbying power of the banking industry, which may push for less regulation after the immediate harm of the banking crisis is forgotten in the public sphere.

Finally, security markets liberalization seems to be affected negatively by the shock. The lowest level is significantly reached after four years. This is a bit surprising given that security markets constitute an alternative to the traditional bank financing and thus would be expected to be liberalized further after a banking crisis so that the harmful effects of the bank failures on domestic lending could be eased.

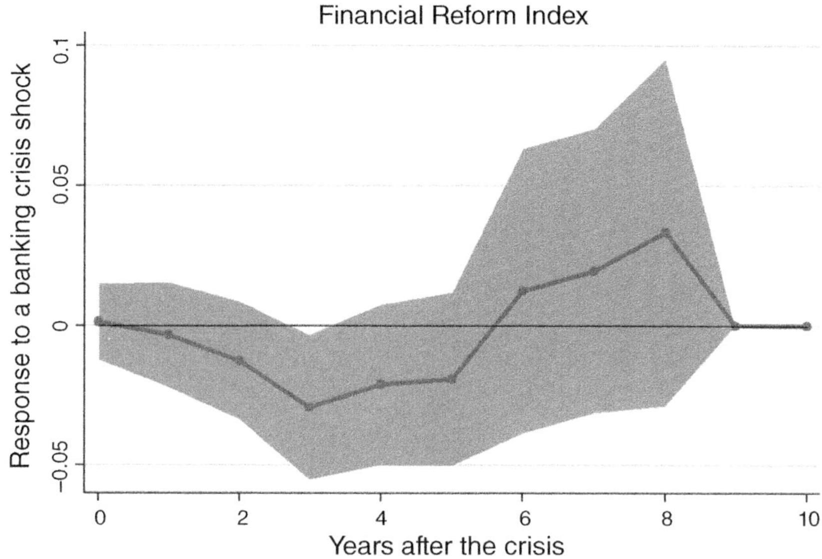

Figure 6.5 European Union sample: impulse-response functions of average financial reform to a banking crisis shock. The figure shows the estimated LPs from Equation (6.2) using the average financial reform as the endogenous variable and banking crises as the exogenous shock. The shaded area represents the 90 per cent confidence intervals.

This does not seem to be the case in Figure 6.5, which leads us to think that the negative attitude and public distrust in the aftermath of a banking crisis pushes policy makers to reverse financial reforms even in distantly related areas, creating a sort of contagion effect across various policy dimensions.[13]

Again, we repeat the impulse-response estimations for the EU subsample and plot the results in Figures 6.6 and 6.7. As in the earlier section, the evidence here is almost always insignificant implying that the negative relationship between crises and financial reforms may not hold for European countries. The sample size is again a potential problem, as confidence intervals seem to get wider at longer horizons

[13] Part of the security market subindex is composed of a question related to how well-developed security markets are and short-selling bans that are usually introduced around financial crises could affect this component. However, it is hard to argue that such temporary bans on short-selling can explain the persistence of the impulse responses up to four years.

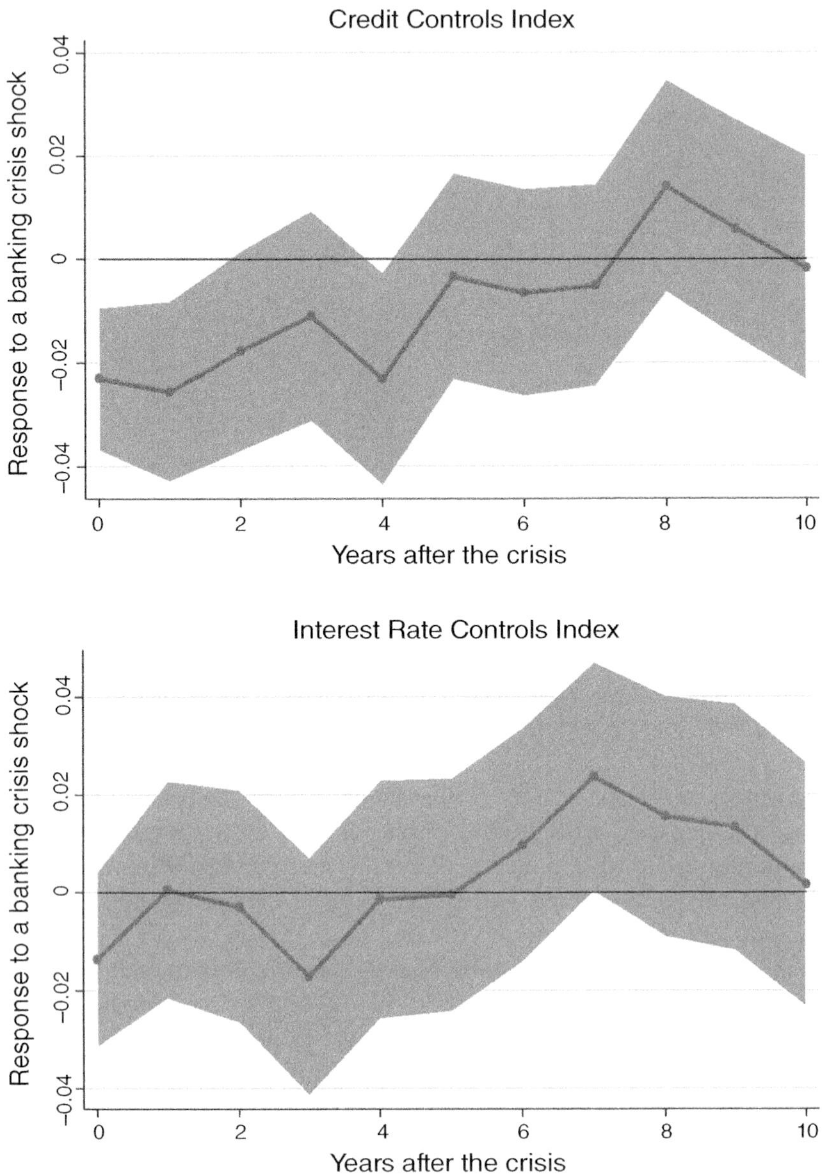

Figure 6.6 Global sample: impulse-response functions of financial reform areas to a banking crisis shock. The figure shows the estimated LPs from Equation (6.2) using the financial reform subindices as the endogenous variable and banking crises as the exogenous shock. The shaded area represents the 90 per cent confidence intervals.

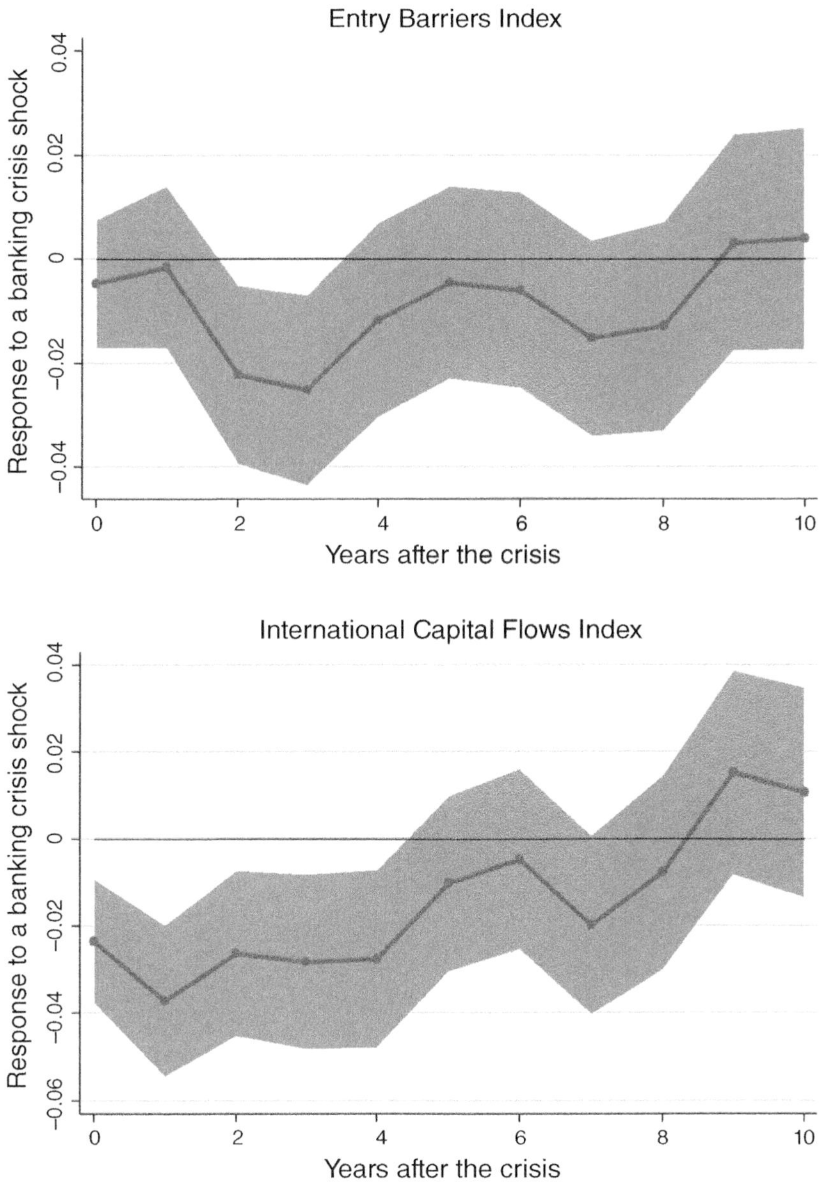

Figure 6.6 (*cont.*)

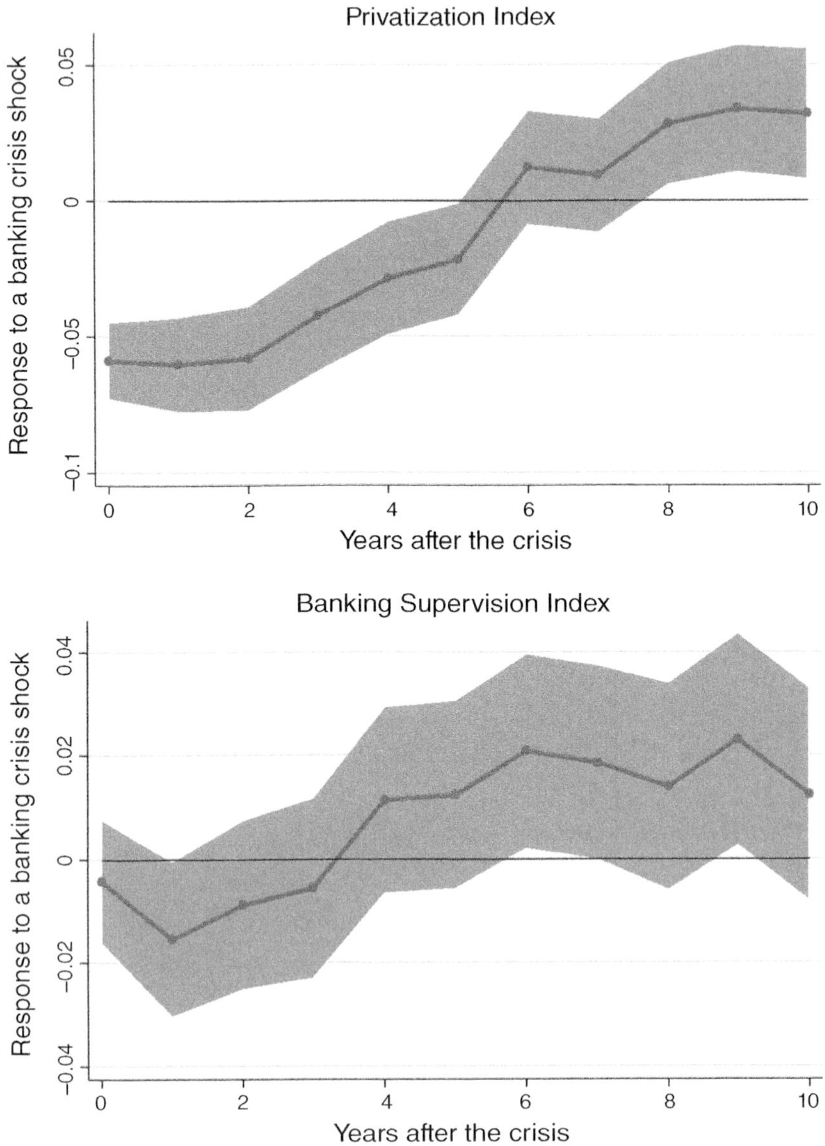

Figure 6.6 (*cont.*)

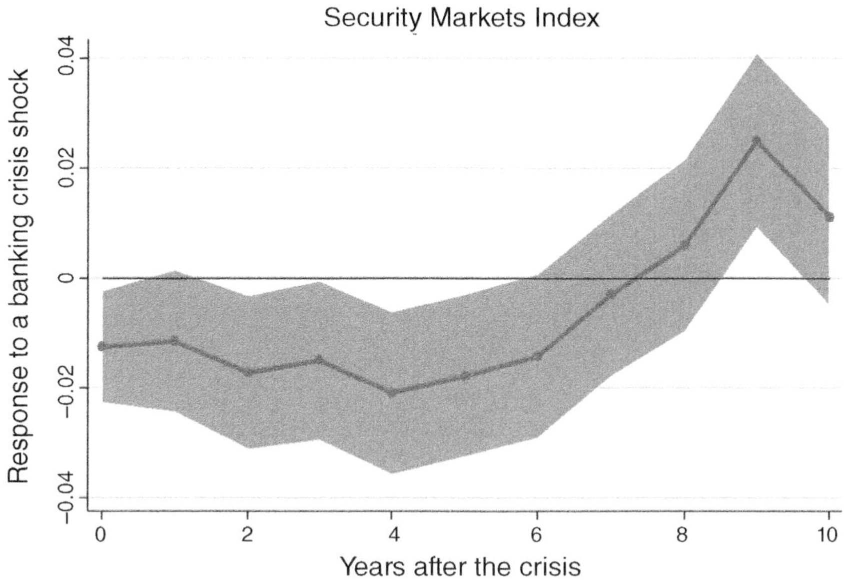

Figure 6.6 (*cont.*)

in these plots. On the other hand, the estimates for the contemporaneous relationship are sufficiently close to zero, suggesting at least that the lack of evidence for the negative initial reaction to crises may not be due to sample size but because of the institutional factors relevant to the EU sample.

6.4.3 Robustness Checks

For the panel analysis, we have done various robustness checks in the following way: (1) when defining the financial crises (*POSTcrisis* and *PREcrisis*), dummies are turned off for the start dates and the years immediately before and after the start dates in order to make sure that we do not pick up any temporary policy response to the crisis; (2) in addition to the previous exclusion, we also exclude the years that fall within both *PREcrisis* and *POSTcrisis* periods; (3) as an alternative to the list of financial crises in Laeven and Valencia (2018), we try with the Reinhart and Rogoff (2011) dataset, which has a smaller country coverage.

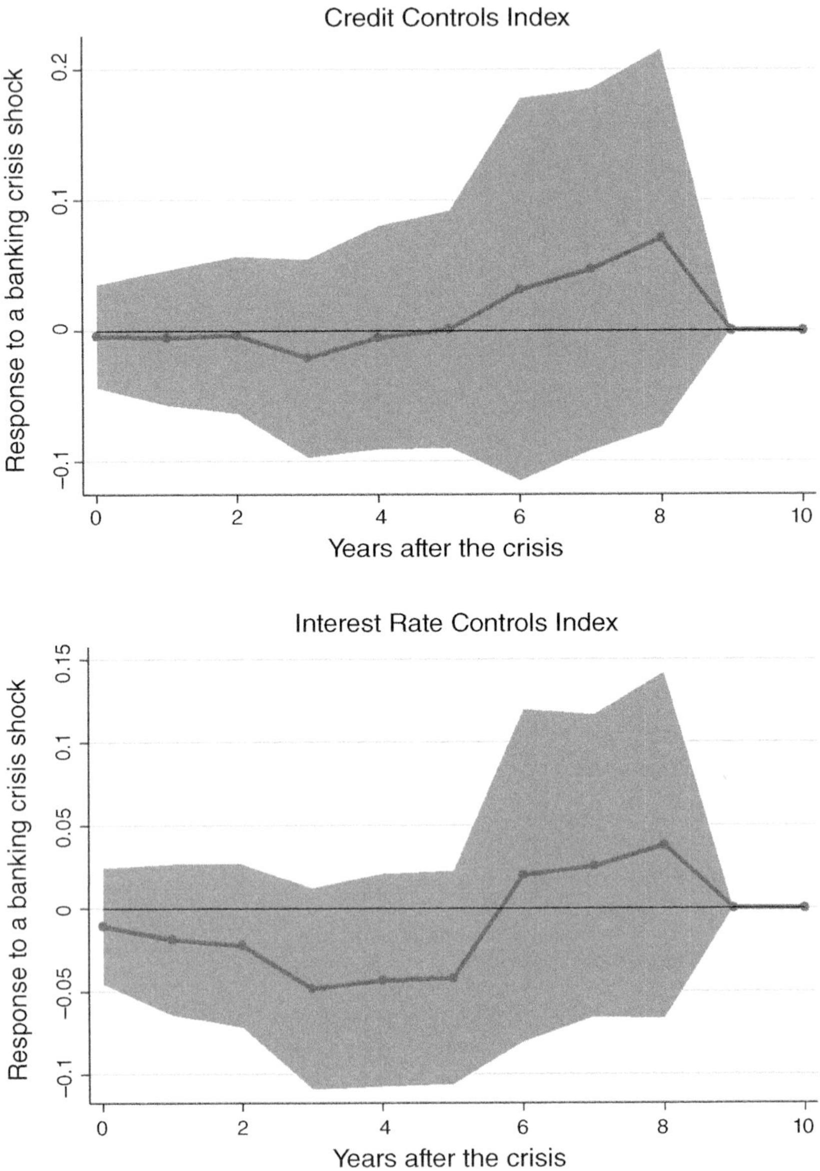

Figure 6.7 European Union sample: impulse-response functions of financial reform areas to a banking crisis shock. The figure shows the estimated LPs from Equation (6.2) using the financial reform subindices as the endogenous variable and banking crises as the exogenous shock. The shaded area represents the 90 per cent confidence intervals.

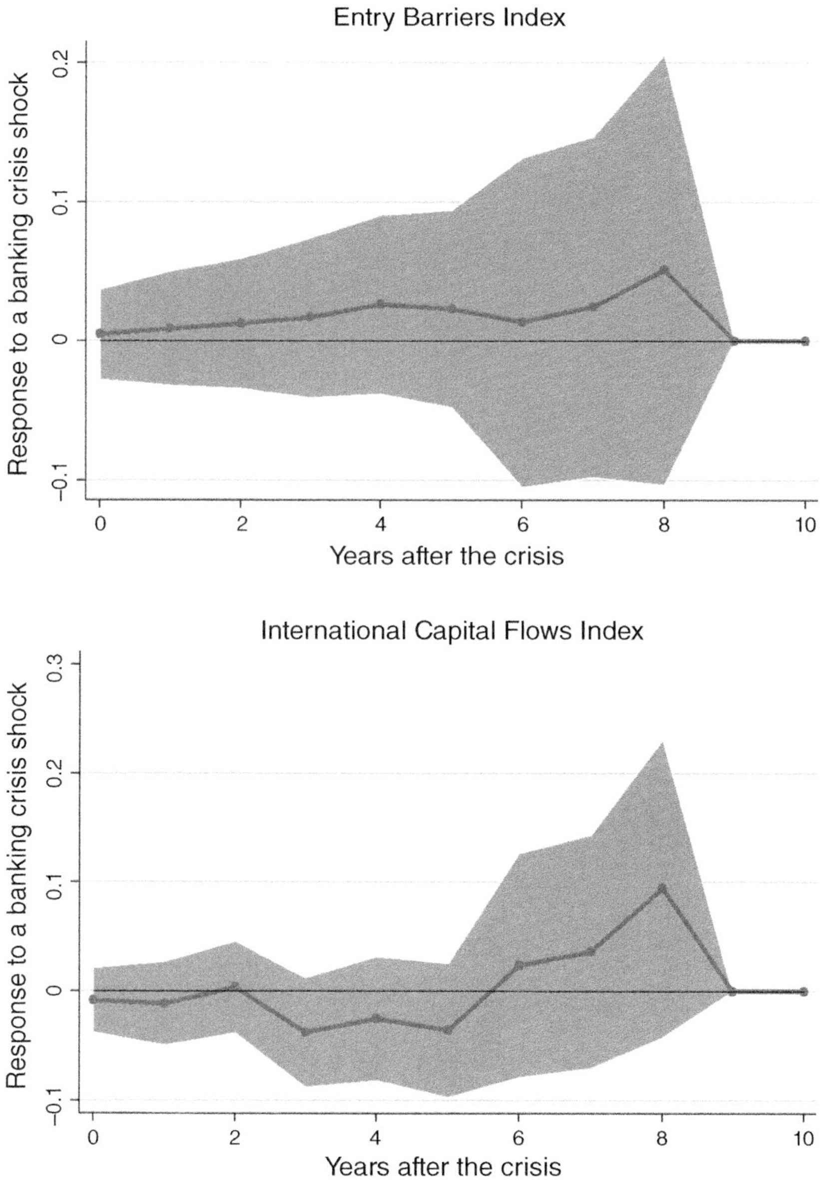

Figure 6.7 *(cont.)*

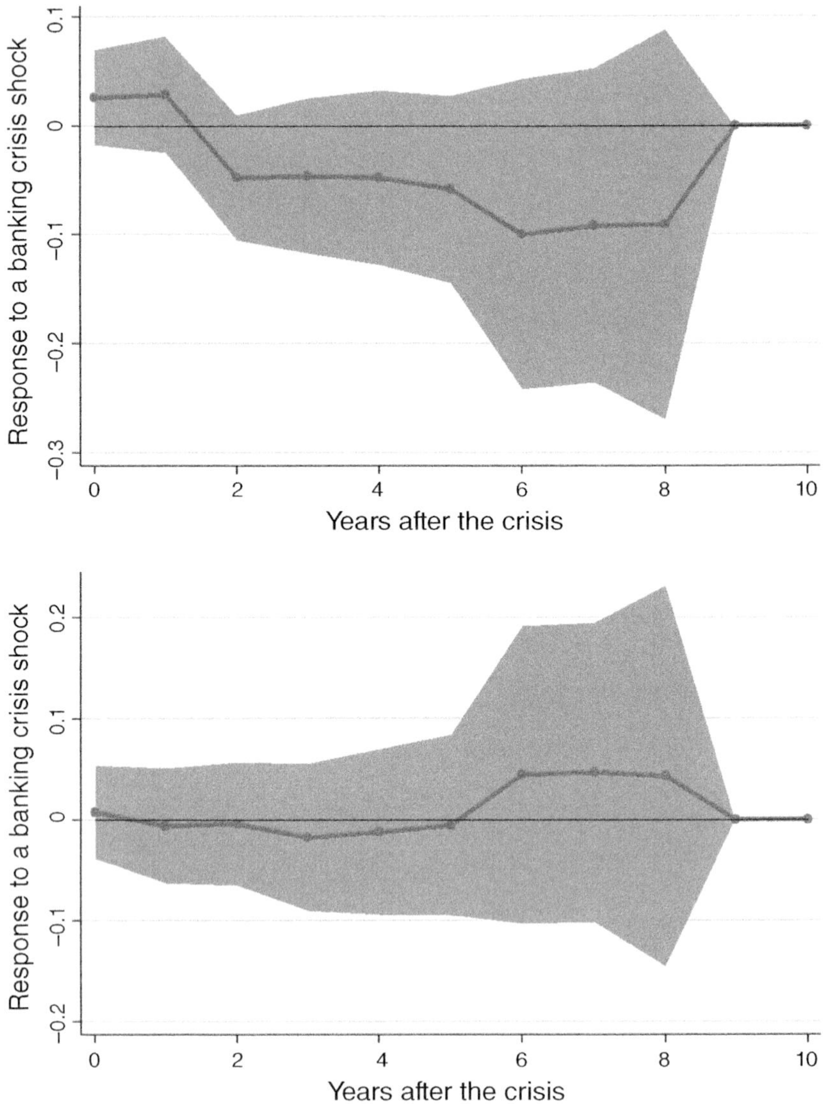

Figure 6.7 (*cont.*)

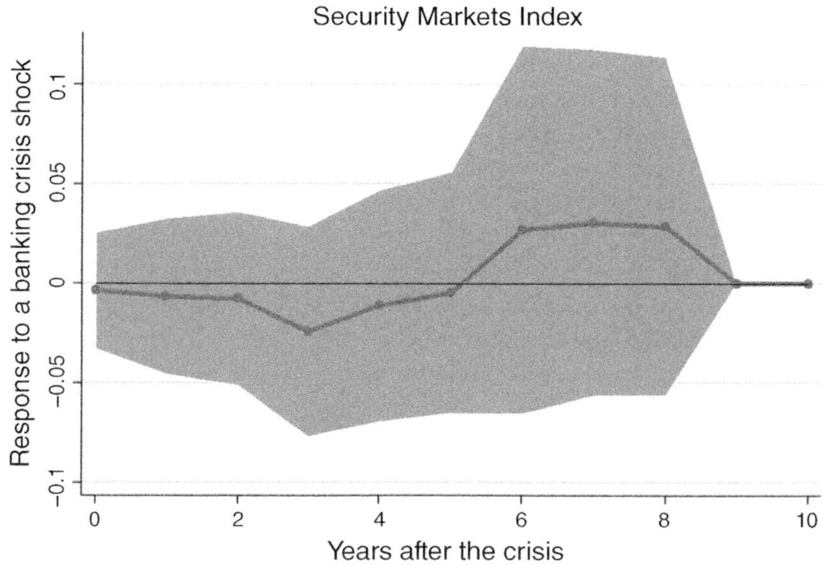

Figure 6.7 (*cont.*)

For the local projections generating impulse responses, we have tried (1) different lag structures; (2) dropping time trends; and (3) clustering standard errors at the country level.

And in general, we have rerun the analysis only with the original financial reform dataset (from Abiad et al., 2010), which ends in 2005 and covers ninety-one countries.

None of these robustness checks implies qualitative changes in our findings.

6.5 Conclusion

The literature on the determinants of structural reforms generally suggests that turbulent periods should play a key role in changing the policy equilibrium and thus spurring liberal reforms. Despite various theoretical mechanisms that may support this prediction, the empirical evidence in the literature so far seems to have been mixed at best. Using a recent comprehensive dataset on financial reforms across ninety-four countries for the period between 1973 and 2015, we test the validity of this prediction for the financial sector specifically in the aftermath of financial crises.

We provide evidence that financial crises in general lead to reversals in financial market liberalization in the short term; however, countries struck by a crisis gradually catch up with the others in the long term. In fact, such difference in the short-term vs. long-term dynamics might be one of the underlying reasons why the evidence in the previous literature is so weak regarding the 'crises-beget-reform' hypothesis.

Empirically we use two complementary approaches. First, by using a quasi-difference-in-differences methodology in a panel setting, we compare the level of financial liberalization between the two periods immediately before and after a financial crisis, which helps us capture the causal impact of the financial crisis itself. Our findings suggest that, even though small on average in terms of economic magnitude, all types of financial crises have a negative effect on the reform process. These reversals are the strongest in the case of sovereign debt defaults followed by currency crises whereas banking crises seem to trigger relatively more modest reversals.

Second, we explore the dynamic relationship between financial crises and various areas of financial reform by using a flexible methodology estimating the impulse-response functions via local projections (Jordà, 2005). On average, we find that a banking crisis leads to a rapid reduction in the degree of overall financial liberalization, with the liberalization process kicking in after about three to four years and the overall negative effects gradually dying out in the long term. This is also true for various aspects of the reform process. We show that government ownership in the banking sector increases substantially as bailouts become necessary. Controls on the domestic credit as well as on the international capital flows are introduced in the very short term, possibly to stop potential bank runs and restore confidence in the financial system. Moreover, negative public and policy sentiment during banking crises seems to spread even towards the regulation of alternative sources of finance as asset (security) markets also suffer from the deliberalization process. All these subareas of financial liberalization eventually recover from the initial state interventions, and countries catch up with others five to six years after a financial crisis.

When repeated on the smaller EU sample, our analysis turns out to be less fruitful, and we find a lack of evidence on the deliberalization process after crises. On the one hand, it is possible that the small sample size here prevents us from reaching statistical significance. On the other hand, the EU single market and common currency, as an institutional anchor, might prevent its members from reducing market liberalization after financial crises, thus decreasing the size of the estimates in this subsample. A contributing factor could be the potentially large lobbying power of commercial banks in Europe, since the banking sector composes a big chunk of the overall financial system in many European countries. It is possible that a stronger banking sector might have more resources to be able to resist potential government interventions in the aftermath of financial crises. Lastly, since most of the countries in this subsample are democracies, it is possible that their policy reactions are structurally different from others, which may lead to the divergences we detect in this subsample. It could be an interesting endeavour for future research to investigate these potential channels within the EU context and understand their relative importance in determining policy responses after financial crises.

References

Abiad, A. and Mody, A. (2005). 'Financial Reform: What Shakes It? What Shapes It?' *American Economic Review*, Vol. 95, No. 1, 66–88.

Abiad, A., Detragiache, E. and Tressel, T. (2010). 'A New Database of Financial Reforms', *IMF Staff Papers*, Vol. 57, No. 2, 281–302.

Alesina, A., Ardagna, S. and Trebbi, F. (2006). 'Who Adjusts and When? The Political Economy of Reforms', *IMF Staff Papers*, Vol. 53, No. 1, 1–29.

Bruno, M. and Easterly, W. (1996). 'Inflation's Children: Tales of Crises that Beget Reforms', *American Economic Review*, Vol. 86, No. 2, 213–217.

Chinn, M. D. and Ito, H. (2006). 'What Matters for Financial Development? Capital Controls, Institutions, and Interactions', *Journal of Development Economics*, Vol. 81, No. 1, 163–192.

Denk, O. and Gomes, G. (2017). 'Financial Re-Regulation since the Global Crisis? An Index-Based Assessment', OECD Economics Department Working Papers, No. 1396.

Drazen, A. and Easterly, W. (2001). 'Do crises Induce Reform? Simple Empirical Tests of Conventional Wisdom', *Economics & Politics*, Vol. 13, No. 2, 129–157.

Drazen, A. and Grilli, V. (1993). 'The Benefit of Crisis for Economic Reforms', *American Economic Review*, Vol. 83, No. 3, 598–607.

Friedrich, C., Schnabel, I. and Zettelmeyer, J. (2013). 'Financial Integration and Growth – Why is Emerging Europe Different?' *Journal of International Economics*, Vol. 89, No. 2, 522–538.

Giuliano, P., Mishra, P. and Spilimbergo, A. (2013). 'Democracy and Reforms: Evidence from a New Dataset', *American Economic Journal: Macroeconomics*, Vol. 5, No. 4, 179–204.

Green, D. (1995). *Silent Revolution: The Rise of Market Economics in Latin America*. Cassell.

Jordà, Ò. (2005). 'Estimation and Inference of Impulse Responses by Local Projections', *American Economic Review*, Vol. 95, No. 1, 161–182.

Krueger, A. (1993). *Political Economy of Policy Reform in Developing Countries*. MIT Press.

Laeven, L. and Valencia, F. (2013). 'Systemic Banking Crises Database', *IMF Economic Review*, Vol. 61, No. 2, 225–270.

Laeven, L. and Valencia, F. (2018). 'Systemic Banking Crises Revisited', IMF Working Paper, No. 206.

Langfield, S. and Pagano, M. (2016). 'Bank Bias in Europe: Effects on Systemic Risk and Growth', *Economic Policy*, Vol. 31, No. 85, 51–106.

Loayza, N., Ouazad, A. and Rancière, R. (2018). 'Financial Development, Growth, and Crisis: Is There a Trade-off?' NBER Working Paper, No. 24474.

Lora, E. (1998). 'What Makes Reforms Likely? Timing and Sequencing of Structural Reforms in Latin America', Working Paper, No. 424. Inter-American Development Bank.

Mendoza, E. G., Quadrini, V. and Rios-Rull, J. V. (2009). 'Financial Integration, Financial Development, and Global Imbalances', *Journal of Political Economy*, Vol. 117, No. 3, 371–416.

Mian, A., Sufi, A. and Trebbi, F. (2014). 'Resolving Debt Overhang: Political Constraints in the Aftermath of Financial Crises', *American Economic Journal: Macroeconomics*, Vol. 6, No. 2, 1–28.

Mian, A., Sufi, A. and Verner, E. (2017). 'Household Debt and Business Cycles Worldwide', *Quarterly Journal of Economics*, Vol. 132, No. 4, 1755–1817.

Nelson, J. (1990). *Economic Crisis and Policy Choice: The Politics of Adjustment in the Third World*. Princeton University Press.

Pepinsky, T. B. (2012). 'Do currency Crises Cause Capital Account Liberalization?' *International Studies Quarterly*, Vol. 56, No. 3, 544–559.

Perotti, R. (1999). 'Fiscal Policy in Good Times and Bad', *Quarterly Journal of Economics*, Vol. 114, No. 4, 1399–1436.

Prati, A., Massimiliano, G. O. and Papageorgiou, G. (2013). 'Which Reforms Work and under What Institutional Environment? Evidence from a New Dataset on Structural Reforms', *Review of Economics and Statistics*, Vol. 95, No. 3, 946–968.

Ramey, V. A. and Zubairy, S. (2018). 'Government Spending Multipliers in Good Times and Bad: Evidence from US Historical Data', *Journal of Political Economy*, Vol. 126, No. 2, 850–901.

Reinhart, C. M. and Rogoff, K. S. (2011). 'From Financial Crash to Debt Crisis', *American Economic Review*, Vol. 101, No. 5, 1676–1706.

Romer, C. D. and Romer, D. H. (2017). 'New Evidence on the Aftermath of Financial Crises in Advanced Economies', *American Economic Review*, Vol. 107, No. 10, 3072–3118.

(2018). 'Why Some Times Are Different: Macroeconomic Policy and the Aftermath of Financial Crises', *Economica*, Vol. 85, 1–40.

Williamson, J. (1994). *The Political Economy of Policy Reform*. Institute for International Economics.

7 *Structural Reforms and Fiscal Sustainability*

DAVIDE FURCERI AND JOÃO TOVAR JALLES

7.1 Introduction

There is a broad consensus on the desirability of making markets more efficient, across several economies, so as to increase competitiveness and improve future growth prospects (European Commission, 2013; IMF, 2016; OECD, 2012).[1] In the current policy context, advancing structural reforms is of paramount importance to address the decline in productivity growth – the key long-term driver of living standards – which fell sharply following the global financial crisis and has remained sluggish ever since (IMF, 2017).

Growing focus is also placed on the link between structural reforms and public finances, to address the growing public indebtedness across the world since the global financial crisis. In this context, a better knowledge of the implications of structural reforms for public finances is required to better design and prioritize packages of growth-enhancing reforms. Two broadly opposite views have been expressed in the recent debate on the relations between fiscal policy and structural reforms (Buti et al., 2008). The first view suggests that structural reforms and improvements in fiscal stance are hardly compatible, so that policy authorities may be left with a dilemma. According to this view, excessively tight constraints to fiscal policy may be incompatible with reform objectives and reduce the political capital of government to implement reforms. Another view suggests that fiscal discipline and reforms not only are not incompatible but tend to go hand in hand.

[1] * The authors are grateful to Paul De Grauwe for useful comments and to participants at the Conference on European Integration and Structural Reforms that took place in London in May 2018. The usual disclaimer applies, and any remaining errors are the authors' sole responsibility. The views expressed are those of the authors and do not necessarily represent those of the International Monetary Fund (IMF) or its policy.

In addition, reforms can improve debt sustainability by increasing output, the tax base, and, therefore, reducing debt-to-GDP ratios.

In addition to these views, two key considerations must be taken into account. First, the budgetary effects of structural reforms may materialize over different horizons, requiring an analysis of their impact over time. Second, the channels of transmission can be complex because the effect of reforms on fiscal positions may depend on initial conditions. These aspects warrant a systematic analysis of the interaction between fiscal policy and structural reforms.

This chapter contributes to the existing empirical literature on this topic by examining the effect of structural (domestic and external finance, trade, and product market) reforms on public debt for a sample of ninety advanced and developing countries spanning between 1973 and 2003. More specifically, we rely on the Ostry et al. (2009) cross-country dataset of major regulatory policy changes and estimate the dynamic response of public debt to these reforms using the local projection method (Jordà, 2005).

The results suggest that over the medium term – that is, four to six years after the reform takes place – reforms (with the exception of capital account) contribute to lower the debt-to-GDP ratio. This effect depends on the initial debt-to-GDP at the time of the reform. Our findings are robust to the inclusion of all reforms simultaneously and to an instrumental variable approach that uses political economy drivers of reforms as instruments.

The remainder of the chapter is organized as follows. Section 7.2 reviews the relevant literature. Section 7.3 presents the data and some stylized facts, and it also outlines the empirical methodology. The following section discusses the empirical results, including a battery of sensitivity and robustness checks. The last section concludes.

7.2 Literature Review

The sign of the relation between structural reforms and fiscal outcomes is theoretically uncertain, and several arguments have been developed to ascertain whether reforms can yield negative or positive impacts on fiscal outcomes.

The first relates to the budgetary effects of structural reforms. On the one hand, the implementation of some structural reforms might entail direct budgetary costs, which will weigh negatively on fiscal sustainability (Razin and Sadka, 2002). Some reforms could also negatively affect public finances indirectly through changes in prices. There is also the possibility that structural reforms impact the cyclical components of budgets through their temporary output effects (Hughes-Hallett et al., 2004). They could also contribute positively to sounder public finances in an indirect manner, i.e., by strengthening incentives to work and invest over time and thus increasing potential output and growth. This generates a positive denominator effect that strengthens fiscal sustainability. On the other hand, structural reforms can have direct budgetary saving effects, impacting positively on fiscal sustainability. This impact, however, can vary across types of reforms (IMF, 2016).

The second argument refers to political economy considerations.[2] In some instances, structural reforms may require political capital from the government, which may not be always available (Eichengreen and Wyplosz, 1998), and can be politically costly as they may negatively affect certain special-interest groups (Blanchard and Giavazzi, 2003; Boeri, 2005; Saint-Paul, 1996). The government in office may decide to incur into budgetary costs in two ways to "sweeten" the (potentially negative) effect of reforms. One is by directly compensating reform-losers with targeted tax cuts and transfers/subsidies (Pierson, 2001).[3] The other is by engaging into an accommodating fiscal stance to boost employment and help easing resistance for reforms (Deroose and Turrini, 2005).[4] Both these options, while easing the short-term costs

[2] For some structural reforms, however, indirect long-run fiscal gains need to be weighed against their short-run direct fiscal costs, because those costs are only partly recouped over time as output rises (IMF, 2017). More importantly, according to Deroose and Turrini (2005) there is a trade-off between structural reforms and budgetary objectives: an excessive focus on short-term budgetary discipline could act as a constraint on the pursuit of reforms that could improve public finances in the long run. This occurs when reforms worsen the budgetary position in the short run while gains appear mainly after some time. Theoretical chapters analyzing the trade-off between budgetary objectives and structural reforms include the works by Beetsma and Debrun (2003, 2005) and Razin and Sadka (2002).

[3] The liberalization and privatization of economic activities in several Eastern European countries during the transition process was often followed by the temporary provision of government subsidies to permit the restructuring of firms. On the revenue side, economic reforms were quite often implemented together with tax cuts.

[4] A supportive fiscal stance may be needed in the short term to obviate to the temporary widening output gap associated with reforms (Hughes-Hallett et al.,

of reforms in the transition dynamics, imply a short-run deterioration of the budget balance and so require sufficient fiscal space to be deemed feasible (IMF, 2016).

Finally, the sign and magnitude of the budgetary effects can ultimately depend on reforms' credibility and design (Heinemann, 2005). A government can gain credibility by committing to medium-term budgetary discipline and by signaling seriousness to implementing tough policies (Tavares, 2004). This in turn could raise investors' and consumers' confidence, generating positive effects on economic activity, reducing the political cost of reforms, and eventually improving the fiscal stance both through numerator and denominator effects (Deroose and Turrini, 2005; Tavares, 2004).[9]

A few theoretical papers have directly studied the relationship between structural reforms and fiscal policy. Campoy and Negrete (2010) model the interrelations between budget deficits and structural reforms in a monetary union by considering the international spillovers generated by both policies. They show that efforts to achieve fiscal policy coordination within the Eurozone reduce member countries' incentives to carry out much-needed structural reforms and turn out to be welfare-reducing. Papageorgiou and Vourvachaki (2017) set up a dynamic general equilibrium model calibrated for the Greek economy to study the impact of product and labor market reforms. Results show that reforms produce important long-run GDP gains that materialize earlier, the faster the reforms are implemented. When implemented jointly with fiscal consolidations, structural reforms may amplify the short-run costs of fiscal tightening. Muller et al. (2016) constructed a dynamic theory of sovereign debt and structural reforms with interacting frictions. According to them, higher debt levels deter reforms because most of the gains accrue to foreign lenders in the form of capital gains on the outstanding debt. Finally, Sajedi (2018) suggests that the fiscal costs and benefits of reforms are generally small, although larger reforms entail larger rises in deficit-to-GDP in the short run. Moreover, reforms in labor markets have little effect on public finances in the long run, but their short-run costs can be counterbalanced if combined with product market reforms. Furthermore, reforms

2004; Saint-Paul, 2002). This argument is strengthened by the claim that some reforms may lower the effectiveness of automatic stabilizers, thereby requiring discretionary fiscal policy to step in, in order avoid a suboptimal degree of fiscal stabilization (Mabbett and Schelkle, 2007).

implemented when monetary policy is constrained can be contractionary in the short run, resulting in higher deficit-to-GDP ratios.

Empirically, some papers have related structural reforms to fiscal adjustment programs. Kumar et al. (2007) found that structural reforms in the areas of health care, unemployment benefits, and pensions have supported fiscal consolidations. Tagkalakis (2009) investigates the role played by labor and product market institutions in determining the likelihood of initiating and of successfully concluding a fiscal adjustment. Using data for sixteen Organization for Economic Cooperation and Development (OECD) countries he found that a less generous unemployment benefit system contributes to the success of fiscal consolidation. On the other hand, product market deregulation and more flexible employment protection legislation do not contribute positively to fiscal consolidation. Heylen et al. (2013) found that consolidation policies are more successful when they are accompanied by product market deregulation.

More closely related to our chapter, Deroose and Turrini (2005) do not find strong empirical support to the view that labor market, product market, or pension reforms were associated with short-term budgetary costs in advanced economies. Evidence points to a slight deterioration in budgets that is not always statistically different from zero. Moreover, recent empirical analysis on a sample of advanced economies over forty years suggests that most labor and product market reforms can create fiscal space over the medium term (IMF, 2017). Across advanced economies, major episodes of deregulation of retail trade, professional services, and network sectors led to large increases in GDP and higher government revenues, which in turn lowered public debt-to-GDP ratios. In contrast, major reforms of job protection for regular workers had a limited impact on public finances, reflecting their small and statistically insignificant effects on output, as well as the absence of upfront fiscal costs.

7.3 Data Issues and Methodology

7.3.1 Structural Reforms Database

This chapter's analysis relies on Ostry et al.'s (2009) structural reforms dataset, which identifies major policy changes for a sample of ninety countries, twenty-nine advanced and sixty-one developing economies

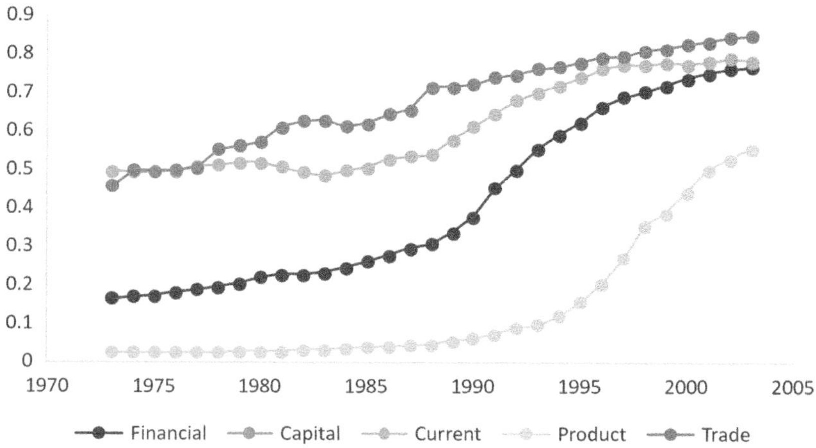

Figure 7.1 Evolution of all structural reform indicators, full sample.
Source: Ostry et al. (2009)

over three decades, between 1973 and 2003.[5] The database covers the following policy areas: domestic finance, external finance, trade, and product market.[6] Financial sector indicators pertain to domestic financial markets – including banking and securities markets – as well as the external capital account. Real sector structural indicators include measures of trade (average tariff rates, current account) and product markets (telecommunications and electricity markets). All indicators are scaled to vary between zero and unity, with higher values representing greater liberalization.

Figure 7.1 sums up the different structural reforms' cross-country and time-series patterns for the entire sample. On average, trade reforms display a gradual liberalizing trend throughout the entire period, while both capital and current account reforms tightened slightly in the late 1970s and early 1980s. Both domestic finance and product market reforms witnessed relatively little action until the late 1980s, but they picked up a liberalizing path very fast afterward.

The average patterns shown in Figure 7.1 hide several heterogeneities between income groups (Figure 7.2). For domestic finance and product market reforms, the aggregate average patterns translate well the behavior of the different income groups. However, capital account

[5] Country groups are classified according to the IMF World Economic Outlook (WEO).

[6] It does not cover labor market reforms, where progress has been typically more modest, probably due to possible political costs associated with these reforms.

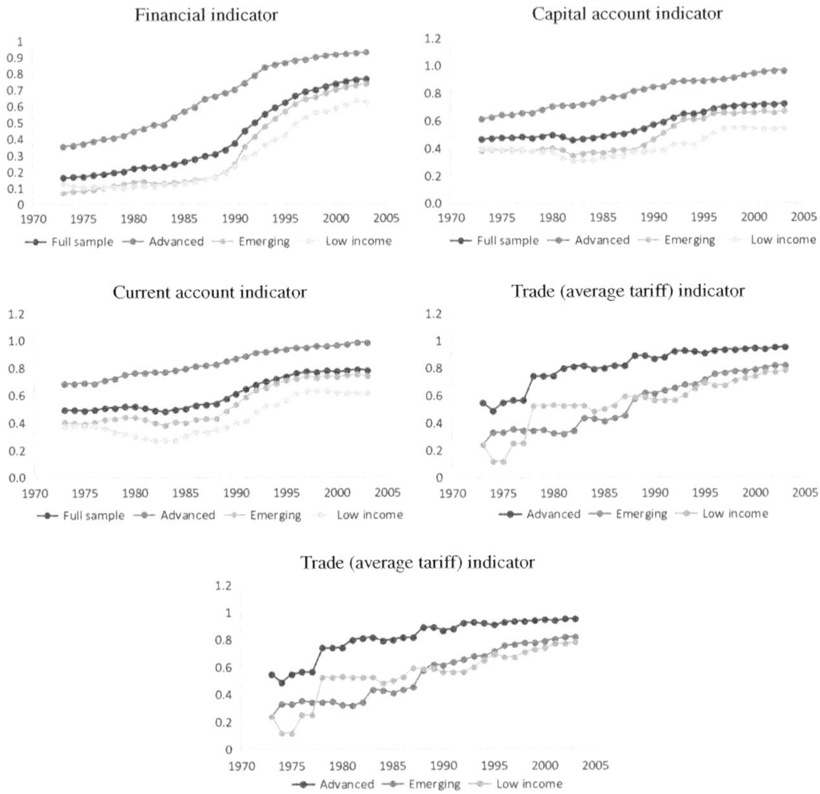

Figure 7.2 Evolution of all structural reform indicators by income group.
Source: Ostry et al. (2009)

reforms show different trends: in advanced economies, liberalization has been the norm since the early 1970s, while in emerging and low-income countries, this movement only began in the later 1980s and mid-1990s, respectively. A similar picture emerges from current account reforms. The time dynamics of trade reforms is more volatile, but in all income groups the trend has been toward increased liberalization, particularly since after the early 1980s.

7.3.2 Debt and Other Data

Our main dependent variable is the (gross) public debt-to-GDP ratio (in percent). Data on debt and other control variables (see the next section) are retrieved from the IMF's WEO database. Summary statistics are presented in the Appendix Table 7.1A.

7.3.3 Empirical Methodology

The empirical analysis consists in estimating and tracing out the average evolution of the public debt-to-GDP ratio in the aftermath of major policy changes. The statistical method follows the approach proposed by Jordà (2005) to estimate impulse-response functions. This approach has been advocated by Auerbach and Gorodnichencko (2013) and Romer and Romer (2017), among others, as a flexible alternative to vector autoregression (autoregressive distributed lag) specifications since it does not impose dynamic restrictions. It is also particularly suited to estimating nonlinearities in the dynamic response. Our main regression specification is estimated as follows:

$$y_{i,t+k} - y_{i,t-1} = \alpha_i + \mu_t + \beta_k R_{i,t} + \theta X_{i,t} + \varepsilon_{i,t} \tag{7.1}$$

in which $y_{i,t+k}$ is the public debt-to-GDP ratio in country i in period $t + k$; α_i are country fixed effects included to control for unobserved cross-country heterogeneity; μ_t are time effects to control to control for global shocks; and $R_{i,t}$ is our reform shock indicator. $X_{i,t}$ is a set of controls including two lags of the debt-to-GDP ratios, two lags of the reform variable, and two lags of real GDP growth to account for the possibility that reforms are implemented to address weak economic conditions.[7]

Equation (7.1) is estimated via ordinary least squares (OLS) for each $k = 0,..,6$ with robust standard errors clustered at the country level. Impulse-response functions are computed using the estimated coefficients β_k, and the confidence bands associated with the estimated impulse-response functions are obtained using the estimated standard errors of the coefficients β_k. While we believe that our empirical setup addresses endogeneity concerns related to omitted variable bias, in order to further mitigate such concerns, we also reestimate our specifications using an instrumental variable (IV) approach, drawing our instruments from the political economy literature on the drivers of reforms (refer to Section 7.4.2 for further details).

[7] Results remain qualitatively unchanged to alternative lag structure specifications.

7.4 Empirical Results

7.4.1 Baseline

Figure 7.3 presents the results obtained by estimating Equation (7.1). It shows the response of the debt-to-GDP ratio to major reform episodes – defined as a change in the reform indicator equivalent to two standard deviations of the annual change – and its associated 90 percent confidence bands. The results suggest that reforms contribute to lower the debt-to-GDP ratio in the medium term – that is, four to six years after the reform takes place. In particular, the medium-term debt effect of major reforms ranges between –2 percentage point (for trade reforms) and –4 percentage points (for domestic finance reforms). Finally, the effect is more precisely estimated for financial reforms. While these effects can be considered economically small, as we will show later, they tend to be magnified in countries with higher initial debt-to-GDP ratios.

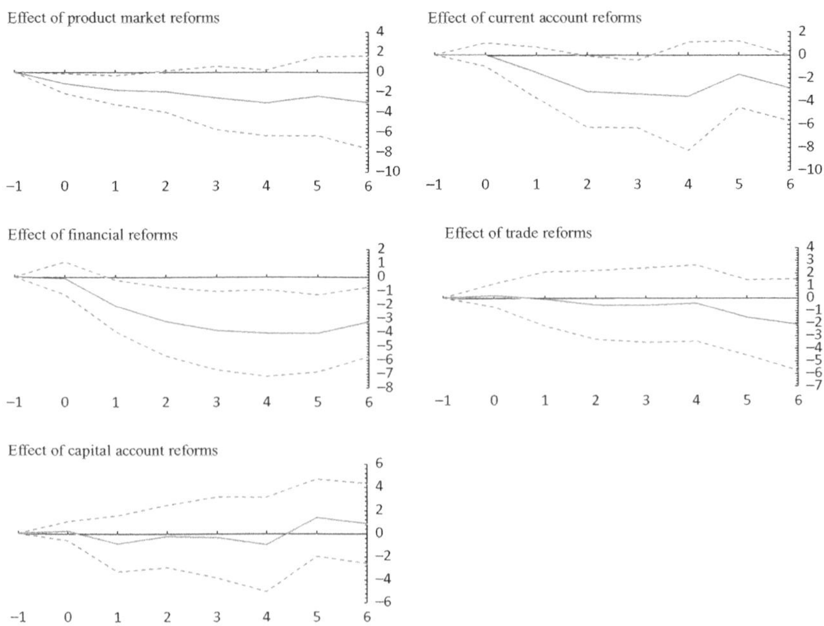

Figure 7.3 The effect of structural reforms on public debt (percent of GDP).
Note: Estimates based on Equation (7.1). Solid line denotes the public debt effect of reforms. Dotted lines indicate 90 percent confidence interval based on standard errors clustered at the country level.

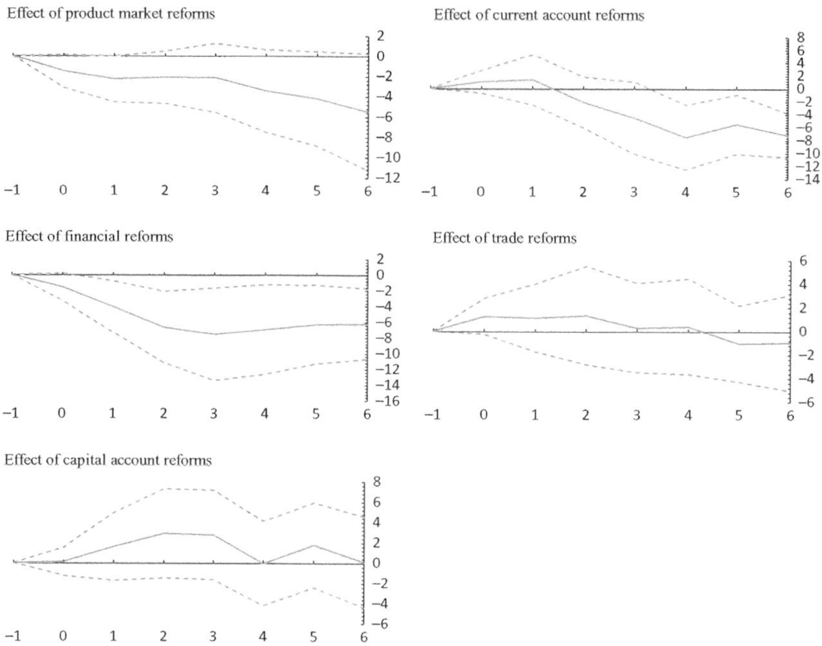

Figure 7.4 The effect of structural reforms on public debt using lagged GDP as denominator.

Note: Estimates based on Equation (7.1). Solid line denotes the public debt effect of reforms. Dotted lines indicate 90 percent confidence interval based on standard errors clustered at the country level.

Following Auerbach and Gorodnichenko (2017), we also redid the estimations by measuring the debt ratio with respect to lagged GDP. Lagging the denominator by one period is done to ensure that the contemporaneous reaction of the ratio to a structural reform shock is driven by changes in debt rather than output. The results displayed in Figure 7.4 yield qualitatively similar results to those presented in Figure 7.3.

These results, however, may mask heterogenous effects across income groups. To check whether this is the case, we run separate estimation of Equation (7.1) for advanced economies and developing countries. The results reported in Figures 7.5a and 7.5b suggest that while trade reforms have larger effects in advanced economies, financial reforms tend to have more significant effects in developing economies.

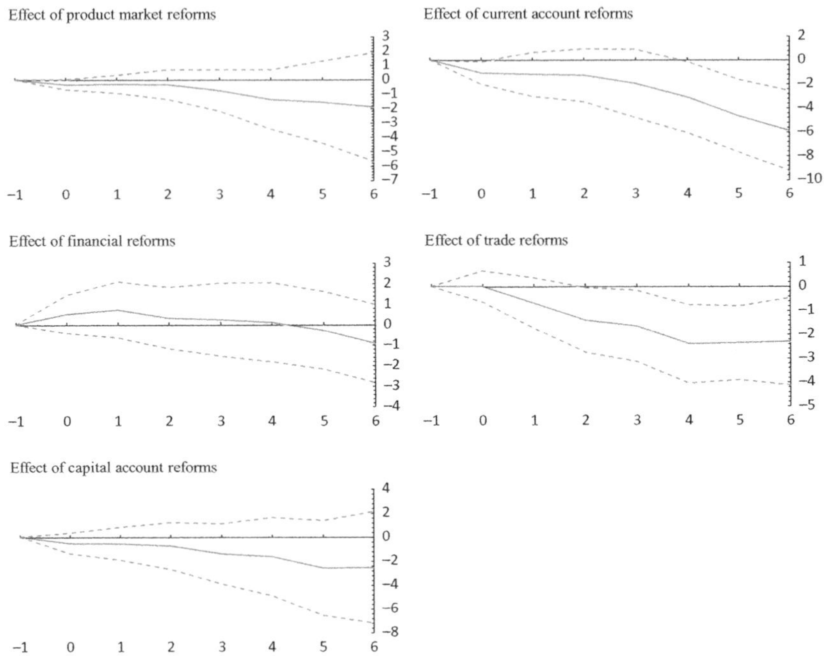

Figure 7.5a The effect of structural reforms on public debt (percent of GDP) (%), advanced economies.

Note: Estimates based on Equation (7.1). Solid line denotes the public debt effect of reforms. Dotted lines indicate 90 percent confidence interval based on standard errors clustered at the country level.

7.4.2 Robustness Checks

7.4.2.1 Omitted Variable Bias

The previous analysis considers the impact of structural reforms one at a time, raising potential concerns about omitted variables – reforms could be carried out across different areas at the same time. We reestimate our main regression Equation (7.1) by including reforms in all areas simultaneously.[8] Figure 7.6 shows the effects on public debt and confirms that such augmentation of the vector of controls does not change the basic thrust of our results.[9]

[8] The vector $X_{i,\,t}$ in Equation (7.1) was augmented to include up to two lags of all other reforms.

[9] Estimates could also be biased in the event of reform reversals (i.e. tightening or major tightening). In practice, however, this bias is negligible, as there are only a

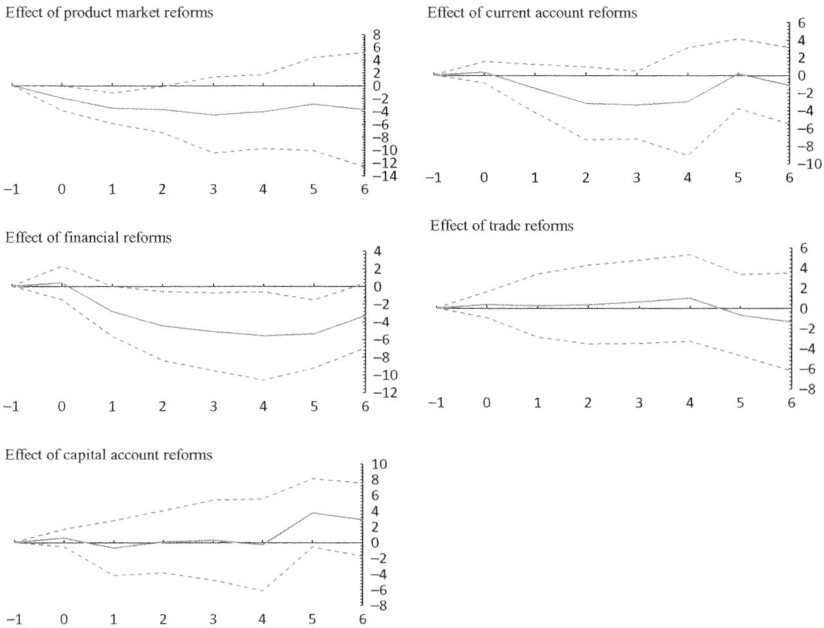

Figure 7.5b The effect of structural reforms on public debt (percent of GDP) (%), developing countries.
Note: Estimates based on Equation (7.1). Solid line denotes the public debt effect of reforms. Dotted lines indicate 90 percent confidence interval based on standard errors clustered at the country level.

7.4.2.2 Instrumental Variables

Even though, as discussed earlier, we believe that our empirical setup addresses endogeneity concerns, we still check the robustness of our results to an IV approach that instruments our structural reform indicators. The literature has put forward several theories to rationalize why and when reforms (do not) happen. We focus on one main broad factor examined in the literature: *political institutions* (see Duval et al., 2018) for a recent contribution). Specifically, we use the following set of political economy variables as external instruments which we divide in four categories. First, we focus on ideology of the governing party or parties, and we use discrete variables to distinguish

very few such cases. Furthermore, the results are robust to focusing exclusively on reform episodes (and excluding reform reversals).

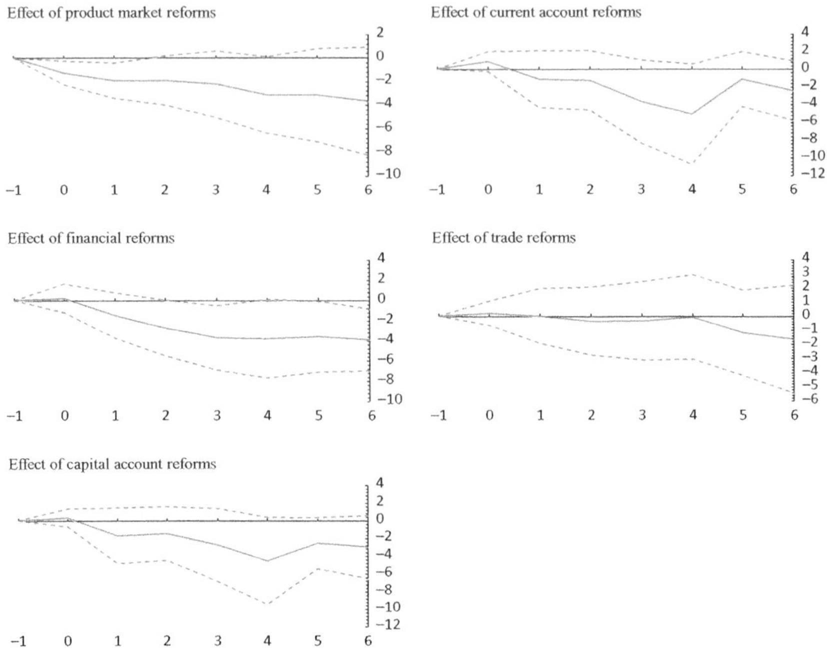

Figure 7.6 The effect of structural reforms on public debt (percent of GDP), controlling for reforms in all other areas.
Note: Estimates based on Equation (7.1). Solid line denotes the public debt effect of reforms. Dotted lines indicate 90 percent confidence interval based on standard errors clustered at the country level.

between left, center and right (3, 2, and 1, respectively) (*Parties*).[10] Second, we investigate the importance of political system, by exploring whether reforms happened more often in the context of parliamentary, assembly-elected, or presidential form of governments (using discrete variables: 2, 1, and 0, respectively) (*System*).[11] Third, we consider the role of party fragmentation and use a continuous variable bounded between 0 (no fragmentation) and 1 (maximum fragmentation) to capture the number of political parties in the lower house of the

[10] Right-wing governments are more conductive to market-oriented reforms (Alesina and Roubini, 1992).

[11] Persson (2002) argues that in countries with presidential forms of government reforms face less effective opposition to implement reforms than in countries with a parliamentary system.

legislative assembly (*Fragmentation*).[12] Fourth, we investigate whether reforms are more likely to happen in an environment characterized by stronger democratic institutions (measured as polity IV and normalized between 0 and 1) (*Democ*).[13] Data on these variables are taken from the World Bank Database of Political Institutions.

By means of a two-stage least squares estimator, we reestimate Equation (7.1) using up to two lags of the political economy exogenous instruments described previously. To check the validity of our instruments and assess the strength of our identification, we rely on the Kleibergen–Paap and Hansen statistics. The underidentification tests that the excluded instruments are "relevant" (meaning correlated with the endogenous regressors). Our obtained statistics generally reject the null that the different equations are unidentified (Stock–Yogo critical values were applied). Then the Hansen test statistics reveal that the instrument sets contain valid instruments (i.e., that they are uncorrelated with the error term, and that the excluded instruments are correctly excluded from the estimated equation) is not rejected. The results reported in Figure 7.7 are similar to, and not statistically different from, those obtained using OLS, confirming that endogeneity is not a serious concern in our setup.

7.4.3 *Initial Level of Debt*

In this subsection, we explore whether the initial level of public debt affects the magnitude of the response of structural reforms. In our second regression specification, the dynamic response is allowed to vary with the initial level of public debt-to-GDP ratio:

$$y_{i,t+k} - y_{i,t-1} = \alpha_i + \mu_t + \beta_k^L F(z_{i,t-1}) R_{i,t} + \beta_k^H \left(1 - F(z_{i,t-1})\right) R_{i,t} + \theta M_{i,t} + \varepsilon_{i,t} \tag{7.2}$$

[12] In countries where with higher political fragmentation the government may find it more difficult to implement reforms (Haggard and Webb, 1994; Roubini and Sachs, 1989).

[13] While democracy can hinder reforms if special interests prevail on the general welfare, democratic rulers are typically more sensitive to the interest of the public, and so more prone to implement reforms that benefit a large share of the population (Giuliano et al., 2013).

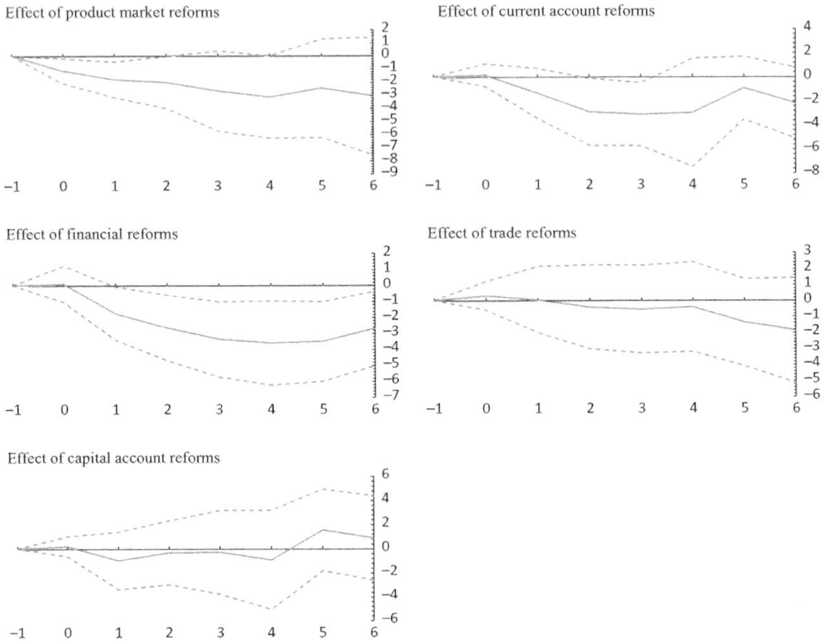

Figure 7.7 The effect of structural reforms on public debt (percent of GDP), instrumental variables.
Note: Estimates based on Equation (7.1) with a two-stage least squares estimator. Instruments used comprised on four political economy variables (up to their second lag) – see main text for details. Solid line denotes the public debt effect of reforms. Dotted lines indicate 90 percent confidence interval based on standard errors clustered at the country level.

with

$$F(z_{it-1}) = \frac{\exp(-\gamma z_{it-1})}{1+\exp(-\gamma z_{it}-1)}, \gamma > 0$$

in which z_{it} is an indicator of the initial level of public indebtedness (proxied by the public debt-to-GDP ratio) of the economy normalized to have zero mean and unit variance. F_{it} is a smooth transition function used to estimate the impact of reform shocks in low-indebted versus high-indebted countries. We set $\gamma = 1$. M is the same set of control variables used in the baseline specification, but now including also two lags of $F(z_{i,\,t-1})$. As before, Equation (7.2) is estimated using OLS for each $k = 0,..,6$ with robust standard errors clustered at the country

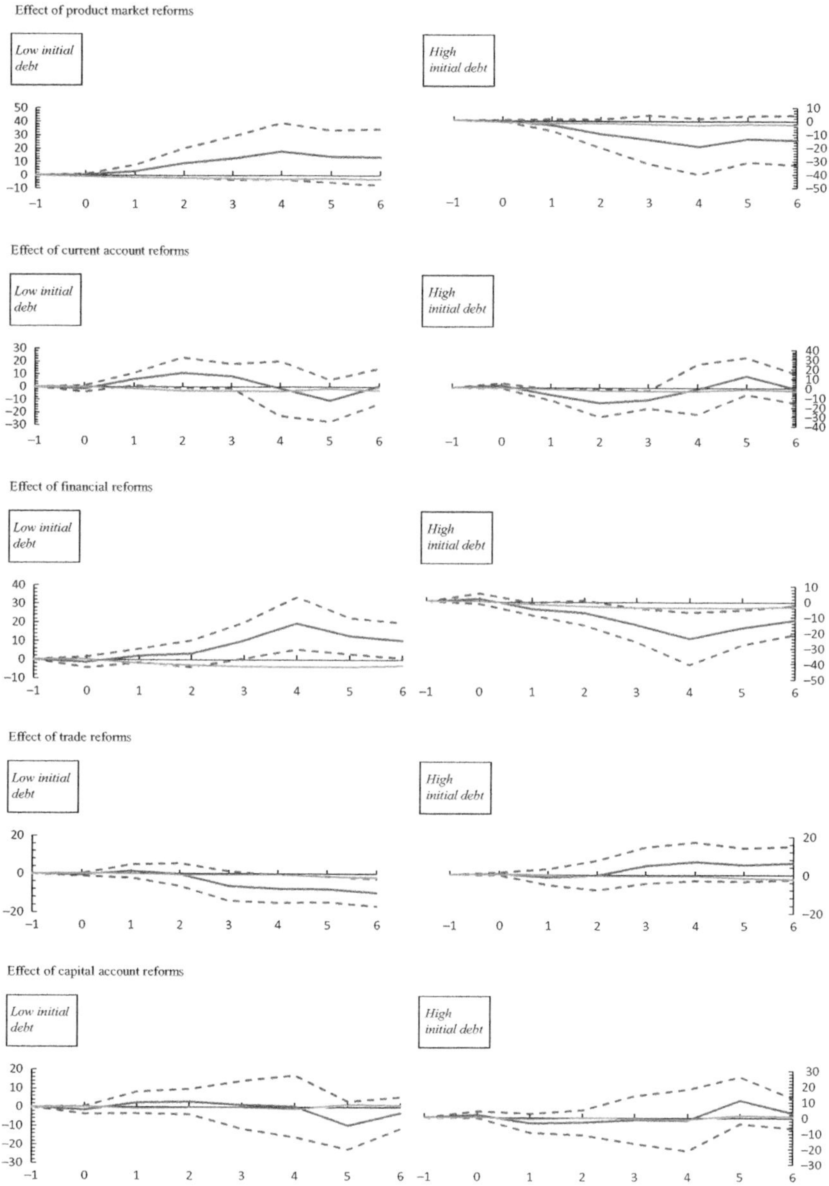

Figure 7.8 The effect of structural reforms on public debt (percent of GDP) depending on initial indebtedness level.

Note: Estimates based on Equation (7.2). Effects under low (high) initial indebtedness level are shown here using F = 0 (F = 1). The solid line denotes level, and impulse response functions are computed using the estimated coefficients β_k.

This approach is equivalent to the smooth transition autoregressive model developed by Granger and Terävistra (1993). The advantage of this approach is twofold. First, compared with a model in which each dependent variable would be interacted with a measure of the level of public indebtedness, it permits a direct test of whether the effect of reforms varies across different regimes such as low and high initial debt. Second, compared with estimating structural vector autoregressions for each regime, it allows the effect of reforms to change smoothly by considering a continuum of states to compute the impulse-response functions, thus making the response more stable and precise.

Looking at Figure 7.8, we can observe that the effect of financial and product market reforms tends to be larger and economically significant (above 10 percentage points) when enacted in countries with higher debt levels. For the remaining reforms, responses are surrounded by some degree of uncertainty.

7.5 Conclusion

This chapter estimated the short-term impact of structural reforms in different policy areas on the public debt-to-GDP ratio applying a local projection method to a dataset of major reforms in advanced and developing economies spanning between 1973 and 2003.

The results suggest that over the medium term – that is, four to six years after the reform takes place – reforms contribute to lower the debt-to-GDP ratio. While the magnitudes of these effects are on average small, they tend to be larger and economically significant in countries with high initial debt. The findings are consistently robust to the inclusion of all reforms simultaneously and to the instrumental variable approach, which uses political economy drivers of reforms as instruments.

Figure 7.8 (*cont.*) the public debt effect of reforms. The solid light gray line denotes the unconditional (baseline) public debt effect of reforms. The solid darker gray line denotes the conditional public debt effect of reforms. Dotted lines indicate 90 percent confidence interval based on standard errors clustered at country level.

The empirical results should be treated with care: the set of structural reforms considered have often been accompanied by other fiscal and monetary measures that cannot be fully controlled for in the analysis. Moreover, the empirical estimates capture the average historical impact of major reforms on a proxy of fiscal sustainability. As such, they do not explicitly account for inherent uncertainty and cross-country heterogeneity regarding key variables (for example, fiscal multipliers, government funding costs, etc.). Furthermore, our empirical analysis of the impact of structural reforms on fiscal sustainability suffers from an inevitable problem of self-selection bias: the reforms observed are only those that have not been blocked in the political process, that is, many reforms projects may have been blocked exactly because of their (short-term direct) budgetary impact, but the analysis does not take that into account. All in all, while some generalizations can be made in what concerns the link between structural reforms and fiscal sustainability in the short to medium term, caution is warranted, as there is no one size fits all.

References

Alesina, A. and Roubini, N. (1992). "Political Cycles in the OECD," *Review of Economic Studies*, Vol. 59, No. 4, 663–688.

Andres, J., Arce, O. and Thomas, C. (2014). "Structural Reforms in a Debt Overhang," Documentos de Trabajo No. 1421, Banco de Espana, Spain.

Auerbach, A., and Gorodnichenko, Y. (2013). "Output Spillovers from Fiscal Policy," *American Economic Review*, Vol. 103, No. 3, 141–146.

Auerbach, A. and Gorodnichenko, Y. (2017). "Fiscal Stimulus and Fiscal Sustainability," NBER Working Paper No. 23789, Boston, Cambridge.

Autor, D. H., Kugler, A. R.. and Kerr, W. D. 2007. "Do Employment Protections Reduce Productivity? Evidence from U.S. States," *Economic Journal*, Vol. 117 , No. 521, 189–217.

Bassanini, A. and Duval, R. (2006). "Employment Patterns in OECD Countries: Reassessing the Roles of Policies and Institutions," OECD Economics Department Working Paper, No. 486.

Bean, C. (1998). "The Interaction of Aggregate Demand Policies and Labor Market Reform," *Swedish Economic Policy Review*, Vol. 5, No. 2, 353–382.

Beetsma, R. and Debrun, X. (2003). "Reconciling Stability and Growth: Smart Pacts and Structural Reforms," CEPR Discussion Paper No 3930.

(2005). "The New Stability and Growth Pact: A First Assessment," Mimeo, University of Amsterdam.

Bentolila, S. and Bertola, G. (1990). "Firing Costs and Labour Demand: How Bad Is Eurosclerosis?" *Review of Economic Studies*, Vol. 57, No. 3, 381–402.

Blanchard, O. and Giavazzi, F. (2003). "Macroeconomic Effects of Regulation and Deregulation in Goods and Labour Markets," *Quarterly Journal of Economics*, Vol. 118, No. 3, 879–907.

Boeri, T. (2005). "Reforming Labor and Product Markets: Some Lessons from Two Decades of Experiments in Europe," IMF WP/05/97.

et al. (2006). *Structural Reforms without Prejudices*. Oxford University Press.

Buti, M., et al. (2008). "Defying the 'Juncker Curse': Can Reformist Governments Be Reelected?" European Economy: Economic Papers No. 324, May.

Cacciatore, M. and Fiori, G. (2016), "The Macroeconomic Effects of Goods and Labor Market Deregulation," *Review of Economic Dynamics*, Vol. 20, No. 1, 1–24.

Cacciatore, M., Duval, R., Fiori, G. and Ghironi, F. (2016a). "Short-Term Pain for Long-Term Gain: Market Deregulation and Monetary Policy in Small Open Economies," *Journal of International Money and Finance*, Vol. 57, 86–114.

(2016b). "Market Reforms in the Time of Imbalance," *Journal of Economic Dynamics and Control*, Vol. 72, 66–93.

Calmfors, L. (2001). "Unemployment, Labour-Market Reform and Monetary Union," *Journal of Labor Economics*, Vol. 19, No. 2, 265–289.

Campoy, J. C. and Negrete, J. C. (2010). "Structural Reforms and Budget Deficits in a Monetary Union: A Strategic Approach," *B.E. Journal of Economic Analysis & Policy*, Vol. 10, No. 1, 1–31.

Cingano F., Leonardi, M., Messina, J. and Pica, G. (2010). "The Effects of Employment Protection Legislation and Financial Market Imperfections on Investment: Evidence from a Firm-Level Panel of EU Countries," *Economic Policy*, Vol. 25, 117–163.

Deroose, S. andTurrini, A. (2005). "The Short-Term Budgetary Implications of Structural Reforms: Evidence from a Panel of EU Countries," CEPR Discussion Paper No. 5217.

Devries, P., Leigh, D., Guajardo, J. and Pescatori, A. (2011). "A New Action-Based Dataset of Fiscal Consolidation," IMF Working Paper No. 11/128, International Monetary Fund, Washington.

Draghi, M. (2015), "Monetary Policy and Structural Reforms in the Euro Area," presented at Prometeia, Bologna, Italy, December 14.

Duval, R. and Furceri, D. (2017). "The Effects of Labor and Product Market Reforms: The Role of Macroeconomic Conditions and Policies," *IMF Economic Review*, Vol. 66, No. 1, 31–69.

Duval, R., Furceri, D. and Jalles, J. T. (2017). "Job Protection Deregulation in Good and Bad Times," IMF Working Paper No. 17/277, Washington.

Duval, R., Furceri, D. and Miethe, J. (2019). "The Needle in the Haystack: What Drives Labor and Product Market Reforms in Advanced Economies," IMF Working Paper (forthcoming).

Duval, R., Furceri, D., Hu, B., Jalles, J. and Nguyen, H. (2018). "A New Narrative Database on Product and Labor Market Reforms in Advanced Economics," IMF Working Paper.

Eggertsson, G., Ferrero, A. and Raffo, A. (2014). "Can Structural Reforms Help Europe?" *Journal of Monetary Economics*, Vol. 61, 1–22.

Eichengreen, B. and Wyplosz , C. (1998). "The Stability Pact: More than a Minor Nuisance?" *Economic Policy*, Vol. 26, 65–104.

Escolano, J. (2010). "A Practical Guide to Public Debt Dynamics, Fiscal Sustainability, and Cyclical Adjustment of Budgetary Aggregates," IMF Technical Note and Manual, International Monetary Fund, Washington.

Eslava M., Haltiwanger, J,, Kugler, A. and Kugler, M. (2004). "The Effects of Structural Reforms on Productivity and Profitablity Enhancing Reallocation: Evidence from Colombia," *Journal of Development Economics*, Vol. 75, No. 2, 333–371.

European Commission, (2013). "The Growth Impact of Structural Reforms," in Quarterly Report on the Euro Area, No. 4, 17–27.

Giuliano, P., Mishra, P. and Spilimbergo, A. (2013). "Democracy and Reforms: Evidence from a New Dataset," *American Economic Journal: Macroeconomics*, Vol. 5, No. 4, 179–204.

Granger, C. W. J. and Teräsvirta,. T. (1993). *Modelling Nonlinear Economic Relationships*. Oxford University Press.

Griffith, R. and Harrison, R. (2004). "The Link between Product Market Reform and Macro-Economic Performance," Economic Paper, n° 209, European Commission.

Griffith, R., Harrison, R. and Macartney, G. (2007). "Product Market Reforms, Labour Market Institutions and Unemployment," *Economic Journal*, Vol. 117, No. 519, 142–166.

Haggard, S. and Webb, S. B. (ed.) (1994). *Voting for Reform: Democracy, Political Liberalization, and Economic Adjustment*. Oxford University Press.

Haltiwanger, J. C., Jarmin, R. S. and Miranda, J. (2010). "Who Creates Jobs? Small vs. Large vs. Young," NBER Working Papers 16300, National Bureau of Economic Research.

Heinemann, F. (2005). "How Distant Is Lisbon from Maastricht? The Short-Run Link between Structural Reforms and Budgetary Performance." In S. Deroose, E. Flores, and A. Turrini (ed.), *Proceedings from the ECFIN Workshop "The Budgetary Implications of Structural Reforms,"* December 2.

Heylen, F., Hoebeeck, A. and Buyse, T. (2013). "Government Efficiency, Institutions, and the Effects of Fiscal Consolidation on Public Debt," *European Journal of Political Economy*, Vol. 31, 40–59.

Hughes-Hallett, A., Hougaard Jensen, S. E. and Richter, C. (2004). "The European Economy at the Cross Roads: Structural Reforms, Fiscal Constraints, and the Lisbon Agenda," unpublished manuscript, Vanderbilt University.

International Monetary Fund (2013). "World Economic Outlook. Transitions and Tensions," October.

(2016). "World Economic Outlook, Time for a Supply Side Boost? Macroeconomic Effects of Labor and Product Market Reforms in Advanced Economies," chapter 3, April.

(2017). "Labor and Product Market Reforms in Advanced Economies: Fiscal Costs, Gains and Support," Staff Discussion Note, 17/03, March.

Jordà, O. (2005). "Estimation and Inference of Impulse Responses by Local Projections," *American Economic Review*, Vol. 95, No. 1, 161–182.

Jordà, P. and Taylor, A. (2016). "The Time for Austerity: Estimating the Average Treatment Effect of Fiscal Policy," *Economic Journal*, Vol. 126, No. 590, 219–255.

Krugman, P. (2014), "Structural Deformity," *New York Times*, November 20.

Kumar, M., Leigh, D. and Plekhanov, A. (2007). "Fiscal Adjustments: Determinants and Macroeconomic Consequences," IMF Working Paper 07/196.

Mabbett D. and Schelkle, W. (2007). "Bringing Macroeconomics Back into the Political Economy of Reform: The Lisbon Agenda and the 'Fiscal Philosophy' of EMU," *Journal of Common Market Studies*, Vol. 45, No. 1, 81–103.

Muller, A., Storesletten, K. and Zilibotti, F. (2016). "The Political Color of Fiscal Responsibility," *Journal of the European Economic Association*, Vol. 14, No. 1, 252–302.

Nickell, S., Nunziata, L. and Ochel, W. (2005). "Unemployment in the OECD since the 1960s: What Do We Know?" *Economic Journal*, Vol. 115, No. 500, 1–27.

OECD (2012). *Economic Policy Reforms 2012: Going for Growth*, OECD Publishing.

Ostry, J. D., Spilimbergo, A. and Prati, A. (2009). "Structural Reforms and Economic Performance in Advanced and Developing Countries," IMF Occasional Paper No. 268, International Monetary Fund, Washington.

Papageorgiou, D. and Vourvachaki, E. (2017), "Macroeconomic Effects of Structural Reforms and Fiscal Consolidations: Trade-Offs and Complementarities," *European Journal of Political Economy*, Vol. 48, 54–73.

Persson, T. and Tabellini, G. (2002). *Political Economics: Explaining Economics Policy*. MIT Press.

Pierson, P. (ed.) (2001). *The New Politics of the Welfare State*. Oxford University Press.

Razin, A. and Sadka, E. (2002). *Labor, Capital and Finance: International Flows*. Cambridge University Press.

Rodrik, D. (1996). "Coordination Failures and Government Policy: A Model with Applications to East Asia and Eastern Europe," *Journal of International Economics*, Vol. 40, No. 1–2, 1–22.

(2015). "The Mirage of Structural Reform," *Project Syndicate*, October 8.

Romer, C. and Romer, D. (1989). "Does Monetary Policy Matter? A New Test in the Spirit of Friedman and Schwartz," in O. J. Blanchard and S. Fischer (ed.), *NBER Macroeconomics Annual 1989*. MIT Press, pp. 121–170.

Romer, C. and Romer, D. (2010). "The Macroeconomic Effects of Tax Changes: Estimates Based on a New Measure of Fiscal Shocks," *American Economic Review*, Vol. 100, No. 3, 763–801.

(2015). "New Evidence on the Impact of Financial Crises in Advanced Countries," NBER Working Paper No. 21021, National Bureau of Economic Research, Cambridge, MA.

(2017). "New Evidence on the Aftermath of Financial Crises in Advanced Countries," *American Economic Review*, Vol. 107, No. 10, 3072–3118.

Roubini, N. and Sachs, J. (1989). "Political and Economic Determinants of Budget Deficits in the Industrial Economies," *European Economic Review*, Vol. 33, No. 5, 903–938.

Saint-Paul, G. (1996). "Exploring the Political Economy of Labor Market Institutions," *Economic Policy*, Vol. 23, 265–315.

(2002). "Distribution and Growth in an Economy with Limited Needs," CEPR Discussion Papers, 2834, CEPR Discussion Papers.

Sajedi, R. (2018). "Fiscal Consequences of Structural Reform under Constrained Monetary Policy," *Journal of Economic Dynamics and Control*, Vol. 93(C), 22–38.

Tagkalakis, A. (2009). "Fiscal Adjustments and Asset Price Movements," Working Papers 104, Bank of Greece.

Tavares, J. (2004). "The Open Society Assesses its Enemies: Shocks, Disasters and Terrorist Attacks," *Journal of Monetary Economics*, Vol. 51, No. 5, 1039–1070.

Van Schaik, T. and van de Klundert, T. (2013). "Employment Protection Legislation and Catching-Up," *Applied Economics*, Vol. 45, No. 8, 973–981.

Appendix

Table 7.1A *Summary statistics.*

Variable	Observations	Mean	Standard deviation	Minimum	Maximum
Public debt-to-GDP ratio	5,515	51.28	36.52	0	246.17
Real GDP growth	5,510	3.76	5.10	–96.95	71.53
Financial reforms	2,809	0.01	0.04	–0.28	0.33
Capital account reforms	2,805	0.01	0.06	–0.50	0.50
Current account reforms	2,805	0.01	0.06	–0.69	0.50
Trade reforms	2,385	0.01	0.06	–0.64	0.84
Product market reforms	2,809	0.02	0.14	–1	1.5
Growth expectations	3,323	4.27	3.64	–6.32	122.59
Parties	4,784	1.24	1.25	0	3
System	4,844	0.83	0.95	0	2
Fractionalization	4,256	0.79	0.27	0.02	1
Democ	4,600	4.98	4.18	0	10

Table 7.2A *Country coverage.*

Advanced economies	Emerging markets		Low-income countries
Australia	Albania	Namibia	Bangladesh
Austria	Algeria	Pakistan	Bolivia
Belgium	Argentina	Paraguay	Burkina Faso
Canada	Azerbaijan	Peru	Cameroon
Czech Republic	Belarus	Philippines	Côte d'Ivoire
Denmark	Botswana	Poland	Ethiopia
Estonia	Brazil	Romania	Ghana
Finland	Bulgaria	Russia	Kenya
France	Chile	South Africa	Kyrgyz Republic
Germany	China	Sri Lanka	Lesotho
Greece	Colombia	Swaziland	Madagascar
Hong Kong SAR	Costa Rica	Thailand	Malawi
Ireland	Dominican Republic	Tunisia	Mozambique
Israel	Ecuador	Turkey	Nepal
Italy	Egypt	Ukraine	Nicaragua
Japan	El Salvador	Uruguay	Nigeria
Korea	Georgia	Venezuela	Senegal
Latvia	Guatemala		Tanzania
Netherlands	Hungary		Uganda
New Zealand	India		Uzbekistan
Norway	Indonesia		Vietnam
Portugal	Jamaica		Zambia
Singapore	Jordan		Zimbabwe
Spain	Kazakhstan		
Sweden	Lithuania		
Switzerland	Malaysia		
United Kingdom	Mexico		
United States	Morocco		

Source: Ostry et al. (2009).

8 Transitions in the EU Labour Market before and after the Crisis

The Role of Reforms

CORRADO MACCHIARELLI, VASSILIS MONASTIRIOTIS AND NIKOLITSA LAMPROPOULOU

8.1 Introduction

This chapter provides an update on labour market transitions in the European Union (EU) since the financial crisis, offering an examination of the EU-Labour Force Survey (EU-LFS). We compare for some indicators the results before the crisis, also building on the existing precrisis results in Ward-Warmedinger and Macchiarelli (2014), in order to get insights on how well European economies have recovered from the crisis and whether, and to what extent, their labour markets have reached their precrisis fluidity. In particular, we analyse year-on-year labour market transitions and their evolution over the years 2004–2016, across three key labour market statuses (employment, unemployment and inactivity), providing aggregate breakdowns by country, age groups, gender and the individual's level of education based on the EU-LFS. Following this, we use country-specific measures of transition rates and a synthetic index of mobility (between labour market statuses) in order to draw comparisons across countries and over time. For the discussion and further analysis of the results, we complement these data with qualitative and macroquantitative information about the different countries of the EU, allowing us to split the countries into different groupings corresponding to different social systems, and we cross the information with structural indicators (employment protection legislation [EPL], product market regulation [PMR], use of part-time contracts, unemployment benefits, out-of-work maintenance schemes and employment incentives). This allows us to analyse aggregate labour market changes (changes in participation, unemployment and inactivity rates) to offer an overview of labour market trends by country and for the EU as a whole, as well as to draw conclusions about the functioning of labour markets in Europe with regard to their flexibility (speed/extent of transitions and extent of mobility/churn) and how this evolved over time since the crisis.

We show that all EU countries, which we classify as Mediterranean, Continental, Central Eastern and Nordic, exhibit a high degree of employment persistence and persistence of inactivity (out of the labour force), which show little cyclicality. The dynamics concerning unemployment duration, however, appear more varied. Our evidence shows that unemployment duration is by far lowest in the Nordic countries and highest, postcrisis, in the Mediterranean countries. Unemployment persistence increased with the crisis everywhere and, with the exception of the Central and Eastern European countries, it continued to rise also after 2012.

Overall, our results sketch a picture of significant country heterogeneity in the intensity and direction of the labour market transitions across the EU. As expected, the crisis did have an impact on labour market transitions and employment/unemployment persistence, but in most cases, the effect of the crisis was smaller than the size of country differences observed in any one period (precrisis, during the crisis and postcrisis). Countries known for their institutional rigidities in the labour market, such as those of the Mediterranean, have been found to have less favourable labour market flows and higher unemployment duration. At the same time, we found no evidence that this links directly to the degree of employment protection, the main labour market institution associated with labour market rigidity. Instead, part-time employment seems to have played (even if rather marginally) a positive role for containing unemployment persistence, while product market regulations appear as a much more significant influence on adverse labour market flexibility. In any case, and despite the relative recovery of the European economies postcrisis, we conclude that the degree of labour market flexibility has not fully recovered to precrisis levels.

8.2 Relevant Literature

The contribution of flows into and out of unemployment to the cyclicality of unemployment has attracted a great deal of attention in the analysis of labour market dynamics since the crisis (Shimer, 2012). Recent articles have mainly found a relatively equal contribution of inflows and outflows to the unemployment stock (Elsby et al., 2009; Fujita and Ramey, 2009). Elsby et al. (2009) questioned the validity of the assumption of the usual steady-state decomposition for unemployment that forms the basis of a number of theoretical models. In particular, they calculated the relative contributions to unemployment using a neat decomposition based on the identity describing the dynamics of unemployment in which inflow and outflow rates are separable. In the same vein, Kilponen and Vanhala (2009) argued that European countries generally have low unemployment inflow and outflow rates, which contributed to high rates and unemployment persistence. Petrongolo and Pissarides (2008) identified the relative role of inflow and outflow rate from unemployment in explaining labour market dynamics, and concluded that the relative contribution of each depends on labour market institutions. Finally, Brandolini et al. (2006) emphasised the need to acknowledge the group of nonparticipants (or *potentially* unemployed) when looking at labour market dynamics; accordingly, the distinction provided for by the International Labour Organisation (ILO) definition of unemployment is only 'artificial', and indeed nonparticipants and unemployed do not differ substantially in their job search activity.[1]

Fujita and Ramey (2009), as well as Fujita (2011), find evidence for differences in the timing of these effects, with the effect of the inflow rate being more prevalent during the early phase of a recession, and the effect of the outflow rate being more important in the middle of a downturn.

Yet these studies have generally focused on the US labour market and relied on aggregate data, thus neglecting potential composition effects, i.e., differences in the sociodemographic structure of the employed and unemployed. An exception to this is the recent study by Daouli et al. (2015) for Greece, which has found that the cyclicality in the relative importance of inflows and outflows over the business

[1] While this is beyond the scope of this chapter, one could break down the inactivity further. For example, one could single out the group of marginally attached workers (those willing to work but not actively looking for a job). In general, this group is more attached to the labour market than others. This should be reflected in their transition rates. Some recent work on the issue using the Hornstein–Kudlyak–Lange Non-Employment Index is available in the Labour Market and Wage Developments in Europe Annual Report (LMWD, 2017). Source : https://publications.europa.eu/en/publication-detail/-/publication/2df2eaca-b3b0–11e7–837e-01aa75ed71a1/language-en.

cycle varies with individual-level heterogeneity. For example, although the unemployment inflows in Greece are a phenomenon that mostly concerns female workers, in the post-2008 period the relative position of male workers has worsened. On the other hand, although the unemployment outflows are a phenomenon that concerns primarily male unemployed individuals, in the post-2008 period the relative position of females has improved. Moreover, younger workers face increased risk of moving from employment to unemployment both in the precrisis and the crisis periods, while the relative risk for younger (fifteen to twenty-four) and older (forty-five to fifty-four) workers has increased in the crisis years.

Regarding the effect of institutional factors on mobility, a number of papers have focussed on establishing the persistence of unemployment and its duration using longitudinal data (Boeri and Garibaldi, 2009; Brandolini et al., 2006; Petrongolo and Pissarides, 2008, for Europe; Elsby et al., 2009; Kilponen and Vanhala, 2009, for OECD countries).[2] These papers document an overall increase in labour market mobility during the last two decades before the crisis, with differences in the extent of mobility across countries being attributed to institutional factors such as labour and product market regulation, active labour market policies and union density.

Boeri and Garibaldi (2009) asked, for instance, why the decrease in unemployment does not show up as increased satisfaction in the labour market, attributed to the increased risk of job loss as the result of higher labour market turnovers (see also Green, 2010). The effect of EPL on labour market turnover, especially among young people, is analysed in Gangl (2003), whereas, Nicoletti and Scarpetta (2000) look at the effect of EPL and PMR on employment at large. Boeri et al. (2000), find a 'potentially' significant impact of EPL and PMR on labour market outcomes and structure. Nickell and Layard (1999), focussing on the link between labour market institutions and economic performance, equally conclude that policy should be focussed on encouraging product market competition, as a way to 'eliminate the negative effects of unions'. Other papers have analysed the effect of institutions on EU labour market efficiency on the whole, as measured by employment (Kruppe et al., 1998; see also Siebert, 1997) or,

[2] See, among other things, Fujita and Ramey (2006); Shimer (2005; 2012) for the United States.

indirectly, through the effects of unemployment benefits and employment protection legislation in the provision of insurance against labour market risk (see Boeri et al., 2003). The remaining pertinent literature has also focussed on the effect of currency union on labour market reforms in Europe, within this framework, highlighting how structural reforms motives are strengthened by high unemployment (see Duval and Elmeskov, 2006).

Despite this broad literature, comprehensive analyses of labour market transitions across the EU member states are limited, and thus also limited is the evidence base concerning the cyclicality of these transitions (especially in relation to the recent crisis), the possible differences in transition dynamics across countries and country groups and, ultimately, their link to labour market flexibility and their contribution to attaining high levels of employment and employment participation. In this chapter, we examine these issues through an extensive analysis of available data from the EU LFS. Drawing on this, we perform a microdata-based analysis of the labour market transitions in a large number of European countries and investigate how these transitions have been affected by the recent financial and economic crisis, by providing an assessment of labour market transitions at the precrisis plateau (2004–2008), during the crisis' early phase and in the crisis' peak (2009–2013) and ensuing recovery (2014–2016) (see Figure 8.1 in the next section).

A focus on the behaviour of labour market transitions around periods in which actual unemployment has risen or fallen sharply may inform on the factors behind shifting mobility flows, as well as other factors contributing to periods of prolonged economic slowdown and/or unemployment persistence (i.e., *hysteresis*). The results can also have implications for the active labour market policies' effectiveness, 'not least in the context of current economic conditions' and the radical structural reforms taking place, particularly in some countries (see Ward-Warmedinger and Macchiarelli, 2014).

8.3 Data and Methods

In our exercise, we use the EU-LFS for the purpose of analysing trends in key labour market indicators and in flows/transitions across the three key labour market statuses of employment, unemployment and inactivity. For these analyses, following common practice we use the annual files of the survey, relying on retrospective questions about each individual's labour market status one year ago. Our sample consists of individuals in their working age (aged fifteen to sixty-four).[3] For the discussion and further analysis of the results, we complement these data with qualitative and macroquantitative information from the OECD about the different countries of the EU, allowing us to split the countries into different groupings corresponding to different social systems.

Data quality and availability issues necessitate that some countries are excluded from parts of the analysis: this is both for sample-size reasons (e.g., Luxemburg), data coverage issues (e.g., data for Malta become available from 2009 onwards), and data availability issues (e.g., some variables are not recorded for countries such as Germany, the United Kingdom and Ireland).

In light of these limitations, the United Kingdom, Germany (DE), and Ireland (IE) are excluded from the analysis owing to a lack of data.[4] The remaining countries are grouped as follows:

Central Eastern, including Bulgaria (BG), Croatia (HR), Czech Republic (CZ), Estonia (EE), Hungary (HU), Latvia (LV), Lithuania (LT), Poland (PL), Romania (RO), Slovakia (SK) and Slovenia (SI)

Nordics, including Denmark (DK), Finland (FI), the Netherlands (NL) and Sweden (SE)

Continental, including Austria (AT), Belgium (BE), France (FR) and Luxemburg (LU)

Mediterranean, including Cyprus (CY), Greece (GR), Italy (IT), Malta (MT), Portugal (PT) and Spain (ES).

[3] Evidently, this demographic includes people with very different intensities of labour market attachment. For example, people in the fifty-five+ age group may have options for early retirement schemes; while those under twenty-five may withdraw from the labour market for educational reasons. We examine this issue of differentiation of transitions on the basis of age (as well as other individual characteristics such as gender and levels of education) later.

[4] Due to missing data, some countries are also excluded when computing aggregated results. Based on the LFS, data are not available for Germany, the United Kingdom and Ireland on the overall sample, for France, Austria and Spain for the 2004–2005 period, for Sweden for the 2004–2006 period, for Bulgaria and Netherlands for the 2004–2007 period and for Malta for the 2004–2008 period.

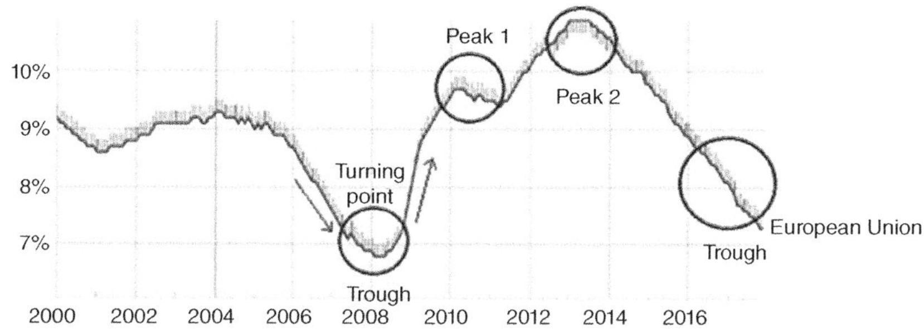

Figure 8.1 The Unemployment rate in the EU.
Source: Eurostat data

This grouping clusters countries according to social policy models,[5] drawing on the definition of Boeri (2002), Sapir (2006) and Ward-Warmedinger and Macchiarelli (2014).[6]

Our analysis covers the period from prior to the crisis (2004–2008) and up to 2016. For much of the analysis, we focus on three subperiods, i.e., 2004–2008, 2009–2013 and 2014–2016. In doing so, we update the work of Ward-Warmedinger and Macchiarelli (2014), who analyse labour market transitions in the EU for the ten years preceding the Great Recession (1998–2008). Looking at 2004–2008 as a reference precrisis period is motivated by the idea that the slack in real economic activity affected the EU labour markets with some lag, with the worsening of unemployment figures mainly starting from 2009; this is the case since the impact on the labour market is typically perceived on average later than the shock in real activity (e.g., GDP; see NBER, 2008). The subperiods we derive are consistent with the peak-trough dates (i.e., turning points) we obtain by using a simple dating procedure on the EU individual unemployment rate series (Table 8.1A). In choosing the dates of business-cycle turning points, we follow standard procedures and chronologically identify the dates of peaks and troughs that frame economic recession or expansion. For instance, the period from a peak to a trough is a recession, and the period from a trough to a peak is an expansion (see Figure 8.1).

[5] Country weighting in each country grouping is based on the gross domestic product (GDP) share of each country over the total for each group.

[6] The latter definition differs from the one used in Ward-Warmedinger and Macchiarelli (2014) in that it does not classify countries according to euro area membership or not.

From the EU-LFS, we construct raw probabilities of moving or remaining in any labour market status, together with an index of mobility (Shorrocks, 1978). Particularly, we consider nine possible transition probabilities across the statuses of employment, unemployment and out of the labour market (inactivity). The (ex-post) probability of remaining in any particular labour market status is defined on the basis of the number of individuals being in that particular status *A* in both years (*t*) and (*t* + *1*), as a percentage of the number of individuals in the same status *A* in the year (*t*). Conversely, the probability of moving from one labour market status to another is defined as the ratio of the probability of remaining in any labour market status *A*, as defined previously, over the probability of an individual in status *B* in period (*t*) turning to status *A* in the period (*t* + *1*).

More formally, the probability of moving across $n = 3$ labour market statuses between year (*t*) and year (*t* + *1*) is a (3 *x* 3) matrix in which each individual element (P_t^{AB}) records the transition probability, with *A*, *B* = employment (*E*), unemployment (*U*), or inactivity (*I*):

$$P_t^{AB} = Pr\{S_{t+1} = B \mid S_t = A\} = \frac{AB_{t,t+1}}{A_t} \tag{8.1}$$

The probability of a transition from an origin state *A* to a destination state *B* is given by the number of workers making that transition over a given period, divided by the stock of individuals in the origin state at the start of that period. For example, if we denote the number of employed workers *E* in a given year (*t*) who are unemployed *U* in the subsequent year (*t* + *1*) by EU_t, the associated transition rate equals the following:

$$P_t^{EU} = \frac{EU_{t,t+1}}{E_t} \tag{8.2}$$

Based on the decomposition outlined before, we finally construct, for each country (*j*), a measure of mobility using Shorrocks' (1978) mobility index, which is defined as follows:

$$M_{jt} = \frac{\left[n - trace\left(P_{jt}^{AB}\right)\right]}{n - 1} \tag{8.3}$$

where *n* is the number of states (in this case, employment, unemployment and inactivity) and *trace* is the trace of a three-by-three square transition matrix P defined to be the sum of the elements on the main diagonal. By definition, the mobility index is bounded between [0,1], where a value of zero implies no probability of leaving any labour market status and a value of one implies full mobility.

At this stage, it should be noted that flows from and into the labour market are very different between them. In fact, people moving from inactivity to unemployment are different from people moving from inactivity to employment, as the former reenter the labour market but do not find a job immediately. In this vein, distinguishing between flows into and out of inactivity can be retained in the probability of *successfully* reentering the labour market (Theeuwes et al., 1990; Ward-Warmedinger and Macchiarelli, 2014). The latter is defined as

$$SL_{jt} = \frac{P_{jt}^{IE}}{P_{jt}^{IE} + P_{jt}^{IU}} \tag{8.4}$$

which is the percentage of people *successfully* entering the labour market (P_{jt}^{IE}), i.e., flows from inactivity to employment, as a percentage of the number of people entering the labour market as a whole.

Analogously, we note how people leaving unemployment to get back into employment are different from those who, once separated from their job, stop searching for a new one (i.e., they move from unemployment into inactivity). Thus, *unsuccessful* unemployment exits are computed as (see also Ward-Warmedinger and Macchiarelli, 2014):

$$FL_{jt} = \frac{P_{jt}^{UI}}{P_{jt}^{UI} + P_{jt}^{UE}} \tag{8.5}$$

which is the percentage of people withdrawing from the labour market, as a percentage of people generally leaving unemployment (moving either back into employment or inactivity).[7]

The deriving country- and period-specific measures of mobility and/or labour market transitions are subsequently depicted visually with the use of graphs and tables, allowing us to present in a comparative way both changes over time within countries and cross-country differences/heterogeneity in a static sense. Finally, we draw on the country

[7] It should be noted, however, that *unsuccessful* labour market outcomes may not represent labour market withdrawals per se, as flows into inactivity also capture shifts into retirement or education.

distinctions described earlier to draw conclusions about how the observed patterns (both static and dynamic) may link to specific institutional or other characteristics on the national political economies of the EU.

8.4 Empirical Results

8.4.1 Transition Probabilities and Labour Market Exits/Entries

Table 8.1 provides a snapshot of average transition probabilities, over time and across countries, between the three core labour market statuses during the period 2004–2016 for all country groupings and for the three subperiods considered.

Starting with the information concerning stability (diagonal elements), the table shows that the (weighted) average probability of being employed in year *t-1* and year *t* is quite high and broadly similar across country groups: 94 per cent on average in Central Eastern countries; around 93 per cent in Continental and Mediterranean countries; and around 89 per cent in Nordic countries. Importantly, this probability seems to change little over time (e.g., during/after the crisis). While this is in part an issue of scale (even in deep crisis, most people remain in employment), it also clearly suggests that much of the unemployment movement during the crisis period had to do with other types of labour market flows, such as transitions from unemployment to employment (declining job-finding rates) and transitions from inactivity to unemployment (the so-called added worker effect). As we shall explain later, this seems to be only marginally explained by the use of part-time contracts.[8] In turn, the probability of remaining unemployed shows much more variation (and is of course lower): it is around 66 per cent in Central Eastern European countries; around 62 per cent in

[8] While it is tempting to interpret this as the probability of *remaining* employed in two consecutive periods, also looking at the role of part-time contracts and contract with no minimum hours guaranteed (the so-called zero hour contracts), we note that the data used here provide information only for the start and end of each annual period considered. As a result, while we know for an individual with EE status that they were employed at the time of the survey in year *t* and one year before in *t-1*, we do not know whether that individual was employed for this entire period. It is possible – especially in labour markets with high prevalence of seasonal employment and short-term contracts – that an individual may switch labour market status (even several times) over a year.

Table 8.1 *Transition probabilities.*

			Labour market status year t											
			Central Eastern			Nordics			Continental			Mediterranean		
Labour market status	Year *t-1*	*2004–2008*	E	U	I	E	U	I	E	U	I	E	U	I
		E	0.936	0.028	0.036	0.898	0.016	0.086	0.933	0.033	0.034	0.936	0.032	0.032
		U	0.282	0.624	0.094	0.211	0.318	0.471	0.321	0.597	0.083	0.314	0.588	0.098
		I	0.045	0.021	0.934	0.102	0.020	0.878	0.038	0.013	0.949	0.035	0.025	0.940
		2009–2013	E	U	I	E	U	I	E	U	I	E	U	I
		E	0.927	0.037	0.036	0.893	0.027	0.081	0.923	0.041	0.035	0.914	0.054	0.031
		U	0.252	0.697	0.051	0.375	0.356	0.269	0.308	0.594	0.097	0.214	0.704	0.082
		I	0.032	0.017	0.952	0.094	0.028	0.878	0.044	0.021	0.936	0.024	0.031	0.945
		2014–2016	E	U	I	E	U	I	E	U	I	E	U	I
		E	0.945	0.024	0.031	0.888	0.032	0.079	0.920	0.043	0.037	0.930	0.044	0.026
		U	0.280	0.666	0.054	0.345	0.430	0.226	0.280	0.639	0.080	0.208	0.712	0.080
		I	0.031	0.014	0.954	0.109	0.037	0.855	0.040	0.020	0.940	0.021	0.031	0.948

Note: E = employed; U = unemployed; I = inactive so that EE = remains in employment between one year and the next; UU = remains in unemployment, II = remains in inactivity. Observations are weighted according to the GDP share in each country over the group aggregate. Elements showing a probability of remaining in the same labour market state (employment, unemployment and inactivity) are in bold.
Sources: EU-LFS microdata, authors' computations.

Continental countries; but sizeably lower at around 37 per cent in the Nordic countries; and much higher in the Mediterranean countries (over 70 per cent in the post-2009 years).[9] By comparison, the probability of remaining inactive is much higher across country groups – typically at between 94–95 per cent in the Central Eastern, Continental and Mediterranean countries, and at slightly below 90 per cent in the Nordic countries.

Concerning the transition dynamics (off-diagonal elements), we also observed some differences across groups. From Table 8.1, the probability of moving from unemployment to employment is lowest in the Mediterranean countries, especially during and after the crisis; it is around 25–30 per cent in the Central Eastern European and Continental countries; and it is sizeably higher, at 35 per cent postcrisis, in the Nordic countries. In the Central Eastern, Mediterranean and Continental countries, this probability is much lower than the probability of remaining in unemployment, compared to Nordic countries. In the case of Nordic EU countries, the picture is consistent with relatively fast hiring and firing dynamics, compared to other EU social models. Inversely, the probability of transition from unemployment to inactivity is much higher in the Nordic countries (between 22 per cent and 47 per cent – compared to below 10 per cent in all other groups).[10]

Comparisons of labour transition probabilities over time show that in the Central Eastern, Nordic and Mediterranean countries the number of people remaining in unemployment has increased between the crisis (2009–2013) and the precrisis (2004–2008) periods, whereas it has remained broadly stable in Continental countries (Table 8.1).[11] For Nordic countries, of those individuals unemployed in period *t-1*, the percentage remaining unemployed in period *t* increased from

[9] Those results are broadly consistent with Ward-Warmedinger and Macchiarelli (2014), where it is shown that the probability of remaining in unemployment is about 40 per cent in both Denmark and Sweden.

[10] It is possible that these differences reflect institutional differences in the process of retirement. Examining these in detail is, however, beyond the scope of the present analysis.

[11] The probability of remaining in unemployment has increased in Czech Republic, Hungary, Poland, Romania and Slovakia over the last decade, but has fallen in the Baltic countries (Estonia, Latvia and Lithuania). In Latvia and Lithuania, the fall in the probability of remaining in unemployment was accompanied by a higher probability of transiting from unemployment to inactivity over time, while for Estonia this probability remained roughly similar across time.

32 per cent to 36 per cent between the precrisis and the crisis periods. For Central Eastern countries, the same number increased instead from 62 per cent to 70 per cent.[12] The same number increased in Mediterranean countries, from 59 per cent to 70 per cent. By contrast, the probability of remaining inactive increased over the crisis period in Central Eastern countries, while it remained broadly stable in Mediterranean and Nordic countries. It decreased slightly in Continental countries.

Finally, the probability of remaining in employment decreased in all country groups. However, there are again differences in the scale of the decline: measured in terms of percentage points, the decline in the Mediterranean countries is twice as large as in the Central Eastern and Continental countries and four times as large as in the Nordic countries. In all cases, the size of the observed changes is lower than the observed rise in unemployment, reflecting the fact that – despite the existence of a significant number of layoffs – the main part of the unemployment increase is accounted for by a sharp reduction in hiring rates (rise in unemployment persistence) and secondarily from an increase in flows from inactivity into unemployment (added worker effect).

Looking at the percentage of people entering successfully the labour market (*successful labour market entries*) – which are transitions from inactivity to employment as a share of the sum of transitions out of inactivity – we find that this percentage has decreased in Central Eastern countries (from 68 per cent to 65 per cent), the Nordics (from 83 per cent to 77 per cent), Continental and Mediterranean countries (from 74 per cent to 68 per cent and from 58 per cent to 43 per cent, respectively) over the crisis period (see Table 8.2). At the same time, however, the percentage of *unsuccessful unemployment exits* – i.e., the percentage of people transitioning from unemployment to inactivity as a share of all transitions out of unemployment – has strongly decreased in Central Eastern countries (from 25 per cent to 17 per cent) as well as in the Nordic countries, whereas it has increased in all other countries, particularly in the Continental European countries (by about 3.5 percentage points [p.p.]), with the strongest increase recorded in Mediterranean countries (about 4 p.p.).

[12] Macchiarelli and Ward-Warmedinger (2014) discuss how changes in the institutional arrangements and labour market composition (also in the light of labour market migration to Western Europe stemming from the EU accession in 2004) have contributed to this high number precrisis.

Table 8.2 *Successful and unsuccessful labour market outcomes.*

	Central Eastern	Nordics	Continental	Mediterranean
		Successful labour market entries		
2004–2008	0.683	0.836	0.741	0.580
2009–2013	0.653	0.769	0.677	0.433
2014–2016	0.687	0.748	0.670	0.411
		Unsuccessful unemployment exits		
2004–2008	0.250	0.691	0.205	0.237
2009–2013	0.168	0.418	0.240	0.275
2014–2016	0.162	0.395	0.223	0.278

Note: Following Theeuwes et al. (1990) a successful labour market entry is computed as the percentage of people *successfully* entering the labour market as a percentage of the total number of people entering the labour market. Analogously, an unsuccessful unemployment exit is the percentage of people withdrawing from the labour market, as a percentage of people leaving unemployment (see also Ward-Warmedinger and Macchiarelli, 2014).
Sources: EU-LFS microdata, authors' computations.

Over the 2014–2016 period, the probability of successfully entering the labour market returned to crisis levels only in Central Eastern European countries and in the Nordic countries (excluding the Netherlands). The same probability has remained broadly stable in Continental Europe, whereas it worsened further in the Mediterranean countries. Unsuccessful unemployment exits have nevertheless decreased in the Nordic and Continental EU countries, whereas they remained broadly stable in the Central Eastern and Mediterranean countries. In Mediterranean countries, in particular, while the probability of leaving the labour market has not changed much since the crisis, the likelihood for a person from outside the labour market to join employment has decreased. All in all, the 2014–2016 can hardly be dubbed 'recovery' for some countries as those years have not necessarily yet determined an inversion of the crisis' trend, with countries being far away from the levels of successful and unsuccessful labour market outcomes observed before the crisis.

8.4.2 Changes across Periods

Turning to changes between the crisis period (2009–2013) and the last part of the sample (2014–2016), the transitions show lower unemployment persistence in Central Eastern EU countries. The remaining countries display higher unemployment persistence. Looking at the peak-to-trough transitions based on the results in Table 8.1A, we are able to identify some clear developments across the selected Mediterranean and Central Eastern countries, with much of the variation being evident in the probability to remain unemployed over time (see Figure 8.2). Those countries show large peak-to-trough movements in unemployment persistence.[13]

During the period 2014–2016, the probability to remain in inactivity has not changed significantly in any of the country groupings, apart from the Nordic countries. The probability to remain in employment has increased noticeably only in Central Eastern countries, and to a lesser extent in Mediterranean countries.

Turning to the transitions between different labour market statuses in Figure 8.3 (calculated as the difference between the weighted average transition for a country grouping/subperiod, compared to the previous subperiod), unemployment-to-employment flows have increased by about 15 percentage points over the crisis in Nordic European countries, while they declined by 3 p.p. in Central Eastern countries and more strongly in Mediterranean countries.[14] Flows in the opposite direction (i.e., employment to unemployment) have increased by 3 p.p. in Mediterranean countries, while they remained broadly stable in all remaining countries.

The figures also show that changes from unemployment to inactivity have overall not changed as much since 2014 in Continental and Mediterranean countries, whereas they decreased in Central Eastern countries (by 4.5 p.p.) and in the Nordics (by almost 20 p.p.). Finally, Figure 8.3 suggests that transitions from inactivity into employment have remained broadly constant in all countries. Turning to the 2014–2016 period, the transitions from unemployment to inactivity have decreased in Nordic countries and, to a lesser extent, in Continental countries.

[13] The remainder of the results are available upon request from the authors.

[14] Country-specific results point to the fact that flows from employment to unemployment or inactivity do not vary much across countries, whereas movements from unemployment to employment or inactivity as well as transitions from inactivity to employment show more pronounced cross-country variation.

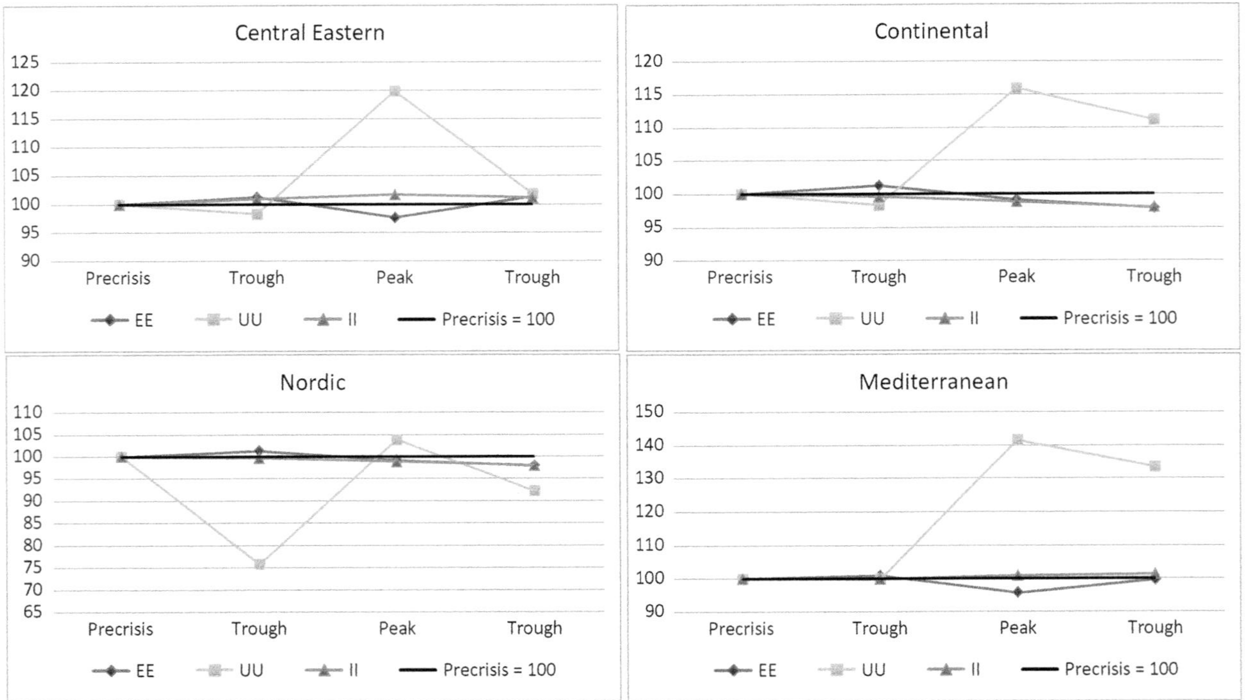

Figure 8.2 Changes in the persistence of employment, unemployment and inactivity.

Sources: EU-LFS microdata, authors' computations. The changes in the persistence of employment, unemployment and inactivity in the graphs are based on unweighted country pooling.

a) Crisis (2009–2013) minus precrisis (2004–2008)

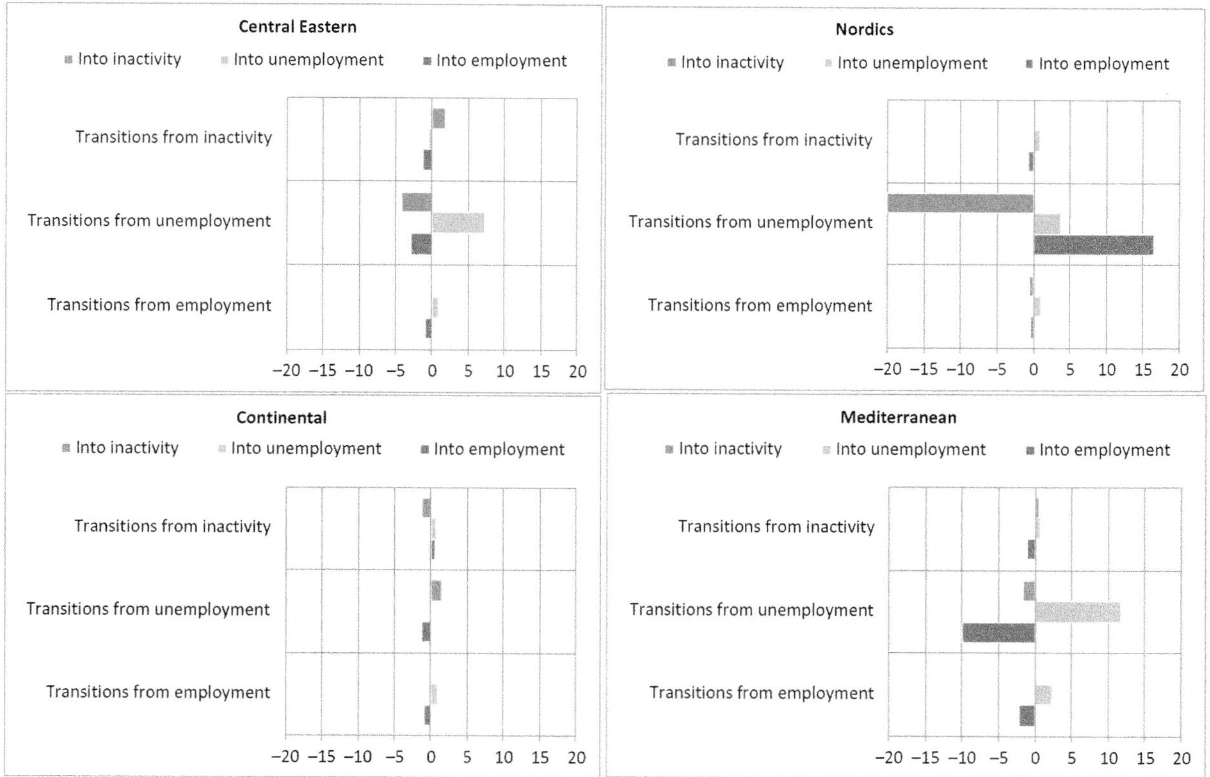

Figure 8.3 Changes in transition probabilities over time.
Sources: EU-LFS microdata, authors' computations.

b) Recovery (2014–2016) minus crisis (2009–2013)

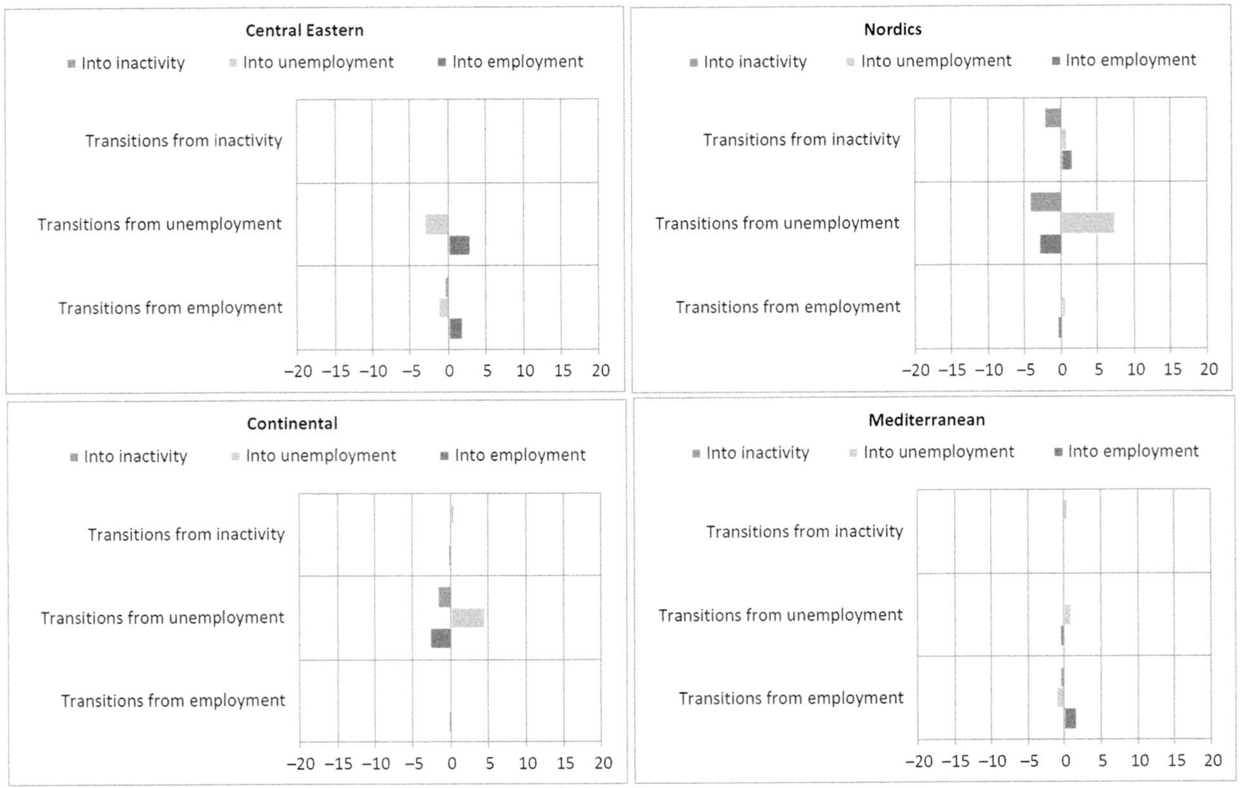

Figure 8.3(*cont.*)

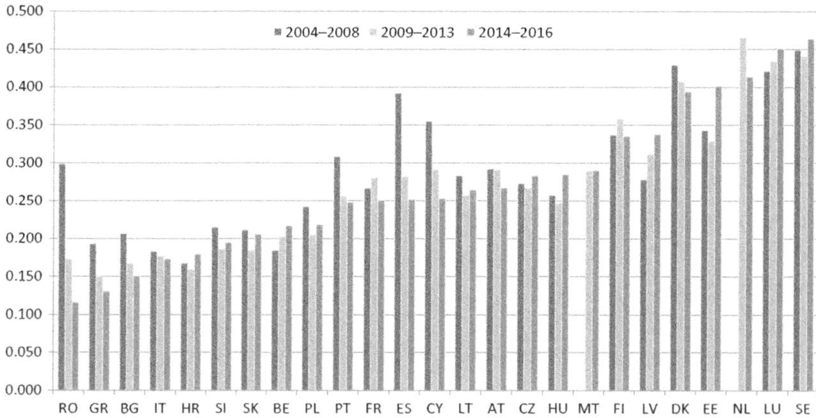

Figure 8.4 Mobility index in the EU.
Sources: LFS microdata, authors' computations.

8.4.3 Labour Mobility and Worker Heterogeneity

Figure 8.4 provides a summary measure (the Shorrocks' index explained earlier, see Equation (8.3)) of labour market mobility. Importantly, the index summarises the extent of the transitions between different economic activity statuses (employment, unemployment and inactivity).[15]

The mobility index reflects an increase in labour market churning over the crisis period in Nordic and Continental countries. On the contrary, the Shorrocks' summary index for the period 2009–2013 reveals a decrease in labour market mobility compared to the precrisis period both in the Mediterranean and the Central Eastern European countries. The drop in mobility since the crisis may suggest a less efficient matching of individuals with jobs, as evidenced by the increase in the probability to remain in unemployment.[16] For Mediterranean

[15] As summarised before, the Shorrocks' index is a proxy index for mobility. For example, with respect to the results in Tables 8.2 and 8.3, the decrease in state persistence over time (i.e., the reduction of the elements on the main diagonal from 1998–2003 to 2004–2008) implies an increase in the mobility index across the two subperiods.

[16] Mobility clearly depends on the level of unemployment. In a country with high employment, you would also expect low mobility between states (as those not in employment are probably those with the least attractive characteristics). This interpretation is different for a country with low employment as it could point to

countries, a lower mobility over time analogously reflects an increase in the likelihood to remain unemployed over time. In the Nordic and Continental countries, mobility increased over the crisis period, essentially as the result of a fall in the probability of remaining in employment, unemployment and inactivity overall.[17]

Looking at the results in Figure 8.4, labour markets in Estonia, Luxembourg, the Netherlands and Spain, together with Denmark, Finland and Sweden, are more flexible on average. For the latter mobility is twice as high relative to Belgium, Bulgaria, Croatia, Greece, Hungary, Italy, Latvia, Poland, the Slovak Republic and Slovenia. A group of countries reporting intermediate mobility is represented instead by Austria, Cyprus, the Czech Republic, Finland, France, Lithuania and Portugal. Cyprus, Romania and Spain recorded the highest drops in mobility since the crisis.

The mobility index also confirms that, in Continental countries, mobility was particularly high for people under fifty-four and highly educated people, and has overall increased over the crisis, as the result of a lower likelihood to remain in employment, unemployment and inactivity.

From Figure 8.5, in Nordic countries, people between the ages of sixteen and twenty-four are the most mobile on average, albeit their mobility has decreased over time, particularly during the crisis. Such behaviour is always driven by a lower probability of remaining in employment, unemployment and inactivity compared to Continental and Mediterranean countries (see Table 8.2A Annex).

In Nordic countries, highly educated individuals generally display both a higher probability of remaining in employment and a lower probability of remaining in unemployment and inactivity over time, while female workers display a lower probability of remaining in both employment and unemployment over time (Table 8.2A).[18]

rigidities or disincentives to work. Note also that high transitions should not necessarily be good as in a highly segmented labour market dominated by short-term contracts, as this may mean that individuals regularly switch between employment and unemployment (e.g., Spain or France).

17 In Figure 8.1A (Annex), we decompose the changes in the overall mobility index by country groupings through the contribution of mobility by individual characteristics.

18 It should be noted, however, that successful exits of females from unemployment into employment are typically lower than those of males. This is because females also have a higher probability of moving from unemployment into inactivity compared to males.

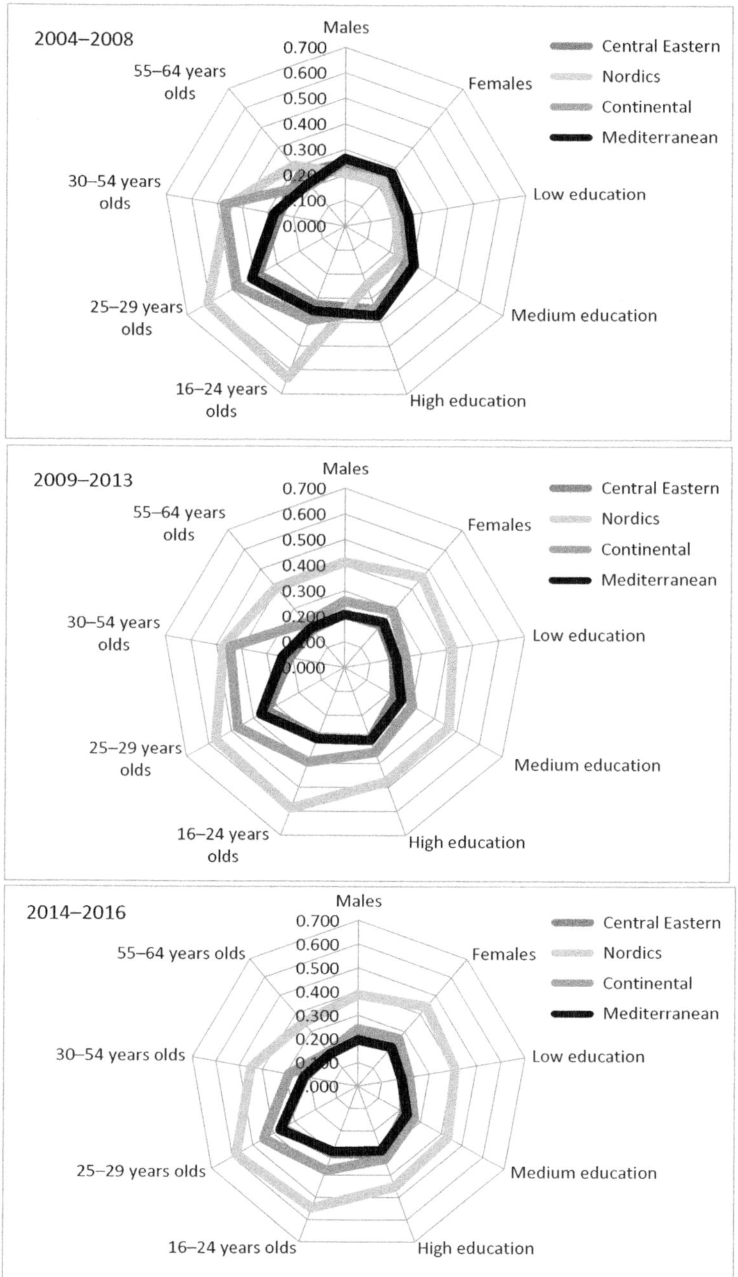

Figure 8.5 Mobility index by worker group.
Sources: LFS microdata, authors' computations

In Central Eastern European countries, mobility is higher for females, highly educated people and workers between the ages of twenty-five and twenty-nine, though this pattern has overall decreased over time. In these countries, the higher mobility of women is driven by a lower probability of remaining in employment and unemployment over time. Highly educated individuals in the Central Eastern EU countries are more mobile through a lower probability over time of remaining in inactivity and unemployment.

Figure 8.5 also shows that on average highly educated individuals and people between the ages of twenty-five and twenty-nine are the most mobile across labour market statuses. Moreover, while for Denmark, Sweden, and the Continental and Mediterranean countries, mobility of all worker groups has increased over the last decade (particularly for females), there is no clear pattern for the disaggregated Central Eastern European countries (Table 8.2A).

The mobility index by worker groups suggests an overall increase of mobility in the Nordics since the crisis but not elsewhere (Figure 8.5). Although examining this in much depth is beyond the scope of this analysis, we can deduct from our previous analysis that this is probably related to the increase in flows from employment into unemployment as well as from inactivity into both unemployment and employment.

8.6 The Role of Reforms

Disaggregating the labour market patterns on the basis of individual and country characteristics revealed that individual heterogeneity plays a role: national labour markets have developed differently during the crisis, with countries such as Greece, Italy, Portugal and Spain still displaying high unemployment rates of up to 21 per cent, and countries such as Austria, Germany, Luxembourg and the Netherlands denoting substantially lower rates, below 5 per cent, based on the Eurostat.

There is a consensus that the aim of reducing unemployment and increasing employment in Europe could be achieved through structural reforms at the level of the nation-state, i.e., reforms that contribute to removing barriers to the smooth and efficient functioning of product, capital and labour markets would help ensure the economic growth sustainability. Such reforms could also improve the efficiency and effectiveness of public finances' expenditure (Ilzkovitz and Dierx, 2011), as is also extensively discussed by the European Governance literature on the 'need for bribes' hypothesis (Mabett and Shelkle, 2007). The functioning of a regulated labour market depends on various factors, such as the model of the welfare state, the structure of the economy, the culture of a society, etc., the majority of which are idiosyncratic and tend to differ greatly from one country to another. The flexibility of the labour market and mobility of labour (both across sectors and jobs) are decisive factors for an economically wealthy and stable European labour market – but certainly not the only factors.

In the economics literature (Biroli et al., 2010; Boeri, 2005), the usual product market regulation and employment protection legislation indicators are used as measures of structural reforms in the product and labour markets. Based on these indicators among the Eurozone countries, product market regulation in 2008 was the strictest in Greece and Poland, while being relatively loose in Ireland and the United Kingdom. The process of product market liberalization between 2003 and 2008 was most rapid in new member states such as Hungary and Poland, but also in Spain. On the other hand, in Belgium, Luxemburg, the Nordic countries, Slovakia and the United Kingdom, the pace of product market liberalisation was relatively slow. Moreover, employment protection legislation in 2008 was relatively strict in southern euro area countries such as France, Greece, Portugal and Spain, while being looser in the United Kingdom, suggesting that, on average, the labour markets in countries with relatively strict product market regulation and employment protection legislation precrisis were relatively slower in recovering.

Looking at specific country cases unveils yet more heterogeneity. Reforms in Germany led to a recalibration of the country's labour market model, with elements of both the Anglo-Saxon model (less generous benefit systems and lower levels of protection against dismissal) and the model of 'flexicurity' (combining a fully developed social security system with labour market policies aimed at activating the unemployed and making the labour market more flexible). The so-called Hartz reforms also included greater liberalisation of flexible working arrangements such as the 'atypical' jobs, temporary employment, self-employment, part-time work and fixed-term employment contracts in order to increase the capacity of the labour market

(Eichhorst, 2013). In the course of the crisis, Greece also adopted significant labour market reforms aiming at reducing labour costs in order to boost its competitiveness and increase the ability of firms to adjust to shocks. These reforms included measures that made the wage bargaining system more decentralised, reduced employment protection for permanent employees by lowering firing costs, while the setting of the minimum wage was turned over to the government away from the social partners (Kosma et al., 2017). In the Spanish labour market, reforms have been oriented towards an increase in flexibility as well. Activation is the most recent instrument to be introduced into the Spanish labour market and seems to be following the European Employment Strategy, whereas passive policies have been progressively reduced. Empirical evidence shows that there is a strong tendency to increase the intensity of active labour market policies (ALMP). Spain and the rest of southern European countries show poor levels of ALMP expenditure, whereas Continental countries are leading the way (Ramon Ballester, 2005). Italy also undertook the Jobs Act reform in 2014–2015 in order to foster employment, simplify bureaucratic procedures for temporary contracts and turn Italian labour market institutions in the direction of flexicurity (keeping in mind the greater constraints on public expenditure). The reforms relaxed employment protection legislation for permanent contracts and reduced the use of atypical contracts, which are typically characterised by weak employment protection and low social benefits. According to the OECD indicators, Italy's employment protection legislation is less restrictive than in France and Germany. Moreover, the focus of passive policies shifted from job to worker protection, which facilitated the reallocation of workers to more productive occupations, together with unemployment insurance, the coverage of which was extended (Pinelli et al., 2017).

Milan et al. (2013) examined the impact of the employment protection legislation on hiring and firing decisions by the smallest firms (one to four employees) in the EU-15 countries. They found that the strictness of EPL is negatively related to the probability that employers take on new employees. On the other hand, they find that strict EPL lowers the number of job dismissals. In other words, although employees are better off in an environment of strict EPL (i.e., their rights are better protected), unemployed individuals may find it harder to find a job in such an environment as employers face higher rigidities, particularly whenever firms are forced to downsize due to external shocks. Although the authors cannot clearly conclude whether hiring or firing decisions dominate as a result of lower EPL, they conclude that lowering EPL is linked with higher labour turnover among the smallest of firms. Equally, Noelke (2016) analysed the effect of employment protection legislation on youth unemployment and employment rates in Western Europe over the period 1980–2008. In this case, EPL is differentiated between job security provisions and regulations on temporary contracts. The evidence shows that deregulating temporary contracts at high levels of job security provisions has significantly increased youth unemployment rates and decreased youth employment rates.

In what follows, we complement this discussion by looking at macroeconomic trends in mobility together with the evolution of structural indicators (EPL, PMR, etc.). Our objective is to understand whether part of the observed changes in mobility can be broadly explained by some 'macro' explanatory factors (see also Macchiarelli et al., 2018). This would also help explain what is behind such heterogeneity in mobility indexes and feeds into the discussion of the policy implications stemming from our findings. The mobility observed in some countries can be linked to the use of time-limited contracts and part-time work, and vice versa.

Looking at the simple cross-sectional correlations in Table 8.3 and Figure 8.6, we show that, broadly speaking, those countries where mobility increased over time are also those where the percentage of part-time work increased. The relationship is stronger post-2008. In addition, we find the usual negative relationship between the unemployment rate and mobility, with such a relationship remaining broadly stable before/after 2008. This suggests the fact that a high degree of labour market turnover is not necessarily benefitting labour markets, to the extent that those movements interact with shifts out of employment, and into unemployment and inactivity. Focussing on the structure indicators in Table 8.3, mobility does not seem to be related with the strictness of EPL, however measured (individual dismissal or temporary contracts). We find evidence instead of PMRs not being positively related to labour market turnovers, particularly precrisis.[19]

[19] PMR is a composite indicator produced by the OECD to measure the extent to which product market regulations (such as licensing) introduce rigidities to the

Table 8.3 *Unconditional correlations between mobility index and structure indicators.*

		Direct-job creation	Empl. incentives	EPL (individual dismissals)	EPL (temporary contracts)	Mobility index	Out-of-work maintenance schemes	PMR	Part-time contracts	Unempl.
2004 – 2008	Direct-job creation	1.000	–0.025	–0.270	0.568	0.000	0.406	–0.123	0.033	–0.030
	Employment incentives	–0.025	1.000	–0.083	0.173	**0.638**	0.478	–0.337	0.482	–0.239
	EPL (individual dismissals)	–0.270	–0.083	1.000	0.075	–0.021	-0.114	0.228	–0.236	–0.070
	EPL (temporary contracts)	0.569	0.173	0.075	1.000	0.115	0.384	0.053	0.316	–0.083
	Mobility index	0.000	**0.638**	–0.021	0.115	1.000	0.290	**–0.561**	0.263	**–0.416**
	Out-of-work maintenance	0.406	0.478	–0.114	0.384	0.290	1.000	–0.403	0.684	–0.219
	PMR	–0.123	–0.337	0.228	0.053	**–0.561**	–0.403	1.000	–0.445	0.631
	Part-time contracts	0.033	0.482	–0.236	0.316	0.263	0.684	–0.445	1.000	–0.381
	Unemployment	–0.030	–0.239	–0.070	–0.083	**–0.416**	–0.219	0.631	–0.381	1.000

2009 – 2013	Direct-job creation	1.000	−0.151	−0.264	0.061	0.067	0.030	−0.045	−0.077	−0.091
	Employment incentives	−0.151	1.000	−0.130	0.034	**0.457**	0.055	0.104	0.145	−0.159
	EPL (individual dismissals)	−0.264	−0.130	1.000	−0.182	0.020	0.047	−0.056	0.110	0.009
	EPL (temporary contracts)	0.061	0.034	−0.182	1.000	−0.162	0.336	0.272	−0.051	0.151
	Mobility index	0.067	**0.457**	0.020	-0.162	1.000	0.159	**-0.455**	**0.551**	**−0.415**
	Out-of-work maintenance	0.030	0.055	0.047	0.336	0.159	1.000	−0.310	0.493	0.215
	PMR	−0.045	0.104	−0.056	0.272	**−0.455**	−0.310	1.000	−0.614	0.404
	Part-time contracts	−0.077	0.145	0.110	−0.051	**0.551**	0.493	−0.614	1.000	−0.443
	Unemployment	−0.091	−0.159	0.009	0.151	**−0.415**	0.215	0.404	−0.443	1.000

Note: The panel is based on period averages which, based on the available data, includes AT, BE, BG, CY, CZ, DK, EE, ES, FI, FR, GR, HR, HU, IT, LT, LU, LV, MT, NL, PL, PT, RO, SE, SI and SK. Data after 2014 are not consistently available for all the indicators.
Sources: LFS microdata, authors' computations.

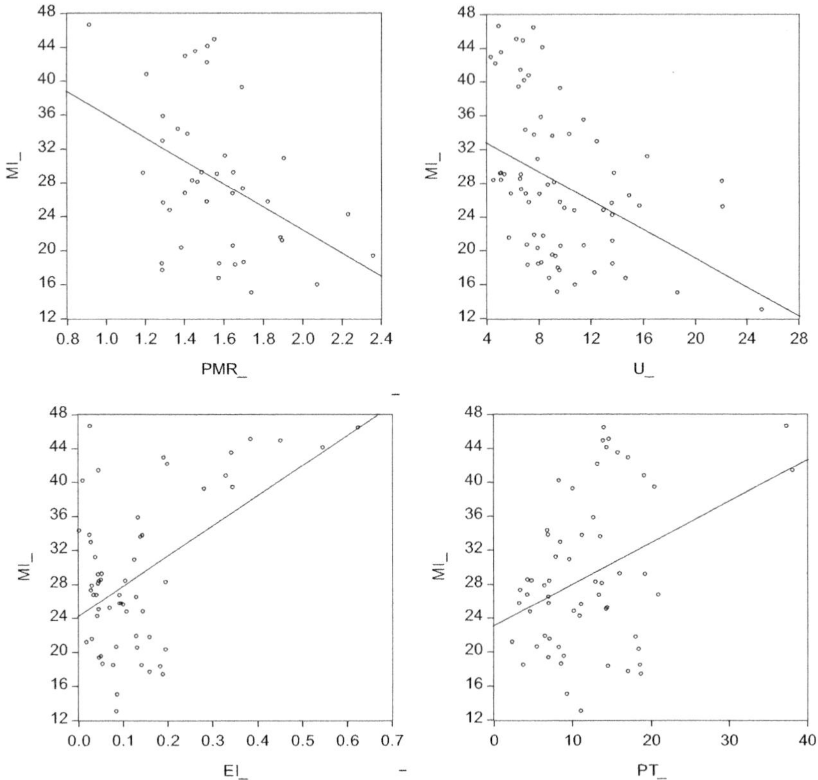

Figure 8.6 Cross-plot of mobility index and selected structure indicators.
Note: Product market regulation (PMR); unemployment (U); employment Incentives (EI); use of part-time contracts (PT).
Sources: LFS microdata, authors' computations

Some active labour market policies did not interact with mobility either, with the exception of employment incentives, which positively correlate with mobility indices across countries, a relationship that has weakened since 2009.

A note of caution is due. The results presented here present general associations between pairs of indicators (as they are based on unconditional cross-plots among indicators) and thus they should not be

economy (product market). There is wide evidence in the literature that often rigid product markets pose more constraints to economic adjustment and growth than rigidities observed in the labour market. Our results here are in line with this received wisdom.

taken as indicative of any causal links between, say, the structural indicators and the labour market transition measures. An analysis of the latter (causal links) would require econometric estimation of a structural model and a good identification strategy to unveil causality. Given a range of data limitations (short time horizon, lack of sufficient variation in some institutional indicators, high degree of collinearity between indexes), we consider this to be beyond the scope of this chapter. We note, however, that the patterns found in our correlation analysis generally survive in simple OLS regressions using subsets of the indicators considered here (results available upon request from the authors), and in any case they do reflect the general-equilibrium picture for the measures considered.

8.7 Conclusions

The frequencies at which individuals change their labour market status – and, inversely, the persistence of specific labour market outcomes at the individual level – give an indication of the flexibility of their labour market. Using individual-level microdata from the EU-LFS, this chapter analysed aggregate labour market transitions across the countries of the EU over 2004–2016, covering the period from before the eruption of the global financial crisis to the economic recovery past the Eurozone crisis. By comparing transition dynamics both across countries and country groups and over time, we were able to identify country differences in this degree of flexibility and to examine how the crisis episodes, associated to the global financial crisis and the Eurozone crisis, impacted the European labour markets.

Our analysis showed that all EU countries, across country groups, exhibit a high degree of employment persistence and persistence of inactivity, which show little cyclicality. The dynamics concerning unemployment persistence, however, as well as transitions from and into unemployment, appear more varied. Concerning unemployment persistence, our evidence shows that this is by far the lowest in the Nordic countries and highest, postcrisis, in the Mediterranean. Unemployment persistence increased with the crisis everywhere, and with the exception of the Central and Eastern European countries, it continued to rise also postcrisis. Transitions from employment to unemployment also increased with the crisis everywhere, with the trend recovering after the crisis in Central and Eastern Europe and the Mediterranean but continuing to rise elsewhere. In turn, successful labour market entries (defined as moves from inactivity into employment) and successful employment transitions (defined as moves from unemployment into employment) are highest in the Nordics and least favourable in the Mediterranean. Particularly for the latter group of countries, 2014–2016 can hardly be dubbed a period of 'recovery', as those years have not necessarily yet determined an inversion of the crisis' trend, with countries being far away from the levels of successful and unsuccessful labour market outcomes observed before the crisis.

Disaggregating these patterns on the basis of individual characteristics revealed that individual heterogeneity plays a role, with male and highly educated workers experiencing more favourable transitions from unemployment into employment on the whole (including during the crisis period), although this was stronger in some groups (e.g., Nordics) than others (e.g., the Mediterranean). Among all groups and periods, age seemed to be the main factor accounting for the largest differences in labour market transitions. Concerning the case of unemployment persistence, for example, this was found to be higher for young individuals (sixteen to twenty-four and twenty-five to twenty-nine years old) in the Nordics, well above any other category; more mature workers in the Continental countries (thirty to fifty-four years old); and the twenty-five to twenty-nine year olds in the Mediterranean and in Central and Eastern Europe. Inversely, overall mobility was found to be higher – and increasing with the crisis – for people under fifty-four and for highly educated people in Continental countries; for younger individuals and again for the highly educated in Central and Eastern Europe and the Mediterranean; and highest for the sixteen to twenty-four year olds – but not for the highly educated – in the Nordics.

The descriptive analysis concentrated in turn on the relationship between labour market mobility and various labour markets institutions, such as part-time contracts, product market regulation, employment protection legislation and employment incentives. We found that mobility is on the whole inversely related to the degree of product market regulation, positively related to the prevalence of part-time contracts and employment incentives schemes but has no relation with the degree of employment protection in the labour market.

Overall, our results sketch a picture of significant country heterogeneity in the intensity and direction of the labour market transitions across the EU. As expected, the crisis did have an impact on labour market transitions and employment/unemployment persistence, but in most cases, the effect of the crisis was smaller than the size of country differences observed in any one period (precrisis, during the crisis and postcrisis). Countries known for their institutional rigidities in the labour market, such as those of the Mediterranean, have been found to have less favourable labour market transitions and higher unemployment persistence. At the same time, we found no evidence that this links directly to the degree of employment protection, the main labour market institution associated with labour market rigidity. Instead, part-time employment seems to have played a positive role (even if rather marginally before 2009) for containing unemployment persistence, while product market regulations appear as a much more significant influence on adverse labour market transitions (and lower labour market mobility in particular). In any case, and despite the relative recovery of the European economies postcrisis, the degree of labour market flexibility (and the rates of labour market transitions) has not fully recovered to their precrisis levels.

Drawing on these results, it appears that the policy message emanating from this chapter is that efforts to increase labour market 'fluidity' should continue: unemployment persistence remains high in much of the EU postcrisis, while labour market transitions are not equally satisfactory in all countries or for all groups of workers. Enhancing this fluidity in the labour market, however, and especially facilitating convergence across countries in their extent of unemployment persistence, labour market churn or transitions into employment, does not seem to be conditioned on raising labour market flexibility in the traditional sense (namely, reducing employment protection). Rather, policy should aim at more nuanced and country/context-specific measures, including ones that fall outside the labour market.

Acknowledgements

Part of the analysis reported here draws on a Research Note produced for the European Commission's Social Situation Monitor under funding provided by the Directorate-General for Employment, Social Affairs and Inclusion (Macchiarelli et al, 2018, Transitions in the EU labour market: structure, crisis and recovery – Grant No. VT/2017/0341).

References

Ballester, R. (2005). 'European Employment Strategy and Spanish Labour Market Policies', *Documents de Treball del Departament d'Economia*, No. 14, 1–31.

Biroli, P., Mourre, G. and Turrini, A. (2010). 'Adjustment in the Euro Area and Regulation of Product and Labour Markets: An Empirical Assessment', CEPR Discussion Paper Series, No. 8010, September.

Boeri N., Scarpetta, S. and Nicoletti, G. (2000). 'Regulation and Labour Market Performance', in G. Galli and J. Pelkmans (ed.), *Regulatory Reform and Competitiveness in Europe: Horizontal Issues*. Edward Elgar Publishing.

Boeri, T. (2002). 'Let Social Policy Models Compete and Europe Will Win', paper presented at a Conference hosted by the Kennedy School of Government, Harvard University, 11–12 April.

(2005). 'Reforming Labor and Product Markets: Some Lessons from Two Decades of Experiments in Europe', IMF WP/05/97, May.

Boeri, T., Conde-Ruiz, J. I. and Galasso, V. (2003). 'Protecting against Labour Market Risk: Employment Protection or Unemployment Benefits?' CEPR Discussion Paper No. 3990. Available at SSRN: https://ssrn.com/abstract=443067.

Boeri, T. and Garibaldi, P. (2009). 'Beyond Eurosclerosis', *Economic Policy*, Vol. 24, No. 59, 409–461.

Brandolini, A., Cipollone, P. and Viviano, E. (2006). 'Does the ILO Definition Capture All Unemployment?' *Journal of the European Economic Association*, Vol. 4, No. 1, 153–179.

Daouli, J., Demoussis, M., Giannakopoulos, N. and Lampropoulou, N. (2015). 'The Ins and Outs of Unemployment in the Current Greek Economic Crisis', *South-Eastern Europe Journal of Economics*, Vol. 13, No. 2, 177–196.

Duval, R. and Elmeskov, J. (2006). 'The Effects of Emu on Structural Reforms in Labour and Product Markets', ECB Working Paper No. 596. Available at SSRN: https://ssrn.com/abstract=887083.

Eichhorst, W., (2013). *The European Labour Market: Success through Flexibility and Mobility*. Konrad-Adenauer-Stiftung.

Elsby, M. W., Michaels, R. and Solon, G. (2009). ‚The Ins and Outs of Cyclical Unemployment', *American Economic Journal: Macroeconomics*, Vol. 1, No. 1, 84–110.

Fujita, S. (2011). 'Dynamics of Worker Flows and Vacancies: Evidence from the Sign Restriction Approach', *Journal of Applied Econometrics*, Vol. 26, No. 1, 89–121.

Fujita, S. and Ramey, G. (2006). 'The Cyclicality of Job Loss and Hiring' (No. 06-17). Federal Reserve Bank of Philadelphia, Working Paper (No. 06-17).

(2009). 'The Cyclicality of Separation and Job Finding Rates', *International Economic Review*, Vol. 50, No. 2, 415–430.

Gangl, M. (2003). 'The Only Way Is Up?: Employment Protection and Job Mobility among Recent Entrants to European Labour Markets', *European Sociological Review*, Vol. 19, No. 5, 429–449.

Green, F. (2010). 'Well-Being, Job Satisfaction and Labour Mobility', *Labour Economics*, Vol. 17, No. 6, 897–903.

Ilzkovitz, F. and Dierx, A. (2011). 'Structural Reforms: A European Perspective', *Reflets et perspectives de la vie économique*, Vol. 50, No. 3, 13–26.

Kilponen, J. and Vanhala, J. (2009). 'Productivity and Job Flows: Heterogeneity of New Hires and Continuing Jobs in the Business Cycle', Research Discussion Paper (No. 15/2009), Bank of Finland.

Kosma, T., Papapetrou, E., Pavlou, G., Tsochatzi, C. and Zioutou, P. (2017). 'Labour Market Adjustment and Labour Market Reforms in Greece during the Crisis: Microeconomic Evidence from the Third Wave of the Wage Dynamics Survey', Working Paper 227, Bank of Greece

Kruppe, T., R. Rogowski, and Schömann, K. (1998). *Labour Market Efficiency in the European Union: Employment Protection and Fixed-Term Contracts*. Routledge.

Leulescu A., Agafitei, M. and Mercy, J. L. (2013). 'Statistical Matching: A Case Study on EU-SILC and LFS', Eurostat, European Commission, Luxembourg.

Mabbett, D. and Schelkle, W. (2007). 'Bringing Macroeconomics Back into the Political Economy of Reform: The Lisbon Agenda and the "Fiscal Philosophy" of EMU', *Journal of Common Market Studies*, Vol. 45, No.1, 81–103.

Macchiarelli C., Monastiriotis, V. and Lampropoulou, N. (2018). 'Transitions in the EU Labour Market: Structure, Crisis and Recovery', Report – DG-EMPL, European Commission.

Millán, A., Millán, J. M., Román, C. and van Stel, A. (2013). 'How Does Employment Protection Legislation Influence Hiring and Firing Decisions by the Smallest Firms?' *Economics Letters*, Vol. 121, No. 3, 444–448.

NBER (2008). 'Business Cycle Dating Committee', National Bureau of Economic Research, www.nber.org/cycles/jan08bcdc_memo.pdf.

Nickell, S. and Layard, R. (1999). 'Labor Market Institutions and Economic Performance', in O. Ashenfelter and D. Card (ed.), *Handbook of Labor Economics*, edition 1, volume 3, chapter 46, Elsevier, pp. 3029–3084.

Noelke, C. (2016). 'Employment Protection Legislation and the Youth Labour Market', *European Sociological Review*, Vol. 32, No. 4, 471–485.

Petrongolo, B. and Pissarides, C. A. (2008). 'The Ins and Outs of European Unemployment', *American Economic Review*, Vol. 98, No. 2, 256–262.

Pinelli, D., Torre, R., Pace, L., Cassio, L. and Arpaia, A. (2017). 'The Recent Reform of the Labour Market in Italy: A Review' (No. 072), Directorate General Economic and Financial Affairs (DG ECFIN), European Commission.

Sapir, A. (2006). 'Globalization and the Reform of European Social Models', *JCMS: Journal of Common Market Studies*, Vol. 44, No. 2, 369–390.

Shimer, R. (2005). 'The Cyclical Behavior of Equilibrium Unemployment and Vacancies', *American Economic Review*, Vol. 95, No. 1, 25–49

(2012). 'Reassessing the Ins and Outs of Unemployment', *Review of Economic Dynamics*, Vol. 15, No. 2, 127–148.

Shorrocks, A. F. (1978). 'The Measurement of Mobility', *Econometrica: Journal of the Econometric Society*, Vol. 46, No. 5, 1013–1024.

Siebert, H. (1997). 'Labor Market Rigidities: At the Root of Unemployment in Europe', *Journal of Economic Perspectives*, Vol. 11, No. 3, 37–54.

Theeuwes, J., Kerkhofs, M. and Lindeboom, M. (1990). 'Transition Intensities in the Dutch Labour Market 1980–85', *Applied Economics*, Vol. 22, No. 8, 1043–1061.

Ward-Warmedinger, M. and Macchiarelli, C. (2014). Transitions in labour market status in EU labour markets. *IZA Journal of European Labor Studies*, Vol. 3, No. 1, 17.

Appendix

Table 8.1A *Peaks and troughs in unemployment for selected EU countries.*

Precrisis peak	Precrisis trough	Crisis peak 1	Crisis peak 2	Postcrisis trough
AT = 2004	AT=2008	AT = 2009	AT = 2011	AT = 2016
BE = 2005	BE = 2008	BE = 2010	BE = 2011	BE = 2014
BG = 2004	BG = 2008	BG = 2013	-	BG = 2016
CY = 2005	CY = 2008	CY = 2014	-	CY = 2016
CZ = 2005	CZ = 2008	CZ = 2010	-	CZ = 2016
DE = 2005	DE = 2008	DE = 2009	-	DE = 2016
DK = 2004	DK = 2008	DK = 2011	-	DK = 2015
EE = 2004	EE = 2007	EE = 2010	-	EE = 2015
ES = 2004	ES = 2007	ES = 2013	-	ES = 2016
FI = 2004	FI = 2008	FI = 2010	FI = 2012	FI = 2015
FR = 2004	FR = 2008	FR = 2009	FR = 2010	FR = 2015
GR = 2004	GR = 2008	GR = 2013	-	GR = 2016
HR = 2004	HR = 2008	HR = 2014	-	HR = 2016
HU = 2005	HU = 2007	HU = 2010	-	HU = 2016
IE = 2004	IE = 2007	IE = 2012	-	IE = 2016
IT = 2004	IT = 2007	IT = 2014	-	IT = 2016
LT = 2004	LT = 2007	LT = 2010	-	LT = 2016
LU = 2004	LU = 2007	LU = 2009	LU = 2010	LU = 2015
LV = 2004	LV = 2007	LV = 2010	-	LV = 2016
-	-	MT = 2009	-	MT = 2016
NL = 2005	NL = 2008	NL = 2014	-	NL = 2016
PL = 2004	PL = 2008	PL = 2013	-	PL = 2016
PT = 2005	PT = 2008	PT = 2013	-	PT = 2016
RO = 2004	RO = 2008	RO = 2011	-	RO = 2015
SE = 2005	SE = 2007	SE = 2010	-	SE = 2016
SI = 2005	SI = 2008	SI = 2013	-	SI = 2016
SK = 2004	SK = 2008	SK = 2010	-	SK = 2016
UK = 2006	UK = 2007	UK = 2011	-	UK = 2016

Sources: Eurostat data, authors' computations.

Table 8.2A *Transition probabilities by worker group.*

Labour market status year t − 1		Central Eastern			Nordics			Continental			Mediterranean		
Males		E	U	I	E	U	I	E	U	I	E	U	I
2004–2008	E	**0.947**	0.029	0.025	**0.929**	0.016	0.056	**0.941**	0.030	0.029	**0.945**	0.029	0.026
	U	0.300	**0.625**	0.074	0.213	**0.485**	0.302	0.337	**0.600**	0.063	0.340	**0.586**	0.074
	I	0.048	0.022	**0.930**	0.093	0.019	**0.888**	0.039	0.012	**0.949**	0.039	0.024	**0.937**
2009–2012	E	**0.934**	0.039	**0.027**	**0.908**	0.029	0.063	**0.930**	0.041	0.029	**0.917**	0.057	0.027
	U	0.263	**0.698**	0.039	0.390	**0.378**	0.233	0.310	**0.615**	0.075	0.223	**0.724**	0.053
	I	0.032	0.019	**0.949**	0.081	0.029	**0.890**	0.043	0.021	**0.936**	0.026	0.030	**0.944**
2013–2016	E	**0.953**	0.024	0.023	**0.903**	0.031	0.065	**0.925**	0.045	0.030	**0.933**	0.044	0.023
	U	0.291	**0.670**	0.039	0.355	**0.460**	0.185	0.286	**0.652**	0.062	0.220	**0.727**	0.053
	I	0.031	0.016	**0.953**	0.101	0.036	**0.863**	0.042	0.020	**0.938**	0.024	0.030	**0.947**
Females		E	U	I	E	U	I	E	U	I	E	U	I
2004–2008	E	**0.923**	0.028	0.049	**0.858**	0.017	0.125	**0.923**	0.037	0.040	**0.922**	0.035	0.042
	U	0.263	**0.623**	0.114	0.209	**0.257**	0.534	0.306	**0.593**	0.102	0.292	**0.589**	0.119
	I	0.043	0.020	**0.937**	0.109	0.021	**0.870**	0.037	0.014	**0.949**	0.032	0.026	**0.941**
2009–2012	E	**0.918**	0.035	0.047	**0.873**	0.024	0.103	**0.915**	0.042	0.043	**0.911**	0.052	0.038
	U	0.240	**0.695**	0.065	0.366	**0.338**	0.296	0.307	**0.573**	0.120	0.205	**0.683**	0.112
	I	0.031	0.016	**0.953**	0.105	0.027	**0.867**	0.044	0.021	**0.935**	0.023	0.032	**0.945**
2013–2016	E	**0.935**	0.024	0.041	**0.871**	0.033	0.096	**0.914**	0.041	0.045	**0.925**	0.044	0.031
	U	0.267	**0.661**	0.072	0.337	**0.401**	0.261	0.275	**0.625**	0.101	0.195	**0.695**	0.110
	I	0.031	0.013	**0.955**	0.116	0.037	**0.847**	0.039	0.020	**0.941**	0.020	0.031	**0.949**
Low education		E	U	I	E	U	I	E	U	I	E	U	I
2004–2008	E	**0.881**	0.049	0.070	**0.851**	0.026	0.123	**0.904**	0.046	0.049	**0.919**	0.039	0.042
	U	0.186	**0.699**	0.115	0.170	**0.310**	0.520	0.242	**0.666**	0.092	0.269	**0.623**	0.109
	I	0.021	0.007	**0.972**	0.042	0.013	**0.945**	0.017	0.009	**0.974**	0.017	0.016	**0.968**

2009–2012	E	**0.853**	0.075	0.072	**0.836**	0.039	0.124	**0.889**	0.060	0.051	**0.886**	0.071	0.043
	U	0.160	**0.782**	0.059	0.302	**0.376**	0.322	0.223	**0.670**	0.108	0.177	**0.738**	0.085
	I	0.012	0.006	**0.982**	0.039	0.019	**0.943**	0.019	0.013	**0.967**	0.011	0.018	**0.972**
2013–2016	E	**0.884**	0.054	0.062	**0.823**	0.047	0.130	**0.880**	0.063	0.056	**0.905**	0.057	0.037
	U	0.188	**0.756**	0.056	0.270	**0.435**	0.294	0.193	**0.714**	0.093	0.165	**0.749**	0.086
	I	0.010	0.007	**0.983**	0.051	0.024	**0.925**	0.015	0.012	**0.974**	0.008	0.015	**0.977**
Medium education		E	U	I	E	U	I	E	U	I	E	U	I
2004–2008	E	**0.939**	0.030	0.031	**0.895**	0.016	0.089	**0.934**	0.034	0.032	**0.943**	0.031	0.027
	U	0.313	**0.600**	0.086	0.218	**0.373**	0.409	0.357	**0.569**	0.073	0.350	**0.559**	0.090
	I	0.058	0.033	**0.909**	0.134	0.026	**0.840**	0.053	0.019	**0.927**	0.069	0.044	**0.886**
2009–2012	E	**0.928**	0.040	0.032	**0.891**	0.029	0.081	**0.922**	0.044	0.034	**0.921**	0.054	0.025
	U	0.270	**0.682**	0.048	0.409	**0.330**	0.261	0.346	**0.562**	0.092	0.244	**0.680**	0.076
	I	0.036	0.023	**0.941**	0.117	0.035	**0.848**	0.057	0.028	**0.915**	0.047	0.061	**0.893**
2013–2016	E	**0.946**	0.026	0.028	**0.884**	0.035	0.081	**0.914**	0.049	0.038	**0.934**	0.045	0.021
	U	0.291	**0.656**	0.053	0.339	**0.420**	0.241	0.305	**0.620**	0.076	0.235	**0.694**	0.071
	I	0.034	0.018	**0.948**	0.122	0.042	**0.836**	0.047	0.026	**0.927**	0.041	0.059	**0.900**
High education		E	U	I	E	U	I	E	U	I	E	U	I
2004–2008	E	**0.961**	0.012	0.027	**0.930**	0.010	0.060	**0.953**	0.022	0.025	**0.960**	0.020	0.021
	U	0.413	**0.512**	0.074	0.251	**0.341**	0.407	0.432	**0.490**	0.078	0.414	**0.506**	0.080
	I	0.125	0.043	**0.832**	0.205	0.026	**0.770**	0.114	0.025	**0.861**	0.130	0.081	**0.789**
2009–2012	E	**0.956**	0.018	0.027	**0.927**	0.017	0.056	**0.946**	0.027	0.027	**0.946**	0.033	0.021
	U	0.376	**0.579**	0.045	0.429	**0.346**	0.225	0.419	**0.497**	0.084	0.303	**0.621**	0.076
	I	0.094	0.039	**0.867**	0.188	0.037	**0.775**	0.115	0.035	**0.850**	0.086	0.083	**0.831**
2013–2016	E	**0.963**	0.013	0.024	**0.920**	0.023	0.056	**0.944**	0.028	0.028	**0.954**	0.028	0.018
	U	0.399	**0.551**	0.050	0.432	**0.434**	0.133	0.390	**0.543**	0.067	0.296	**0.630**	0.074
	I	0.091	0.029	**0.881**	0.203	0.055	**0.742**	0.109	0.035	**0.855**	0.079	0.081	**0.840**

Table 8.2A (*cont.*)

		Labour market status year t											
15–24 year olds		E	U	I	E	U	I	E	U	I	E	U	I
2004–2008	E	**0.886**	0.062	0.052	**0.729**	0.034	0.236	**0.856**	0.085	0.059	**0.885**	0.074	0.041
	U	0.345	**0.557**	0.098	0.281	**0.155**	0.564	0.419	**0.509**	0.072	0.370	**0.556**	0.073
	I	0.063	0.039	**0.898**				0.114	0.037	**0.849**	0.088	0.060	**0.852**
2009–2012	E	**0.861**	0.084	0.055	**0.692**	0.053	0.255	**0.828**	0.104	0.068	**0.830**	0.130	0.040
	U	0.299	**0.640**	0.061	0.417	**0.288**	0.296	0.384	**0.528**	0.088	0.227	**0.707**	0.066
	I	0.049	0.037	**0.914**	0.115	0.040	**0.845**	0.103	0.045	**0.853**	0.049	0.079	**0.872**
2013–2016	E	**0.898**	0.053	0.050	**0.671**	0.055	0.274	**0.827**	0.111	0.062	**0.842**	0.116	0.042
	U	0.361	**0.588**	0.051	0.258	**0.397**	0.345	0.364	**0.552**	0.084	0.241	**0.697**	0.062
	I	0.055	0.033	**0.912**	0.115	0.050	**0.835**	0.096	0.042	**0.862**	0.045	0.077	**0.878**
25–29 year olds		E	U	I	E	U	I	E	U	I	E	U	I
2004–2008	E	**0.958**	0.025	0.016	**0.901**	0.021	0.078	**0.921**	0.053	0.026	**0.926**	0.049	0.026
	U	0.266	**0.655**	0.080	0.259	**0.169**	0.572	0.444	**0.495**	0.061	0.392	**0.539**	0.069
	I	0.086	0.041	**0.872**	0.323	0.045	**0.632**	0.277	0.092	**0.631**	0.177	0.115	**0.709**
2009–2012	E	**0.949**	0.033	0.018	**0.881**	0.034	0.085	**0.902**	0.067	0.030	**0.886**	0.090	0.024
	U	0.244	**0.720**	0.037	0.475	**0.363**	0.162	0.396	**0.519**	0.085	0.272	**0.672**	0.056
	I	0.062	0.031	**0.906**	0.308	0.075	**0.617**	0.248	0.117	**0.636**	0.132	0.158	**0.710**
2013–2016	E	**0.963**	0.022	0.015	**0.872**	0.044	0.084	**0.894**	0.075	0.031	**0.898**	0.081	0.021
	U	0.271	**0.689**	0.040	0.444	**0.390**	0.166	0.373	**0.559**	0.068	0.278	**0.668**	0.054
	I	0.066	0.029	**0.904**	0.311	0.111	**0.578**	0.241	0.105	**0.654**	0.143	0.157	**0.700**
30–54 year olds		E	U	I	E	U	I	E	U	I	E	U	I
2004–2008	E	**0.958**	0.025	0.016	**0.933**	0.014	0.053	**0.959**	0.027	0.014	**0.954**	0.028	0.018
	U	0.266	**0.655**	0.080	0.231	**0.567**	0.202	0.333	**0.610**	0.057	0.301	**0.605**	0.094

	I	0.086	0.041	**0.872**	0.186	0.043	**0.772**	0.100	0.046	**0.854**	0.060	0.050	**0.889**
2009–2012	E	**0.949**	0.033	0.018	**0.936**	0.024	0.040	**0.950**	0.035	0.015	**0.934**	0.051	0.015
	U	0.244	**0.720**	0.037	0.395	**0.366**	0.239	0.323	**0.606**	0.071	0.215	**0.713**	0.072
	I	0.062	0.031	**0.906**	0.185	0.060	**0.755**	0.103	0.063	**0.834**	0.053	0.069	**0.878**
2013–2016	E	**0.963**	0.022	0.015	**0.934**	0.030	0.037	**0.947**	0.037	0.016	**0.947**	0.041	0.012
	U	0.271	**0.689**	0.040	0.388	**0.445**	0.166	0.286	**0.652**	0.062	0.211	**0.722**	0.067
	I	0.066	0.029	**0.904**	0.200	0.080	**0.720**	0.090	0.059	**0.851**	0.047	0.074	**0.879**
55–64 year olds		E	U	I	E	U	I	E	U	I	E	U	I
2004–2008	E	**0.865**	0.017	0.118	**0.884**	0.016	0.099	**0.849**	0.022	0.128	**0.905**	0.017	0.078
	U	0.144	**0.635**	0.221	0.133	**0.407**	0.461	0.075	**0.742**	0.184	0.141	**0.676**	0.183
	I	0.025	0.005	**0.970**	0.048	0.006	**0.946**	0.005	0.003	**0.992**	0.008	0.010	**0.982**
2009–2012	E	**0.877**	0.029	0.094	**0.890**	0.024	0.087	**0.864**	0.027	0.109	**0.896**	0.032	0.071
	U	0.134	**0.758**	0.108	0.321	**0.364**	0.315	0.104	**0.701**	0.195	0.110	**0.729**	0.161
	I	0.015	0.003	**0.982**	0.051	0.014	**0.935**	0.010	0.006	**0.984**	0.012	0.010	**0.978**
2013–2016	E	**0.908**	0.021	0.071	**0.892**	0.032	0.076	**0.876**	0.027	0.096	**0.920**	0.028	0.052
	U	0.146	**0.750**	0.104	0.255	**0.499**	0.246	0.105	**0.767**	0.128	0.103	**0.746**	0.151
	I	0.013	0.005	**0.982**	0.074	0.019	**0.908**	0.009	0.007	**0.984**	0.011	0.012	**0.977**

Note: E = employed; U = unemployed; I = inactive so that EE = remains in employment between one year and the next; UU = remains in unemployment, II = remains in inactivity. Observations are weighted according to the GDP in each country over the group aggregate. Elements showing a probability of remaining in the same labour market state (employment, unemployment and inactivity) are in bold.

Sources: LFS microdata, authors' computations.

Table 8.3A *Mobility index across country and worker group.*

		CEE EU countries										
		BG	CZ	EE	LV	LT	HU	PL	RO	SK	SI	HR
Total	2004–8	0.207	0.273	0.343	0.278	0.283	0.257	0.242	0.298	0.212	0.215	0.168
	2009–12	0.167	0.267	0.329	0.312	0.257	0.247	0.205	0.174	0.184	0.186	0.160
	2013–16	0.151	0.284	0.401	0.338	0.265	0.285	0.219	0.116	0.206	0.195	0.180
Males	2004–8	0.218	0.265	0.315	0.262	0.287	0.240	0.241	0.299	0.203	0.203	0.176
	2009–12	0.166	0.263	0.311	0.297	0.268	0.232	0.207	0.172	0.173	0.182	0.159
	2013–16	0.151	0.290	0.383	0.307	0.268	0.270	0.210	0.117	0.192	0.196	0.179
Females	2004–8	0.197	0.285	0.379	0.299	0.281	0.276	0.246	0.296	0.222	0.229	0.163
	2009–12	0.169	0.275	0.354	0.329	0.247	0.264	0.205	0.179	0.197	0.192	0.162
	2013–16	0.151	0.279	0.424	0.375	0.265	0.300	0.229	0.116	0.221	0.195	0.181
Low-education	2004–8	0.185	0.211	0.331	0.266	0.278	0.224	0.204	0.310	0.136	0.236	0.174
	2009–12	0.167	0.228	0.297	0.309	0.240	0.237	0.169	0.192	0.134	0.186	0.167
	2013–16	0.142	0.213	0.401	0.319	0.210	0.290	0.177	0.135	0.134	0.196	0.153
Medium-education	2004–8	0.248	0.310	0.366	0.294	0.310	0.295	0.261	0.302	0.255	0.223	0.180
	2009–12	0.187	0.291	0.361	0.320	0.282	0.271	0.215	0.171	0.202	0.195	0.165
	2013–16	0.165	0.311	0.427	0.336	0.277	0.293	0.221	0.115	0.224	0.199	0.190
High-education	2004–8	0.259	0.378	0.394	0.362	0.337	0.367	0.363	0.325	0.391	0.311	0.214
	2009–12	0.212	0.375	0.379	0.388	0.353	0.317	0.314	0.186	0.372	0.270	0.227
	2013–16	0.206	0.408	0.445	0.445	0.382	0.334	0.325	0.121	0.371	0.256	0.268
16–24 years olds	2004–8	0.230	0.376	0.439	0.385	0.386	0.311	0.333	0.295	0.291	0.450	0.298
	2009–12	0.205	0.362	0.459	0.397	0.377	0.327	0.303	0.179	0.256	0.404	0.263
	2013–16	0.196	0.398	0.524	0.467	0.402	0.376	0.301	0.131	0.290	0.458	0.307
25–29 years olds	2004–8	0.313	0.384	0.456	0.398	0.456	0.366	0.400	0.390	0.357	0.444	0.277
	2009–12	0.235	0.418	0.437	0.449	0.462	0.358	0.358	0.215	0.342	0.394	0.315
	2013–16	0.223	0.504	0.580	0.511	0.494	0.409	0.361	0.151	0.401	0.425	0.398
30–54 years olds	2004–8	0.246	0.270	0.354	0.288	0.321	0.261	0.229	0.364	0.207	0.159	0.115
	2009–12	0.181	0.256	0.357	0.321	0.286	0.268	0.198	0.187	0.185	0.149	0.126
	2013–16	0.161	0.255	0.429	0.338	0.287	0.316	0.231	0.119	0.214	0.170	0.147
55–64 years olds	2004–08	0.204	0.279	0.344	0.217	0.249	0.267	0.258	0.345	0.236	0.241	0.134
	2009–12	0.164	0.279	0.328	0.298	0.251	0.218	0.148	0.187	0.180	0.224	0.137
	2013–16	0.140	0.239	0.378	0.282	0.228	0.225	0.171	0.106	0.177	0.187	0.132

Notes: Measures are based on the Shorrocks' mobility index. The table refers to twenty-five EU countries: Estonia (EE), Finland (FI), France (FR), Greece (GR), Hungary (HU), Italy (IT), Latvia (LV), Lithuania (LT), (SK), Slovenia (SI), Spain (ES) and Sweden (SE).

Sources: LFS microdata, authors' computations.

Nordics				Continental				Mediterranean					
NL	FI	DK	SE	BE	FR	LU	AT	GR	ES	IT	CY	PT	MT
0.000	0.337	0.429	0.449	0.184	0.267	0.421	0.292	0.193	0.392	0.183	0.355	0.309	0.000
0.466	0.358	0.407	0.441	0.203	0.281	0.435	0.291	0.150	0.282	0.177	0.292	0.256	0.290
0.414	0.336	0.394	0.464	0.217	0.250	0.451	0.267	0.130	0.252	0.174	0.253	0.248	0.291
0.000	0.303	0.414	0.427	0.189	0.261	0.417	0.271	0.218	0.380	0.183	0.350	0.304	0.000
0.433	0.332	0.399	0.423	0.207	0.266	0.403	0.265	0.158	0.265	0.168	0.285	0.252	0.264
0.377	0.313	0.376	0.449	0.216	0.244	0.428	0.242	0.132	0.243	0.163	0.244	0.251	0.269
0.000	0.372	0.443	0.471	0.182	0.273	0.427	0.319	0.183	0.405	0.186	0.360	0.315	0.000
0.496	0.388	0.417	0.460	0.200	0.295	0.467	0.325	0.146	0.300	0.189	0.298	0.260	0.355
0.449	0.359	0.412	0.482	0.220	0.257	0.474	0.300	0.130	0.261	0.188	0.261	0.245	0.331
0.000	0.291	0.436	0.386	0.167	0.228	0.404	0.278	0.176	0.371	0.157	0.327	0.295	0.000
0.477	0.320	0.401	0.387	0.191	0.237	0.419	0.269	0.147	0.269	0.156	0.280	0.249	0.263
0.442	0.286	0.396	0.417	0.206	0.210	0.451	0.232	0.128	0.230	0.150	0.233	0.242	0.256
0.000	0.389	0.435	0.497	0.211	0.292	0.416	0.311	0.202	0.441	0.220	0.364	0.330	0.000
0.487	0.400	0.436	0.477	0.229	0.311	0.443	0.306	0.158	0.329	0.206	0.296	0.296	0.385
0.416	0.376	0.417	0.490	0.239	0.270	0.451	0.279	0.137	0.289	0.202	0.243	0.289	0.392
0.000	0.388	0.485	0.503	0.281	0.361	0.499	0.321	0.276	0.479	0.300	0.469	0.437	0.000
0.496	0.397	0.449	0.496	0.260	0.369	0.487	0.353	0.202	0.359	0.269	0.374	0.334	0.458
0.443	0.369	0.434	0.518	0.271	0.337	0.493	0.326	0.166	0.330	0.266	0.353	0.324	0.466
0.000	0.587	0.722	0.610	0.335	0.392	0.506	0.457	0.270	0.510	0.242	0.446	0.418	0.000
0.546	0.568	0.702	0.607	0.343	0.400	0.504	0.417	0.235	0.383	0.231	0.412	0.373	0.397
0.456	0.525	0.700	0.637	0.334	0.380	0.562	0.408	0.235	0.360	0.236	0.391	0.376	0.472
0.000	0.549	0.637	0.623	0.388	0.504	0.475	0.400	0.310	0.595	0.288	0.534	0.472	0.000
0.537	0.552	0.600	0.622	0.388	0.493	0.616	0.416	0.281	0.491	0.281	0.479	0.423	0.338
0.548	0.540	0.591	0.652	0.379	0.458	0.700	0.415	0.296	0.462	0.295	0.471	0.446	0.426
0.000	0.404	0.447	0.498	0.188	0.304	0.425	0.288	0.169	0.415	0.187	0.345	0.307	0.000
0.484	0.441	0.415	0.498	0.223	0.317	0.451	0.304	0.138	0.320	0.193	0.271	0.246	0.255
0.429	0.433	0.389	0.533	0.240	0.276	0.493	0.285	0.127	0.282	0.197	0.231	0.232	0.248
0.000	0.237	0.315	0.340	0.124	0.215	0.303	0.254	0.167	0.318	0.155	0.249	0.208	0.000
0.506	0.276	0.317	0.339	0.116	0.237	0.400	0.258	0.157	0.256	0.162	0.198	0.209	0.324
0.392	0.255	0.287	0.360	0.126	0.187	0.419	0.220	0.105	0.227	0.149	0.181	0.198	0.291

Austria (AT), Belgium (BE), Bulgaria (BG), Croatia (HR), Cyprus (CY), Czech Republic (CZ), Denmark (DK), Luxemburg (LU), Malta (MT), the Netherlands (NL), Poland (PL), Portugal (PT), Romania (RO), Slovakia

9 On the Complementarity between Labour Market Regulation and Tax Reforms in the European Union

ANGELO MARTELLI, NAURO F. CAMPOS, MICHAEL GANSLMEIER, YUEMEI JI AND ORKUN SAKA

9.1 Introduction

In the last decade, several European Union (EU) countries have suffered from low economic growth, weak productivity and declining competitiveness.[1] Structural reforms that deregulate the labour market are thought to promote economic and employment growth. Cross-country analyses indicate that a lower labour tax wedge reduces unemployment in the long run (see Lehmann et al., 2014; OECD Taxation and Employment, 2011). A close look at the experiences of countries such as Spain and Italy shows a high degree of complementarity between changes in taxation and in labour market regulation. Yet their effects on employment growth remain understudied. This chapter tries to address this issue.

There is a large literature on labour market reforms and taxation policies. While scholars mostly agree that economies with flexible labour markets and low taxation rates sustain employment and economic growth, the cross-country heterogeneity of these effects remains a puzzle. One argument that supports the heterogeneity in reform effects is related to the complementarity of different reforms. To put it differently, an economy can benefit from a structural reform in one specific area, if another area has already been liberalized or is also undergoing reform in the same direction.

In the past, much effort has been devoted to understanding the interaction between labour and product market reforms. This chapter

[1] We thank seminar participants at the London School of Economics (LSE) Structural Reforms Workshop on 11 May 2018 for valuable comments on a previous version. This work was supported by the Economic and Social Research Council grant ES/P000274/1. The usual disclaimer applies.

aims to investigate this complementarity issue by looking at two other important reform areas in the recent EU reform agenda, i.e., labour market reforms and changes in taxation. To estimate the size of the complementarity effects, we cover a large number of EU countries (including new member states that joined after 2004) and also use the most recent data in our econometric analysis.

The chapter is organized as follows. Section 9.2 motivates our analysis with a brief overview of the recent reform experiences of Italy and Spain. Section 9.3 critically reviews the literature on whether reforms are substitutes or complementary. Section 9.4 presents our data and methodology. Section 9.5 discusses our econometric estimates. Section 9.6 concludes.

9.2 Reform Experience of Italy and Spain

Italy and Spain provide two very interesting cases in recent years, where reform complementarity may have played a key role in reducing labour market dualism and fostering employment growth.

In the Italian Jobs Act of 2014–2015, new regulations on lowering firing costs and making them less uncertain were combined with generous hiring subsidies. The Jobs Act made employment protection legislation less restrictive when compared to France and Germany, both on open-ended and temporary contracts according to the Organisation for Economic Cooperation and Development (OECD) indicators.

One of the objectives of the reform is to make the Italian labour market more efficient and less segmented. The data shown in Figures 9.1 and 9.2 seem to confirm that this objective has been achieved.

Figure 9.1 shows the contribution to employment growth by different types of labour contract since 2014. The increase in employment growth seems to be associated in particular with an increased use of permanent contracts. This is to a large extent explained by the tax subsidies put in place by the government to promote new permanent contracts or incentivize employers to transform existing fixed-term contracts to permanent ones. In Figure 9.2, we show the data on the composition of new contracts. The data from the National Social Security Agency (INPS) shown in Figure 9.2a and the data from the Ministry of Labour in Figure 9.2b both confirm that the number of new permanent contracts turn positive after 2015. Figure 9.3 shows

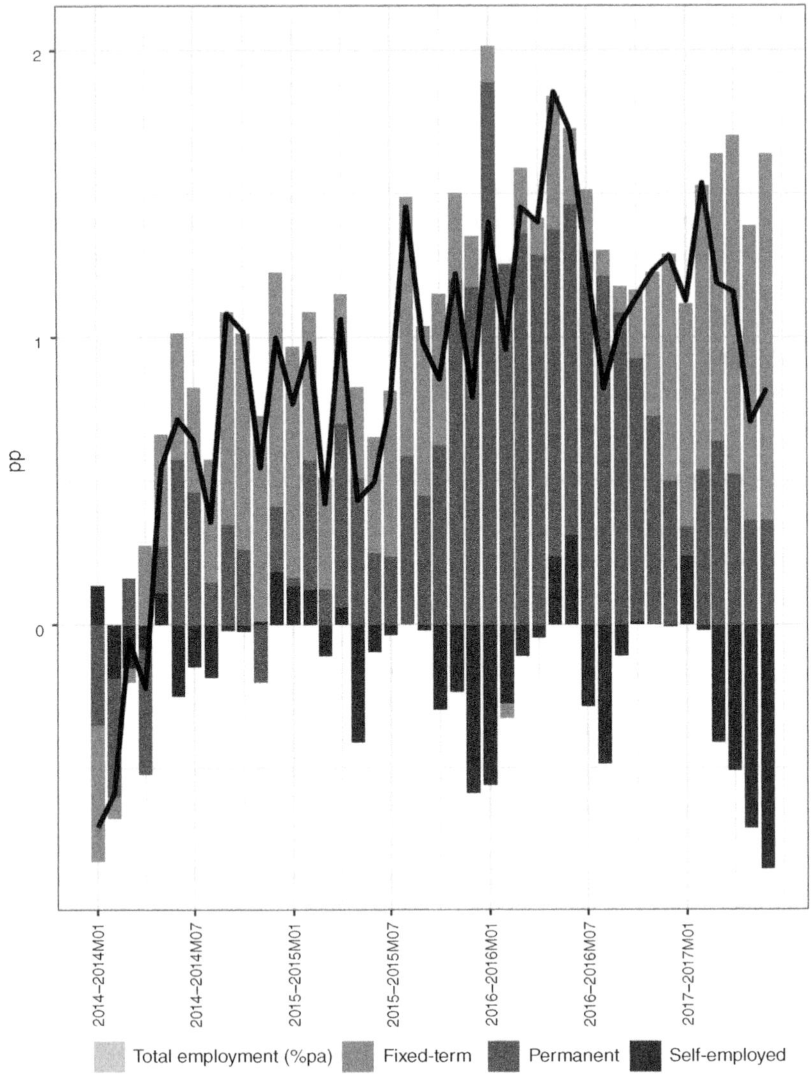

Figure 9.1 Contribution to y-o-y employment growth by contractual status, 2014M1–2017M6.

Source: Data elaborated from European Commission, DG for Economic and Financial Affairs (2017).

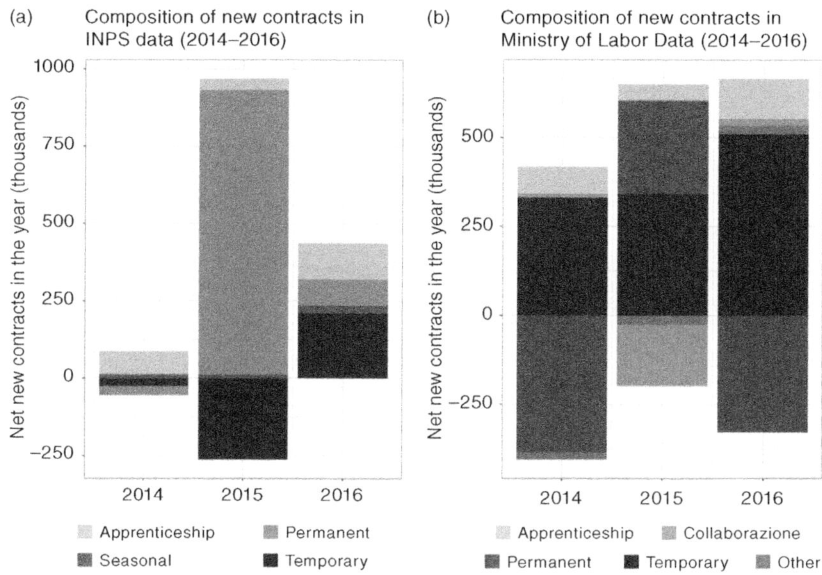

Figure 9.2 Composition of new contracts in INPS data (a) vs. composition of new contracts in Ministry of Labour data, 2014–2016 (b).
Source: Data elaborated from European Commission, DG for Economic and Financial Affairs (2017)

that after the introduction of hiring incentives at the beginning of 2015, the number of net new permanent contracts have increased sharply and remained at a higher level also later on due to both activations and conversions.

Using microdata for one Italian region and econometric analysis, Sestito and Viviano (2018) are able to disentangle the impacts of the different reforms. The authors conclude that the two reforms contributed to doubling the monthly rate of conversion of fixed-term jobs into permanent positions. Around 40 per cent of new total gross hires with permanent job contracts occurred because of the incentives, whereas 5 per cent can be attributed to the new firing regulations.

Moving to the Spanish Labour Market Reform of 2012, one can observe similar patterns. The crisis hit job creation hard and trends for new permanent contracts have started to diverge since then. In 2013, firms with fifty employees or fewer accounted for more than three-fourths of all new permanent contracts concluded within that month. The effect of the reform was also reflected in the share of permanent

(a)

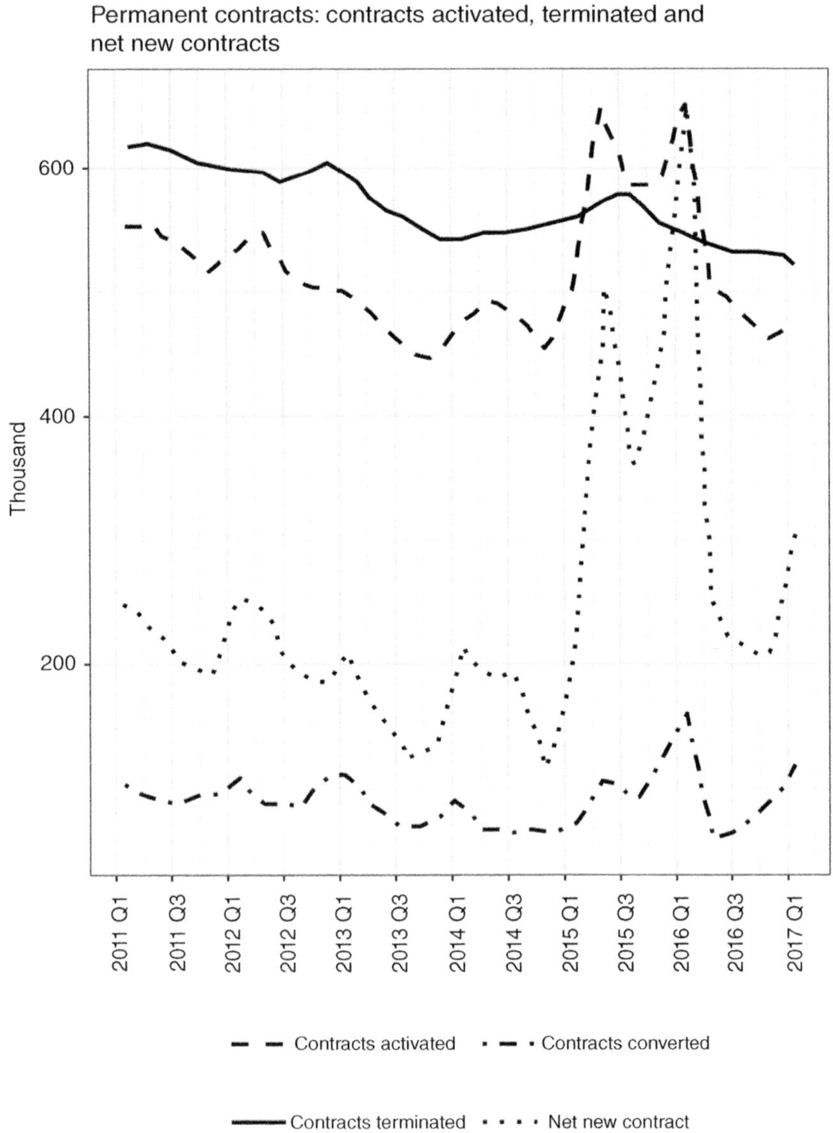

Figure 9.3 Permanent contracts vs. temporary contracts.

Source: Data elaborated from European Commission, DG for Economic and Financial Affairs (2017)

(b)

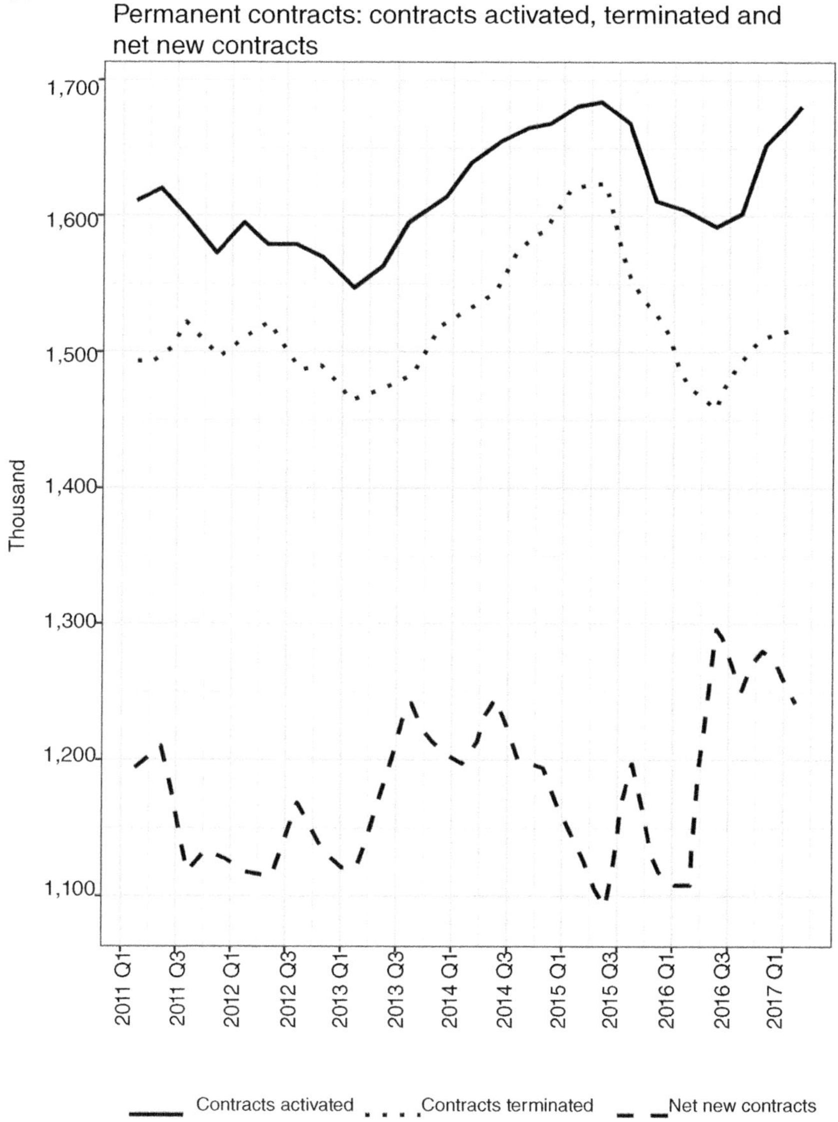

Figure 9.3 (*cont.*)

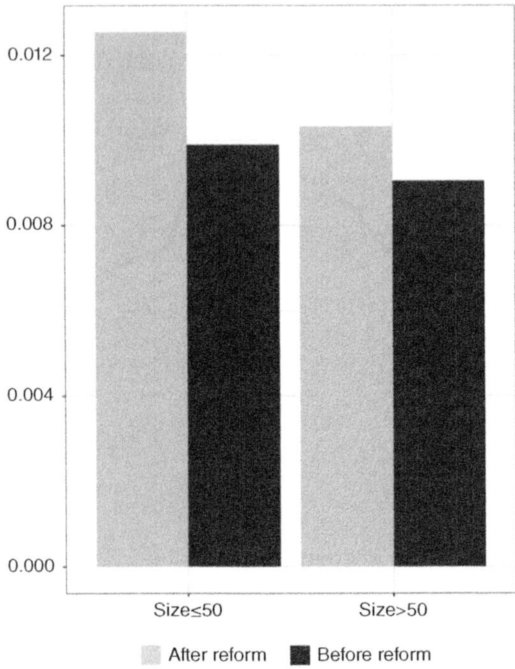

Figure 9.4 Exit from unemployment to permanent employment by firm size. Monthly probability for individual transition for unemployment durations smaller or equal than six months.
Source: OECD (2014)

contracts in all new contracts, which increased by 30 per cent. As can be observed from Figure 9.4, the reform had a major impact on transitions from unemployment to permanent employment, particularly in small establishments rather than in large ones.

Moreover, in Figure 9.5, we see that there has been an increase in the transition towards permanent employment significantly more for those who had a temporary contract prior to becoming unemployed, while the effect remains insignificant for those who previously held a permanent contract.

Both the Italian and Spanish reform experiences suggest that a combination of changes in taxation, represented for instance by hiring incentives, together with the introduction of a new contractual form may have positive effects on employment growth and could tackle the dualism and segmentation patterns present across many European labour markets. For example, the reform efforts in France moved in a

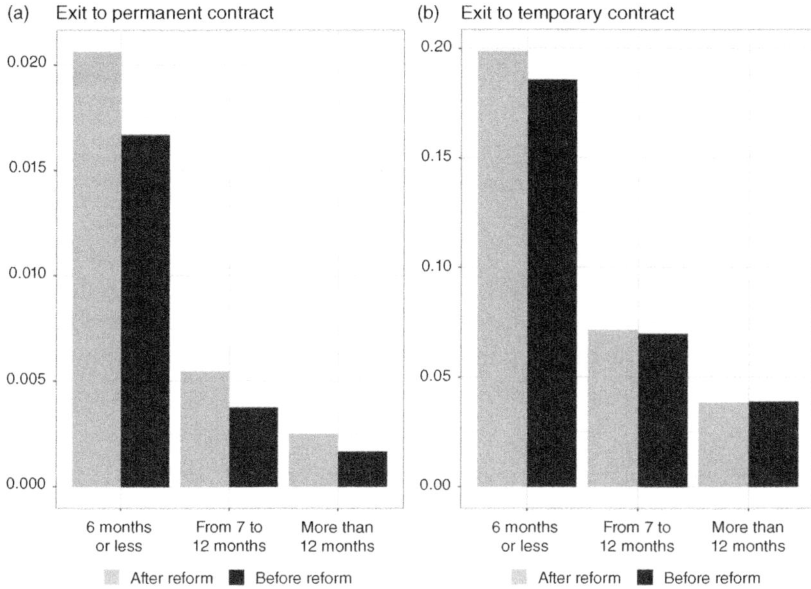

Figure 9.5 Exit to permanent contract (a) vs. exit to temporary contract (b).
Source: OECD (2014)

similar direction. The problem in the current analysis is that we do not know the actual causal effects of these reform efforts. There are many other factors, one important factor being related to the business cycle. Figure 9.6 shows the dynamics of output and employment for the years between 2008 and 2017 in Italy and Spain, respectively. Although the employment rates in Italy and Spain seem to be highly correlated to the gross domestic product (GDP) growth, it is difficult to conclude if the recovery of employment is due to structural reforms or to the business-cycle fluctuations. This chapter will try to take the latter factor into account in our econometric analysis of the role of reforms. Moreover, this chapter will also shed light on the complementarities between labour market and tax reforms. Before we move to a robust econometric analysis on testing this issue in Sections 9.4 and 9.5, we will discuss the theoretical and empirical literature at first.

9.3 Literature Review

The objective of this section is to provide a systematic overview of the efforts at analysing the relationship between different structural reforms and its impact on employment.

Berger and Danninger (2007) develop a theoretical model of reforms complementarity and sequencing. They study why making labour markets more flexible can benefit employment if an employer-friendly regime enhances competition amongst firms and raises the labour demand curve. In this context, we discuss the various ways of identifying reform complementarity and related measurement issues.

Consider a simple labour demand and supply model, where a closed economy is currently at equilibrium A with a high degree of labour legislation rigidity (Figure 9.7). Policy makers then decide to reduce the strictness of labour regulation, which leads to a shift of the labour supply curve. The new equilibrium at B is characterized by a lower real

(a)

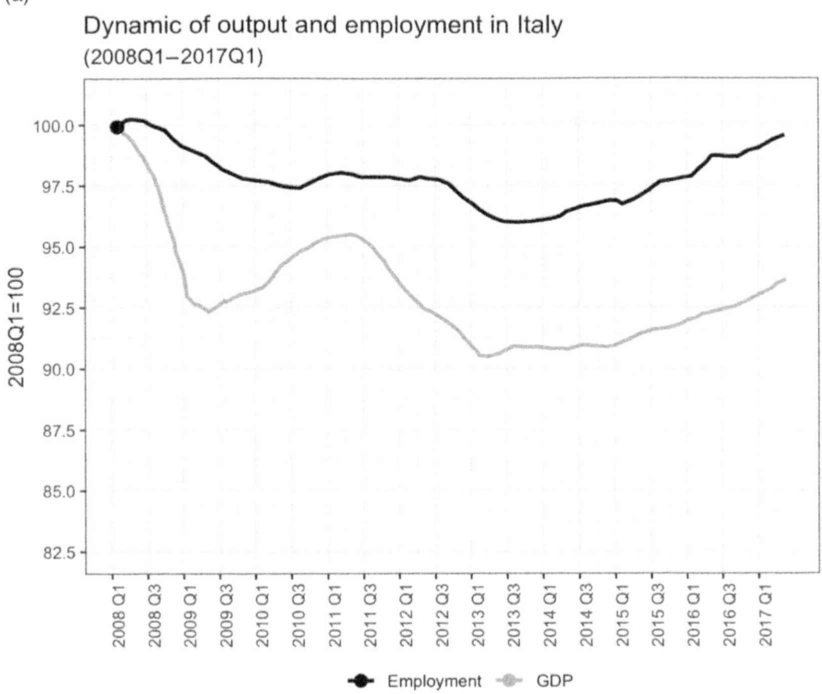

Figure 9.6 Dynamic of output and employment in Italy and Spain.

Source: Data elaborated from European Commission, DG for Economic and Financial Affairs (2017). Employment and GDP data from Federal Reserve Bank of St. Louis

(b)

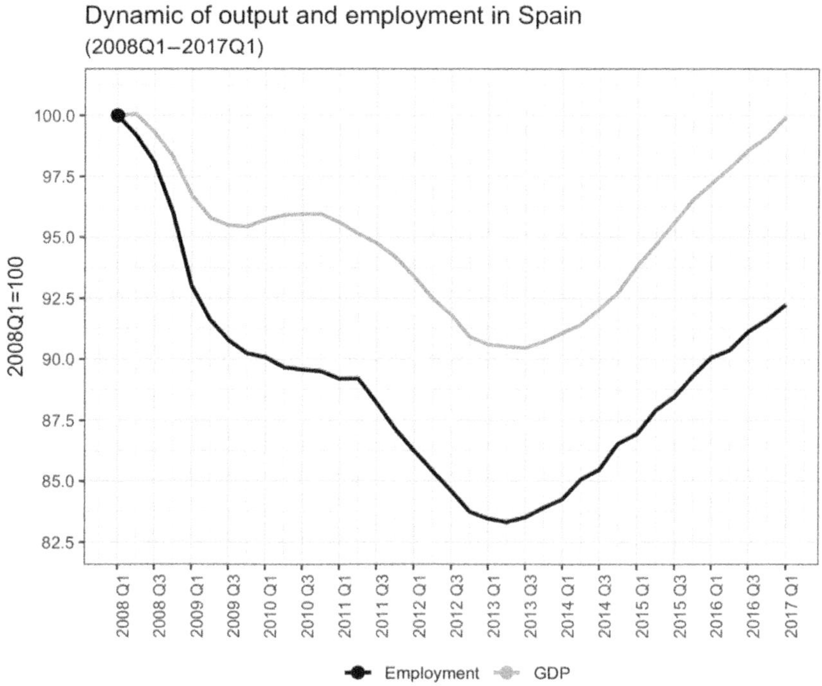

Figure 9.6 (*cont.*)

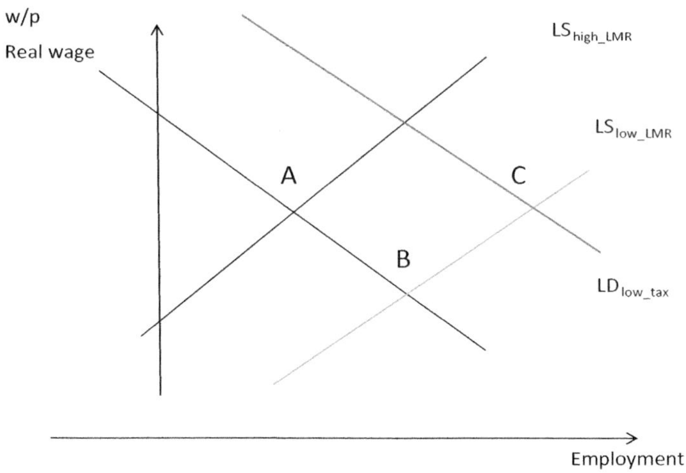

Figure 9.7 Employment, labour market regulation and taxation.

wage and a higher employment rate than the previous equilibrium, point A. This positive effect on employment is enhanced by lowering taxes on labour. The latter has the effect of shifting the demand for labour to the right. We obtain a new equilibrium in point C where labour market reform and taxation have complementary effects on employment.

The complementarity argument of structural reforms dates back to Lipsey and Lancaster's theory of second best (1956), which states that liberalizing one particular policy area without removing market imperfections in other related domains can hinder the economy from fully benefitting from these liberalizations. Scholars such as Foster and Sonnenschein (1970) as well as Rader (1976) build on this theoretical claim and argue that a proportional reduction of market distortions has positive welfare effects thus supporting the notion that applying structural reform strategies entail a radial reduction of market imperfections.

These ideas have been explored by many to understand the complementarity between labour market reforms and imperfections in other markets (e.g., product market, financial markets) and institutional condition (e.g., taxation).

One complementarity that has been extensively explored is that between labour and product markets. Selected studies on reform complementarity and their main features are summarized in Table 9.1. Various theoretical works (such as Amable and Gatti, 2004; Bassannini and Duval, 2006; Berger and Danninger, 2007; Blanchard and Giavazzi, 2003; Koeniger and Vindigni, 2003; Krueger and Pischke, 1997; Kugler and Pica, 2006) show positive interaction effects between labour and product markets. Product market deregulation that allows the entry of new firms should increase the labour demand of firms. This allows the economy to benefit from the liberalized labour market in creating more employment.

Not all economists agree with this view. For example, Amable and Gatti (2004) argue that there is substantial uncertainty about such complementarity. Using a model of dynamic efficiency wages combined with monopolistic competition in product markets, they show that increased product market competition may increase or decrease the level of employment. An increase in employment protection may have complementary or offsetting effects.

Table 9.1 *Selected studies on reform complementarity and their impact.*

Studies	Complementarity measurement	Dependent variable	Country and time coverage	Method	Reform pairs	Results
Amable et al. (2007)	Interactions between reform measures	Unemployment, inactivity, jobless rates	18 countries (1980–2004)	PCSE, GLS, FEVD	Labour, product, financial	Substitution effects between LMR and PMR (significant)
Bassanini and Duval (2006)	Interactions between reform measures	Employment, unmployment	21 OECD countries (1982–2003)	OLS, FGLS, IV	Labour, taxation, product	Complementarity between LMR, PMR and taxation (significant)
Belot and Van Ours (2001)	Interactions between reform measures	Unemployment rate	18 OECD countries (1960–1994)	OLS, FE	Labour, taxation	Complementarity between tax and replacement rate as well as EPL and centralization (significant)
Belot and Van Ours (2004)	Interactions between reform measures	Unemployment rate	17 OECD countries (1960–1999)	OLS, FE	Labour, taxation	Complementarity between tax and replacement rate as well as EPL and centralization (significant)
Berger and Danninger (2005)	Interactions between reform measures	Employment growth	OECD countries (1990–2004)	FE, RE, IV, GMM	Labour, product	Complementarity between LMR and PMR (significant)
Bicaba (2011)	Herfindahl–Hirschman concentration index	FDI, Portfolio investments	91 countries (1973–2004)	OLS, IV	Financial, banking, product, trade	Complementarity significant on FDI but not on portfolio investment flows

Table 9.1 (*cont.*)

Studies	Complementarity measurement	Dependent variable	Country and time coverage	Method	Reform pairs	Results
Chang et al. (2009)	Interactions between reform measures	GDP per capita growth	82 countris (1960–2000)	OLS, GMM	Labour, trade	Complementarity between LMR and trade (significant)
Coricelli and Maurel (2011)	Reciprocal of HH index of reforms	Depth of crisis, length of crisis	EU10 and CIS countries (1989–2005)	OLS, FE	Financial, trade	Complementarity between trade and financial reforms (significant)
De Macedo et al. (2014)	Policy dispersion indicator, HH index of reforms, range between reform levels	Crisis depth, crisis length	130 countries (1994–2006)	OLS, FE, RE, 2SLS,	Product, trade, financial, banking	Complementarity between reforms (significant); stronger in developing countries
Fiori et al. (2012)	Interactions between reform measures	Employment rate	20 OECD countries (1980–2002)	OLS, GLS, IV	Labour, product	Substitution effects between LMR and PMR (significant)
Freud and Bolaky (2008)	Interactions between reform measures/ institutions	GDP per capita growth	126 countries (2000–2004)	OLS	Trade, fiancial, product, labor	Complementarity between trade and PMR (significant)

Spilimbergo et al. (2009)	Interaction between reform measures	GDP per capita growth	91 countries (1960–2005)	OLS	Trade, product, financial	Liberalization of trade and domestic financial markets before external capital account lead to more rapidly growth (significant)
Sachs (2015)	Interactions between reform measures	Unemployment rate	17 OECD countries (1982–2005)	BMA	Labour, product, public ownership	Complementarity between EPL and unemployment benefit coverage/public ownership; complementarity between entry barriers and public ownership
Piton and Rycx (2018)	Interaction between reform measures	Unemployment rate	24 European countries (1998–2013)	OLS, FE, IV	Labour, product	Complementarity between EPL and PMR

Notes: 2SLS = two-stage least squares; BMA = Bayesian model averaging; FE = fixed effects; FEVD = fixed-effects vector decomposition; FGLS = feasible generalized least squares; GLS = generalized least squares; GMM = generalized method of moments; IV = instrumental variable; OLS = ordinary least squares; PCSE = panel-corrected standard error; RE = random effects.

The empirical evidence in this regard remains inconclusive. Estevão (2005) shows that wage moderation – measured by the productivity and unemployment level adjusted wage change – is more effective in stimulating growth if it occurs in countries with more deregulated product markets. The implication is that insufficient competition limits the benefits of labour market reforms. Annett and Debrun (2004) find that, within the euro area, product market reforms Granger-cause labour market reforms, and there is a spillover effect from product market deregulation into labour market deregulation. De Macedo et al. (2014) and Sachs (2015) explore the same issue in developing and transition countries. Piton and Rycx (2018) analyse data for twenty-four European countries over 1998–2013 and find that product market deregulation overall reduces the unemployment rate, whereas labour market deregulation is detrimental to employment in the short term while beneficial in the long run. Amable et al. (2007) find that decreasing product market regulation makes deregulation in labour markets a detrimental policy for employment, suggesting these deregulation policies are not complementary but rather substitutes. These authors indicate that the overall impact of labour market deregulation on employment growth is negative at low levels of product market reforms.

A second complementarity that has been explored in previous studies is the one between labour reforms and financial market imperfections. Wasmer and Weil (2004) consider a macroeconomic model where imperfections on both labour and credit markets interact. Imperfections rely on informational and search frictions and are modelled using matching functions. Entrepreneurs must find credit before setting up a firm, and they must find workers before producing. Credit market imperfections delay the setting up of firms and make the whole process more expensive, which ultimately depresses labour demand and contributes to raising the unemployment rate above the level that would have resulted from the existence of labour market imperfections alone.

A third complementarity that has been studied is between labour and other policy and institutions. The more employment-friendly the overall policy and institutional framework, the greater the impact of a labour reform in promoting employment. Bassanini and Duval (2006) look at employment patterns in OECD countries and assess the role of specific interactions across policies and institutions. They find that any reform that lowers unemployment is likely to be complementary with reforms that go in the same direction (such as unemployment benefits and public spending on active labour market programmes, statutory minimum wages and the tax wedge). They estimate that a 10 percentage point reduction in the tax wedge, a 10 percentage point reduction in unemployment benefits or a decline in product market regulation by two standard deviations lead to a drop in the unemployment rate of about 2.8, 1.2 and 0.7 percentage points, respectively. This suggests that well-designed reform packages would yield greater employment gains than separate, 'piecemeal' reforms, although the magnitude of such reform complementarities is found to be moderate for the average OECD country.

Finally, the most relevant issue in our case is the complementarity between labour market reforms and the taxation policy. Some earlier studies (Daveri and Tabellini, 2000; Elmeskov et al., 1998) find that the effects of the tax wedge and employment protection legislation (EPL) are detrimental for unemployment in intermediate bargaining regimes where 'insiders' have stronger bargaining power and can more easily resist attempts by employers to transfer the burden of payroll taxes and/or turnover costs onto wages. Belot and Van Ours (2001) investigate the interaction between labour market institutions and taxation in eighteen OECD countries during 1960–1994. Their results show a positive interaction between the tax rate and the replacement rate. Bassanini and Duval (2006) have interesting results: tax incentives appear to affect the job prospects of those groups 'at the margin' of the labour market. High implicit taxes on continued work (embedded in old-age pension schemes and other social transfer programmes) deter older workers from continuing to work beyond certain age. Moreover, low tax incentives for part-time work are associated with lower female employment rates. Gal and Theising (2015) confirm that elements of the tax benefit system, activation policies and wage-setting institutions are robust policy determinants of the aggregate employment and unemployment rates.

9.4 Methodology and Data

The empirical strategy consists in an adaption of the unrestricted dynamic model of employment growth from Berger and Danninger (2005). Here we emphasize the pivotal role played by interaction effects between taxes and labour market regulation. The empirical model is described as in Equation (9.1);

$$\Delta E_{it} = \alpha + \alpha_1 \Delta E_{i,t-p} + \alpha_2 R_{TAX_t} + \alpha_3 R_{LMR_t} + \gamma R_{TAX_t} * R_{LMR_t} + \delta X_{it} + \varepsilon_{it} \qquad (9.1)$$

where ΔE_{it} is the employment rate change for country i in period t, $\Delta E_{i,t-p}$ is the lagged (with a length of p) employment change for country i, R_{TAX_t} is the tax reform in period t, R_{LMR_t} labour market reforms in period t and X_{it} a set of control variables. The key parameter of interest is γ, concerning the complementarity.

Some variations on the current empirical model will also be included in our analysis to check the robustness of our results. Standard panel econometric models such as fixed effects, random effects, the instrumental variable (IV) approach and Arellano–Bond models are employed to estimate the potential complementarity effects. These alternative panel regression models allow us to explore both the cross-time and cross-country variations in the data and to mitigate the potential endogeneity problems.

We compile data from various sources with the aim to cover all EU28 countries for the period from 1990 until 2015. Regarding the dependent variable (i.e., employment growth rate, of total sample and of sample by gender), we mainly use the ILOStat database from the International Labour Organization (ILO). The database provides detailed information on employment data back to the 1980s and also provides us with information on employment for different genders. For labour market reforms, we use the European Commission's LABREF database, which contains information on labour market policy reforms for all EU28 countries between 2000 and 2011. The LABREF dataset provides information about the intensity of a given reform, the direction of a reform (increasing or decreasing labour market flexibility) and the classification of reforms into five (from the original eight) broad labour market policy domains, namely (1) EPL, (2) unemployment benefits, (3) active labour market policies (ALMP), (4) welfare benefits and (5) early withdrawal. Using the LABREF dataset, we created country-level variables that count the number of reform policy domains in a given year. Here, we focus on the reforms that are 'structural' in nature. In contrast to single-reform datasets, one might also look at policy indicators that enable a more precise assessment of labour market policies. In this regard, the OECD has provided the Employment Protection Legislation database, which includes various index-based measures of labour market policies. These policies include three aspects: 'protection of regular workers against individual dismissal'; 'regulation of temporary forms of employment'; and 'specific requirements for collective dismissals'. The dataset covers seventy-four countries between 1985 and 2013.

Regarding tax reforms, we gathered data from three different sources. First, previous research on tax reforms has predominantly used the OECD Taxing Wages dataset. This includes various measures of the taxation system of a country such as average income tax rate, marginal tax rate and average rate of social security contributions. Since family type has important consequences on taxation, the OECD differentiates their tax measures into (1) one-earner, (2) two-earner married couple and (3) single persons. In Table 9.2, we list the variable ID, description and source.

9.5 Results

This section presents our econometric estimates focusing on whether the labour and tax reforms are complementary with respect to employment growth in Europe. In each table, we will have the following model specifications. In columns (1) and (3), country and year fixed effects; (2) and (4), random effects; (5), IV approach with lagged GDP growth as instrument for lagged dependent variable; and (6), Arellano–Bond estimator. In the baseline specification with country and year fixed effects (Table 9.3), three results stand out. First, a decline of the *EPL_collective* and *EPL_individual* indices that come alone (i.e., without tax reform) increases employment significantly. This is not the case with the *EPL_temporary* index. Second, a decline in the *average_tax_wedge*, in isolation, increases employment significantly. Third, these effects are reinforced significantly when they occur together, i.e., when employment protection is reduced while the tax wedge is reduced at the same time. Our results are comparable in terms of coefficient sign with the findings by Bassanini and Duval (2006), who report that the interaction of tax wedge and EPL drives the unemployment rate significantly downwards. In Tables 9.4 and 9.5, we analyse the male and female samples separately using the similar regressions of Table 9.3. We find very comparable results. The effects of the *EPL_collective* and *EPL_individual* indices are similar, and so is the interaction term.

Table 9.2 *Data descriptive and data sources.*

Variable ID	Variable	Variable description	Source
emp_t_r emp_m_r emp_f_r	Annualized employment growth rate (total, male, female)	Employment growth rate based on total employment (in thousands)	ILOStat from the International Labour Organisation (2018)
emp_t_r5 emp_m_r5 emp_f_r5	Employment growth rate averaged over five years (total, male, female)	Employment growth rate averaged over five years based on total employment (in thousands)	ILOStat from the International Labour Organisation (2018)
EPL_individual (eprc_v1)	Strictness of employment protection – individual dismissal (regular contracts)	Consists of eight data items concerning regulations for individual dismissals	OECD Employment Protection database
EPL_temporary (ept_v1)	Strictness of employment protection – temporary employment	Consists of six data items concerning strictness of regulation on the use of fixed-term and temporary work agency contracts	OECD Employment Protection database
EPL_collective (epc)	Strictness of employment protection – collective dismissals (additional provisions)	Consists of four data items concerning additional costs and procedures involved in dismissing more than one worker at a time	OECD Employment Protection database

labref_net	Aggregated Index of labour market reforms (all sub-indices)	Number of liberalizing reforms minus number of deliberalizing reforms	LABREF reform database; Turrini et al. (2015)
labref_epl_net	Index of labour market reforms of EPL	Number of liberalizing EPL reforms minus number of deliberalizing EPL reforms	LABREF reform database; Turrini et al. (2015)
Average_tax_wedge	Average tax wedge	Average sum of personal income tax and employee plus employer social security contributions together with any payroll tax less cash transfers	OECD Taxing Wages database
GDP_r	Real GDP growth rate	Real GDP growth	International Monetary Fund (IMF) World Economic Outlook (WEO)

Table 9.3 *Total employment growth, employment protection legislation subindices (OECD) and average tax wedge.*

	(1)	(2)	(3)	(4)	(5)	(6)
	5-year employment growth fixed effects	5-year employment growth random effects	1-year employment growth fixed effects	1-year employment growth random effects	5-year employment growth IV	1-year employment growth Arellano–Bond
EPL_collective	–6.850***	–4.370***	–5.778**	0.0305	0.733	–6.798***
	(1.237)	(1.208)	(2.581)	(1.385)	(0.769)	(2.552)
EPL_individual	–7.593***	–5.482***	–7.041**	–1.084	1.717*	–4.655
	(1.733)	(1.655)	(3.348)	(1.444)	(0.917)	(4.767)
EPL_temporary	1.968	2.178**	1.424	0.684	–0.424	–1.325
	(1.767)	(0.954)	(2.342)	(0.742)	(0.447)	(3.226)
average_tax_wedge	–1.624***	–1.007***	–1.441***	–0.0529	0.212*	–1.519**
	(0.234)	(0.184)	(0.468)	(0.180)	(0.111)	(0.621)
EPL_collective * average_tax_wedge	0.257***	0.144***	0.245**	0.00410	–0.0194	0.327***
	(0.0482)	(0.0370)	(0.0948)	(0.0377)	(0.0211)	(0.109)

EPL_individual * average_tax_wedge	0.306***	0.232***	0.234**	0.0316	−0.0555*	0.167
	(0.0541)	(0.0551)	(0.107)	(0.0480)	(0.0304)	(0.166)
EPL_temporary * average_tax_wedge	−0.0328	−0.0336	−0.0121	−0.0192	0.000712	0.0778
	(0.0466)	(0.0270)	(0.0646)	(0.0213)	(0.0121)	(0.0944)
Observations	190	190	236	236	245	226
R-squared	0.665		0.504		0.466	
Number of countries	22	22	22	22	22	22
Country and Year FE	Yes	No	Yes	No	No	No

Notes: Arellano–Bond test for AR(1) in first differences: $z = -3.4$ $Pr > z = 0.0006$. Arellano–Bond test for AR(2) in first differences: $z = -0.9$ $Pr > z = 0.3720$. OECD sample. The dependent variable is the total average employment growth rate over five years for columns (1), (2) and (5), while we take the simple employment growth rate over one year for columns (3), (4) and (6). *$p < 0.1$, **$p < 0.05$, ***$p < 0.01$. Standard errors are reported in parentheses.

One important issue related to identification is that the labour market legislation measurement may affect the estimation results of complementarity interactions between the labour market reforms and tax changes. To check the robustness of our previous results, we use the LABREF reform dataset from the European Commission. Using the information from the dataset, we generated count-based policy indices that are used in regressions shown in Table 9.6. Thus, labref_net consists of all labour market policy domains, and it is defined as the difference between the number of liberalizing and deliberalizing labour market reforms per year in a given country; thus it is positive, if the number of liberalizing reforms is larger than the number of deliberalizing reforms. In contrast to the EPL measures from OECD, high values refer to the liberalization of labour markets. In other words, the coefficients of the interaction term have to turn out negative in order to be in line with the results from Tables 9.3 through 9.5.

In Table 9.6, we report results from the alternative measure of labour market reforms we previously described. The coefficients related to the complementarity hypothesis are negative in almost all regressions. However, most of the estimates are not statistically significant. In Table 9.7, we replace the labour market reform measure with the EPL domain measures. The results in the six regressions indicate conflicting information. Results in columns (1) through (4) show positive complementary effects that are in line with the findings from Table 9.3: liberalizing EPL reforms that are coupled with tax cuts plays a positive role in promoting employment growth. Results in columns (5) and (6) do not support this conclusion. The results in Tables 9.6 and 9.7 indicate that the positive impact of tax and labour market reform is not conclusive. Our results may depend on how the key reforms are measured. We believe further research is necessary to tackle this issue.

9.6 Concluding Remarks

The analysis presented in this chapter examined whether and to what extent changes in labour market regulation can be seen as complementary to tax reforms in increasing employment across the European Union. By adapting the unrestricted dynamic model of Berger and Danninger (2007), we tried to disentangle the individual from the combined effects of these two reforms. Our yearly panel covers a

Table 9.4 *Male employment growth, employment protection legislation subindices (OECD) and average tax wedge.*

	(1)	(2)	(3)	(4)	(5)	(6)
	5y growth with FE	5y growth with RE	1y growth with FE	1y growth with RE	5y growth IV	1y growth AB
EPL_collective	–7.362***	–3.968***	–5.439*	0.866	1.513	–6.991**
	(1.326)	(1.302)	(2.940)	(1.606)	(1.016)	(3.022)
EPL_individual	–7.593***	–4.750***	–5.974	-0.234	3.532***	–4.727
	(1.873)	(1.735)	(3.800)	(1.659)	(1.211)	(6.150)
EPL_temporary	1.989	2.114**	1.016	0.520	–0.944	–1.477
	(1.911)	(0.973)	(2.652)	(0.855)	(0.590)	(4.337)
average_tax_wedge	–1.711***	–0.865***	–1.399***	0.0856	0.425***	–1.651**
	(0.252)	(0.192)	(0.532)	(0.208)	(0.146)	(0.790)
EPL_collective * average_tax_wedge	0.280***	0.124***	0.255**	–0.0199	-0.0455	0.358**
	(0.0515)	(0.0390)	(0.108)	(0.0437)	(0.0278)	(0.141)
EPL_individual * average_tax_wedge	0.310***	0.200***	0.186	0.000463	–	
0.116***	0.155					
	(0.0585)	(0.0580)	(0.121)	(0.0552)	(0.0401)	(0.209)

Table 9.4 (*cont.*)

	(1)	(2)	(3)	(4)	(5)	(6)
	5y growth with FE	5y growth with RE	1y growth with FE	1y growth with RE	5y growth IV	1y growth AB
EPL_temporary * average_tax_wedge	−0.0309	−0.0331	0.00404	−0.0153	0.00974	0.0946
	(0.0504)	(0.0278)	(0.0732)	(0.0247)	(0.0160)	(0.126)
Observations	190	190	236	236	245	226
R-squared	0.651		0.487		0.109	
Number of countries	22	22	22	22	22	22
Country and Year FE	Yes	No	Yes	No	No	No

Notes: Arellano–Bond test for AR(1) in first differences: $z = -3.47$ $Pr > z = 0.0005$. Arellano–Bond test for AR(2) in first differences: $z = -0.67$ $Pr > z = 0.4984$. OECD sample. The dependent variable is the male average annual employment growth rate over five years for columns (1), (2) and (5), while we take the simple employment growth rate over one year for columns (3), (4) and (6). $^{*}p < 0.1$, $^{**}p < 0.05$, $^{***}p < 0.01$. Standard errors are reported in parentheses.

Table 9.5 *Female employment growth, employment protection legislation subindices (OECD) and average tax wedge.*

	(1)	(2)	(3)	(4)	(5)	(6)
	5y growth with FE	5y growth with RE	1y growth with FE	1y growth with RE	5y growth IV	1y growth AB
EPL_collective	−6.475***	−4.763***	−7.058***	−0.914	−0.312	−7.694***
	(1.212)	(1.176)	(2.530)	(1.330)	(0.553)	(1.786)
EPL_individual	−7.785***	−6.263***	−9.034***	−2.098	−0.744	−7.119**
	(1.682)	(1.627)	(3.325)	(1.413)	(0.659)	(3.340)
EPL_temporary	2.372	2.311**	2.292	0.911	0.293	−0.442
	(1.718)	(0.955)	(2.341)	(0.719)	(0.321)	(2.493)
average_tax_wedge	−1.544***	−1.131***	−1.688***	−0.210	−0.0736	−1.739***
	(0.227)	(0.182)	(0.459)	(0.175)	(0.0795)	(0.459)
EPL_collective * average_tax_wedge	0.237***	0.162***	0.269***	0.0312	0.0161	0.334***
	(0.0472)	(0.0366)	(0.0927)	(0.0363)	(0.0151)	(0.0806)
EPL_individual * average_tax_wedge	0.304***	0.260***	0.322***	0.0680	0.0272	0.280**
	(0.0523)	(0.0540)	(0.106)	(0.0471)	(0.0218)	(0.123)

Table 9.5 (*cont.*)

	(1)	(2)	(3)	(4)	(5)	(6)
	5y growth with FE	5y growth with RE	1y growth with FE	1y growth with RE	5y growth IV	1y growth AB
EPL_temporary average_tax_wedge	−0.0467	−0.0363	−0.0361	−0.0247	−0.0117	0.0375
	(0.0454)	(0.0269)	(0.0646)	(0.0205)	(0.00872)	(0.0706)
Observations	190	190	236	236	245	226
R-squared	0.666		0.477		0.771	
Number of countries	22	22	22	22	22	22
Country and year FE	Yes	No	Yes	No	No	No

Notes: Arellano–Bond test for AR(1) in first differences: $z = -3.3$ $Pr > z = 0.0010$. Arellano–Bond test for AR(2) in first differences: $z = -0.55$ $Pr > z = 0.5808$. OECD sample. The dependent variable is the female average annual employment growth rate over five years for columns (1), (2) and (5), while we take the simple employment growth rate over one year for columns (3), (4) and (6). $^{*}p < 0.1$, $^{**}p < 0.05$, $^{***}p < 0.01$. Standard errors are reported in parentheses.

Table 9.6 *Employment growth, employment protection legislation (labref_net) and tax changes (average_tax_wedge): annualized five-year growth.*

	(1)	(2)	(3)	(4)	(5)	(6)
	5y growth with FE	5y growth with RE	1y growth with FE	1y growth with RE	5y growth IV	1y growth AB
labref_net	0.000806	0.00613	0.0513	0.214*	0.00829	0.170
	(0.0781)	(0.0922)	(0.119)	(0.124)	(0.0693)	(0.180)
average_tax_wedge	−0.121**	−0.0492**	−0.108	−0.0285	0.0197*	0.146
	(0.0519)	(0.0201)	(0.0775)	(0.0183)	(0.0114)	(0.112)
labref_net * average_tax_wedge	−0.000760	−0.000815	−0.00336	−0.00659*	−0.000505	−0.00598
	(0.00227)	(0.00271)	(0.00353)	(0.00371)	(0.00209)	(0.00542)
Observations	220	220	275	275	286	266
R-squared	0.433		0.438		0.320	
Number of countries	22	22	22	22	22	22
Country and Year FE	Yes	No	Yes	No	No	No

Notes: Arellano–Bond test for AR(1) in first differences: $z = -3.27$ $Pr > z = 0.0011$. Arellano–Bond test for AR(2) in first differences: $z = -0.51$ $Pr > z = 0.6039$. EU sample. The dependent variable is the total average annual employment growth rate over five years for columns (1), (2) and (5), while we take the simple employment growth rate over one year for columns (3), (4) and (6). $^{*}p < 0.1$, $^{**}p < 0.05$, $^{***}p < 0.01$. Standard errors are reported in parentheses.

Table 9.7 *Employment growth, employment protection legislation (labref_epl_net) and tax changes (average_tax_wedge).*

	(1)	(2)	(3)	(4)	(5)	(6)
	5y growth with FE	5y growth with RE	1y growth with FE	1y growth with RE	5y growth IV	1y growth AB
labref_epl_net	0.000806	0.00613	0.0513	0.214*	0.00829	0.170
	(0.0781)	(0.0922)	(0.119)	(0.124)	(0.0693)	(0.180)
average_tax_wedge	−0.121**	−0.0492**	−0.108	-0.0285	0.0197*	0.146
	(0.0519)	(0.0201)	(0.0775)	(0.0183)	(0.0114)	(0.112)
labref_epl_net * average_tax_wedge	−0.000760	−0.000815	−0.00336	−0.00659*	−0.000505	−0.00598
	(0.00227)	(0.00271)	(0.00353)	(0.00371)	(0.00209)	(0.00542)
Observations	220	220	275	275	286	266
R-squared	0.433		0.438		0.320	
Number of countries	22	22	22	22	22	22
Country and year FE	Yes	No	Yes	No	No	No

Notes: Arellano–Bond test for AR(1) in first differences: $z = -3.3$ $Pr > z = 0.0009$. Arellano–Bond test for AR(2) in first differences: $z = -0.63$ $Pr > z = 0.5241$. EU sample. The dependent variable is the total average annual employment growth rate over five years for columns (1), (2) and (5), while we take the simple employment growth rate over one year for columns (3), (4) and (6). $^{*}p < 0.1$, $^{**}p < 0.05$, $^{***}p < 0.01$. Standard errors are reported in parentheses.

period from 1990 to 2015, and we use various datasets for our reform variables. The results point at a positive and significant interaction effect. We also observe differentiated effects depending on employment protection subdomains and type of labour market reform, with the LABREF datasets providing a more mixed picture. Our interpretation is that while labour market reforms, like the loosening of employment protection, makes the supply side of the economy more flexible and increases employment, this effect on employment growth is reinforced significantly when demand is also stimulated. The latter is accomplished by tax reductions. Thus the complementarity of labour market reforms and tax reforms may be understood as the former stimulates supply while the latter gives a boost to demand.

While we are aware that the evidence above has a number of limitations, there are several policy-relevant implications that revolve around the key role played by complementarity. This is confirmed to be a fundamental but often understudied aspect in the reform debate, perhaps with the exception of the case of the interaction between product and labour market regulation. As highlighted in the evidence on Italy and Spain, complementarity has delivered enhanced labour market outcomes, and this seems to be the case also in more recent reform attempts such as those undertaken in France, where complementarity between labour market reforms and tax incentives for new forms of labour contracts has been considered extensively in the legislative efforts.

References

Amable, B. and Gatti, D. (2004). 'Product Market Competition, Job Security, and Aggregate Employment', *Oxford Economic Papers*,Vol. 56, No. 4, 667–686.

Amable, B., Demmou, L. and Gatti, D. (2007). 'Employment Performance and Institutions: New Answers to an Old Question', IZA Discussion Paper, No. 2731.

(2011). 'The Effect of Employment Protection and Product Market Regulation on Labour Market Performance: Substitution or Complementarity?' *Applied Economics*, Vol. 43, No. 4, 449–464.

Annett, T. and Debrun, X. (2004). 'Implementing Lisbon: Incentives and Constraints', in A. Annett, M. Estevão, H. Faruqee, X. Debrun and J.-J. Hallaert (ed.), *Euro Area Policies: Selected Issues*, IMF Country Report No. 04/235. International Monetary Fund, pp. 42–81.

Baker, D., Glyn, A., Howell, D. R. and Schmitt, J. (2005). 'Labor Market Institutions and Unemployment: Assessment of the Cross-Country Evidence', in D. R. Howell (ed.), *Fighting Unemployment. The Limits of Free Market Orthodoxy*. Oxford University Press.Vol. 3, pp. 72–113.

Bassanini, A. and Duval, R. (2006). 'Employment Patterns in OECD Countries', OECD Economics Department Working Papers 486.

Belot, M. and Van Ours, J. C. (2001). 'Unemployment and Labour Market Institutions: An Empirical Analysis', *Journal of the Japanese and International Economies*,Vol. 15,No. 4, 403–418.

(2003). 'Interactions between Institutions Matter', *CESifo DICE Report*, Vol. 1, No. 2, 3–6.

(2004). 'Does the Recent Success of Some OECD Countries in Lowering Their Unemployment Rates Lie in the Clever Design of Their Labour Market Reforms?' *Oxford Economic Papers*, Vol. 56, No. 4, 621–642.

Berger, H. and Danninger, S. (2007). 'The Employment Effects of Labour and Product Market Deregulation and Their Implications for Structural Reform', *IMF Staff Papers*, Vol. 54, No. 3, 591–619.

Berger, M. H. and Danninger, M. S. (2005). 'Labour and Product Market Deregulation: Partial, Sequential, or Simultaneous Reform?' No. 5-227, International Monetary Fund.

Bicaba, Z. T. (2011). 'Do Financial Reforms Complementarity and Reforms Sequence Matter for International Capital Inflows?' Proceedings of the German Development Economics Conference, Verein für Socialpolitik, Research Committee Development Economics, Berlin.

Blanchard, O. and Giavazzi, F. (2003). 'Macroeconomic Effects of Regulation and Deregulation in Goods and Labour Markets', *Quarterly Journal of Economics*, Vol. 118, No. 3, 879–907.

Blanchard, O. and Wolfers, J. (2000). 'The Role of Shocks and Institutions in the Rise of European Unemployment: The Aggregate Evidence', *Economic Journal*, Vol. 110, No. 462, 1–33.

Calderón, C. and Fuentes, R. (2006). 'Complementarities between Institutions and Openness in Economic Development: Evidence for a Panel of Countries', *Cuadernos de economía*, Vol. 43, No. 127, 49–80.

Chang, R., Kaltani, L., and Loayza, N. V. (2009). 'Openness Can Be Good for Growth: The Role of Policy Complementarities', *Journal of Development Economics*, Vol. 90, No. 1, 33–49.

Coe, D. T. and Snower, D. J. (1997). 'Policy Complementarities: The Case for Fundamental Labour Market Reform', *Staff Papers*, Vol. 44, Vol. 1, 1–35.

Coricelli, F. and Maurel, M. (2011). 'Growth and Crisis in Transition: A Comparative Perspective', *Review of International Economics*, Vol. 19, No. 1, 49–64.

Daveri, F. and Tabellini, G. (2000). 'Unemployment, Growth and Taxation in Industrial Countries', *Economic Policy*, Vol. 15, No. 30, 48–104.

Debrun, X. and Annett, A. 2004, *Implementing Lisbon: Incentives and Constraints, Chapter II in Euro Area Policies – Selected Issues* International Monetary Fund.

de Macedo, J. B. and Martins, J. O. (2008). 'Growth, Reform Indicators and Policy Complementarities', *Economics of Transition*, Vol. 16, No. 2, 141–164.

de Macedo, J. B., Martins, J. O. and Rocha, B. (2014). 'Are Complementary Reforms a "Luxury" for Developing Countries?' *Journal of Comparative Economics*, Vol. 42, No. 2, 417–435.

Díaz-Vázquez, M. D. P. and Snower, D. J. (1996). 'Employment, Macroeconomic Fluctuations and Job Security' (No. 1430), CEPR Discussion Papers.

Duval, R. and Furceri, D. (2018). 'The Effects of Labour and Product Market Reforms: The Role of Macroeconomic Conditions and Policies', *IMF Economic Review*, Vol. 66, No. 1, 31–69.

Elmeskov, J., Martin, J. and Scarpetta, S. (1998). Key Lessons for Labour Market Reforms: Evidence from OECD Countries' Experience.

Estevão, M. M. M. (2005). 'Product Market Regulation and the Benefits of Wage Moderation' (No. 5-191), International Monetary Fund.

European Commission, DG for Economic and Financial Affairs, (2017). 'The Recent Reform of the Labour Market in Italy: A Review', European Economy Discussion Paper 072, December.

Fella, G. (2000). 'Efficiency Wage and Efficient Redundancy Pay', *European Economic Review*, Vol. 44, No. 8, 1473–1490.

Fiori, G., Nicoletti, G., Scarpetta, S. and Schiantarelli, F. (2012). 'Employment Effects of Product and Labour Market Reforms: Are There Synergies?' *Economic Journal*, Vol. 122, No. 558, F79–F104.

Foster, E. and Sonnenschein, H. (1970). 'Price Distortion and Economic Welfare', *Econometrica: Journal of the Econometric Society*, Vol. 38, 281–297.

Freund, C. and Bolaky, B. (2008). 'Trade, Regulations, and Income', *Journal of Development Economics*, Vol. 87, No. 2, 309–321.

Gal, P. and Theising, A. (2015). 'The Macroeconomic Impact of Structural Policies on Labour Market Outcomes in OECD Countries: A Reassessment', OECD Economics Department Working Paper.

Gatti, D., Rault, C. and Vaubourg, A. (2010). 'The Financial Determinants of Unemployment: Do They Interact with Labour Market Institutions?' (Vol. 273). William Davidson Institute Working Paper.

Griffith, R., Harrison, R. and Macartney, G, (2006). 'Product Market Reforms, Labour Market Institutions and Unemployment', *Economic Journal*, Vol. 117, No. 519, C142–C166.

Koeniger, W. and Vindigni, A. (2003). 'Employment Protection and Product Market Regulation', IZA WZB Economics Seminar Series.

Krueger, A. B. and Pischke, J. S. (1997). 'Observations and Conjectures on the US Employment Miracle', (No. w6146), National Bureau of Economic Research.

Kugler, A. and Pica, G. (2006). 'The Effects of Employment Protection and Product Market Regulations on the Italian Labour Market: Labour Market Adjustments in Europe', IZA Discussion Paper No. 948.

Lehmann, E., Lucifora, C., Moriconi, S. and Van der Linden, B. (2014). 'Beyond the Labour Income Tax Wedge: The Unemployment-Reducing Effect of Tax Progressivity', IZA DP No. 8276.

Lipsey, R. G. and Lancaster, K. (1956). 'The General Theory of Second Best', *Review of Economic Studies*, Vol. 24, No. 1, 11–32.

Loayza, N. V., Oviedo, A. M. and Servén, L. (2005). *Regulation and Macroeconomic Performance*. World Bank.

Lora, E. A. (2000). 'What Makes Reforms Likely? Timing and Sequencing of Structural Reforms in Latin America', IDB Working Paper No. 355.

Nickell, S., Nunziata, L. and Ochel, W. (2005). 'Unemployment in the OECD since the 1960s: What Do We Know?' *Economic Journal*, Vol. 115, No. 500, 1–27.

Nicoletti, G. and Scarpetta, S. (2006). 'Regulation and Economic Performance: Product Market Reforms and Productivity in the OECD', *Institutions, Development, and Economic Growth*, Vol. 13, 81.

Nsouli, M. S. M., Rached, M. M. and Funke, M. N. (2002). 'The Speed of Adjustment and the Sequencing of Economic Reforms: Issues and Guidelines for Policymakers', (No. 2-132), International Monetary Fund.

OECD (2011). *Tax Policy Studies, Taxation and Employment*. OECD Publishing.

(2014). 'The 2012 Labour Market Reform in Spain: A Preliminary Assessment', June.

Orszag, J. M. (1998). 'Anatomy of Policy Complementarities', *Swedish Economic Policy Review*, Vol. 5, 11–33.

Piton, C. and Rycx, F. (2018). 'The Unemployment Impact of Product and Labour Market Regulation: Evidence from European Countries', IZA Discussion Papers 11582, Institute of Labor Economics (IZA).

Rader, T. (1976). 'The Welfare Loss from Price Distortions', *Econometrica: Journal of the Econometric Society*, Vol. 44, No. 6, 1253–1257.

Roland, G. (2000). *Transition and Economics: Politics, Markets, and Firms*. MIT Press.

Sachs, A. (2015). 'Unemployment, Institutions, and Interdependencies: Identifying Successful Reforms', *Journal of Economic Policy Reform*, Vol. 18, No. 1, 34–50.

Sakyi, D., Villaverde, J., Maza, A. and Reddy Chittedi, K. (2012). 'Trade Openness, Growth and Development: Evidence from Heterogeneous Panel Cointegration Analysis for Middle-Income Countries', *Cuadernos de Economía*, Vol. 31, 21–40.

Sestito, P, and Viviano, E. (2018). 'Firing Costs and Firm Hiring: Evidence from an Italian Reform', *Economic Policy*, Vol. 33, No. 93, 101–130.

Spilimbergo, M. A., Prati, M. A. and Ostry, M. J. D. (2009). 'Structural Reforms and Economic Performance in Advanced and Developing Countries', (No. 268), International Monetary Fund.

Turrini, A., Koltay, G., Pierini, F. et al. (2015). 'A Decade of Labour Market Reforms in the EU: Insights from the LABREF Database', *IZA J Labor Policy*, Vol. 4, No. 12. doi:10.1186/s40173-015-0038-5.

Wacziarg, R. and Wallack, J. S. (2004). 'Trade Liberalization and Intersectoral Labour Movements', *Journal of International Economics*, Vol. 64, No. 2, 411–439.

Wasmer, E. and Weil, P. (2004). 'The Macroeconomics of Labour and Credit Market Imperfections', *American Economic Review*, Vol. 94, No. 4, 944–963.

PART III

Case Studies

10 *Structural Reforms in Europe*
Lessons from Early Experiences

ORKUN SAKA, ANGELO MARTELLI, MICHAEL GANSLMEIER, YUEMEI JI, NAURO F. CAMPOS AND PAUL DE GRAUWE

10.1 Introduction

This chapter focuses on a set of major reform episodes that occurred across both financial and labour markets in four European countries in the 1980s and 1990s.[1] The countries under analysis are Denmark, France, Greece and Portugal. This series of case studies was carefully chosen because they certainly represent among the most intense reform efforts in the two domains we have focused on and because they are distant enough from major crises and spillover effects from interconnected countries. Because of the methodology we are implementing, Synthetic Control Method, the analysis of these early reform experiences allows us to have pre- and posttreatment periods that are long enough to investigate the effects on our outcomes of interest: growth and inequality for both domains, and bank deposit per capita and employment to population ratio for financial and labour market reforms respectively. The results are very mixed in nature, showing that the relationship between structural reforms and several macro measures, also in the long run, may not yield the intended results and an institutional embedding to explain differences in performance is necessary.

Billmeier and Nannicini (2013) started to use the synthetic control method in the reform-growth literature by estimating the effect of trade liberalization on real GDP per capita. Hereby, they have estimated all liberalization episodes between 1965 and 2005 for countries in the

[1] We thank seminar participants at the London School of Economics (LSE) Structural Reforms Workshop on 11 May 2018 for valuable comments on a previous version. This work was supported by the Economic and Social Research Council grant ES/P000274/1. The usual disclaimer applies.

Middle East, Asia, Africa and Latin America. Overall, their results indicate a positive impact of trade liberalization, although the effect varies across countries. It seems that the reform effects of countries that liberalized at a later state – e.g., African countries in the 1990s – do not reach conventional significance levels.

In line with these results, Terzi and Marrazzo (2017) investigated the effect of real and financial structural reforms on economic growth. Conducting synthetic controls for twenty-two countries between 1961 and 2000, they found that the overall impact of liberalizing the national economy is positive, although heterogeneous treatment effects exist between advanced and emerging economies. To be more specific, advanced economies seem to materialize the benefits earlier but to a smaller extent compared to emerging countries.

Duval et al. (2018) used the synthetic approach to identify the effect of labour and product market regulation on economic performance. Hereby, reforms in four out of six countries turned out to have a positive impact. Interestingly, the labour market reforms in Denmark and New Zealand in the early 1990s seem to have no positive impact on economic growth.

In contrast to these studies, a positive impact of flat tax reforms could be documented by Adhikari and Alm (2016), who found that the adoption of flat tax systems spurs economic growth in eight Eastern and Central European countries between 1994 and 2005. Seven of these cases reach conventional significance levels. The average treatment effect of all eight countries estimates that the adoption of flat tax systems increases average gross domestic product (GDP) per capita by 18.2 per cent.

10.2 Methodology

10.2.1 Synthetic Control Method (SCM)

First proposed by Abadie and Gardeazabal (2003) and later developed by Abadie et al. (2010, 2015), SCM is a program evaluation tool that estimates the effect of a treatment (in this chapter, a structural reform) on a given unit (e.g., country) at a certain point in time. This data-driven case study approach comes along with two major advantages: first, the data-driven selection of comparison groups can be considered as a more objective way of choosing adequate control units. Second,

SCM estimates the trajectory of a counterfactual scenario for the treated unit by producing a weighted average of the outcomes of the untreated units in the control group. Unit-specific nonnegative weights are determined by employing an optimization method that aims to minimize the pretreatment distance between the outcome of the treated unit and the weighted average outcome of the control units. Thus, these optimal weights are projected over the posttreatment period in order to synthetically create a counterfactual outcome and determine the magnitude of the treatment effect for the treated unit.

The SCM has often been used in empirical studies in the field of structural reforms.[2] The overall goal in this literature is to determine the effect of a reform in a given country by estimating the difference between 'what has happened with the reform' (i.e., observed growth experience of the reforming country) and 'what would have happened without the reform' (i.e., growth experience of a synthetic counterfactual composed of nonreforming countries) in the time period following the reform introduction. Structural reforms in areas such as trade and labour market policies have been typical examples in recent empirical SCM studies (Billmeier and Nannicini, 2013; Terzi and Marrazzo, 2017). The present analysis aims to build on these studies by estimating the impact of financial market and labour market reforms in selected European countries.

10.2.2 Model Specification

In all our estimations, we define several model parameters. First, in each of our case studies, the year in which a specific type of reform was introduced is represented by T_0 and the pretreatment period covers the twenty years between T_{-20} and T_{-1}. As Abadie et al. (2015) have argued, a sufficiently long pretreatment period is crucial for identification as it ensures that the unobservable time-varying shocks would be captured by the synthetic counterfactual.[3] Ending the optimization period at T_{-1} has the advantage that the immediate effects of the

[2] SCM has been used extensively in the empirical literature. See Ferman et al. (2018) for a review.

[3] Due to data availability however, the pretreatment period we employ could not be extended further.

treatment do not influence the donor composition.[4] Second, the post-treatment period lasts from T_0 until T_9, meaning that not only can we estimate the instantaneous effect, but we can also plot the dynamic effects of reforms over time.

In order to pick which reform episodes to focus on, we need a consistent dataset of reforms over countries and time. Arguably, the financial reform dataset first coined by Abiad et al. (2010) and then partly extended by Denk and Gomes (2017) is the most prominent and comprehensive dataset in that respect. Thus, we combine these two datasets and compute the largest yearly changes in the aggregate financial liberalization index for the countries in the European Union from 1973 to 2015. Focusing on the positive changes, we select the four largest financial liberalization episodes in the history of the EU, namely France 1984, Denmark 1988, Portugal 1992 and Greece 1993. Although Italy adopted major financial liberalization policies in 1993, we do not take the country into account because of the European Exchange Rate Mechanism (ERM) crisis.[5] On the labour market side, we select the same treated countries as in the financial side in order to draw direct comparisons between the effects of financial and labour market reforms on the same set of countries. According to the Institute of Labour Economics (IZA) dataset, the aforementioned countries undertook structural labour market reforms in the following years: France 1986, Denmark 1995, Portugal 1996 and Greece 1990.

We are especially interested in how financial liberalization affects (1) log GDP per capita, (2) labour share of GDP and (3) bank deposit per capita for financial reforms and employment level for labour reforms. The first indicator will tell us about the economic growth rate of the country, and the second is a proxy for the level of economic inequality, while the last one is a measure of development in the related sector.

In order to improve the matching between the donor and the treated countries and thus enhance the reliability of the estimated counterfactual, we control for the following covariates: population, population growth, investment share of real GDP per capita, openness ((export + import)/GDP), percentage of secondary schooling

[4] In the SCM literature, donors are simply the control units that are assigned positive weights in determining the synthetic outcome. Control units can only be assigned a nonnegative weight, including zero.

[5] In this case, it is methodologically impossible to isolate the effect of the reform from the coinciding ERM crisis.

completed, percentage of tertiary schooling completed and financial (or labour) reform index. Although some covariates may receive more loadings than others, they are generally useful to assign donor weightings to countries that are similar to the treated unit along key country characteristics. However, controlling for further covariates does not guarantee the creation of a suitable counterfactual because of the following two reasons: first, the estimated synthetic country (for example, Italy) should not be a linear combination of donor countries only located at the minimum and maximum of the dependent variable and/or covariates (for example, Sweden and Ghana). Second, donor countries that have experienced major economic turmoil and/or undertaken structural reforms themselves would bias the treatment effect. In order to limit such concerns, it is conventional to manually exclude some units from the potential donor pool beforehand. In our case, we drop countries that either (1) experienced one or more financial crises between T_{-5} and T_4; or (2) adopted major (financial or labour) reforms in the 1970s, 1980s and 1990s; or (3) have a population at $T_0 < 1$mio; or (4) belong to the 25 per cent poorest countries among all donor pool countries (based on GDP per capita).

In addition to these exclusions, the SCM algorithm requires fairly good data coverage. Thus, countries that have no data for at least one of the predictors for the entire pretreatment period have to be dropped. In addition, countries with any missing values for the dependent variable between T_{-20} and T_9 are removed as well.

10.3 Results

10.3.1 Financial Reforms

10.3.1.1 French Banking Act in 1984

The French banking system entered the 1980s with a heavy regulatory hangover. There was a credit-ceiling arrangement, called *encadrement du crédit*, that forced limits on the amount of lending that banks could provide to the private sector. The policy was adopted in order to limit the money growth, which had led to multiple devaluations of the domestic currency between 1974 and 1976. In addition, the government had many subsidized schemes that were granted exemptions from these restrictive credit-ceiling rules. Hence, subsidized lending started dominating the credit markets and there were as many as 250 different subsidy programmes by 1984.

The socialist government in power undertook further bank nationalizations in 1982 despite having already had a significant presence in the banking sector, increasing its share to more than 50 per cent. Interest rates were also regulated by the central bank to such an extent that some observers claim that they played a minimal role in capital allocation (Naouri, 1986).

Given this background, the Banking Act of 1984 came as a major reform shock for the French financial system. In essence, it eliminated entry barriers in the banking industry, simplified the framework for commercial banking activities and modernized the prudential rules that levelled the playing field across different types of banks. Immediately after the Act, the subsidized loans were eliminated, and the previous credit-ceiling arrangements were abolished. These developments are also captured by the dataset we employ (Abiad et al., 2010) and major positive (liberalizing) changes are reported in the interest rate, entry barriers and banking supervision aspects of the aggregate financial reform index.

The literature studying this specific reform episode generally focused on the efficiency gains that these reforms brought along. For instance, an early survey showed that reforms triggered efficiency concerns among bank managers in France, especially in terms of reducing costs and better monitoring for the credit performance (Rémy and Sergent, 1986). Discussing the positive externalities of these banking reforms on capital markets development in France, Melitz (1990) concluded that they decreased the historical bank dependence of the real sector and changed the financial profile of the country more towards an Anglo-Saxon model. At the micro level, Bertrand et al. (2007) provided empirical evidence that bank lending started flowing to more productive firms following these reforms.

From this cited literature, one could optimistically expect to see a positive effect of this reform package on macro outcomes such as the growth rate of the country. Our results, reported in Figure 10.1, shed a different light, however. Figure 10.1a illustrates that the growth rate of the GDP per capita in France was not able to keep up with its synthetic counterpart after the reforms were introduced, suggesting a negative causal impact of reforms on economic growth. In line with this underperformance, Figure 10.1b shows that the postreform share of labour in the economy decreased, suggesting a substantial uptick in economic inequality involving a redistribution from labour to capital.

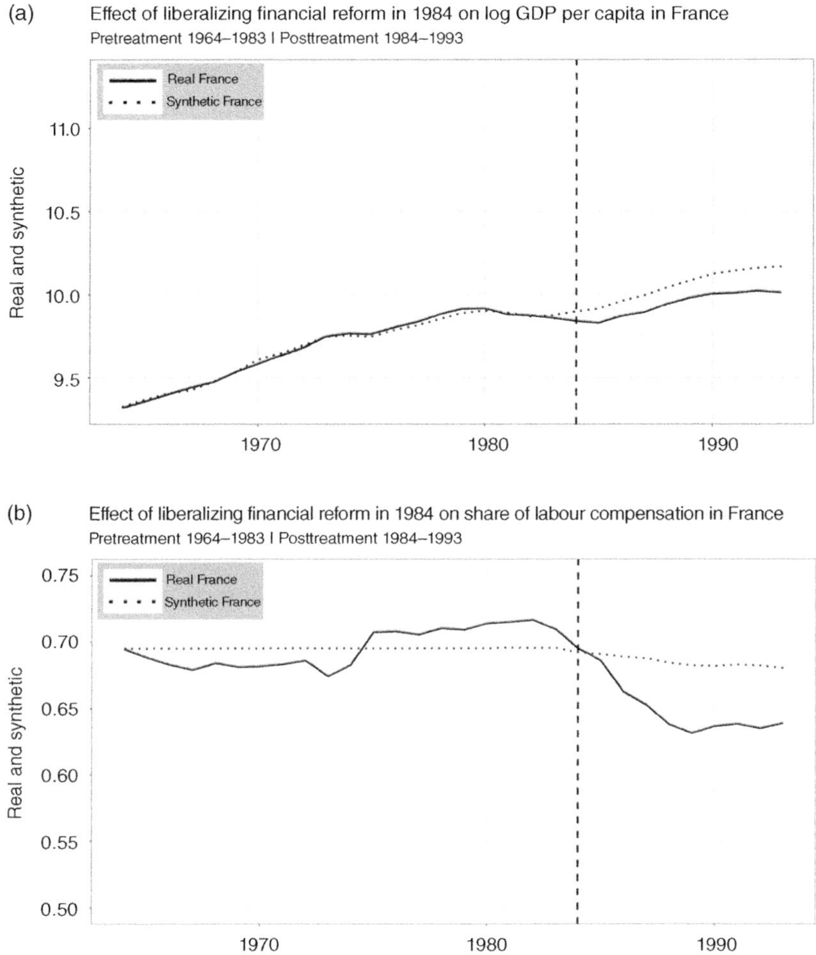

Figure 10.1 The effects of 1984 financial reforms in France. The figure shows the realized (solid line) and synthetic (dotted line) outcomes in France from 1964 to 1993. The dashed line indicates the reform year in 1984.

Finally, it seems from Figure 10.1c that banking reforms were not able to improve the deposit conditions at French banks, at least not as much as the level of France's counterparts represented by the synthetic trend.

These results lead us to conclude that, although it may have fixed certain failures in credit markets, the French Banking Act of 1984 was not particularly successful at the macro level. This in itself constitutes an interesting

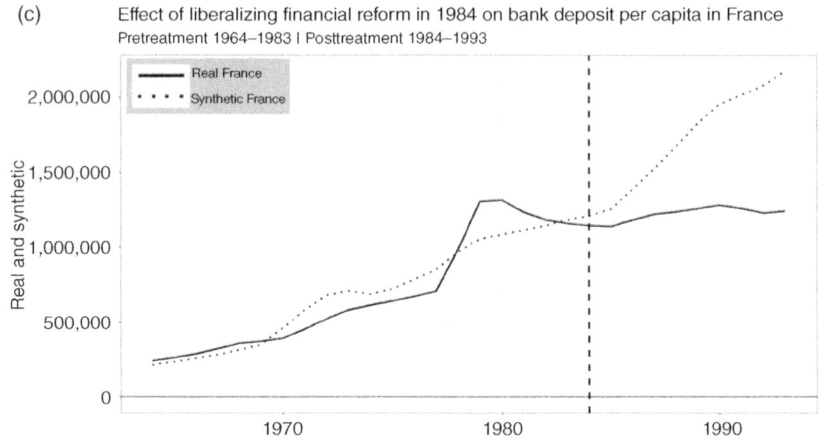

Figure 10.1(*cont.*)

finding where micro and macro outcomes do not seem to have tended towards the same direction. What was crucially different regarding the French Banking Act was the big-bang nature of the reforms, which introduced different dimensions of financial liberalization all at the same time.

10.3.1.2 Danish Financial Liberalization Wave in 1988

The financial system in Denmark was already well integrated with the rest of the world starting from late 1950s onwards and most of the internal liberalization had already taken place in the early 1980s (Jonung, 2008). Hence, 1988, the year during which our dataset indicates a large reform was introduced, cannot be considered categorically the same as the 1984 period in France that was discussed in the previous section. In 1984, France was at low levels of liberalization in most dimensions and tried to liberalize its financial system all at once with a big-bang-like reform effort. In contrast, Denmark was already at a more liberalized level and was taking gradual steps for further reforms in the beginning of 1980s so that 1988 was not a substantially different year than others in terms of the magnitude of reform it brought.

Our dataset shows that the main areas of reform in Denmark during this period was not about interest rates or credit controls, which were almost fully liberalized by that point; but they were about international capital flows and entry barriers in the banking sector. This reform push led

Denmark to open up to foreign banks and also to hot money flows that were vastly feared a decade ago. Alongside foreign bank entry, the country modernized its regulatory framework and updated its banking supervision laws.

Figure 10.2 shows us how these changes affected the key macro outcomes in Denmark. First, GDP per capita seems to have

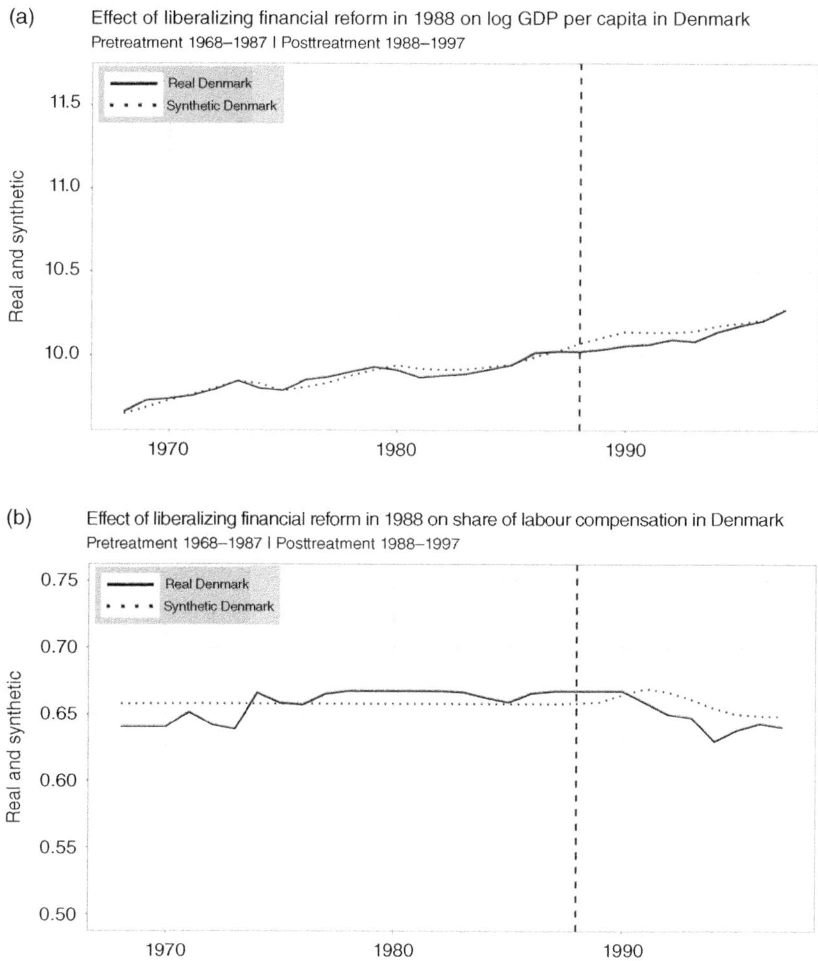

Figure 10.2 The effects of 1988 financial reforms in Denmark. The figure shows the realized (solid line) and synthetic (dotted line) outcomes in Denmark from 1968 to 1997. The dashed line indicates the reform year in 1988.

(c)

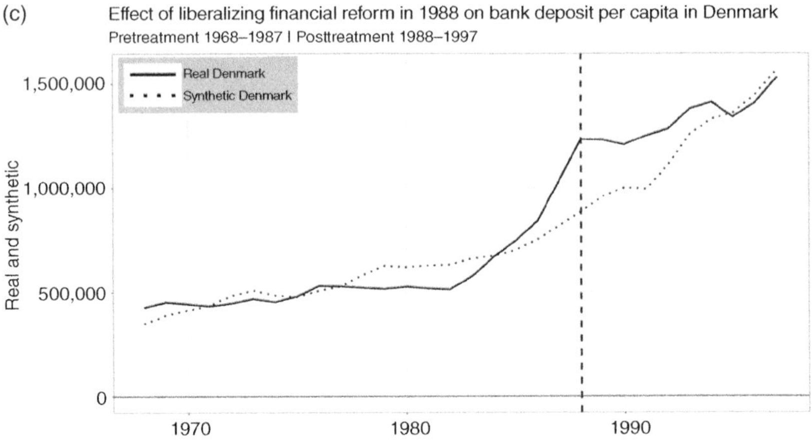

Figure 10.2(*cont.*)

underperformed in the short term; however, it later caught up in the longer term, after which the effect becomes invisible. Similar to what happened in France in 1984, the labour share of the Danish GDP follows a downward trend after the reforms and – even though the counterfactual trend is also in the negative direction – the difference between the real and synthetic series gets larger, indicating increasing inequality after the reform introduction (an increasing redistribution from labour to capital). Finally, it is harder to interpret the results for the bank deposit per capita trend since the matching between the real and synthetic series is not great during the prereform period, leading us to doubt the identification of the treatment effect. All in all, the Danish liberalization wave does not seem to have triggered a major positive change in any of the macroeconomic indicators that we investigate.

10.3.1.3 Bank Privatizations in Portugal in 1992

After the revolution in 1974 and the subsequent heavy state involvement in almost all parts of the economy, Portugal experienced the 1980s with restrictive financial regulations and a large part of its banking system being under government control. Restrictions on the amount of credit and on interest rates were common during this period. Furthermore, commercial and investment banks had different regulatory treatments and were legally separated. The range of activities that commercial banks could engage in was also restricted, leading to low levels of competition, innovation and efficiency (Lagoa et al., 2013).

In the late 1980s and early 1990s, Portugal changed its track in economic management. After the country became a member of the European Economic Community in 1986, there was a need to integrate its economy into the European Common Market. Therefore, the country started relaxing its banking regulatory framework, opening up its borders for private capital and allowing foreign banks to come and operate in the country. Between 1990 and 1994, the number of banks in the country almost doubled.

Specifically, in 1992, there were several aspects of financial liberalization that were initiated. During this year, our dataset indicates that the last set of controls on the interest rates and banking entry barriers were eliminated while the financial supervision was improved. But most importantly, the first phase of the banking privatizations was put into practice within this year. This was a crucial point since it was the first push to curb the direct state influence on financial institutions that had been there since the 1974 revolution that had irreversibly nationalized the banking sector by writing it down in the country's constitution.

Figure 10.3 illustrates the net effect of this reform episode. In the short term, it is hard to say there was an effect on economic growth; however, it seems that Portugal positively differentiated itself from its counterfactual in the longer horizon, albeit not substantially (Figure 10.3a). There is also a positive change in terms of economic inequality as illustrated by the stable trend for Portugal and the downward trend for its counterfactual. Finally, bank deposits also show an increasingly positive differentiation between Portugal and its synthetic and mainly point to the faster development of the financial system after the reform efforts.

Overall, compared to the past two cases in France and Denmark, the 1992 reform in Portugal sheds a more positive light on the costs and benefits of financial liberalization. The most important differentiating aspect of this period was the long-waited privatization of the banking system, which is likely to be the main reason lying behind the more positive patterns in Figure 10.3. Such large-scale privatizations did not occur in the previous cases. Although the interaction of different financial reforms, complementarity among them, and their

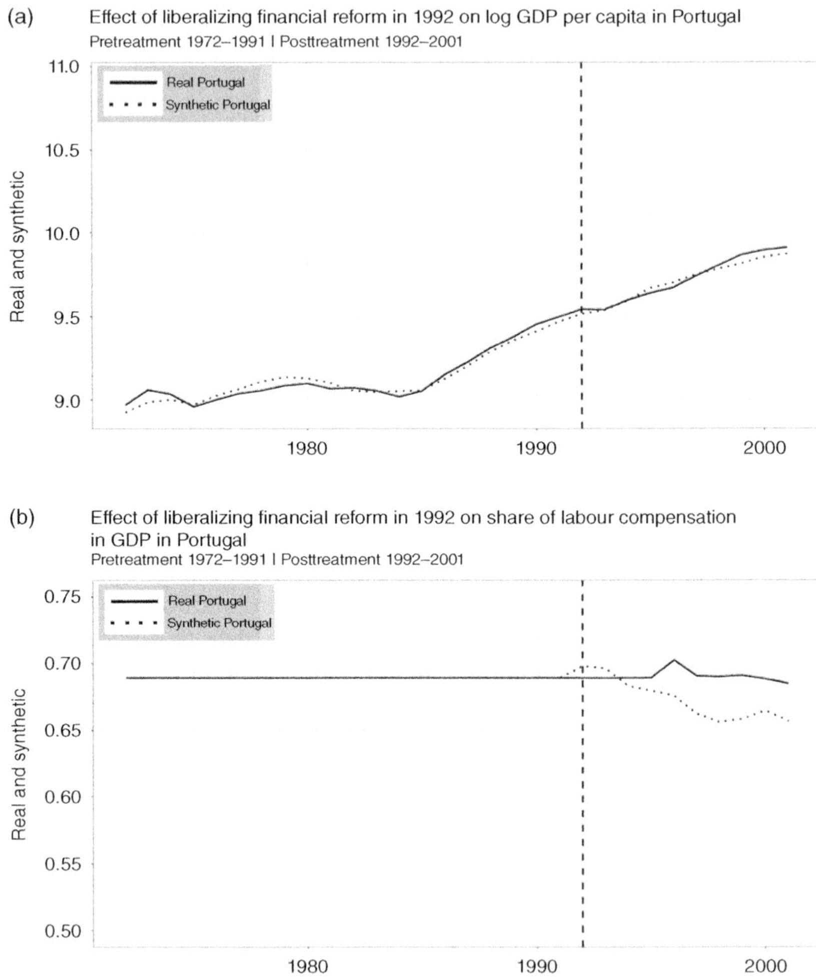

Figure 10.3 The effects of 1992 financial reforms in Portugal. The figure shows the realized (solid line) and synthetic (dotted line) outcomes in Portugal from 1972 to 2001. The dashed line indicates the reform year in 1992.

sequence must be important, Portugal illustrates a scenario where cutting off the ownership links between the state and the banking sector may indeed be fruitful for the country's macroeconomic performance in the long run. It is worth noting that in contrast to France and Denmark, Portugal did not experience a redistribution from labour to capital.

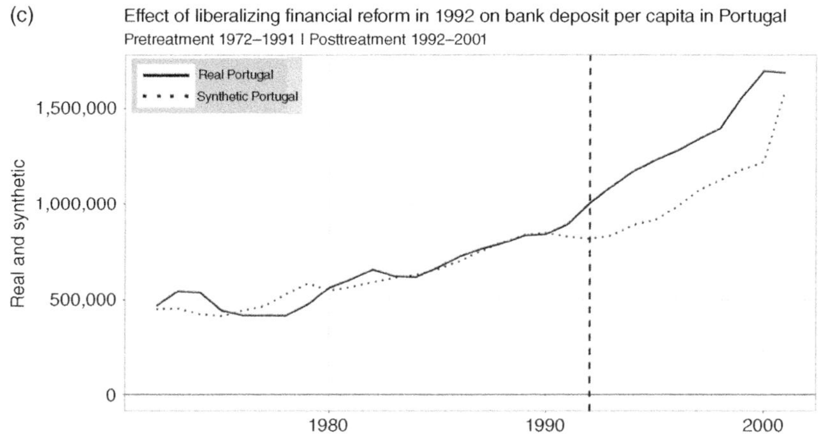

Figure 10.3(*cont.*)

10.3.1.4 EC Directives in Greece in 1993

In order to adopt several European Council (EC) directives in August 1992, the Greek government passed a Banking Law, which brought several changes to the country's financial system starting from 1993. First of all, the adopted directives had many aspects that related to the liberalization of the securities market. They aimed to increase the scale and variety of the instruments in the capital markets as well as better governance of the stock markets. Within the same year, the minimum rate requirement on deposits (determined by the Bank of Greece) was abolished. Lastly, the compulsory investment requirement of commercial banks in government paper was lifted. This meant banks could freely buy government paper, thus demanding higher yields in times of higher risk and providing better incentives for the government to be fiscally prudent.

Figure 10.4 shows the macro effects of these reforms. There seems to be a bit of an underperformance in Greek economic growth (compared to its synthetic counterfactual), though the size of the effect seems to be marginal. For labour share, it is hard to say if there is an effect whatsoever. And for the financial development, it seems that bank deposits grew more slowly in Greece; however, it is difficult to be conclusive since the prereform matching between the synthetic and the real series does not seem to be at the ideal level.

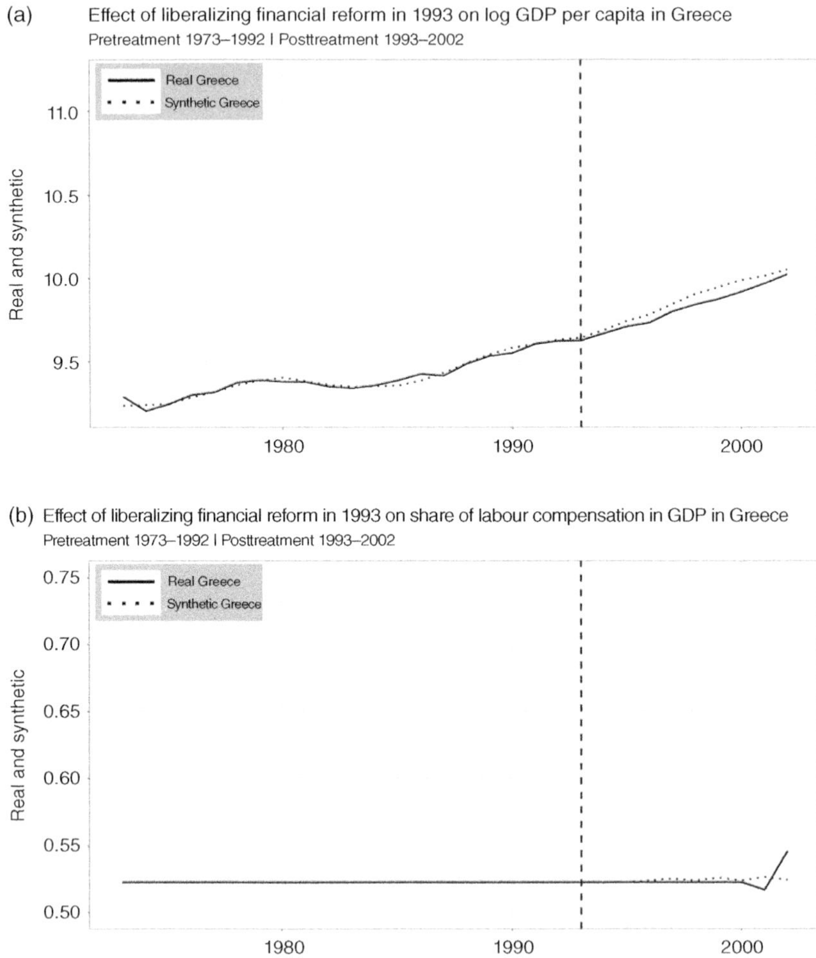

Figure 10.4 The effects of 1993 financial reforms in Greece. The figure shows the realized (solid line) and synthetic (dotted line) outcomes in Greece from 1973 to 2002. The dashed line indicates the reform year in 1993.

10.3.2 Labour Reforms

10.3.2.1 France 1986

The labour market reform of 1986 in France was deliberalizing in nature according to the fRDB-IZA Social Reforms database. On the one hand, there was an increase in unemployment benefits; on the

(c)

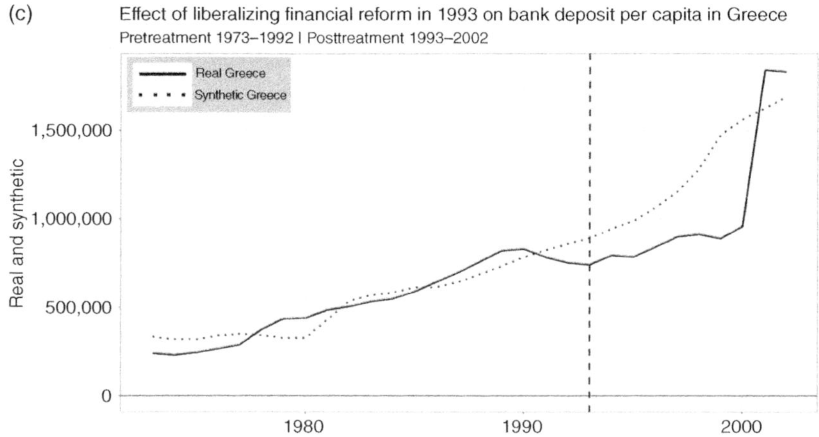

Figure 10.4(*cont.*)

other hand, the reform tackled the use of fixed-term contracts (Contrats à durée determine, or CDDs), which had been introduced in 1979 and that had already seen a first reduction in their scope in 1982. With the 1986 reform the twelve conditions under which firms could use CDDs were replaced by a general rule prohibiting firms from using them to fill a permanent position. According to Blanchard and Landier (2002), which considered data for young workers since the early 1980s, the aforementioned measures increased turnover, without a substantial reduction in unemployment duration; moreover, the effect on welfare for this cohort seems to have been negative.

Looking at our synthetic results in Figure 10.5 and starting from the effect the 1986 reform had on log GDP per capita, we see that France performed consistently worse compared to the synthetic group in the posttreatment period. The gap between the two is actually widening in the later years, implying that the increase in benefits led to negative income effects. This result is in line with the previously mentioned literature where the authors show that the welfare effects of these measures appear to have been negative.

Moving to the effect the reform had on inequality, here proxied by the share of labour compensation in GDP, we discover that the delib-eralization led to a substantial decrease in the share of labour

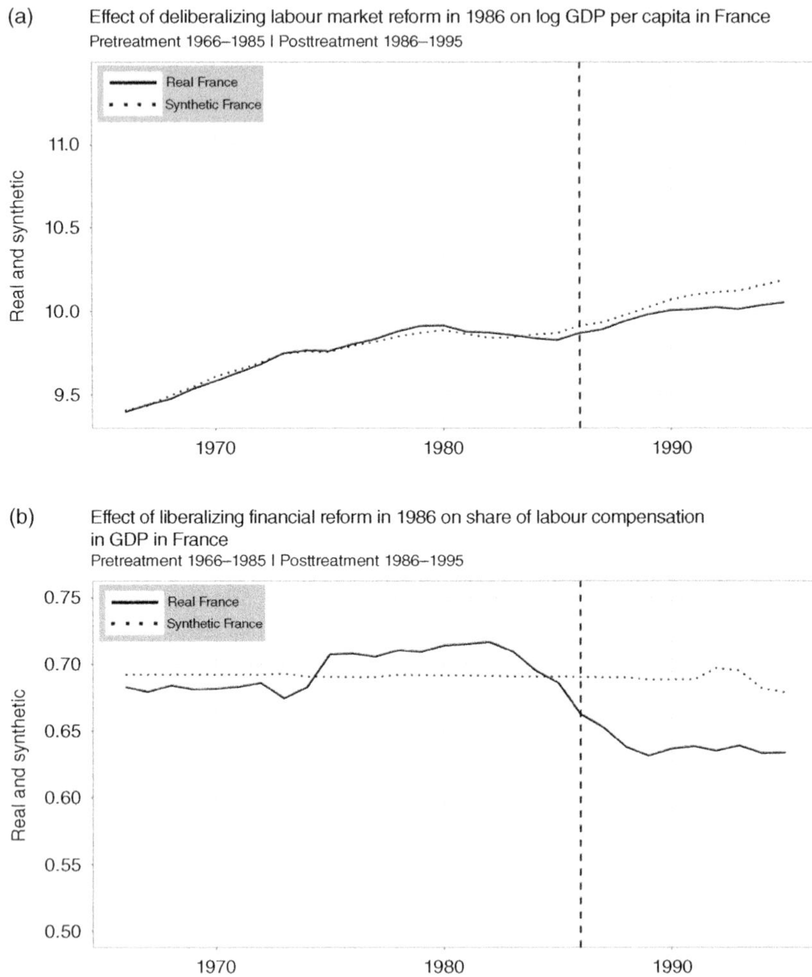

Figure 10.5 The effects of 1986 labour reforms in France. The figure shows the realized (solid line) and synthetic (dotted line) outcomes in France from 1973 to 2002. The dashed line indicates the reform year in 1993.

compensation of roughly 5 per cent from 0.69 to 0.64. This is quite surprising as many of these reforms introduced by the French socialist government explicitly aimed at forcing a redistribution from capital to labour. However, we have to note that the quality of the pretreatment matching for this particular measure is particularly poor, thus we need to interpret results with caution.

(c) Effect of deliberalizing labour market reform in 1986 on employment–population ratio in France
Pretreatment 1966–1985 I Posttreatment 1986–1995

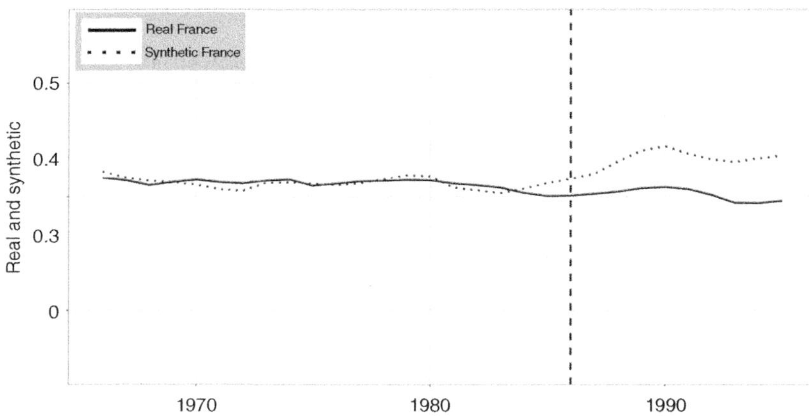

Figure 10.5(*cont.*)

Finally, when we look at the effect of the reform on the employment–population ratio, the results, which in this case display a very good prematching performance, show that the reform measures led to an inferior performance for France compared to the synthetic counterfactual. This indicator, which does not suffer from short-term fluctuations or seasonal variations, is likely to be directly affected by the increase in unemployment benefits and changes in the use of fixed-term contracts. We have a very slight increase in the ratio for France in the years following the reform, but this trend is inverted for the later years with the number of people employed divided by the total number of people of working age falling after 1990 and a gap between real and synthetic of roughly 4 per cent.

10.3.2.2 Denmark 1995

When we look at the main changes in labour market policy over 1994–1995 in Demark, a number of measures were adopted to tackle in particular the shortages of skilled labour experienced in those years (EU Commission, Employment and Social Affairs, Labour Market Studies Denmark, 1996). The main liberalizing drive was motivated by two complementary objectives: to reduce both structural unemployment and registered unemployment. The labour market policy involved among other things a reduction of the benefit period, a doubling of the period required to acquire unemployment entitlements, earlier activation schemes, introduction of a right and duty to training or education for unskilled unemployed persons under twenty-five years of age after six months of unemployment.

Analysing the effects the reform had on GDP per capita, in Figure 10.6, we observe that the pretreatment has a very good matching. After the threshold, Denmark performed slightly better than the

(a) Effect of liberalizing labour market reform in 1995 on log GDP per capita in Denmark
Pretreatment 1975–1994 I Posttreatment 1995–2004

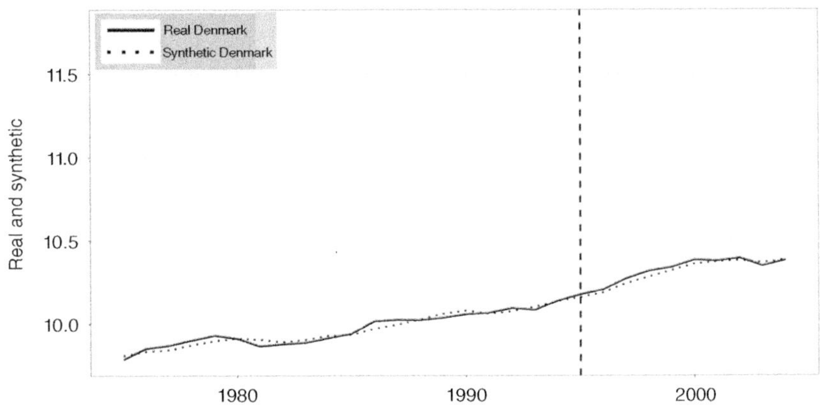

(b) Effect of liberalizing financial reform in 1995 on share of labour compensation in Denmark
Pretreatment 1975–1994 I Posttreatment 1995–2004

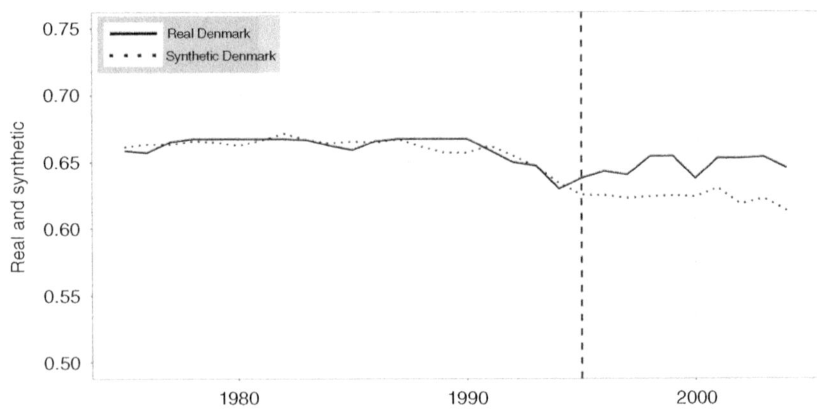

Figure 10.6 The effects of 1995 labour reforms in Denmark. The figure shows the realized (solid line) and synthetic (dotted line) outcomes in Denmark from 1973 to 2002. The dashed line indicates the reform year in 1993.

(c) Effect of liberalizing labour market reform in 1995 on employment–population ratio in Denmark
Pretreatment 1964–1983 I Posttreatment 1984–1993

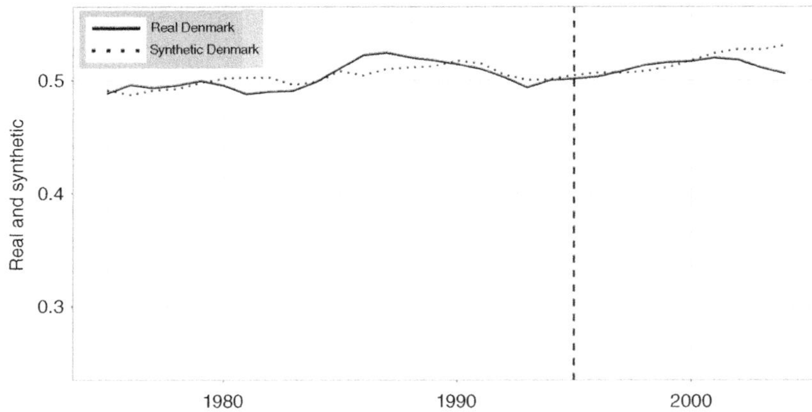

Figure 10.6(*cont.*)

synthetic counterfactual up to 2000, after which the gap disappears. The difference between Denmark and its synthetic counterfactual is so small as to be insignificant.

Moving to assess the performance in terms of employment to population ratio, we see that again Denmark improves very slightly up to 2000, but then there is a major reversal compared to the synthetic after this year with a significant deterioration in this indicator. The liberalization measures thus were not long-lasting with the opposite effect than the intended one observed after 2000.

Finally, when looking at our measure of inequality, we have that the reform actually led to an improvement in the indicator when comparing Denmark to the synthetic counterfactual, highlighting that the measures reversed the drop experienced by the country from 1990. It seems therefore that while the liberalization applied stricter conditions to access benefits and reduced their duration, the boost in activation and upskilling led to a redistribution favouring labour.

10.3.2.3 Portugal 1996

In 1996, as part of the Short-Term Social Pact, Portugal introduced a set of liberalizing measures for a more flexible organization of working time. In particular, the reform involved a great use of temporary work agency employment and focused on reducing job demarcation (Duval et al.,

2018). This was a major change in the patterns of industrial relations in Portugal, therefore we expect the effects on our indicators to be substantial.

Starting from the effect on GDP per capita in Figure 10.7, we observe that the liberalization led to much higher performance for

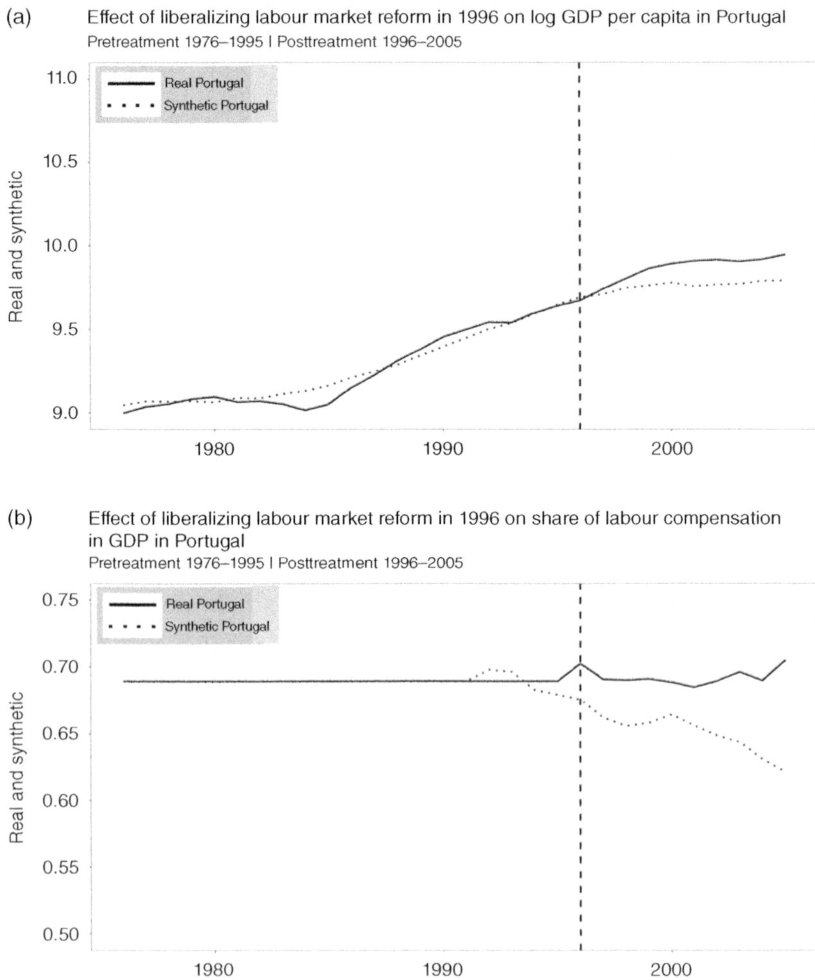

Figure 10.7 The effects of 1996 labour reforms in Portugal. The figure shows the realized (solid line) and synthetic (dotted line) outcomes in Greece from 1973 to 2002. The dashed line indicates the reform year in 1993.

(c) Effect of liberalizing labour market reform in 1996 on employment–population ratio in Portugal
Pretreatment 1976–1995 I Posttreatment 1996–2005

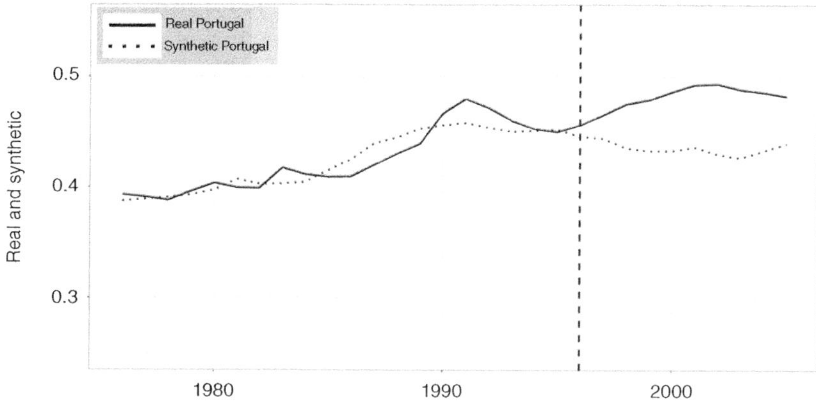

Figure 10.7(*cont.*)

the country compared to the synthetic counterfactual. The gap between the two increased significantly in the three years after 1996, roughly a 15 per cent rise, and remained stable after that, marking almost a permanent upward shift in the standards of living for the country. The positive effect of the reform with an upheaval of the organization of labour is therefore quite remarkable.

When looking at the measure for inequality, despite some problems with the matching for the pretreatment period, we can highlight that also in this case the difference is very large. While Portugal's share of labour compensation remained very high, also compared to the other countries we analysed, we see a major decline in the synthetic counterfactual. This provides empirical evidence that despite the liberalization drive, which increased extensively flexibility, Portugal managed to redistribute from capital to labour.

Lastly, when we look at the employment-to-population ratio, we note that despite the noise in the pretreatment period, the introduction of the reform measures led to a marked increase in our indicator. The liberalization thus impacted employment positively, which was one of the desired objectives of the reform efforts. The gap actually increases for a prolonged period, up to 2002 roughly, when the trend changes direction.

10.3.2.4 Greece 1990

Another major labour market reform was undertaken in Greece in 1990, when the previous system of inflation indexation was abandoned and industrial relations saw the introduction of a new legislation that drastically reduced direct government influence in collective negotiations (EU Commission, Employment and Social Affairs, Labour Market Studies Greece, 1996). As for other European countries at the time, the pattern of misalignment between real wages and changes in productivity or unemployment was a common feature, with governments playing a major role in the wage formation process. The 1990 reform efforts on the one hand tried to eliminate this interventionism while at the same time changing the regulation on the duration of unemployment benefits; however, this latter development was viewed by experts as a move towards less flexibility.

When we analyse the effects on GDP per capita, in Figure 10.8, we observe that the Greek performance is slightly worse than the synthetic counterfactual, but with the difference between the two being almost unnoticeable. This trend seems to reverse in the second half of the 1990s, with Greece seeing an increase in living standards compared to the synthetic.

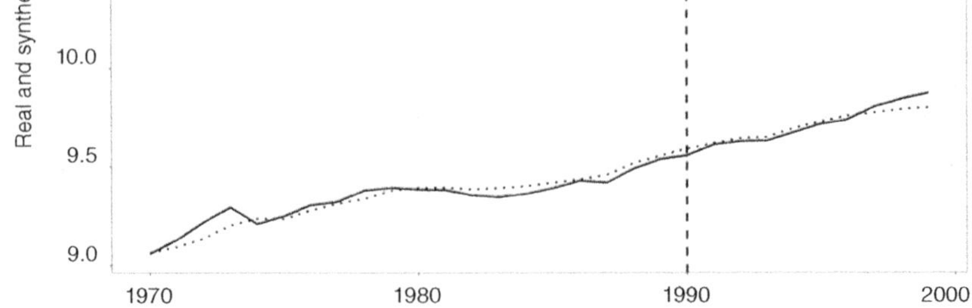

Figure 10.8 The effects of 1990 labour reforms in Greece. The figure shows the realized (solid line) and synthetic (dotted line) outcomes in Greece from 1973 to 2002. The dashed line indicates the reform year in 1993.

(b) Effect of deliberalizing labour market reform in 1990 on share of labour compensation in GDP in Greece
Pretreatment 1970–1989 I Posttreatment 1990–1999

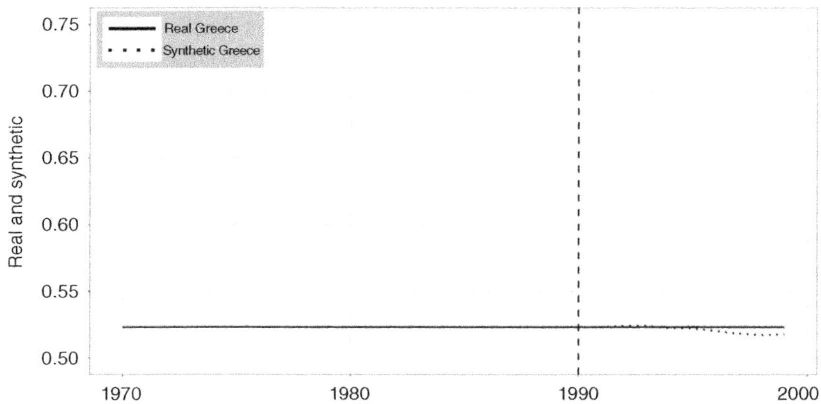

(c) Effect of deliberalizing labour market reform in 1990 on employment–population ratio in Greece
Pretreatment 1970–1989 I Posttreatment 1990–1999

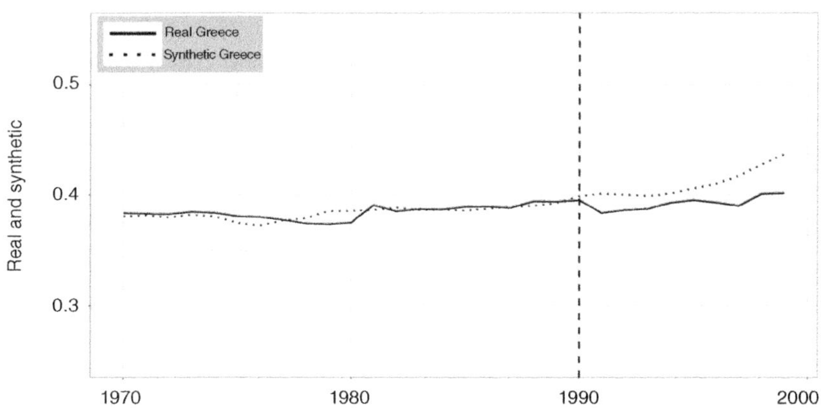

Figure 10.8(*cont.*)

It is rather hard to make any inference from the graph for inequality since the performance of this measure is rather poor. What we observe, however, is a minor improvement in the late 1990s compared to the synthetic.

Finally, when we look at the employment-to-population ratio, the reform seems to have had a more negative performance compared to the synthetic, with the gap increasing with time, especially when closer to the 2000s. This might have to do with the extension of the unemployment benefits duration, but it is hard to disentangle this effect from the reorganization of the industrial relations with less state interventionism in the collective bargaining system.

10.4 Conclusions

The series of reform episodes we have explored in this chapter has delivered a mixed picture on the relationship between structural reforms in the financial and labour market realms and the set of outcomes under investigation, including growth and inequality. Using a Synthetic Control Approach, we have selected four countries of interest (France, Denmark, Portugal and Greece) and picked reform efforts that occurred in the 1980s and 1990s, which has given us ample opportunity to observe their effects over a long posttreatment period and avoid potential interferences from major crises or spillovers. A number of interesting patterns emerge from the analysis. However, because of the mixed nature of the results and because the reforms were both liberalizing and deliberalizing in their direction, it is difficult to draw a set of conclusions that can be valid across the four countries and for the two reform domains. Put differently, although we obtain a number of interesting results, it remains true that financial reforms and labour market reforms are generally not good predictors of subsequent development of economic growth and inequality.

References

Abadie, A. and Gardeazabal, J. (2003). 'The Economic Costs of Conflict: A Case Study of the Basque Country', *American Economic Review*, Vol. 93, No. 1, 113–132.

Abiad, A., Detragiache, E. and Tressel, T. (2010a). 'A New Database of Financial Reforms', *IMF Staff Papers*, Vol. 57, No. 2, 281–302.

Abadie, A., Diamond, A. and Hainmueller, J. (2010b). 'Synthetic Control Methods for Comparative Case Studies: Estimating the Effect of California's Tobacco Control Program', *Journal of the American Statistical Association*, Vol. 105, No. 490, 493–505.

(2015). 'Comparative Politics and the Synthetic Control Method', *American Journal of Political Science*, Vol. 59, No. 2, 495–510.

Adhikari, B. and Alm, J. (2016). 'Evaluating the Economic Effects of Flat Tax Reforms Using Synthetic Control Methods', *Southern Economic Journal*, Vol. 83, No. 2, 437–463.

Bertrand, M., Schoar, A. and Thesmar, D. (2007). 'Banking Deregulation and Industry Structure: Evidence from the French Banking Reforms of 1985', *Journal of Finance*, Vol. 62, No. 2, 597–628.

Billmeier, A. and Nannicini, T. (2013). 'Assessing Economic Liberalization Episodes: A Synthetic Control Approach', *Review of Economics and Statistics*, Vol. 95, No. 3, 983–1001.

Blanchard O. and Landier, A. (2002). 'The Perverse Effects of Partial Labour Market Reform: Fixed-Term Contracts in France', *Economic Journal*, Vol. 112, No. 480, F214–F244,

Denk, O. and Gomes, G. (2017). 'Financial Re-regulation since the Global Crisis? An Index-Based Assessment', OECD Economics Department Working Papers, No. 1396.

Duval, R., Furceri, D., Hu, B., Jalles, J.T. and Nguyen, H. (2018), 'A Narrative Database of Major Labor and Product Market Reforms in Advanced Economies', IMF Working Paper.

EU Commission, Employment and Social Affairs, (1996). 'Labour Market Studies Greece'.

EU Commission, Employment and Social Affairs, (1996). 'Labour Market Studies Denmark'.

Ferman, B., Pinto, C. and Possebom, V. (2018). 'Cherry Picking with Synthetic Controls', Working Paper.

Jonung, L., (2008). 'Lessons from Financial Liberalisation in Scandinavia', *Comparative Economic Studies*, Vol. 50, No. 4, 564–598.

Lagoa, S., Leão, E., Mamede, R. and Barradas, R. (2013). 'Report on the Financial System in Portugal', Financialisation, Economy, Society and Sustainable Development (FESSUD) Project.

Melitz, J. (1990). 'Financial Deregulation in France', *European Economic Review*, Vol. 34, No. 2–3, 394–402.

Naouri, J. C. (1986). 'La réforme du financement de l'économie', *Revue Banque*, Vol. 459, 211–221.

Rémy, C. and Sergent, B. (1986). 'La banque en Europe: Les dix prochaines années', *Revue Banque*, Vol. 457, 37–42.

Terzi, A. and Marrazzo, P. M. (2017). 'Wide-Reaching Structural Reforms and Growth: A Cross-Country Synthetic Control Approach', (No. 82a). Center for International Development at Harvard University.

11 Fiscal Consolidation and Inequality

The Distributive Effects of Fiscal Reforms in Greece and Portugal

FABIAN MUSHÖVEL

11.1 Introduction

On 20 August 2018, Greece concluded its third Economic Adjustment Programme (EAP) following eight years of painful reforms and the largest government bailout in history. With economic recovery now under way, Greece follows the path of Portugal, Ireland and Cyprus, which have all received financial assistance by their European partners and the International Monetary Fund (IMF) in the wake of the sovereign debt crisis in the Eurozone periphery. All four countries in return had to implement far-reaching fiscal and structural reforms monitored by the supranational Troika of European Commission, IMF, and European Central Bank. While much of the debate has so far focused on the success of the reform programs in increasing the four countries' resilience to future shocks, bringing back economic growth and lowering public deficits and debt-to-GDP ratios to sustainable levels, the distributional impact of the reforms remains understudied. In particular, the deep cuts in public expenditure to achieve primary budget surpluses, as well as the substantive structural reforms aimed at increasing labour market flexibility, raise the question of whether the burden of the adjustment was shared equally or whether the reforms have led to deeper income inequality and more heavily segmented labour markets.

This chapter presents evidence from a comparative case study of the Greek and Portuguese EAPs, covering the duration of the Portuguese programme from 2011 to 2014, and the reforms under the Greek programmes between 2010 and 2017. The case study answers the questions of how the EAPs affected (1) the redistributive capacities of the welfare states of the recipient countries and (2) the distribution of incomes. It does so by combining the use of household income data taken from the latest waves of European Union Statistics on Income and Living Conditions (EU-SILC) panel data with data obtained through simulations run with tax-benefit microsimulation tool EUROMOD. Although the data offer some insights regarding the effects of structural reforms on inequality, the analysis focuses on fiscal policy reforms and their effects on the distribution and redistribution of incomes.

The evidence presented in this chapter shows that contrary to previous examples of deep fiscal consolidation and structural reforms, (1) inequality has remained stable throughout the reform process; (2) despite fiscal consolidation pressures, redistribution through the welfare state has increased and (3) controlling for the effects of the recession, the reforms of the EAPs had inequality-reducing first-order effect, which at times were large enough to offset the inequality increases induced by the recession through, e.g., higher unemployment.

Based on these findings, this chapter offers insights into the interplay between the design and composition of fiscal consolidation measures and their distributive effects: whether fiscal consolidation is achieved mainly through spending cuts or revenue increasing measures seems less crucial to the distributive impact of those measures than their exact design. In fact, the evidence suggests that adverse effects on relative inequality can be averted through increasing the proportion of the adjustment burden that is put on higher incomes, as well as the degree to which the most vulnerable income groups are protected or compensated.

The chapter is structured as follows. The following section provides a review of the economic literature on the interplay of fiscal consolidation programmes and inequality, particularly regarding composition and design of such reforms. The third section outlines methodological considerations, including case selection, datasets, inequality measurements and the use of tax-benefit microsimulation techniques. In the last section, the empirical findings are presented and discussed.

11.2 Literature Review

This section serves as a review of the existing economic literature on the distributive effects of such measures. In the past, research on phases of fiscal adjustment has largely focused on the determinants of success of the adjustment efforts. Much work has therefore been done in particular since the early 1990s on the effects of different variables of fiscal adjustment programmes, such as their size and composition. Most prominently, Alesina and Perotti (1995, 1996) and McDermott and Wescott (1996) have shown that expenditure-based fiscal consolidation programmes have a higher likelihood of success as well as being more sustainable fiscally in the long run.

The effects of such programmes on economic inequality, however, have only recently begun to climb further up on the research agenda. Studies in the past have distinguished between fiscal adjustment programmes in advanced economies, in which such programmes were implemented by national governments, and developing economies, usually as a condition for financial assistance from the IMF.

With regard to phases of fiscal adjustment in developing economies as part of a programme supervised by a supranational institution, Oberdabernig (2013) analyses the distributional effects of IMF programmes in eighty-six countries between 1982 and 2009. The study finds that in the majority of cases, the programme implementation correlated significantly with an increase in inequality, as well as poverty. However, the study ascertains that from 2000 onwards, this trend is reversed, and IMF programmes between 2000 and 2009 correlate with falling levels of inequality and poverty. This coincides with the adoption of the Poverty Reduction and Growth Facility (PRGF) by the IMF, although the author states that the analysis does not provide a clear confirmation that the PRGF in fact caused the change in the distributive effects of IMF programmes.

With regard to fiscal adjustment programmes in advanced economies, more detailed studies are available looking into the overall effects of such programmes, as well as differentiating between different designs and their respective distributional impacts. Agnello and Sousa (2014) analyse eighteen industrialised countries from 1978 to 2009, finding that periods of fiscal consolidation correlate with substantive increases in income inequality. Of particular relevance to the analysis at hand is the finding that the composition of the fiscal adjustment programmes is indeed vital for their impact on income inequality: the authors show that spending cuts lead to higher levels of income inequality, while measures that focus on increasing government revenues, such as tax increases, seem to compress the income distribution. A different study by Ball et al. (2013) finds that both expenditure-based and revenue-based consolidation programmes have inequality-increasing effects, although the effects of the former are more pronounced. A later study by Woo et al. (2017) confirms this in addition to finding that by altering the composition of the fiscal consolidation measures with regard to the progressivity of tax reforms and targeted social benefits, the inequality-increasing effects of the fiscal consolidation measures can be offset to a certain degree.

The general finding that the composition of fiscal consolidation programmes is key to their distributive effects is conceptually plausible: on the one hand, spending cuts tend to include cuts in social expenditure, which limits the redistribution of market incomes, and disproportionately affect lower income groups, thus explaining the inequality-increasing effects of fiscal consolidation programmes that are heavily expenditure based. On the other hand, tax increases can have inequality-reducing effects when they move within an already progressive system of taxation, as is usually the case with income tax reforms, as well neutral distributive or even inequality-increasing effects, when reforms are designed so that lower income groups are negatively affected, as tends to be the case with increases in value-added tax (VAT) rates. Therefore, it is important to register from the literature that there is a strong, but exclusively empirical, case for expenditure-based fiscal consolidation programmes to be inequality increasing, with more mixed evidence for revenue-based programmes.

Nevertheless, based on these past empirical studies, it is reasonable to expect increases in levels of income inequality during phases of fiscal adjustment. Following the empirical argument, the effect is likely to be larger in cases where fiscal adjustment is based heavily on expenditure cuts rather than revenue-increasing measures. This is of particular importance for the analysis at hand since the literature seems to identify a trade-off between a higher likelihood of success and sustainability of fiscal adjustment programmes on the one hand and progressive distributional outcomes on the other, since the former requires relying on expenditure cuts, while the latter is jeopardised by those exact expenditure-cuts. It is noteworthy, however, that the findings on IMF programmes post-2000 seem to suggest that this trade-off can be circumvented to some degree and that progressive distributive effects can in fact be achieved in spite of an expenditure-based approach to fiscal consolidation. This caveat is given additional weight by the lack of theoretical arguments in the literature outlining why a particular composition of fiscal consolidation programmes should necessarily lead to certain distributive effects. Despite the strong empirical case we have outlined here, it is therefore possible that fiscal consolidation may in fact go together with falling levels of inequality if designed accordingly.

11.3 Methodological Considerations

11.3.1 The Composition of the Fiscal Adjustment Programmes: the Logic behind the Case Selection of the Greek and Portuguese Programmes

The previous section has shown that there is a consensus in the literature that expenditure-based fiscal consolidation is more sustainable than revenue-based consolidation. Consulting the memoranda of understanding (MoU) that preceded the EAPs yields that the policy makers of the Troika and the national authorities agreed on a course of action that strongly reflects these findings. Outlining the planned policy reforms to achieve the intended fiscal consolidation, both the MoU of the Greek and the Portuguese programmes contain a similar focus on expenditure-based fiscal consolidation measures. In fact, both MoU stipulate that the fiscal consolidation effort would be based on expenditure cuts by a ratio of two to one vis-à-vis revenue-increasing measures (see European Commission, 2010, 2011; see Figure 11.1).

In that sense, based on the economic literature on the effects of expenditure-based fiscal consolidation programmes, it is reasonable to expect similar effects of the Greek and Portuguese programmes, i.e. rising levels of inequality.

However, both in the case of Greece and Portugal, the Troika was faced with unforeseen difficulties during the implementation phase of the EAPs, which resulted in substantial changes of the prescribed policy measures from the original MoU vis-à-vis those were eventually implemented. In the Greek case, a much deeper than anticipated recession, wiping out a quarter of the Greek economy throughout the duration of the crisis, strained public finances more than expected. The targets of the fiscal consolidation effort in the EAP were revised repeatedly and substantially, and a second programme was set up in 2012.[1] The

[1] It also became evident that the strategy of outlining general long-term policy prescriptions and fiscal consolidation targets was not productive amid the

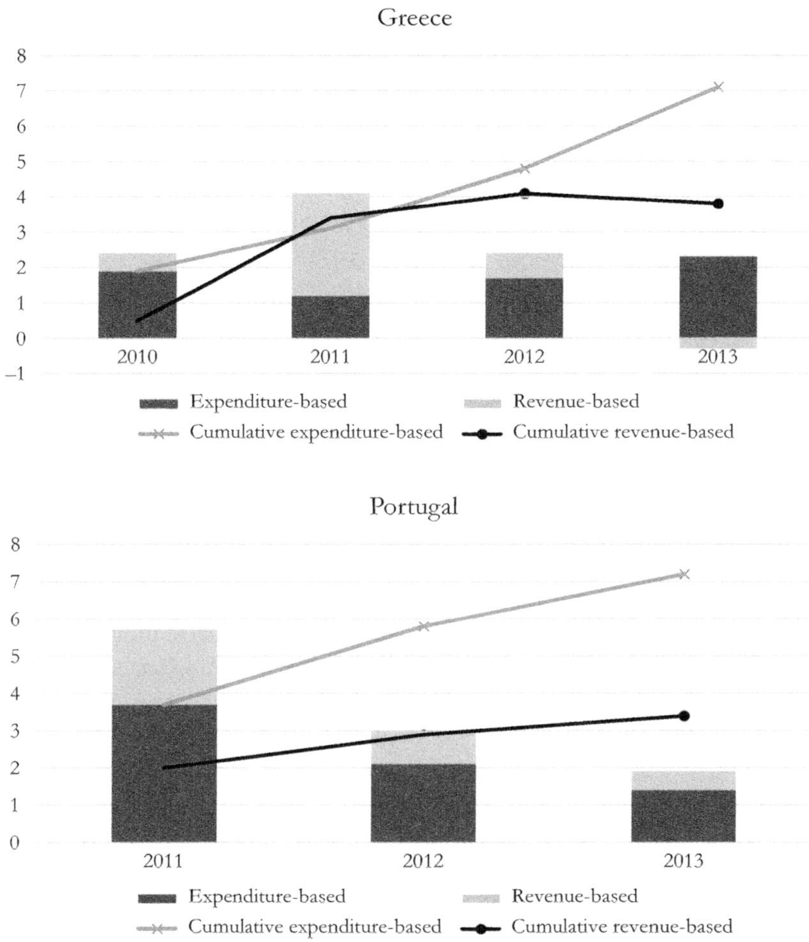

Figure 11.1 Projected austerity measures prescribed in the MoU per year, as per cent of GDP.
Source: European Commission (2010; 2011)

general strategy of basing the consolidation effort largely on expenditure-based measures, however, was maintained since the beginning of the adjustment process: the Troika's response to Greece missing

deterioration of the macroeconomic environment, and the Troika abandoned it in favour of continuously updated medium-term fiscal strategies (MTFS). This is why detailed information on the composition of the prescribed consolidation measures is not part of the subsequent programme revisions.

its fiscal targets in 2010, 2011 and 2012 was demanding further efforts to close fiscal gaps in earlier years, i.e., ever deeper spending cuts. When further revisions became necessary in subsequent years, the reform prescriptions were corrected, but maintained the two-to-one expenditure-revenue ratio.[2]

By comparison, the Portuguese programme was met with much fewer difficulties due to the relatively smaller downturn of the Portuguese economy. However, while the overall targets for the budget consolidation were met, the Troika departed substantively from its strategy outlined in the MoU and employed in the Greek case regarding the composition of the budget consolidation measures: because a large part of the consolidation effort in Portugal was initially based on one-off measures, the Troika shifted its focus to more sustainable consolidation measures after 2011. In doing so, it became evident that cuts in government expenditure were difficult to enforce, while revenue-increasing measures proved more effective than initially assumed. This led to both the Portuguese government and the Troika officially abandoning the objective of a two-thirds expenditure-based programme by 2013. The measures implemented throughout the Portuguese programme were overall much more revenue based than (1) the measures envisioned in the MoU and (2) the measures implemented in the Greek case. In fact, by the end of the Portuguese EAP, revenue-based measures were more than twice as high as initially planned in the MoU (see Figure 11.2).

[2] The second revision of the first EAP in December 2010 brought the first wave of additional measures that amounted to an additional 2.5 per cent of GDP in 2011, bringing up the consolidation effort to 5.7 per cent of GDP in that year, and an additional 5 per cent throughout 2012–2014, two-thirds of which were to be expenditure based. In mid-2011, the Greek government adopted the first MTFS outlining the details of the increased consolidation targets for 2012–2014. However, already later in that year, it became evident that the additional austerity measures were not enough to meet the fiscal target for 2012, resulting in heavier frontloading of those measures agreed on in October 2011. In total, the consolidation effort in 2010 and 2011 amounted to 8.4 per cent and 7.7 per cent of GDP respectively, with another 5.5 per cent planned for 2012. After the second EAP was agreed on and the adjustment period for Greece extended by two years, the MTFS for 2013–2016 was adopted, including savings of 7.2 per cent of GDP over 2013–2014, only 1.9 per cent of which was revenue based. From 2014 onwards, fiscal consolidation targets were met, and no additional consolidation measures were necessary.

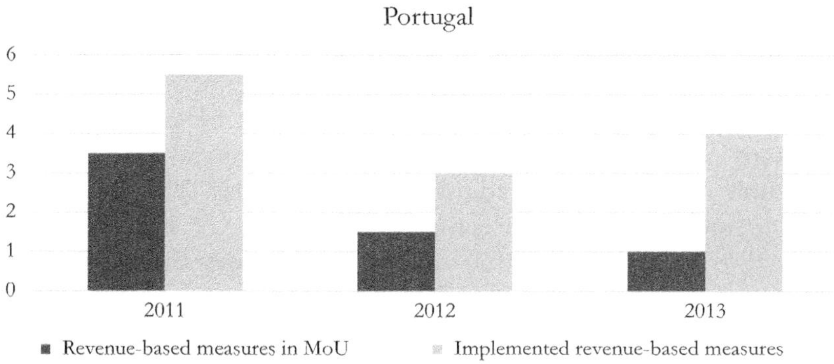

Figure 11.2 Revenue-based measures in the MoU vs. actually implemented measures, per year, in billion €.
Source: European Commission, 2016

Against these data, a comparative case study of the distributive effects of the Greek and the Portuguese programmes makes sense: as the economic literature outlined earlier in this section agrees, there is empirical evidence for fiscal consolidation programmes to lead to increases in relative inequality. Such increases depend on the exact composition and design of the reform measures, with a stronger empirical case for expenditure-based phases of fiscal consolidation resulting in more pronounced increases in inequality. Based on the empirical – albeit not theoretical – evidence, it is therefore reasonable to expect the Greek EAP, which followed a strongly expenditure-based approach, to result in higher levels of inequality. Such expectations are more difficult to formulate for the Portuguese EAP, which deviated from its originally expenditure-based approach sharply throughout the duration of the programme, eventually putting a stronger focus on revenue-increasing measures. Such programmes were in the past found to have differing distributive effects, with some leading to increases in inequality, while others were less regressive and resulted in a compression of the income distribution. For both the Greek and Portuguese EAPs, it is important to note that, despite the empirical case for the former being likely to have inequality-increasing effects, the exact design of the reform measures is crucial in determining their distributive effects. The comparative case study of these two different programmes will therefore yield further insights into the exact distributive effects of fiscal consolidation measures of differing composition and design.

11.3.2 Measuring Inequality: A Review of Commonly Used Indicators

This section of the chapter serves to outline the indicators used to measure inequality and how it was affected by the fiscal consolidation measures in the economic adjustment programmes. While there is a vast literature on the conceptual underpinnings of the notion of inequality (Sen, 1980, 1992), this chapter focuses on the income dimension of inequality rather than wealth or consumption. This is firstly because, although especially inequality of wealth has become the object of increased attention in academic research in recent years, not least through the work of Atkinson (2015), Piketty (2014) and Saez and Zucman (2014), the great majority of the existing literature and the numerous indicators that attempt to measure inequality refer to the income dimension of inequality. This reflects a number of difficulties in the measurement of wealth inequality, such as a lack of reliable information on the distribution of wealth.

Many attempts have been made in the past to develop an indicator that satisfactorily measures income inequality.[3] However, so far all of the established indicators fall short of satisfying all of the desired properties of an inequality indicator, the most important of which are symmetry, normalisation, transfer, continuity, replication and scale invariance, transfer sensitivity, subgroup consistency, decomposability and ease of interpretation (Anand, 1983; Shorrocks, 1988). Mostly due to its high ease of interpretation, the indicator that emerged as the most commonly used is the Gini coefficient, which is in turn based on the Lorenz curve. This uses the Gini coefficient as the prime indicator for income inequality.

Visually, the Gini coefficient represents the area between the Lorenz curve and the 45° line of equality divided by the area below the line of equality, with the Lorenz curve plotting the cumulative proportions of income of the poorest x per cent of the population, for different values of x. The Gini coefficient therefore always takes values between 0 and 1, 0 being absolute equality and 1 being an extreme case where one person earns all the income (Cowell, 2011). In this analysis, the Gini

[3] For more detailed discussions of various advantages and shortcomings of different inequality indicators see Anand (1983); Atkinson (1970); Foster (1985); Foster and Sen (1997); Kakwani (1980); Sen (1973, 1992); Shorrocks (1988).

coefficient is calculated on the basis of equivalised disposable household incomes. This is because market income, i.e., income before taxes and benefits, does not capture a state's redistributive efforts, which is the central object of analysis in this chapter, and the household, rather than the individual, is the unit that redistribution through the tax-benefit system is based on. The Gini coefficient is calculated annually by aggregating monthly data.

For completeness reasons, the analysis based on the Gini coefficient presented in Section 11.4 is carried out in the same manner for a second inequality indicator, the S80/S20 ratio. This is because the Gini coefficient is a suitable measure for changes in the middle of the income distribution but is rather insensitive towards changes at the bottom and top ends of the income distribution. The S80/S20 ratio is calculated by dividing the aggregate income of the top quintile of the income distribution by the income of the bottom quintile, and has emerged as a commonly used addition to the Gini coefficient in measuring inequality because it is particularly sensitive towards changes at the tails of the income distribution. Equivalent to the Gini coefficient, the calculations are based on annual equivalised disposable household incomes.

11.3.3 Presentation of the Datasets

The inequality levels measured by the Gini coefficient presented here are based on panel data from the Survey of Income and Living Conditions carried out by Eurostat (EU-SILC). The data are collected in the year after the reference period.[4] In most countries, data collection is based on household surveys; however, a small number of countries rely on a combination of administrative registers and representative interviews with household members (Iacovou et al., 2012). While it must be stated that these differences in the collection process and the sampling procedure create minor issues of comparability between different countries, it is by far the largest, most accurate dataset that exists for the analysis of income inequality in the EU, and is widely used in academic research. The data that are ascertained through the EU-SILC waves provide household disposable income data on a monthly level, which is aggregated to annual levels, and equivalised through the modified

[4] Exceptions are the United Kingdom and Ireland, where data are collected during the reference period and twelve months after the reference period respectively.

Organisation for Economic Cooperation and Development (OECD) equivalence scale to account for different household sizes (Eurostat, 2015).

The analysis in this chapter is complemented by findings based on European tax-benefit microsimulation tool EUROMOD at the University of Essex. Microsimulation tools are frequently used by researchers to account for time lags in the data availability, and allow calculations of household incomes based on previous waves of household income survey data (EUROMOD is based on EU-SILC data) by adjusting household incomes depending on changes in the tax-benefit system. This is done by making use of additional data provided by national statistical offices and other institutions such as central banks, accounting for distortionary effects, such as earnings growth (Bank of Greece, 2013), tax evasion (Matsaganis et al., 2012), rise in unemployment (Figari et al., 2010) and non-take-up of social benefits (Matsaganis and Leventi, 2014). EUROMOD has been validated on both the micro and macro level and tested in various applications. For further information on the tool, see Figari et al. (2012) and Bargain (2006).

However, the advantages of using tax-benefit microsimulation tools go further than filling time lag-induced gaps in the data availability. As EUROMOD contains all tax-benefit policies of a given EU country in a given year, its key added value is that it allows for a simulation of the effects of hypothetical policy changes. For the purpose of this chapter, this allows us to assess the distributive effects that particular policy reforms such as changes in unemployment benefits or pensions have on the income distribution in a given year by changing the policies in the model and applying it to the same income data. This in turn enables the use of indicators such as the Gini coefficient that capture the distributive impacts of policy measures against a counterfactual scenario that can be constructed with EUROMOD where said policy changes are absent (see also Duclos and Araar, 2006; Reynolds and Smolensky, 1977). For the scope of this chapter, this method creates crucial insights in addition to the analysis with EU-SILC data because it allows us to exclude the effects of the recession on income inequality through increased unemployment and isolate the effects of the policy reforms.

In this context, it needs to be stated that while the analysis with EUROMOD provides useful additions to the analysis of inequality indicators based on real data, it is restricted to 'first-order' distributive effects of policies. The concept of first-order distributive effects relates to direct effects of policy reforms on the income distribution, e.g., the direct effects of a reform in the tax system on the different income deciles. This neglects 'second-order' distributive effects of the analysed policy reforms, which affect inequality indirectly through affecting other economic indicators such as employment. This gains importance in cases where policy reforms have sufficiently large effects to change the economic outlook of a country, e.g., if a reform in unemployment benefits affects gross incomes in such a way that aggregate demand falls sufficiently to trigger an increase in unemployment, this will affect inequality in addition to the direct effects the reform had in the first place. However, preliminary results of studies that are working on resolving this issue indicate that in the cases analysed for this chapter, second-order effects are comparably small and thus unable to offset first-order effects. Moreover, it is unclear that second-order effects would necessarily be unidirectional, as the reforms are ultimately aimed at sustainably expanding economic activities and would thus facilitate employment, particularly when compared to a possible counterfactual without reforms.[5]

11.3.4 The Approach of This Chapter

The following section of the chapter contains the empirical analysis, which is divided into two parts. In the first part, income inequality levels measured by the Gini coefficient are given for the years of the programme duration in Greece and Portugal, as well as the preceding years. These are based on EU-SILC data provided by Eurostat. This analysis is completed by a comparison of levels of inequality measured by the Gini coefficient of disposable household incomes with inequality of market incomes, i.e., incomes of households before transfers through taxes and benefits (including pensions). This analysis provides an approximation for the redistributive capacities of the welfare state of the two case study countries.

This analysis provides a comprehensive picture of how inequality and redistribution have developed throughout the duration of the Greek and Portuguese EAPs. However, income inequality is influenced by a variety of different factors, which is why the second part of the

[5] For an insightful discussion of how structural reforms affect the distribution of incomes, see Campos et al. (2017).

section provides supporting data created with EUROMOD, which isolates all of these effects and assesses the direct effects of the policy reforms in the EAPs. This is done by comparing income inequality levels measured by the Gini coefficient under a reform scenario and a counterfactual scenario. In the reform scenario, the effects of all policy reforms that were implemented as part of the Greek and Portuguese EAPs are simulated. In the counterfactual scenario, the tax-benefit systems of both Greece and Portugal are held constant from the year prior to the respective programme inception and applied to the same income data as the reform scenario. In the Greek case, the counterfactual scenario contains the tax benefit system of 2009 (the year before the first Greek EAP began), which is applied to the years of the programme implementation (2010 through 2017). In the Portuguese case, tax-benefit policies from 2010 are applied to the years of the Portuguese EAP (2011 through 2014).

11.4 Empirical Analysis

11.4.1 The Development of Income Inequality in the Eurozone

In assessing the distributive impacts of the fiscal consolidation measures outlined in the economic adjustment programmes, this chapter first shows how inequality measured by the Gini coefficient developed between 2005 and 2016, including the years of the EAPs in Greece and Portugal (see Figure 11.3). The evidence shown at this point is based on the Gini coefficient calculated with EU-SILC data. Two major findings can be derived from this analysis:

The Gini coefficient of disposable household incomes has stagnated with minor fluctuations in both countries. Some qualifications need to be made at this point: (1) in Greece, there is some increase in the Gini coefficient of disposable household income between 2010 and 2012, after which inequality remains constant for the following years. Compared to earlier years, inequality levels during the Greek EAPs stay at similar levels. (2) In Portugal, inequality of disposable household income remains constant from the beginning of the EAP onwards. However, the downward trend that inequality levels had been following in the years prior to the beginning of the EAP was interrupted. (3) The results for Greece are corroborated using the S80/S20 ratio (see Figure 11.4) as a second inequality indicator. For the Portuguese case, however, the

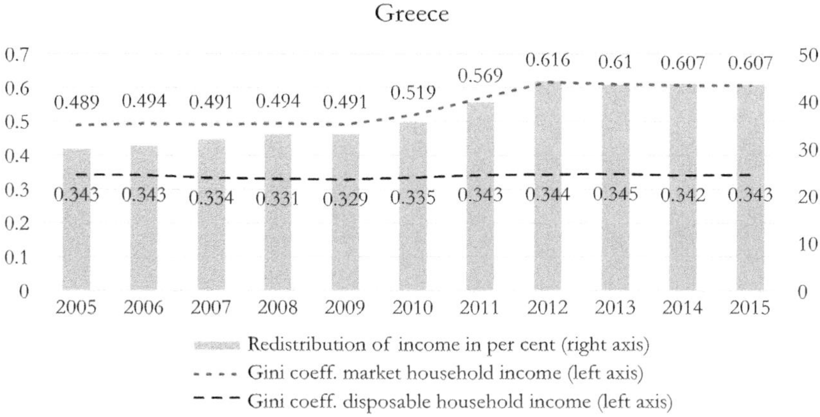

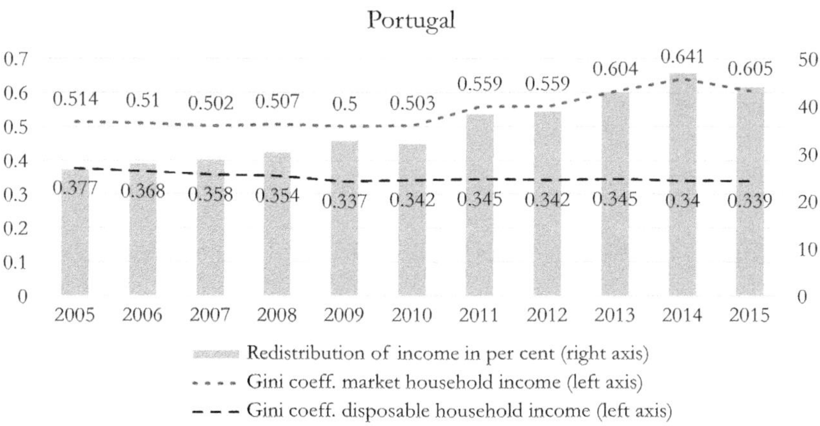

Figure 11.3 Gini coefficient of disposable and market household incomes.
Source: Eurostat (EU-SILC survey [ilc_di12; ilc_di12b])

S80/S20 ratio shows increases in the years 2011–2014, thereby continuing a trend that began in the year prior to the inception of the EAP. It was only in the last year of the EAP that the S80/S20 ratio fell again. In absolute terms, the S80/S20 ratio remains below pre-2008 levels throughout the entire duration of the EAP. The changes in the S80/S20 ratio suggest that there have been changes at the tails of the income distribution that are not captured by the Gini coefficient.

Conversely, inequality of market household incomes has increased substantively with the inception of the EAPs in both Greece and Portugal. While this can be attributed to the recession and the increase

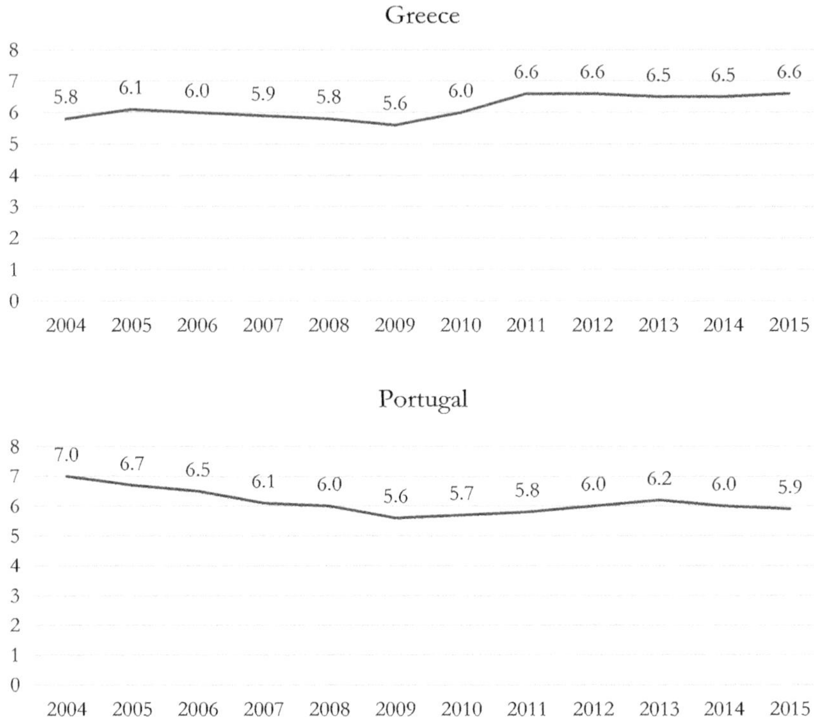

Figure 11.4 S80/S20 ratio of disposable household incomes.
Source: Eurostat (EU-SILC survey)

in unemployment, it is a somewhat surprising finding in conjunction with the previous finding of stagnating levels of disposable income inequality. The widening gap between the two is illustrated in Figure 11.3 by the grey bars representing the percentage difference between inequality of market and disposable household income. In the Greek case this difference has increased from 33 per cent in the year before the EAP began (2009) to 43 per cent from 2013 onwards. In the Portuguese case, the difference increased from 33 per cent in 2010 to 47 per cent by the time the programme had been concluded (2015). In both cases, there was therefore sufficient redistribution to offset the entirety of the increase in market income inequality induced by the recession.

Based on these findings, it follows that the increases in inequality as expected based on the review of the economic literature described in

Section 11.2 failed to materialise. This is true for both the Greek and the Portuguese case. In addition, the growing gap between market and disposable household income shows that the redistributive functions of the welfare state have remained intact in both Greece and Portugal. In fact, more income has been redistributed throughout the duration of the EAPs than in the years prior to that. Moreover, considering the different composition of the Greek and Portuguese EAPs, the data show that both the strongly expenditure-based fiscal consolidation efforts in Greece and the revenue-based consolidation in Portugal have led to remarkably similar outcomes regarding inequality of disposable household incomes and the redistribution of income.

11.4.2 A Tax-Benefit Microsimulation Approach to Assessing the Distributive Effects of Fiscal Consolidation Measures

While the data presented in Figures 11.3 and 11.4 give some valuable insight into the interplay between fiscal consolidation and income inequality, showing that contrary to previous findings inequality has not increased throughout the duration of the EAPs, these results may have been caused by a number of different factors. The use of microsimulation allows for a more nuanced and straightforward assessment of whether the reforms of the tax-benefit system prescribed in the EAPs have in fact served to alleviate market-induced increases in income inequality during the recession. To that end, this chapter presents a counterfactual scenario constructed with EUROMOD, showing 'what would have happened in the absence of the fiscal consolidation measures' (Sutherland et al., 2013, p. 6). This method excludes the effects of the wider recession on the income distribution, thus allowing for an analysis of the tax-benefit reforms in an isolated manner. More concretely, in the counterfactual scenario the tax-benefit system remains unchanged from the year prior to the respective programme inception throughout the implementation period of the adjustment programme. Thus, the counterfactual shows how disposable income inequality would have developed if market incomes in the various years throughout the programmes had been redistributed through the tax-benefit system that was in place in the year prior to the programme inception, i.e., before the reform efforts prescribed by the Troika began (i.e., 2009 for Greece, 2010 for Portugal).

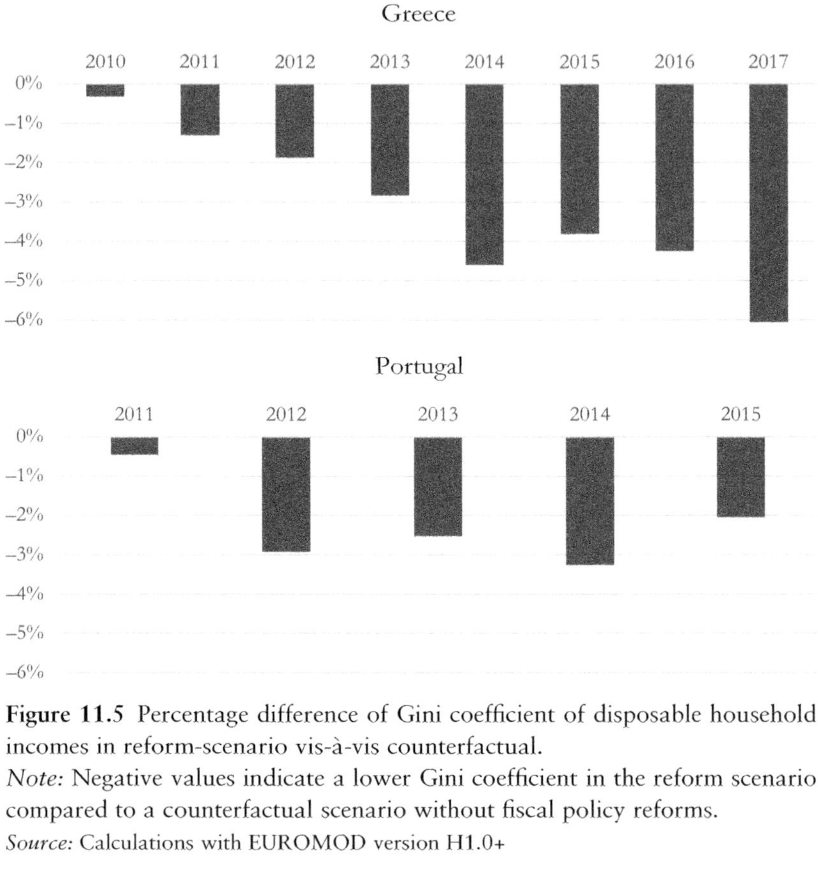

Figure 11.5 Percentage difference of Gini coefficient of disposable household incomes in reform-scenario vis-à-vis counterfactual.
Note: Negative values indicate a lower Gini coefficient in the reform scenario compared to a counterfactual scenario without fiscal policy reforms.
Source: Calculations with EUROMOD version H1.0+

This exercise yields that the reform measures in the EAPs did in fact produce lower levels of income inequality when compared to a simulated counterfactual of unchanged tax-benefit policies from before the EAPs began (see Figure 11.5). The reforms in the Greek EAPs produced a Gini coefficient of disposable household income of 6 per cent below that in the counterfactual by the year 2017. The reforms of the Portuguese EAP resulted in a Gini coefficient of disposable household income of between 2 per cent and 3 per cent below that in the counterfactual between 2012 and 2015. These data confirm that the fiscal consolidation measures in the EAPs had an inequality-reducing effect, which at times must have been large enough to offset the increases in market income inequality throughout the duration of the EAPs. Moreover, the most progressive reforms were implemented as part of the

Greek EAPs, which stands in opposition to the expectation that expenditure-based fiscal consolidation measures should lead to higher levels of inequality than revenue-based measures.

In order to provide a higher level of detail as to how exactly the reforms in the EAPs in Greece and Portugal have affected inequality, the next part of this section presents data produced with EUROMOD that simulates the effects of different classes of policies on each income decile. The data show the percentage changes in income per policy class and decile due to the reforms.

In Figure 11.6, these data are presented cumulatively, i.e., as the sums of the annual percentage changes in income per decile as a result of the policy reforms. The cumulative data does not account for changes in original incomes, which the annual percentage changes refer to and therefore need to be interpreted accordingly. The underlying annual changes in income due to the policy reforms can be found in Appendices A (Greece) and B (Portugal).

For the Greek case (see Figure 11.6 and Appendix A for annual breakdowns), this exercise yields the following important insight: the most progressive, i.e., inequality-reducing reform measures have been in the class of means-tested benefits. Particularly in the years 2012–2013, 2013–2014, 2015–2016 and 2016–2017, changes in means-tested benefits led to substantive increases in disposable household income of the lowest income decile. In the years 2012–2013 and 2013–2014, this was true for the whole bottom half of the income distribution. Other classes of policy reforms produce mixed distributive outcomes with, e.g., changes in direct taxation leading to a reduction of high incomes in 2011–2012, and a reduction of low incomes in 2012–2013.

The analysis of the Portuguese EAP (see Figure 11.6 and Appendix B) yields very different results compared to the Greek EAPs. While changes in means-tested benefits had the largest inequality-reducing effect in the Greek case, they had the largest inequality-increasing effects in the Portuguese case. In the years 2010–2011 and 2012–2013, changes in means-tested benefits led to substantive reductions in incomes of the bottom half of the income distribution. Direct taxes, on the other hand, have compressed the income distribution, leading to large reductions of incomes in the top half of the income distribution in the years 2010–2011 and 2012–2013, although incomes of the two top deciles were increased through changes in direct

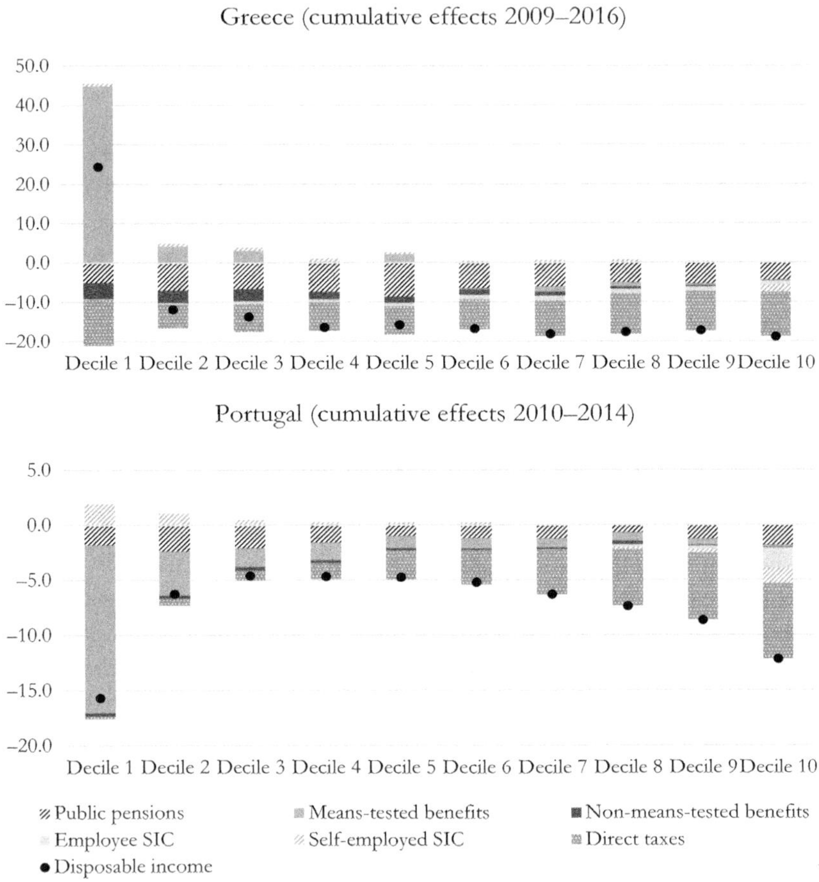

Figure 11.6 Percentage change in income due to the reforms in the EAPs per decile by policy class.
Source: Calculations with EUROMOD version H1.0+

taxation in the year 2011–2012. Changes in public pensions had an inequality-reducing effect in the year 2011–2012 and the opposite effect in the year 2012–2013.

Beyond the distributive effects of the reforms by policy class, it is striking that despite the fact that both the Gini coefficient and the S80/S20 ratio show falling or at least stagnating levels of inequality throughout the Portuguese EAP, the decomposition by decile reveals the following: middle-income groups have remained somewhat shielded from the adverse effects of expenditure cuts and tax increases, resulting in an aggregate reduction of incomes for the second through to the seventh income deciles of between 4 per cent and 6 per cent. The eighth and ninth deciles have seen income losses of between 7 per cent and 9 per cent due to the reforms throughout the duration of the EAP. The biggest aggregate losses of incomes are registered for the very bottom and top deciles, with the first income decile losing 15.7 per cent of their income throughout the EAP as a direct effect of the reforms, and the tenth decile losing 12.2 per cent.

Regarding the effects by policy class, it makes sense to look at two findings from this analysis in more detail: (1) the fact that changes in means-tested benefits had the largest inequality-reducing effects in Greece, while the opposite was the case for Portugal; and (2) the fact that changes in public pensions reduced income inequality in Portugal in one year (2011–2012), and increased it by the same margin in the following year (see Appendix B).

In order to analyse the first finding, the following part of the section compares spending levels on means-tested benefits and non-means-tested benefits in both Greece and Portugal (see Figure 11.7). The data show that in Greece, government expenditure on means-tested benefits has increased after the year 2012 to levels above those of 2009. Considering that the indexation refers to absolute expenditure levels and that in the same period the Greek economy has shrunk substantively, this signifies a large increase in government expenditure on means-tested benefits. The large increases in spending on means-tested benefits coincide with inequality-reducing effects that changes in means-tested benefits had on the income distribution measured with EUROMOD (see Figure 11.6). At the same time, spending on non-means-tested benefits decreased to almost one-third of 2009 levels from 2014 onwards. In fact, some of the benefits that used to be non-means-tested were simply made means-tested as part of the reforms in the EAPs for Greece. In comparison, spending on means-tested benefits in Portugal dropped to almost half of the 2010 spending level by the end of the EAP, whereas spending on non-means-tested benefits fluctuated between 10 per cent below and above 2010 spending levels. This suggests that the inequality-increasing effect of changes in means-tested benefits in Portugal stems from a simple reduction in government spending on means-tested benefits, the opposite of which was the case in Greece.

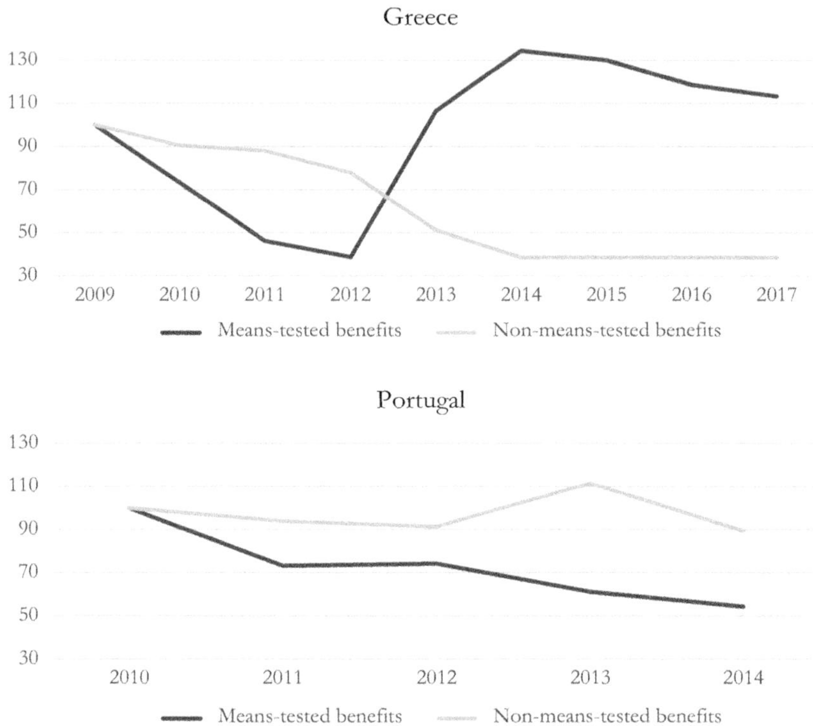

Figure 11.7 Government expenditure on means-tested and non-means-tested benefits Index (Greece: 2009 = 100; Portugal: 2010 = 100).
Source: Calculations with EUROMOD version H1.0+

To analyse the second finding, i.e., that changes in public pensions were inequality-reducing in 2011–2012 in Portugal but inequality-increasing in 2012–2013, requires a qualitative account of the pension reform that was part of the Portuguese EAP. As part of an effort to cut government expenditure on pensions by an overall 1.5 per cent of GDP, the EAP for Portugal prescribed a suspension of the indexation for all but the lowest pensions, increasing the retirement age, and introducing a temporary 'Extraordinary Solidarity Contribution' on pensions above a specified threshold. In addition, the thirteenth and fourteenth monthly payments to pensioners were cut. Overall, the design of the pension reform seems to have put the bulk of the consolidation burden of 1.5 per cent of GDP on higher pensions. However, in 2013 the Portuguese constitutional court ruled against the pension reform requiring most of the original pension system, such as the thirteenth and fourteenth monthly payments, to be reinstated. Both events, the implementation of the pension reform in 2011–2012 and the ruling of the courts and subsequently almost complete reinstatement of the old pension system in 2013, coincide with the substantive changes in the distributive effect of pensions observed in the previous part of this section, reducing inequality in 2011–2012, and increasing inequality in 2012–2013.

11.4.3 Compliance with the Fiscal Policy Prescription in the EAPs

As the results presented in the previous part of this section show, the policy reforms prescribed in the EAPs lead to stagnating or even falling levels of income inequality, while the respective redistributive capacities of the countries' tax-benefit systems increased, or were at least triggered to a larger extent while not being curtailed by the reforms. In addition, the reforms' direct distributive effects were inequality reducing. However, this leaves the question whether the Troika was in fact the driving force behind a set of reforms that was progressive by design, or in contrast to that, whether national governments altered the policies outlined in the EAPs before implementing them in order to shield their electorates from potentially regressive reforms. In order to assess this, a qualitative analysis of the quarterly reviews of the EAPs for Greece and Portugal is necessary.

In the Greek case, overall compliance with the EAPs can be described as high, even though the fiscal targets were frequently missed due to the deteriorating macroeconomic environment. However, the reviews of the EAPs offer the insight that in the early stages of the first EAP, the Greek government had a larger degree of discretion in implementing the reform prescriptions of the Troika. After missing the fiscal targets outlined in the MoU, the Troika abandoned this rather hands-off approach in favour of more micromanagement. Instead of outlining general fiscal aims and leaving the design of the actual policy reforms to the national authorities, the Troika introduced the concept of medium-term fiscal strategies by mid-2011. In doing so, the Troika had to approve the Greek reform efforts on a quarterly basis, ensuring that the Troika's reform prescriptions would be followed to a higher degree. The fact that this change in strategy coincides with more inequality-reducing reforms after an initial spike in inequality levels suggests that the hypothesis that the Greek government altered some of the reform prescriptions in order to shield its electorate from potentially inequality-increasing reforms cannot be substantiated.

In the case of Portugal, the initial reform prescriptions were changed more substantially than in the Greek case. The focus of the consolidation effort shifted from largely expenditure-based measures to more revenue-based measures. However, the Troika was involved in all of those changes, as an analysis of the reviews of the Portuguese EAP as well as the Post-Programme Surveillance Report indicate. The most prominent case where the implemented reforms deviated from those prescribed in the EAP was the comprehensive pension reform, which had large inequality-reducing effects, and which was reversed by the Portuguese courts (see Section 11.4.2). This suggests that similar to the Greek case, the reforms were progressive by design rather than due to the national governments changing the reforms to increase their progressiveness.

In fact, the wording of the reform prescriptions in the EAPs reveals that there was at least some sensitivity among the Troika towards the social dimension of the fiscal adjustment effort. In the EAP for Greece, there are several passages referring to the social impact of the programme: [while] 'incomes and social security policies need to buttress the fiscal adjustment effort and restoration of competitiveness ... the government is committed to fairness in the distribution of the adjustment burden' (European Commission, 2010, p. 41), and further: 'The lowest-income and lowest-pension earners, as well as the most vulnerable and those requiring family support, will all be protected and compensated for the adverse impact of the adjustment policies' (ibid., p. 28). Similar passages can be found in the Portuguese EAP.

11.4.4 Discussion of the Findings

This section has shown that not only did inequality not increase throughout the duration of the Greek and Portuguese EAPs, but the reforms prescriptions actually had inequality-reducing direct effects. Considering that both Greece and Portugal were not only plagued by high public debt when the economic adjustment programmes were implemented, but also by a severe economic recession, this finding is all the more puzzling. During the recession, in the programme countries the respective economies had low economic growth rates, and at times shrank substantively, while unemployment rose, which was expected to put an upward pressure on income inequality, and which is illustrated by the increases in market income inequality observed in this section (see Figure 11.3). Despite this, redistribution has in fact gone up in both countries, which is illustrated by the fact that despite the increases in market income inequality, disposable income inequality has remained stable throughout the crisis.

The fact that the EAPs relied heavily on expenditure-based measures in the case of Greece was expected to exacerbate the inequality-increasing effects through cuts in the social budget, which should have undermined the state's capacity to mitigate upward pressures on inequality levels, stemming from higher unemployment, by means of redistribution. As this has evidently not occurred, based on the findings presented in this section, this suggests that the fiscal consolidation measures outlined in the economic adjustment programmes were in fact progressive in their distributive impact and thus managed to offset the upward pressure on inequality levels induced by the economic recession and rising levels of unemployment, as confirmed by the data from the simulations presented in Figure 11.5.

The a priori expectations for the Portuguese programme were less clear-cut due to the weaker empirical case of revenue-based programmes causing inequality levels to move in one particular direction. The empirical analysis in this chapter showed that at the aggregate level, much like in the Greek case, inequality has remained stable throughout the adjustment process with only minor fluctuations, and that this was due to the progressive direct effects of the reforms, as evidenced through the simulations presented in Figure 11.4. However, one key difference between the Greek and the Portuguese cases, despite aggregate inequality indicators such as the Gini coefficient and the S80/S20 ratio showing similar results, is revealed when decomposing the direct distributive effects of the reforms by deciles. In the Greek case, the bottom decile of the income distribution in fact saw substantive increases in their incomes due to the reforms vis-à-vis the simulated nonreform scenario, while the top decile saw the largest losses. In the Portuguese case, it was the middle-income groups that were somewhat protected from the adverse effects of the adjustment process, while both the bottom- and top-income deciles saw the largest aggregate income losses due to the reforms. Neither the Gini coefficient nor the

S80/S20 ratio would have picked this up, as the Gini coefficient is in any case rather insensitive towards changes at the tails of the income distribution, and the S80/S20 ratio only looks at the relative ratio between the two top and bottom deciles, thus not capturing the previously outlined changes in the income distribution as the long as the ratio between top and bottom deciles in relative terms remains stable.

While further research analysing the exact reasons for the different distributive effects of the Greek and Portuguese EAPs by deciles is necessary, one potentially powerful explanatory factor is offered by the scholarship on electoral dynamics and the median voter theorem: in its original formulation, based on Downs (1957) and Meltzer and Richard (1981) show that in the policy-making process, particularly in matters regarding redistribution and the welfare state, governments seek to represent to the best of their ability the median voter, i.e., the hypothetical voter in the middle of the income distribution. While Meltzer and Richard use the median voter theorem to explain how governments are pushed for ever more redistribution, thus accounting for the growth of the public sector, their model was later developed further to describe the position of the decisive voter in the income distribution, which in turn offers an explanation as to which income groups governments tend to cater to in decisions regarding redistribution (Bassett et al., 1999). Based on this scholarship and assuming that all conditions of the model hold, it is reasonable to assume governments to be most concerned with protecting voters in the middle of the income distribution whom they perceive as essential to their ability to govern successfully and secure reelection.

One possible argument based on the findings presented in this chapter could be that the median or decisive voter dynamic has remained more powerful in Portugal than in Greece. This is based on the Portuguese government and public sector pushing back more effectively against the reform prescriptions of the Troika and overall retaining a higher degree of autonomy, while the Troika essentially stripped away most decision-making power from the Greek authorities, as outlined in Section 11.4.3. Following a historical institutionalist view, one could argue that both elected policy makers and historically grown institutions follow the dynamics of the decisive voter. This in turn is a possible explanation for why middle-income groups in Portugal, i.e., those of the decisive voter, remained rather shielded from the adverse effects of the adjustment process through interventions from the

Portuguese government and courts, while both the very bottom and very top deciles, i.e., those furthest away from the decisive voter, saw the largest reductions in their incomes. These hypotheses based on an application of the median voter theorem would therefore form a promising basis for further research to determine the origins of the different distributive effects by deciles of the Greek and Portuguese EAPs.

More generally, the findings presented here leave the conclusion that against what previous studies have found empirically regarding the distributive effects of fiscal consolidation measures, there is no such thing as an automatism between a certain composition of fiscal consolidation measures and their distributive effects. The evidence presented in this section rather suggests that policy makers have different choices available in designing policy reforms, which lead to different distributional outcomes. The fact that after the Troika took a more micromanaging approach in the implementation of the Greek EAPs, the inequality-reducing effects of the reforms increased, and that this was largely achieved by making formerly non-means-tested benefits means-tested is one piece of evidence for this: even though the overall EAPs for Greece remained strongly expenditure based, spending on means-tested transfers increased, illustrating that even in the face of high pressure to cut government expenditure, there is room for manoeuvre regarding expenditure on social transfers with progressive distributional outcomes.

11.5 Conclusion

This chapter aimed to establish the distributive effects of fiscal consolidation measures in the Eurozone crisis based on a comparative case study of the Greek and Portuguese Economic Adjustment Programmes. While the Greek EAPs were found to be heavily expenditure based, the Portuguese EAP was revised in its composition and ultimately relied more on revenue-increasing measures rather than expenditure cuts. While previous studies have found that fiscal consolidation leads to higher levels of income inequality, which is exacerbated when the consolidation is largely based on expenditure measures, the chapter has shown evidence that this was not the case in either the Greek or the Portuguese case.

In fact, inequality of disposable household income has been found to stagnate throughout the duration of the EAPs rather than increase. In addition to this, inequality of market income has increased substantively in both Greece and Portugal, suggesting that the redistributive capacities of the countries' welfare states have remained intact or even been strengthened. Based on data created through simulations with tax-benefit microsimulation tool EUROMOD, the chapter has found that in addition to this general development of inequality indicators, the fiscal consolidation measures themselves had inequality-reducing direct effects in both countries.

Based on the empirical findings of previous studies, it was the progressiveness of the Greek programme that was particularly puzzling. In explaining this puzzle, the chapter has shown that expenditure-based fiscal consolidation is possible without crippling the welfare state's redistributive capacities. An analysis of the impact of different classes of policies has yielded that Greece has managed to avoid large increases in inequality by making large parts of formerly non-means-tested benefits means-tested. In doing so, higher-income groups were then exempt from these benefits, while lower-income groups were compensated. At the same time, expenditure on non-means-tested benefits for high-income groups tends to be higher than for low-income groups, which makes this approach not only more progressive but also more effective in reaching the targets of fiscal consolidation.

Furthermore, the distributive effects of the Greek and Portuguese programmes, while progressive when measured through inequality indicators based on aggregate figures, display large differences when decomposing the effects by income deciles. While in Greece very low-income groups were shielded from the adverse effects of the adjustment, in Portugal it was middle-income groups that saw the most protection. The chapter offers a possible explanation of this by proposing that the dynamics based on the median voter theorem remained intact in Portugal, where authorities and institutions pushed back more effectively against the Troika's reform prescriptions, but not in Greece, where the Troika essentially took over policy-making competences. Further research is necessary to test this hypothesis.

Lastly, since the effects and the design of the policy reforms say little about who was key for their progressive nature, the chapter tested whether they were simply a result of the recipient countries' governments not implementing the reform prescriptions. However, the chapter found that compliance with the programmes was high, and that the inequality-reducing effects of the reforms were largest in those instances where the Troika was most closely involved in the consolidation process. This suggests that the reform prescriptions were inequality reducing by design.

References

Agnello, L. and Sousa, R. (2014). 'How Does Fiscal Consolidation Impact on Income Inequality?' *Review of Income and Wealth*, Vol. 60, No. 4, 702–726.

Alesina, A. and Perotti, R. (1995). 'Fiscal Expansions and Adjustments in OECD Countries', *Economic Policy*, No. 21, 205–248.

(1996). 'Fiscal Adjustments in OECD Countries: Composition and Macroeconomic Effects', NBER Working Chapter (5730).

Anand, S. (1983). *Inequality and Poverty in Malaysia: Measurement and Decomposition*. Oxford University Press.

Atkinson, A. (1970). 'On the Measurement of Inequality', *Journal of Economic Theory*, No. 2, 244–263.

(2015). *Inequality: What Can Be Done?* Harvard University Press.

Ball, L., Furceri, D., Leigh, D. and Loungani, P. (2013). 'The Distributional Effects of Fiscal Consolidation', IMF Working Chapter 13/151.

Bank of Greece (2013). *2012 Governor's Report*. Bank of Greece.

Bargain, O. (2006). *Microsimulation in Action: Policy Analysis in Europe using EUROMOD*. Emerald.

Bassett, W. F., Burkett, J. P. and Putterman, L. (1999). 'Income Distribution, Government Transfers, and the Problem of Unequal Influence', *European Journal of Political Economy*, Vol. 15, No. 2, 207–208. https://doi.org/10.1016/S0176-2680(99)00004-X.

Campos, C., De Grauwe, P. and Ji, Y. (2017). 'Structural Reforms, Growth and Inequality: An Overview of Theory, Measurement and Evidence', IZA Discussion Chapter, November.

Cowell, F. (2011). *Measuring Inequality*. Oxford University Press.

Downs, A. (1957). 'An Economic Theory of Political Action in a Democracy', *Journal of Political Economy*, Vol. 65, No. 2, 135–50. https://doi.org/10.1086/257897.

Duclos, J.-Y. and Araar, A. (2006). *Poverty and Equity: Measurement, Policy and Estimation with DAD*. Kluwer Academic.

European Commission (2010). *The Economic Adjustment Programme for Greece*. Directorate-General for Economic and Financial Affairs Publications.

(2011). 'The Economic Adjustment Programme for Portugal', Directorate-General for Economic and Financial Affairs Occasional Chapters (79).
(2013). 'The Second Economic Adjustment Programme for Greece. Second Review – May 2013', Directorate-General for Economic and Financial Affairs Occasional Chapters.
(2016). 'Post-Programme Surveillance Report for Portugal'.

Eurostat (2015). 'Eurostat Statistics Explained'. Retrieved 12 March 2016, from 'Definitions': http://ec.europa.eu/eurostat/statistics-explained/index.php/Living_standard_statistics.

Figari, F., Salvatori, A. and Sutherland, H. (2010). 'Economic Downturn and Stress Testing European Welfare Systems', ISER Working Chapter Series No. 2010-18.

Figari, F., Skew, A., Iacovou, M. and Sutherland, H. (2012). 'Approximations to the Truth: Comparing Survey and Microsimulation Approaches to Measuring Income for Social Indicators', *Social Indicators Research*, Vol. 105, No. 3, 387–407.

Fitoussi, J.-P. and Saraceno, F. (2013). 'European Economic Governance: The Berlin–Washington Consensus', *Cambridge Journal of Economics*, Vol. 37, No. 3,479–496.

Foster, J. (1985). 'Inequality Measurement', in H. P. Young (ed.), *Fair Allocation*. American Mathematical Society.

Foster, J. and Sen, A. (1997). 'On Economic Inequality after a Quarter Century', in A. Sen (ed.), *On Economic Inequality (Expanded Edition)*. Clarendon Press.

Iacovou, M., Kaminska, O. and Levy, H. (2012). 'Using EU-SILC Data for Cross-National Analysis: Strengths, Problems, and Recommendations', ISER Working Chapter Series No. 2012-03.

Kakwani, N. C.(1980). *Income Inequality and Poverty*. World Bank.

Matsaganis, M. and Leventi, C. (2014). 'Poverty and Inequality during the Great Recession in Greece', *Political Studies Review*, No. 12, 209–223.

Matsaganis, M., Leventi, C. and Flevotomou, M. (2012). 'The Crisis and Tax Evasion in Greece: What Are the Distributional Implications?' *CESifo Forum*, Vol. 13, No. 2, 26–32.

McDermott, C. J. and Wescott, R. F. (1996). 'An Empirical Analysis of Fiscal Adjustments', *Staff Chapters (International Monetary Fund)*, Vol. 43, No. 4, 725–753.

Meltzer, A. H. and Richard, S. F. (1981). 'A Rational Theory of the Size of Government', *Journal of Political Economy*, Vol. 89, No. 5, 914–27. https://doi.org/10.1086/261013.

Oberdarnig, D. (2013). 'Revisiting the Effects of IMF Programs on Poverty and Inequality', *World Development*, No. 46, 113–142.

Piketty, T. (2014). *Capital in the Twenty-First Century*. Harvard University Press.

Reynolds, M. and Smolensky, E. (1977). *Public Expenditure, Taxes and the Distribution of Income: The United States, 1950, 1961, 1970*. Academic Press.

Saez, E. and Zucman, G. (2014). 'Wealth Inequality in the United States since 1913: Evidence from Capitalized Income Tax Data', NBER Working Chapter No. 20625.

Sen, A. (1973). *On Economic Inequality*. Clarendon Press.

(1980). 'Equality of What?' in S. M. McMurrin (ed.), *Tanner Lectures on Human Values, I*. Cambridge University Press.

(1992). *Inequality Reexamined*. Russell Sage Foundation.

Shorrocks, A. F. (1988). 'Aggregation Issues in Inequality Measurement', in W. Eichhorn (ed.), *Measurement in Economics: Theory and Applications in Economic Indices*. Physica Verlag.

Sutherland, H., Avram, S., Figari, F., et al., (2013). 'The Distributional Impact of Fiscal Consolidation in Nine Countries', EUROMOD Working Chapter No. EM 2/13.

Woo, J., Bova, E., Kinda, T. and Zhang, Y. (2017). 'Distributional Consequences of Fiscal Adjustments: What Do the Data Say?' *IMF Economic Review*, Vol. 65, No. 2, 273–307.

Appendix

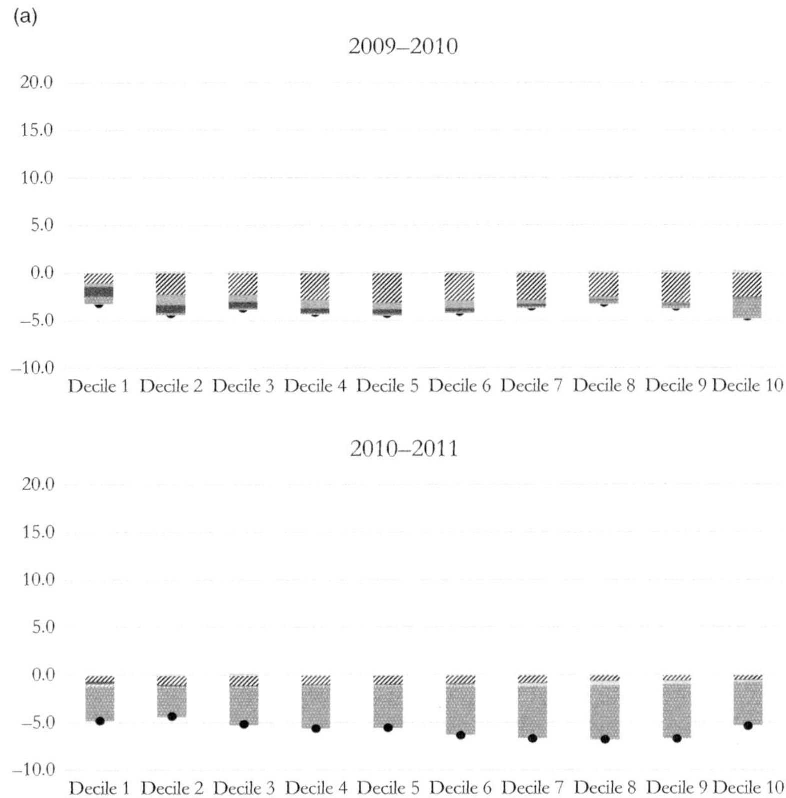

Appendix A Percentage change in income due to the reforms in the EAPs per decile by policy class and year.
Source: Calculations with EUROMOD version H1.0+

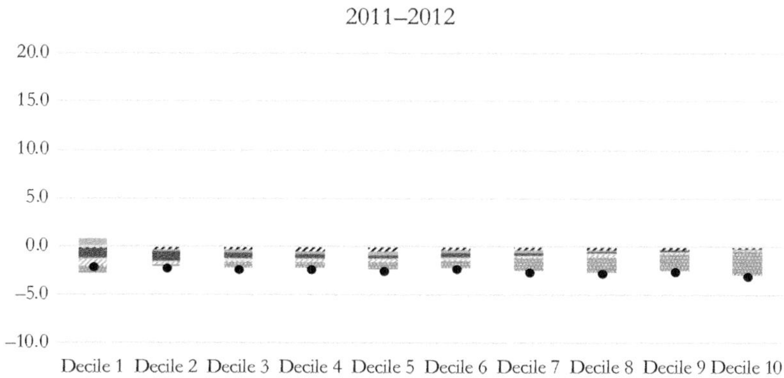

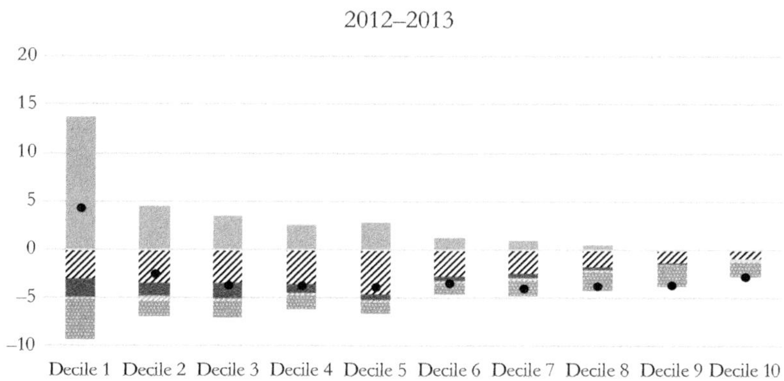

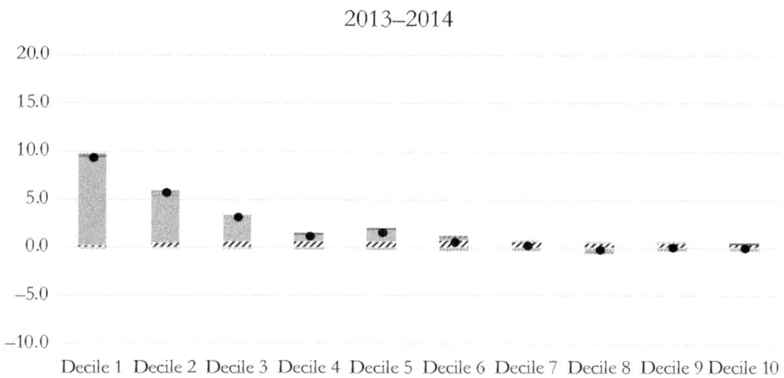

Appendix A (*cont.*)

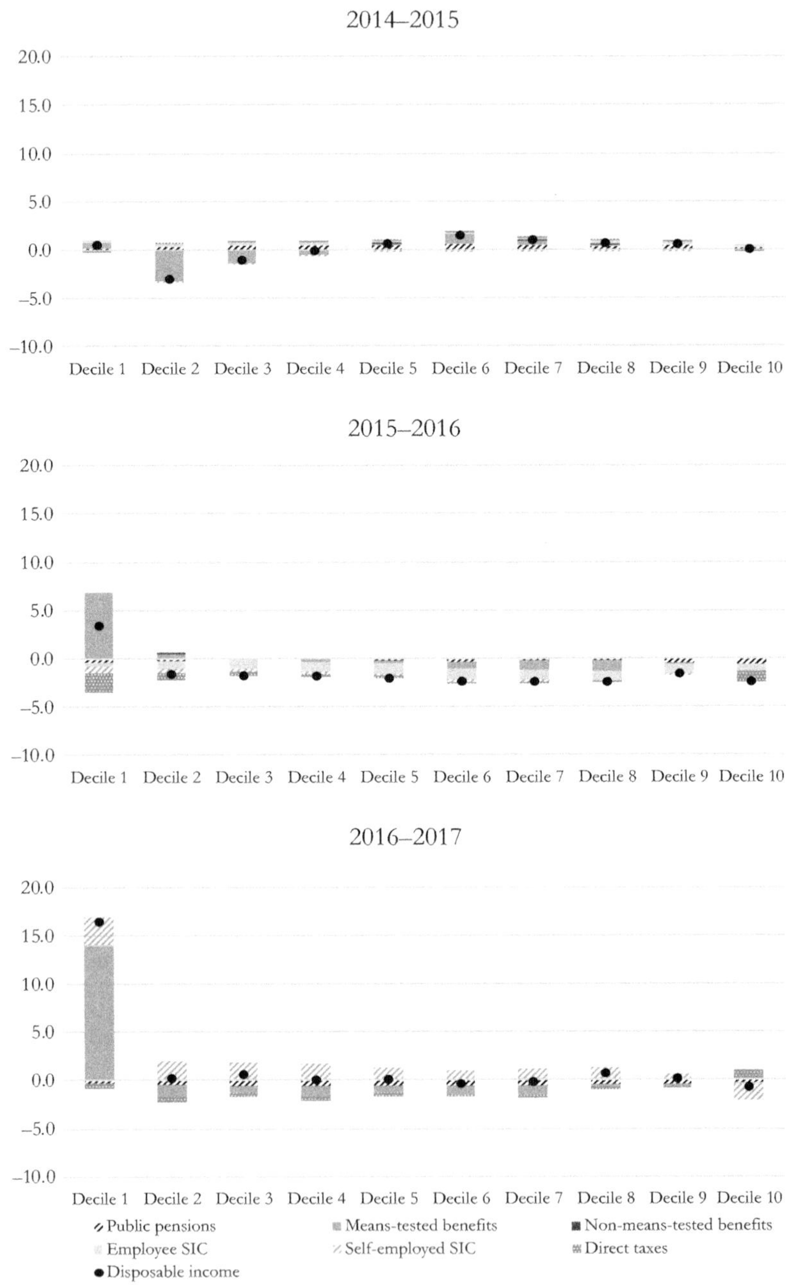

Appendix A (*cont.*)

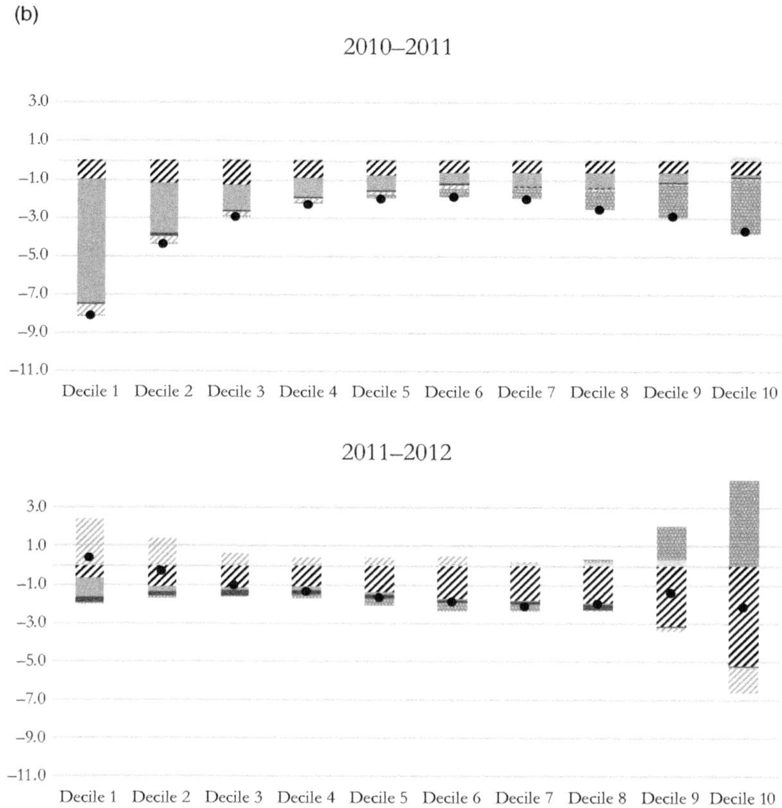

Appendix B Percentage change in income due to the reforms in the EAPs per decile by policy class and year.
Source: Calculations with EUROMOD version H1.0+

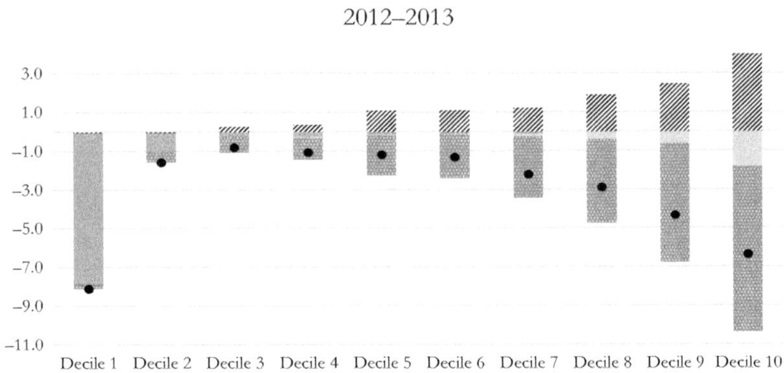

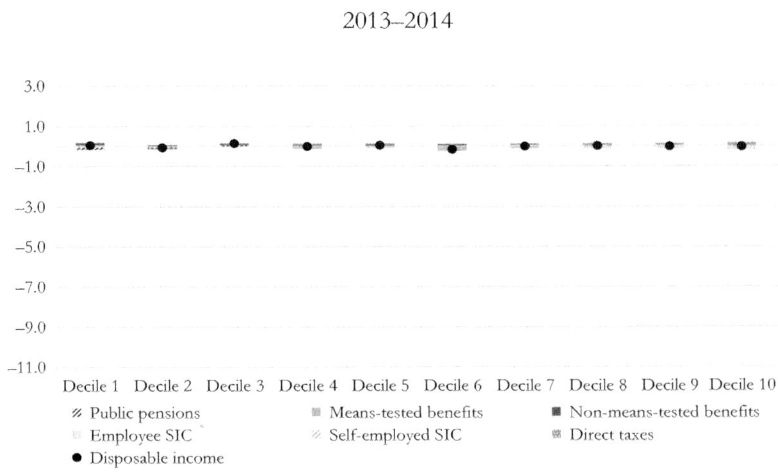

Appendix B (*cont.*)

12 *How Openness to Trade Rescued the Irish Economy*

KIERAN MCQUINN AND PETROS VARTHALITIS

12.1 Introduction

The remarkable recovery in the Irish economy since 2013 has surprised most observers.[1] Having been particularly impacted by the international financial crisis of 2007–2008, Irish economic activity has, since 2013, grown significantly, outpacing the rest of the Euro area. Indeed, the recent performance of the Irish economy is reminiscent of the earlier 'Celtic Tiger' era; between 1995 and 2007, the Irish economy, on average, grew by 7.3 per cent per annum – over three times the Euro area average for the period. Unemployment, which had been stubbornly high in the Irish economy through the 1980s and early 1990s, averaged just over 4.5 per cent between 2000 and 2007. However, given the emergence of a property-related credit bubble by 2007, the economy was particularly susceptible to the international financial crisis of 2007 and 2008. The Irish real estate boom saw the construction sector, both residential and commercial, assume a disproportionate influence on domestic economic activity by 2007. As a result, with the emergence of a toxic negative feedback loop between the sovereign and the Irish banking sector, formalised by the Irish government guaranteeing the liabilities and assets of the banking sector in

[1] We thank the editors of this volume Nauro Campos, Paul De Grawe and Yuemei Ji. We would also like to thank Alan Barrett, Adele Bergin, Abian Garcia-Rodriguez, Ilias Kostarakos, Martina Lawless, Conor O'Toole, Dimitris Papageorgiou, Apostolis Philippopoulos, Stelios Sakkas, Iulia Siedschlag and seminar participants at the ASSET 2018 conference and at the London School of Economics in the '2nd Workshop on Structural Reforms in the EU' 2018 for useful comments. The model used in this chapter was developed as part of a joint research programme between the Economic and Social Research Institute (ESRI) and the Department of Finance and Revenue Commissioners, and we are grateful for the helpful comments of the programme steering committee. The views expressed herein are our own and do not necessarily reflect the views of ESRI or the Department of Finance and Revenue Commissioners.

September 2008, the economy experienced one of the sharpest contractions among Euro area countries. Unemployment went from over 4 per cent to 14.5 per cent in just three years, while Irish output fell by 8 per cent between 2007 and 2009.

The underlying difficulties in the financial sector, given the property bubble, and the resulting fiscal burden on the state, saw Ireland enter a programme of support in October 2010 with the European Union, the European Central Bank and the International Monetary Fund (IMF) (commonly referred to as the 'Troika'). As with most programmes of support, the Irish state was committed to fulfil certain 'objectives' in order to satisfy the terms and conditions for the subsequent financing provided (see European Economy, 2011). These objectives centred on restoring financial stability, fiscal policy reform and structural reforms. While most of the attention concerning the performance of the Irish programme has centred on the first two objectives (see Schoenmaker, 2015, for a review of financial sector measures, and McCarthy, 2015, for an overview of the role played by fiscal consolidation), very little attention has been devoted to the role played by structural reforms in the Irish recovery.

However, structural reforms have long been heralded by international institutions such as the IMF, the European Commission and particularly the Organisation for Economic Cooperation and Development (OECD), among others, as a means of improving the growth potential of individual economies. Consequently, the obligation to undertake such reforms is frequently an important condition of support programmes extended to individual countries. Given the subsequent substantial performance of the Irish economy, it is now appropriate to assess whether the structural reforms proposed in the original adjustment programme were a contributing factor to this recovery. Clearly, if the adoption of certain structural reforms were influential in influencing the recovery, the programme of support given to the Irish state could serve as a successful template for other struggling European countries.

In this chapter, using a dynamic stochastic general equilibrium (DSGE) modelling framework, we critically appraise the performance of the Irish economy over the period 2008–2014. Using a model[2] with a tradable and nontradable sector, we examine whether the

[2] The model is a variant of the Fiscal Irish General Equilibrium Model (FIR-GEM), which is a small open economy DSGE model for fiscal policy analysis in Ireland; see Varthalitis (2019).

reason for the Irish recovery was a rebalancing of the Irish economy, post-2008, away from the disproportionate influence of the construction (nontradable) sector and back to the more productive tradable sector. Using the same framework, we contrast this with the role that structural reforms played in the Irish recovery. Our results suggest that the financial crisis acted as a rebalancing mechanism for the Irish economy, with the tradable sector contracting less and recovering quicker than the nontradable sector. Our model-based simulations indicate that the Irish recovery is mostly export driven with structural reforms playing a very minor role in stimulating growth in the immediate period after the crisis.

Our chapter contributes to the literature on the Irish crisis and recovery and on structural reforms in the context of DSGE models. On the one hand, a strand of the literature empirically assesses the Irish crisis and recovery;[3] see, e.g., Barry and Bergin (2019) and Whelan (2014). Here, by contrast, we examine the empirical facts through the lenses of a general equilibrium model. To the best of our knowledge, this is the first work that provides a unified narrative of the Irish crisis and recovery using this framework. On the other hand, there is a vast literature that studies structural reforms[4] under various DSGE setups; see, e.g., Cacciatore et al. (2012), Eggertsson et al. (2014), Forni et al. (2010), Gerali et al. (2014), Gomes et al. (2013), Koliousi et al. (2017), Papageorgiou and Vourvachaki (2018) and Sajedi (2018). In our chapter, we focus on the Irish economy and examine the potential role of structural reforms over the 2008–2014 recovery.

The rest of the chapter is laid out as follows. In the next section, we review the performance of the Irish economy over the period 1990–2014, focusing on three subperiods. In Section 12.3 we present our theoretical model in an informal setup. Section 12.4 solves the model and describes the various simulated scenarios, while Section 12.5 discusses the results of the modelling simulations. A final section offers some concluding comments.

[3] For a detailed report on the various aspects of Irish crisis and recovery, see also CESifo (2014).

[4] Several theoretical and econometric studies have been conducted for structural reforms. Selective references include Babecký and Campos (2011), De Grawe and Ji (2017), Fatas (2016) and Whelan and McQuinn (2018). For an exhaustive and critical overview of the literature on structural reforms, see Campos et al. (2018) and references therein.

12.2 The Irish Economy: 1990–2014

In reviewing Irish economic performance over the period 1990–2014, we examine three particular subperiods. Initially, we examine the role of openness to trade in Irish income levels converging with those of the richest EU countries between 1990 and 2001; then we discuss the Irish credit and housing bubble that led to the emergence of imbalances in the Irish economy between 2001 and 2007. Finally, we examine the role the international financial crisis played post-2008 in rebalancing Irish economy with exports, in particular being a key driver of post-crisis Irish macroeconomic dynamics.

12.2.1. Convergence through Trade Openness

The remarkable economic performance of the Irish economy since the late 1980s and early 1990s is well documented. Ireland's real cumulative gross domestic product (GDP) growth summed to 128 per cent from 1988 to 2007, implying an annual average growth of 6.4 per cent. The reasons for the exceptional growth have been examined in length in Fitzgerald (2000), Honohan and Walsh (2002), Whelan (2014) and more recently Klein and Ventura (2018). Here, we focus on the role played by international trade and trade openness in influencing Irish growth during this period.

As can be seen in Figure 12.1, trade as a share of GDP in Ireland had already been among the highest in the European Union since the late 1980s early 1990s. However, from the early 1990s onwards, external trade[5] accelerated sharply, rendering Ireland one of the most open to trade economies globally. In 2001, international trade[6] was 1.7 times Ireland's GDP, while the analogous figures in select core and periphery EU countries were below 0.8 with the exception of the Netherlands.

The trajectory of GDP per capita closely follows the path of international trade as illustrated in the left panel of Figure 12.1. It is the exceptional degree of trade openness, among other factors, that underpins Ireland's economic convergence with the richest EU countries in the late 1990s and, as we argue in this section, it is this openness that appears to be a key driver of the Irish recovery after the global financial crisis.

[5] Much of Ireland's trade is in electronics, pharmaceuticals, other chemicals and medical instrumentation; see Barry and Bergin (2012) for more details.

[6] As indicator of trade openness, we employ the sum of imports and exports as a share of GDP, which is widely used. See, e.g., OECD (2011).

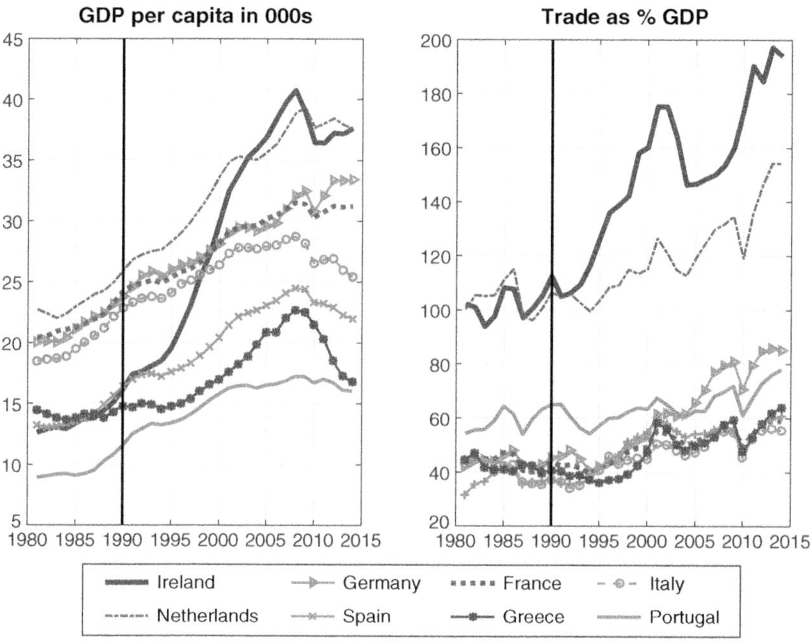

Figure 12.1 Trade openness and GDP per capita of the Irish economy since the 1990s.

Note: Trade is defined as the sum of exports and imports.

Source: Eurostat

In general, the change in Ireland's trading performance over the period 1990–2001 is quite remarkable. In Figure 12.2, we plot some key international variables, showing exports (imports) to GDP ratio increases from 40 per cent (40 per cent) in 1990 to 92 per cent (80 per cent), while the foreign direct investment (FDI) to GDP ratio goes from 1.26 in 1990 to 25.8 in 2001. Finally, over the same period, the Irish trade balance went from 0 per cent to 12 per cent. As a result, over this period the tradable sector, mostly dominated by foreign affiliated firms, expanded significantly vis-à-vis the nontradable sector.

12.2.2 Emergence of the Irish Property Bubble: 2004–2007

The emergence of the Celtic Tiger in the mid-1990s resulted in a significant increase in Irish living standards, with real incomes growing considerably. With declining interest rates due to accommodative

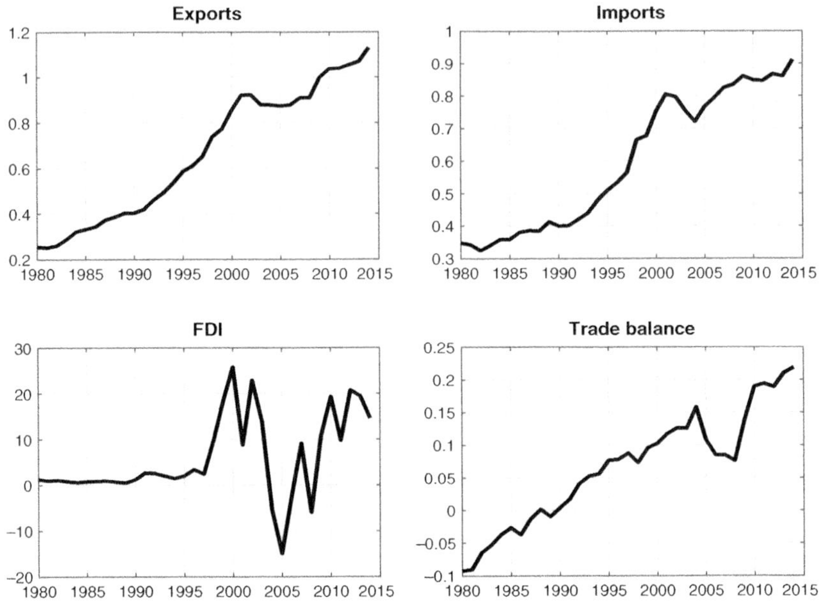

Figure 12.2 Other Irish international macro variables (as per cent of GDP).
Notes: Exports/imports of goods and services; FDI is measured as inward inflow.
Sources: United Nations Conference on Trade and Development (UNCTAD) and OECD

monetary policy at the same time, the domestic property market experienced a substantial increase in affordability and consequently demand. Additionally, the housing stock per capita in Ireland was by the mid-1990s one of the lowest in Europe.[7] Real Irish house prices grew by nearly 9 per cent per annum between 1995 and 2007.

While the initial phase of increased activity in the housing market 1995–2003 is typically attributed to developments in underlying fundamentals in the market, the period 2004–2007 is characterised by the emergence of a credit-based property bubble (see McCarthy and McQuinn, 2017, for more on this). The increased ability of Irish financial institutions to borrow from credit institutions abroad, coupled with the easing of credit conditions in the domestic market,

[7] In 2000, in an OECD cross-country sample of dwellings per 1,000 inhabitants, the Irish housing market had the fifth lowest number of dwellings per population out of a sample of thirty-one countries.

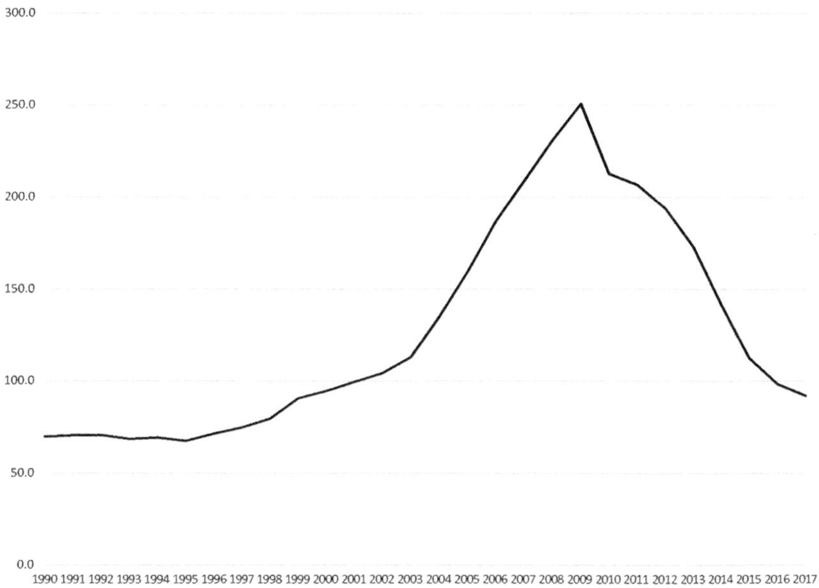

Figure 12.3 Credit to gross national income (%): 1990–2017.
Note: Own calculations.
Sources: Central Statistics Office (CSO) and Central Bank of Ireland

saw a significant increase in mortgage and construction credit issued. The dramatic increase in credit vis-à-vis GDP in the Irish economy can be observed in Figure 12.3.

As a result, house construction levels soared with annual house completions averaging 84,000 units between 2004 and 2006. This resulted in the investment to GDP ratio in Ireland rising to 29.1 per cent in 2006 (relative to 22.0 per cent in the EU). Between 2003 and 2007, investment in housing in Ireland averaged 12 per cent of GDP, more than double the European average. Employment levels in construction increased by 75 per cent between 2000 and 2007. As a result, by early 2008, approximately one in eight workers was employed in the construction sector in Ireland, relative to one in 12 in the EU. Consequently, the significant increase in construction-related activity resulted in productive resources in the domestic economy being reallocated towards the nontradable sector (see also Section 12.2.3).

The international financial crisis of 2007 and 2008 led to a swift decline in investor confidence in Irelands' property sector given concerns about a price bubble and significant oversupply. The housing market collapse began in 2008, with prices declining on average by 10 per cent in nominal terms in each of the years to 2013. Annual house completions dropped by 91 per cent (from a peak of 93,000 units in 2006) to a low of 8,300 units in 2013. Finally, the number of persons employed in the construction sector dropped by two-thirds.

12.2.3 Post-2008: The International Financial Crisis as a Rebalancing Mechanism?

In this section, we examine the effect of the international financial crisis of 2007–2008 on the structure of the Irish economy at that time and on its subsequent economic performance. The evidence suggests that post-2008 the Irish economy rebalances away from the disproportionate impact of the nontradable sector back to the tradable sector. This happens due to the combination of the collapse of the construction sector, which reduces the size of the nontradable sector and the increase in exports, which sees a sizeable increase in the tradable sector.

To examine the effect of the crisis on the structure of Irish economy, we decompose GDP growth into two main components: domestic demand and net exports. As can be seen in Figure 12.4, from 2001 to 2007 the main driver of real GDP growth is domestic demand mainly fuelled by the credit and construction boom. In particular, domestic demand (represented by the black bars) contributes more than 80 per cent to annual real GDP growth. However, after 2008–2009, domestic demand falls significantly due to the collapse of the housing bubble and does not recover until 2014. On the other hand, pre-2008 net exports contribution to real GDP growth is either small or negative, but it increases in the first years after the crisis compensating for the collapse of domestic demand.

Using this decomposition, 2008 emerges as a turning point not only for real GDP growth but also for its constituent components. Before 2007, it is evident real GDP growth is primarily domestic demand–driven whereas from 2008 onwards net exports substitute domestic demand as the main determinant of growth.[8] From 2001 to 2007, the contribution of domestic demand averages 5.1 per cent, whereas for 2008–2014 the equivalent figure is –0.02 per cent. In contrast, net

[8] Notice that in 2014 domestic demand seems to contribute relatively more to GDP growth. This can be mostly attributed to the partial recovery of domestic investment that collapsed in 2008. Thus, any pickup observed is from a very low base.

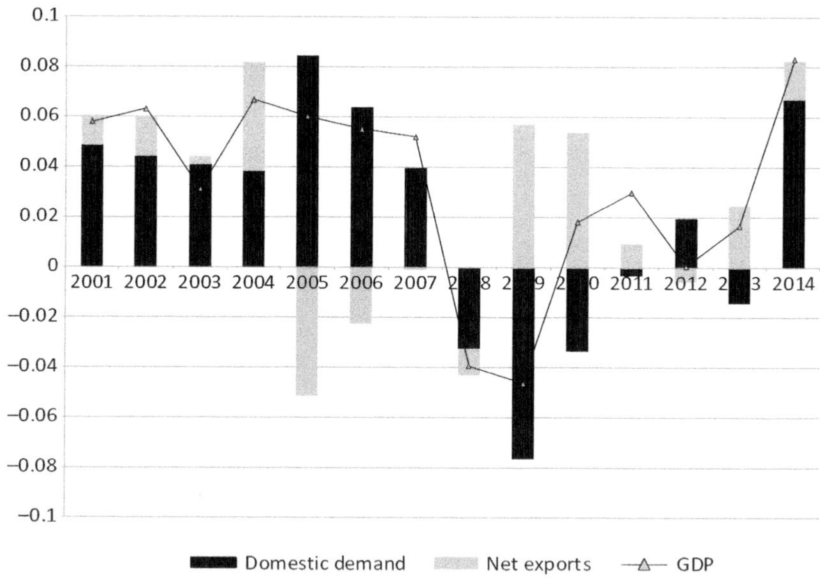

Figure 12.4 Contribution of domestic demand and net exports to real GDP growth (2001–2014).
Note: Year-over-year (y-o-y) growth rates.
Source: Eurostat; GDP and main components, chain-linked volumes (2010)

exports contribution averages −1 per cent between 2001 and 2007 and then 2.04 per cent between 2008 and 2014.

Similar evidence can be inferred from decomposing total output (measured in gross value-added terms) into two sectors: tradable and nontradable. We choose this categorisation for two reasons: first, it is of particular relevance for our study of the Irish crisis and recovery; Ireland is a small open economy (SOE) that relies on international trade, thus decomposing output into tradable and nontradable sectors enables us to disentangle the effect of exports, which operates through the tradable sector from any other effects (e.g., fiscal policy and structural reforms). Second, it allows us to establish a link between the empirical part of the chapter and the theoretical DSGE model that we develop in the second part.

Figure 12.5 plots gross value added (GVA) in the tradable and nontradable sectors[9] from 2001 to 2014. The tradable sector was less impaired by the crisis than the nontradable sector. In particular, it

[9] We allocate all NACE activities for Irish economy to two sectors, i.e., tradable and nontradable, following Bergin et al. (2017).

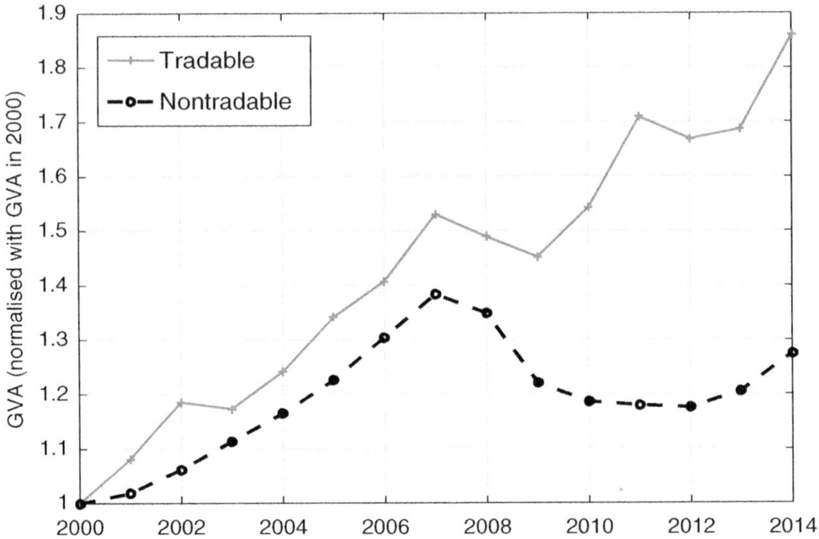

Figure 12.5 Tradable and nontradable GVA (2001–2014).
Source: Eurostat; GVA-chain-linked volumes (2010); total: all NACE activities

declines temporarily and recovers sharply towards its precrisis trend. In contrast, the nontradable sector enters a prolonged period of recession while it converges slowly towards a lower trajectory. Thus, sectoral outputs respond asymmetrically in the aftermath of the crisis. In the postcrisis period, the share of the tradable sector expands while the share of the nontradable shrinks.

In Figure 12.6, we show that the increase in tradable output is accompanied by a resource reallocation of productive factors, such as investment and employment, towards the expanding sector of the economy. Moreover, sectoral investment and employment shares indicate the nature of the underlying imbalances in the Irish economy, namely, the misallocation of resources towards the overheated nontradable sector and out of the tradable sector over 2001–2007 and the reversal of this trend after 2008 crisis (for example, the employment and investment share increases in the tradable sector post-2008; see the black square lines).

12.2.4. The Role of Structural Reforms over 2008–2014

So far our analysis focuses on the export-driven narrative of Irish recovery. Given the importance attached to structural reforms in

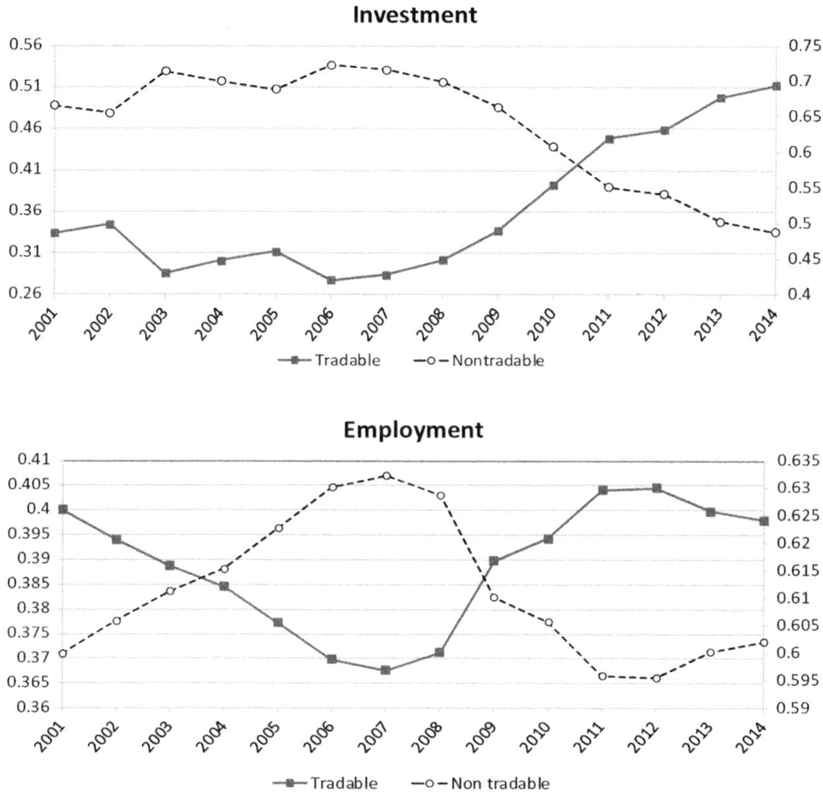

Figure 12.6 Share of productive factors in the tradable and nontradable sector.
Notes: Shares are computed divided by total employment in private tradable and nontradable sectors, while we exclude public employment.
Source: CSO and ESRI database

driving the recovery of economies, in this section we examine the performance of the Irish economy in adopting structural reforms post-2008 as measured by OECD product and labour market deregulation indicators.

In particular, in the top panel of Figure 12.7 we present the broad product market regulation (PMR) indicator for Ireland, comparing it with OECD and EU averages. PMR indicator measures liberalisation in product markets in a scale ranging from 0 to 6, where 0 stands for perfect competition and 6 for fully regulated product market. PMR averages scores from three subindicators, i.e., state control, barriers to

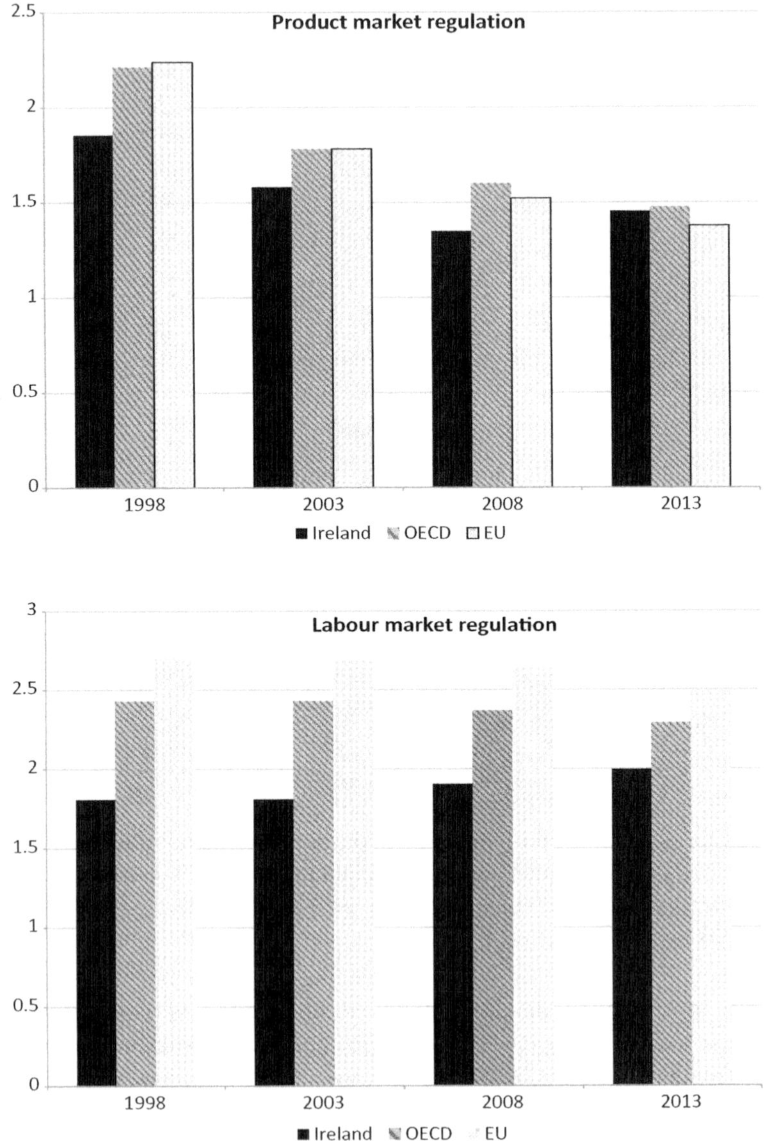

Figure 12.7 Product and labour market OECD indicators. top panel: economywide product market regulation index (PMR); bottom panel: employment protection legislation indicator (individual and collective dismissals, regular contract).
Source: OECD

entrepreneurship and barriers to trade and investment. Similarly, in the bottom panel we present an employment protection legislation (EPL) indicator for Ireland and averages for the OECD and EU. EPL measures flexibility in labour markets on a scale from 0 to 6, where 0 implies a flexible labour market and 6 a rigid labour market. As can be seen in Figure 12.7, Ireland ranks higher in product and labour market flexibility than OECD and EU averages for all years of the OECD sample.[10] Thus, according to the classification, Ireland had already been a relatively flexible economy when the 2008 crisis occurred. Focusing on the period of interest and comparing PMR and EPL values in 2008 with their values in 2013, it is evident no further liberalisation in product and labour markets can be observed. Actually, these indices slightly increase between this period, suggesting a slight deterioration in product and labour market flexibility. Thus, we can infer that there are no clear signs of major structural reforms occurring in the Irish economy during this period. Later in the chapter, using our modelling framework we perform simulations to examine the impact of potential structural reforms on the performance of the Irish economy post-2008.

12.3 Theoretical Analysis

In this section, we outline the small open economy DSGE model used to simulate the alternative scenarios that could serve as possible explanations for Irish economic performance post-2008. Then we compare the model-based simulations of each scenario to assess quantitatively which of those scenarios can replicate most closely the actual empirical outcomes highlighted in Section 12.2.

Therefore, initially we present the SOE-DSGE model in an informal setup. The model is then solved numerically for a data-mimicking steady-state solution, and the alternative simulated scenarios are presented. Finally, we assess the different scenarios quantitatively using model-based simulations of the main Irish macroeconomic variables.

[10] In 2013, Ireland ranks below the EU average in the PMR indicator. This can be attributed mostly to the increase in the subindicator 'state control', which was influenced by state ownership of Irish banks after the bailout programme was launched in 2011.

12.3.1. A DSGE Model for Ireland

The model is a variant of the Fiscal Irish General Equilibrium Model (FIR-GEM). Full details of the model in a formal setup are discussed in Varthalitis (2019). Here we outline the main features in an informal setup. The present model is a small open economy DSGE model with a tradable and nontradable sector calibrated for the Irish economy[11]; since Ireland is member of the Eurozone, we assume a monetary regime of fixed exchange rates while monetary policy is conducted by the European Central Bank (ECB) as in Philippopoulos et al. (2017). The small open economy consists of three building blocks: households, firms and government. Each block of the model is now discussed.

12.3.1.1 Households

The economy is populated by *N* number of households. Each household aims to maximise a welfare function, i.e., their expected lifetime utility, by choosing their consumption and investment plans as well as their working schedule given fiscal policy. Their expected lifetime utility depends positively on the composite final consumption good and the public good and negatively on hours worked (or positively on leisure). The final composite good that enters the utility function of each household is assumed to be a composite good made up of the domestic composite good and imported goods from the rest of the world; similarly the domestic composite good is made up of tradable and nontradable goods produced domestically. Regarding their income and assets, households rent physical capital and supply differentiated labour services to firms of the tradable and nontradable sector. Also, they enjoy market power for their own labour supply, meaning that they can set wages with a markup over their marginal rate of substitution between consumption and hours worked. In addition, they can borrow/lend government bonds and internationally traded financial assets. Finally, Irish households are subject to consumption, labour and capital taxes while they receive lump-sum public transfers.

[11] General equilibrium models calibrated for Ireland include Clancy and Merola (2014), Klein and Ventura (2018) and Lozej et al. (2017).

12.3.1.2 Production

There are two sectors of production, the tradable and the nontradable sector. Both sectors have a similar structure. In each sector, there are two types of firms: the final good distributors and the intermediate good producers. The intermediate good producers enjoy market power for their own goods, meaning that they can set prices with a markup over their marginal cost. To produce intermediate goods, they rent physical capital and labour services from households. Final good distributors combine the different varieties of intermediate goods to produce a single good that can be used by households either for consumption or investment purposes. This holds for each sector; thus the SOE produces tradable and nontradable composite goods.

12.3.1.3 Government

The government levies consumption, labour and capital taxes on domestic households and borrows from domestic households and foreign investors to finance government purchases of private goods and public transfers to households. The national fiscal authority follows simple feedback rules, meaning that its independently set policy instruments react to a small number of easily observable macroeconomic indicators. The fiscal instruments used include the ratios of government spending and public transfers to GDP, the tax rates on consumption, capital and labour income. These fiscal instruments react to deviations in the public debt to GDP ratio from its target value and the output gap (see Schmitt-Grohe and Uribe, 2007, for similar rules).

12.3.1.4 Modelling Exports

A small open economy setup means that a country is small in world product and financial markets. Thus, it cannot influence variables such as world interest rates and prices. As noted by Schmitt-Grohé and Uribe (2003), in order to achieve a dynamically stable solution and a well-defined steady state, we must endogenise the world interest rate at which the small open economy borrows from the international financial markets. We do this by assuming that the interest rate a country borrows from international capital markets with is an increasing function of the country's net foreign liabilities.[12] Regarding world prices,

[12] Alternatively, we can assume that interest rate is an increasing function of debt to GDP when this ratio exceeds a specific threshold. Both are common

typically it is assumed that the terms of trade defined as the relative price of exports in terms of imports are exogenous and follow an autoregressive process, while exports are an endogenous variable (see Schmitt-Grohé and Uribe, 2017). In our case, we aim to mimic the increase in exports observed in Irish data; thus, it is more convenient to assume that exports are exogenous and in particular follow a law of motion while we allow the terms of trade to become an endogenous variable. That is, exports are a function of three components: exports in the previous period, an exogenous innovation and of deviations in the terms of trade from its steady-state value. The exogenous innovation can capture changes in the world economy that are exogenous to the Irish economy (for more details on the shock and its rationale, see Subsection 12.4.2.2.), while the latter term ensures dynamic stability and allows exports to have an endogenous feedback from changes in relative prices (as in, e.g., Philippopoulos et al., 2017)). That is, *ceteris paribus*, a decrease in the relative price of Irish exports with respect to prices in the rest of the world results in an increase in Irish exports.

12.3.1.5 Structural Reforms in DSGE Setup

Finally, in order to model the potential implications of structural reforms being implemented, we assume that structural reforms refer to policies that make the product and labour market more flexible and competitive. Thus, in order to study structural reforms in a DSGE model, we depart from the assumption of fully competitive markets and introduce product and labour market imperfections.

In particular, we introduce the standard Dixit–Stiglitz-type monopolistic competition in both product and labour markets. As a result, prices are set with a markup over marginal cost, and wages are set with a markup over the marginal rate of substitution between consumption and hours worked. Prices and wages in Ireland are generally acknowledged as being relatively flexible; see, e.g., OECD (2009) for price and wage flexibility and Babecky et al. (2010) for a comparison of wage rigidities within Europe. The structural reforms proposed are mainly

assumptions in the related literature – see, e.g., Bi (2010), Economides et al. (2017); Garcia-Cicco et al. (2010), Philippopoulos et al. (2017) and Schmitt-Grohe and Uribe (2003) – and is supported by a number of empirical studies – see, e.g., European Commission (2012).

concerned with competition policy and activation measures in the labour market.[13] Thus, markups in our model can be interpreted as capturing a lack of competition and other structural rigidities in product and labour markets such as barriers to entrepreneurship and investment, the degree of regulation in labour markets and the general lack of labour market mobility. In this setup, structural reforms can take the form of reductions in price and wage markups.[14] The size, pace, timing and reversal or not of this reduction depends on the implementation of the reforms.

12.4 Numerical Solution of the Model

For the purposes of examining our alternative scenarios, we initially obtain a numerical steady solution. Then, to examine the impact of alternative simulated scenarios, we observe the deviation from this solution of each particular scenario.

12.4.1 Steady-State Solution

As we wish to examine the performance of the Irish economy post 2008, the model is calibrated using relevant Irish data over the period 1995–2008. In particular, most of the structural parameters of the model are calibrated so that the numerical solution mimics key macro and international macro ratios in the Irish data, while fiscal policy instruments are set as per the actual data. The steady solution of the model is presented in Table 12.1. The model replicates some key data ratios and as such will be used as the reference point to evaluate the various scenarios subsequently performed.

[13] For a discussion on proposed selected structural reforms in Ireland, see Irish Government Economic and Evaluation Service (2014) and OECD (2009).

[14] For a similar approach to modelling structural reforms, see, e.g., Andrés et al. (2017), Gomes et al. (2013), Papageorgiou and Vourvachaki (2017), and Sajedi (2018). However, there are different modelling approaches; see, for example, Cacciatore et al. (2016), who modelled structural reforms as reductions in the size of sunk entry costs in product markets and as a reduction in unemployment benefits and workers' bargaining power in labour market, while De Grawe and Ji (2017) study structural reforms that increase flexibility in price and wage setting in the context of a New Keynesian behavioural model.

Table 12.1 *Steady-state solution.*

Variable	Model	Data
Consumption as a share of output	0.45	0.47
Total public debt as a share of output	0.42	0.42
Trade balance as a share of output	0.1	0.1
Exports to Imports ratio	1.4	1.2
Tradable to nontradable wage ratio	1.5	1.5

12.4.2. Simulated Scenarios

We now subject the economy to certain exogenous shocks so as to mimic the Irish crisis of 2008–2009 while at the same time simulating alternative scenarios to assess different possible explanations of the Irish recovery. In order to replicate the Irish crisis and capture the decline of around 9 per cent in Irish GDP over 2008–2009, we implement a negative total-factor productivity (TFP) shock[15] on the tradable and nontradable sector.[16] To replicate the increase in the Irish debt-to-GDP ratio, which soared from 42 per cent in 2008 to 110 per cent in 2010, we also assume an initial debt shock.

Given these external shocks, we simulate three different scenarios to assess quantitatively possible explanations for the significant Irish recovery over the period 2008–2014. In the next subsection, we consider three main scenarios, namely the baseline, the export-driven recovery and the structural reforms scenario.

[15] McQuinn and Whelan (2018), in examining the growth performance of EU countries, generate estimates of TFP for 12 member countries. In the Irish case, McQuinn and Whelan (2018) find that TFP fell during the crisis. Although the 2007–2008 world financial crisis affected Ireland in many different ways, our aim is to start from the crisis and focus on its aftermath; thus we assume that these different adverse effects are reflected in adverse TFP shocks (see, e.g., Chari et al. (2007) for a methodological treatment of this issue).

[16] Notice that although the negative TFP shocks that hit the tradable and nontradable sectors are ex-ante symmetric, our model endogenously generates asymmetric output responses in the two sectors. These responses resemble the actual responses in Irish data, meaning a relatively higher contraction in the nontradable sector vis-à-vis the tradable sector.

12.4.2.1 The Baseline Scenario (Fiscal Adjustment)

This scenario is used as the reference scenario for comparison purposes. We refer to the scenario as the baseline one because it consists of commonly accepted facts of the Irish crisis, i.e., the exogenous shocks that resulted in the Irish crisis and the fiscal consolidation policies subsequently implemented. This baseline scenario quantifies the impact of exogenous shocks mimicking the impact of the 2008 crisis on the Irish economy if only fiscal consolidation policies were implemented while other structural or exogenous shocks are 'switched off' or not implemented.

We simulate this scenario as follows. The economy departs from the steady-state solution reported in Table 12.1 in 2008. On impact, the economy is subjected to exogenous shocks that mimic the key features of the Irish crisis. In particular, negative TFP shocks are implemented on the tradable and nontradable sectors, reflecting a contraction in total and sectoral outputs. In addition, we assume an initial debt shock mimicking the substantial increase in the debt-to-GDP ratio. Then we assume that a fiscal policy is implemented consisting of an expenditure-based fiscal consolidation programme similar to the one actually implemented by the Irish government over the period 2009–2014 (for more details, see Larch et al., 2016).

This is implemented through the feedback policy coefficients in the associated fiscal feedbacks rules so that the main Irish tax-spending instruments resemble their observed path in the data.[17] Thus, transition dynamics are driven by data-mimicking exogenous shocks while fiscal policy reacts to debt imbalances so as to reduce the level of public debt.[18] It should be noted that the model is dynamically unstable when fiscal policy does not react to debt levels. Thus, some fiscal action was necessary to ensure fiscal sustainability. Section 12.5 computes simulated paths of key endogenous variables of the model under this scenario. The other scenarios are in addition to this baseline scenario.

[17] This implies spending cuts of 4 percentage points on impact, temporary increases in consumption and labour taxes of around 0.8 per cent and 2 per cent respectively, while the capital tax rate is set constant to its relatively low level with respect to the rest of Eurozone data average.

[18] Five exogenously set fiscal instruments are assumed to follow feedback rules, namely government consumption and transfers to GDP ratio, consumption, labour and capital tax, while debt adjusts residually to satisfy the government budget constraint.

12.4.2.2 Export-Based Recovery

In this scenario, we aim to examine the impact of an increase in Irish exports given the exogenous shocks that lead to the contraction in output, the increase in debt and the fiscal consolidation programme implemented by the Irish government. Comparing this scenario with the baseline, we can disentangle the role played by the increase in exports.

We simulate this scenario as follows. Starting from the baseline scenario, we assume an exogenous increase in exports in line with the increase observed in Irish data over the period 2008–2010. This exogenous increase can be attributed to changes in the world economic environment at that time, e.g., the recovery of the main trading partners of the Irish economy and the related favourable movements (for Irish exporters) of the Euro with respect to the US dollar and British sterling. As with the baseline scenario, the economy departs from the 2008 data-mimicking steady-state solution. Then, when the economy is subjected to the exogenous, negative TFP shock and a debt shock, the Irish government is assumed to initiate a fiscal consolidation package as in the baseline scenario. However, now Irish exports recover in line with the Irish data. Exports increase on impact, mimicking the increase in the observed Irish data, and then return gradually to their precrisis value following an autoregressive process. The parameter influencing the persistence of exports is calibrated so as to replicate the average increase in exports from 2008 to 2014.[19] Therefore, in this scenario the transition dynamics are driven by the exogenous shocks also assumed in the baseline scenario plus the increase in exports over the period 2008–2014. As before, the government adopts fiscal consolidation policies resembling the actual fiscal policy undertaken over 2008–2014.

12.4.2.3 Structural Reforms-Based Recovery

We then simulate a scenario to quantify the impact of structural reforms on the Irish recovery. As before, structural reforms are modelled in addition to the baseline scenario while we now switch off the impact due to exports. Comparing this scenario with the baseline, we

[19] We have experimented with various values for the autoregressive parameter that governs exports' persistence, and we report that our main qualitative results hold.

can quantify, separately, the effect of the structural reforms. To assess the effect of product and labour market reforms separately, we simulate reforms in one market at a time.[20]

We now assume that product market reforms are implemented when the exogenous TFP and debt shocks impact the economy and when the government implements its fiscal consolidation package. That is, price markups in tradable and nontradable sectors decrease by 3 percentage points (p.p.) and 5 p.p., respectively, and then return gradually to their precrisis value following an autoregressive process. The parameter influencing the persistence of structural reforms is set at a very high value[21]; thus reforms in our model are fully implemented on impact and are almost permanent in their impact. We limit our analysis to the first few years (2008–2014) after the crisis, as we are interested in the short-run effects of structural reforms on the Irish recovery. Given that our modelling implies that reforms are fully implemented on impact, our results set an upper limit for the potential short-run positive effects of structural reforms.[22]

12.5 Quantitative Assessment of the Various Simulated Scenarios

In this section, we present model-based simulations for the alternative scenarios described earlier in the chapter. In order to disentangle the effects and mechanisms of each different explanation, we simulate one scenario at a time. We start by computing the effect of total and sectoral outputs for each scenario, because this facilitates comparisons with the empirical analysis in Section 12.2. Then, we employ model-based simulations of several endogenous variables of our model to shed light on the propagation mechanism of each alternative scenario.

[20] We have also performed simulations with structural reforms in both product and labour markets, and we report that our main qualitative results do not change, but as expected we observe some quantitative differences.

[21] Since we don't find clear-cut empirical evidence of extensive structural reforms over 2008–2014 (see Section 12.2.5), we consider this scenario as counterfactual. To this end, the size of the markups reduction, persistence and timing follows the related literature.

[22] We report that we have experimented with the pace and timing of reform implementation, and the qualitative results do not change. Similarly, we model labour market reforms (LMR) as a decrease in wage markups of the tradable and nontradable sector.

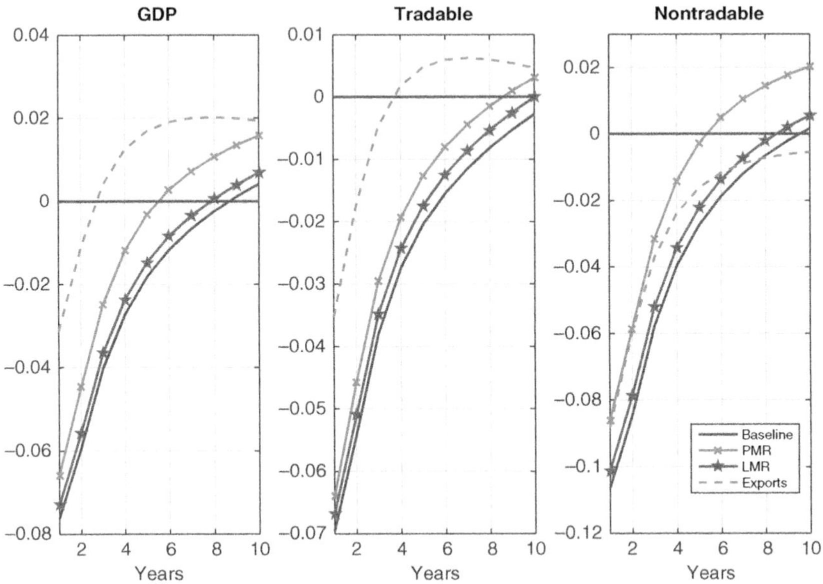

Figure 12.8 GDP and sectoral output.
Note: Variables are percentage deviations from their steady-state value.

In doing so, we provide a unified framework to develop an economic narrative of the Irish recovery, establishing links with the empirical facts when necessary.

12.5.1 Effect on GDP and Sectoral Output

Figure 12.8 presents the simulated implied paths of total and sectoral outputs in the tradable and nontradable sectors. The solid horizontal black line represents the point of departure, i.e., the solution reported in Table 12.1, while the black solid lines represent the baseline scenario, the light grey dashed lines the export-based recovery scenario and the grey cross and black square lines reflect the structural reforms in product and labour market, respectively.

Comparing across alternative scenarios, we observe that, in the export-driven recovery scenario, the GDP recession is smaller on impact and the recovery is faster in the aftermath of the crisis. On the other hand, the simulated response functions under the structural reforms in product markets or in labour markets suggest that these reforms are most unlikely to reflect the significant recovery observed in the Irish data. Comparison between product/labour market reforms scenarios with the baseline scenario implies that such reforms could not have substantially mitigated the recessionary effects of the exogenous shocks that impacted the Irish economy. This is more striking in the short run (over the first three years after the negative shocks), where structural reforms scenarios implied that response functions do not deviate substantially from the baseline scenario. Thus, a key message from our model-based simulations is that only the export-driven recovery scenario can mimic the significant recovery in total output.

As discussed in Section 12.2.3, a key feature of the Irish quick recovery is its sectoral decomposition between the tradable and nontradable sectors. Our model-based simulations allow us to break down the GDP recession and recovery into its sectoral components, i.e., tradable and nontradable output, under the different scenarios. This analysis provides further evidence that support the export-based recovery scenario; that is, simulations generated by the latter mimic closely the actual path of sectoral outputs in the Irish data. In addition, the rapid recovery in Irish GDP can be attributed mostly to an analogous recovery of the tradable sector of the Irish economy due to an increase in exports while the nontradable sector enters a relatively more prolonged recession and recovers on a slower basis (see Figure 12.5 in Section 12.2.3). Both structural reform scenarios generate simulations for sectoral outputs that do not resemble their actual paths observed in the Irish data.

12.5.2 Underlying Mechanisms

To understand the key underlying mechanism of each scenario, we now present the associated impulse response functions of other key endogenous variables. Figure 12.9 plots the associated simulated paths of the output share of tradable and nontradable output, the real wage in the tradable and nontradable sector, the relative price of tradable with respect to the price of nontradable sector, the trade balance and the exports to GDP ratios under the various scenarios. Similar to Figure 12.8, the baseline scenario is illustrated by the black solid lines, the export-driven scenario by the light grey dashed lines while the structural reforms in product and labour markets are denoted by the grey cross and black square lines respectively. Since the export-driven

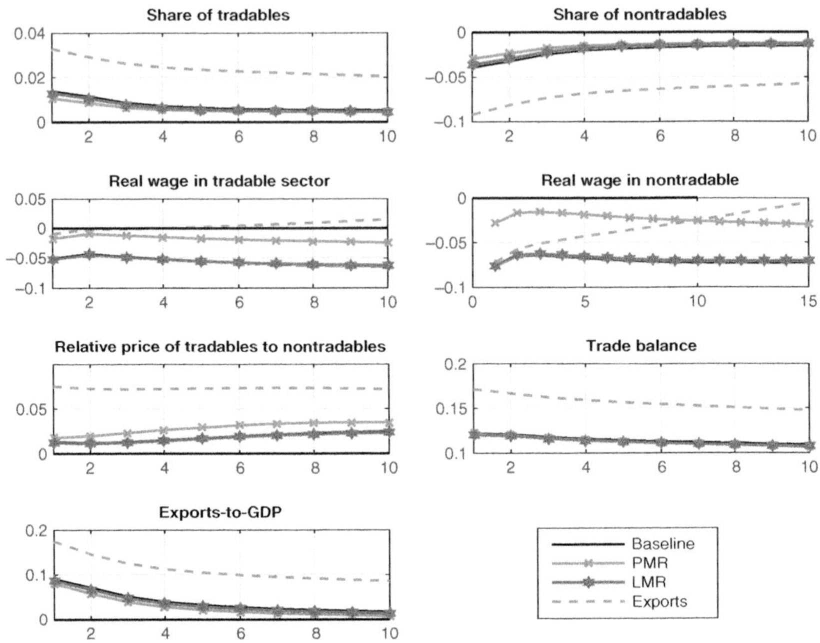

Figure 12.9 Implied response functions of other macroeconomic variables.
Note: Variables are percentage deviations from their steady-state value.

scenario moves in line with the actual postcrisis Irish data, in what follows we develop our economic narrative around this scenario while for reasons of comparison we refer to the other scenarios to illustrate any differences.

Under the export-driven scenario, the Irish crisis seems to act as a rebalancing mechanism for the Irish economy; the tradable sector contracts less and recovers much faster than the nontradable sector. As a result, the share of the tradable sector increases vis-à-vis the share of the nontradable sector, as can be seen in the first row of Figure 12.9. The severe negative shock impacts the nontradable sector of the economy disproportionately while the negative effect is mitigated in the tradable sector due to the exogenous increase in exports; the latter can be seen by the last subplot of Figure 12.9, where the exports-to-output ratio, under the export-driven recovery scenario, increases significantly more than in the structural reforms and baseline scenarios. In the baseline and structural reform scenarios, the significant loss in output and reductions in price and wage markups do result in an increase in

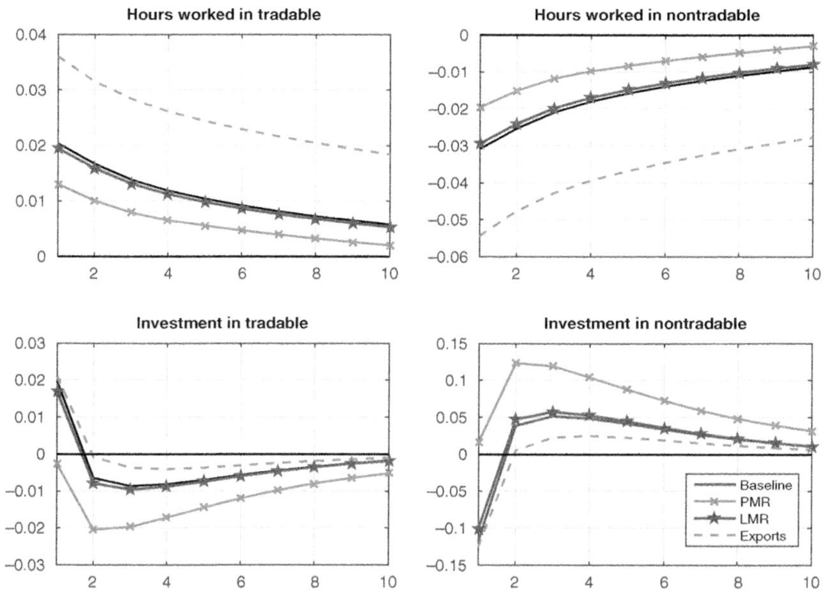

Figure 12.10 Shares of production factor inputs in tradable and nontradable sectors.
Note: Variables are percentage deviations from their steady-state value.

exports by reducing domestic prices vis-à-vis the rest of the world prices, and hence improving competitiveness. However, in magnitude terms, this is not significant enough to generate the implied response functions that reflect the actual path of Irish exports and of other endogenous variables during the recovery.

The increase in the exports-to-output ratio in the former scenario is calibrated to replicate the increase in exports observed in the data over the period 2008–2014. In our model, due to the expansion of the tradable sector vis-à-vis the nontradable sector, productive resources such as investment and employment reallocate towards the tradable sector of the economy and away from the nontradable sector. This can be seen in Figure 12.10, where we plot shares of hours worked and investment in physical capital with respect to their aggregates in the tradable and nontradable sectors. Shares of hours worked and investment in the tradable sector increase on impact, while the analogous shares in the nontradable sector decrease. Thus, in our model, the 2008 crisis acts as a rebalancing mechanism in all scenarios studied;

however, this is even more striking under the export-driven recovery, where the increase in exports underpins the asymmetric sectoral response.

In summary, our model-based simulations show that the path of exports plays a qualitatively and quantitatively important role in explaining the post-2008 dynamics of the main Irish macroeconomic variables.

Regarding competitiveness, under the export-driven scenario any increase in overall competitiveness arises due to the decline in real wages and prices in the nontradable sector of the economy due to the large negative effect of the crisis in this sector. This is also reinforced by the reallocation of demand and resources towards the tradable sector. The associated simulated paths of real wages in the tradable and nontradable sector as well as the relative price of tradables to nontradables (see the light grey dashed lines in the associated subplots in Figure 12.9) illustrate the underlying dynamics of the reallocation. The relative price of tradables to nontradables increases, indicating a fall in prices of the nontradable sector. Real wages in the nontradable sector experiences a sharp decrease at the outset of the shock in contrast to real wages in the tradable sector, which slightly decrease when the shock occurs. Real wages then remain constant in the short run and subsequently grow higher than their precrisis levels. The latter trend is also evident in the actual data.[23]

12.6 Conclusions

In a well-cited review of Irish economic performance, Honohan and Walsh (2002) argue that the surge in Irish economic activity witnessed from the early 1990s reflected the sizeable movement in the labour force away from traditional sectors of the economy, such as agriculture, towards the information technology and pharmaceutical sectors. The young Irish workforce being English-speaking with a relatively high educational attainment levels were ideally suited for the rapidly growing information technology using sectors from the early 1990s.

[23] For example, the average real wage growth per employee in the tradable sector over 2001–2007 was 2 per cent and remained positive to 2.1 per cent over 2008–2014. On the other hand, the average real wage growth per employee in the nontradable sector was 2.2 per cent and –1.1 per cent over 2001–2007 and 2008–2014 respectively.

However, the resulting export lead growth, which characterised the initial phase of the Celtic Tiger, gave way to a credit-fuelled bubble driven by activity in the nontraded sector. By 2007, the construction sector exerted a disproportionately large influence on domestic economic activity.

Using a DSGE framework, our simulations indicate that the international financial downturn of 2007–2008 prompted a significant rebalancing within the Irish economy; capital and labour resources, which had been attracted to the bubble-driven returns of the construction sector between 2001 and 2007, were subsequently redeployed towards the more productive export sector.

The relatively modest contributions of structural reforms to the recovery experienced in the Irish economy raise interesting policy issues. Institutions such as the IMF, the OECD and the European Commission place a significant emphasis on the capacity for structural reforms to improve the medium-term growth prospects of individual economies. While this is undoubtedly the case, policy makers must be wary of issuing a one-size–fits-all series of policy recommendations to countries experiencing significant difficulties; the reemergence of the Irish economy over the period 2008–2014 was for a particular set of circumstances not necessarily transferable to other countries such as Greece, Portugal or Spain. Countries like Spain experienced a similar boom in the residential sector preceding 2007; however, the much more open nature of the Irish economy meant it was significantly better placed to benefit from the subsequent rebalancing of resources from the nontraded to the traded sectors.

References

Andrés, J., Arce, Ó. and Thomas, C. (2017). 'Structural Reforms in a Debt Overhang', *Journal of Monetary Economics*, Vol. 88, 15–34.

Babecký, J. and Campos, N. (2011). 'Does Reform Work? An Econometric Survey of the Reform-Growth Puzzle', *Journal of Comparative Economics*, Vol. 39, 140–158.

Babecký, J., Du Caju, P., Kosma, T., Lawless, M., Messina, J. and Rõõm, T. (2010). 'Downward Nominal and Real Rigidity: Survey Evidence from European Firms', *Scandinavian Journal of Economics*, Vol. 112, No. 4, 884–910.

Barry, F. and Bergin, A. (2012). 'Inward Investment and Irish Exports over the Recession and Beyond', *World Economy*, Vol. 35, No. 10, 1292–1303.

(2019). "Export Structure, FDI and the Rapidity of Ireland's Recovery from Crisis", The Economic and Social Review, Vol. 50, No. 4, pp. 707–724.

Bergin, A., Conroy, N., Garcia-Rodriguez, H. D., Mc Inerney, N., Morgenroth, E. and Smith, D. (2017). 'COSMO: A New Core Structural Model for Ireland', ESRI Working Papers No. 553.

Bi, H. 2010. 'Optimal Debt Targeting Rules for Small Open Economies', mimeo.

Cacciatore, M., Duval, R. and Fiori, G. (2012). 'Short-Term Gain or Pain? A DSGE Model-Based Analysis of the Short-Term Effects of Structural Reforms in Labour and Product Markets', OECD Economics Department Working Papers, No. 948, OECD Publishing, Paris.

Cacciatore, M., Fiori, G. and Ghironi, F. (2016). 'Market Deregulation and Optimal Monetary Policy in a Monetary Union', *Journal of International Economics*, Vol. 99, 120–137.

Campos, N., De Grawe, P. and Ji, Y. (2018). 'Structural Reforms, Growth and Inequality: An Overview of Theory, Measurement and Evidence', in N. Campos, P. De Grawe and Y. Ji (ed.), *The Political Economy of Structural Reforms in Europe*. Oxford University Press, pp. 1–44.

CESifo (2014). 'Ireland's Recovery from Crisis', *CESifo Forum*, Vol. 15, No. 2, 3–31.

Chari, V. V., Kehoe, P. and McGrattan, E. (2007). 'Business Cycle Accounting', *Econometrica*, Vol. 75, 781–836.

Clancy, D. and Merola, R. (2014). 'EIRE Mod: A DSGE Model for Ireland', *Economic and Social Review, Economic and Social Studies*, Vol. 47, No. 1, 1–31.

(2017). 'Countercyclical Capital Rules for Small Open Economies', *Journal of Macroeconomics*, Vol. 54, 332–351.

De Grauwe, P. and Ji, Y. (2017). *Structural Reforms and Monetary Policies in a Behavioural Macroeconomic Model.* Centre for Economic Policy and Research.

Economides, G., Papageorgiou, D. and Philippopoulos, A. (2017). 'The Greek Great Depression: A General Equilibrium Study of Its Drivers', in I. Bournakis et al. (ed.), *Political Economy Perspectives on the Greek Crisis*. Palgrave Macmillan, pp. 205–220.

Eggertsson, G., Ferrero, A. and Raffo, A. (2014). 'Can Structural Reforms Help Europe?' *Journal of Monetary Economics*, Vol. 61, 2–22.

European Commission,(2012). 'Public Finances in EMU – 2012', Report No. 4/2012, European Economy Series.

European Economy (2011). 'The Economic Adjustment Programme for Ireland', European Economy Occasional Paper 76, February.

Fatas, A. (2016). 'The Agenda for Structural Reforms in Europe', in F. Caselli, M. Centeno, and J. Tavares (ed.), *After the Crisis: Reform, Recovery, and Growth in Europe*. Oxford Scholarship Online.

Fitzgerald, J. (2000). 'Ireland's Failure and Belated Convergence', ESRI Working Paper No. 133.

Forni, L., Gerali, A. and Pisani, M. (2010). 'Macroeconomic Effects of Greater Competition in the Service Sector: The Case of Italy,' *Macroeconomic Dynamics*, Vol. 14, 677–708.

Garcia-Cicco, J., Pancrazi, R. and Uribe, M. (2010). 'Real Business Cycles in Emerging Economies', *American Economic Review*, Vol. 100, No. 5, 2510–2531.

Gerali, A., Notrapietro, A. and Pisani, M. (2014). 'Macroeconomic Effects of Simultaneous Implementation of Reforms after the Crisis', Bank of Italy Working Paper No. 997.

Gomes, S., Jacquinot, P., Mohr, M. and Pisani M. (2013). 'Structural Reforms and Macroeconomic Performance in the Euro Area Countries: A Model-Based Assessment', *International Finance*, Vol. 16, 23–44.

Honohan, P. and Walsh, B. (2002). 'Catching Up with the Leaders: The Irish Hare', *Brookings Papers on Economic Activity, 2002*, Vol. 33, No. 1, 1–78.

Irish Government Economic and Evaluation Service, (2014). 'Quantification of the Economic Impacts of Selected Structural Reforms in Ireland', IGEES Working Paper.

Klein, P. and Ventura, G. (2018). 'Taxation, Expenditures and the Irish Miracle', 2018 Meeting Papers 282, Society for Economic Dynamics.

Koliousi, G., Miaouli, N. and Philippopoulos, A. (2017). 'Liberalization of Product and Labor Markets: Efficiency and Equity Implications', *Journal of Macroeconomics*, Vol. 53, 92–106.

Larch, M., Malzubris, J. and Santacrose, S. (2016). 'Fiscal Consolidation in Ireland: Recent Successes and Remaining Challenges', European Economy Economic Brief 011.

Lozej, M., Onorante L. and Rannenberg, A. (2017). 'Countercyclical Capital Regulation in a Small Open Economy DSGE Model', Research Technical Papers 03/RT/17, Central Bank of Ireland.

McCarthy, J. (2015). 'Fiscal Consolidation and Structural Reforms: The Irish Perspective', presentation to the German Finance Ministry conference, Berlin, March.

McCarthy, Y. and McQuinn, K. (2017). 'Credit Conditions in a Boom and Bust Property Market: Insights for Macro-Prudential Policy', *Quarterly Review of Economics and Finance*, Vol. 64, 171–182.

McQuinn, K. and Whelan, K. (2018). 'Europe's Long-Term Growth Prospects: With and without Structural Reforms', in N. Campos, P. De

Grawe, and Y. Ji (ed.), *The Political Economy of Structural Reforms in Europe*. Oxford University Press.

OECD (2009). *OECD Economic Surveys: Ireland 2009*. OECD Publishing.

(2011). *Trade Openness, in OECD Science, Technology and Industry Scoreboard 2011*. OECD Publishing.

Papageorgiou, D. and Vourvachaki, E. (2017). 'Macroeconomic Effects of Structural Reforms and Fiscal Consolidations: Trade-offs and Complementarities', *European Journal of Political Economy*, Vol. 48, 54–73.

Philippopoulos, A., Vassilatos, V. and Varthalitis, P. (2017). 'Fiscal Consolidation in an Open Economy with Sovereign Premia and without Monetary Policy Independence', *International Journal of Central Banking*, Vol. 13, No. 4, 260–306.

Sajedi, R. (2018). 'Short-Run Costs of Structural Reforms: What Role for Fiscal Policy?' in N. Campos, P. De Grawe, and Y. Ji (ed.), *The Political Economy of Structural Reforms in Europe*. Oxford University Press.

Schmitt-Grohe, S. and Uribe, M. (2003). 'Closing Small Open Economies', *Journal of International Economics*, Vol. 61, No. 1, 163–185.

(2007). 'Optimal Simple and Implementable Monetary and Fiscal Rules', *Journal of Monetary Economics*, Vol. 54, No. 6, 1702–1725.

(2017). *Open Economy Macroeconomics*. Princeton University Press.

Schoenmaker, D. (2015). 'Stabilising and Healing the Irish Banking System: Policy Lessons', presentation to the Central Bank of Ireland-CEPR-IMF Conference 'Ireland – Lessons from Its Recovery from the Bank-Sovereign Loop', Dublin, January.

Varthalitis, P. (2019). 'FIR-GEM: A SOE-DSGE Model for Fiscal Policy Analysis in Ireland', ESRI Working Paper No. 620.

Whelan, K. (2014). 'Ireland's Economic Crisis: The Good, the Bad and the Ugly', *Journal of Macroeconomics*, Vol. 39, 424–440.

13 *Goulash Labour Market Structural Reforms*

Hungary, 1986–2016

NAURO F. CAMPOS

13.1 Introduction

Labour market reforms are notoriously difficult to study, especially when compared to other reforms such as trade liberalization or product market deregulation.[1] Labour reforms have a broader range in that they directly affect the whole working population while, e.g., trade reforms directly affect mostly the tradables sector. This may explain why labour reforms are extensively debated, often hard-fought, approved in bundles and often contain agreed upon implementation lags. Their effects are wide, deep and take a long time to set in.

This chapter investigates structural labour market reforms in Hungary from 1986 to 2016. This is an important period because it encompasses the collapse of the Soviet Union, European Union (EU) accession in 2004 and the global financial crisis. By the same token, Hungary is a country attracting huge interest because of its role in the recent populist wave (Mudde, 2017).

Using the narrative approach by tracking changes in labour laws, our analysis identifies three main labour market reforms in Hungary: in 1992 and 2002 aimed at increasing, and in 2012 at decreasing, employment protection. We then study the effects of these reforms using a unique data set of Hungarian workers. We find that (1) the skill premium almost doubled from 6.4 per cent in 1986 to 12.3 per cent in 2016, but peaking in 2004; (2) the gender wage gap decreased to a third with the difference in

[1] I thank László Bruszt, Fabrizio Coricelli, Romain Duval, Michael Ganslmeier, Yuemei Ji, Jeffrey Nugent and István Székely for valuable comments on a previous version. Financial support from the Economic and Social Research Council (ESRC) grant no. ES/P000274/1 is gratefully acknowledged. This chapter would not have been possible without the support of Janos Köllo and the assistance of Balazs Munkacsy from the Institute of Economics of the Hungarian Academy of Sciences in Budapest. I am entirely responsible for all remaining errors.

log wages declining from 0.31 in 1986 to 0.13 in 2004, with no changes thereafter and (3) gender discrimination practically halved as the unexplained component from the Oaxaca decomposition of the difference in log wages decreased from 0.27 in 1989 to 0.15 after 2004.

The chapter is organized as follows. Section 13.2 provides background on Hungary and details on the implementation of labour market reforms. Section 13.3 introduces our data set and methodological and estimation features. Section 13.4 discusses our estimates of the changes in returns to education and gender between 1986 and 2016. Section 13.5 concludes.

13.2 Labour Market Reforms in Hungary

The objective of this section is twofold. One is to briefly describe the main macroeconomic developments in Hungary during the period 1986 to 2016, and the other is to identify and discuss the key relevant labour market structural reforms.

Hungary is one of the postcommunist countries with a long history of promarket reforms as well as of gradualism. The root of these early reforms may be found in the Hungarian Uprising of 1956, which to be quelled required a Soviet military intervention. For the thirty-two years from 1956 until his retirement in 1988, the country was led by János Kádár, who is credited with the implementation of 'goulash communism', so named because it was concerned more about household consumption than, say, investment in heavy industry (Benczes, 2016.) In 1968, Kádár implemented the New Economic Mechanism (NEM), an extensive reform program that liberalized international trade and allowed for much freer forms of enterprise (cooperatives) and the emergence of a large 'second economy' allowing peasants and workers to produce agricultural goods for the market. NEM worked well until the 1973 oil shock, when large parts of these reforms were halted. They were restarted only in the early 1980s despite concerns about rising external debt.

Economic liberalization preceded political change. In early 1989, the Hungarian government decided to turn off the power of the electrified wall borders with Austria and in late summer allowed Hungarian citizens to travel to Western Europe. In October 1989, Parliament passed legislation for multiparty parliamentary election. These took place in 1990, resulting in a centre-right coalition government under Prime Minister (PM) Antall. The 1994 election produced a centre-left coalition under PM Horn, who incidentally was the last communist foreign affairs ministry, responsible for cutting down the wall in the summer of 1989. It was followed by a centre-right coalition led by PM Viktor Orbán between 1998 and 2002, by a centre-left coalition from 2002 to 2006 (Medgyessy-Gyurcsány), by another centre-left coalition from 2006 to 2010 (Gyurcsány-Bajnai) and then finally by three centre-right coalition governments all led by PM Orbán in 2010–2014, 2014–2018 and 2018 to the present.

Hungary enjoyed an initial advantage in its transition from centrally planned to a market economy: even under planning, parts of the economy were liberalized. Small firms could be privately owned and operated (Kornai, 1986). Even considering the propitious initial conditions, the Hungarian private sector developed fast: in 1998, it accounted for 80 per cent of GDP. Compared to other Visegrad countries (i.e., Czech Republic, Poland and Slovakia), the performance of the Hungarian economy was slightly smoother. Halpern and Wyplosz (1998) note that the real shock came not with the fall of the Berlin Wall but later with the collapse of CMEA and the Soviet Union in 1991. Output fell less than in these other countries, although growth rates were also lower. The period 1990–1994 marks what has been called by Kornai (1994) the 'transformational recession', as output declined by around 20 per cent and industrial production by 35 per cent (Figure 13.1a). Moreover, the country faced large fiscal and current account imbalances (the current account deficit rose to 10 per cent GDP in 1993 and 1994).

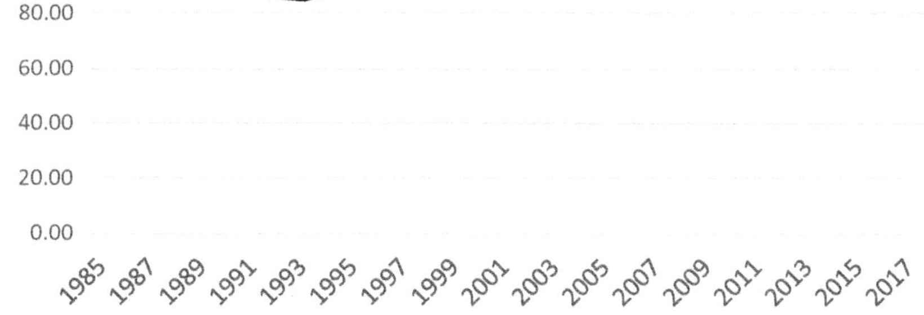

Figure 13.1a Hungary GDP, 1985–2017 (1990 = 100).

Source: Author's calculations using data from the Hungarian Central Statistical Office

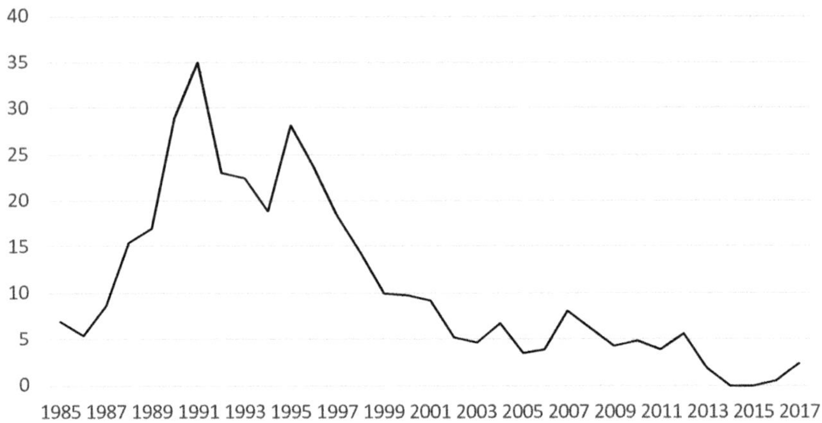

Figure 13.1b Inflation rate in Hungary, 1985–2017 (consumer price index, per cent).

Source: Author's calculations using data from the Hungarian Central Statistical Office

In 1995, the Bokros package, the biggest fiscal austerity programme in postcommunist Hungary, was launched. Inter alia, it comprised import surcharges, a 9 per cent devaluation of the Hungarian forint (plus the introduction of a crawling peg exchange rate regime), a rigid wage policy and reduction of government expenditures. This led to government deficit and unemployment declines and the acceleration of economic growth. Real wages fell by 26 per cent between 1988 and 1996, which was partly a consequence of rigid wage policies during the stabilization program and the persisting two-digit inflation. This was coupled with the intensification of a successful case-by-case privatization that shored up a large inflow of foreign direct investment (FDI) (Brown et al., 2016; Kaminski, 2000).

Thanks to various reforms under communism, the change in relative prices was not as dramatic as in other former centrally planned economies. Inflation reaches its highest value in 1991 (35 per cent) and then another peak of 28 per cent in 1995. In the following years, it continuously declined and has, since 1998, never again reached double-digits (Figure 13.1b).

Although Hungary was unique in starting the transition with a legal framework in place to cope with unemployment (Boeri and Pulay, 1998), it does not differ from others in that the disappearance of the strict central planning wage setting system was swift (Székely and

Figure 13.1c Unemployment rate in Hungary, 1992–2017.
Source: Author's calculations using data from the Hungarian Central Statistical Office

Ward-Warmedinger, 2018).[2] Figure 13.1c shows that unemployment was negligible in the pretransition years, but increased rapidly, reaching peak in 1993 (705,000 or 12.9 per cent registered, 11.9 per cent International Labour Organisation [ILO]/Labour Force Survey [LFS] unemployment rate).[3] The unemployment rate declined from 1994 until EU accession. Part of the explanation is that many workers left the labour force (e.g., early retirement) while training programs were introduced (Boeri and Terrell, 2002).[4] The unemployment rate of women was lower than that of men, but male unemployment decreased more rapidly than female unemployment, with the highest incidence of unemployment among younger workers. Unemployment rose again after EU accession in 2004 and particularly so with the

[2] The government's attempts at setting up collective bargaining had limited success: 'The new Hungarian system of wage setting is based on the principle of bargaining freedom, but actual wage evolution is far more dependent on employers' decisions and the immediate impact of market forces than on collective agreements with low coverage and poor contents' (Koltay, 2002, p. 61).

[3] See Commander et al. (1995) on the relationship between unemployment and restructuring in Hungary.

[4] O'Leary (1997) studies the impacts of active labor market policies in Hungary, in general, and specifically the impact of retraining and public service employment (PSE) on reemployment and earnings.

global financial crisis in 2008 (Valentinyi, 2012). After 2013, it declined to levels unseen since before the transition started.

Declining labour force participation is an important feature of the Hungarian labour market. The potential supply of labour has been declining in recent history. The number of people available for work has been influenced by many factors. Vodopivec et al. (2005) compute an index of the generosity of unemployment benefits for Central and Eastern European countries in the 1990s and find that these benefits are the most generous in Hungary and Slovenia, and the least generous in Estonia. The number of working pensioners has also declined. More than 600,000 people who are under the retirement age and another 320,000 persons of retirement age left the labour force in the first half of the 1990s. The age of retirement was fifty-five for women and sixty for men until a pension reform in 1997 introduced gradual increases in the retirement age for both men and women. After the changes, retirement age increased to sixty-two for both males and females. Note the decline in labour force participation slowed down by the end of the 1990s.

Kattuman and Redmond (2001) provide an analysis of the early rise of income inequality in Hungary. They find that in Hungarian fashion, inequality rose only moderately (irrespectively of the measure of inequality) but followed a more erratic behaviour: increase in 1987–1989, decrease between 1989 and 1991 and rise again afterwards (when mean income decreased, but so did dispersion). Most of the changes in the distribution of income occurred at the low and high tails.[5] Income taxes helped to reduce inequality in the early transition years, but their impact was eroded as income from sources other than employment became more important, e.g., transfers and benefits became important sources of income for most Hungarian households in those years.

Structural reforms in the transition were seldom implemented alone (Campos and Horvath, 2012). It is important to keep in mind the distinction between structural reforms that affect the labour market (like privatization and trade liberalization) from those designed to

[5] Jarvis and Pudney (1995) study redistributive policies in the early Hungarian transition. They argue that although a progressive income tax (PIT) and a value-added tax (VAT) were introduced in 1988, their redistributive impact has been reduced by the successive reforms to a point that inequality increased between 1988 and 1992 (to a level comparable to the United Kingdom's).

change it directly. Even so, it remains quite difficult to pinpoint major reforms specially when one is interested in distinguishing between de jure and de facto reforms.

Here we focus on de jure reforms and do so with the narrative approach that has been used previously in this literature.[6] We apply it to the most comprehensive compendium of labour laws we are aware of, namely the ILO NATLEX depository.[7] The way we use the narrative approach in this chapter is to collect and read all labour laws that were enacted by Hungarian governments from 1989 to 2017, and following Campos and Nugent (2018), focus on working time, employment contracts, hiring and firing legislation. We then establish whether the intended effect of each law is either to increase or to decrease employment protection. Finally, we try to identify periods in which there is more legislative activity in this area, and we also try to identify the overall direction or intended effects of these efforts. We also provide various illustrative examples.

Using the narrative approach, we identify three main clusters of labour market reforms in Hungary: in 1992 and 2002 aiming at increasing, and in 2012 at decreasing, employment protection. The first and third of these reforms were enacted by centre-right governments, while the 2002 reform was enacted by a centre-left government. In 1992, a new Labour Code was adopted, and it was in force until 2012 when a new Labour Code came in the immediate aftermath of the 2011 Constitution. Although the period of the 2002 reform may be remembered by the doubling of the minimum wage between 2001 and 2002, there were various other important changes.

It may be surprising that only the third and last major reform we identify aims at lowering the extent of employment protection in Hungary. One would expect that the transition from communism to a market economy entails a decrease in employment protection. Some would argue that a similar expectation should apply to such a

[6] Ciminelli et al. (2018) and Duval et al. (2018) offer measures of reform using the narrative approach, but unfortunately they do not include Hungary. Campos and Nugent (2018) also use the narrative approach to labour market reforms and do include Hungary, but the frequency of their indexes is not annual, but five-year averages instead.

[7] Cf. www.ilo.org/dyn/natlex/natlex4.countrySubjects?p_lang=en&p_country=HUN.

structural reform, that is, that it would mostly involve liberalizing the labour market. But this is not what we see in Hungary until 2012. One example that illustrates this unexpected finding is that the 1992 Labour Code increased the annual leave entitlement, from twelve to twenty working days.

The 1992 reform is perhaps the most significant of the three in terms of magnitude. It was mostly driven by changes in working time, in hiring and in firing legislation. Major changes occurred regarding the regulation of working time: there was an increase in annual leave entitlements; in public holidays entitlements; in overtime work premia; in weekend working premia, regarding stricter limits on overtime working; and a reduction of normal working hours (from forty-eight to forty per week). As for hiring and firing, the 1992 reforms included an increase in the legally mandated notice period (from fifteen to thirty days), redundancy compensation and the imposition of various procedural constraints on dismissals. In terms of forms of employment, the main change was that a five-year maximum limit was set for fixed-term contracts, while no such limits existed before 1992.

The 2002 reform is mostly driven by the changes in employment contracts. Chiefly among them are the laws that gave part-time workers and fixed-term workers the right to equal treatment with full-time workers. Because alternative labour contracts were not common in the early years of the transition from communism, most of the changes from the 1992 reform applied to full-time workers. The 2002 reform broadly extend these rights.

Although it is interesting that the Organization for Economic Cooperation and Development (OECD) employment protection legislation indicator corroborates the 2002 but not the 1992 reform we identify in this chapter, our choice of 2002 needs some more explanation. In 2002, a narrow election victory led to a centre-left government coalition that proposed these important laws when coming into office, but they were only approved in 2003 due to the government's tight parliamentary majority. This 2002 reform is also noteworthy because it contrasts with the 'goulash populist' approach (Benczes, 2016) of the previous centre-right government coalition led by MP Orbán from 1998 to 2002, which doubled the minimum wage after shortening the maximum duration of unemployment benefits and making eligibility more restrictive (e.g., requiring participation in public works.)

It is also important to note that between the 1992 and the 2002 reform there were reforms, but they were mostly related to nondiscrimination. In 1997, Decree 38 amended the rules (in place since 1968) regarding nondiscrimination in employment regarding gender, age, nationality, race, religion, etc. The other important change happens in 2001, when Act 60 transposes the Protocol to the UN Convention on the Elimination of All Forms of Discrimination against Women into Hungarian law. Notice that there are, in NATLEX, only six laws under equality of opportunity and nondiscrimination, but they are dated before 2001, and all except the two aforementioned ones are related to ethnic minorities.

The 2012 reform is encapsulated by the New Labour Code that followed from the new 2011 Constitution. Different from the previous two reforms, the 2012 aims at reducing the level of employment protection, and the main components of this reform were firing legislation and working time regulations. The 2012 Labour Code halves the premium for weekend working and increases by a quarter the legal limit for overtime work (in hours). As for dismissals, the major change is that it eliminates the disciplinary procedures requirements established in 1992 and that employees' right to contest dismissal were curtailed.

Adams et al. (2016) offer a quantification of the ILO data for 117 countries from 1970 until 2013. Higher values of their index reflect more labour regulation. They cover five main areas (full- or part-time contracts, hiring, firing, representation/unions and strike legislation) with a total of forty quantitative components. Originally these are all on a 0 to 1 scale, so we simply average them and think of reforms as changes over time in this index. The index for Hungary broadly confirms the three main reforms we identified using the narrative approach here. It suggests that the reforms we identify for 1992 and 2002 were aimed at increasing regulation, while the one for 2012 aimed at decreasing regulation, and that the first reform is 'bigger' than the other two, which are of comparable 'size', although of opposite 'directions'. Yet an important advantage of this measure is that it allows for cross-country comparisons. Figure 13.2 shows it for Hungary and for relevant comparator groups of EU (excluding Hungary), Visegrad, Northern, Southern and Western EU averages for all the years for which the index is available.[8]

[8] We define Northern EU as Sweden, Finland, Latvia, Lithuania, Estonia and Denmark; Western EU as Belgium, France, Ireland, Luxembourg, the Netherlands

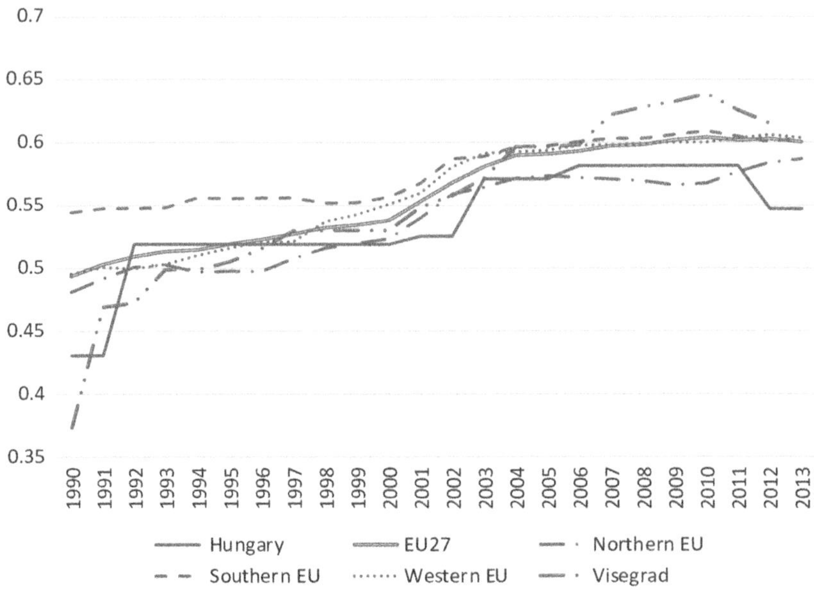

Figure 13.2 Labour Regulation Index: Hungary and comparators, 1990–2013.
Source: Author's calculations using data from Adams et al. (2016)

In comparative perspective, the level of employment protection in Hungary seems to have been consistently low. Except for the years between 1992 and 1995, the values of their index for Hungary have been substantially below the EU average confirming that indeed the Hungarian labour market seems to be less regulated or more flexible when compared to the EU average. The index shows that for most of the period between 1990 and 2013, the Southern EU group had the highest levels of employment protection. After the global financial crisis, there seems to have been some convergence between Southern and Western EU countries, although the Northern EU countries still show a lower level of employment regulation and the average value of their index for Hungary resembles this latter group more than any of the others.

and the United Kingdom; Southern EU as Italy, Spain, Greece, Malta, Cyprus and Portugal; and Visegrad as Czech Republic, Slovenia, Slovakia and Poland.

13.3 Data and Methodology

The data used in this chapter are from the Wage and Earnings Survey of the National Labour Centre in Hungary. Its repeated cross-sections are narrow and long: they cover a handful of variables for a very large number of wage earners. They contain information on wages, location, education, age, gender and other demographic details. They are unique, representative and carefully recoded data that start in 1986 and in three-year intervals end in 2016. The frequency of the data collection became annual in the late 1990s, but for convenience we use it for estimation at three-year intervals. The years we use in the estimations are 1986, 1989, 1992, 1995, 1998, 2001, 2004, 2007, 2010, 2013 and 2016. They cover the late-communist and early-transition periods, the years before and after the accession to the European Union (in 2004) as well as the period before and after the global financial crisis. With assistance from the National Labour Centre and the Hungarian Central Statistical Office, we ensured that variables were coded consistently over time, which involved substantial recoding of the pre-1992 data (Campos and Zlabkova, 2001).

Wage equations are estimated using the standard Mincer specification:

$$\ln(w_i) = \beta_1 S_i + \beta_2 E_i + \beta_3 E_i^2 + \beta_4 G_i + \beta_5 X_i + \varepsilon_i \qquad (13.1)$$

where i denotes the individual, w is wages, S is years of schooling (or type of education), E is potential labour market experience, G is gender and X contains a set of variables to control for industry, institutional and spatial differences.

The wages refer to their monthly value (in forint). They are the sum of the official base wage plus other payments such as overtime work, shift work, rewards and other special payments.

We use two measures of schooling. The first is a vector of six dummy variables that denote the highest type of schooling completed. The school types include primary, three types of secondary (vocational, technical and general), college and university. The second measure of schooling is an estimate of years of school attainment. This is created by converting the data on highest school type completed into years of schooling. Its average value increased from 9.6 years of schooling in 1986, to 11.9 years in 2004, to 12.0 years in 2010 to finally 12.2 years in 2016.

Potential labour market experience is constructed by subtracting the number of years of schooling from the age of the wage earner. Average age in the sample was 38.2 years in 1986. The average age has risen in every single year. It reached 41.5 in 2004 and 43.0 in 2016. Potential experience shows a similar trajectory except for the initial years. The average (weighted) potential labour market experience was 22.5 years in 1986, but it declines slightly to 22.3 in 1989, which is the year of the fall of the Berlin Wall, and then it declines again to 21.6 in 1992, from which point it starts to increase. It reaches 23.6 years of potential experience for the average wage earner in 2004 and finally 24.8 in 2016.

The variable for gender is to control for differences across the sexes. Note the share of females increases throughout the period of analysis. In the 1986 sample, 43.1 per cent of the wage earners were women. This (weighted) share increases to 47.8 in 1992, and then to 50.6 per cent in the year Hungary joined the European Union (2004). It has since declined to 48.9 in 2016.

The set of control variables designated by *X* includes variables to account for important spatial and sectoral differences. It has a set of industry dummies as well as a dummy variable for large firms (those with more than 300 employees). The sectoral classification has changed in 2001, but this has little impact in our estimates because we use repeated cross sections.[9]

Our estimations also include a dummy variable for each of the administrative counties of Hungary and for the capital, Budapest. These spatial variables control for any county-specific variation, for example regarding wages and prices. The county dummy variables will also control for region-specific differences in labour markets, which are potentially important since unemployment rates tend to be lower in Budapest. These spatial (county) dummy variables also control for the

[9] Before 2001, it covered the following sectors: agriculture; industry; construction; transport and communications; trade; services; health and social services; and public services. After 2001, the sectoral classification became as follows: agriculture, forestry and fishing; mining and quarrying; manufacturing; electricity, gas, water supply and waste management; construction; wholesale and retail trade; accommodation and food service activities; transport, storage and communications; financial and insurance activities; real estate, renting and professional, scientific, technical and administrative activities; education; human health and social work activities; and art, entertainment, recreation and other community, social and personal services.

potential measurement problem that a year of schooling may result in different levels of human capital accumulation over different regions if there are differences in schooling quality across regions.

The county, firm size and industry fixed effects substantially reduce the potential for omitted-variable bias. Having data that were collected using the same survey instrument shores up the credibility of measured changes. These are important advantages to using the Wage and Earnings Survey data.

The main disadvantage of using this data source is that the choice of variables is small. Consequently, the ability to address violations of ordinary least squares (OLS) assumptions is limited. If education is correlated with the residual, which can occur for instance if people select into (or out of) the sample based on some characteristic correlated with education, then the OLS estimator is biased. This source of bias is typically corrected by modelling the selection decision, which requires data on the individuals who have opted out of the wage market. Yet we cannot use this approach because the survey provides information only on wage earners.

In addition to examining the effects of labour market reforms on rates of return to education and experience, we also study gender differences. The canonical approach to deal with this issue is by Oaxaca (1973). Using the separate regression estimates for male and female wage functions, it decomposes the observed gender wage gap into two components, namely that from differences in education and experience levels (and any other explanatory variable) of men and women and that which cannot be explained from the model. The latter is often interpreted as resulting from labour market 'discrimination'.

The Oaxaca decompositions assume the OLS regression line runs through the mean and the difference in the mean of log wages between men and women can be written as

$$\overline{\ln(w_m)} - \overline{\ln(w_f)} = (\bar{X}_m - \bar{X}_f)\beta^* + [(\hat{\beta}_m - \beta^*)\bar{X}_m + \left(\beta^* - \hat{\beta}_f\right)\bar{X}_f] \tag{13.2}$$

where β^* is the hypothetical wage structure that would exist in the absence of discrimination. The first term on the right-hand side of Equation (13.2) represents the portion of the wage difference that is explained by differences in endowments across men and women. The second term on the right-hand side represents the portion of the wage difference that is due to the different wage structures for men and women. This is the part of the wage differential that cannot be explained by the model and is potentially due to discrimination.

Notice that if there is any omitted variable that, say, has a positive effect on wages, and if men are more highly endowed with this characteristic, then the results from the decomposition would overestimate discrimination. Alternatively, if some of the factors that are in the model are themselves affected by discrimination, then the analysis could well underestimate discrimination. For example, if women are more likely to be fired in economic downturns, or if they have less access to the types of schooling deemed more valuable by the market, then the decomposition may underestimate discrimination.

13.4 Structural Reforms and the Labour Market

The objective of this section is to investigate the development of the labour market in Hungary using a unique data set covering the period from 1986 to 2016. As noted, three major structural labour market reforms were implemented in Hungary around the years 1992, 2002 and 2012. The first two intended to increase, and the last one to decrease, employment protection. In this section, we would like to see whether these three key changes have discernible and identifiable effects in terms of returns to education, experience, industry and gender.

Table 13.1 provides fixed-effects estimates of Equation (13.1) for all firms with more than fifty employees from 1986 to 2016. The results show that the returns to a year of schooling almost doubled from 1986 (6.4 per cent) to 2016 (12.3 per cent). Notice that the rate of return to education peaks at almost 14 per cent in the year 2004, which is of course the year in which Hungary officially joined the European Union. The estimate hovers around 13 per cent until 2013 and decreases to about 12 per cent in 2016. This very fast rise in returns to education until 2004 reinforces the notion that central planners undervalued education and that the market can correct this undervaluation. The acceleration until 2004 and its subsequent levelling off afterwards illustrates the power of the prospect of EU membership as an external anchor.

While most Eastern European countries have education levels similar to Western European countries, average wages continue to be

Table 13.1 *Returns to years of schooling, 1986–2016: fixed-effects estimation of Equation (13.1).*

	1986	1989	1992	1995	1998	2001	2004	2007	2010	2013	2016
Potential years of schooling	0.064	0.078	0.096	0.112	0.117	0.132	0.138	0.130	0.134	0.135	0.123
	(0.0004)	(0.0004)	(0.0007)	(0.0007)	(0.0007)	(0.0010)	(0.0009)	(0.0009)	(0.0009)	(0.0008)	(0.0007)
Sex (male)	0.281	0.279	0.154	0.141	0.136	0.179	0.199	0.200	0.207	0.182	0.191
	(0.0022)	(0.0022)	(0.0042)	(0.0036)	(0.0038)	(0.0037)	(0.0037)	(0.0037)	(0.0037)	(0.0033)	(0.0032)
Potential experience	0.028	0.026	0.029	0.025	0.025	0.018	0.020	0.020	0.024	0.025	0.024
	(0.0003)	(0.0003)	(0.0007)	(0.0006)	(0.0007)	(0.0007)	(0.0007)	(0.0007)	(0.0007)	(0.0006)	(0.0005)
Potential experience squared	–0.040	–0.037	–0.036	–0.028	–0.030	–0.026	–0.033	–0.036	–0.042	–0.042	–0.043
	(0.0007)	(0.0007)	(0.0015)	(0.0013)	(0.0015)	(0.0016)	(0.0014)	(0.0014)	(0.0014)	(0.0012)	(0.0011)
Firm size: $\geq$ 300 employees	0.007	0.001	–0.014	–0.138	–0.162	0.159	0.136	0.138	0.140	0.120	0.129
	(0.0055)	(0.0019)	(0.0054)	(0.0034)	(0.0034)	(0.0043)	(0.0041)	(0.0040)	(0.0041)	(0.0036)	(0.0035)
Number of observations	145,886	383,720	48,261	371,882	334,207	74,763	78,902	82,266	77,089	84,451	91,953
R-squared	0.449	0.408	0.427	0.402	0.402	0.429	0.455	0.449	0.469	0.489	0.479

Notes: The dependent variable is the log of monthly wages using Wage and Earnings Survey (WES) of the National Labor Centre in Hungary. The sample consists of all firms with fifty or more employees. Numbers in parentheses are standard errors robust to heteroscedasticity of unknown form. The county, firm size and industry dummies are jointly significant. They are suppressed from the table for the sake of brevity. Industry classification differs after 2011. All listed point estimates are significant at $p < 0.001$.

lower. Estimated returns to schooling are measured as percentage changes in wages. If markets are fully liberalized, rates of return will be higher than in Western Europe until there is convergence in wage levels.

Table 13.1 also provides evidence of decreasing returns to experience, which peak in 1992 and decline until about 2002. This result appears to support the notion that labour market experience acquired under communism loses value after the introduction of major economic reforms although these results do not clarify whether trade liberalization or privatization instead play major roles at this point in time (Campos and Jolliffe, 2007).

Table 13.1 also shows results in terms of gender and firm size. As for gender, it suggests that the uncorrected or raw wage difference in favour of males was larger during communism than after its collapse. Wages in larger firms seem to have been substantially lower in the years before 2000, perhaps reflecting privatization and the rapid decline of the state sector.

While returns to a year of schooling generally rose over 1986–2016, the wage premium to primary, and to a lesser extent vocational and technical schooling, actually declined (Table 13.2). Wage earners who completed secondary general education but especially college or university, experienced the largest percentage changes in the wage premium. This finding supports the view that more generalist education may enhance an individual's ability to adapt to a rapidly changing environment.

The returns to college and university education shown in Figure 13.3 reveal various inflection points, two of which interestingly overlap with the first two major reforms we identified. The 1992 reform coincides with an inflection point in the growth of the returns to college and university education, while these returns seems to peak at the time of the 2002 reform. As stressed in the discussion in Section 13.2, there other various factors at play here that make it rather difficult to link these developments to the two individual reforms.

It is important also to look at whether different sectors behave differently in this context. As noted previously, the industrial classification in the data set has changed in 2001, so these changes have to be examined with caution especially because it seems that the patterns are quite different before and after 2001. It is thus quite difficult to tell whether this is driven by changes in the coding of industries or by the

Table 13.2 *Wage premiums by school type, 1986–2016 fixed-effects estimation of Equation (13.1).*

	1986	1989	1992	1995	1998	2001	2004	2007	2010	2013	2016
Primary	0.085 (0.0049)	–0.040 (0.0059)	0.089 (0.0104)	0.074 (0.0130)	0.084 (0.0203)	0.221 (0.0240)	0.163 (0.0180)	0.124 (0.0228)	0.078 (0.0239)	0.130 (0.0341)	0.074 (0.0466)
Vocational (sec. school)	0.209 (0.0053)	0.083 (0.0064)	0.272 (0.0146)	0.224 (0.0132)	0.212 (0.0206)	0.356 (0.0240)	0.318 (0.0180)	0.284 (0.0228)	0.235 (0.0238)	0.311 (0.0340)	0.223 (0.0466)
Technical (sec. school)	0.380 (0.0054)	0.372 (0.0063)	0.255 (0.0111)	0.545 (0.0137)	0.552 (0.0208)	0.601 (0.0243)	0.566 (0.0183)	0.528 (0.0231)	0.467 (0.0240)	0.513 (0.0341)	0.387 (0.0466)
General (sec. school)	0.304 (0.0059)	0.242 (0.0065)	0.516 (0.0108)	0.490 (0.0140)	0.510 (0.0210)	0.634 (0.0243)	0.599 (0.0184)	0.590 (0.0232)	0.523 (0.0241)	0.542 (0.0342)	0.449 (0.0467)
College	0.554 (0.0068)	0.530 (0.0064)	0.825 (0.0111)	0.855 (0.0139)	0.870 (0.0208)	1.206 (0.0257)	1.169 (0.0197)	1.073 (0.0239)	1.044 (0.0246)	1.069 (0.0343)	0.922 (0.0468)
University	0.719 (0.0058)	0.749 (0.0067)	1.034 (0.0126)	1.078 (0.0151)	1.151 (0.0219)	1.488 (0.0263)	1.434 (0.0203)	1.260 (0.0243)	1.238 (0.0249)	1.261 (0.0345)	1.111 (0.0469)

Notes: The dependent variable is the log of monthly wages using WES of the National Labor Centre in Hungary. The sample consists of all firms with fifty or more employees. Numbers in parentheses are standard errors robust to heteroscedasticity of unknown form. The county, firm size and industry dummies are jointly significant. The other variables from Equation (13.1) are suppressed for the sake of brevity. Industry classification differs after 2011. All listed point estimates are significant at $p < 0.001$.

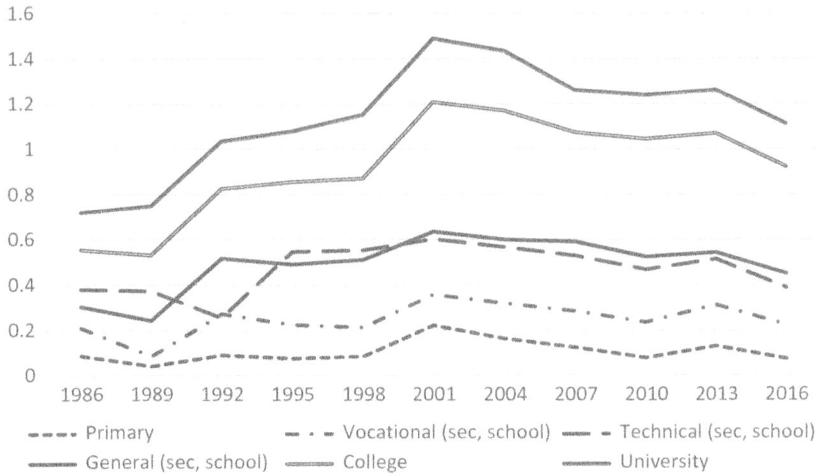

Figure 13.3 Returns to education in Hungary (1986–2016) by type of education.
Source: Author's estimates from Table 13.2

labour market structural reforms implemented in 2002. Figure 13.4 plots our estimates of the returns to one year of education in eight different industrial sectors between 1986 and 2016 using the 'old' classification. Until 2001, the largest returns to schooling are found in the services, trade and transportation industries. This is consistent with the notion that the planned economy undervalued skilled labour used in the production of nonphysical goods and services. After 2001, there seems to be a convergence of returns across industrial sectors with the exception of public services, which exhibits substantially lower returns to schooling than any of the other seven sectors after 2001.

Now we turn to a discussion of the gender aspects. We first discuss our results from estimating male and female wage regressions, and then we study the Oaxaca decomposition results. There is a huge amount of recent research on the gender wage gap (Altonji and Blank, 1999; Blau and Lawrence, 2017) with the objective of trying to understand its underlying causes but at the same time with a shift in emphasis away from the study of large cross-sections towards an emphasis on how the gap changes over time. Here we investigate male–female differences in the labour market in Hungary from 1986 to 2016.

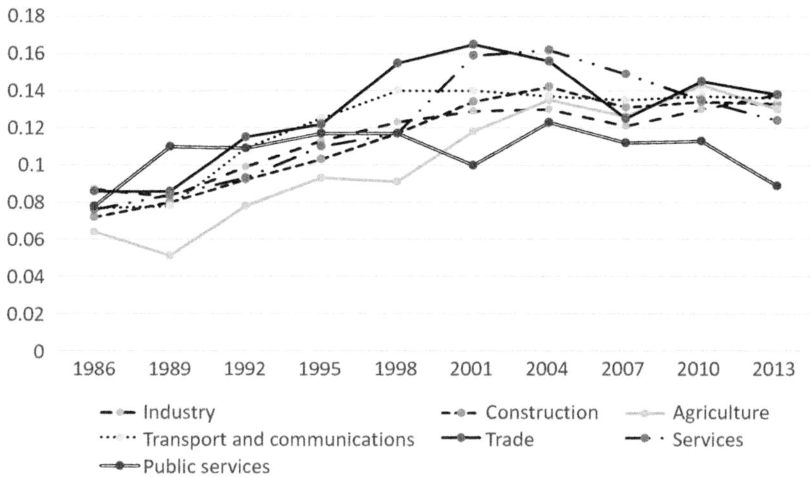

Figure 13.4 Returns to education in Hungary (1986–2013) by industrial sector.

Source: Author's calculations using Equation (13.1) and pre-2001 industry classification

Panel A of Table 13.3 presents the industry and country fixed-effects estimates of Equation (13.2) for males, and Panel B lists these estimates for female wage earners. While the estimates for the male and female wage equations differ, there seem to be no clear patterns in their difference over time and few stark differences in a given year.

Table 13.4 provides an Oaxaca decomposition of the log wage gap for the years from 1986 to 2016 using the pooled-sample, OLS estimate as the nondiscriminatory wage structure. As before, these estimates control for firm size, industry and county, thus minimizing as much as possible concerns about omitted variables biases. The first column shows that the male–female difference in log wages has declined substantially from 0.31 in 1986 to 0.11 in 2016, and the second column provides standard errors that indicate that the difference is highly significant.

The column labelled 'Part of the Gap Explained by the Model, Total', provides an estimate of the first term on the right-hand side of Equation (13.2). The estimates from Table 13.4 indicate that in 1986, the male–female log wage difference would have been only 0.03 if males and females were paid according to the same wage structure. In other words, about 10 per cent of the actual log wage difference of 0.31 can be explained by the econometric model. This estimate

Table 13.3 *Returns to school by sex, 1986–2016, fixed-effects estimates of wage Equation (13.1).*

	1986	1989	1992	1995	1998	2001	2004	2007	2010	2013	2016
					Panel A: Males						
Primary	0.105	0.024	0.115	0.106	0.170	0.217	0.165	0.089	0.070	0.117	0.094
	(0.0023)	(0.0037)	(0.0091)	(0.0126)	(0.0192)	(0.0280)	(0.0214)	(0.0271)	(0.0305)	(0.0367)	(0.0294)
Vocational (sec. school)	0.191	0.097	0.235	0.219	0.309	0.354	0.314	0.252	0.227	0.301	0.258
	(0.0023)	(0.0038)	(0.0114)	(0.0126)	(0.0191)	(0.0279)	(0.0212)	(0.0270)	(0.0304)	(0.0365)	(0.0293)
Technical (sec. school)	0.315	0.429	0.260	0.481	0.589	0.561	0.509	0.441	0.400	0.442	0.388
	(0.0026)	(0.0048)	(0.0092)	(0.0131)	(0.0194)	(0.0283)	(0.0216)	(0.0273)	(0.0306)	(0.0367)	(0.0294)
General (sec. school)	0.238	0.205	0.472	0.438	0.529	0.635	0.562	0.522	0.499	0.492	0.470
	(0.0034)	(0.0046)	(0.0095)	(0.0143)	(0.0203)	(0.0284)	(0.0218)	(0.0275)	(0.0308)	(0.0368)	(0.0296)
College	0.517	0.425	0.821	0.848	1.038	1.115	1.066	0.932	0.946	0.971	0.901
	(0.0034)	(0.0051)	(0.0109)	(0.0142)	(0.0202)	(0.0296)	(0.0229)	(0.0280)	(0.0311)	(0.0370)	(0.0299)
University	0.691	0.735	1.019	1.067	1.291	1.410	1.326	1.113	1.088	1.155	1.099
	(0.0034)	(0.0055)	(0.0111)	(0.0143)	(0.0204)	(0.0301)	(0.0234)	(0.0284)	(0.0316)	(0.0374)	(0.0301)
Potential experience	0.034	0.021	0.031	0.029	0.027	0.019	0.022	0.022	0.027	0.023	0.022
	(0.0002)	(0.0003)	(0.0006)	(0.0006)	(0.0007)	(0.0007)	(0.0006)	(0.0006)	(0.0006)	(0.0006)	(0.0005)
Potential experience squared	–0.001	–0.000	–0.000	–0.000	–0.000	–0.000	–0.000	–0.000	–0.000	–0.000	–0.000
	(0.0000)	(0.0000)	(0.0000)	(0.0000)	(0.0000)	(0.0000)	(0.0000)	(0.0000)	(0.0000)	(0.0000)	(0.0000)
Number of observations	429,535	387,278	67,440	161,106	148,966	76,033	95,848	91,433	84,924	86,431	92,485
R-squared	0.307	0.229	0.419	0.418	0.440	0.441	0.460	0.443	0.467	0.484	0.483
	1986	1989	1992	1995	1998	2001	2004	2007	2010	2013	2016

				Panel B: Females							
Primary	0.081	–0.028	0.124	0.054	0.187	0.161	0.087	0.111	0.063	0.158	0.078
	(0.0024)	(0.0040)	(0.0080)	(0.0129)	(0.0171)	(0.0298)	(0.0180)	(0.0196)	(0.0263)	(0.0349)	(0.0431)
Vocational (sec. school)	0.208	0.048	0.340	0.206	0.323	0.258	0.186	0.230	0.179	0.278	0.176
	(0.0029)	(0.0045)	(0.0111)	(0.0133)	(0.0175)	(0.0300)	(0.0181)	(0.0197)	(0.0263)	(0.0349)	(0.0431)
Technical (sec. school)	0.359	0.274	0.288	0.507	0.662	0.522	0.459	0.476	0.439	0.491	0.358
	(0.0028)	(0.0045)	(0.0091)	(0.0133)	(0.0174)	(0.0301)	(0.0184)	(0.0199)	(0.0264)	(0.0350)	(0.0431)
General (sec. school)	0.291	0.188	0.516	0.460	0.630	0.541	0.465	0.514	0.466	0.521	0.394
	(0.0029)	(0.0046)	(0.0083)	(0.0133)	(0.0175)	(0.0302)	(0.0185)	(0.0201)	(0.0266)	(0.0351)	(0.0432)
College	0.585	0.388	0.827	0.834	0.977	1.073	0.982	0.970	0.927	0.957	0.818
	(0.0043)	(0.0050)	(0.0091)	(0.0136)	(0.0177)	(0.0326)	(0.0203)	(0.0214)	(0.0274)	(0.0354)	(0.0436)
University	0.788	0.713	1.053	1.095	1.276	1.323	1.224	1.167	1.158	1.174	1.027
	(0.0037)	(0.0057)	(0.0106)	(0.0143)	(0.0185)	(0.0340)	(0.0217)	(0.0227)	(0.0285)	(0.0361)	(0.0439)
Potential experience	0.025	0.021	0.027	0.026	0.024	0.018	0.018	0.016	0.020	0.020	0.019
	(0.0002)	(0.0003)	(0.0005)	(0.0005)	(0.0006)	(0.0008)	(0.0006)	(0.0006)	(0.0007)	(0.0006)	(0.0006)
Potential experience squared	–0.000	–0.000	–0.000	–0.000	–0.000	–0.000	–0.000	–0.000	–0.000	–0.000	–0.000
	(0.0000)	(0.0000)	(0.0000)	(0.0000)	(0.0000)	(0.0000)	(0.0000)	(0.0000)	(0.0000)	(0.0000)	(0.0000)
Number of observations	376,652	546,004	69,389	368,822	338,194	50,874	68,715	65,823	61,025	61,135	64,906
R-squared	0.346	0.284	0.453	0.443	0.441	0.439	0.468	0.482	0.487	0.482	0.488

Notes: The dependent variable is the log of monthly wages using WES of the National Labor Centre in Hungary. The sample consists of all firms with fifty or more employees. Numbers in parentheses are standard errors robust to heteroscedasticity of unknown form. The county, firm size and industry dummies are jointly significant. They are suppressed for the sake of brevity. Industry classification differs after 2011. All listed point estimates are significant at $p < 0.001$.

Table 13.4 *Oaxaca decomposition of gender wage gap, 1986–2016 based on estimation of Equation (13.2).*

	Log wage gap	Standard error wage gap	Part of gap explained by the model			Unexplained 'discrimination'	Standard error
			Total	Education	Experience		
1986	0.31	(0.001)	0.03	–0.001	0.000	0.27	(0.001)
1989	0.29	(0.001)	–0.01	0.000	0.001	0.27	(0.001)
1992	0.19	(0.003)	0.02	–0.001	–0.001	0.16	(0.002)
1995	0.18	(0.003)	0.01	0.001	–0.001	0.14	(0.002)
1998	0.17	(0.003)	0.01	–0.003	–0.001	0.12	(0.002)
2001	0.15	(0.004)	0.00	0.004	0.000	0.15	(0.003)
2004	0.13	(0.004)	–0.02	0.001	0.000	0.15	(0.003)
2007	0.13	(0.003)	–0.03	0.000	0.000	0.16	(0.003)
2010	0.11	(0.003)	–0.04	0.000	0.000	0.16	(0.003)
2013	0.10	(0.003)	–0.03	0.000	0.000	0.14	(0.003)
2016	0.11	(0.003)	–0.03	–0.001	0.000	0.15	(0.003)

Notes: Dependent variable is the log of monthly wages using WES of the National Labor Centre in Hungary. The sample consists of all firms with fifty or more employees.

fluctuates over the thirty-year period but show that by 2016 the male–female log wage difference would have been –0.03 if males and females were paid on the same wage structure. The estimates in the columns labelled 'Education' and 'Experience' measure what portion of the log wage gap is explained by the male–female differences in these human capital characteristics. They show that for both 1998 and 2016, if men and women were paid according to the same wage structure, the market would value more highly experience and education held by women.

The penultimate column in Table 13.4 lists how much of the difference in male–female log wages cannot be explained by the econometric model. The estimate of the male–female difference in log wages that cannot be explained by the model is typically described as resulting from discrimination. It is the difference between the actual log wage gap and that part of the gap that is explained by the model. In 1986, the unexplained component of the log wage differential was 0.27, or 68 per cent of the difference. By 2004, the unexplained component dropped by almost half to 0.13 but captured the bulk of the wage difference. Another way to consider this is to note that from 1986 to 2004 the male–female difference in log wages declined by an amount of 0.18, and this decline is almost fully matched by the drop in that part of the unexplained portion of the log wage differential. What we call the 2002 reform overlaps with EU accession in 2004. Both the wage gap and discrimination decrease rapidly until 2004. The levelling off after 2004 illustrates the power of the prospect of EU membership as an external anchor. Reforms have not only allowed markets to function more freely but have also encapsulated the role of the EU as an external anchor. The prospect of joining the EU may have motivated the government to ensure (through the passing of antidiscrimination legislation) that remuneration practices of the public sector were as nondiscriminatory as possible. However, after 2004 other forces come into play. One can hypothesize that the EU anchor is the main driver responsible for decreasing the gap until 2004, and from that point in time onwards, Beckerian competition driven by greater trade openness and FDI or by complementary improvements in product market regulations becomes the main force at play instead of the EU anchor. Future research should focus on this hypothesis.

In addition to examining the Oaxaca decomposition over the full sample, we also carry out this analysis by firm ownership, i.e., for public and private firms.[10] Becker's theory of discrimination argues that the market punishes discrimination in private enterprises, but no similar force exists for public firms. The results show that while the wage gap in public diminished quicker than in private firms, the discrimination component has remained more or less stable in both types of firms.

13.5 Conclusions

This chapter offers case study econometric evidence that tries to throw light on structural labour market reforms in Hungary, which is a country that has received relatively little attention so far. Using the narrative approach, our analysis identifies three significant labour market reforms in Hungary: in 1992 and 2002 aiming at increasing, and in 2012 at decreasing, employment protection. We then study the effects of these reforms using a unique, representative and carefully recoded data set that starts in 1986 and extends, in three-year intervals, until 2016, thus covering the fall of communism in 1989, the accession to the European Union in 2004 and the global financial crisis. We find that over these thirty years the skill premium almost doubled, the gender wage gap decreased to a third and gender discrimination practically halved.

The empirical evidence discussed in this chapter supports the view that reforms have led the economy to better respond to market forces in providing large returns for human capital investments. The evidence also suggests that wage earners are responding to the changes in the market. The results also show a large and statistically significant decline in the male–female difference in log wages over time as well as a large and statistically significant decline in the amount of the log wage difference that cannot be explained by the econometric model, i.e., 'discrimination'. We conclude that highly educated and female

[10] Public firms include state-owned enterprises, public services as well as public administration. Many firms are not clearly classified as public or private by the National Employment Office and are excluded from the analysis (for instance, the data include wage earners in charities and nongovernmental organizations). Finally, because central planning was still in force in 1986 and 1989, there are no firms classified as private for these years, and this is why this information is only available from 1992 onwards.

workers seem to have been the main beneficiaries from the labour market reforms in Hungary from 1986 at least until 2010.

There are various lessons and suggestions for future research. One is about the value of case study evidence. We think this is an important approach because it allows us to simultaneously address three key research questions about structural reforms. Namely, what are the economic and political conditions that help the implementation of reforms? What are their main impacts? And how do their sequencing and reversals affect their impacts? Traditional econometric studies tend to focus on one or two of these. A case study also allows us to go deeper in identifying and measuring structural reforms as well as in tracking key development in the labour market. Yet we must recognize a drawback from this greater granularity: it makes the link between reforms and their outcomes more nuanced and difficult to establish. One important direction for further research is to try to tighten these links in a case study context.

The structural reforms literature usually focuses on macro outcomes such as employment, growth and inequality (Campos and Nugent, 2018). In this chapter, we focused instead on more micro or labour market outcomes such as returns to education, experience, sector and gender. Another suggestion for future research is to try to strengthen these links. One way to do so would be to go deeper into education and discrimination inequalities by using other methods, such as quantiles regressions and the range of other decomposition approaches (Blau and Kahn, 2017). Spatial econometric methods may also prove useful in further exploring the dynamics of the gender wage gap in terms of different industrial sectors, ownership (public, private and foreign) and across age cohorts. For the case of Hungary, this will require additional data work, both in terms of bringing in a range of other available data sources (such as the Labour Force Survey that has been running since 1992) as well as digging deeper into the WES to further improve the match of the industrial classification over time, the definition of weights and the firm ownership classification.

References

Adams, Z., Bishop, L. and Deakin, S. (2016). *CBR Labour Regulation Index: Dataset of 117 Countries*. Centre for Business Research.

Altonji, J. and Blank, R. (1999). 'Race and Gender in the Labor Market', in O. Ashenfelter and D. Card (ed.), *Handbook of Labor Economics: Volume 3C*, Elsevier, North-Holland, 3143–3259.

Benczes, I. (2016). 'From Goulash Communism to Goulash Populism: The Unwanted Legacy of Hungarian Reform Socialism', *Post-Communist Economies*, Vol. 28, No. 2, 146–166.

Blau, F. and Kahn, L. (2017). 'The Gender Wage Gap: Extent, Trends, and Explanations', *Journal of Economic Literature*, Vol. 55, No. 3, 789–865.

Boeri, T. and Pulay, G. (1998). 'Labor Market Policy Reforms and the Fiscal Constraint', in L. Bokros and J.-J. Dethier (ed.), *Public Finance Reform during the Transition: The Experience of Hungary*. World Bank, pp. 317–336.

Boeri, T. and Terrell, K. (2002). 'Institutional Determinants of Labor Reallocation in Transition', *Journal of Economic Perspectives*, Vol. **16**, No. 1, 51–76.

Brown, D., Earle, J. and Telegdy, A. (2016). 'Where Does Privatization Work? Understanding the Heterogeneity in Estimated Firm Performance Effects', *Journal of Corporate Finance*, Vol. 41, No. 2, 329–362.

Campos, N. and Horváth, R. (2012). 'Reform Redux: Measurement, Determinants and Growth Implications', *European Journal of Political Economy*, Vol. **28**, No. 2, 227–237.

Campos, N. and Jolliffe, D. (2007). 'Earnings, Schooling and Economic Reform: Evidence from Hungary (1986–2004)', *World Bank Economic Review*, Vol. **21**, No. 3, 509–526.

Campos, N. and Nugent, J. (2018). 'The Regulation of Labour in Developed and Developing Countries since 1960', in N. Campos, P. De Grauwe and Y. Ji (ed.), *The Political Economy of Structural Reforms in Europe*. Oxford University Press, pp. 75–88.

Campos, N. and Zlabkova, D. (2001). 'The Wrong Mix: A First Look at Occupational Mobility during the Hungarian Transition', CERGE-EI Prague, DP 59.

Ciminelli, G., Duval, R. and Furceri, D. (2018). 'Employment Protection Deregulation and Labor Shares in Advanced Economies', IMF WP 18/186.

Commander, S., Kollo, J., Ugaz, C. and Vilagi, B. (1995). 'Unemployment, Restructuring, and the Labor Market in Eastern Europe and Russia: Hungary', in S. Commander and F. Coricelli (ed.), *Unemployment, Restructuring, and the Labor Market in Eastern Europe and Russia*. World Bank, pp. 1–38.

Duval, R., Furceri, D., Hu, B., Jalles, J. and Nguyen, H. (2018). 'A Narrative Database of Major Labor and Product Market Reforms in Advanced Economies', IMF WP/18/19.

Halpern, L. and Wyplosz, C. (1998). 'The Hidden Hungarian Miracle,' in L. Halpern and C. Wyplosz (ed.), *Hungary: Towards a Market Economy*. Cambridge University Press, pp. 1–19.

Jarvis, S. and Pudney, S. (1995). 'Redistributive Policy in a Transition Economy: The Case of Hungary', CEPR DP 1117, January.

Kaminski, B. (2000). 'Industrial Restructuring as Revealed in Hungary's Pattern of Integration into European Union Markets', *Europe-Asia Studies*, Vol. 52, No. 3, 457–487.

Kattuman, P. and Redmond, G. (2001). 'Income Inequality in Early Transition: The Case of Hungary 1987–1996', *Journal of Comparative Economics*, Vol. 29, No. 1, 40–65.

Kertesi, G. and Köllo, J. (2003). 'Fighting "Low Equilibria" by Doubling the Minimum Wage? Hungary's Experiment', IZA DP 970.

Koltay, J. (2002). 'Wage Setting: Institutions and Practices', in K. Fazekas and J. Koltay,(ed.), *The Hungarian Labour Market*. Institute of Economics, pp. 54– 62.

Kornai, J. (1986). 'The Hungarian Reform Process: Visions, Hopes, and Reality', *Journal of Economic Literature*, Vol. 24, No. 4, 1687–1737.

(1994). 'Transformational Recession: The Main Causes', *Journal of Comparative Economics*, Vol. 19, No. 1, 39–63.

Mudde, C. (2017). 'Eastern Europe's Populists, Racists, and Extremists', in A. Fagin and P. Kopecky (ed.), *The Routledge Handbook of East European Politics*. Routledge, pp. 254–263.

O'Leary, C. (1997). 'A Net Impact Analysis of Active Labour Programmes in Hungary', *Economics of Transition*, Vol. 5, No. 2, 453–484.

Székely, I. and Ward-Warmedinger, M. (2018). 'Reform Reversals: Areas, Circumstances and Motivations', *Comparative Economic Studies*, Vol. 60, No. 4, 559–582.

Valentinyi, A. (2012). 'The Hungarian Crisis', in *EEAG Report on the European Economy*, European Economic Advisory Group, pp. 115–130.

Vodopivec, M., Worgotter, A. and Raju, D. (2005). 'Unemployment Benefits Systems in Central and Eastern Europe: A Review of the 1990s', *Comparative Economic System*, Vol. 47, No. 4, 615–651.

Vonyó, T. (2010). 'Socialist Industrialisation or Post-War Reconstruction? Understanding Hungarian Economic Growth, 1949–1967', *Journal of European Economic History*, Vol. 39, No. 2, 253–300.

Žídek, L. (2014). 'Evaluation of Economic Transformation in Hungary', *Review of Economic Perspectives*, Vol. 14, No. 1, 55–88.

Conclusions

The financial crisis of 2007–2008, which led to the Great Recession of 2008–2009 and triggered the sovereign debt crisis in the euro area in 2010, has led to a lot of soul searching among professional economists. With the benefit of hindsight, it can now be said that these crises were misdiagnosed in two ways. First, many economists interpreted these crises to have increased the need for more flexibility in labour and product markets. Structural reforms aimed at making both labour and product markets more flexible were seen as the tools to boost economic activity and to launch countries into a higher growth path. Thus, although the initial shocks were understood to have originated from a financial and banking implosion, which led to a collapse of aggregate demand in 2009, many economists surprisingly advised to fix the supply side.

This therapeutic analysis was very influential. It was enshrined in forceful policy advice by major international institutions like the International Monetary Fund (IMF), the Organization for Economic Cooperation and Development (OECD) and the European Commission. Central banks joined the chorus of advisors urging governments to 'reform their economies'. This was especially strong in the euro area, where the IMF, the European Commission and the European Central Bank (the 'Troika'), enforced supply-side structural reform programmes on the countries of the periphery as the price to pay for financial support.

A second misdiagnosis consisted in seeing 'government profligacy' as one of the root causes of the crises. Government debt accumulation had become unsustainable and had to be checked. This view then led to the policy prescription that countries should institute drastic austerity programmes aiming at reducing government debt. The popularity of these austerity prescriptions in official circles was enhanced by the theory of non-Keynesian effects of fiscal consolidation claiming that highly indebted governments could by reducing government spending generate so much confidence that the private sector would start investing again, thereby pulling the country out of the recession. One drawback that did not receive sufficient attention at the time was that these policies made it much harder to compensate the losers from these structural reforms, thus compromising how well the reforms could potentially work.

This second misdiagnosis completely misunderstood the nature of the crisis. The latter was the result of a typical boom-bust cycle that capitalism regularly generates. A period of optimism and euphoria leads private agents to finance consumption and investment by excessive bank credit. When the crash comes, massive deleveraging is necessary, leading to a deep recession. This forces responsible governments to sustain economic activity and to bail out failing banks. This leads to an explosion of government debt.

All this was very well understood by older writers such as Keynes, Fisher, Minsky and Kindleberger, to name a few. It was, however, collectively forgotten by a significant part of the economics profession and policy makers.

This collective amnesia then led to the application of programmes combining austerity and structural reforms. The question that arises today is how successful these programmes have been.

In this book, we have focused on the question of how successful structural reform programmes have been in boosting economic growth and employment. It should be kept in mind that quite often this question can only be answered successfully when it is analyzed together with the macroeconomic policies that were instituted at the same time.

Here are some of the conclusions that can be extracted from the different chapters of this book. First, structural reform programmes have very divergent effects on economic growth, employment and income inequality. Sometimes they promote growth and employment; sometimes they have opposite effects. The same holds true for its effects on inequality. The case studies in this book illustrated that similar structural reform programmes in one country have very different effects on inequality than in other countries. Sometimes they reduce inequality, sometimes they increase it or have no discernible effects. Thus, more generally, structural reforms are poor predictors of subsequent changes in economic growth, employment and inequality.

A second conclusion from this book is that the effects of structural reforms very much depend on 'initial conditions'. The latter can be institutional in nature. It can also be the business cycle conditions. In this connection, it appears that structural reforms instituted during a recession may actually aggravate the recession. These initial conditions often are the macroeconomic policies that are pursued jointly with structural reforms. For example, it appeared from one of the chapters in this book that liberalization of employment protection legislation has enhanced positive effects on employment if accompanied by a reduction of taxation of labour. In that case, a supply-side measure is reinforced by a demand-boosting policy.

From the preceding analysis, it follows that the dogmatism that has been driving policy makers in urging for structural reforms under any condition is misplaced. We know too little about how these reform programmes affect the economy, and about the initial conditions that have to be satisfied to generate the desired results. This book has shed some light on these issues, but it is clear that more research will have to be done before we can conclude with confidence that structural reforms are always good for us.

Index